GUIDANCE AND PERSONNEL
SERVICES IN EDUCATION

Guidance and Personnel Services in Education

By

ANNA Y. REED

Professor Emeritus in New York University
Resident Lecturer at Cornell University

Ithaca, New York
CORNELL UNIVERSITY PRESS
1947

FIRST PRINTING, AUGUST, 1944
SECOND PRINTING, DECEMBER, 1944
THIRD PRINTING, JUNE, 1947

Cornell University Press

London: Humphrey Milford
Oxford University Press

PRINTED IN THE UNITED STATES OF AMERICA
BY THE VAIL-BALLOU PRESS, INC., BINGHAMTON, N. Y.

PREFACE

THIS volume is the result of the study and experiences which have completely monopolized the author's interest and which have provided her with both work and play, throughout the some thirty-five years during which the theories and practices of the organized guidance and personnel movement have been making their imprint on the social and economic life of the country, and recording their story in the literature of the day.

Preparation of the volume has been a long-anticipated pleasure—a pleasure which has been augmented by the opportunity which delay has given for association with many mature students who were traveling in the same general direction but by a variety of routes. The seminar hours which have been passed in the company of these fellow travelers, where the give and take of true scholarship has always prevailed, have been a continuous spur to achievement and a challenge to maximum effort. The author acknowledges her indebtedness to, and thanks, all those students who, by their own high standards of scholarship and by their critical judgment of hers, have been indirect contributors to the pages which follow.

Obligations to business men and to business publications, which have given her much practical information to share with these same students, have been recognized at different places throughout the book. The benefits derived from business contributions, without which no guidance program and no treatment of guidance procedures can be complete, will be obvious to readers.

The purpose of the book is to present, as inclusively as the limitations of a single volume permit, the whence, how, and where of the guidance and personnel movement and to question its whither: (1) to tell a unified story, from the original records, of how four segments of a guidance movement came into being during the first decade of the twentieth century and are now waiting for co-ordination and integration; (2) to present the universally recognized principles, practices, tools, and techniques which are essential to the proper understanding and performance of the guidance function; (3) to take stock of the present assets and liabilities of guidance and personnel services, to point out fundamentals and permanent values which are progressively facilitating the fulfillment of

v

the "promise of America," and to note deficiencies which are calling for authoritative attention.

The book does not purport to be a definitive study. The guidance movement has not, as yet, been sufficiently tested by time for any writer safely to attempt a definitive report and to be dogmatic as to best procedures, or egotistical regarding the value of his own contribution. The frequent use of "must" or "should" in some chapters may leave the impression of dogmatism. It was sometimes difficult to find less positive substitutes; and among the many things which experience has taught this counselor none have been more valuable than the knowledge that in dealing with human problems *there is no one best way,* but many good, or better, or best ways; and that each counselor is personally responsible for never utilizing a *good* way when there is a *better*—or a *better* way when there is a *best.*

Although the volume is designed primarily to serve as a textbook, handbook, or guide for the use of graduate classes and seminars in universities, it is hoped that college and public-school teachers, social workers, and administrators, as well as general readers, community counselors, and placement officers may find some helpful suggestions for the better performance of their own personnel responsibilities. For all readers, it is hoped that it may be informative, illuminative, and provocative.

Now and then, in connection with the more generally accepted guidance and personnel procedures, the reader will find something new in approach or method of attack, in heretofore unpublished material, in interpretation, or in method of presentation. But the uniqueness of the volume, and therefore its major contribution and its most permanent values, will be found in content which is either entirely omitted from, or very inadequately treated in, other publications dealing with the same subject. Much of the source content of Part I is not elsewhere available. The author is not aware of any other work which traces the origin of the various guidance and personnel activities of the early twentieth century to a common philosophy based on world-wide social and economic conditions. Nor is she familiar with any other publication which has described the agencies fostering these activities in such fashion that interrelationships are revealed and each agency assigned to its proper position in the total picture.

In Part IV, Chapter XV deals with Placement, a topic usually mentioned only incidentally, while Chapter XVI includes a section on Counseling the Superannuated or Older Worker, a topic usually ignored. Part V, "Organization and Administration," presents an old topic in a new dress. The author is hopeful that its content may be somewhat disturbing to administrative authorities and sufficiently provocative to bring constructive results.

Part VI, "Retrospect and Prospect," summarizes *where,* and raises a question as to *whither.* It is the only section which has given specific attention to guidance and personnel problems related to the present war. A conscious effort has been made to avoid reflecting the problems of the moment. Rather has the author tried to present constants which carry over from one period to the next, helping youth to acquire knowledges, skills, attitudes of mind, and emotional controls which have permanent values and which permit him, and those who counsel him, to take depression, or war, or other emergencies in their stride. The role of a firmly grounded, well-poised, currently informed guidance or personnel service does not change materially during emergencies. Fundamentals remain fundamentals; they are dateless, but accents will shift, ultimate objectives may be held in abeyance, and temporary essential informational data must be acquired and intelligently used.

In anticipation of my retirement from active service as Chairman of the Department of Personnel Administration, School of Education, New York University, in 1940, Richard J. Bailey, who had been my colleague at the University, and I planned to collaborate in the preparation of a series of books which had long been under consideration. Three projects were outlined during the winter of 1940. Some progress had been made in the preparation of this, our first volume, when war intervened and Dr. Bailey's acceptance of a commission as psychologist in the U. S. Maritime Service forbade his continued collaboration. The loss of his assistance, together with the great amount of material which was considered in determining what should be included and the rapidly changing national conditions which have necessitated frequent alterations, accounts for the fact that the volume was not completed until April, 1943. In October, 1943, before the final typescript went to the publisher, it was checked with special reference to statements of fact which time might have rendered inaccurate. Should the reader find some such statement which was overlooked, he is asked to accept both the explanation and the apology of the author.

I am under obligation to Lynn A. Emerson, Professor of Industrial Education, Cornell University, for preparing the charts and to A. L. Winsor, Professor of Psychology, also of Cornell University, for advice on, and the reading of, the portions of the text which deal with the Analysis of the Individual.

Finally, I am grateful to publishers and organizations which have graciously permitted me to use copyrighted material. Their names will be found in the footnotes which identify the passages quoted. The American Management Association deserves special mention for its exceptional generosity.

ANNA Y. REED

Ithaca, New York
January 1944

CONTENTS

ix

PART I
Guidance and Personnel Services Prior to 1916

CHAPTER I
Local Experiments in Youth Guidance

CHAPTER II
Guidance and Personnel Services on the College Level

CHAPTER III
Organizations Interested in Guidance and Personnel Services

CHAPTER IV
Interpretative Summary of Source Material

"In using the word modern I refer to the 1930–37 streamlined version since guidance models prior to 1930 are disappearing even in the hands of the second-hand dealers through junking rather than resale."—DONALD G. PATERSON, 1938.

"Documentary evidence is at hand to prove that all the significant principles, practices, and techniques in use in 1940 were also in use in 1908. Progress has been made in the refinement of the old rather than in the introduction of anything new."—ANNA Y. REED, 1940.

CHAPTER I

Local Experiments in Youth Guidance

SOCIAL movements as a rule do not originate; they evolve. They are not set down full-fledged among us, even though such may appear to be the case. Rather, from very small and unimportant beginnings, modified as they progress by social and economic conditions and in their tangible form adapted to the cultural milieu in which they find their expression, they evolve very slowly until eventually there are observable evidences that a new movement has come into being. It is these tangible evidences of the crystallization of a movement which are often accepted, and dated, as the genesis or origin of the movement. Hence it is logical that such services as guidance should be credited by the casual student to one or more apparently spontaneous events or happenings which others have accepted as beginnings, or primary causal factors. In reality, they are symbols of a change which has been taking place in the established cultural pattern.

No study of the combination of social and economic factors which eventually found its expression in organized guidance services in various places in this country has as yet been made. The present writer made a cursory beginning in 1922 and a second attempt in 1932. Both resulted in the collection of much valuable historical data and both indicated that the time had not yet come for such a study—that in order to grasp the full significance of the organized movement a longer time perspective was necessary. What had passed was a revealing prologue; but the ramifications and points of contact were found to be many, the subtle influences most difficult to analyze and interpret. The undertaking was deferred for another decade.

For the purpose of this book it is sufficient to state that, both in its inherent and unconscious and in its purposeful and organized forms, guidance, since the dawn of history, has been an important factor in the growth and adjustment of individuals irrespective of the status of scientific thinking or of prevailing social and economic conditions. The fact that for many centuries guidance received no special recognition and was characterized by no distinctive nomenclature does not justify the assumption that it was nonexistent. But it is a long and time-consuming task to review the story of man in his activities as a social being, to trace the emergence of the principles upon which modern guidance and personnel work is

advancing, and finally to uncover how, as the nineteenth century was near-
ing its close, the time was ripe in practically all the civilized nations of the
world for the practical expression of these principles in what is today
called "guidance." No such task is attempted here. On the other hand, the
responsibility of students within the field for approaching the history of
the movement from the long-term point of view, rather than from the
comparatively recent evidence that somebody, somewhere, was doing
something about guidance in a more or less organized way, is recognized.[1]

During the closing years of the nineteenth century the civilized world
replied affirmatively to the age-old question, Am I my brother's keeper?
Society had accepted the theory of the unity of humanity and the brotherhood of man and was ready to begin translation of the theory into practice.
During the same years psychologists were busily engaged in translating
into practice the theory of individual differences. Thus it happened that
on the eve of the new century two theories—the one sociological and the
other psychological, and both fundamental to the introduction of organized guidance activities—had crystallized sufficiently to attract attention to the desirability of their practical application, and a number of
experiments had already been undertaken.

The years 1900 to 1910 were banner years for the expression of these
newly accepted theories in terms of social and philanthropic efforts to
service humanity better, especially the "ill-fed, ill-clothed, and ill-housed"
segment of humanity. Although New York and Boston have been rather
generally credited with pioneering leadership, when the complete story
of the guidance movement is written it will reveal that between 1900 and
1916 a number of other cities were thinking and working along the same
lines and recording their efforts in the annals of women's clubs, chambers
of commerce, city clubs, the Association of Collegiate Alumnae, and other
service organizations. A comparison of the history of these local interests
reveals the fact that much of the early experimentation in these United
States, as well as in foreign countries, owed its origin to similar economic
and social conditions which tended to reveal similar guidance opportunities and needs. These identical problems, arising simultaneously in widely
separated communities, were in some cases responded to by similar but
entirely unrelated programs; in other cases, publicized programs were
transplanted in toto or with modifications. Part I is concerned with the
presentation of basic data upon which to determine to what extent there
were fundamental principles and characteristic features common to all

[1] A history of the guidance and personnel movement from its inception to the present
time is in preparation. A few points of particular significance to educators are presented
in this volume.

guidance experiments; which of these have proved their worth and been continuously retained and which have been discarded; and what new principles and practices have come into being with the passage of time.

In order to satisfy the demands of various types of students two approaches to the beginnings of the organized guidance movement are offered. Chapter I presents the beginnings through the media of contemporary documents dealing with a series of experiments in different sections of the country, thus offering the reader an opportunity to interpret some of the original records for himself. This is the scholar's way. But the presentation of a sufficient volume of source material to reconstruct the history of the movement would be space-consuming and inappropriate in the light of the purpose of this work. Hence Chapters II and III are largely condensations of factual data taken from the sources. The second approach is offered in Chapter IV wherein the author's interpretation of the sources cited in previous chapters has been supplemented by the interpretation of such other source material as is essential to round out the picture.

The experiments chosen for presentation in Chapter I have been selected to represent all sections of the country, to show motivating influences, fundamental principles, uniformity and variation in tools, techniques, and procedures, character of sponsorship, outstanding personalities and agencies, and types of problems involved in organization and administration.

The year 1908 is the first milepost in the history of guidance as a conscious process in the United States. By that date, two programs, one in Boston and one in New York, had made sufficient progress to result in local organization, to focus national attention upon the beginnings of a tendency to recognize the desirability of assistance in personal adjustments in all the areas of life, and to indicate the necessity of including occupational information and early work experience, accompanied by employment supervision, as factors in twentieth-century education.

BOSTON

The Boston experiment was social-philanthropic in character; the Civic Service House was the center of its activities; Mrs. Quincy A. Shaw was its financial sponsor; and Frank Parsons was its guiding genius. Parsons described its origin, purpose, methods, and early development in detail in a volume published in 1909 after his death.[2] This book gave us our first

---

[2] *Choosing a Vocation* (New York: Houghton Mifflin Co., 1909). Much of the same material appeared in the *Arena*, XL (1908), 3–16, 171–183. All references in this book, however, are to the 1909 edition.

definition in the guidance field (vocational guidance is "the choice of a vocation, adequate preparation for it, and the attainment of efficiency and success" [3]) and touched upon practically every phase of modern guidance service. Periodic rereading of the volume leaves one ever more impressed with the wide range of Parsons' knowledge and experience [4] and with his unusual understanding of the individual as well as of the strengths and weaknesses of education and industry. He showed thorough familiarity with co-operative courses, the places where they had been tried, and their results, and he recommended the extension of such "Public Half-Work High Schools" as a means of guaranteeing youth both a practical and an academic education. He anticipated what recent years have so strongly emphasized that today neither the man in the street nor the educator in the school can have failed to recognize its importance:

A man cannot be fully successful, nor secure against the changes constantly oc-curring in industry, unless he knows a good deal besides the special knowledge immediately applicable to his business.[5]

Parsons was also thoroughly informed regarding the status of the testing movement and knew where the most reliable experimentation was going on. He made several pronouncements on the value of tests; he indicated how, when, and what tests might be used by counselors: and he added:

Nevertheless it must not be forgotten that all such indications are only straws, hints to be taken into account with all the other facts of the case. The handicap of slow decision or imperfect memory may be more than overcome by superiority in industry, earnestness, vitality, endurance, common sense, sound judgment, etc.[6]

Parsons' conception of vocational guidance was based on the broadest possible interpretation of the term; all-round manhood was the true aim, "making a living only one arc of the circle." His general suggestions for an individual if he were to attain success were in keeping with this con-ception: systematic and scientific training of body and brain, memory, reason, and character according to individual differences. Broad general culture, industrial education, and some practical experience were con-sidered to have both individual and social values. His conception of guidance procedures and the relation of the adviser to the advisee were

[3] *Choosing a Vocation*, p. 4.
[4] Parsons was a graduate of the engineering college of Cornell University; he had served on the engineering staff of a railroad; and he had been a teacher in a district school, a city director of art instruction, a practicing lawyer in Boston, a writer of legal textbooks, a university lecturer on English and law, a professor of history in a western agricultural college, and a lecturer on municipal government.
[5] Parsons, *op. cit.*, p. 12.
[6] *Ibid.*, p. 8.

definitely expressed. Three procedures on the part of the person seeking advice were involved: (1) the getting of a clear understanding of himself —an understanding of his abilities, aptitudes, interests, ambitions, resources, and limitations and their causes; (2) the getting of a knowledge of occupations and their opportunities and requirements; and (3) true reasoning on the relationship between these two series of facts.[7] The major function of the counselor was to render skilled assistance in securing accurate information and to aid the counselee in "true reasoning" so that he would make wise decisions for himself: "No person may decide for another what occupation he should choose, but it is possible to help him so to approach the problem that he shall come to wise conclusions for himself."[8]

If counselors were to perform their functions adequately, Parsons felt that they must be experts, "trained as carefully for the work as men are trained for medicine and law," and that they must be equipped with "every facility science can devise for the testing of the senses and capacities and the whole physical, intellectual and emotional make-up."[9] Parsons specifically mentioned the use of schedules, questionnaires, self-analysis, personal records, case studies, employee efficiency records, forms and weighted rating scales, descriptive material for traits, and minimum hiring specifications. A second series of equipment comprised lists of community resources; tables of training opportunities with date, length of course, admissions, costs, and opportunities to earn while studying; tables showing the location of industries and the movement of demand; classifications of industries showing the human traits essential for general and special groups; apprenticeship possibilities; employment agencies, including news ads and employers' forms; and hiring specifications and rating systems.[10]

The major technique whereby Parsons' entire guidance procedure was brought to a focus was the counseling or integrating interview. Such an interview, repeated as often as necessary, was similar in character to the final step in 1943 clinical guidance procedure, while the modern "case conference" was an integral part of Parsons' program for the preparation of counselors. Group conferences, forerunners of present-day "career conferences," were approved, conducted, and found to be valuable both as sources of vocational information and in opening the way for personal interviews.

Meyer Bloomfield was Parsons' colleague in instituting the Boston ex-

[7] *Ibid.*, p. 5.
[8] *Ibid.*, p. 4.
[9] *Ibid.*, p. 22. Parsons recommended the use of both psychology and phrenology.
[10] *Ibid.*, *passim.*

periment. When Parsons died in 1909 Bloomfield assumed responsibility
for the original bureau and became the chief instrumentality in expanding
its local services as well as in spreading the gospel to other communities.
Bloomfield did an excellent job. The tangible results of his activities, both
in the educational and in the business world, are sufficient proof of the
debt which the modern personnel movement owes to his promotional and
organizational abilities. Vocational guidance was born at the psychological
moment in our economic and social history. It contained a strong practical
and emotional appeal. Bloomfield knew how to translate this appeal into
terms of educator, employer, and mass action. He was a born promoter
at a time when promotional ability was needed. Enthusiasm for vocational
guidance spread from coast to coast. Events moved rapidly both locally
and nationally. Four specific results of Parsons' program, as fostered and
expanded by Bloomfield, were:

1. *The establishment of the Vocation Bureau of Boston, 1909.* The
Vocation Bureau was a co-operative and philanthropic agency, the parent
of several other local efforts, especially the Public School Bureau of Boston. There is considerable material available on the functions of the
Vocation Bureau, not the least interesting of which is a very attractive
brochure, issued in 1915, which describes the character and scope of its
services and gives a rather colorful review of its accomplishments in local,
national, and international fields.[11] If those who have access to all the
original documents think it hardly legitimate to attribute all of these
accomplishments to the Vocation Bureau, they will at least concede that
by 1910 the Bureau had become the center of much guidance activity and
that, judged by modern standards, its basic principles and practices were
a fundamentally sound foundation for later development. Boston traveled
a long distance in the right direction between 1909 and 1915.

2. *The establishment of the Public School Bureau of Boston, 1912.* The
Public School Bureau was the outgrowth of an earlier Committee on Vocational Guidance, admittedly stimulated and to a large extent directed by
the Vocation Bureau. The origin and activities of the Public School Bureau
are fully described in the reports of the committee and in those of the superintendent of schools for 1910, 1912, and 1913. A cumulative record card was
in use, although its major purpose was not developmental growth. By
1906 the High School of Commerce was giving systematic instruction in
business opportunities, with information based on annual occupational
surveys, and the committee had recommended "a place for vocational in-

11 See the Vocation Bureau, Boston, *Vocational Guidance and the Work of the Vocation
Bureau of Boston* (Boston: The Bureau, 1915), pp. 8–11; also, the *Twenty-fifth Annual
Report of the Commissioner of Labor,* 1910 (Washington, 1911), pp. 419–497.

formation of an educational character in the regular school curriculum."
Placement and employment supervision were operating in 1909 by means
of summer "apprenticeship," which gave boys and girls insight into the
relation of their school tasks to their life work. In 1913, as one method of
providing counselors with accurate vocational information, "moving pictures were used to illustrate the printing and binding of a book." Counselors' duties varied: some individuals were primarily educational
counselors; others were more concerned with vocations; one "teacher-
adviser" was provided for each forty pupils, and "homeroom teachers"
had rather definite guidance responsibilities. Nor was provision for the
education of parents forgotten. In his 1910 report the superintendent
noted that the School and Home Association had made plans for interesting parents in the problem of vocational selection.

3. *The First National Conference on Vocational Guidance, 1910.* The
first national vocational guidance conference was called by the Boston
Chamber of Commerce and the Vocation Bureau of Boston and met November 15 and 16, 1910.[12] Forty-five cities sent delegates. Manufacturers,
employees, businessmen, social workers, and educators participated in the
discussions. Among the names appearing on the conference program either
as speakers, participants, or sponsors, the following continued to be interested in the guidance movement in subsequent years: Stratton D.
Brooks, Superintendent of the Boston Public Schools; E. W. Weaver, Boys'
High School, Brooklyn, New York; Florence M. Marshall, Director of the
Girls' Trade Education League of Boston; Meyer Bloomfield; David
Snedden, Massachusetts Commissioner of Education; Robert A. Woods
of the South End House; Frank M. Leavitt, Delegate from the University
of Chicago; Frederick P. Fish, Chairman of the Massachusetts Board of
Education; A. Lincoln Filene; Henry C. Metcalf; Jane Addams of Hull
House; G. Stanley Hall of Clark University; Graham Taylor and George
H. Mead of the University of Chicago; and Homer Folks, Secretary of the
State Charities Aid Association, New York. Significant attitudes and ideas
included the interest expressed by businessmen in the subject of expert
vocational counseling; the generally expressed opinion that vocational
guidance was a public-school function; the importance of vocational guidance, its aims and fundamental principles; and its ethical and economic
implications. Charles W. Eliot restated his views, previously expressed
before the National Education Association, on the value of the life-
career motive.[13]

[12] The account which follows is based on an original program of the conference.
[13] "The Value During Education of the Life-Career Motive," in National Education
Association of the United States, *Journal of Proceedings and Addresses,* 1910, pp. 133–141.

4. *The organization of the Boston Employment Managers Association, 1911.* From its inception the Vocation Bureau of Boston had worked in close co-operation with employer and employee groups. The necessity for such co-operation if vocational guidance were to be effective was evidenced by the participation of the Chamber of Commerce in the calling of the first conference. Additional proof is given of the friendly relations between educational, philanthropic, and business organizations by the fact that Bloomfield was the mastermind in the organization of the Employment Managers Association.

NEW YORK

A second effort in the direction of organized guidance, an effort which was sufficiently publicized by 1908 to attract national attention, originated in New York City *within* the public school system but *without* official endorsement. It was sponsored, and in its origin largely financed, by the High School Teachers' Association under the leadership of Eli W. Weaver of the Boys' High School of Brooklyn. For some time prior to the inclusion of other people in the work Weaver had been actively engaged in guiding individual boys as occasion arose and he continued until his death in 1922 to be an increasingly valuable contributor to the sane development of vocational guidance.

Data relative to the origin and development of organized guidance in New York City are found in the reports of the superintendent of schools, of the High School Teachers' Association, and of private organizations supporting philanthropic bureaus, in press items, and in press reports.

The purposes, methods, and accomplishments of the New York project are well presented in the first report of the Student Aid Committee, Eli W. Weaver, Chairman. This report was included in the 1909–1910 report of the High School Teachers' Association of New York City. Teachers, without additional remuneration, were reported to be serving as counselors in a number of high schools; bulletins on vocational opportunities were available; a career plan including special study of his own capacities was required of each student as a part of the English course; vocational addresses by outside speakers were in vogue; and provision was made for employer contacts, for placement, and for employment supervision.

In connection with the placement activities, which were an important part of the New York program, it is interesting to note that the Association anticipated by more than a decade the U. S. Boys' Working Reserve, established April 20, 1917, as part of our junior war-emergency program. In 1908 the Department of Agriculture of the State of New York, the Bureau of Information and Statistics, issued a bulletin entitled: "Bulletin

on Extra Help for the Harvest: The Successful Experiment of Employing
High School Boys on New York Farms during the Season of 1907."

In April, 1908, Weaver reported 2500 boys registered for the second
summer. This agricultural project was abandoned, but other types of
summer services better adapted to city boys and offering a better opportunity for employment supervision were substituted.

Still more significant, in this first report, than the program which the
Association was attempting to carry out was the expression of need for a
more effective central organization:

It seems hardly expedient to carry on this work unless a more effective organization can be inaugurated. . . . In the report of the association for 1909 your
committee recommended to the authorities that the vocation advisers of the
schools should be allowed some time to attend to this work and that facilities
should be afforded them to keep proper records. The school authorities have become interested and the work has commended itself to Superintendent Maxwell,
Associate Superintendent Stevens and the Committee on High Schools, and a
request has been made for the preparation of a detailed plan for the organization of a school vocation bureau.[14]

The "detailed plan" which the school authorities sought was incorporated in this first report, and the *Eleventh Annual Report of the Superintendent of Schools,* 1909, contained Maxwell's opinion relative to its
desirability:

. . . Some work of a most beneficent character has already been done along these
lines by a self-appointed committee of high school teachers, under the chairman-
ship of Mr. E. W. Weaver, of the Boys' High School, Brooklyn. The work thus
happily commenced should be officially recognized and greatly amplified. The
Board of Education would do well to organize a vocation or employment bureau
with Mr. Weaver, who has shown a rare capacity for such work, at its head. . . .

Maxwell's recommendation for a central bureau was not endorsed by
the board, but an appropriation of $250 was granted each high school for
expenditure in connection with its guidance program.

There were three immediate results of the efforts of the New York
Teachers' Association.

1. *The New York City Vocational Guidance Survey, February–July,
1911.* Typical school districts were included in this survey and the results
were published in the *Fourteenth Annual Report of the City Superintendent of Schools,* 1912.

2. *The organization of a number of local agencies to deal with guidance and placement.* One of the outstanding characteristics of the guidance
movement in New York was the large number of decentralized guidance

14 High School Teachers' Association of New York City, *Bulletin,* IV (1909–1910), 27–30.

efforts which sprang up in the early period. They rendered certain very desirable community services but, in the final analysis, handicapped centralization and hindered the logical development of a unified, publicly supported service. The beginnings of this decentralization are early apparent. Louise C. Odencrantz in 1913 found sixty-two organizations doing placement work or offering guidance in connection with placement.[15] This excessive decentralization, which was in direct conflict with the recommendations of both Superintendent Maxwell and the High School Teachers' Association, was credited according to the records to disagreement regarding the directorship. Whatever the cause, it was most unfortunate that New York City permitted so many good beginnings to overshadow the importance of centralization and thereby lost her opportunity for national leadership in a field which she might otherwise have claimed and which, on many other counts, was legitimately hers.

3. *The Second National Conference on Vocational Guidance, New York City, October 23–26, 1912.* Discussions during the conference covered the entire field of guidance service including a rather complete summary of experimental activities. The proceedings were privately published and are valuable to students who seek to follow the history of the guidance movement.[16] Although a decision to form a national association was arrived at during the conference, final action was delayed until the meeting of the Third National Conference in Grand Rapids in 1913.

CINCINNATI

Superintendent Dyer's reports for the years 1907 and 1910 show persistent concern for the personal problems of young wage-earners. His report for 1911 indicated that the administrative authority was definitely committed to vocational guidance and had made a decentralized beginning of introducing it into the public-school system. The type of program advocated for educational and vocational guidance between 1911–1913 was formulated by Frank P. Goodwin, Director of the Department of Civil and Vocational Service. It comprised: (1) study of the individual and use of personnel record cards; (2) systematic effort to keep the life-career motive before high-school pupils; (3) collection of occupational information including information on the personal factors which make for success in different lines of work; (4) knowledge of opportunities for advanced training, especially college training; and (5) better adaptation of school

15 "Placement Work for Women and Girls in New York City," *Manual Training and Vocational Education*, XVII (1915), 169–177.
16 *Proceedings of the Second National Conference on Vocational Guidance, New York, Oct. 23–26, 1912* (privately printed).

courses to the vocational needs of pupils.[17] Goodwin cited six conditions which made for successful vocational guidance in a large high school: (1) the appointment of a director with time for supervision; (2) a school organization which will permit the close personal contact of each pupil with at least one teacher of the right type; (3) the exercise of an intelligent and sympathetic helpfulness on the part of the teacher; (4) a logical analysis of the personal characteristics of each pupil; (5) an understanding of the relation of the school work to the life-career motive; and (6) the adaptation of school work to the vocational needs of the community.[18]

Philanthropy, as in so many other cities, played a major part in establishing organized guidance in Cincinnati. In 1907 the Schmidlapp Fund "to uplift, and to strengthen the lives of young women who are compelled to be self-supporting" was established.[19] In the fall of 1909 it instituted, in co-operation with the local Child Labor Committee, a privately financed Vocation Department,[20] which, from the administrative angle, was a public school vocation bureau from its inception. Mrs. Helen T. Woolley, a nationally known psychologist, was director of this bureau. Under her supervision a psychological laboratory for mental and physical testing was established. Vocational advising, placement work for boys and girls, and issuance of work certificates were other responsibilities of the bureau.

Although in the early years of the guidance movement Cincinnati instituted several phases of guidance service, its real claim to national leadership was based upon a research program in the field of individual differences and the relation of these differences to employment influences. Mrs. Woolley's study, undertaken in 1911 to compare the rate of development, mental and physical, of children in industry and those in school, was a model of painstaking psychological research.[21] The findings were somewhat disappointing to the sponsors of the study, but in methods of research and as an example of the desirability of conducting psychological laboratories in connection with guidance bureaus, it made an admirable contribution to the progress of personnel methods and to knowledge of the comparative influences of school and employment on fourteen- to eighteen-year-old youths.

[17] See Goodwin's address before the Ohio State Teachers' Association, Dec. 19, 1913, in Meyer Bloomfield, ed., *Readings in Vocational Guidance* (Boston: Ginn and Co., [c1915]), pp. 129–140.
[18] *Ibid.*, p. 140.
[19] See the letter of gift, dated January 1, 1908, which followed the trust agreement of the preceding year.
[20] The annual reports of the Schmidlapp Bureau, Edith W. Campbell, Director, cover the history of the early work in Cincinnati from 1909 to 1920.
[21] The findings were published by Mrs. Woolley in *An Experimental Study of Children* (New York: Macmillan Co., 1926).

GRAND RAPIDS

The introduction of vocational guidance into the Grand Rapids, Michigan, school system,[22] and the course of its development after introduction, were due almost entirely to the initiative of Jesse B. Davis, Principal of the Central High School, to the enthusiasm which he inspired in his high-school teaching corps, and to the co-operation which he was able to secure from the Chamber of Commerce, the Public Library, the Y.M.C.A., and other civic and social organizations. Two important phases of the guidance movement were accented in the Grand Rapids program: (1) personality culture and character development and (2) vocational information in connection with regular curriculum subjects. The recorded history of the Grand Rapids work begins in 1909, but the fundamental experience upon which formal procedure was based was, here as elsewhere, founded upon several years of experience in connection with general educational responsibilities. Davis' objectives, his methods, his program, and his standards for evaluating results indicated that vocational guidance in his mind was intimately related to guidance in toto. Although the term "personnel service" was unknown in 1909, Davis recognized its underlying principle—the unitary character of human problems and the necessity for a unit program of advisory service.

Because of its outstanding features, because of its high-school origin, because no preliminary surveys preceded or accompanied introduction, because no private financial support was received, it has sometimes been erroneously assumed that guidance efforts were confined to the Central High School and that no centralized bureau was advocated or established. Documentary evidence contradictory to such an assumption is available. In 1910 Davis made a plea for a community "vocation bureau" and enumerated its tentative aims: (1) to establish a closer relationship between the high schools and the business world; (2) to advise with the school authorities regarding the practical side of school work; (3) to aid in giving the pupils some idea of the demands and opportunities of the various vocations in life; (4) to form a kind of employment bureau for those who must leave school on or before graduation; and (5) to lend a moral influence toward the enforcement of child labor laws and more favorable conditions of employment.[23]

[22] The record of development in Grand Rapids is found in the reports of the Board of Education for 1908–1909, 1909–1910, 1910–1911, and 1911–1912, and in Jesse B. Davis, *Moral and Vocational Guidance* (New York: Ginn and Co., 1914).

[23] *Annual Report of the Board of Education,* 1910, pp. 37–39.

Educational, civic, and social guidance were included in Davis' program although he definitely defined the aims of vocational and moral guidance only.

The purpose of the work is to unfold to the pupil a better understanding of himself, to awaken a moral consciousness that will lead to stronger character; . . . to prepare himself in mind and heart for his life calling; . . . to lead the pupil to a conception of the moral responsibilities that will be his from the point of view of his future relation to business or professional associates, in his social relations to the community in which he lives, and as a citizen toward the law.[24]

In June, 1913, Davis was appointed Director of Vocational Guidance for the city,[25] and in October of the same year the Board of Education established a vocation bureau with an office in the city hall. Grand Rapids had established a centralized system of guidance.

PHILADELPHIA

The records and reports of the Consumers' League of Philadelphia (later known as the Consumers' League of Eastern Pennsylvania) and of the Public Education Association of Philadelphia furnish the data for the initial chapter of the story of guidance in Philadelphia. By 1912 the public schools had entered the picture, and still later the White-Williams Foundation, the Y.M.C.A., the Chamber of Commerce, and similar community agencies were actively interested.

The activity of the Consumers' League [26] derived from its interest, expressed in 1909, in the Labor Law for Women and Minors. To assist in the enforcement of this law the Industrial Betterment Bureau was established in 1910, with the double purpose of reporting law violations and of affording guidance and placement for youth just starting out to work. The records of the placement office contain many significant comments by young applicants.

Where there was a real economic need and where the boy or girl was especially promising, the League arranged for scholarships. "Each week, reports from the teachers are regularly received and examined before the weekly three dollars is sent to the parent, and for absence without a good cause, a proportionate amount is deducted."

24 *Ibid.*, 1911–1912, pp. 30–31.
25 See the *Annual Report of the Superintendent*, 1912–1913, pp. 29–30.
26 See the *Tenth Annual Report of the Consumers' League of Philadelphia*, 1910. Page references cannot be given in many citations such as this to early documents relating to the beginning of the guidance movement because the material is not generally accessible. The author has typed copies of many of these reports in her files where they may be consulted by students and scholars.

The League outlined the educational and vocational needs of young wage-earners and suggested a program to meet them:

For many months the Consumers' League has been urging some educational agencies to start some organized work on this basis, and it seems probable that before another annual report this will have been done.[27]

Three years later it stated:

Although the work of the Bureau in individual cases is encouraging, it is obvious that the problem of vocational direction and employment cannot be solved by any private agency. The responsibility rests first and last upon the schools. Children should be given careful vocational guidance.[28]

The second private organization to become interested in vocational guidance, to make definite contributions to its furtherance, and to assert that the school was the proper agency "both for financing and directing the work" was the Public Education Association of Philadelphia, James S. Hiatt, Secretary. Hiatt defined vocational guidance as

. . . that new educational force which attempts to bridge the gap between the school and the proper life work of the child. Of course, the idea of careful guidance of boys and girls into the occupations best fitted for them is as old as industry itself[;] . . . the new feature in Vocational Guidance is the attempt . . . to connect the work of guidance directly with the schools.[29]

Hiatt offered to make a study of the entire field and to present the results to the school authorities for their help in the solution of "this vital matter." The study was made and is one of the most attractively presented of the early vocational guidance surveys.[30]

The Department of Compulsory Education was reorganized in 1911 in response to the demands of the labor law of 1909. Continuation schools, trade schools, promotions by subjects, and other timely educational innovations received the attention of educational authorities. Superintendent M. G. Brumbaugh recognized the importance of vocational guidance as a factor in the solution of the many personal problems which were encountered by school eliminates and recommended some sort of vocational bureau to "wisely advise all pupils" who desire to leave school.[31] In 1914 the Board of Education established a Department of Vocational

[27] *Eleventh Annual Report,* 1911.

[28] *Fourteenth Annual Report,* 1914.

[29] *An Introduction to Vocational Guidance* (Philadelphia: Public Education Association, [?1911]).

[30] Public Education Association, *Annual Report, 1911–1912: A Year of Cooperative Service for the Schools.* See also James S. Hiatt, *The Child, the School, and the Job,* reprinted by the Public Education Association from the *City Club Bulletin* of Dec. 27, 1912.

[31] *Annual Report of the Superintendent of Schools,* 1912, pp. 13–14.

Education and Guidance with John C. Frazee as Director.[32] A School Placement Bureau was instituted in 1915.

CHICAGO

Organized experimental work in vocational guidance in Chicago in 1911 was the logical outgrowth of a program of child welfare, civic betterment, and educational progress which had commanded the attention of a number of civic and social agencies over a considerable period of time. Leadership radiating from the Chicago School of Civics and Philanthropy and from the University of Chicago inspired and guided lay interest, first, in conducting a series of preliminary research projects and, second, in interpreting the findings of such investigations in terms of facilities for meeting the needs revealed.

The Committee on Public Education of the City Club of Chicago, Professor George H. Mead, Chairman, comprised three subcommittees one of which was the Sub-Committee on Vocational Guidance. City Club bulletins and reports for 1911 and 1912 revealed a background of interest and information which made the organization a desirable member of the Joint Committee on Vocational Supervision established in 1913.[33]

The Chicago Association of Commerce was primarily interested in practical vocational education and the type of legislation best adapted to secure such education. Interest in vocational guidance per se is recorded in the 1912 report of Dr. Nathaniel Butler, Chairman of the Committee on Vocational Education.[34] Before the close of the year various speakers, including Mrs. Woolley from Cincinnati, appeared before the Association, and an appropriation was granted to employ a man, Raymond Charles Booth, to carry on guidance work for boys. Interest in the work continued, and the scope of the activities is described in considerable detail in the reports for 1913, 1914, 1915, and 1916.[35] In 1916 active interest ceased and financial support was withdrawn.[36]

The report for 1913 noted that the Board of Education had given official recognition to the work by delegating to District Superintendent William M. Roberts the supervision of all efforts in guidance; that a part-

[32] See Superintendent J. P. Garber's *Report to the State Department of Education*, 1915.

[33] Unpublished material in the files of the City Club was placed at the disposal of the author in 1921. Copies were made of material desired for historical purposes.

[34] See the Chicago Association of Commerce, *Annual Report*, 1912, pp. 56–58.

[35] Typed copies of these reports were made available to the author through the courtesy of the Committee on Education. Abstracts of the reports and news items relative to the progress of the work appeared from time to time in *Chicago Commerce*, published by the Association.

[36] *Chicago Commerce*, XI (April 7, 1916), 40.

time plan with two boys on a single job was being experimented with, and that summer placement on farms was about to be tried in order to give impetus to agricultural education along practical lines. The Vocational Bureau of the Buffalo Chamber of Commerce had been visited, and a report had been made. The report for 1914 stated that all records were being cleared through the offices of the Board of Education and that the Association was urging the board to make provision for a vocational guidance bureau in the regular budget. Attention was called to the pamphlet, "What Occupation Shall I Choose?" which had been prepared as a co-operative enterprise with special assistance from the Public Library and which was being distributed among the schools with the approval of the Board.

The 1915 report contained recommendations relative to the establishment of a vocational guidance bureau to be maintained and managed under the public schools. This request was endorsed by the Joint Committee on Vocational Supervision and the Chicago Woman's Aid. It emphasized the general agreement by all who had considered the subject "that the problem of vocational guidance should be worked out by boards of education rather than through private philanthropic agencies." Announcement of the organization of the "Employment Advisers' Club," comprising about twenty employment managers of leading concerns, in the establishment of which the Association's committee participated, was also contained in this report.

Work by women's organizations in the interest of vocational guidance for girls preceded the activities of the Association of Commerce and established precedents which were followed by that organization in introducing service for boys. The reports of women's clubs show an interest continuously and variously expressed prior to the first use of the term "vocational guidance." Manual training, domestic science, educational and industrial legislation, juvenile delinquency, juvenile courts, and the like were all live topics in club circles. Fortunately for the development of the guidance movement, the interests and abilities of women's organizations were unified and directed by the Department of Social Investigation of the Chicago School of Civics and Philanthropy. In December, 1911, this department made a report to the Chicago Woman's Club, the Chicago Association of Collegiate Alumnae, and the Women's City Club entitled, "Finding Employment for Children who Leave the Grade Schools to go to Work." [37] Subtitles are significant: Section I, "The School and the Working-Child; A Plea for Employment Supervision in City Schools; Section II, "Preliminary Report on Opportunities of Employment in Chicago Open to Girls

[37] Chicago School of Civics and Philanthropy, *Report*, 1911.

Under Sixteen." This study was made under a subsidy from the Russell Sage Foundation. Additional experimental investigation was financed by the women's organizations previously mentioned, and a beginning of interviewing, guidance, and placement was made by Anne Davis in a room provided by the Board of Education in the Lucy L. Flower Technical High School:

The Superintendent of Schools recommends that Sophonisba P. Breckenridge and Edith P. Abbott of the Chicago School of Civics and Philanthropy be given permission to occupy a room in the Lucy L. Flower Technical High School for the purpose of meeting students of the school and giving them advice about methods and opportunities of earning a livelihood, thus making the beginning of a "Vocation Bureau." . . . Granted use of room. . . .[38]

Thus the board gave official endorsement to vocational guidance. On January 22, 1913, two very significant recommendations were made to the board by Superintendent Ella Flagg Young.

1. That the Board accept the offer made by various organizations to extend the work in vocational guidance begun at the Lucy L. Flower High School to other schools of the city "subject to direction by the Superintendent of Schools" and that Assistant Superintendent Roberts be in charge.

2. That women counselors be appointed in each "mixed" high school for the social guidance of girls. . . . The boys have a counselor and a friend in the principal who directs and advises them in affairs of personal and organized social nature arising outside the class room; . . . the girls have no woman teacher to whom they can go in similar circumstances.[39]

She recommended selection of "a woman teacher who shall teach three regular classes and shall under the direction of the principal, give special attention to the organized social life of the girls, said woman counsellor to be paid three hundred dollars ($300) extra. . . ."

In March, 1913, the board entered upon a period of active support of vocational guidance.[40] District Superintendent Roberts made lengthy reports, and Superintendent Young on June 25, 1913, sent a communication to the board which indicated that she was not allowing board initiative to lag. She prophesied that a corps of teachers in this new field would soon be necessary and recommended that an examination for "teachers of vocational guidance" be authorized, such examination to be held July 1, 1913.[41] Although there was increased interest on the part of the board, that body did not assume full responsibility for vocational guidance until 1916. On

[38] *Proceedings of the Board of Education of the City of Chicago*, 1911–1912, p. 80.
[39] *Ibid.*, 1912–1913, p. 703.
[40] See the *Circular of Announcement of the Department of Vocational Supervision* (Series 3, No. 18) issued by the Board of Education, May 1, 1913.
[41] *Proceedings*, 1912–1913, p. 1398.

March 1 of that year the superintendent submitted a detailed list of appointments with the salary schedule for the first staff of the Public School Bureau of Vocational Guidance:

The Secretary presented the following communication from the Superintendent of Schools:
(29193–F).
Bureau of Vocational Guidance—Appoint Advisers and Adjust Salaries.
The Superintendent of Schools reports that consideration has been given to the plan for organization of the Department of Vocational Guidance, in accordance with authority granted under date of February 2, 1916, (Report No. 28987) and the following recommendations and appointments are submitted to the Board for approval.[42]

The report met with unanimous approval, and four appointments were made: Anne S. Davis and Raymond Booth as vocational advisers at $1500 each and Bertha Van Hove and Ethel Kawin as assistant vocational advisers at $1260 each. Mr. Booth did not accept the appointment.

St. Louis

Early interest in the guidance movement in St. Louis coincided in time with its beginnings in other cities but differed as to origin and outcome. While private initiative instigated many local guidance efforts and resulted in more or less tangible experimentation which eventually led to educational co-operation, educational administration took the initiative in St. Louis. The beginnings of the movement centered around Superintendent Ben Blewett, who was much interested in the findings of the Massachusetts Commission on Industrial and Technical Education, 1905; E. George Payne of Harris Teachers College; and E. E. Lewis, who made a very complete survey of eliminated pupils the findings of which were included in the superintendent's report for 1911–1912. The reports for 1910, 1911, and 1912 indicate considerable interest and some development in the broader field of personnel problems, but administrative interest did not ripen until some years later into a definite bureau under trained leadership.

Minneapolis

Minneapolis' initial contribution to the literature of vocational guidance comprised reports on two surveys: *A Vocational Survey of Minneapolis,* published by the Minneapolis Teachers' Club in 1913, and the *Report of the Minneapolis Survey for Vocational Education,* published

---

42 *Proceedings,* 1916, p. 2358.

under the auspices of the National Society for the Promotion of Industrial Education in 1916.

The 1913 survey was conducted by a commission representative of differing interests. Financial support was received from the Teachers' Club and from Unity House, a philanthropic organization. The scope of the study and its findings were similar to those of other early elimination or vocational guidance surveys. Its pronouncements and the recommendations which resulted were accepted and put in motion by the Board of Education:

Vocational guidance has three functions to perform: it must exhibit the world to which boys and girls must go; it must know the child, his powers, his desires, and his weaknesses; then it must strive to fit the child for the job and the job to the boy.[43]

A careful, continuous survey of business and industries was recommended, the results to be made available for guidance purposes in homes and in school. *"This the Board of Education should do."*

In order to know the child better the teachers must learn to be more observant; weaknesses or defects must be ascertained; a cumulative record must be kept; and homes should be visited.

"The Board of Education should organize a Department of Vocational Guidance, with experts to advise youth."

The Board of Education responded almost immediately to both of the demands which the 1913 survey made: it organized a Department of Vocational Guidance very similar to that suggested in the survey, and wheels were set in motion which resulted in the Vocational Education Survey of 1915. This second survey was a bona fide vocational education survey. The report of the findings made no attempt to outline any program for guidance or to influence the development of the program which had been instituted, but it did contain one short chapter describing the Public School Department with both its immediate and tentative plans and its relation to the effective use of the later survey findings.[44]

The significant features of the Minneapolis plan in comparison with other local plans are found in the title, "Department of Attendance and Vocational Guidance"; in the functions, which included duties connected with the school census and attendance, employment certification and supervision, and "incidental placement" and vocational guidance; and in suggestions for a "juvenile employment exchange," for changes in the

[43] *Vocational Survey*, 1913, pp. 67–68.
[44] Pp. 628–632.

curriculum to provide for suitable study of vocations, and for the preparation of a corps of vocational assistants.

HARTFORD

The Hartford Vocational Guidance Committee was the direct outgrowth of the activities of the Consumers' League of Connecticut.[45] As early as 1907–1908 the League was occupied with investigations looking toward revision of labor legislation. In 1909 a new child-labor law was passed, and the League, believing that the expansion of educational opportunities was fully as important as restrictive labor legislation, financed a study of foreign educational systems in order to secure suggestions for the educational solution of juvenile employment problems in the United States. The results of the study were published in 1911,[46] and in November of the same year the Vocational Guidance Committee was formed.[47] It included representatives from the Board of School Visitors, Principals' Club, High School Committee, Civic Club, Juvenile Commission, and Consumers' League, the last organization having initiated the work in Hartford. The original purpose of the committee "was to make an intensive study of the conditions surrounding the fourteen to sixteen year old worker. . . . No effort had been made to consider their individual needs or to formulate a constructive program of readjustments for the institutions that specifically affected their interests."

A local industrial survey, which included an investigation of occupational distribution of juvenile workers, a study of training opportunities for working minors, and a series of elimination interviews for the purpose of analyzing personal problems in detail, was conducted and the findings made public. An elaborate program, "How Vocational Guidance May Solve This Problem in Hartford," was suggested, and methods for carrying it out were offered.

The report of the General Committee for 1911–1913 closed as follows:

Vocational Guidance in Hartford has up to the present concerned itself only with the fourteen to sixteen year old worker. After studying the problem of these children, it tried to provide wise, practical supervision for them and sometimes material assistance in obtaining positions. When education, social service and industry have readjusted their forces in order to care more effectively for these

[45] Typed copies of the records of the Consumers' League are in the author's files.
[46] See *A Glance at Some European and American Vocational Schools for Children Between 12 to 16 Years of Age: The Results of an Investigation Made by the Consumers' League of Connecticut*, 1909–1910 (Hartford: The League, 1911).
[47] See *Vocational Guidance in Hartford, Connecticut: Report of the General Committee and Vocational Counselor*, 1911–1913, p. 3.

children, the heaviest burden of supervision will be lifted from the shoulders of the vocational counsellor. Vocational Guidance from that time on will probably take two lines of development.

(1) As a piece of educational work it is primarily interested in the individual child. Therefore, it may still provide guidance for children through the labyrinth of vocational and academic courses so their educational and vocational life may be as nearly as possible an expression of their own personalities.

(2) It may concern itself with more pretentious and scientific investigation of the occupations open to minors of a more advanced age with the intention of providing guidance for the older workers.

The *Third Annual Report of the Juvenile Commission* mentions the city's interest in vocational guidance and the employment of a trained vocational counselor in November, 1912, for a period of six months. Her salary was paid by contributions from clubs and private individuals.

DE KALB

The Township High School, De Kalb, Illinois, affords an early example of small town experimentation in vocational guidance. Principal F. M. Giles reported on local problems and his attempted methods of solution before the organization meeting of the National Vocational Guidance Association in Grand Rapids, October, 1913.[48] At that time, according to Giles, the program had been going on for "a number of years." [49]

The program consisted of two parts: (1) Systematic courses of instruction in vocational opportunities, in preparation for which students were told that their occupational decision should rest upon two things, knowledge of themseves and their abilities and knowledge of social conditions.

It will be noticed that we do not decide for the individual. We throw the burden back upon the student. Our purpose is to furnish the individual with the material for a more intelligent decision, not to make the decision for him.

(2) Instruction in personal characteristics, which Giles liked to think of as applied ethics and which he believed had permanent value in establishing ideals.

OMAHA

The Omaha Vocation Bureau was opened in 1915. It is included here because it owed its origin to the Association of College Alumnae. Space was furnished by the Board of Education, but the office was open only

[48] See U. S. Bureau of Education, *Vocational Guidance* (Bulletin, 1914, no. 14; Washington, 1914), pp. 52-59.
[49] *Ibid.*, p. 52.

three hours daily because of limited funds and the necessity for spending much time investigating local opportunities. A résumé of the first year's work [50] shows that it included both guidance and placement; that the Omaha Public Library was a valuable co-operating agency; that educational guidance was assumed to be comprised in vocational guidance; and that registration was open to youth who had already left school as well as to those still in school. Statistics of interviews, employers' calls, placements, etc., were included in the report, and the problem of evaluating accomplishments was clearly stated:

It is impossible to record in figures the principal work of the Bureau, because it has to do with the welfare of the individuals we touch—a thing which only time can measure. . . . The outstanding fact made clear by our year's work is that Omaha boys and girls, like those of other cities, need information which will show them the nature of the many things which are possible, and which will enable them to direct their study wisely and to make a considered and intelligent choice of vocation.

Total expense, for which the Association was responsible, was $560.13. This was increased to $694.50 for the second year.

On September 1, 1916, the Board of Education assumed entire control; the services of the bureau were confined almost entirely to the granting of employment certificates, and applicants for placement who were over twenty-one were sent to the Federal and Municipal Employment Bureau. The Health Supervision Department of the public schools was considered an important adjunct since a visit to that office "makes the youth realize that physical fitness is one of the first essentials to success." Part-time programs were arranged, usually on the basis of half the day for work and half for school, but a small group of boys worked alternate weeks. The director made a strong plea for employment supervision: "Those interested in the progress of vocational guidance in the United States are convinced that the supervision of the youth at work is a necessity for the protection of society, and is an important part of the educational system." [51]

Southern Cities

The most complete and authentic information on the history of organized guidance in southern cities is found in the report of a vocational survey of New Orleans conducted by David Spence Hill [52] together with

---

[50] The Vocation Bureau Under the Direction of the Association of Collegiate Alumnae, Omaha, *Summary of Work in 1916*.

[51] *Ibid.*

[52] *Vocational Survey for the Isaac Delgado Central Trades School* (2 pts.; New Orleans: Commission Council, 1916).

an address by Hill before the National Vocational Guidance Association, December, 1914.[53]

In search of a reply to the question, "What is being done about organized vocational guidance in the South?" Hill sent a letter of inquiry to forty-one superintendents in fourteen states. Fourteen superintendents replied; twelve indicated no definite effort was being made in the direction of organized guidance. Hill concluded that aside from New Orleans there was as yet little interest in such work. He quoted, however, several interesting comments which show that some rather keen thinking was being done on the subject.

Birmingham reported two committees: a Committee on Vocational Education, representing the United States Chamber of Commerce, held joint meetings with the Vocational Guidance Committee of the public schools. The superintendent considered the work of the latter committee

. . . exceedingly valuable, not simply in the way of securing information but in the practical assistance it has afforded hundreds of young people whose work in school, whose choice of studies and future lifework have been determined after serious consideration and consultation.

From Superintendent Horn of Houston, Texas, came the following:

I have always believed theoretically in the idea of vocational guidance, but I have never felt quite sure that the work has been so developed, up to the present, as to make it particularly valuable. In other words, we have been waiting for you, and some other gentlemen, to do a little more experimenting before our own city goes into it. I am interested in the subject, however, and should be glad to know anything that may be of value as to results obtained.

And from Little Rock, Arkansas:

We are studying the question thoroughly and shall be ready to make some recommendations later.

NEW ORLEANS

The primary concern of the Division of Educational Research of the Public Schools of New Orleans was the collection of information upon which to determine the needs of the city with reference to both vocational education and vocational guidance. Documentary evidence, furnished by Hill, indicates that in 1914 there was no separate bureau for vocational guidance, but for two years, under the auspices of the schools and with the co-operation of civic organizations, definite preliminary work had been done. Among other accomplishments directly connected with the

[53] "The Problems of Vocational Guidance in the South," *Proceedings of the Fourth National Conference of the National Vocational Guidance Association*, 1915, pp. 36–44.

guidance phase of the undertaking were the following: The Y.W.C.A. had published a booklet intended to help young women to suitable occupations; the Consumers' League had collected, for local use, data concerned with labor conditions; school surveys of various types for use in analyzing and meeting pupil and community needs were going on; and a psychological clinic pooling information secured from teacher, psychologist, social worker, and physician had demonstrated its effectiveness for a two-year period. Of the latter it was reported: "So far this laboratory method has been applied chiefly to exceptional children in an effort to determine their capacity for education and possible aptitudes for vocations."

In his address before the National Vocational Guidance Association, Hill warned against certain dangers which were apparent in the vocational guidance movement:

It is indeed a difficult matter either for an individual or an organization to guide human beings successfully into their life work, so manifold and elusive are individual differences, so spotted with shoals are economic opportunities, so inadequate our expensive, slow-moving educational machine . . . and so ignorant are we of human nature. It is a delusion to believe because a proposition seems logical that the conclusion will prove satisfactory when applied to the individual human organism. It is a question whether theoretical defective vocational guidance is harmful or worse than no guidance at all. On the other hand, our leaders and our efficient workers, many of them, have found their life work through the school of unchosen experience, that costliest of schools in which the survivors are a handful as compared with the multitudes who have succumbed to its curriculum. The waste of potential human productiveness, the presence of poverty, the absence of skill and knowledge in industry, the pretense in the professions, the misfits, and the wreckage of hopes, ambitions and love itself—some of these of late may be charged to the lack of organized vocational guidance, a necessity evoked by the complexity of our present civilization.

The report on the vocational survey contained a section, "Recommendations Concerning Vocational Guidance," which included a tentative but very complete plan for a "Cooperative Bureau of Vocations." There were two specific recommendations:

1. The facts of the report should be made the basis of further and carefully defined plans for vocational guidance, both formally by a Bureau of Vocational Guidance within the public schools and also informally as between parents, teachers, and boys.

2. Any serious student of this problem understands that such a bureau of Vocational Guidance demands the highest degree of skill and tact for its administration. It is far more than an "employment agency." Bloomfield, Leavitt, Richards, Book, Prosser, and others, have sufficiently indicated the scope and conduct of such organized work. . . . A scientific bureau would organize and promote the work of the placement of boys and girls over sixteen years of age in all of its phases, as: (1) Training for wise choice of occupation; (2) studying and disclos-

ing industrial, commercial and professional *opportunities;* (3) studying the individual's physical and mental *capacities and needs;* (4) *promoting vocational training* for successful occupation; (5) promoting cooperation between employers, employees and civic organizations.[54]

Additional comments on the type of individual not qualified to conduct a guidance service appeared at the close of Section III of Hill's plan:

With the recognition of the necessity of some kind of definite efforts at vocational guidance throughout the country certain dangers are apparent in the movement. In the first place there are *quacks* not remote in principles and practice from phrenologists, astrologers and fortune tellers. More reliable, but not good leaders, are the *illuminists* who, really understanding by investigation something of the problems and methods of good, organized guidance, nevertheless almost unconsciously come to pose as self-authorized authorities, speaking *ex cathedra*. Then there are the *amateurs* and *job-seekers*, who collecting bundles of questionnaires, card indices and notes at six-weeks summer schools, return to the grade of high school work of the local community, presently to appear as "lecturers" and even "specialists" and prospective directors and counselors for a local bureau.

CALIFORNIA

The general situation in California in the early period is described in the *Report of the Commissioner of Industrial and Vocational Education*, 1914–1916. Since many high schools failed to report on educational and vocational guidance, no statistical statement was made. Los Angeles, Oakland, and San Francisco, as well as many smaller cities, provided educational and vocational guidance, "the courses at San Jose and Pomona standing out most prominently." The Commissioner stressed the importance of educational guidance courses, maintaining that "vocational guidance when applied to one attending school always involves educational guidance." From his point of view, "there is probably more danger of getting lost in the maelstrom of the curriculum of the high school or college than there is of getting lost in the world of occupations."

Educational guidance courses are described. In content they are much like the more recent orientation courses with one recitation period per week for one semester. Courses in "life career study" are also mentioned. "These are usually credit courses utilizing one recitation daily for one semester." But class work is not sufficient:

Since only the most general information relating to occupations, individual capacities and the requirements for success in life may be attained through class instruction, individual study and individual counsel will be necessary to meet the needs of a majority of the pupils. . . . The term *vocational guidance* does not truly indicate the import of this subject. Knowledge, counsel and individual choice rather than guidance should control the selection of a vocation.

[54] Hill, *Vocational Survey*, pt. 2, pp. 298–302.

And again:

In a democracy the final choice of an occupation must rest with the one who would enter the same, and with no other.

The *Report* mentioned the great interest which had been aroused in the state, partially owing to summer courses for counselors which had been given for three consecutive years (the first two summers by Bloomfield at the University of California). Then very significantly the Commissioner commented: ". . . Vocational guidance as a propaganda has swept the state. On the other hand, vocational guidance as a practical subject is in its infancy."

SALT LAKE CITY

Salt Lake City is a good example of an early attempt to afford educational guidance through the introduction of a high-school advisory program.[55] This program was rather an innovation in 1909 although it is common today. The program was instituted by the high-school teachers with the "hearty concurrence of the Superintendent." A letter explaining the plan and its purpose was addressed to parents on March 29, 1909. Closer relationship between the home and school in order to serve pupils better was the purpose. Each teacher was assigned about twenty-five pupils, who became her special wards. By means of home visitation and personal conferences she was to ascertain all the facts necessary to a thorough understanding of each individual and, in co-operation with the parent, to act as a guide and counselor to the pupil in the pursuance of his high-school course.

SEATTLE

The first guidance venture in Seattle was, as in so many other cities, semiphilanthropic in origin. There was, however, one major difference which makes it desirable to include Seattle in this group of representative beginnings: the philanthropic element in the other cities was contributed by one or more civic organizations which assumed responsibility for the salaries of those engaged in the project; the Seattle project had no organized support; it was the result of educational initiative;[56] and the unremunerated service of the single worker supplied the philanthropic element.

The Experimental Seattle School Guidance Bureau, operating under the Board of Education, 1913–1916, was the outgrowth of the interest of Principal J. A. Reed and his wife, Anna Y. Reed, in the relationship which

[55] See the *Bulletin of the State University of Iowa*, n.s. no. 85, 1914; also a letter in the private files of the author.
[56] Office space and stenographic services were provided by the Board of Education.

might exist between school retardation and elimination, and truancy, delinquency, and later criminality. During 1906 and 1907 Mr. and Mrs. Reed were in New York City where discussion of many of the new psychological, sociological, and economic theories was centered and where considerable practical experimentation was going on. Mrs. Reed remained in the East until the fall of 1909 when she returned to Seattle and at once instituted the series of research projects which led to the survey of 1913 and the establishment of a bona fide school bureau in 1916.

The first investigation was a case study of 1800 youths who for one reason or another had been brought before the King County Juvenile Court. Analysis of these cases revealed that in an alarming number of instances there was a direct line of progression in the direction of criminality: school failure and retardation were accompanied by truancy and minor delinquencies; school elimination was followed by repeated shifts in employment, unemployment, and increasingly serious delinquencies; appearance before the Juvenile Court, sometimes several appearances, was accompanied by repeated probation and eventually commitment to the city parental school. This exhausted the city's correctional resources, but state facilities comprised an industrial school, a reformatory for young men, and a penitentiary. Sometimes each in turn registered the same individual.

The findings of this study aroused the interest of Governor Hay, who was legitimately proud of the state institutions and much interested in enhancing their correctional value, while Superintendent Cooper, of Seattle, was quick to grasp the import of the neglected responsibilities of education as revealed by the study. Both officials requested Mrs. Reed to continue her work in the areas under their respective jurisdictions. Both requests were complied with as an unremunerated public service.

The second study was made as the personal representative of the governor. It involved a case study of all the records for, supplemented by one or more personal interviews with, each inmate of each of the three state correctional institutions. The objectives were: (1) to determine the extent of recidivism and, so far as possible, its causal factors and (2) to ascertain what additional educational facilities and service the state should provide and how it might improve its correctional procedures. Two reports were published by the state, one in 1911 and the other in 1912. Many inadequacies in the home, school, and community were revealed, and several suggestions for change in institutional procedures were acted upon.

The third investigation was undertaken in 1913 and was conducted under the auspices of the Seattle Board of Education. Its findings and recommendations were published in two special reports in addition to brief interim reports included in the annual reports of the superintendent of schools. The first special report [57] was a survey similar in character to other early vocational guidance surveys. It revealed three definite lines in which the school product was found to be deficient: academic knowledge, character qualities, and personality including personal hygiene, courtesy, and refinement in speech and manner. Superintendent Cooper expressed the hope that the findings of the report would help the schools to minister more suitably to youth while in school and would lead to the conclusion "that the protection and supervision of the educator should follow the working child into his new surroundings and help in the solution of the problems involved in his daily life."

The questions to which the second school study sought replies were: Is vocational guidance in connection with the school system desirable? What should be its aims and methods? How should it be organized and how related to the established lines of education?

The interim report of April, 1916, covered the first question and it was immediately answered in the affirmative by the decision of the board to establish a department of vocational guidance in connection with the educational system, the expense of such a bureau to be a legitimate charge against the school budget. The other questions to which the second study sought replies were answered in detail in the report published by the board, November, 1916.[58] A few statements from the section, "Aims and Methods of Vocational Guidance," throw light upon the status of both theory and practice in 1916:

Vocational guidance is a bit of new and popular phraseology which carries with it a variety of meanings and is open to a variety of interpretations.

In the minds of some it is an indefinite something which is too intangible to attempt to define, much less to utilize. It is something to be avoided. In the minds of others it is decidedly definite but means nothing more scientific than free employment. Somewhere between these two extremes there is to be found a logical, purposeful, vocational guidance program which will sooner or later be incorporated in our educational system.

. . . The *aim* of vocational guidance is to give the pupil a better understanding of himself and of the world in which he lives; to open his eyes to the opportunities of life and help him to prepare for the field in which he can render his best service; to develop his judgment so that he may reason clearly and logically on the relationship between himself and his environment. In other words it has been my constant policy to guide pupils to *find* themselves so that at maturity they may know how to *guide* themselves.

[57] Anna Y. Reed, *Seattle Children in School and in Industry* (Seattle: Board of School Directors, 1915).

[58] Anna Y. Reed, *Vocational Guidance Report, 1913–1916* (Seattle: Board of School Directors, 1916).

The best *methods* of vocational guidance are still to be developed. Up to date we have depended upon individual rather than general methods, which, in order to bring success must be based upon a logical combination of two things—correct psychological interpretation of the aptitudes and abilities of the individual concerned and correct sociological interpretation of his social, civic and industrial environment.

Type of pupils and the material part of the method employed may be explained, but explanation of that part of method which is due to personal contact between mind and mind, to individual interpretation of another's motives, abilities and ambitions, and that subtle influence which can often create ambitions and develop abilities where none exist, is far in the future. It is a matter of personality and can neither be explained nor taught.[59]

Educational guidance and vocational guidance were both specifically dealt with in this report.

[59] *Ibid.,* pp. 13–14.

CHAPTER II

Guidance and Personnel Services on the College Level

THE introduction of organized guidance into the field of higher education must be attributed to somewhat different causes than those that were found in connection with its origin for the noncollege groups.

The sociological theory, which found practical expression in philanthropic bureaus designed to serve underprivileged youth, was of comparatively little importance on the college level although "Student Aid" was fairly common and the occupational surveys made by the Association of Collegiate Alumnae were expected to enlarge occupational prospects for women. Service to college men and women rather than philanthropy was the controlling motive. The psychological factor was also less dominant on the college level. This was logical since in its initial investigations the psychology of individual differences was concerned primarily with substandard youth. The sifting process, involving individual interest in college work, financial ability to attend college, and the ability to furnish acceptable admission credentials, kept the college group without the purview of the psychologist until the findings relative to the biologically and economically handicapped groups pointed to the desirability of the inclusion of the more privileged group. It must not be overlooked, however, that quite some time before the beginnings of organized guidance had attained the status of personnel service, here and there in the history of higher education statements are found which prophesy a day when the services of clinical psychology will be available for all students and which indicate that such an innovation will be welcome to college authorities. Perhaps President Harper, of the University of Chicago, most forcefully uttered this prophecy and the importance of its fulfillment.

This [the scientific study of the student] will be made (1) with special reference to his character . . . to find out whether he is responsible or careless, or shiftless, or perhaps vicious; (2) with special reference likewise to his intellectual capacity; (3) with reference to his special intellectual characteristics to learn whether he is independent or original; (4) with reference to his special capacities and tastes; (5) with reference to the social side of his nature.[1]

[1] *The Trend in Higher Education* (Chicago: University of Chicago Press, 1905), p. 320.

This feature of twentieth-century college education will come to be regarded as of greatest importance, and fifty years hence will prevail as widely as it is now lacking. It is the next step in the evolution of the principle of individualism, and its application will, in due time, introduce order and system into our educational work, where now only chaos is to be found.[2]

A third difference between the origin of the college and the noncollege movement is found in their geographical confines. The practical application of newly crystallized psychological, sociological, and economic theories on the noncollege level was international in scope: the majority of the civilized nations of the world, 1900–1908, were interested in practical experimentation. So far as this writer has been able to ascertain, student personnel service on the college level, as it has developed in the United States, has no counterpart in the universities of the Old World. It originated in the United States and has been confined to the United States.[3]

In addition to differences in the origin and purposes of guidance service for college and noncollege groups, there are also interesting differences, and some similarities, in the origin and purposes of such services for college men and for college women.

GUIDANCE FOR COLLEGE WOMEN

Guidance efforts in the interest of college women were fostered by two specific groups and for entirely different purposes. One group was within the institutions, the other without. The former consisted of authorities in charge of men's institutions to which women, immediately after the War between the States, were seeking admission in increasing numbers. As expansion of coeducation seemed inevitable, especially in the state universities of the West, administrative authorities openly voiced their concern for the social, moral, and physical welfare of women were the doors of men's universities to be opened to them. By intercommunication they sought to secure administrative opinion relative to the probable dangers and the best methods of forestalling the undesirable results which they anticipated. Official reports afford a variety of statements some of which are full of humor for the reader of today, although they filled the authorities with fears and misgivings in the late 1850's and the 1860's.[4] President

[2] *Ibid.*, p. 325.

[3] See James F. Findlay, *The Origin and Development of the Work of the Dean of Men in Higher Education* (unpublished thesis, New York University, 1940), pp. 84–90.

[4] See "Report on the Admission of Females," Sept. 29, 1858, in *Proceedings of the Board of Regents, University of Michigan*, 1858. Those who desire additional information and do not have access to the original, see Lulu Holmes, *A History of the Position of Dean of Women in a Selected Group of Co-educational Colleges and Universities in the United States* (New York: Teachers College, Columbia University, 1939), pp. 5–7.

Hopkins, of Williams, thought "the difficulty would be social"; Horace Mann, of Antioch, was forced to admit that "the dangers of it are terrible"; while President Finney, of Oberlin, suggested, "You will need a wise and pious matron with such lady assistants as to keep up sufficient supervision. . . ."

The doors began to open. The first solution of the administrator's problem was the Lady Principal, Warden, Lady Assistant, Matron, or the like, who had full supervision of the social life of the students, their physical well-being, and their general welfare. Lady Principals and others of the same genus were forerunners of Advisers and Deans of Women. They were employed primarily to help solve the administrator's problems. By 1900 the influx of students with variegated cultural backgrounds and a multiplicity of motives for college attendance, the inadequate housing facilities, the increasing importance of social activities, and the smörgåsbord menu of college catalogues had enhanced the complexities incident to the "welfare of women." The times demanded a new type of Lady Principal. The transition was gradual, the functions frequently being the same as those performed prior to the change of title, but the modern story of the Dean of Women began with the use of the new title —at Chicago in 1892 and at Michigan in 1896. In 1903 the first national convention was called and eighteen members attended.[5] The demand for deans increased rapidly after 1913, and it seems justifiable to assume that the needs of the students had become an equal if not more important factor than the needs of the administrator. True to their original purpose, however, deans are still expected to handle, according to the most recent studies, educational problems, disciplinary duties, and extracurricular activities.

The second significant effort in the direction of special guidance services for college women had as its immediate concern vocational and educational rather than social objectives. It originated with the Association of Collegiate Alumnae. This organization has been mentioned among the civic and philanthropic agencies which participated in the establishment of certain local vocation bureaus, later taken over by public-school systems. Its interest in the guidance movement, however, did not originate in the field of public education. Some years before the earliest record of either philanthropic or public-school activity, this organization had been actively interested in the vocational and educational problems of college women

[5] See Mary Ross Potter, "History of Conferences of Deans of Women to the Organization of the National Association in 1917," Fourteenth Yearbook of the National Association of Deans of Women, 1927, pp. 212–227.

and it had attacked several phases of modern personnel work through the avenue of surveys.[6]

Activity between 1882, the date of the birth of the Association, and 1900 was concentrated on securing facts relative to three questions brought to the fore by the increasing tendency to admit women to college on the same basis as men: Were women physically capable of meeting college requirements? Did college education unfit women for homemaking? Were women intellectually capable of mastering collegiate requirements?

The Association went about its task in a thoroughgoing manner. By 1890 it had completed a full series of surveys on college elimination, occupational distribution, training and employment opportunities, and health. The occupational distribution survey of 1894 found that 451 college women were distributed among 68 different occupations. These early surveys indicated the direction in which educational and vocational guidance service should proceed.

Between 1890 and 1910 such topics as Occupational Guidance through Curricula Selection and Adjustment, Occupational Information upon Which to Base Vocational Choice, Wage Scales Per Se and in Comparison with Men, Analysis of Labor Turnover, Establishment of Placement Bureaus, etc., received major attention. The Women's Educational and Industrial Union of Boston published *Vocations for the Trained Woman* in 1910. The same year a Committee on Vocational Opportunities was organized under the leadership of Elizabeth Kemper Adams.

Collegiate bureaus of occupations were encouraged and frequently subsidized.[7] The best known of these bureaus were: The Bureau of Vocational Information, New York City, with which both Emma Hirth and Beatrice Doerschuk were connected; The Women's Educational and Industrial Union of Boston of which Florence Jackson was long the director; The Collegiate Bureau of Occupations of Chicago, usually thought of in connection with the name of Helen Bennett; The Southern Women's Educational Alliance of Richmond with O. Latham Hatcher in charge. Denver, Minneapolis, Philadelphia, Cleveland, Kansas City, Los Angeles, and Pittsburgh also supported such bureaus. On regular schedule or by special invitation speakers were sent out from these bureaus to conduct confer-

[6] See Bertha M. Scullin, *The Contribution of the American Association of University Women to the Development of Vocational Guidance for College Women* (unpublished thesis, University of Chicago, 1923).

[7] This chain of collegiate bureaus formed what was known as the Intercollegiate Bureaus of Occupations, and considerable attention was given to their activities in the current journals of the Association. While the majority did not survive their World War I experiences, a number are still functioning successfully.

ences and act as visiting counselors for colleges in their vicinity. They prepared and distributed vocational information circulars and did excellent placement work when placement was included among their functions. It was with much regret that those who had been closely connected with their objectives and accomplishments saw them, after the United States entered World War 1, absorbed into the Women's Division of the United States Employment Service and discarded with that agency in the postwar federal house cleaning.[8]

The Association, as an organization, has made comparatively little contribution to vocational guidance service since 1915. In evaluating its early service one is impressed with the fact that it originally attacked a specialized guidance problem. One problem led to another, the scope of its interest broadening to meet the needs revealed, until, in the progressive development of its service, it had made a definite contribution to every area of guidance. Its work was efficiently planned and well carried out, and its contributions have had a lasting influence on personnel service for college women.

GUIDANCE FOR COLLEGE MEN [9]

Those who are familiar with the general outline of higher education on both continents will remember that guidance was an undifferentiated educational service in medieval universities; that the development of the whole man, his moral, social, emotional, and spiritual, as well as his intellectual qualities, was a responsibility of the university and an obvious essential to a complete education.

A similar pattern of inherent guidance services is found in connection with the development of early collegiate institutions in the United States. The number of students was comparatively small; vocational outlets for college men were few and well known; and vocational choice was usually a precollege decision, its fulfillment the reason for college attendance. The elective system was unknown; departmental hawkers had not yet cast their shadow over the educational world; and both student personnel and faculty personnel comprised a single sex. Under such conditions it was relatively easy for students with serious intellectual interests and definite vocational goals to secure presidential or faculty advice in attaining their goals and, at the same time, to receive the sort of intangible guidance which contributed mightily to the education of the whole man.

[8] See the *Journal of the Association of Collegiate Alumnae: The News Letter*, XIII (Nov., 1919), p. III.

[9] The thesis of James F. Findlay, previously referred to, is the best single source for material on the origin and development of the office of Dean of Men.

But changes in the social and economic life of the United States brought changes in the college atmosphere, accompanied by changes in student-faculty relationships, and these changes, in their turn, called attention to the desirability of more adequate provision for the individual needs of the student body. The major factors which were fundamental causes of these changes were common to all types of colleges, segregated as well as coeducational. Among them may be mentioned: (1) the influx of students from different cultural backgrounds and with widely divergent objectives, (2) the lack of predetermined vocational goals at a time when individual responsibility for choice of electives was paralleled by wider opportunities for vocational choice, (3) the expansion of fraternity and other extraclassroom activities, (4) inadequate housing facilities, (5) subject departmentalization and faculty specialization which tended to lessen the value of faculty members as advisers, and (6) the increase in class size with sufficient divergence in interests and abilities of students to require concentration on their intellectual development to the neglect of the development of other qualities formerly deemed an essential part of education.

Organized guidance service was one of the special provisions instituted to meet the demands of the new conditions prevalent in college circles, especially in the rapidly growing state universities of the West which, by virtue of public support, were practically always coeducational. Service was instituted on a sex basis—a woman serving women and a man serving men—although in the early history of the movement the officials did not often recognize the needs of men and of women at the same time. Surveys of the beginnings and development of this form of educational service reveal some interesting similarities and some equally interesting dissimilarities in the movement as it affected women and men.

One similarity of importance is found in the single broad purpose of guidance service. It was, and is, generally agreed that the object of all student personnel work, whether in the interests of one sex or the other, is service to the individual in all the areas of life, with a major responsibility to effect such co-ordination of educational services as promises to result in integration of personality and in the balanced development of the whole man.

A second similarity is found in the fairly common use of "Dean" to designate the official in charge of student personnel work, variations in usage being more common with reference to men than with reference to women. "Dean" is an inheritance from the past.[10] In the course of history it has, at various times, been used with a military, civil, ecclesiastical, or

[10] *Ibid.*, pp. 15–17.

educational significance, but it has always connoted authority—authority over the group concerned. The original occasion for the introduction of the term into the vocabulary of higher education in the United States was the increased volume of registration which necessitated relief for the presidential load. Administrative duties were divided, and the dean of the college assumed part of the responsibilities. Sometimes, indeed usually, guidance of students, which had been an inherent responsibility of the president, fell to the lot of the new dean, where it was still regarded as an inherent responsibility. When further subdivision of responsibilities occurred, it often happened that the supervision of student relationships was the major function allotted to one person. It was logical that "Dean" should be a part of this one person's title regardless of the qualifying phrase—"of students," "of men," "of student affairs," and the like. The Dean of Women arrived at her designation earlier in point of time and by a somewhat shorter route. There was no gradual or intermediate subdivision and delegation of responsibilities. With the first appointment of a Lady Principal, the president automatically delegated functions which were administrative, authoritative, and advisory, and with the change in title these duties were passed on to the Dean of Women.

A third similarity is found in the hybrid character of the functions performed. Since presidents are essentially administrators, even though they may perform a variety of functions which are not administrative in character, it was quite natural that there should have been no clear-cut classification of their various responsibilities. It was equally logical that, when the time came for division of responsibilities, the sharing official should be given an administrative title with hybrid functions.[11] In this one procedure may be found the roots of the "rather illy coordinated functions" mentioned by Dean Coulter at the 1937 meeting of the National Association of Deans and Advisers of Men.[12]

Certain dissimilarities in origin and development help to explain divergencies in present-day viewpoints, practices, and results:

(1) When a coeducational institution opened its doors to women, there was immediate need for the appointment of a lady principal or dean. Such appointments were regarded by college alumnae as a major step forward in the direction of equality of opportunity for women. There was no such specific causal factor influencing the appointment of deans

[11] For a list of twenty-three activities included in student personnel service, see *The Student Personnel Point of View* (American Council on Education Studies, ser. I, vol. I, no. 3; Washington, 1937), pp. 3–4.

[12] *Secretarial Notes: Nineteenth Annual Conference*, p. 40.

of men. The demand came slowly; appointments were neither heralded abroad nor was there any organization similar to the Association of Collegiate Alumnae which actively interested itself in forcing the appointment of such officials as a condition of "accreditment." The men's movement developed more slowly and had a better chance to grow up.

(2) The dean of women came into the college picture as an administrative officer. She inherited disciplinary responsibilities as well as the rights and privileges of inherent guidance. The students had no voice in the matter and in some cases were outspoken in their resentment of the assumption that women were in need of a special caretaker. The administrative, authoritative, and disciplinary aspect of the dean's work was so definitely in the foreground of everyone's consciousness that it seriously handicapped her effectiveness as a counselor. The dean of men came into the picture under more auspicious conditions. During the transition from sole dependence upon inherent guidance to definite provision for personnel service, voluntary service had been so ably carried on by men whose personalities peculiarly fitted them for such service that the confidence of the students was already won. There is abundant evidence to indicate that "the demands of the students for a dean" were voiced fully as audibly as was the call of administration for relief.[13] Therefore the men's movement was more definitely a personnel movement with emphasis on student counseling rather than on student control.

(3) The dean of men, almost without exception, came from within the faculty;[14] the dean of women, of necessity, came from without the institution. The potentialities of the dean of women were always a question; the effectiveness of the dean of men was tested before appointment. History has placed too many names on the roster of student-favored deans to require laboring this point: Briggs of Harvard is there, Clark of Illinois, Straub of Oregon who performed the duties unofficially from 1878 to 1920, Coulter of Purdue, and Goodnight of Wisconsin. President Eliot in his characterization of Dean Briggs has given an admirable description of these unofficial advisers who were serving students in the areas of life no longer automatically included in university responsibilities and at the same time laying the foundation for the type of personnel service which advised with students rather than controlled students:

I had discovered that he possessed a high honesty, a readiness to give himself to others, and a certain charming kindliness of character which made men at ease in his presence and encouraged them to be confidential with him. . . . I feel

[13] Findlay, *op. cit.*, p. 47.
[14] *Ibid.*, p. 91.

sure, however, that my chief reason for appointing him was this: I had discovered that students were going to him for counsel on every kind of problem, and I thought they might keep on going to him, even if he was the dean.[15]

Students whose primary interest lies in the field of college personnel work may supplement this brief overview of the beginnings of organized work with a study of various types of surveys such as the Stanford series of 1911, 1912, and 1913; with analysis of the activities of faculty, alumni, and student committees; and with recommendations for the establishment of collegiate personnel services in the various areas of life. They may also continue their study of the history of the movement by means of the reference list which follows Part I.

[15] R. W. Brown, *Dean Briggs* (New York: Harper and Bros., 1926), p. 197.

CHAPTER III

Organizations Interested in Guidance and Personnel Services

IT WOULD be impossible to mention all the agencies which made contributions to the beginnings of organized guidance services in these United
States. As our story has progressed, attention has been called to several
agencies which fostered, and sometimes subsidized, local guidance efforts,
e.g., the National Child Labor Committee, the National Consumers
League, the National League of Compulsory Education Officials,[1] chambers of commerce, and women's clubs. The Y.M.C.A. and the Y.W.C.A.
made important practical contributions on the youth and adult level and
in the college field. Another group of organizations closely related to, marginal to, or dealing with some specific phase of guidance includes among
others the National Committee for Mental Hygiene, the National Association of Visiting Teachers, the American Child Health Association, the
National Education Association, and the American Association of Public
Employment Offices. Three types of agencies which have maintained a
more or less continuous interest in the progress of guidance and personnel
and which are bound to be so intimately associated in the future advancement of the movement that close co-ordination of their activities is of
paramount importance will be specifically discussed.

THE NATIONAL EDUCATION ASSOCIATION

Examination of the *Proceedings and Addresses* of the National Education Association covering a long period of years reveals a sporadic rather
than a continuously sustained interest in or support of the movement.
President Eliot's address, "The Value During Education of the Life-
Career Motive," was delivered at the annual meeting of the Association in Boston, July, 1910.[2] This meeting antedated by a few months the
first national conference on vocational guidance which met in the same
city. Since there was no widespread knowledge of the guidance objective
at this date, it may be assumed that Eliot's address represented his own

---

[1] Now known as the National League to Promote School Attendance.

[2] As previously noted, it was restated in November before the National Conference
on Vocational Guidance.

previously expressed viewpoint on education and the co-operative interest of all agencies in Boston rather than particular interest on the part of
the National Education Association.

By 1912 the first wave of national interest was at its peak and the N.E.A.
program at Chicago reflected this interest. Jesse B. Davis made two addresses. Reporting on the Grand Rapids program in an address entitled
"Vocational and Moral Guidance through English Composition in the
High School," Davis indicated that from his point of view vocational
guidance meant the gradual unfolding of the pupil's better understanding of himself and assistance of the pupil in selecting and preparing for
his own best field of service as a social being. His second address, "The
Use of the Library in Vocational Guidance," aroused considerable interest
among both educators and librarians. Charles A. Prosser spoke before
the Industrial Education Section on "Vocational Guidance." Prosser cited
two essentials in any plan for vocational guidance; a greater knowledge
of the child and a close co-operation with agencies outside the school.
Frank M. Leavitt, of the University of Chicago, and John C. Brodhead,
of Boston, participated in the discussion. Meyer Bloomfield spoke on the
guidance program in Boston and stressed once more that "decision must
come from within." A Committee on Vocational Education and Vocational
Guidance was appointed at this meeting.

In 1913 the N.E.A. met in Salt Lake City and the Committee made a
tentative report. A subcommittee to make a special study of vocational
guidance was appointed. It was comprised of Meyer Bloomfield as vice-
chairman, Edith Campbell, Alice Barrows, James Hiatt, and Jesse B.
Davis.[3] G. P. Knox spoke on "How Should the School System Contribute
to an Intelligent Choice of Vocation on the Part of the Pupil?" Once again
prominence was given to the undesirability of attempting to determine a
pupil's choice rather than of assisting him to choose intelligently. While
Knox stated that experience only would give the necessary wisdom to conduct vocational guidance, he made a number of suggestions which he
felt were essential to success. Among them were the following: The child
must be considered physically, mentally, and temperamentally. The environment must always be investigated. Vocational guidance must be
linked up with other directive forces, and since there should be no duplication of effort, it should be directed by one person. Guidance was a matter
of education as well as of information. The counselor should be the
teacher, either the one in the classroom or the principal. The consultation

[3] In 1921 when the author was making a determined effort to collect historical material
covering the early period of the guidance movement, she could learn of no action or
report by this committee though she searched the records and interviewed its members.

must always be individual in character, and the parents must be reached.

Following the 1913 meeting interest in vocational guidance, as evidenced by N.E.A. programs, declined. Major spokesmen for the movement did not attend the 1914 meeting. Its outstanding advocate at the 1915 session was Frank E. Spaulding, of Minneapolis. Interest was at low ebb in 1916 and few of the leaders were in attendance. In 1917 the author was the most prominent representative of the movement present. "Guidance" did not again appear on N.E.A. programs until 1920, when Frank M. Leavitt, Associate Superintendent of Schools, Pittsburgh, representing the Junior Division of the United States Employment Service, spoke on "Vocational Guidance and Placement." Leavitt's theme was the necessity for an efficient placement service in connection with public-school guidance services.

A number of factors contributed to the short-lived interest of the National Education Association in the vocational guidance movement. Without going into detail, for the ramifications are many, perhaps the most logical explanation is to be found in the fact that in its organization year, 1913, and in the years immediately following, the National Vocational Guidance Association was more closely affiliated with the activities of the National Society for the Promotion of Industrial Education than with agencies primarily concerned with traditional education. There is considerable evidence to support such an interpretation in spite of the fact that there is equally reliable evidence that the National Society did little or nothing to foster the guidance movement.

The recently renewed and much more active interest of the N.E.A. in guidance and personnel, especially on the secondary level, has received considerable publicity and may well be studied by educators who desire to connect the early history of its efforts with its present activities.[4]

BUSINESS ORGANIZATIONS

Changes in our social and industrial organization which played so large a part in focusing the attention of education and philanthropy upon the need for organized guidance were also responsible for calling the attention of employers to the desirability of more practical education, of provision for guidance in the selection of training programs, and for improvement in methods of employee selection. In several cities chambers of commerce instituted, or co-operated in instituting, public-school guid-

[4] U. S. Office of Education, *Occupational Information and Guidance Service 1941–42* (Misc. 2913; Washington, [1942]). This is a four-page leaflet which gives full information on the Service and its program, a list of states having guidance officials in state departments, and a list of publications.

ance bureaus. Boston, Chicago, Buffalo, Cleveland, and Minneapolis furnish examples of active and effective interest on the part of businessmen's organizations.

The National Society for the Promotion of Industrial Education, organized in 1907, was an employer movement in the interests of more practical and more purposeful public education. The organization was the direct result of the Massachusetts Industrial Survey of 1905, the findings of which when published in 1906 had aroused the interest of both educator and employer. The activities of the Society included a number of vocational surveys emphasizing job analysis and job specification. Publication of the results of these surveys made a valuable contribution to available vocational information. But the major purpose of the organization was to secure the enactment of federal legislation which would foster vocational education. This objective was achieved with the passage of the Smith-Hughes Bill in 1917. Alvin Dodd, now president of the American Management Association, was secretary of the Society and largely responsible for the efficiency with which its affairs were conducted.

It took the National Society for the Promotion of Industrial Education ten years to get legislation which provided for vocational training under the auspices of public education. Ad interim, through the medium of another organization, employers who were training or were planning to train their own employees made another attempt to improve vocational efficiency within their own domain and to influence courses in educational institutions in such a manner that they might more fully meet the needs of industry. The National Association of Corporation Schools was formed at a conference of representatives of such schools at Dayton, Ohio, in 1913. A Committee on Vocational Guidance was chosen, and its report, well worth reading, was published in 1916.[5]

PUBLIC EMPLOYMENT OFFICES

In contrast to the lagging interest of the National Education Association, which appears to have been somewhat derelict in grasping the possibilities of the guidance movement, employment agencies, both public and philanthropic, made larger contributions to the practical application of guidance principles than has usually been recognized by educators. Perhaps this was due to the fact that the initial years of the guidance movement were concurrent with the years of aggressive interest in the betterment of humanity by means of legislative enactments. Child-labor laws, which legislated youth out of industry, combined with compulsory

[5] "Report of Committee on Vocational Guidance," in the National Association of Corporation Schools, *Proceedings of Fourth Annual Convention*, 1916, pp. 273–468.

education laws to legislate youth into school. These enactments received the unquestioning approval of educators, who challenged the desirability of "placement" as an invitation to law evasion. Lest there may be some carry-over of this feeling, a few historical facts are presented to give placement its legitimate position in the guidance picture.

The American Association of Public Employment Offices was organized in 1913, the year of the organization of the National Vocational Guidance Association. The list of members enrolled in the one compares very favorably, intellectually and professionally, with the list enrolled in the other, while the annual proceedings of the former, in comparison with those of the latter, reveal that employment officials were much more concerned with the social waste and the social danger connected with the "school discard" than were the schools themselves. The Massachusetts Employment Law was passed in 1906, and at the very first national meeting in 1913 Walter Sears advocated state provision for "minors with a vocational counselor in charge."

In 1914 the Cleveland City-State Employment Bureau made special provision for vocational guidance and placement of juniors. And in May, 1914, W. M. Leiserson, Superintendent of Wisconsin Employment Offices, stated that public employment experience indicated two major classes of maladjusted workers, unguided school children and immigrants.

Quotations from the *Annual Proceedings* of the organization for 1913, 1914, and 1915 reveal that attempts to meet the emergency demands of the educational discard were affording a practical basis upon which public employment officials were working out the fundamental principles of guidance and placement:

If the job is a preparatory school for more responsible work, it would be a mistake to put into it a man who is incapable of learning to do the more difficult work. The man should not be sacrificed to the job nor the job to the man.

In the first place so very many workers are so poorly equipped to earn their living and are in such a discontented and unsettled state that it is almost impossible to keep them employed in one place for any length of time. The need of vocational guidance for the young is clearly shown every day in our work.

Ohio is the first state that has gone so far as to recognize the value of vocational guidance and to try a plan of combining the State-City labor exchange of Cleveland with the vocational guidance bureau operating under the commissioner of labor and the industrial commission.

The young clerical workers without any experience or training are a more hopeless proposition. Feeling themselves superior to factory work, and yet unprepared either in education or special training for any office work, they are almost impossible to place. Some few can, after much persuasion, be directed into the lighter kinds of factory work, but there is still a great oversupply of these clerical workers. Perhaps the schools are somewhat to blame for laying greater emphasis upon the dignity of mental labor than upon that of manual labor. Perhaps also some would be deflected from this overcrowded field if they knew more about the small chance ahead for the unskilled clerical worker, who can hardly expect a brighter future than the most unskilled factory worker.

In 1918 a study of public employment offices, undertaken by the Bureau of Labor Statistics in 1915, was published.[6] This study recognized the existence of school bureaus and gave a brief account of the work under way in Chicago and Philadelphia. One paragraph is indicative of the narrow vision which influenced the original practices of school bureaus:

When an application for help is received which is found to offer no possibility of advancement for the boy or girl who might be sent to fill it, or if the opportunity for employment is not the kind of work or trade that will help the child's chance for a future, the application is referred to the juvenile department of the Illinois Free Employment Bureau. There is no sort of cooperation between this office and any commercial bureau.

The *Proceedings of the American Association of Public Employment Offices* for 1916 comprised ninety-two pages. Twenty pages were devoted to four addresses on guidance and placement: Alvin E. Dodd, "Vocational Education and Juvenile Placement Departments"; W. W. Zurbrick, "Vocational Guidance as a Public School Function"; Rachel Gallagher, "Vocational Guidance and the Juvenile Placement Work of a Public Labor Exchange"; and G. D. Halsey, "Cooperation between Employers and the Schools in Vocational Guidance."

One should not close the story of the various agencies which participated in the beginnings of organized guidance in the United States without some reference to the juvenile court movement. Interest in juvenile delinquents who appeared before juvenile courts in Seattle and Chicago has been previously mentioned as a spur to local guidance efforts. The year 1899 marks the beginning of legislative recognition of juvenile delinquencies as maladjustments to be solved by educational rather than by criminal procedures, although the instrumentality for carrying forward these procedures was judicial rather than educational. Students of the cases coming before the juvenile courts in this early period were agreed that many maladjustments which originated in the home, school, or community came to a focus during initial work experiences. They also agreed that sympathetically directed work experience was a desirable medium through which adjustments might be satisfactorily accomplished. But the schools did not consider work experience as a part of education, hence

---

6 John G. Herndon, Jr., *Public Employment Offices in the United States* (Bulletin of the U. S. Bureau of Labor Statistics, no. 241, Employment and Unemployment series; Washington, 1918).

placement offices, public and philanthropic, were called upon to care for the court discard as well as for the school discard. One very significant report is quoted:

An agency of no small importance engaged in the distribution of labor in Indianapolis is the employment bureau of the Children's Aid Association. This bureau grew out of the juvenile court, and its first work was securing positions for boys on probation. It now finds positions for children of both sexes from 14 to 21 years of age. It investigates positions very thoroughly, the manager visiting all factories, stores, etc., before children are placed in them. She also visits the homes of children in order to become acquainted with their needs and capabilities. The children's bureau has the confidence of employers, many of whom rely upon it entirely for boys needed.[7]

In 1909 this bureau placed 500 youths; in 1911 the total was 1191.

[7] F. B. Sargent, *Statistics of Unemployment and the Work of Employment Offices* (U. S. Labor Bureau Bulletin, no. 109, misc. ser. 1; Washington, 1913), p. 45.

CHAPTER IV

Interpretative Summary of Source Material

EVIDENCE has been submitted which indicates that all geographical sections of the United States, all levels of the educational system, and various types of organized groups—educational, philanthropic, civic, and business—were sharing in a world-wide movement which was the outgrowth of the crystallization of certain sociological and psychological theories, and of interest in their practical application. Among the several forms in which practical experimentation was attempted, one was designated "Vocational Guidance."

The first wave of interest in vocational guidance began about 1900, reached its crest between 1908–1912, and then, during World War I when interest was centered on other objectives, was largely static. Thus it is justifiable to assign the beginnings of organized guidance to the years 1900–1916 and to consider these years a logical first period in the history of the organized guidance movement.

The topical and interpretative summary which follows will, it is hoped, afford a general picture of the status of the movement in 1916 and at the same time furnish basic facts for clearer understanding of its development during the later periods of its history.

TIME AND PLACE OF FIRST EXPERIMENTATION. Sufficient evidence has been presented to discredit the statement that vocational guidance began in 1908 in Boston, or in New York, or in any other city at any specific time. The decade from 1900 to 1910 witnessed several local beginnings, but no evidence has as yet been uncovered to validate the claim of any specific city to being the first. Careless repetition of the statement that "Boston was the first" merely because it was widely publicized first, or first used the phrase, "vocational guidance," has resulted in the multiplication of errors without the establishment of fact.

MOTIVATION. Two major sources of motivation have been revealed— the one humanitarian, the other civic betterment, which in some instances was characterized by self-interest on the part of the agencies concerned.

NOMENCLATURE. The social sciences have the misfortune to possess no technical vocabulary. Guidance shares in this misfortune. In recent

years, therefore, it has offered a tempting battleground for verbal con-
flicts which, thus far, have been either futile or confusing rather than
clarifying. The *casus belli* is inherent in the terminology usages of this
early period. The terms found in the sources studied in Chapter I are
"vocational guidance," "educational guidance," "guidance," "social guid-
ance," "health guidance," "moral guidance," and "character guidance." [1]
"Vocational adjustment," "vocational advice," "vocational supervision,"
and "vocational direction" were also used. The terms used to designate individuals who performed guidance services were "dean," "adviser," "counselor," "educational counselor," "vocational counselor," "homerooom
teacher," "teacher-adviser," and "teachers of vocational guidance," the
last found but once and that in the Chicago call for an examination for
such officials in 1913.

The evidence indicates that "vocational guidance" rather than "guidance" was the parent name, and that Parsons was the first to use the term
to characterize services which had been going forward simultanously in
several cities. As time passed and the use of modifiers with the word "guidance" increased, some who felt that this use of a phrase expressive of only
one aspect of guidance as a substitute for or as synonymous with the more
general term "guidance" was illogical advocated certain changes in usage.
They supported their contention by expressing fears lest the continued
differentiation of areas might result in the disintegration of services, failure to co-ordinate findings relative to individuals, and ultimate disintegration of personalities.

Others desired to retain the original phrase, in what they considered
to be its original connotation, indicating that "vocational guidance" had
enough adjustment responsibility in its own area without attempting to
function in all the other areas. They also felt that the use of a modifier to
indicate that some specific area was of immediate concern or was the major
field in which an organization was prepared to offer services was legitimate,
provided it was recognized that any area of guidance must of necessity
be more or less concerned with the whole man and that no definite line
of demarcation could completely set off one area of service from other
areas. Still others have watched with some uneasiness the taking over of
this original expression by every conceivable commercial agency and its

---

[1] "Personnel service" is a war-period expression. "Guidance counselor" and "clinical
guidance counselor" are awkward and indefensible combinations of terms which have
characterized recent years. "Individualized education" is found in educational phraseology during the years under consideration, but it is open to challenge as guidance usage
in any period. President Eliot in 1892 had prophesied this sort of education for all public-
school pupils, and E. E. Slosson had used such a term in 1909 with reference to college
education.

degeneration into a propaganda term.[2] They would be glad to discard the phrase any time a more suitable substitute is found.

Analysis of the source materials in the light of these more recent discussions seems to indicate that the acrimonious claims and counterclaims are due not only to the use of "vocational" as a modifier but also to failure to interpret correctly the early functions included under this phrase, i.e., to the recent assumption that the guidance functions performed could be determined by inference from nomenclature in isolation rather than in its context.

The documents which tell the story of the early history have been examined with special reference to the relation between nomenclature and functions, and three somewhat different usages of the term "vocational guidance" have been found:

The first is exemplified by Parsons who took pains to elaborate his *vocational* definition so that it might be definitely understood that vocational was but "one arc of the circle." "All around manhood was the aim"; the medium, vocational guidance. This is the most clear-cut usage of "vocational guidance" in the generic sense which has been found. Nor does it differ materially from our present-day definition of "personnel work," which has as its goal the all-round development of a person.

Davis is a good representative of the second and somewhat more limited usage. "Vocational guidance" was his most inclusive and most frequently used expression, and his title was Director of Vocational Guidance. But the title of his book was "Vocational and Moral Guidance," while educational and civic guidance found important places in his program. Perhaps Davis, as well as many others, accepted Parsons' term and used it in a semigeneric sense without giving validity of usage any special consideration. The author admits that this was her unconsidered practice, and her usage undoubtedly would fall in this division.

The third usage was usually found in connection with a dominant interest in vocational education where the term was used to limit the scope of guidance. In this sense "vocational guidance" was a service which helped youth to choose an industrial training program and "to bridge the gap between school and work." It made no provision for those who were interested in academic courses. Many examples of this limited sense have been found, and many were expected since the beginnings of the guidance movement were concurrent with the peak of the agi-

[2] Present-day pronouncements which may well be considered in connection with the 1914–1916 California statement on "guidance as a propaganda" (see p. 26) include Henry M. Wriston's reference to guidance as "that last refuge of the confused educator" ("Democracy and a Self-reliant Culture," *Journal of Adult Education*, XII [1940], 241) and George H. Geyer's introductory remark in an address before a recent California meeting to the effect "that there is much more lip service than real action in all the fields of vocational guidance" (*Occupations*, XIX [1941], 305). See also the author's address, "Is Guidance a Racket?" published in *Vital Speeches*, IV (1938), 636–638 and in *N.E.A. Proceedings*, LXXVI (1938), 625–630.

tation for industrial education. Had Parsons left us nothing but his formal definition, it would seem justifiable to classify his usage with this group.[3]

Probably no one would deny that all three usages are legitimate, although not all are equally logical. Each has played an important part in the evolution of the guidance movement and he who would interpret that part correctly should familiarize himself with the terms and their contexts as given in the early documents. On the other hand, there is no reason why the movement should continue to be designated by titles which have outlived their usefulness, or which were chosen without due consideration. Most of those who are interested in the field would welcome any suggestion which would help to clarify objectives, define functions, and delimit the field through the use of a better name.

DEFINITIONS AND AIMS. Very few clear-cut definitions of either "guidance" or "vocational guidance" have been found. But statements of aims are fairly common, and sometimes definition and aim are combined in a single statement.[4] Parsons defined "vocational guidance" formally and narrowly but at once qualified his definition by a very inclusive statement of aims. Davis did not define "vocational guidance" but his statement of aims was much more inclusive than "vocational" implies. It comprised practically all the objectives of education. The author once stated that "vocational guidance" was "a bit of new and popular phraseology which carries with it a variety of meanings and is open to a variety of interpretations." [5] She then offered a statement of aims which put her use of the terms in the same category with that of Davis. There seems, however, to be a rather significant difference in the Seattle conception of the relation between "guidance" and "education" and that of recent writers who regard "education" as "guidance" and make the terms synonymous. In the Seattle report guidance was a "facilitating agency," aiding in the developmental growth of the individual in all the areas of life; it was the handmaid (or, to use another figure, a servicing station) of education rather than its equivalent. Hiatt's and Brumbaugh's definitions dealt with the vocational aspect of guidance and were in harmony with their statement of aims and

---

[3] A number of articles which appeared in *Occupations* under the National Occupational Conference regime, as well as some of the printed matter on the "Superintendents' Tour," seemed to indicate adherence to this conception of vocational guidance as the handmaid of vocational education, e.g., "Occupational Adjustment: School Superintendents Devise Program," *Occupations*, XV (1937), 833–837.

[4] One wonders if this was a logical characteristic of a new movement which had not yet found its bearings sufficiently for its supporters to define its terms, or if it was an unconscious avoidance of defining the unknown, accompanied by an equally unconscious statement of aims, which were easy to formulate.

[5] Reed, *Vocational Guidance Report*, p. 13.

with the title, Director of Vocational Education and Guidance, which was adopted in Philadelphia. California mentioned vocational guidance as "a propaganda" while several authorities stressed the dual aim of vocational guidance, social and individual.

There was universal agreement that the ultimate aim of all guidance was self-guidance, that no man may decide for another. One hesitates, therefore, to cite the single danger signal which warned that such agreement might not be permanent. The peculiar significance of the warning is due to the fact that it came from the pen of a psychologist who was in charge of one of the first psychological laboratories connected with the guidance movement. Hill, in his New Orleans report, stressed the desirability of caution in dealing with "human nature" and the undesirability of assuming that propositions, because they seem logical, "will prove satisfactory when applied to the individual human organism." He also listed several dangerous types of counselors (see p. 25). Did Hill fear that members of his own profession might sometime be tempted to try to substitute the decision of clinical counselors, based on psychological tests, for the decision of the individual, based on what Parsons described as "all the assistance which science and experts can give"?

FUNCTIONS OF VOCATIONAL GUIDANCE. Any attempt to make a classification of functions, tools, and techniques which would be mutually exclusive is bound to be a disappointment. Yet there is a marked distinction between a function and a tool and between a tool and a technique.[6] None of these words were common in the early period; "aims," "duties," "materials," and "methods" were the usual substitutes. Therefore, the classification which follows is based upon the author's interpretation of each specific word in its context, the different terms having been given their usually accepted sense: a "function" is a duty or a task to be performed; a "tool" is an instrument useful in performing the duty; and a "technique" is a method used to accomplish the objective. Obviously, the making of a cumulative record is a function, but later the record may become a useful tool in the counseling process; the personal interview may be a tool for fact-finding or, with a different objective in view, it may be a counseling technique.

---

[6] Recent years have witnessed increasing confusion in the use of these terms. For instance, in *Students and Occupations* (New York: Henry Holt and Co., 1937) E. G. Williamson on page xiii says that for several decades "vocational information alone was assumed to be an adequate *method* of vocational guidance," and on page xix he declares that "we must become aware of weaknesses in vocational information as a *technique* of guidance." Similarly Ruth Strang mentions counseling as one of the most important *tools* of guidance (in *Report of Committee on Teacher Education of the Association of Colleges and Universities of the State of New York*, 1940).

There was rather uniform agreement among early authorities that the all-inclusive function of guidance was comprised in securing information about the individual, securing information about opportunities of various types, and assisting the individual to interpret both series of information in terms of his own problems and needs. However, the majority of the local experiments previously mentioned report certain specific guidance responsibilities in elaboration of the more general functions. These specific responsibilities are illuminating because of their variety. No frequency tabulation is offered since the items listed were chosen for diversity of characteristics rather than for similarities:

(1) Moral, civic, vocational, educational, and ethical counseling were usually or frequently mentioned. So too were character and health counseling. Personality development was mentioned once.

(2) Counseling with reference to social problems was mentioned twice in public schools and often in colleges.

(3) The placing of applicants and employment supervision were mentioned several times, and placement bureaus were common on the college level.

(4) Summer employment and co-operative courses as exploratory methods of guidance were favored.

(5) Courses in educational guidance similar in content to certain types of present-day orientation courses and life-career classes or courses in occupations were functioning.

(6) Vocational addresses and conferences were common.

(7) Cumulative records and case histories were mentioned, but not frequently. Their preparation was a function, but in the final analysis they were tools.

(8) Home visitation and assistance of parents in performing guidance functions were included.

(9) Leadership among teachers and in the community appeared a few times where directors of guidance were available.

(10) Local surveys on all levels of education, initial and continuous, were usually considered a guidance responsibility.

(11) The taking of a school census, work certification, enforcement of labor and education laws were occasionally included.

(12) Financing and granting scholarships was a function of several philanthropic agencies.

(13) Psychological testing and in two cities the operation of a psychological clinic were noted.

(14) The preparation and dissemination of educational and vocational information in various forms were common functions.

(15) Making a list of community resources available for guidance purposes was fairly universal.

TOOLS ESSENTIAL FOR GUIDANCE SERVICES. The most inclusive statement of the tools essential for the counselor is given by Parsons and there has been little to add since he offered his tabulation. They comprised: (1) tools used in the analysis of the individual—schedules, self-analysis blanks, questionnaires, health histories, psychological tests, records, case histories, and interviews for fact-finding—and (2) materials concerned with educational and occupational information—all types of statistical surveys including distribution of workers, vocational information, job specifications, weighted rating scales, lists of training opportunities, apprenticeship possibilities, employment agencies, and community resources. Refinement of tools rather than addition of tools has characterized the later periods of the guidance movement. That improvements were in progress during the early period is indicated by the fact that under "functions of guidance" there have been found such items as the preparation of "cumulative records" which in recent years have come to be important guidance tools.

TECHNIQUES FOR COUNSELING. Four techniques were in vogue during the period under consideration:

(1) The personal interview for integrative and counseling purposes.

(2) Group discussions, group conferences, and addresses which were designed to function as guidance for participants or attendants.

(3) Case studies and case conferences which included the counselee among the participants.

(4) Clinical services which included interpretation of the findings for the counselee.

LEADERS IN THE EARLY PERIOD OF ORGANIZED GUIDANCE. An effort has been made, both in the selection of early experiments and of material to characterize such experiments, to bring into the story the names of the individuals who were most closely connected with the early beginnings of the movement. This has been done partly in order to supply a deficiency in information which has been found to be rather common among novices in the field. Many do not realize that names familiar to them through repeated appearance in recent literature were not the names of the founders and original spokesmen for the movement. It is well, for example, for the student of today and tomorrow to realize that William M. Leiserson, now chairman of the National Mediation Board, has in one capacity or another been a contributor to guidance and personnel from the beginning of the movement. It is suggested that both the early and the more recent activities of the leading participants whose names appear in Chapter I be made a class assignment whenever library facilities permit.[7]

[7] There are, of course, many individuals whose names do not appear in Chapter I who made major contributions to the progress of the movement. Examples of such omissions are Edward L. Thorndike, Leonard P. Ayres, Howell Cheney, and Thomas Mac-Cracken. Their contributions were in somewhat different lines from those dealt with in this overview, and it has been impossible to include all areas of activity. Considerable attention was given to surveys and research projects in one of the author's earlier books, *Human Waste in Education* (New York: Century Co., 1927), where a number of the names omitted here will be found.

PRINCIPLES OF GUIDANCE. Chapter I has indicated that the organized guidance movement was based upon two fundamental theories which were gradually accepted as principles: the principle of individual differences and the humanitarian principle of universal brotherhood. These two theories served as working hypotheses for many agencies interested in their practical application. By 1916 experiment and experience had revealed and formulated a number of principles, analysis of which leads to the conclusion that the majority are logical corollaries of the two major principles. These secondary principles, crystallizing under different local conditions and expressed in somewhat different terms, were concerned with most of the problems involved in the conduct of guidance services—the aims and objectives of guidance, the character of the guidance function, the relationship of counselor to counselee, the qualifications of counselors, and the like. Those which appear most frequently in the sources or have been most persistent in their demand for attention throughout the later as well as during the earlier years of the movement include: [8]

1. Guidance is an integral part of education. It begins in the home and continues throughout school life and initial work life. It serves as a facilitating and integrating agency in all areas of life.

2. Vocational guidance has a social and an individual aim. It is a co-operative factor in the social economy of the time. It is a direct responsibility of the educational system.

3. Individuals, both youth and adult, face many problem situations.

4. The unitary character of individual problems and the necessity for unity in performing guidance functions must be recognized.

5. Persistent and consistent recognition of individual differences is essential to guidance service. Progress in analysis of the individual is dependent upon progress in the psychology of individual differences.

6. Self-evaluation is an important factor in individual growth.

7. A scientific attitude and the use of scientific methods is essential in dealing with human problems.

8. The humanitarian or service motive is fundamental to successful guidance.

9. The major function of the counselor is to assist the individual in securing all possible information upon which to base his decision.

10. Cumulative records are essential to individual guidance.

11. Making contacts with others is important both for personality growth and for personality integration.

12. Ultimate decision in any area of life rests with the counselee.

13. Educational administration must assume responsibility for guidance service. Centralized control and decentralized execution is desirable.

[8] Each student at some point in his study should challenge the legitimacy of omissions and inclusions in this list and should determine for himself the extent to which each principle (or practice) has been accepted or rejected. He should also be prepared to add any new principles which his study may reveal.

14. Leadership must be delegated to specially prepared personnel. The entire faculty must participate.

15. Guidance services properly performed should keep the educational system in close contact with community needs and its guidance facilities.

16. Adequate time for the performance of guidance functions is a prerequisite to success.

SELECTION, CERTIFICATION, AND PREPARATION OF COUNSELORS. From the very beginning of the organized movement the necessity for carefully selected and properly prepared counselors has been recognized as prerequisite to success. Discussion of the selection, preparation, and qualifications of such officials received major attention in many of the early articles. Chapter III of Parsons' book described a school for vocational counselors which was sponsored by the Boston Young Men's Christian Association. Admission qualifications included mature judgment (the applicant must be twenty-five years of age unless very mature earlier), good manners and address, character and personality inviting respect and confidence, both a good general education including history, civics, and economics, and a specialized preparation in the principles and methods of modern psychology (at least a high-school education or its equivalent was required). Practical experience of specified kinds was also prerequisite to admission, two years or more in teaching, in business, or in social work. These experiences involving human contacts were supposed to give the applicant a knowledge of human nature, the motives, interests, and ambitions that dominate the lives of others, a sympathetic understanding of youth, a knowledge of the requirements for success, familiarity with educational opportunities, and such knowledge of scientific method as would enable him to understand how facts are secured, classified, and used for drawing justifiable conclusions. The length of the course was one, two, or three terms depending upon the applicant. The content of the course comprised lectures, addresses by businessmen, case conferences, laboratory practice at least three hours a week, discussions, use of tests, analysis of facts, and criticism of conclusions drawn from facts. A certificate of proficiency was issued whenever practical results indicated that registrants were qualified to test the abilities and capacities of young men and apply good judgment, common sense, and scientific method to the problems involved.[9]

[9] In a recent article dealing with modern requirements, Donald G. Paterson of the University of Minnesota mentioned Parsons' program and added, ". . . One may now look with amusement at the training program proposed by Frank Parsons in 1909" ("The Genesis of Modern Guidance," *Educational Record*, XIX [1938], 42). Amazement would seem to be the more appropriate term, and one wonders if Mr. Paterson has not yielded to the common temptation to take programs out of their setting and evaluate them in a "modern frame of reference." Students are advised to compare Parsons' program in the

Parsons' program, which, so far as our records show, was the first specific training course offered in the field, was soon followed by others. Meyer Bloomfield gave courses at Harvard in the summer of 1911 and in his 1915 brochure reported "nearly a score of colleges, universities and other institutions" conducting special or part-time courses in vocational guidance. His own activities included two summers at the University of California, three courses at Harvard, two at Boston University where "a special professorship of vocational guidance had been established," and one each at Indiana University and the State Normal School, Greeley, Colorado. The Women's Educational and Industrial Union of Boston, in connection with Simmons College, offered a full-year, thirty-credit-hour course in 1914–1915.[10] The course was open to experienced teachers who were granted leaves of absence for the purpose of preparing to become counselors. The description of the course listed six major subjects: (1) Educational, Industrial, and Social Investigation; (2) Statistics, i.e., methods of handling and interpreting data; (3) Industrial Relations of Minors; (4) Elements of Psychology and of Education or Economics; (5) Applied Psychology; and (6) Practice in Methods.

The courses given by the Beacon Vocation Bureau of Boston, J. Adams Puffer, Director, are a good example of the training offered by agencies to which Bloomfield may have been referring when he mentioned "other institutions." This bureau gave a number of different courses of lectures for teachers' institutes and normal schools. Announcements for 1912 and 1913 report engagements in twelve states. One of the twelve topics in a course of lectures on vocational guidance was "The Equipment of a Counselor."

The first course for deans of women was given at Columbia University under the direction of Paul Monroe in 1916.

Training courses for employment executives in business and industry paralleled training courses for educators and philanthropists. The first course of which this author has a record was offered by Frank B. Gilbreth, Providence, Rhode Island, in the summer of 1913 "for a selected group of teachers and thinkers who desire to understand the science of management and to become acquainted with the most recent developments in the theory and practice." The course lasted two weeks and there was no fee. It consisted of lectures, laboratory work, and visits to various plants. Gilbreth's reason for a selected registration is interesting: ". . . The type of

light of 1909 teacher requirements with the present-day requirements for both teachers and counselors and decide for themselves how much relative progress has been made in the selection and preparation of counselors.

10 Circulars, course outlines, and other data used in this section are on file in the author's library.

work to be done demands a mind that has a thorough training not only in acquiring, but also in transferring knowledge and experience. The problem of management is, in its final analysis, one of teaching."

The Tuck School of Administration and Finance of Dartmouth College in 1915 under Harlow S. Person instituted a program for the training of employment executives. Person's statements regarding the functions, qualifications, and preparation of employment personnel are illuminating in the light of similar topics which were being simultaneously discussed with reference to educational personnel.[11] Qualifications were discussed from the standpoint of personality, mental characteristics and knowledge, and experience. Person's requirements are valuable comparative material for those who are interested in the early history of training programs and the qualifications of workers. A knowledge of psychology and of the possibilities and limitations of psychological laboratories in selecting and classifying employees was one requirement. A knowledge of public and private educational facilities, of vocational guidance, and of employment agencies and the degree of efficiency with which each accomplishes its aims was another. "Our system of training must involve at an early stage, and at later stages, mechanism for selecting and rejecting . . . candidates for training." Supplementary business apprenticeship with business firms "can offer much in support of the processes of the school and college."

A number of the reports cited in Chapter I called attention to the need for trained workers; Chicago held an examination for counselors in 1913; the author's recommendations to the Seattle Board called for examinations for counselors and attendance officers. The uncanny foresight of Hill of New Orleans in warning against poorly trained but presumptuous workers has already been mentioned.[12]

ORGANIZATION AND ADMINISTRATION. The documents upon which this summary of early guidance services is based have revealed that prior to 1916 guidance projects had been instituted under philanthropic, educational, business, and civic or governmental auspices. Each agency faced problems concerned with administration and organization regardless of whether its activities comprised all or only one area of guidance service. Two methods of administration prevailed, by committee or by a single official acting under the general direction of a board, president, secretary, or superintendent. The majority of the philanthropic bureaus were in-

---

11 See Harlow S. Person, "University Schools of Business and the Training of Employment Executives," *Proceedings of Employment Managers' Conference* (Bulletin of U. S. Bureau of Labor Statistics, whole no. 196, Employment and Unemployment ser. 3; Washington, 1916), pp. 30–38. This is the best article available on this subject and may be studied by educators with profit.

12 See p. 25.

stituted under the committee system; some public-school and college bureaus also operated under the committee system, and practically all the
public placement bureaus were required to work under local advisory
committees. The Seattle Public School Bureau, from its inception, was
conducted by a director who was responsible to the board and superintendent; there was no committee either within or without the schools.
Business projects were uniformly an integral part of the administrative
program of the house.

In this day of committee popularity, especially committees comprised
of representatives of this, that, or the other, there is no need to discuss
the advantages and disadvantages of conducting experiments under such
auspices. It is pertinent, however, to call attention to certain logical reasons why, during the transition from guidance as a philanthropy to guidance as a function of education, certain public-school and college bureaus
should have been carried on under the committee plan:

(1) The example of the philanthropic agencies.

(2) The backwardness of educational administration in recognizing
guidance as an educational function. A self-appointed committee was the
only recourse of interested parties.

(3) The necessity of having committees in order to secure financial support.

(4) The ability of committees comprised of representatives from various
organizations to attract moral and financial support and at the same time
to educate their constituency.

Whatever part any one or more of these reasons may have played in
the carry-over of committee control to the beginnings of guidance under
educational auspices, a study of the sources seems to indicate that comparatively few of the early school bureaus would have materialized without
philanthropic pressure and committee services. In fact it is hard to find a
single prominent philanthropic agency which did not attempt to force
upon public education assumption of responsibility for organizing and
financing guidance services. In the final analysis, although by 1916 there
was a definite trend in the direction of administration by educational
authorities, the responsibility was, it would seem, "fastened upon" education rather than welcomed by education.[13]

In some communities the committee system was continued under
educational auspices; in others local retiring committees concluded their

---

[13] In 1915 W. R. Smith declared in an article that appeared in *Teaching*, a periodical
published by the State Normal School, Emporia, Kansas, ". . . By the usual process of
elimination it [vocational guidance] is certain to be fastened upon [educational systems]"
(I, 27).

experiments with recommendations for a rather definite program under the supervision of a director, an assistant superintendent, or some other educational officer, who would be responsible for the unification of all guidance efforts either within or without the educational system. Boston and Chicago furnished examples of supervision by some member of the superintendent's staff; Grand Rapids appointed Jesse B. Davis Director of Vocational Guidance for Grand Rapids; Philadelphia appointed a Director of Vocational Education and Guidance; and Minneapolis, a Director of Attendance and Vocational Guidance. As a volunteer director of the initial guidance work in Seattle, the author in her final recommendations to the Board of Education did not favor the assignment of guidance service to an assistant superintendent and cited four reasons for believing that guidance would be more successful if supervised by a director whose functions could be definitely differentiated from the universally recognized functions of assistant superintendents:

(1) The duties of an assistant superintendent differ markedly from those of a director of guidance.

(2) A well-equipped vocational guidance director can command a higher salary than the average assistant superintendent.[14] Salary complications would be avoided by the appointment of a director.

(3) Employers, and the public in general, regard the old-line educational officers as deficient in practical knowledge and experience. A new type of officer would receive better business co-operation.

(4) Experience has indicated that employers will deny valuable, and often confidential, vocational information to officials who are members of a Board of Superintendents and might feel free to discuss such information with their colleagues.[15]

Problems of organization were faced by all agencies which instituted guidance services, educational, philanthropic, civic, and business. There was, however, considerable difference among various agencies regarding the number, type, and difficulty of the problems. Major problems centered around such more or less interrelated questions as:

(1) What should be the objectives of the service?

(2) To whom should its facilities be available—to all who apply or to a limited group? If the latter, how should the group be limited, by age, sex, education, economic status, religious affiliation, membership in some club or organization, or what?

(3) What functions should be performed?

[14] This statement was true only in the early years of the movement.
[15] *Vocational Guidance Report*, p. 17.

(4) What form of organization, centralized or decentralized, would be best adapted to accomplishment of the purposes?

The objectives of organized guidance service, regardless of what type of organization offered the service, were usually very definitely stated during the early period.[16] Bureaus under philanthropic auspices were instituted to meet the revealed needs of the clientele to be served; therefore, the answers to questions of age, sex, economic status, etc., were predetermined. The same statement is applicable to "business" whether it was acting in a philanthropic or in a corporate capacity. One or more of the functions as tabulated from contemporary records (see pp. 53 f.) were performed by each agency, the number and character being dependent upon the contribution which each promised to make toward realization of the ultimate objective. Now and then as conditions changed, an agency was found to have discarded one function or added another. Centralized or decentralized control was not a problem to newly established agencies concerned only with the performance of guidance functions, but if an individual agency did face a control problem, it was usually too easily resolved to warrant its inclusion among problems.

Answers to the same series of organizational questions were far more difficult for long-established agencies, instituted to attain other, even though intimately related, objectives and already performing a considerable variety of other functions. Such agencies, when they entered the guidance field, were obliged to reinterpret or enlarge their objectives, to expand their list of functions, and frequently to revise their administrative set-up in order adequately to meet the demands of their enlarged responsibilities. The Young Men's Christian Association is a good example of this type of philanthropic agency. Although the guidance objective was in harmony with the general objective of the Y.M.C.A., although it may well be considered as an inherent factor in all Y.M.C.A. activities, and although the Y.M.C.A. was one of the first agencies definitely to commit itself to guidance service, this organization was a well-established agency prior to the beginnings of organized guidance and of necessity was obliged to reinterpret some of its older activities in terms of guidance and to deal with some rather difficult organization and integration problems.

Corporate business, too, for much the same reasons faced problems in reinterpretation of objectives, integration of employee relations, and

---

[16] In 1913 the National Vocational Guidance Association had a very clear-cut objective; at the present time a marked cleavage exists among its members both as to objectives and as to a name which is in harmony with the objectives.

centralized or decentralized control of personnel functions. Business organizations had always selected, paid, trained, promoted, demoted, and discharged men. But during the period under consideration, influenced in common with other institutions by evolving sociological, psychological, and economic theories and the beginnings of their practical application, business came to recognize that "Employment Management," "Management of Men," or "Human Engineering" were integral factors in "Management." The character of administrative and executive functions in their relation to personnel was reinterpreted to conform to newly accepted theories; new functions were introduced; employment executives were appointed and their selection, qualifications, training, and responsibilities were major topics of conference discussion.

Guidance was no less, and possibly more, an inherent function of education than it was of philanthropic agencies and corporate business. But however serious the difficulties of assimilating the new responsibilities and reinterpreting the old may have been for established philanthropic and business institutions, evidence indicates that organization difficulties reached a climax in the case of education. The difficulties began with the transfer of certain "going" guidance activities from philanthropy to education. Education was an old, well-established institution; its major objective was the imparting of knowledge, with guidance an inherent factor therein; its clientele comprised school attendants, voluntary or involuntary; its functions were in harmony with its objectives, and the performance of these functions was confined to the school year and the school day; line organization prevailed. It was apparent immediately after the one "going" concern was "fastened upon" the other "going" concern, that they were not always to travel together harmoniously, and this in spite of the fact that their goal was supposed to be the same and the one to be inherent in the other.

It has been very easy for those whose primary interest centered in guidance to criticize educational administration for the dilatory manner in which it has dealt with organized guidance. It has been less easy to appreciate the exceedingly difficult task which educators faced when organized guidance was definitely "fastened upon" a local educational system. Certain guidance responsibilities had been taken over; but there were no helpful precedents relative to the best administrative procedures, and it was necessary to struggle with a dual problem of integration—integration of guidance services with all other forms of educational service and integration of guidance services on all levels and in all subdivisions of the educational system. There is no evidence that the full implication of these organization problems was anticipated prior to the "taking over."

What were the objectives of guidance in connection with the educational system? Education has never been very clearheaded as to the objectives of education and it has not been more so as to the objective of guidance. To say that guidance and education are synonymous is begging the question. Education has not been specific as to the place of guidance in the total educational picture; guidance was an unwelcome child at birth and it is still the orphan of education, both in public schools and colleges.

Who were to be the beneficiaries of organized guidance under educational auspices? Where philanthropy had been entirely free to determine its clientele and had been very liberal in extending its services to both youth and adult, school attendants and nonattendants, many boards of education felt constrained by law to limit service to school attendants. This was the attitude of the Seattle board in 1913. In her final report to the board the author made a strong plea for the extension of services to out-of-school youth "who might, through the instrumentality of these services, be offering public education its last opportunity to help them on life's journey." When the Omaha bureau was transferred to education its community characteristic was lost. Other similar instances are on record. On the college level, faculties were often explosively jealous of any extension of "their" services to "outsiders."

Granting the legitimacy of confining the use of school funds to school attendants or alumni, we have the right to assume that educational institutions would service their entire clientele within their own domain. This they did not do on any level of education. Expense was, of course, a strong influencing factor. Determination of the groups to be served was always a problem. The most commonly selected groups were elementary groups approaching the end of compulsory education, high-school pupils, college freshmen, college seniors, subnormals, physical defectives, college and public-school failures, discipline cases, and the like. Grand Rapids seems to have offered one of the most inclusive programs for all school attendants and for school eliminates, although much of the school program was group work carried on by the classroom teacher with Principal Davis himself shouldering leadership responsibilities. Hill in the New Orleans report noted services to special groups but hoped that they would be extended to all when the program was fully worked out.

Since objectives were not very clear, determination of functions on the basis of objectives was hardly to be expected. Immediately after transfer to public education a sort of hit-or-miss method of adding to, or discarding from, functions previously performed by philanthropy began, and is still in process. On the college level the deans of women and deans of men rapidly acquired a hybrid list of functions, and there is little evidence that any function once acquired was later discarded. The acquisitive character of college personnel is best evidenced by its present most vocal sponsors who have recently revealed a willingness to absorb all college functions not definitely either "business or instruction," or "all that have to do with the individual." Since instruction may be offered to groups, while translation of instruction into education is purely an individual process, this sort of function determination does not seem very logical. In a few instances the list of college personnel functions has grown to such an extent that it now includes such items as "curriculum revision," "supervision of instruction," and "dishonorable dismissal of students."

What is still more disturbing than this continuous tendency to increase the heterogeneous character of the guidance function is the apparent unwillingness, or inability, of spokesmen for the movement to delimit the field, if there be a field, and to allocate to it functions which differentiate it from other fields of educational service. There seems to be little interest in this phase of guidance service, but until some active and intelligent effort along this line has been made, it is hopeless to assume that personnel service is, or can become, a profession; that it will be an established occupational field; or that it will attract the high type of educator which effectiveness demands.

A comparison of the list of functions allotted to guidance during the early period with those found in present-day lists indicates that initial functions centered around a much more definitely defined field than do the functions included today. Counselor training programs, offered by instructors who have given little or no attention to the why, whence, where, and whither of guidance, have added to the confusion. Several textbooks written by or for the use of such instructors contribute their bit to the confusion; e.g., one text, indicating by its title that it is designed to deal with "personnel services" or "guidance activities" and promising the reader that it is a "definitive" study, includes in its content practically all the functions performed in secondary schools or colleges; a second text purporting to deal with "campus activities" or "extracurricular activities" and promising to describe "clearly the scope and organization" of such activities, forgets all about its good intentions and describes rather unclearly practically the same functions which the first text had described in its "definitive" study of personnel. Under present conditions it is possible for a truly enthusiastic, nonstop writer to publish as many as three books without making much change in content—School Administration, Guidance Activities, and Extracurricular Activities.[17] It is all very dis-

[17] An examination of several textbooks carrying such titles will be very helpful to students.

concerting, especially to those who have been interested in guidance over a long period of years.

From its first introduction into the educational system, both in public schools and in colleges, the problem of centralized or decentralized control has been a moot question which time has intensified rather than lessened. Several programs for organized guidance services prior to 1916 included centralized direction and supervision of all guidance activities, with leadership of the teaching corps in the more effective performance of its guidance functions a major responsibility. Grand Rapids, as has been indicated, seems most nearly to have established a centralized program. But decentralization was the rule: the "teacher-adviser," a common term in the early period, was left to do the best she could without benefit of co-operation, co-ordination, or leadership.[18] The Boston school committee set up a centralized program which included leadership among the teachers; the New York superintendent recommended such a program; the Minneapolis Teachers' Club formulated one for such units as were recommended; the Seattle report envisaged co-ordination of all school, home, and community activities and centralized supervision and leadership of the teaching corps. Programs for central leadership and control rarely materialized although the title of director might be given to some individual who was placed in charge of some phases of guidance. On the whole one must conclude that public-school guidance services were not on a very secure foundation when the United States joined the Allies in 1917. A decline in their effectiveness was noticeable before 1916 and was logically credited to a combination of causes, some of which will be revealed as our study progresses.

On the college level, with no more definite objectives and with a larger accumulation of activities, there was even less co-ordination of functions and centralization of direction and leadership. All sorts of official and unofficial guidance services were to be found on almost any college campus, most of the officially recognized services being for women with a sharp

18 In recent years it has become increasingly common—perhaps because as a people we are inclined to uncritical repetition of the statements of others rather than to acceptance of responsibility for factual documentation of our own statements—to hear or read pronouncements to the effect that only recently have teachers participated in guidance services, or that guidance by experts has prevailed until recent years, or that until the last few years guidance was regarded as a function independent of education. Such statements are not true. The evidence of a vast amount of source material invalidates them. In fact there were few projects in the early years of organized guidance which, in one way or another, failed to recognize the importance of teacher participation, and in many cases the teaching corps carried the entire responsibility. Before further repetition of such statements is made it is well to ask, Who were these "experts" and where did they come from?

line between services for men and for women. It is suggested that those whose major interest is in college personnel services keep in mind the early differences in the objectives of deans of men and deans of women, in the methods of their selection, in their preselection preparation, and in the possible effect of these differences on the development of these two deanships in their relation to an all-university student personnel service.

EVALUATION IN THE EARLY PERIOD. The perspective which is essential to evaluation or measurement of the accomplishments of any social service was not attained during the early period of the guidance movement. There is, however, in the source materials some evidence that those actively engaged in the work were questioning the effectiveness of their service. Parsons was hopeful regarding ultimate results; he noted that the work was growing in extent and utility and regretted that society did not make more adequate provision for the development of its human resources. Weaver, who made great personal sacrifices to carry on his project, when asked if he felt that his sacrifices and efforts were warranted by the returns replied:

> Providence has been very kind. It has sent a few who feel that I have been helpful to tell me so, and it has kept from me the many who must have felt that they had received no benefit. The few appreciative consultants have encouraged me to go on; had all of the latter reported I fear I should have become discouraged. Just what has been done to help our fellow travelers only time and eternity can tell.[19]

Weaver was always a very modest estimator of his own services and an unusually generous one of the services of others.

The Association of Collegiate Alumnae in its résumé of the first year's work in Omaha confirmed Weaver's final statement:

> It is impossible to record in figures the principal work of the Bureau, because it has to do with the welfare of the individuals we touch—a thing which only time can measure.[20]

The author early recognized that guidance had many of the same characteristics which handicapped scientific procedures in education and prevented accurate measurement or even tentative appraisal of results, and she shared the point of view of Weaver and the Omaha report:

> It is well to recognize that educational administration is handicapped by its limited knowledge of definite standards as to aims of education, methods of ac-

---

[19] From a memorandum of a private conversation between Eli W. Weaver and the author in Brooklyn, N.Y., March, 1917.

[20] See *Summary of Work in 1916.* In recent years, as a tendency to measure results in terms of mechanical devices has increased, Harry D. Kitson has reiterated these early statements as warnings of the dangers inherent in neglect of the spiritual phase of results which still defy measurement.

complishing its aims and accurate standards for measuring results. It is well to realize that perfecting our knowledge in these lines depends upon progress in psychology and sociology, sciences which are still in their infancy. It is well to remember that custom standards rather than scientific standards still dominate the educational field. But, if we would be optimistic, it is also well to remember that the demand for education on a scientific basis is increasing, and that the discouragements of today are full of promise for tomorrow. Because we cannot definitely define the aims of vocational guidance and the results to be attained by it, because we cannot test accurately the value of our efforts in character development, shall we refuse to use the beginnings of scientific knowledge and such empirical information as we do have in helping to develop this new phase of modern education? [21]

She further stated:

In many instances casual remarks indicate how our schools have helped or hindered these boys on life's journey; . . . just what we have accomplished . . . I do not know—perhaps it is not intended that we shall know—but I believe that the effort is worth continuing and I have faith enough in humanity to believe that the results will be commensurate with the responsibility.[22]

Both philanthropic and educational bureaus made reports on the more material phases of their work in the form of statistical summaries of interviews, tests administered, placements made, numbers returned to school, etc.,[23] but it seems to have been fairly generally recognized that there was an unmeasurable residue of effectiveness which might never be open to accurate appraisal. Paterson, alone, so far as this writer has knowledge, has been willing to assume responsibility for a definite statement relative to the value of guidance services not only before 1916 but also before 1930. In an article in the *Educational Record* Paterson made the following pronouncement:

In using the word modern I refer to the 1930–37 streamlined version since guidance models prior to 1930 are disappearing even in the hands of the second-hand dealers through junking rather than resale.[24]

It is hoped that each student will find this brief history of the beginnings of organized guidance a satisfactory background upon which to consider the inherent and relative values of the tools, techniques, principles, and practices presented in the following chapters. It is also hoped that knowl-

[21] *Vocational Guidance Report*, p. 10.
[22] *Ibid.*, p. 17.
[23] Recent personnel surveys such as those by Howard M. Bell, *Youth Tell their Story* (Washington: American Council on Education, 1938) and by Ruth E. Eckert and Thomas O. Marshall, *When Youth Leave School* (New York: The Regents' Inquiry, McGraw-Hill Book Co., 1938), include many of the topics dealt with in the early surveys. See the author's compilation in *Human Waste in Education*. A comparison of the findings, item by item, is enlightening. Just what progress has been made between 1910 and 1944?
[24] *Loc. cit.*

edge of the whence and why of guidance may help him to determine its how and where, and will be of use to him in formulating his own philosophy of personnel service, deciding what functions may legitimately be comprised therein, and how to proceed in organizing a service which will be in harmony with the best practices of the day and at the same time adapted to local needs. And, finally, it is hoped that students will find in this early source material an inspiration to leadership in determining the whither of the guidance and personnel movement.

SELECTED SUPPLEMENTARY READING

Beatty, Albert James. *Corporation Schools.* Bloomington, Ill.: Public School Publishing Co., 1918. The status of vocational education and the activities of corporation schools prior to the enactment of the Smith-Hughes Law.

Bloomfield, Meyer, ed. *Readings in Vocational Guidance.* Boston: Ginn and Co., [ᶜ1915]. A valuable collection of source material for the years prior to 1915.

Brewer, John M. *The Vocational Guidance Movement: Its Problems and Possibilities.* New York: Macmillan Co., 1918. A review of the history to 1918. The author's point of view in 1918 may be compared with his more recent outlook as expressed in *Education as Guidance* (New York: Macmillan Co., 1932).

——, et al. *History of Vocational Guidance: Origins and Early Development.* New York: Harper and Bros., 1942. A recent, and the only, reference book on the history of vocational guidance. The balanced picture implied in "history" is to some extent marred by overemphasis on the familiar and by errors of fact in the unfamiliar, which might have been prevented by more generous use of contemporary documents.

Henderson, Charles Richmond. *Citizens in Industry.* New York: D. Appleton and Co., 1915. A good account of the progress of the humanitarian movement during the early years of the guidance movement.

Lescohier, Don D. *The Labor Market.* New York: Macmillan Co., 1919. The broadest in scope, most reliable, most readable, and most generally available publication on the history of public employment and related problems. At the time of writing the author was a member of the faculty of the University of Wisconsin. Previously he had been Superintendent of the Minnesota Public Employment Office and Chief Statistician for the State Department of Labor and Industries.

Perry, Clarence Arthur. *Wider Use of the School Plant.* New York: New York Charities Publication Committee, 1910. An account of early efforts to extend school services to meet community needs.

Rosenberry, Lois K. (Mathews). *The Dean of Women.* New York: Houghton Mifflin Co., 1915. A pioneer effort to explain the problems of women in coeducational institutions written by a former dean of women of the University of Wisconsin.

Ryan, W. Carson, Jr. *Vocational Guidance and the Public Schools.* Washington, 1918. (U. S. Bureau of Education Bulletin, 1918, no. 24.) A questionnaire study of the status of guidance in secondary schools, with special emphasis on placement.

Schneider, Herman. *Education for Industrial Workers.* Yonkers, N.Y.: World Book Co., 1915. Deals with co-operative schools and courses.

Small, George D. *The Dean of Men's Viewpoint: An Annotated Bibliography of References of Interest to Deans and Advisers of Men.* Urbana, Ill.: National Association of Deans and Advisers of Men, 1940. (Offset.) A very valuable bibliography for those who desire to make a thorough study of the functions of deans of men.

Stevenson, George S., and Smith, Geddes. *Child Guidance Clinics: A Quarter Century of Development.* New York: Commonwealth Fund, 1934. Deals with the history and present status of child guidance clinics.

Talbot, Marion, and Rosenberry, Lois K. (Mathews). *The History of the American Association of University Women, 1881–1931.* Boston: Houghton Mifflin Co., 1931.

Woolley, Helen T., and Fischer, Charlotte R. *Mental and Physical Measurements of Working Children.* Princeton, N.J.: Psychological Review Co., 1914. (The Psychological Monographs, vol. XVIII, no. 1.)

PART II
Information on Educational and Occupational Opportunities and Community Resources

CHAPTER V
Information on Educational Opportunities

CHAPTER VI
Information on Occupational Opportunities

CHAPTER VII
Information on Community Resources

CHAPTER VIII
Classifying, Indexing, and Filing Informational Material

A FIRST PREREQUISITE TO COUNSELING:

"Information about educational and occupational opportunities, and knowledge of community resources available in determining upon goals, and in attaining them."—FRANK PARSONS, 1908.

"Appraisal of various possible activities in the light of the interests, aptitudes, abilities, and services demanded of the individual."—DAVID G. RYANS, 1941.

CHAPTER V

Information on Educational Opportunities

PART I has indicated how, in the course of our social and economic progress, a new movement, crystallizing under the dominance of science and the machine on the one hand and under the aegis of philanthropy, education, and industry on the other, came into being and was christened "Vocational Guidance." It has also indicated how, since its baptismal name was not sufficiently inclusive to compass its activities or suggest the necessary implementation for its conduct, its alter ego, Guidance, was usually implied in spite of the limiting prefix. Since this and the following chapters are concerned with present-day principles and practices and with all aspects of guidance or personnel service, the use of "vocational guidance" as a synonym of "guidance" will be discontinued and "personnel service" will be used interchangeably with "guidance service," although their acceptance as synonyms is open to question.

It is perhaps fair to the reader that, at this point, the author should explain her own point of view regarding nomenclature. She does so in the hope and expectation that no student who has not given careful attention to this subject and arrived at independent conclusions will accept it as his own (1) because it is tentative and because it is hoped that in the near future more appropriate phrases may be discovered and both of these terms eliminated, and (2) because true scholarship forbids the unchallenged acceptance of the pronouncements of others. At the present time she thinks of "guidance service" as more inclusive than "personnel service" in scope, in available resources, and in methods. It may include guidance through the example of parents, teachers, and others, and guidance which comes incidentally from the reading of a book, attendance at a lecture, participation in some community service, and the like. Guidance may derive from group activities such as assembly or homeroom programs, club conferences, and classroom discussions, and it may also derive from counseling interviews implemented with the best of tools and techniques. It may be offered either consciously or unconsciously in a great variety of ways and under many conditions. Services of this type lie all around each one of us not only in our infancy but throughout our entire life.

"Personnel service," on the other hand, seems much more specific; it is never unconsciously offered and is always personal in character and application; the personal interview is its major technique. It is intensive and exclusive where guidance is extensive and inclusive. It has at its command all the types of information mentioned in Parsons' first and second series, supplemented by the most refined tools for the analysis of the individual —very dangerous tools in the hands of untrained or semitrained teacher-counselors who function in the broader, less specific, less professional, and less scientific areas of "guidance." Personnel service does not include such administrative functions as organization and supervision of cocurricular activities, of homeroom and assembly programs, or the performance of bona fide disciplinary functions. It does not include teaching functions exemplified in homeroom guidance classes, orientation classes, and classes in occupational information. Personnel service puts a high value on organized activities as tools for the growth or adjustment of individuals, and on the knowledge acquired in various forms of guidance classes as a basis for personal decisions. It is eager to utilize its tools, techniques, and opportunities for the solution of potential disciplinary problems while they are still in the realm of personal adjustment through aiding the individual to exercise self-control and self-discipline, but if and when external disciplinary action becomes necessary, it feels that responsibility should be assumed by the administrative authorities and not by the personnel worker.

Perhaps in the future guidance services may be differentiated on the basis of quantity and quality—100 per cent quantity being available through the co-operation of home, school, and church. Just to be guidance-conscious is a step in advance; participation within the limits of parental and teacher ability is an additional step in advance. Quality of service would reach its peak in the exercise of a type of professionalism which is most nearly approached by personnel service. In the meantime, if personnel service would divest itself of several functions which are properly administrative or instructional and limit its field to personnel or counseling functions, the name would be less objectionable, and it might become a sufficiently differentiated field of educational service to prophesy eventual professional status.

Parts II and III deal with tools essential for guidance service. Parsons was very specific regarding guidance procedures. He specified two kinds of information which should be collected and be at hand for the use of counselor and counselee before the third step, counseling, could safely be taken:

1. Information about educational and occupational opportunities and their requirements, and knowledge of community resources available in determining upon goals, and in attaining them.

2. Information about the individual including his aptitudes, abilities, interests, etc.[1]

Pronouncements taken from one of the most recent efforts to clarify guidance thinking and improve guidance procedures are offered for comparison. Two out of "at least three preliminary procedures intrinsically associated with any guidance endeavor" are stated to be:

1. Self-appraisal of one's interests, aptitudes, and abilities.

2. Appraisal of various possible activities in the light of the interests, aptitudes, abilities, and services demanded of the individual.[2]

These statements span the entire life of the organized guidance movement. Their agreement, supported by the fact that study of the intervening years has revealed universal accord regarding both series of prerequisites, is indicative of their fundamental importance. Variations in emphasis have been found, and should continue to be found, in order to service properly the different clienteles for whom counseling is offered. Parsons and Ryans both recognized "all the arcs of the circle." Parsons dealt, in the main, with adults who for the most part sought assistance in meeting employment problems. Therefore, his first set of prerequisites is very specifically inclusive of occupational and educational information and of community resources. His second series was as inclusive as conditions in 1908 permitted, but analysis of the individual was approached, in the main, from an adult angle: it was analysis of abilities already developed or of immediate assets upon which to capitalize.

Ryans' report is concerned with youth still under institutional supervision. The groups with which he is concerned did not take the initiative in soliciting guidance; their elders were anxious to find the most desirable methods of servicing them. Developmental possibilities and growth programs dominate the picture. Those who have advised with a variety of individuals, youth and adult, employed and unemployed, men and women, physically handicapped and physically sound, and the like, will realize that procedures must differ as to tools and techniques as well as to the extent to which detailed self-appraisal is possible. However, since nothing in logic or experience indicates that these two series of fundamental facts will not remain fundamental in the years to come, every individual who advises with other individuals, whether as parent, priest, teacher, friend, counselor, social worker, or employer, will need to be informed regarding the types of data included in both series; where and how such data may be secured; and how they may be prepared for use.

[1] *Choosing a Vocation,* p. 5.

[2] David G. Ryans, *The First Step in Guidance: Self-Appraisal; A Report on the 1940 Sophomore Testing Program* ([New York: Cooperative Test Service of the American Council on Education, c1941]), p. 7.

Part II is concerned with the what, where, and how of the data included in the first series of Parsons' prerequisites—educational and occupational opportunities and their requirements and various community, state, and national services available for the assistance of individuals who seek to develop their potentialities and bring them to fruition in a personally satisfying and socially useful occupational life. It comprises an overview of the sources from which such data may be obtained, discusses criteria for determining the value of each type of source and its content, and stresses the critical ability which should characterize those who collect such material or who use it in connection with advisory or instructional duties.

Possible Methods of Collecting Information on Educational Opportunities

Information relative to educational opportunities should be available to residents of every community through the instrumentality of some local agency or agencies. The public schools would seem to be the logical agency for pooling, classifying, and disseminating such information, although on the adult level the public libraries occupy an equally strategic position. Irrespective of what agency may perform clearance functions, there is a specific opportunity for community co-operation in the collection, evaluation, and keeping up-to-date of this type of information. Parents' clubs, or parent-teacher associations, might well be interested in assuming responsibility for information on nursery schools and child guidance clinics, both from the point of view of child registrants and of opportunities for the preparation of community young people for such service. Another group might concentrate on special schools on the elementary level, indicating the type of normal or atypical children who would profit from differentiated services.

Secondary schools of many types, both public and private, local and widely distributed geographically, are increasing in number and are offering scholarships of various kinds to pupils who promise to fulfill both individual and social objectives. Men's service clubs and other commercial and business organizations are in a position to aid in procuring information on the opportunities offered by corporation or company schools. The women's college clubs have always been interested in college opportunities, and the long list of scholarships offered by their own organizations might be extended to include other similar offerings. Decentralized educational services of this type are quite common, especially in the larger cities, but we are unable to cite a single instance of a unified service which pools all the information on educational opportunities available for all ages, all levels of ability, and all types of individuals. Decentralized services are very helpful but they would be much more effective and much less wasteful of time and money if community clearance and division of labor were to be instituted. Pupils, teachers, librarians, and individuals not only profit by participating in the collection of such material but also make a social contribution of considerable value.

The suggestions in this chapter are tentative. It would be undesirable to attempt to set up any arbitrary plan for the collection of information on educational opportunities or for its classification. Each community must determine for itself what information it needs and what agencies and individuals are available to perform accurately and adequately the task of collecting and keeping it up-to-date. It would be equally undesirable to attempt to impose a universal classification and filing system. The volume and range of material to be classified, the clerical assistance available for handling it, and the purposes for which it is to be used are the factors which should determine classification and filing methods.

The first step in the collection of educational information is the enumeration of the immediately available community training opportunities on all levels of education. Such resources will include nursery schools, kindergartens, child guidance or child welfare facilities, boarding homes, special schools for defective children, classes and schools for the physically and mentally handicapped, progressive schools, and various types of private and public elementary and secondary schools, including academic, trade, vocational, continuation, business, and opportunity schools, apprenticeship opportunities, co-operative courses, technical institutes, and all types of colleges and universities.

The great majority of communities will, of course, have few if any educational opportunities beyond the usual resources of the public school. Day nurseries, child guidance clinics, and special schools are usually available only in localities where a large population has warranted their introduction. On the other hand, even though any given community may not support such agencies, it should at least include in its list of resources any regional agencies to which it could turn as need arises. States or their subdivisions frequently provide traveling clinics, furnish transportation to near-by educational centers, and employ visiting teachers, visiting nurses, and psychiatrists who are subject to call, or make regular visits to all communities within their jurisdiction.

The second step in the collection of educational information is the listing of state and national sources from which additional information may be secured if and when needed. It will not usually be deemed desirable to collect a vast amount of information for which there never has been and perhaps never may be a call. On the other hand, whatever types of educational information are needed should be available and should be increased as occasion demands. A few reliable sources from which information may be obtained are suggested. For convenience they have been classified under levels of education although there is of necessity considerable overlapping in their applicability. Because of its importance and because information on such opportunities is less accessible and less well known a separate classification has been made for special education.

SOURCES OF INFORMATION ON EDUCATIONAL OPPORTUNITIES

1. *Preschool, Kindergarten, Elementary Levels.* In nearly every community there comes a time when civic, educational, or social workers desire to establish some agency for special service to its youngest age group, or to know what facilities without the community are available for some child who has suddenly become dependent, ill, neglected, or physically handicapped. Where shall the community or individual turn for assistance in responding to initial demands for information? One or more of the following are reliable first assistants:

The National Association for Nursery Education, Institute of Child Welfare, University of Minnesota, Minneapolis, Minnesota. Disseminates information about nursery schools.

Child Welfare League of America, 130 East Twenty-second Street, New York, New York. Interested in the care and protection of dependent and neglected children. Includes in its membership 165 child-caring agencies, institutions, and public departments in the United States.

U. S. Department of Labor, Children's Bureau, Washington, D.C. Investigates and reports on all matters pertaining to the welfare of children.

Iowa Child Welfare Research Station, University of Iowa, Iowa City, Iowa. Conducts research in the field of child development, disseminates information, and trains research workers and leaders in various branches of child welfare.

Merrill-Palmer School, Detroit, Michigan. An experimental and demonstration nursery school, correlating its work with a practical course in child care for college students.

Expansion of the list is possible for communities which desire to have a more complete file.[3]

2. *Secondary School or Youth Level.* For youths who have exhausted the opportunities of or are misfits in local schools, there are numerous

---

[3] See M. M. Chambers, *Youth-serving Organizations* (1st ed.; Washington: American Council on Education, 1937) for a descriptive directory of national nongovernmental agencies. One such directory will provide all the essential information on the types of services included. Purchasers should ask for the latest edition.

educational opportunities without the community, or in connection with employment either within or without the community. Three sources of information on opportunities for cultural, technical, and semiprofessional education in residential and day schools are cited. Since school directories are frequently revised, dates of publication are omitted:

American School Association, 10 North State Street, Chicago, Illinois. Gives advice on the selection of a private day school, boarding school, military school, camp, etc.

Porter Sargent, 11 Beacon Street, Boston, Massachusetts. Publishes *A Handbook of Private Schools* and other guides to schools and camps in the United States.

American Council on Education, 744 Jackson Place, Washington, D.C. Publishes *American Junior Colleges,* ed. by Walter C. Eells, a recent addition to directories.

Correspondence schools and university extension courses, grouped together because of the similarity of their objectives, are discussed here under secondary school education rather than under college education, to which they equally pertain, because the most recent development in these courses has been the elaboration and enrichment of secondary programs in small or rural communities. Correspondence courses may be taken to get credit toward a college degree, to attain some specific cultural or occupational objective, or to secure high-school credit under a plan of supervised study. They may be taken under extension divisions of universities, under commercial correspondence schools, or under other auspices such as state rehabilitation services and business corporations, which may or may not prepare their own lesson assignments. There is available sufficient published material on correspondence courses of all types to permit the full use of the best of such educational opportunities without anyone's suffering from the abuses of the worst. Counselors in small schools and rural areas will be interested in further study of the supervised correspondence study plan whereby their pupils may receive credit for college admission courses without leaving home, sometimes by cooperation of the university and locally employed teachers and sometimes through the service of itinerant teachers.[4] In a few communities which do not support a high school, this same sort of supervised correspondence study has been arranged for in evening classes which enroll both youth and adult.

Mortality among correspondence course enrollees has been the subject of much study and much criticism. Personal experience has taught the

[4] K. O. Broady, *Enriched Curriculums for Small High Schools* (Lincoln: University of Nebraska, 1938), pp. 71–82.

author that a community counseling service under the auspices of the public schools or the public library should be available to both youth and adult and should be equipped to discuss the educational opportunities available through correspondence courses. Prerequisite to such a service are: (1) knowledge as to which schools are approved, what courses they offer, and their strong and weak points, (2) knowledge of the inherent difficulties in correspondence study, (3) understanding of the inherent weaknesses in human nature which make it difficult to profit by such courses, and (4) skill in assisting potential enrollees to understand the problems involved in the successful completion of such courses and to analyze their own ability and willingness to cope with these problems in order to finish the work satisfactorily. Periodic assistance in meeting the requirements of such courses might be an additional incentive to completion among adult enrollees. Two references to agencies from which information on correspondence study may be secured will be sufficient for ordinary purposes:

National University Extension Association, Indiana University, Bloomington, Indiana. A clearinghouse and bureau of general information on all types of extension service. It maintains a correspondence study directory.

National Home Study Council, 839 Seventeenth Street, Washington, D.C. Under subsidy of the Carnegie Corporation of New York, this organization has inspected and rated 480 schools. Only 46 were approved. The Council's *Home Study Blue Book*, 1941, may be secured free of charge, and the Council will receive and act on complaints against schools whose practices are unethical.

A majority of the states furnish some information on educational opportunities for youth. The two most helpful types of information which come specifically under their jurisdiction are bulletins which describe educational opportunities offered in state-supported institutions and annual lists of private business and other trade or vocational schools which advertise to prepare youth for wage-earning occupations. As an illustration of the method employed in preparing the latter a quotation is given from the 1940 bulletin issued by New York State, which each fall provides school principals with a list of the private business schools registered by the State Education Department during the previous school year:

Registered private schools are visited annually by a representative of the Department. The school plant and facilities are inspected; the program of studies, size of classes, qualifications of the teachers, and the school's reputation for fair and honest dealing with its pupils and the public are investigated. In addition to those important phases of school administration, instruction in the classroom is carefully observed and suggestions are made for the purpose of improving teaching methods and materials. This procedure enables the Department to recommend registered business schools with the confidence that mature and able pupils who attend them may obtain a vocationally valuable business education. The State Education Department's registration requirements are intended to protect the public; in spite of claims to the contrary, few private business schools are able to satisfy them.[5]

Parents and pupils seeking information about private business schools should be advised to observe the following precautions:

(1) Visit and thoroughly inspect the schools in which you are interested; pay especial attention to the classroom equipment and the type of students enrolled.

(2) Do not sign an admission blank or pay money to a school solicitor in your home. Transact all financial business with an officer of the school in the school office.

(3) No reputable school can honestly guarantee you a position as an inducement to enroll. Avoid such schools.

(4) Avoid schools that offer "free books and supplies" or "scholarships," or that pay commissions to pupils for obtaining your enrollment.

(5) Investigate the vocational success of former pupils of the school in which you are interested. Were they able to obtain and hold office positions upon the completion of the course?

(6) If you seek a good business course, you must expect to pay for it. Avoid the "cut-rate school."

Information on educational opportunities may also be secured from the federal government. The U. S. Office of Education publishes two bulletins which are especially helpful to counselors advising on vocational opportunities:

Directory of Federally Aided All-Day Trade and Industrial Education Programs. Washington, 1940. (Misc. no. 2375.) Lists the trades taught and the names and addresses of the public schools in which they are taught.

Private Proprietary and Endowed Schools Giving Trade and Industrial Courses, by Maris M. Proffitt. Washington, 1935. (Bulletin, 1935, no. 8.)

Most professional organizations are equipped to recommend training schools in their field. State departments of education will supply lists of chartered institutions.

3. *College and Adult Level.* Adults who may legitimately expect counseling service relative to educational opportunities can usually be classified under one of four groups: (1) students who have completed secondary

---

[5] New York, Division of Vocational Education, Bureau of Business Education, *Bulletin no. 28*; Albany, N.Y.: State Education Dept., 1940).

education and desire information on collegiate or professional schools and oftentimes information on scholarship possibilities; (2) college graduates who are interested in graduate study, in information on special fields of interest, or in scholarships and fellowships; (3) individuals who have not been interested in formal education beyond compulsory education requirements but who can be induced to seek educational opportunities of an informal type; (4) adults who for one reason or another have not yet mastered the fundamental tools of education.

The type of information of value to the fourth group would of necessity be included under community opportunities; that sought by the third group would be concerned with local opportunities such as library reading lists and with correspondence course opportunities.[6] The information desired by the two groups which are interested in college, professional, or graduate study would include material from a number of sources. In the main it should be sufficient in volume and of such character that the individual alone, or with the help of the counselor, may find replies to certain questions which will be determinants in his choice. A few important questions are suggested and many others will come to mind as counselors deal with individual needs: Which is preferable, a coeducational or a segregated college; a small or large student body? What are the advantages and disadvantages with reference to locality and environment? Admission requirements? Standing in comparison with other institutions? Total expense? Facilities for student aid, scholarships, and the like? Character of the teaching corps? Character of the student body? Status of the alumni and their record after graduation? Living conditions? Health program? Social, moral, and spiritual influences? Advisory system? Outstanding departments? Special facilities for meeting special needs?

A representative list of strictly nonpartisan publications giving data on all institutions will be a first assistant in answering such questions:

Clarence S. Marsh, ed. *American Universities and Colleges.* Washington: American Council on Education, 1940. A factual summary of colleges and universities in America.

Ella B. Ratcliffe. *Accredited Higher Institutions.* Washington, 1938. (U. S. Office of Education Bulletin, 1938, no. 16.) A presentation of the standards of accrediting agencies and associations with lists of professional schools, colleges, and universities.

Walter J. Greenleaf. *Working Your Way Through College and Other Means of Providing for College Expenses.* Washington, 1941. (U. S. Office of Education, Vocational Division Bulletin, 1941, no. 210, Occupational

6 The best single source of information on all types of adult education is the American Association for Adult Education, Teachers College, Columbia University, New York City

Information and Guidance Series, no. 4.) A helpful bulletin which includes assistance in choosing a college.

Ella B. Ratcliffe. *Scholarships and Fellowships Available at Institutions of Higher Education*. Washington, 1936. (U. S. Office of Education Bulletin, 1936, no. 10.)

Catalogues and bulletins of individual colleges and universities elaborate data secured from these more general sources. Secondary schools and libraries will find it convenient to have on hand all the information published by their own state institutions. The extent to which bulletins from other institutions will be needed will depend upon local demands for this type of information. But always, whatever material is "in stock," it must be the latest editions, and those who refer inquirers to such bulletins must be sure that they are up-to-date.

4. *Opportunities for Special Education*. The demand for information on opportunities for special education usually comes from two types of individuals: (1) those who are variants from normal groups to a sufficient extent to warrant the assumption that they will derive most benefit from a type of education specifically adapted to their needs and (2) those who desire to concentrate on preparation for a nonprofessional occupation which is so highly specialized that adequate and rapid preparation is best made in a school confined to a single objective, or through training on the job.

There are many sources of information from which educational opportunities open to individuals comprised in the first group may be ascertained. One for each atypical group is listed, and application to the U. S. Office of Education will bring lists, periodically revised, of residential schools serving these groups:

American Association on Mental Deficiency, Elwyn, Pennsylvania. Promotes the welfare of mentally retarded children. Directs parents or guardians to schools and institutions caring for such children.

American Society for the Hard of Hearing, 1537 35th Street N.W., Washington, D.C. Co-operates with educators, health authorities, parent-teacher groups, etc., in founding local organizations and otherwise assisting young people with impaired hearing.

Braille Institute of America, 1741 North Vermont Avenue, Los Angeles, California. Promotes the welfare of the blind, assists them in obtaining scholarships and in getting established in the business and professional world. Distributes free books to the blind.

International Council for Exceptional Children, 453 Stimson Avenue, Detroit, Michigan. Promotes the welfare and the education of all types of exceptional children, including the handicapped and the gifted.

International Society for Crippled Children, Elyria, Ohio. Assists national, state, and local agencies in providing a program for the care, cure, and education of crippled children.

National Council for the Physically Handicapped, St. Paul, Minnesota. Serves as a clearinghouse for national agencies concerned with persons having physical impairments.

Examples of the type of work for which the student wishing to enter a specialized occupation might desire to prepare are secretarial work, filing, office-machine operating, telephone operating, beauty-parlor operating, waitress work, truck-driving, and some phases of auto-repair and garage service. Short unit courses in public or private schools are the usual method of meeting such needs. Counselors should have at their command a rather complete list of the training opportunities open to youths who desire to enter occupational life with limited formal education. To prepare such a list is one of the most difficult projects connected with an educational opportunity service. Trained research ability of a very high order and wide experience in both the field of education and of occupation is required to discriminate between the offerings of the large number of institutions which thrive on the credulity of parents and pupils and the schools which fully meet their educational obligations.

Some institutions merit high rating for one purpose, low rating for another. Beauty-culture and secretarial schools alone are capable of causing students of such training opportunities unlimited difficulties. If opportunity lists are kept up-to-date, they are money consumers; if not kept up-to-date, they have no value for counseling purposes. If all schools are included without reference to competency or reliability, the lists become mere directories without guidance value. On the other hand, if inclusion in the list be based upon specific criteria for determining efficiency and acceptable ethical practices, there is always the danger of incurring the hostility of directors whose schools are rated substandard; always the question of where substandard should begin; always the possibility of a libel suit if omission from a recommended list can be interpreted as blacklisting. A number of methods of minimizing this sort of difficulty have been tried. Sometimes there is a notation stating that the list is incomplete and that no effort has been made to include all the desirable training opportunities but merely to suggest a list of well-known schools for those who have no personal knowledge as a basis for selection. It is hoped, of course, that choice will be made from the prepared list.

The protection of unsophisticated youth against unethical practices by proprietary schools has been a continuously puzzling problem from the beginning of the guidance movement.[7] The enactment of compulsory continuation school legislation and the issuance of apprenticeship rulings under minimum wage laws closed many opportunities for training on the job and increased the desire of pupils to attend proprietary schools instead of public schools. Abuses were many, and a demand for a state accreditment system or a system of inspection and licensure arose. The New York system whereby one may always be sure of selecting an accredited school gives counselors a list which is approved and relieves them of the dangers involved in censoring their own list. But it does not always give them information on the specific school which is under consideration. Moreover, there is a tendency for neither superior schools nor inferior schools to seek accreditment: the former because their reputations are too well-established for accreditment to have value; the latter because of fear of a refusal of endorsement. This situation leaves an intermediate group of schools which are close enough to the border to make accreditment a commercial asset, and it affords no criteria by which either counselor or individual student may distinguish between the omitted *superior* and the omitted *inferior* schools.

Michigan, a number of years ago, instituted a plan whereby many of the private schools which catered to students of the continuation school age were inspected, licensed, and supervised by the state. As long as standards were maintained, they were allowed to operate as a part of the state educational system and to register students in lieu of continuation schools. Such a system automatically provided an approved list of training opportunities; inspection kept it up-to-date; the training was more practical; and the expense to the state was markedly decreased while the number of occupations for which it could offer training was markedly increased.

[7] For a recent example of philanthropic efforts to protect youth against educational rackets see *Traps for the Unwary*, a six-page pamphlet prepared by the Counseling Service for Juniors of the Westchester County Children's Association, New York State, 1941.

CHAPTER VI

Information on Occupational Opportunities

THE collection of occupational information lends itself less advantageously to community participation than does the collection of information regarding educational opportunities. Special training, wide experience, and unusual tact and judgment are prerequisites to success, especially when dealing with local occupations. Very rarely can communities call to service a volunteer corps equipped to collect this sort of material. This chapter is planned, therefore, on the assumption that it will be of major value to those who are preparing for advisory service—that it will afford them an overview of the sources from which occupational information may be obtained and of the criteria which may be used in evaluating such sources and their content, and that at the same time it will give them an idea of the sort of contribution which is expected of students majoring in occupational research. If its content be mastered and collateral readings be chosen, the student should have acquired:

1. A definite understanding of what is meant by reliable, available, adaptable occupational information.

2. Familiarity with the seven types of occupational information mentioned, and realization of the *plus* which is essential for specialization in the field.

3. A clear conception of the meaning of such terms as "job specification," "job analysis," "job blueprint," "record of usage," "position classification" and "wage standardization" as applied to occupational research.

GENERAL SOURCES OF OCCUPATIONAL INFORMATION

Occupational information may be secured in a number of different ways and from a variety of sources:

1. Direct observation, as a visitor or as an employee, of industrial processes and of business procedures is an excellent method of securing occupational information. The visitor should observe accurately, intelligently, and objectively. The observer-worker should be especially vigilant lest his personal reactions to work experiences and work associations be assumed to be the common reactions of all other workers.

2. Practical experience, at first as an understudy, in placing the product

of educational systems is a second source of occupational information. The placement worker is the liaison officer. He acquires the point of view of employers and employees relative to the same jobs in the same plants. He weighs these opinions in the light of his own knowledge secured from observation. He finds such information very valuable, whether there be sufficient agreement for the facts to be easily established or whether conflict of opinion calls for discrimination in determining truth or in withholding judgment pending further enlightenment.

3. Conferences with employers, employees, personnel officers, placement clerks, and others whose knowledge and experience make their opinions worth while is a third good source of information. Personal prejudice, as well as lack of preparation for accurate observation, often detracts from the value of material secured from such sources. The information derived from a single conference with a single individual or from a single address is best rated "opinion" rather than "fact" until it has been verified. A single affirmation does not establish a fact.

4. Visual aids of all sorts including maps, charts, blueprints, motion pictures, exhibits which show raw material in various stages of processing, demonstrations of work techniques, and the like furnish another group of desirable sources. Within this group the counselor finds both the clever misrepresentation of processes and conditions and the most faithful representation of things as they are. Processes, if shown without partisanship or propaganda, are interesting to a wide range of ages and educational levels and possess a high degree of guidance value.

5. Printed matter of all sorts and of all degrees of reliability and attractiveness forms the largest single source from which to secure counseling material. Public and private libraries, the federal Departments of Commerce and Labor, the U. S. Public Health Service, the Bureau of the Census, chambers of commerce, trade unions, and other similar agencies are sources from which printed material may be secured. Critical evaluation of each piece of material is necessary before it can be accepted as reliable information.

CRITERIA FOR DETERMINING THE VALUE OF OCCUPATIONAL INFORMATION

Not all material is equally valuable for all purposes even though it may be equally valuable per se. There are, however, a few guiding principles which may be used in evaluating occupational material for all purposes, on all educational levels, and for all age groups: (1) it must be reliable; (2) it must be available; (3) it must be adaptable.

The last two criteria are determined fairly easily. Occupational material is of no practical value unless it is accessible and in such shape that it can be used. Adaptability implies that the material is suitable to one of the purposes for which occupational information is commonly used, namely:

1. To broaden pupils' occupational horizon and increase their general knowledge. This purpose is in harmony with both the social and individual aims accepted as a fundamental principle of guidance in the early history of the movement.

2. To help pupils understand community occupations and to appreciate the social significance of each worker's contribution.

3. To help pupils develop right attitudes toward work.

4. To help pupils establish ideals of co-operative service.

5. To arouse pupils' interests and ambitions and to help them in uncovering individual abilities.

6. To help pupils realize the importance of cultivating desirable work habits and personality traits.

7. To help pupils evaluate their qualifications in terms of specific occupational demands.

8. To aid placement officers in distributing labor and in maintaining a well-balanced labor market.

9. To aid school administrators in curriculum determination and revision.

10. To assist business houses in the selection, placement, and progressive training of employees.

If the purpose be to broaden a person's vision of the world's work or to instill proper attitudes toward work, the material chosen would be quite different from that which would be selected to assist someone in choice of an occupation, to aid in employment adjustment, or to suggest curriculum changes. The language and method of presentation should also be in harmony with the purpose. Information helpful to counselors might be entirely unsuitable for pupils. Material which appealed to college students would hardly be appropriate for junior-high-school groups. Material for all purposes will be more satisfactory if descriptions are specific rather than general—if such adjectives as "dirty" and "monotonous" and such terms as "advantages" and "disadvantages," which refer to things not necessarily inherent in the job and which have no significant meaning apart from an individual, are avoided.

The reliability of occupational information is a far more difficult quality to test. We are all naturally credulous. It is much easier to believe everything one sees, hears, and reads than it is to sift the evidence and accept only the truth. Maintaining a critical attitude toward the source and content of occupational information is the first step in developing ability to pass judgment on its reliability. A critical attitude, plus a knowledge and application of the rules of research procedure, would do much to clear away the mass of rubbish which hinders the advance of vocational guidance. Counselors will do well to start out on the assumption that the value of material depends as a rule on three things:

1. *The Character of the Source.* What opportunities for error are inherent in the form, or how might facts secured from any given type of source be influenced by its character? Newspapers, political speeches, war documents, biographies, illustrative material, government and state publications, moving pictures, employer publications, labor-union pronouncements, and the like should all be subjected to question regarding the possible influence of their character on their reliability.

2. *The Character of the Author.* (a) What are his intellectual characteristics? Was he able to observe accurately and describe correctly? A reply involves knowledge of the author's education, the special training which may have prepared him to observe occupational facts, his occupational experiences, his opportunities for observation, and the like. (b) What are his moral characteristics? Is he an honest man? Did he want to know the truth and was he willing to tell it? Efforts to determine the accuracy and good faith of authors center around such factors as their interests; the force of circumstances; their sympathies, vanity, and desire for publicity or for professional recognition; and their abilities as observers in relation to their prejudices and passions. The Character Education Institute, Washington, D.C., some years ago published a list of "Intellectual Immoralities" which are very helpful if kept in mind when preparing one's own research work as well as when passing judgment on the value of the studies of others. The items most important for counselors are the following:

(1) Carelessness in observations; sloppy work.

(2) Inaccuracy in determining units to be counted in statistical research.

(3) Slovenliness in logic, fantastic explanation.

(4) Generalizing beyond one's data.

(5) Confusing opinions with knowledge.

(6) Confidence in the results of research in disregard of weakness in proof and verification.

(7) Poor judgment in research plan and procedure.

(8) Egoism allowed to crowd one to the invention of new theories for personal distinction.

(9) Emotionalism during research; "I believe" instead of "I have proved."

(10) Adjusting theories to popular likes and dislikes.

(11) Rushing into print with a report of research work that justifies no conclusions.

(12) Impatience or unwillingness to proceed step by step through a research.

(13) Indulgence in dense verbiage for the sake of appearing super-learned.

(14) Popularizing tentative generalizations for the sake of personal publicity.

3. *The Influence of Time and Place.* The criteria of time and place are of considerable importance with respect to original value as well as up-to-dateness of occupational material. Trained research workers know that reliable sources usually carry the name of author or investigator and the time of collection of the data as well as the date of writing and of printing. In spite of this generally known requirement, many typed, mimeographed, and even printed pieces of information carry no date, and one is obliged to depend upon the context for time and place. A considerable period of time frequently elapses between fact-finding and publication of findings in government reports. Leaflets on occupations and job analyses should, in every instance, carry the date of research. Otherwise pupils and counselors are bound to find themselves studying processes and analyzing requirements which have already been discarded.

But it must not be assumed that all praise or blame for the accuracy and reliability of occupational information is to be credited to "sources." Counselors, teachers, pupils, or others who interpret sources have an equal, although somewhat different, type of responsibility for accuracy and reliability. Correct interpretation is essential to satisfactory guidance service. One need not go to ancient history to find illustrations of discrepancies between the literal and real meaning of spoken and written words. Statistical evidence, accurate per se, is often made to seem inaccurate by the interpretation put upon it. For example, the *wage-worth-of-school-training myth* grew up around, and continues to receive nourishment from, inadequate interpretation of the relationship between two sets of statistically accurate facts—educational level attained and future financial reward. The persistence of this myth among educators is truly astounding; its usual interpretation for counseling purposes is very dangerous. The most recent example at hand is copied from the *New York Times,* June 15, 1941:

Each year spent in college is worth $18,000, Frank H. Bowles, director of admissions at Columbia University, estimates in "The College Yardstick," a guide to aid high school students in evaluating the educational advantages of the 900 colleges in the United States that award degrees.

Discussing the value of a college education, Mr. Bowles points out that its dividends cannot be counted for many years. "But by the time he is sixty years old, a college graduate has earned, on the average, $72,000 more than a high school graduate," he says. "This means that each college year is worth $18,000."

CLASSIFICATION OF OCCUPATIONAL INFORMATION

There are doubtless many ways in which the various types of occupational information, or the forms in which such information is available, may be classified. If one desires to study the field rather systematically, a rough classification of types of information is usually helpful. Each type can then be taken up in turn and studied more or less thoroughly as time and facilities permit. The following seven-type classification has been used for a number of years in university classes dealing with occupational materials, and the students have reported it valuable: (1) General Occupational Surveys, (2) Occupational Monographs, (3) Statistical Surveys, (4) Employment Opportunity Surveys, (5) Training Opportunities in Employment, (6) Illustrative Material, and (7) Legislative Enactments and Occupational Restrictions.

1. *General Occupational Surveys.*[1] General occupational surveys afford a brief overview of a number of occupations in a single volume under the sponsorship of one or more authors. They do not go into detail and do not expect readers to assume applicability in every respect to every locality. But if the data they do present are accurate and up-to-date, they are very helpful for broadening the occupational horizon and increasing general knowledge, and as a starting point for further study. There are two common methods of preparing such surveys:

(1) *Summaries of the comparable high points of a number of occupations, based on data picked off from more intensive studies of single occupations, are adapted to different purposes and age levels and published in one volume.* Sometimes secondary material is supplemented by personal knowledge or by personal research, but very frequently the bulk of the material collected by this method is secondary in character, and now and then it is three or four times removed from the original source. Therefore its use must be safeguarded by conscious application of the universal rules for documentary criticism cited in the introduction to this chapter.

The major difficulties inherent in the preparation of occupational surveys by this method and in their use are: (1) In order to have value, they

[1] E. A. La Fortune, Director of Guidance of the Ithaca Public Schools, Ithaca, New York, has given valuable assistance in the selection of the various types of material to be included in this chapter. The titles referred to as illustrations are satisfactory examples of different types of material. They must not be assumed to be best publications since those best for one purpose are frequently not the best for another.

should be based upon a wider range of accurate information than it is possible for one, two, or even three persons to possess. (2) Selective ability, even of the highest order, is prone to err in determining relative values. (3) Changing social and economic conditions render such material obsolete before it reaches the market. (4) The high initial cost and the expensiveness of revisions frequently lead to retention and use of such books long after their value is gone. (5) When one such book is selected as a text for occupation-study or for life-career classes, uninformed teachers tend to follow the occupations listed in the text, discouraging constructive interest in the spontaneous study of preferred occupations. (6) If a teacher knows the field well enough to warrant her assignment to such class duty, she knows it too well to depend upon this type of text. If she does not know the occupational field well enough to discard the text, it automatically becomes a dangerous tool in her inexperienced hands.

There are numerous examples of this type of general survey. Lists are found in many easily accessible bibliographies,[2] often without annotations as to value. The three following examples are indicative of the varied characteristics of such survey texts and of the importance of careful evaluation before selection for student use:

Mary R. Lingenfelter and Harry D. Kitson in *Vocations for Girls* [3] discuss thirty-four work fields ranging from semiskilled jobs through the professions, with emphasis on the former. Occupations are grouped according to sex preference: those in which women predominate, those in which the sexes compete on somewhat equal terms, and those usually preferred by men. The material is suitable for high-school or college use. The reading lists include fiction and biography.

A recent volume by Mildred Davey, Elizabeth M. Smith, and Theodore R. Myers, entitled *Everyday Occupations*,[4] is suitable for either junior- or senior-high-school pupils. It deals with typical fields of work from each of the ten census classifications, and within each field a number of jobs are described in detail. Information from other sources has been supplemented by personal investigation, and the material has been tested in counseling situations.

The Choice of an Occupation, published a number of years ago by the Department of Personnel Study of Yale University [5] for the use of Yale

[2] See for example Walter J. Greenleaf, *80 New Books on Occupations* (U. S. Office of Education, Occupational Information and Guidance Service, Misc. no. 2395; Washington, 1940) and *Vocational Guide,* an annotated bibliography of selected current material published monthly by Science Research Associates, 1700 Prairie Avenue, Chicago, Illinois.

[3] New York: Harcourt, Brace and Co., 1939.

[4] Boston: D. C. Heath and Co., 1941.

[5] Ed. by Albert B. Crawford and Stuart H. Clement (New Haven: Yale University, 1932).

students, is a third example. The statements in the introduction are indicative of the scholarship which permeates the volume and which has prolonged the value of the book beyond the usual life of such publications even though certain portions of the material are outdated.

(2) *A second method of preparing occupational surveys is by securing contributions from a number of persons each of whom deals with one occupation.* Each writer may offer a few pages of cursory statements culled from his own experience, or he may prepare a veritable monograph based on the best available experience, his own included. Such material, collected and edited by one person and published in one volume, will form a book of general information. It is obvious that the trustworthiness of each contribution depends upon the "intellectual moralities" of each contributor. Such publications are apt to be very popular, to arouse interest and enthusiasm, and to inspire readers to further study. If not accepted as of more value than their content and method warrant, these books have a place similar to that of the first type of general occupational surveys as background and inspirational material. The first edition of *An Outline of Careers,* edited by Edward L. Bernays,[6] is a good example of a collection of carefully prepared monographs for the use of mature students. *New Occupations for Youth* by T. Otto Nall [7] is a more recent work with less elaborate discussions intended for younger students.

A more scientific approach to the problem of furnishing a bird's-eye view of occupations is found in the *Occupational Outlines* prepared by the Science Research Associates.[8] A set of one hundred outlines dealing with the jobs in which three quarters of all workers earn their living is bound in a substantial loose-leaf binder. The outlines are prepared by methods acceptable to research students. They cover such facts as trends in the field, number of workers, working conditions, wage scales, educational prerequisites, job descriptions, time of hiring, methods of entering, and lines of promotion. There are two material advantages in purchasing occupational information in a loose-leaf binder: removal of individual outlines from the binder permits serving a large number of students simultaneously, and revision of one outline at a time makes upkeep both easy and inexpensive. Counselors who have only ten dollars with which to start their collection of occupational material would do well to consider the desirability of making this volume a first purchase.

2. *Occupational Monographs.* Occupational monographs deal with one

[6] New York: George H. Doran Co., 1927. The recent edition is less complete.

[7] New York: Association Press, 1938.

[8] Louis Eisman, ed., *Occupational Outlines on America's Major Occupations* (Chicago: Science Research Associates, 1940).

vocation, occupational field, or business function. They are usually presented as single studies rather than as collections of information about several occupations and they treat their topic both more intensively and more extensively than is possible in general surveys. There is an increasing tendency to prepare such monographs for guidance purposes with special reference to the interests and needs of different age, level-of-education, and sex groups. If a series of monographs be contemplated, uniformity in form is desirable so that each study may be similar to the others. However, it is to be hoped that the peak in publishing occupational monographs—too often based on purely commercial motives or on a desire to see the name of the author or the school system in print—has been reached. During recent years the demand for occupational information has tended to encourage quantity production at the expense of quality of content; too many ten-cent pamphlets which have no claim to "research" have been foisted on an uncritical public. That does not mean that occupational monographs are not needed. They are. But research monographs are expensive. They require trained ability to collect and criticize the content to be included and to see that the material is properly arranged.

A number of outlines have been prepared as guides to the essential content of monographs.[9] As guides they are helpful in evaluating the various monographs which are available as well as in selecting topics for inclusion if it be decided to venture into the field of publication. The American Council on Education several years ago suggested the following items as desirable for all vocational monographs: (1) definition of the work, (2) type of the work, (3) work relationship with other groups, (4) origin, (5) background and development, (6) organization charts, (7) typical starting point, (8) direct and collateral steps of promotion, (9) opportunity for advancement, (10) primary duties, (11) physical or mental characteristics necessary, (12) physical or mental characteristics handicapping, (13) detailed study of remuneration, (14) earning study of men of same educational level in all work, (15) proportionate representation of college men at different levels, (16) previous preparation needed at start and for advancement, (17) opportunities for obtaining experience, (18) demand for and supply of applicants, (19) the work as training for other fields, (20) cost of training, (21) considerations in choosing a concern, (22) social and other satisfactions inherent, (23) social and other sacrifices involved, and (24) bibliography.

---

9 See "Distinguishing Marks of a Good Occupational Monograph," *Occupations*, XVIII (1939), 129–130, and "Content of a Good Occupational Monograph—The Basic Outline," *Occupations*, XIX (1940), 20–23.

The desirability of these items requires no comment. Personal experience in advisory service for college students influences the author to add three other items: (1) geographical distribution of positions, (2) advice on high-school preparation, and (3) methods of entering. Experience also suggests the desirability of cautioning beginning research workers against too energetic pursuit of salary data. Entree to the best sort of research opportunities has more than once been denied to workers because of their overenthusiasm in attempting to secure what had been decided upon as valuable and essential items of information. Salaries are objective data; if tangible at all they are very tangible, provided the interviewer does not antagonize by overaggressiveness. Approximate salaries afford quite adequate guidance information on the college level, and in many cases statistical consideration of actual earning power at different periods of time could be left for statistical surveys which have salary information as one of their objectives. Wage scales set by labor unions and by wage boards are matters of public knowledge. Perhaps the Council's Item No. 13 might be combined with No. 14 to good advantage.

Opportunity for advancement is another topic which should be dealt with cautiously since advancement is not inherent in occupations and does not automatically come to each employee but is dependent upon the immediate effectiveness of individuals plus their potentialities for service in the particular position open. The fact that oftentimes no advanced position is open to permit the promotion of deserving employees must not be overlooked by those who are preparing youth for intelligent understanding of the principles and practice which control occupational advancements. An opportunity for advancement may not come to one who obviously merits it, but the one unforgivable sin which youth commits against himself is to neglect the preparation essential for advancement so that when the door does open he is unready to enter.

Occupational monographs are available in all stages of accuracy, completeness, and literary perfection. They are prepared to meet the needs of all ages and of all educational levels. Their objectives are sufficiently varied to afford informative and inspirational reading matter, to provide teaching content and lesson plans, or to outline the educational values to be derived from the part-time pursuit of an occupation before the completion of formal education. Some deal with a function such as filing, accountancy, or stenography; others deal with a single occupation or an occupational field.

Electrical Occupations for Boys, by Lee M. Klinefelter,[10] is a very attractive and informative volume which will appeal to the high-school age.

[10] New York: E. P. Dutton and Co., 1937.

It discusses the field of electrical occupations in narrative form, accompanied by many illustrations, and affords a good example of a recent tendency to cover an entire occupational field rather than to describe differentiated occupations within each field in separate monographs.

J. L. Hornung's *Radio as a Career* [11] is another example of practically the same type of monograph, but designed for more mature readers who are closer to their final choice. Both positions which require college preparation and servicing and operating positions which are open to non-college individuals are discussed. The chapter on Home Study (correspondence school study) is timely and important.

The popularity of continuation, part-time, and opportunity schools, coupled with the enactment of the Smith-Hughes Law in 1917, gave considerable impetus to the preparation of occupational monographs dealing with positions open to juniors who were combining school and work. Some were prepared for independent use by youthful wage-earners and would-be wage-earners, but much of the material was prepared for the use of teachers who were dealing with employed youth. *Newsboy Service, A Study in Educational and Vocational Guidance,* published by the present writer in 1917,[12] illustrates a type of local study which was designed to reveal the possible educational values which are inherent in work experience. The study was based on personal interviews with Seattle newsboys, and the findings dealt with the social, moral, economic, physical, educational, and vocational aspects of the work as the newsboys experienced it. It was a revelation to local educators to learn that many of the fundamental knowledges and principles upon which all business systems are built—selecting a location; leasing, buying, and selling locations; wholesaling and retailing; credit and collection; profit and loss; and the like— were well understood by boys still in the elementary schools with a long educational road to travel before they reached textbook discussion of the same topics.

Another later and more specific effort to assist teachers who were interested in part-time pupils was made by the Division of Vocational Education of the University of California during the 1920's. A number of exceedingly valuable monographs were published which by means of outlines, charts, and lesson plans indicated how teachers might relate classroom work to the requirements of different occupations which were open to junior workers.[13] The Series on Commercial Occupations in-

[11] New York: Funk and Wagnalls Co., 1940.
[12] Yonkers, N.Y.: World Book Co., 1917.
[13] See the Part-Time Educational Series published by the University of California, Division of Vocational Education, Research and Service Center, at Berkeley, California, from 1920 to 1930.

cluded such titles as *The Work of Juniors in the Telegraph Service, An Analysis of the Work of Juniors in Banks,* and *An Analysis of Department Store Occupations for Juniors.* Each junior position was analyzed for general facts; duties were listed; required knowledge was arranged in teaching units; sample lesson plans were offered; and lines of promotion were indicated. These monographs, in addition to their valuable content, were models of research which are not outdated as to form and method even today. However, interest in this particular type of monograph for this specific purpose lagged as the compulsory education laws raised the school-leaving age ever higher, and labor laws eliminated much of the previous opportunity for work experience under educational supervision. The utility of the day-continuation school for young wage-earners passed into history, and the occasion for this type of monograph was over. There may, however, be a revival of interest in such material if work experience gains ground as a part of the educational curriculum.

Vocational counselors will, of course, desire to be familiar with all types of monographs, with their differentiated uses, and with the sources from which they may be obtained. A first step in the collection of such material may well be registration on the mailing list of the Occupational Information and Guidance Service of the U. S. Office of Education. Frequent bibliographies, including bibliographies of bibliographies, are published. They suggest many avenues through which occupational information may be secured, and usually they are annotated.[14] A second step might be a canvass of professional organizations to see whether publications are available through their headquarters, e.g., The Nursing Information Bureau of the American Nurses' Association, 50 West Fiftieth Street, New York, or The Engineering Societies, 29 West 39th Street, New York. The American Institute of Mining and Metallurgical Engineers recently issued a vocational pamphlet,[15] prepared in question and answer form for the use of secondary students, which exemplifies the type of information to be secured from such sources.

A third step might consist of a sort of inventory of commercial sources from which reliable monographs might be obtained. Observe carefully the annotations which accompany the listing of such monographs in recognized bibliographies. Cost is always an important consideration, but it is better to have one expensive monograph which tells the truth and is

[14] For example, see their pamphlet entitled *200 Sources of Pamphlet Materials on Occupations* (Misc. no. 2536; Washington, 1941) which is one of the most recent bibliographies. Free or relatively inexpensive material may be secured from the sources mentioned.

[15] Thomas T. Read, *Careers in the Mineral Industries* (New York: American Institute of Mining and Metallurgical Engineers, 1939).

up-to-date than to have a dozen ten-cent pamphlets which have no intrinsic value. It is usually helpful in determining values to compare—as to methods of work, form, content, and reliability—the product of one or more agencies which make monograph preparation a profession with the casually prepared product of avocationalists or opportunists. No agency will turn out uniformly desirable research results; each is bound, now and then, to produce a less desirable study, but those which standardize on the basis of the less desirable are not entitled to counselor support.

3. *Statistical Surveys.* Statistical surveys furnish a third type of occupational information. They are concerned with the collection, tabulation, and analysis of quantitative data regarding the distribution of workers. They include single surveys, specialized as to purpose and content, as well as periodic surveys, repetitive as to purpose and content. In general they are our best sources of information on such items as the distribution of workers among the various occupations by age, sex, color, educational background, and marital status. They include earnings of workers, their geographical distribution, health status, accident incidence, unemployment, and labor turnover. Most of the "Youth Tell Their Story" surveys are single statistical surveys designed to serve a specific purpose. The United States Census Reports and the Directory of Manufacturers compiled by the U. S. Department of Labor are outstanding examples of periodic surveys under federal auspices. Many helpful bulletins reporting statistical surveys are issued by the U. S. Women's Bureau, the U. S. Children's Bureau, the U. S. Employment Service, the U. S. Bureau of Labor Statistics and the Vocational Division of the U. S. Office of Education.[16] These surveys picture broad movements of labor supply and demand, indicate occupational trends, and reveal changes which promise to be permanent and eventually to call for a corresponding shift in the supply of workers.

Since taxpayers have a right to assume that our "planned economy" will recognize the necessity for some relationship between trends in public education opportunities and trends in occupational demands, periodic surveys furnish important data upon which to forecast essential changes in training programs. They also furnish counselors with information to aid youth in making occupational choices from fields where employment opportunities are increasing and where in the coming years his services will be most likely to find a satisfactory outlet. Secondary school pupils,

[16] For example, see *Guidance Bibliography—Trends in Occupations and Vocations* (U. S. Office of Education, Misc. no. 2363–1; Washington, 1940), a two-page list of references on trends. It includes several of the best sources for statistical surveys.

following any one of the excellent patterns which are in print,[17] can easily prepare a decade by decade comparison of occupational trends in their own community. It will tell them which occupations have remained constant, which have disappeared entirely, and what, if any, new occupations are calling for local workers.

In addition to governmental surveys, statistical surveys are prepared by a number of private organizations such as the United States Chamber of Commerce, the National Industrial Conference Board, the National Association of Manufacturers, the American Association of University Women, the National Consumers League, and the National Federation of Business and Professional Women's Clubs. Subdivisions of both governmental and private agencies make statistical surveys on state and community bases, and there are many occupational surveys which deal with the distribution of college and noncollege youth, mentally and physically defective youth, part-time and older workers, and others.

4. *Employment Opportunity Surveys.* The type of statistical survey which is concerned with up-to-the-minute information on the condition of the labor market has been designated an "employment opportunity survey." Such surveys, logically a subdivision of statistical surveys, have been classified separately in order to emphasize their immediate rather than their forecasting value, and their utility for placement counselors rather than for educational counselors. If up-to-date they furnish useful information for a number of purposes: (1) They afford knowledge of the relation between supply and demand, which helps to keep the placement office flexible and makes it a service station for stabilizing employment and for minimizing the undesirable results of technological unemployment. (2) They serve as a final check on occupational choice at the moment of employment and are the only type of survey mentioned which aids an individual to measure his offerings against the demands of particular firms, employers, or companies. (3) Where other types of sta-

---

[17] For example, see Walter Bingham *et al., Occupational Trends in New York City* (Adjustment Service Publication, no. 1, 1933); Emmett H. Welch, *Employment Trends in Philadelphia, 1900–1930* (Harrisburg, Pa.: State Employment Commission, 1933); Alvin H. Hansen and Tillman M. Sogge, *Occupational Trends in Minnesota, 1900–1930* (Minneapolis: University of Minnesota Press, 1933); Ralph G. Hurlin and Meredith B. Givens, "Shifting Occupational Patterns," in *Recent Social Trends* (New York: McGraw-Hill Book Co., 1933), I, 268–324; and H. Dewey Anderson and Percy E. Davidson, *Occupational Trends in the United States* (Stanford University, Calif.: Stanford University Press, 1940). *Survey of Occupational and Educational Trends,* published by the Department of Educational and Vocational Guidance of the Board of Education, Rochester, New York, 1938, gives statistics indicating the replacement needs of industry and business. "Vocations of College Men, 1849–1934" by Mortimer Karpp is a study of the alumni of the College of the City of New York showing trends in types of careers for 8020 alumni during 85 years (*Personnel Journal,* XIII [1934], 158–168).

tistical surveys give information on occupational opportunities en masse or in the abstract, employment opportunity surveys give concrete information regarding immediate, individual opportunities. (4) Because of the frequency with which they must be made, they reveal trends at a comparatively early stage and thus help students to forecast probable employment conditions at the close of a definite training period, educators to realize the need of curriculum change, and the regular clientele of counseling and employment offices to make ready for adjustment requirements. The great majority of such surveys are made for local purposes and have local value only.

The daily tabulations of local placement offices are the best illustration of such surveys and, if they are made simultaneously and the results are immediately pooled, they give a nation- or state-wide picture of the labor market. The U. S. Employment Service and the employment services of various states have rendered valuable service as clearinghouses or tabulating centers for the findings of such surveys. Any efficiently operating clearance systems—intra- and inter-school, state, or other agency—can, by pooling their statistics, furnish a daily, weekly, or monthly survey of labor conditions and of currently available positions and workers. War emergencies usually require very frequent employment opportunity surveys, but under normal conditions they are apt to be infrequent.

In 1918–1919 the clearance system of the U. S. Employment Service made several nation-wide surveys which were completed within twelve hours. At the close of the workday each employment-office superintendent, beginning with those in charge of the smallest local unit, reported to his superior officer in turn—city, state, district—on the excess or shortage of labor within his unit. By midnight national statistics were pooled in Washington and were tabulated in time for publication in the morning papers. Press releases indicated, for the entire nation, where and what positions were open, and where and what labor was available. Complete surveys of this type are expensive, and usually periodic or partial surveys covering one or more occupational units suffice and are made to meet specific needs. Seasonal occupational distribution surveys of the casual labor available as harvest hands—made on the basis of local employment surveys—have been carried on for many years with such efficiency that this particular sort of labor reserve has been mobilized for service in the southwestern states and gradually moved northward for similar service on Canadian ranches.

Employment opportunity surveys in the various fields of education have become fairly common during the last decade owing to the oversupply of teachers coupled with the persistent flooding of the market by teacher-training institutions which were apparently oblivious to the fact that there was such a thing as supply and demand. During the "depression" many employment opportunity surveys were made in the interests of various unemployed groups, engineers, doctors, middleaged persons, youth, married women, and others. The present war program is calling for surveys to locate technical workers of various kinds. Thus it is seen that all employment opportunity surveys are designed to reveal, to maintain, or to restore the balance between supply and demand. They may be instigated either by a surplus of labor coupled with a lack of employment outlets or by excess positions and a shortage of labor.

Although, as has been indicated, the employment opportunity survey has major value for the placement counselor, it is important that all counselors be familiar with its purpose and with its findings. Otherwise educational counselors may tend to stress the production responsibilities of education and fail to recognize that there are also problems connected with the effective distribution of the school and college product and by-product. They also may tend to overlook opportunities to contribute to the improvement of articulation between education and industry and to carry their share of responsibility for the maintenance of a balanced labor market.

5. *Training Opportunities in Employment.* Those who do not differentiate between the functions of education and those of training [18] may challenge the allocation of this topic to Chapter VI, which deals with occupational information, rather than to Chapter V, which deals with educational opportunities. The author, too, has challenged it, and finally accepted it because the content, purpose, and method of vocational training as it is offered on the job and as it is offered in public or proprietary schools differ markedly. Admission procedures, also, are different. In the one case, they follow educational practice: admission and retention are

---

[18] The controversy in educational circles relative to cultural education and vocational education is paralleled in business and industry by discussions about the relation between education and training. An admirable statement of the industrialist's point of view was recently expressed by representatives of the Eastman Kodak Company in an address which has much value for educators who desire to understand the objectives and methods of industrial training and to acquire a more practical basis for co-operation with industry: "What is education for one person becomes training for another who makes use of it directly on his job: or what is education in one locality will be training in another where the schools are not equipped to give it and industry does" (A. B. Gates and N. D. Hubbell, "Industrial Training—Basic Philosophy," a paper given before the Institute on Employment Relations of the National Association of Manufacturers at Burlington, Vermont, August, 1940).

frequently compulsory; instruction is paid for by the public or the individual; and many times there is little or no challenge to the putting forth of the individual's best effort.

In the other instance, employment procedures are followed: previous to admission as a trainee the individual must have been an applicant for a bona fide position to which remuneration is attached; he must have presented school credentials and satisfied physical and other test requirements. If accepted he becomes an employee and is assigned to definite work in a work unit with some personal responsibility for the effective functioning of the entire unit. During a probationary period he is aided to acquire correct attitudes *toward* work, and correct habits *of* work. But before time and money will be spent on "training" other than on the routine instruction necessary for a beginner's job, he must give definite evidence of learning interests and learning abilities. At this point only is selection for training completed and a chance to go forward simultaneously with learning and earning assured. Whatever those on the outside looking in may think, the boy on the inside, looking around and looking back on his previous educational experience, knows that he is in a different situation, and he knows that it is an occupational not an educational situation. "Making good on his own merits" takes on a new meaning, and he realizes that elimination from a job because of inability to compete advantageously with his fellows is quite different from the casual eliminations, absences, and tardinesses to which he had been accustomed in educational circles.

At this point it is well to recall that there are two types of positions entered from the secondary level of education: those that require some pre-employment training and those that require only the fundamentals, plus right attitudes toward work and good work habits. Attention has been called to counselor responsibility for aiding those who enter the first type to select reputable and suitable pre-employment training opportunities. The counselor is no less responsible for aiding those who enter the second type to select companies to which they may apply for employment which includes job training without specific training prerequisites. Local chambers of commerce will usually know what job-training opportunities there are in their own communities. Corporation reports to stockholders frequently describe company training policies and practices, while some of the larger corporations issue pamphlets dealing with training facilities.[19] Trade journals discuss company practices, and

19 Among these are the Ford Motor Company, the General Motors Corporation with its General Motors Institute, the Chrysler Company with its Institute of Engineering, the General Electric Company, the Radio Corporation of America, the Eastman Kodak

industrial, and sometimes popular, magazines publish articles concerned with training opportunities in different plants.[20] Some companies known for their effective training programs receive applications for apprenticeship from every section of the country. Companies seeking outstanding potential competency do not limit their selection area. Counselors who are called upon for this type of occupational information should collect and classify the same sort of information on opportunities for training in employment as has been suggested relative to public and private educational opportunities.[21]

"Corporation training" is the usual term used to designate training on the job. "Company" or "corporation school" is frequently used to designate classes which are sponsored by the company but which do not train for specific jobs. Learners enter on the lowest rung of the company-training ladder. They are production operators doing more or less specialized production work on the job under supervision. During periods of emergency, when the demand for training new workers interrupts too greatly the normal processes of industry, learners are frequently segregated in a "vestibule" school where special production instructors prepare them for transfer to regular production rooms. This is the most intensive, streamlined form of training used by industry, but it is an expensive method; therefore, unless the pressure for production is great and the number of trainees large, learners usually take their places in regular work units. War demands always encourage vestibule methods of training. It was a common method during the last war, and at the present time reports indicate that manufacturing industries are "dusting off" and

---

Company, the Browne and Sharpe Manufacturing Company, the Burroughs Adding Machine Company, and the International Business Machines Company. The 1939–1940 catalogue of the Wyomissing Polytechnic Institute, Wyomissing, Pennsylvania, affords an excellent example of co-operative training programs.

The National Industrial Conference Board with headquarters in New York City has recently issued a study entitled *Training Solutions of Company Problems* (Studies in Personnel Policy, nos. 15 and 18, 1939–1940) which will be helpful to those who do not care to collect catalogues and brochures directly from individual companies. Part A is "Programs Giving Special Attention to Development of Executives and Supervisory Personnel." Part B is "Programs Giving Special Attention to Development of the Skill of Non-supervisory Production Employees." General comments on training and questions for consideration are included.

[20] In 1936 *The American Machinist*, 330 West 42nd Street, New York City, published a series of programs which gave a good picture of training procedures in eight companies prior to the changes required by defense demands. A compilation of these articles entitled *Modern Apprentice Training* is available.

[21] *Practices Relating to Apprentice Training Programs in the Iron and Steel Industry: A Survey and Report* (New York: American Iron and Steel Institute, 1941) gives exceedingly valuable information covering practically all the questions which one would raise relative to apprenticeship.

modernizing the vestibule school of 1917–1918.[22] "Refresher" periods of training and programs for upgrading rusty or older workers fall into the same training category and use many of the methods that are used with learners.

Apprentices are selected much more carefully than learners; sometimes they are selected from learners of proved ability. The age limits are lower, usually applicants must be from eighteen to twenty-one years of age; educational requirements are much more stringent; the training period is longer; and the training content much more inclusive. Among specific preselection requirements, which vary somewhat from company to company, are: (1) a high-school diploma accompanied by a record of achievement, a statement of rank in class, and, if necessary for success in the apprenticeship desired, evidences of special ability in such subjects as science and mathematics; (2) a physical examination; (3) psychological tests; (4) recommendations; (5) a personal interview with each member of a three- to six-man selection committee which must unanimously approve of the applicant as a condition of selection, (6) if chosen for employment, a probationary period before final approval. Any feeling now existing on the part of teachers or counselors that boys of inferior abilities should be advised to enter industry is bound to be radically changed after perusal of the apprenticeship requirements of different companies and realization of the great stress which is put upon the proper selection, induction, and training of employees. The following quotation is an excellent presentation of the industrialist's position with reference to both selection and responsibility for training after selection:

The beginning of all training is the proper selection of the individual. To attempt to teach unqualified individuals is ineffective and wasteful. Before training courses are developed the problem of personnel selection should be thoroughly studied. Every effort must be made to assure the selection of those men who are best suited to the particular job and have better than average chances for success.[23]

Such a statement is equally applicable to the selection of teachers and counselors, and the slogan which accompanies the comment, "Every executive is a teacher," closely parallels the traditional slogan of guidance, "Every teacher is a counselor." It indicates the degree to which education has been woven into the fabric of American business while we still wait for business to be woven into the fabric of American education.

For the information of youth interested in apprenticeship the guidance office should have at hand the new plan for formal apprenticeship spon-

[22] Leonard J. Smith, "Vestibule Training for Today's Needs," *Personnel*, XVII (1941), 247–253.
[23] E. F. Wonderlic, "Training as a Personnel Function," *Personnel*, XIV (1937), 66–72.

sored by the Federal Committee of Apprentice Training which is designed
to afford a well-rounded training for some chosen trade.[24]

There are several other methods or combinations of methods which
afford some degree of job training for beginning workers. In some localities co-operative courses are offered on the secondary level,[25] in others
trade or technical schools offer basic industrial preparation. Some industries think they have a better basis for apprentice selection if they
hire boys for errands or minor shop jobs, and then if they make good in
evening preapprentice classes, they offer them an opportunity for full
apprenticeship. Somewhat different from other job-training programs
mentioned, but well worthy of study, are the Henry Ford Trade School
and the Ford Apprentice School.[26]

Training opportunities on the college level are available for both undergraduates and graduates. In addition to the long-used and very
familiar co-operative courses designed for undergraduate students preparing for certain occupations, a variety of training opportunities are available for full-time or part-time day or evening work in connection with
full-time or part-time study. Under certain conditions employing companies pay all or part of the student's tuition. Opportunities which serve
as tryouts for the undergraduate also offer summer work beginning at the
end of the sophomore or junior year.

On the graduate level it has long been customary for representatives of
industrial and business corporations to make annual visits to such colleges
and universities as experience has shown to be the best sources of recruiting potentially promising executives, engineers, chemists, physicists, and
others who are supposedly grounded in theory and have had at least a
minimum of practical experience. Each "scout" is interested in selecting
for his organization the seniors who seem most likely to justify the time
and expense involved in their selection and training. Selection procedures vary somewhat but all are expensive and time consuming. Routine
procedures are about as follows: College placement officers and recruiting

[24] See *Selecting Trainees for Apprenticeable Occupations* (U. S. Office of Education,
Service Bulletin on Defense Training in Vocational Schools, no. 10; Washington, 1941).
This eight-page leaflet defines apprenticeship, suggests questions helpful in selecting
apprentices, and lists apprenticeships important in defense.

[25] A discussion of such courses in one community may be found in Harold H. Punke's
article, "School and Industry Cooperate in Education: The Jacksonville [Florida] Plan,"
School and Society, LIII (1941), 736–740. Mr. Punke describes the co-operative plan
whereby the co-ordinator has the use of seventy to eighty training agencies. Roughly
90 per cent of the graduates of the program are subsequently employed.

[26] Personal familiarity with many company schools, among them the Ford schools,
leads the author to agree with Nathaniel Peffer who rates the Ford schools as among
the best equipped in the country, not excepting engineering schools ("Educating Workers
at Their Jobs," *Adult Education*, III [1931], 410–414).

agents agree upon visiting dates. The placement office schedules interviews for seniors who desire to confer with representatives of different organizations and sees that personnel records for each interviewee are available for consideration. Or, if the company takes the initiative in determining who shall be granted personal interviews, two visits may be made. During the first visit a company test, which serves as a sieve, may be administered to a large group registered in one or more of the divisions of the university. After the tests are scored, a second visit is made, and in the light of the test results plus a study of all the items on the personnel record the representative determines which seniors he wishes to interview. The character of such tests varies from company to company according to its purpose. Some company tests barely touch upon knowledge in the field of specialization and are almost entirely devoted to testing other knowledges and abilities considered essential to the successful functioning of specialized knowledge. In such cases college records are deemed a sufficiently accurate measure of ability in the field of specialization.

That company testing programs involve many seniors and are carried on in many institutions in order to secure a comparatively small number of recruits is evidenced every season. One company recently stated that it tested 3000 seniors in order to secure 60 satisfied and satisfactory recruits. Another scout, who did no testing, reported an annual interview average of about 250 seniors in order to secure an average of 30 recruits. After preliminary testing and interviewing at the college, seniors whom the company desires to consider and who desire to consider an offer are sometimes invited to visit the plant. This is the final test for both parties; some companies report that out of each two men who visit one is chosen for employment. There is no report available as to how many seniors withdraw their applications after visiting the plant.

After selection by the company and acceptance by the applicant, a period of induction and training follows. Again the procedures are expensive but they are considered vitally important in developing promotional personnel. Young graduate selectees usually lack sufficient practical experience to have immediate value and always they need supplementary instruction in relating their theoretical knowledge to company problems and in applying their knowledge to the specialized needs of the company they serve. Three major methods of inducting college graduates into business organizations are in use: (1) assignment to a regular job, (2) directed work experience, and (3) study-observation. Mr. E. W. Kempton, of the American Wire and Steel Company, has presented a clear-cut picture of each of these methods. After weighing the advantages and disadvantages of each and presenting his conclusions in such fashion that educators may well envy and profit by the industrialists' keen insight into occupational adjustment problems and the necessity for articulation between education and industry, he votes in favor of directed experience.[27]

There are, as in everything else, defects in the college scouting and college training programs, and college counselors should be alert to opportunities for service in connection both with employers' needs and with those of their student clientele. Employers' objectives are very specific. If a given college is found to be an unsatisfactory contact, regardless of the cause they will seek other sources of personnel. The inexperienced student often needs the assistance of an experienced counselor: (1) to help him evaluate the market value of his assets and to understand his liabilities better; (2) to assist him in ascertaining, through study of catalogues and other printed material, the sort of work which is done in various industries and their policies with reference to selection, induction, training, and promotions from within; (3) to help him estimate correctly the salesmanship factor involved in recruitment and to know how to challenge questionable interpretations of statistics or partisan representation of company conditions in comparison with the conditions of other companies. Good salesmen expect to be challenged. They respect intelligently alert challengers and usually regard them as desirable prospects.

When the same student receives several offers, as is frequently the case in a sellers' market when competition for the best prospects is keen, he needs guidance in the type of analysis and comparison which reveals the relative desirability of each opening, both from the immediate and the long-time point of view. As counselors, we may not overlook the fact that guidance in the choice of an employer is often as important as is guidance in the choice of an occupation, and that choice of the wrong employer may negate choice of the right occupation. An industrially illiterate person is useless as a counselor in such situations.

6. *Illustrative Material.* There are many types of useful occupational information which are difficult to classify separately. Since the outstanding feature of much of this material is its illustrative character it has been found convenient to include it under a single topic.

Audio-visual aids, an increasingly fruitful source of occupational information, deserve priority in such a classification. In addition to long-used materials such as maps, charts, posters, blueprints, exhibits, and pic-

[27] "Orienting the College Graduate in Industry," *Personnel*, XVI (1939), 31–39. The same article also appeared in *Proceedings, American College Personnel Association, Sixteenth Annual Meeting*, 1939. See also Eugene M. Stephens, "Coordination of Colleges with Business and Industry," *Personnel*, XIV (1938), 172–179. This article was also published in *Report of Fifteenth Annual Meeting of the American College Personnel Association*, 1938.

tures of all sorts, much information is now to be secured from projected still pictures, motion pictures, and the radio. As has been stated, within this group one finds both deplorable misrepresentations of processes and conditions and accurate presentations of facts.

Current bibliographies of assistance in selecting the latest and best films are available through both public and private agencies. A few are mentioned: The American Council on Education disseminates information regarding available educational films and furnishes complete bibliographies on various aspects of visual aid. The U. S. Office of Education supports a Film Service from which an up-to-date directory of government films may be secured, and it also publishes bibliographies on visual aids. The National Council of the Y.M.C.A., 347 Madison Avenue, New York City, maintains a motion picture bureau, and from the H. W. Wilson Company comes *The Educational Film Catalog,* which is kept up-to-date by means of a quarterly supplement. The *Journal of Business Education* carries a column in each issue entitled, "Film Guide for Business Teachers," and periodically *Occupations* contributes a list of motion pictures useful for the teaching of occupations.

For specific assistance in making discriminating use of the radio as a medium for disseminating vocational information, one turns instinctively to the major broadcasting chains. A characteristic example of the type of material available from these sources is *The Teachers' Manual and Classroom Guide* published annually by the Columbia Broadcasting System for use in connection with the American School of the Air.

But it is not sufficient to have lists of audio-visual aids. Counselors who plan to use these devices for presenting various types of guidance information will do well to consult one or more authorities regarding their specific uses and limitations and to seek advice in selecting the tools and using the methods which experience has shown to be most profitable. For this type of assistance they will turn to such books as Mildred Lincoln Billings' *Teaching About Vocational Life,*[28] which not only indicates how to use these devices for vocational guidance but calls attention to their limitations and to the necessity for care in their preparation and use. In *Visualizing the Curriculum,* by Charles F. Hoban, Sr., Charles F. Hoban, Jr., and Samuel B. Zisman,[29] one finds a very complete and practical discussion of the various ways in which such material may be used to make teaching more concrete. Harry C. McKown and Alvin B. Roberts' *Audio-Visual*

[28] Scranton, Pa.: International Textbook Co., 1937. A second and slightly revised edition has recently appeared under the title, *Group Methods of Studying Occupations* (1941).

[29] New York: Dryden Press, 1937.

Aids to Instruction [30] is a later source of information which is centered on the general use in education of visual aids of all kinds as well as of the radio. Each of these books includes liberal bibliographical material both general and special, and all are to some extent annotated.

Attention is called to the bibliography, rather unique for a textbook, which accompanies Mrs. Billings' revision of her earlier work.[31] It consists of thirty pages of classified sources of information preceded by a "Preview of Bibliography" which affords a section by section table of contents. The explanatory notes regarding the various types of material are indicative of the broad general experience and the firsthand knowledge upon which the entire publication is based. To some extent these sectional notes are a blanket substitute for individual annotations, which are limited and which when used, as in the sections on textbooks for high-school pupils and fiction for young people, are confined to age and grade suitability or to the vocation with which the work of fiction deals. There is no appraisal of the various publications in terms of sources of information, research methods employed, or relative reliability of facts presented.

Job demonstrations, or job performances, either in the schoolroom or in manufacturing plants, if witnessed after a preliminary study of the processes to be seen, supplement other types of information and come a little closer to reality than is possible for even the best of pictures or printed matter.

Material distributed by business organizations ranges in character from purely illustrative material such as posters, charts, and photographs to carefully prepared films and near monographs of outstanding educational value. Material of this type has been available throughout the entire period compassed by the guidance movement. An early, and historically and vocationally instructive, series of monographs was issued by Henry Disston and Sons, of Philadelphia. Among the titles were *The Saw in History*, 1915; *The File in History*, 1920; and *The Pruning Book*, 1921. These pamphlets traced the evolution of the modern tools manufactured by the company from before the dawn of civilization. The sources of information, which were given, included museums, private collections, and historical records. Illustrations were abundant. In 1912 the International Harvester Company issued two pamphlets from data previously published in current magazines: *The Story of Twine* and *The Binder Twine Industry*. The same company published *The Story of Bread*. In

---

[30] New York: McGraw-Hill Book Co., 1940. This is a handbook of procedures for the use of audio-visual aids in connection with instruction in different subjects. Complete bibliographies and source lists are included.

[31] See p. 106 n.

1919 the Goodyear Company published *The Story of the Tire.* A year later two highly prized pamphlets found their way into the author's collection. For one, *The Romance of Lace,* she is indebted to Marshall Field and Company, owners of the Zion lace industry. History, geography, and the growth of an industry as it shifted from hand to machine processes are all within the covers of this small pamphlet and are basic teaching material of the type which educators are always looking for and at the same time frequently overlooking when it is knocking at their very doors. For the other, *Seven Centuries of Brass Making,* she is under obligation to the Bridgeport Brass Company. Artistic in every detail, this beautiful and expensive pamphlet of seventy-eight pages is based on authentic historical data and is thoroughly documented. What an insult to classify such material as "illustrative"!

The postwar period witnessed an increasing volume of this type of occupational information,[32] and, although the number of editions issued would seem to indicate considerable demand and a rather wide distribution, it was largely neglected by educators. This was due, at least partially, to the fact that during the early years of the guidance movement boards of education were definitely opposed to the use by public schools of any material which savored of advertising lest partisanship be charged. Hence, counselors who collected such material were forced to use it somewhat surreptitiously and for one individual at a time. As the years have passed, the attitude of school authorities has changed until today most schools have complete freedom with respect to the collection and use of this valuable type of information.

But freedom to use has entailed responsibilty to exercise discriminating judgment in selecting such material and in helping pupils to evaluate its content. The United Air Lines' Mainliner Teaching Kit, including a *Teacher's Manual of Aviation Aids,*[33] is representative of a definite effort to prepare material specifically for school use. In this case the work was done under the supervision of an educator of many years' experience who was coauthor of one of the early general surveys of occupations.[34] The Boeing School of Aeronautics, Oakland, California, a division of the United Air Lines, publishes a monthly, the *Boeing School News,* devoted

[32] A. D. Inskeep, "Free or Inexpensive Materials for Projects and Social Studies," *Ungraded,* XI (1925), 34–35. This lists by occupations considerable material available in 1925, and *200 Sources of Pamphlet Materials on Occupations,* previously mentioned, lists some recent additions.

[33] Ed. by William A. Wheatley, Director of School and College Relations, United Air Lines, Chicago, Ill., 1940. The purpose of this type of publication is much the same as is that of some of the occupational monographs.

[34] See Enoch Gowin and William Wheatley, *Occupations: A Textbook in Vocational Guidance* (Boston: Ginn and Co., 1916).

entirely to news and pictures about aeronautics. In this day of wishful thinking about integrative material, it is well to give more than passing attention to the practical results of productive thinking along the same lines. Integrative possibilities and values stand out on every page of the best material of this type and should not beckon in vain to social-science teachers. Current magazines, newspapers, and trade journals are good sources of information on which companies distribute such material. School pupils quickly realize its value, learn to watch for sources, and enjoy participating in its collection, classification, and evaluation.

Included in the bibliographies already mentioned and also in those added at the end of Part II are a number of agencies which distribute posters and charts having definite guidance values. Some are concerned with the choice of occupation, job requirements, or the distribution of workers. Others illustrate correct or incorrect methods of applying for jobs, including hints on personal grooming. Still others discuss job attitudes and the like. The American Telephone and Telegraph Company, the Westinghouse Electric Company, and the Bristol-Myers Company are three among many who prepare and distribute such material for counselor use. As an example, the Bristol-Myers charts entitled "Grooming on the Job" present a young man and a young woman both properly groomed for the business world.[35] An explanatory booklet accompanies each chart: for boys, *You Can Win!* for girls, *Make a Good Job of It!* A check list for upkeep and progress is included. Such charts aid in establishing desirable health habits and act as an incentive to maintain or to improve an attractive personal appearance.

Advertising? Surely; very well done, too. Educational? Yes; also very well done. It is very fortunate for teachers and counselors that business is making this sort of material available, for even were educators issuing material equally desirable per se, every experienced counselor knows that dicta coming directly from the business world have an authenticity and a motivating value which is denied educators' pronouncements.

7. *Legislative Enactments and Occupational Restrictions.* Experience indicates that comparatively few teachers and counselors are familiar with the variety of legislative enactments and other types of occupational restrictions which should be considered a part of educational and occupational information. It has not been uncommon in the author's experience to find counselors in secondary schools who were ignorant of the compulsory education laws of their own state, or who admitted that they had never even heard of a minimum-wage law—and this in spite of the fact

[35] These charts may be secured upon request from the Bristol-Myers Co., 45 Rockefeller Plaza, New York City.

that youth of both sexes were daily passing from their jurisdiction to face the handicap or the assistance of such laws. Nor is evidence wanting that adult workers and college students, acting on the advice of advisers, have time and again taken advantage of educational opportunities in the hope and expectation that the skills and knowledges acquired would guarantee employment in certain occupational fields only to discover later that legal enactments, or restrictions of some kind, would curtail or prevent such employment. These bitter disappointments involved an inexcusable oversight on the part of the counselors, provided counselors were consulted.

It is not sufficient for counselors to be familiar with educational opportunities and to aid students in formulating educational programs which meet institutional requirements. They should also be familiar with the occupational outlets for such programs and should be alive to the fact that ignorance of the legislative enactments which control entry to occupations is at times the missing link which destroys the continuity and prevents the functioning of otherwise admirably planned educational programs. A knowledge of the federal, state, and municipal statutes which affect school attendance, control entry to employment, and influence labor relationships is an important asset in both counseling and placement offices. So also is familiarity with the regulations of labor unions [36] and of professional organizations.

Counselors may secure such enactments and regulations directly from the issuing authorities: federal, state, and municipal departments, labor unions, or professional associations. Some exceedingly attractive pamphlets containing essential information for different groups and different purposes come to the author under such titles as *Laws Governing School Attendance and the Employment of Minors; Laws Governing the Employment of Women and Minors;* and *State Laws for the Protection of Minors.* Locally useful enactments and regulations are an essential part of the educational, vocational, and social information which should be available for counseling purposes. The relation of such data to educational and vocational opportunities is of major and increasing importance. A few types of enactments and regulations which have general interest are cited. They are examples, but in no way do they cover the field, which is very broad. Moreover laws are constantly changing, and after each session of Congress and of state legislatures the counselor should check to make sure his legal data are up-to-date and accurate.

1. *Compulsory school attendance and child-labor laws.* These laws de-

---

[36] Counselors who are not familiar with the status of the labor-union movement will find helpful a series of articles presenting different aspects of the unions under the title, "Youth and Labor: A Symposium" (*Occupations,* XVII [1939], 485–498).

termine the age and educational status at which youth may leave school and enter occupational life. The usual age is sixteen but there are many exceptions, and some occupations are forbidden for youth under eighteen or twenty-one. In metropolitan areas where youth residing in one state tend to seek employment in another, many difficulties may be avoided if counselors will familiarize themselves with the laws of both states.

2. *Educational and personal requirements which control enrollment in federal, state, or municipal institutions of all types and admission to civil service examinations.* Residence, citizenship, age, character, economic status, and scholastic record are usually among the items about which information is specifically requested. The requirements for admission to government-controlled schools are included in catalogue data classified under "Educational Opportunities." Notification of civil service examinations will be mailed automatically to any school which asks to be placed on the mailing list.

3. *Accreditment and licensure of private academic, trade, commercial, and other schools.* There are a number of ways of protecting individuals against the unfair practices of unreliable educational agencies. If state departments of education are authorized to set standards for private schools and to accredit or license those which measure up to the requirements, a list of approved schools will be available, and counselors need make no apology for suggesting that it be consulted by students who desire to enroll in a private institution.

4. *Vocational rehabilitation laws.* In 1920 under the general provisions of the Smith-Hughes Law, Congress provided for the vocational rehabilitation of "persons disabled in industry or otherwise." This act provides for federal-state co-operation in "fitting or refitting for remunerative employment" those who are vocationally handicapped because of physical disability. Handicaps may be due to accident, disease, or congenital causes. This provision of the law, so very vital to physically handicapped youth, is not as well known among counselors as it should be. Once the eligibility of a person is established, vocational counseling is indispensable in determining upon a training program. When such a program has been selected, endorsed, and entered upon, rehabilitation is not considered complete until the trainee has been established in suitable employment. Complete information on the operation of the law may be secured from the vocational rehabilitation divisions of state departments of education.

5. *Laws regulating entrance into occupations.* One method of protecting society against individuals who desire to engage in certain occupations but whose services therein, for one reason or another, might be detrimental to society is the setting up of definite personal qualifications as a require-

ment for entry. This is usually called "licensure." We are all more or less familiar with licensure for teachers, doctors, nurses, and a few other professional workers.[37] We are less familiar with the rather long list of non-professional, skilled, and semiskilled workers who are obliged to meet specific personal requirements before they may engage in their chosen work. Material of this type is very important for counselors although as yet it is not available in many states. In 1929 the Commonwealth Club of California issued a research study [38] which opened an entirely new field of occupational information and suggested the desirability of each state making an intensive study of its own legislative enactments and occupational restrictions. Three or four state studies have been made.

One such study, completed in 1939, is especially valuable for informational use.[39] The major purpose of this study was to provide this type of information for the use of counselors and students who were planning educational and vocational programs. At the time of writing L. Paul Miller found that there were sixty-two specifically named jobs or occupations of a nonprofessional character, such as fishing, junk dealing, undertaking, and real estate selling, for which New York legislatures over a long period of years had laid down specific entrance requirements. Fifty-nine of these requirements were still in force. During the session of 1936 bills were introduced affecting thirty-eight occupations; during 1937 admission to forty-two different occupations was affected by bills introduced; and in 1938 there were forty-two different bills which would have affected entrance into twenty-three different occupations.

6. *Laws dealing with conditions of labor.* There are many laws on the statute books which provide for the health, comfort, safety, and general welfare of workers. For lack of a better descriptive term they have been classified under "Conditions of Labor." They deal with hours of work, places of work, fire protection, lighting and heating, lunch periods, use of seats during work hours, lavatory facilities, machinery guards and other safety devices, and protection against dust, lint, fumes, and the like which might cause occupational diseases. Information relative to such enactments and their social objectives are important teaching content for classroom use, but whether or not such information has been a part of previous

37 For a study of this subject, see the *Research Bulletin of the National Education Association*, vol. XVI, no. 4 (1938), entitled *Statutory Status of Six Professions: Accountancy, Architecture, Law, Medicine, Nursing, Teaching.*

38 *Occupational Restrictions: A Study of the Laws of Eighteen Selected States Covering the Requirements for Entering Occupations Therein* (San Francisco: Commonwealth Club of California, 1929).

39 L. Paul Miller, *State Regulation of Entrance into Occupations in the State of New York* (unpublished thesis, New York University, 1939).

classwork, counselors or placement workers should be sure that each advisee is familiar with all the laws of this type which have been put on the statute books for his protection and for the enhancement of his efficiency as a worker.

7. *Workmen's compensation laws.* The first such law was passed in 1911 as a public recognition of the fact that industrial injuries are inevitable under twentieth century methods of production and that the cost of such accidents is a legitimate part of the cost of operating our industrial system. They transfer the burdens resulting from an accident from the workman, who is the victim, to the entire group of consumers, who use the product. This broad purpose, which any child can understand, has been modified and safeguarded in various ways in different states in order to accomplish the main objective with the minimum opportunity for abuse by employer, employee, or accident-chasing lawyer. It is not necessary for counselors to be familiar with all the details of this law. Their main responsibility is to see that their clientele know that there is such a law, understand its purpose, and know where to secure full information immediately if future need arises. Counselors should know whether or not there is special compensation for minors and under what conditions. They should also know for what period of time widows and children receive benefits if husbands and fathers lose their lives in industrial accidents—whether throughout dependency or for a fixed period. These latter items are important for school attendance officers and visiting teachers as well as for counselors.

8. *State minimum-wage laws and orders.* Minimum-wage laws are in force in twenty-five states.[40] As a rule they set wages below which women and minors of both sexes may not be employed. In a few cases boys under eighteen are not included; in Oklahoma both men and women are covered. Usually there are exemptions for learners, apprentices, and physically and mentally handicapped persons. These wage rulings, especially when they have been combined with hour rulings, have caused serious problems for counselors and placement workers. This writer, who was working on the Seattle guidance survey when the Washington minimum-wage law was passed in 1912, included in the report of her findings two sections which dealt with the influence of legislation on Seattle youth, "Minimum Wage and Vocational Efficiency" and "State School and Child Labor Laws and the Making of Unemployables." Case illustrations were given.[41] After six years of experience with the workings of the law in other states

[40] See Florence P. Smith, *State Minimum-Wage Laws and Orders: An Analysis* (U. S. Women's Bureau Bulletin, no. 167; Washington, 1939).
[41] *Seattle Children,* pp. 81–95.

and in the District of Columbia, she again indicated how the law affected certain types of workers.[42]

The federal Fair Labor Standards Act of 1938, usually known as the Wage-Hour Law, is a minimum-wage law for industries engaged in interstate commerce. It fixes a ceiling of forty hours on the standard work week, and a floor of forty cents an hour under wages. It goes into effect gradually, the set floor and ceiling to be reached by 1945, and it carries a child-labor clause, effective from October 24, 1938, for "children" under eighteen years of age.[43] This national law also makes provision for learners and substandard workers.

The general influence of all such laws on the problems of counselors and placement workers is the same: No matter how frequently learning periods are repeated, some substandard workers never attain the minimum efficiency which corresponds to the legislated minimum wage, which of course is designed to reward the efficiency of the average. This type of worker was the "industrial boarder" of former years. He was always partially subsidized by someone, parents, employers, or public relief agencies. Employers, under wage laws, have been loathe to accept chronic learners. There are various easily understandable reasons: the public assumption that employers who are willing to assist in absorbing substandards at an "exemption" wage are trying to exploit labor, the red tape involved in such employment, and the additional supervision and overhead expense involved. Under a legislated wage it is very difficult for counselors to find occupational outlets for substandard workers. It is practically hopeless in a buyer's market. Partial self-support and partial subsidy thus become unemployability and total relief.

At the other end of the scale counselors meet the problem of the superstandard woman. Legislated wages for all women workers have always tended to level off the higher wages commanded by superior ability in order to strike an average with the minimum, which is set for, and often a godsend to, mediocrity.[44]

Another troublesome situation arises from the fact that the law covers men only until they reach eighteen years of age while there is no age release for women. A variety of results confounded counselors and place-

42 See *Junior Wage Earners* (New York: Macmillan Co., 1920), pp. 121, 161–163.

43 See U. S. Dept. of Labor, *A Ceiling for Hours, a Floor for Wages, and a Break for Children* (Washington, [1938]).

44 Official statistics are frequently cited to refute this statement. But years of observation of the effects of the law in different states, plus counseling with many superior women and their employers, both of whom anticipated the results of the law before the employee had time to become a statistic, confirm the statement. All the information has never been officially recorded; in the very nature of things it probably never will be.

ment officers until they had become accustomed to the practical workings of the law. When there is an abundance of labor, men over eighteen may adjust to the current wage, which is apt to fall below the minimum. They will do so, and the pool of unemployed women, who may not work at less than the minimum, will increase. When the condition of the market changes and labor is scarce, men will again command the current wage which is apt to be above the minimum, and women will return to work at the minimum.

A fourth problem, which affects college circles rather seriously, centers about a fairly common ruling that fractions of days must be paid for by the hour, on the basis of the daily wage. Since some hours of the day are much more valuable to employers than others, high-school and college students, whose hours of freedom do not fit the peak load periods in industries open to part-time service, cause school counselors in student-aid divisions considerable anxiety. An excellent recent interpretation of the effect of the federal law of 1938 is Herman Feldman's "The Wage-Hour Law and Job Opportunities." [45]

9. *Laws dealing with the employment of aliens.* Because of the defense program and the immediate need for discriminating judgment regarding the employment of aliens, it might be assumed that this type of legislation is of temporary interest only. This would be an unwarranted assumption. The educational and occupational problems of aliens and their children have always been of concern to counselors although too often they have been ignorant of the enactments which affect the normal absorption of such persons into community occupational life. A fairly recent report of an investigation into this subject is available in libraries.[46] It contains an analysis of the laws enacted by states and of the rulings made by official bodies which discriminate against aliens. The dates of enactment indicate that some of these laws have been on the statute books for years and are without present-day justification.

10. *Laws dealing with the collection of wages and other personal matters.* Legislation regulating payment of wages, titles to homes, insurance contracts, custody of children, status of children whose parents are citizens of different countries, rights and obligations under lease, responsibility for debts, power to withdraw money from banks, divorce and separation, loan-shark regulations, and the like is fairly common. Legisla-

[45] *Occupations,* XVII (1939), 688–693. Very few articles have appeared in print which have revealed the practical working of such laws. The advantages of the law, especially for average workers, are well known, but the great majority of citizens do not yet realize that a way to prevent the exploitation of mediocrity without penalizing so many other types of workers is overdue.

[46] See Harold Fields, "Where Shall the Alien Work?" *Social Forces,* XII (1933), 213–221.

tion applies alike to old and young, rich and poor, but many families whose children are in our public schools lack knowledge of how to proceed in the solution of their problems and are unable to afford legal advice. The collection of small wage payments of from fifteen to fifty dollars is one big item. In order to place legal talent at the disposal of low-income individuals and families, legal aid clinics in connection with law schools and legal aid societies which are contributions of the Bar to community social welfare have grown up throughout the country. There is a National Association of Legal Aid Organizations.[47] Anyone may refer a case to such an organization provided the person involved is unable to meet the usual expense incident to legal advice or litigation. The case is reviewed, and if legal action is justified, a very small deposit is made and the organization takes charge. Among the eighteen thousand individuals with whom the author of this volume has counseled during the ten years from 1929 to 1939, sixty-three, with very diverse problems, were referred to the Legal Aid Society of New York. Accessibility to the services of such an organization is a great asset to counselors.

11. *Legislation affecting the employment of married women.* Economic depressions with their attendant unemployment always focus public attention on the desirability of legislation which would restrict the employment of married women, especially those whose husbands are employed at a wage which removes any claim of need. War emergencies with their attendant demand for additional sources of labor supply always focus public attention on married women as a potential labor reserve. During the recent depression several states introduced legislation intended to limit the employment of married women in public service. Under present conditions radio and press are pleading with the same group to enter public service and conscription is frequently threatened. A knowledge of trends as well as of current practice in both public service and in private business should be of use to counselors advising with college students and adult workers.

12. *The Social Security Act of 1935.* This is a federal grants-in-aid law requiring state co-operation. Therefore, the rules regarding eligibility and the amount of relief or benefit vary widely from state to state. The law provides for assistance to the aged who lack means of support, to children who are homeless, dependent, or neglected, and to the needy blind of any age. Old-age benefits and unemployment insurance are provided on the basis of previous employment or wage-earning history. Ma-

47 See Reginald Heber Smith and John S. Bradway, *Growth of Legal-Aid Work in the United States* (rev. ed., U. S. Bureau of Labor Statistics Bulletin, no. 607; Washington, 1936).

ternal and child welfare provisions include service for crippled children and supplementary services for vocational rehabilitation. Local welfare and social agencies are familiar with eligibility and assistance provisions, and counselors should take advantage of the law for types of pupils who come within its provisions.

OCCUPATIONAL RESEARCH: THE COLLECTION OF INFORMATION FROM THE SOURCES

Teachers and counselors who have familiarized themselves with the seven types of occupational information discussed, who are alive to the various influences which render such material useful or useless, and who have formed the habit of challenging each piece of material which comes to their desks in terms of the character of the source and of the intellectual integrity of the author will accomplish much more than is usually expected of those whose major responsibilities are such that they will, of necessity, always be largely dependent upon occupational information collected and prepared by others. Two cautions bear constant repetition if such generally informed persons are to take sole responsibility for the organized occupational counseling offered by any given community: (1) against using their information too literally since the vocational outlook for each individual is so largely dependent upon his own interests, abilities, industry, and initiative, and (2) against the assumption that occupational information once collected and printed, especially if printed as a text, remains permanently useful. Industrial change is constant and during periods of major reorganization goes forward rapidly.

Research in the occupational field is another matter. Research in any field is an occupation in its own right, and a very highly specialized one with very specific personal qualifications and training requirements. Its function is to secure factual data with reference to any topic under investigation and so to present the findings that opportunities for distortions or misrepresentations will be reduced to the minimum.

Those who aspire to become research scholars in the occupational field must start by realizing that they are on the bottom rung of the occupational information ladder. Therefore, they may well inventory their accomplishments and their immediate assets before they enter the research field or before they assume responsibility for directing the research activities of groups of counselors or teachers. Among the questions which would-be research scholars or directors of research may profitably consider are:

(1) Do I know how to locate occupational material which has already been collected by others?

(2) Have I formulated criteria for testing the reliability of such material?

(3) Do I know how to analyze such material in order to secure background data for a new study?

(4) Do I understand how to make a tentative or working outline?

(5) Have I a plan for research procedure which promises to be successful in securing accurate information directly from the sources, business and industry?

(6) Do I realize the responsibilities involved in directing occupational research?

(7) Do I know how to organize occupational information, keeping in mind the needs of pupils who must soon enter the labor market as well as youth who are looking for further training opportunities?

(8) Do I know where and how to secure job analyses and how to draw off job specifications and records of usage?

(9) Do I know the implications of job classifications for counseling purposes?

(10) Do I realize the importance of applying my appraisal criteria to my own and to my group's results?

(11) Do I know how to aid school administration in understanding the relationship between curricula offerings and their probable occupational functioning?

(12) Have I potentialities for development in the field of occupational research?

He who can answer these questions affirmatively and who has convinced himself that his talents can best be used in research will concentrate on the collection, classification, evaluation, and interpretation of occupational information, or on the supervision of others who are similarly engaged.

Since there is more than a fifty-fifty chance that school directors of local occupational research will be novices in the practical application of research techniques and that their assistants will be mostly untrained workers, it may be helpful to suggest a tentative program for an initial local study. The director is responsible for seeing that all who participate in the study help in making the plan, that it is thoroughly understood by each, and that there is abundant opportunity for periodic discussion and revision of methods and for comparison of findings and their possible and probable interpretations. After the first research project, methods become increasingly automatic so that formal discussions may be minimized. On the other hand, experimentation often results in newer and better methods or in the refinement of the old. A program including the following eight procedures will cover the major essentials of any ordinary occupational research:

(1) Select the occupation, or function, to be studied.

(2) Inventory the available sources of information.

(3) Master the processes and facts revealed and make a working outline.

(4) Inventory the personal qualifications which can be brought to bear upon the project as outlined.

(5) Make a list of the companies locally engaged in the chosen occupation.

(6) Secure the co-operation of the companies selected.

(7) Follow the rules for research.

(8) Classify and file the findings.

The choice of the occupation or function to be studied may be determined by the number of requests for information which have been made by parents, teachers, and pupils; by some problem connected with administrative policy; by placement office needs; by community conditions; or by other reasons. After determining upon the topic, think through its ramifications; consider its possible subtopics; and limit its scope to such aspects as are compassable under the conditions prevailing.

Bibliographies are helpful in inventorying sources. They are supposed to serve as guides in uncovering pertinent material and to act as first assistants to those who desire to analyze the content and arrive at valid judgments regarding the value of the various items. Unfortunately, critical bibliographical work seems to have made little or no appeal to this country's scholars. Perhaps the influence of time and place has tended to lower the intellectual and moral standards of both public and scholar to such an extent that bibliographers along with book reviewers feel no need of the broad knowledge, the critical and analytical abilities, the infinite patience, and the absolute accuracy which characterized the old-fashioned bibliographer and reviewer and resulted in the carefully annotated bibliographies and critical, analytical reviews familiar to historical scholars.

There are bibliographies in the occupational field—not many good ones, however, because most bear the earmarks of superficial knowledge and uncritical scholarship. The standard bibliographies which are available in most libraries are of limited value to counselors because many of the most helpful articles are indexed in such a way that their counseling content is not revealed. A number of special bibliographies are periodically published, such as, *The Occupational Index* (distributed through New York University), *The Vocational Guide* (published monthly by Science Research Associates), *The Bibliography of Economic and Social Study*

Material (available through the National Association of Manufacturers), and the *Bibliography on Occupations* (issued by the Occupational Information and Guidance Service of the U. S. Office of Education).

Counselors, for whose benefit such bibliographies are published, could render a national service by insisting that bibliographers cease to flood the market with lists of useless occupational pamphlets. Some pamphlets are literary in character, some not so literary, but far too many come from the pens of those who have had no personal contact with the occupations they presume to describe. Published for purely commercial purposes, they are compilations culled from other publications without the slightest effort to check on their accuracy or immediate applicability. Those who are solicited to subscribe to current bibliographies have a right to know upon what basis selections have been made and how the authors of the items listed collected their material—directly from the sources by interview, by questionnaire, by observation, by personal participation, or by rewriting the works of others. The National Occupational Conference set a commendable example in this respect when it clearly stated that the content of its occupational pamphlets was not based upon first-hand investigation but upon abstracts from other carefully selected material. The Science Research Associates indicate that their information is secured directly from the sources and tell us by whom the research is made. However although a change in the character of bibliographies would be of material assistance in the location of available data and in the first sifting process it would not exempt the research scholar from conducting his own critical analysis. He will subject each separate document to the canons of external and internal criticism before he accepts it as evidence in the occupational field.

The best sources of information on the specific character of specific jobs and their requirements are business and industrial organizations and the technical reports and publications which deal with the human factor engaged in production and distribution. Much of this material is based on company research or co-operative research carried on by the ablest and best-equipped scholars in the field. Such research studies have been going on with unabating energy over a long period of years, and the author of this volume once again acknowledges her indebtedness to the many business organizations without whose co-operation she would have been unable to maintain an up-to-date file of information for counseling and placement.

The terms most frequently used in connection with the collection and preparation for use of this more scientific and more specific type of occu-

tional information include "job analysis," [48] "difficulty analysis," "job
scription," "job specification," "records of usage," "job classification"
"job zoning," and "wage standardization." "Job analysis," aptly de-
cribed as management's basic tool, is the process of picking a job to pieces
order to find out what is done, how it is done, and what human quali-
ations are necessary to do it successfully. "Difficulty analysis," often in-
uded in "job analysis," stresses the difficulties encountered by those who
rform the tasks. "Job descriptions" and "job specifications," sometimes
ed synonymously, are records of the results obtained from job analysis.
here differentiation in usage is found, a "job description" usually re-
rts analysis findings in narrative but not literary form, while "job speci-
ations" are almost universally recorded in outline form classified under
ch topics as Duties, Qualifications for employment, Working conditions,
d Relation to other jobs.

Job grading and job classification are also based on the findings of
b analysis. They afford a logical and impartial basis whereby busi-
ss houses may classify and group jobs which require approximately
ual ability, or expense for preparation, or effort, or responsibility, or
rvous strain, so that remuneration for the same or equivalent services
ay be as nearly equal as possible. Ratings, promotions, and transfers
well as wage standardization are dependent upon scientific job grad-
g or zoning. Counselors cannot expect to secure full information on
ch topics from business houses, nor do they need it for most educational
rposes.[49] But knowledge of the how and why of such procedures is
ways helpful in advisory and placement work and is bound to call at-
tion to the fact that there are levels below which no wage should fall

[48] These essentially business terms proved so jarring to educator sensibilities that it
s sometimes necessary to resort to camouflage in order to secure educational support.
1928 W. W. Charters, an outstanding educator-experimenter in the field of job
alysis and one well versed in the peculiarities of both educator and employer, de-
ared that since "job analysis" was a term of doubtful respectability in some educational
cles, such synonyms as "activity analysis," "occupational analysis," "duty analysis,"
nctional analysis," and the like had been invented and seemed to imply fewer low
ociations. He added, "But they are all members of the same tribe and are descendants
m old chief Job Analysis" ("The Use of Activity Analysis in Curriculum Construction,"
oceedings of the Sixty-fourth Convocation of the University of the State of New York,
5).
[49] One would not wish to leave the impression that school counselors or directors of
dance service are expected to make, or will be permitted to make, job analyses in
siness houses. Collecting material for such purposes is a highly technical procedure
uiring considerable technical experience. Industrial engineers or others especially
ined for such work are usually employed. Since each plant varies as to tools, conditions
work, qualifications of workers, and "one best ways," a job analysis must be made
ectly from the job or from information furnished by those who work on the job.

as well as levels above which wages may not go no matter how well th
work is done. In one case, the worker cannot live; in the other, the bus
ness cannot survive. All workers are distributed between these two leve]
A number of factors determine the individual's exact position on th
scale. This sort of general knowledge is very helpful during employme
supervision for warning certain types of youth that the end is in sight an
that future advancement requires additional preparation. It is also hel]
ful, if one is familiar with the classifications in vogue in certain compani
and has the confidence of their employing personnel, in securing class
fication above the usual entrance level for outstandingly superior studen
or applicants.

The working outline, the making of which comprises the third step i
research procedure, is based upon analysis of all the data admitted :
"evidence" and the synthesis of major and minor topics in tentative ou
line form.[50] The fourth step is an inventory of the personal qualificatio
of the workers available for attacking the investigations. The qualific
tions of research workers have been discussed in Chapter V. If researe
work is to be successful, the director of the project should insist that eae
co-operator be familiar with the fundamental precepts and that befo
he engages in any specific study he be ready and willing—

(1) To discard all previously conceived ideas as to what facts will l
found.

(2) To make sure that he has secured all the facts. An omitted pe
tinent fact often destroys the value of the project.

(3) To establish the accuracy of his facts.

(4) To analyze the facts and, so far as possible, their causes.

(5) To draw logical and sound conclusions.

(6) To determine the relative value of facts.

(7) To support his conclusions by facts.

(8) To help in the constructive interpretation of facts.

The fifth and sixth steps in the outline of research procedure are co
cerned with securing the co-operation of a selected list of business house
Lists of the companies engaged in the chosen business or industry may l

[50] *The Occupational Research Program of the United States Employment Serv*
(Chicago: Public Administration Service, 1943), by William H. Stead and W. E:
Masincup, which has appeared since the completion of this book, is a valuable guide f
planning and conducting vocational research. It contains a nine-point outline for t
preparation of job descriptions—"national" and "local descriptions" corresponding
"records of usage" and "job specifications," respectively, as the latter terms have be
used in this book. Stead's interindustry vocational classification must not be confus
with intraindustry job classification. His use of job equivalents and job families will
easily understood. Field procedures center around a job analysis schedule.

btained from local classified directories, chambers of commerce, or personnel clubs. The director will check off those which seem to afford the est opportunity for observation and information, keeping in mind the esirability of choosing representative or fair samples: both large and mall, owner- and manager-controlled, well-established and new firms vill be chosen, including those with both inferior and superior equipment nd the like. Current community comment and employee opinions will e of some help in this selection process even though it be opinion more ften than fact. The why of an adverse or too favorable opinion is at imes desirable counselor information.

An effort to secure the consent and co-operation of the houses selected omes next. This may be accomplished through introduction by a mutual riend, by formal introduction from school officials, by written request, r by personal conference. The convenience of the manager or owner hould be consulted, not only for the initial conference but for the time f research if the request to make a study be granted. The manager should e told exactly what is planned, why, and how the findings are to be used. Under no circumstances should general publicity be given to facts or conitions without the consent of the owner or other responsible party. ourtesy demands that he be given an opportunity to review findings and hat any criticisms or suggestions made be given respectful consideration ven though accuracy requires their rejection. Trade secrets are private roperty. As a rule counselors do not find secrets, but when they do they hould remember that protection of their own reputation requires that crets remain secrets.

A short list of Dos and Don'ts, started by the author when she was Diector of the Junior Division of the United States Employment Service and upplemented from time to time, may be suggestive to beginners in the eld of occupational research, job solicitation, or other phases of vocational uidance service which involve visits to industry and business.

os for Visitors to Industry and Business

(1) Have an objective and a plan for its realization.

(2) Be a welcome guest and a courteous one.

(3) Maintain the attitude of the scholar and guest.

(4) Be appreciative. It costs time and money to entertain you.

(5) Be humble. Most counselors are grossly ignorant of business principles, practices, and problems.

(6) Arrive on time and leave on time.

(7) Take your own equipment with you.

(8) Show an intelligent interest in all information given whether
not it seems valuable to you. Guests cannot always control the conver
tion.

(9) Use good judgment in note taking.

(10) Show appreciation for courtesies received by a "thank-you" lett

(11) Check at the entrance of the plant preconceived notions and co
plexes on such subjects as inferiority, superiority, child labor, labor unio
capital, old-age discards, and sex equality. *Forget to claim your prope*
at the exit.

(12) Give a frank opinion if you are *invited to do so* and *your judgme
prompts you to comply.*

(13) Observe absolutely any safety precautions relative to dress, h
dling material, touching machinery, etc.

(14) Avoid visits during busy seasons or on days known to be especia
busy.

(15) Follow the accepted rules for research procedure in collecting a
tabulating material.

(16) Submit your finding first of all to the house from which you secur
your facts.

Don'ts for Visitors to Industry and Business

(1) Don't force yourself in if you are not wanted.

(2) Don't be late and don't change a date and hour once set unless
solutely necessary.

(3) Don't wear your labor or police insignia, at least where it can
seen.

(4) Don't act like a censor of business ethics or a labor inspector.

(5) Don't ask impertinent questions.

(6) Don't ask too many questions; look and listen.

(7) Don't give advice gratis.

(8) Don't jump at conclusions.

(9) Don't scatter your opinions around promiscuously.

(10) Don't betray confidences. It is an unpardonable sin.

(11) Don't interrupt work. Talking to employees on duty may ca
accident, destroy teamwork, or lower piece-rate wages.

(12) Don't introduce unpleasant or controversial topics.

(13) Don't expect free lunches, boxes of candy, a bag of doughnut
dish of ice cream, or a sample pair of hose (and, one might add, do
accept).

(14) Don't comment on what you have observed in other plants. M
of all avoid comparisons.

(15) Don't take along uninvited guests. It is bad manners and bad policy.

(16) Don't use pupils, club women, or other casually interested persons as assistants.

(17) Don't use too many "ests" to indicate approval of what you see. Employers know that there is a limit to "bests," "largests," and "mosts."

(18) Don't presume to rate employer policies and training programs for publication. When educational systems have learned how to rate their own employees and training programs, it will be time enough to attack the same problems in industry.

(19) Don't try to educate or socialize employers.

(20) Don't black-list. You are apt to get yourself and your board of education in trouble.

(21) Don't argue. It will not help in attaining your objective.

The seventh and eighth items require no elaboration since the rules for research and the necessity for recording and filing data have already been discussed. Once the opportunity to make a study directly from the sources has been granted, the universal rules for research should be strictly observed. Reports should be made each evening; the findings should be reviewed in the light of previous findings and knowledge; and possible interpretations should be considered. If gaps in information or weak points in method are revealed, changes in procedure may seem advisable and may be agreed upon for trial on the following day.

When the facts are all in and interpreted, the research proper is completed. Reporting the facts or preparing them for specific uses is editorial work which may or may not be delegated to another individual or group. If the information was secured for general use rather than for some specific purpose, it will probably be recorded on uniform sheets or cards and filed in some convenient place for use as occasion demands. It is the original record. If the placement clerk wants a job specification, it can be drawn off in as much or as little detail as seems best. If the class teacher or counselor desires vocational information for a junior-high-school group, either she or the editorial staff will select the necessary facts and prepare them in a form suitable for adolescent groups. The facts chosen should always depend upon the end in view, and the method of presentation should be adapted to the age and educational level to be served. Pictures and other illustrative material should be classified, filed, and in the larger schools indexed. School librarians frequently assume responsibility for this task, and a good librarian is always a major contributor to the success of research in occupational information.

Counselors who have at their disposal both kinds of information discussed—that secured from the sources mentioned in the seven-point classification and that secured directly from specific jobs—will have appropriate occupational information for every counseling purpose. Since each type of occupational information makes its own peculiar contribution to the implementation of counseling, acquiring and maintaining the right perspective as to the relationship between data secured from these sources and the purposes which each type of material is supposed to serve are exceedingly important.

General occupational surveys are, in the very nature of the case, superficial and apt to be inaccurate in details. But if discriminatingly chosen, they give a bird's-eye view of some relatively large portion of the world's work, lay the foundation for individual limitation of choice, and if their content is attractively presented, they have considerable inspirational, though not much cultural, value.

Monographs vary greatly in character and value. At their worst they are desk-chair rehashes of what was second- or third-rate material to begin with; they are dismal failures for any purpose. At their best, and sometimes it is very difficult to draw the line between the best of the bad and the near best, they are based upon reliable data carefully collected and tested and discriminatingly selected for inclusion. Since they usually include considerable historical, geographical, economic, and sociological information, they have high cultural and integrating value, and they also bring the individual one step farther along his pathway toward ultimate vocational choice. This type of information in its simplest form, supplemented by appropriate illustrative material, has a very important mission in the elementary schools. In the upper grades and on the college level it furnishes comparative data for those who are concentrating on the choice of an occupation either as a preliminary to further education or for immediate entry into occupational life. Many monographs are prepared especially for college students and mature workers. Such material should be brought to students' attention early enough in their college career for them to plan and revise their curricula from time to time as their occupational interests crystallize and their abilities with reference to occupational requirements are better understood.

Records of usage stand next to monographs as aids to individuals who are gradually limiting the range of their occupational choice. For some reason this expression, after a brief popularity in the late twenties, has fallen into disuse in connection with occupational information. For counseling purposes it would seem to provide a desirable intermediate step between the literary monograph and the company-applicable job specification. It is, of course, a hybrid in character. It possesses monograph characteristics to the extent of affording a composite picture of a job requirement which has wide general applicability; it answers the question, What does a man on this sort of job usually do and what qualifications are usually required? Its job specification characteristics are found in the fact that the elements in the composite picture are common to many individual job specifications, that the outline form of presentation is used, that job essentials are given in detail, but that no background data, historical, geographical, economic, or sociological, are included.

Job specifications enter the picture after the occupational choice has been made and preparation has been completed. Since a job specification is taken from the record of a job analysis in a given plant, it is obvious that no job specification can be applicable in all of its details to a similar job in another industrial plant or in an industry as a unit. Therefore, its major function is found in connection with immediate entry to employment. It furnishes a list of essential job requirements and human qualifications which apply only to the job under consideration. It helps the prospective applicant to determine how well qualified he may be for the given job and whether or not he wishes to apply; it helps the personnel department of the company concerned to determine the extent to which each of the various applicants is qualified for the job and which is potentially the most desirable employee.

CHAPTER VII

Information on Community Resources

COMMUNITY resources primarily educational in character have been discussed. According to the character and size of the community, there are, however, many other facilities which are of value to individuals in various areas of their developmental growth. Among such agencies some are designed to serve in the area of physical and mental health; some afford assistance in making social and religious contacts and adjustments, others provide recreational opportunities, and still others act as middlemen in bringing employer and employee together.

Libraries are intimately related to educational facilities and in some communities are classified among public education agencies. Since from the very inception of the guidance movement libraries and librarians have played an important part in the collection and dissemination of occupational information, it is peculiarly fitting that they should be rated as first assistants in any enumeration of community resources available for guidance services. Among the services which they are in a position to render, and do render, more adequately and more effectively than most other community agencies are the collection and classification of all types of occupational information, the maintenance of a special room or shelf for guidance literature, the encouragement of clubs and classes for the study of occupational problems, especially on the adult level, the provision for loan or traveling libraries dealing with occupational material, and the publication of lists of printed material, films, and other visual aids available in the community. A few public libraries provide a counselor versed in community guidance needs who is available for the assistance of teachers, counselors, parents, and others.

Recreational facilities [1] are usually available under both public and private auspices. Park departments and boards of education are the major sponsors of municipal recreations. Private facilities are sponsored by settlements, churches, Y.M.C.A.'s, the Knights of Columbus, boys' clubs, Boy and Girl Scouts, hiking clubs, nature-study clubs, and the like. In industrial

[1] For a study of young people and their recreations, see C. Gilbert Wrenn and D. L. Harley, *Time on Their Hands* (Washington: American Youth Commission of the American Council on Education, 1941).

128

communities industrial organizations frequently carry on a program of recreation. Commercialized recreations are found in every community and usually afford a wide range of choice. All recreational facilities, whether operating under public or private auspices, should be called upon from time to time to review their accomplishments and to re-establish their claims to constructive rather than to subversive or antisocial community influence. Censorship and licensure are common methods of checking on the value of public and commercialized recreations and guaranteeing that only those with a clear record are allowed to operate. Counselors of youth need to be exceptionally well informed regarding recreational facilities and their general character before they venture to suggest the utilization of any particular opportunity for social contacts and social development. And they need to keep their approved list up-to-date.

Rural communities afford fewer organized recreational opportunities for youth, but they have almost untouched possibilities for the development of what were at one time exceedingly popular rural social activities. The home, the school, and the church are the normal centers of social life,[2] and teachers and counselors are in a strategic position to show leadership in community provision for suitable and profitable recreational activities on the home ground. If this responsibility is neglected in this day of easy and quick transportation, the community may lose its hold on young people before the time has come for them to walk safely alone.

Public health services [3] of two types are in vogue in the United States. Most communities make some provision for what are known as the social functions of a health service. These include preventive and protective measures such as periodic examination of school children, examination of employees in food industries, protection of the water supply, etc. A complete list of protective and preventive measures is available through municipal and state departments. The second type of health resources consists of a number of specialized services which are available for the family or the individual—sometimes available through private health agencies and sometimes through both public and private agencies. It is to these specialized services that the counselor turns for guidance and financial

[2] A discussion of the school as a center of community activities may be found in N. L. Engelhardt, Sr., and N. L. Engelhardt, Jr., *Planning the Community School* (New York: American Book Co., 1940). The authors present suggestions for planning the community school in keeping with recent trends and prospective demands. Bernard E. Meland in *The Church and Adult Education* (New York: American Association for Adult Education, 1939) suggests the scope and character of adult education which churches and synagogues are undertaking.

[3] See C.-E. A. Winslow, *The School Health Program* (New York: The Regents' Inquiry, McGraw-Hill Book Co., 1938) and the Educational Policies Commission, *Social Service and the Schools* (Washington: National Education Association, 1939).

assistance in dealing with tubercular, cardiac, and other physical or mental cases. Visiting nurses or visiting housekeepers are frequently provided as a method of dealing with special cases which do not require hospitalization. Welfare departments as well as health departments may be of assistance to counselors in furnishing information regarding the specialized facilities available, and the conditions under which they may be secured.

Welfare agencies, public and private,[4] are numerous and the public ones are multiplying under the grants-in-aid system of the federal government. Public agencies usually assume responsibility for delinquent, dependent, and defective children, for indigent and defective adults, and for those who are on probation or parole through court action or release from institutions. Legal aid in the solution of a variety of problems is provided through the same avenues. School welfare services usually receive a large part of their financial support directly from the corps of the school which they serve. Since many of the pupil needs which they are instituted to relieve are related to the enforcement of the compulsory school attendance laws and the certification of young wage-earners, it is not uncommon to find them under the department of school attendance although now and then they are allocated to a department of child welfare. Their main function is to supply clothing, glasses, braces, or other articles without which the attendance and education of the pupil would be blocked.

In addition to the public welfare services there are many actively interested agencies under private control, orphans' homes, homes for the aged, special clinical stations, big-brother and big-sister organizations affiliated with juvenile and domestic relations courts, and the like. Each agency is a co-operator of inestimable value to counselors but it is impossible to take advantage of such community resources unless one is aware of their existence and acquainted with their functions. In the small communities counselors may secure information directly from the individual organization and establish a school file listing each agency and describing its purpose and resources. In the larger communities such files are usually maintained by a central council or a clearinghouse which is staffed to collect and distribute information about all types of services which the council approves for public use. Where no central agency exists, welfare resources might be studied and information secured, as has been suggested for educational information, through the media of civic and service clubs. The returns might be filed with the public schools, the health department, or

4 See Gaynell Hawkins, *Educational Experiments in Social Settlements* (New York: American Association for Adult Education, 1937), a study of selected social settlements in New York, Chicago, Pittsburgh, Cleveland, and Boston, and Homer Rainey, Mary P. Peckers, and M. M. Chambers, *How Youth Serving Agencies Work Together* (2 pts.; Washington: American Council on Education, 1938–1939).

some other public agency. The values of a central information bureau are many: it prevents duplication of service to individuals and permits prompt response to calls for assistance by rendering unnecessary the canvassing of several agencies in lieu of one. If the community has a genuine and well-sustained interest in the public welfare, the pooling of agency information may reveal unnecessary or duplicate services, or it may show gaps in resources which can be filled by the reorganization of the existing services or by the addition of new ones.

Placement services. A later chapter is concerned with placement as one of the functions of guidance and personnel service. Therefore a brief statement as to the necessity for realizing that provision for placement is a community responsibility and that knowledge of what type of service there is and where it may be obtained is a counselor responsibility is all that is desirable at this point. Free public placement bureaus are usually operated by public schools, by municipalities, by states, and by the federal government. When public agencies combine their resources, one is apt to find a junior division and an adult division. Private agencies, philanthropic or semiphilanthropic in character, may or may not charge registration and placement fees. Among this group are found bureaus under the auspices of the Y.M.C.A. and other service organizations. Commercial agencies of many types and varying degrees of reliability are a third avenue for placement. News ads, trade journals, window signs, and bulletin boards are other media for notifying applicants that opportunities are open. The quality of the service is the important question regarding each available medium. This is especially important when young wage-earners are involved, and counselors should be familiar with the protective legislation which has been enacted in many states to guard against unfair placement practices.

Frequently residential districts and one industry communities lack a sufficient employing clientele to warrant the establishment of a placement office. Adult wage-earners may find their employment outlet through agencies in other cities, through friends, newspaper advertising, trade journals, and similar avenues. But some of the most troublesome problems brought by school counselors to this author's office have been concerned with methods of aiding school pupils who must leave their home community in order to obtain employment. Pending the time when better facilities for junior employment exchanges are available, this responsibility can be partially met by co-operation with such philanthropic bureaus as those of the Y.M.C.A. and by securing a selected list of commercial bureaus which include young workers in their clientele and whose reputation for fair dealing is well established. Moreover it is a well known fact that some business houses prefer to employ junior help directly from surrounding residential towns, and it is possible for any school to establish and maintain personal contacts of this type which will provide outlets for certain types of students.

Listing and utilizing the types of community services which have been discussed has been a common practice from the beginning of organized guidance service. Parsons, in 1908, made constant use of boys' clubs, public libraries, health services, and employment facilities. He reported one case in which a young man was so handicapped by stammering that he was unable to make an occupational adjustment. The man was referred to the Stammerers' Institute for treatment. A 1933 evaluation of counselor service on the college level indicated that students had been referred to twenty different types of agencies, and that counselors had received supplementary information about students from sixteen kinds of agencies.[5]

But it is not sufficient to list and utilize community services. Improving, integrating, and sometimes increasing community services are some of the immediately important steps in service to our entire people, youths and adults. Educators, especially those who function primarily in the personnel areas of education, have a rare opportunity for service in developing as well as in utilizing the resources of their communities for the common good of all their residents.

[5] See E. G. Williamson, H. P. Longstaff, and J. M. Edmunds, "Counseling Arts College Students," *Journal of Applied Psychology*, XIX (1935), 111–124.

CHAPTER VIII

Classifying, Indexing, and Filing Informational Material

THE task of the counselor or research worker is not completed with the collection of the several types of information which have been mentioned as essential to an adequate guidance service. Reliability, adaptability, and availability have been cited as indispensable characteristics of such information. Methods of testing the reliability of each piece of material have been stressed, and attention has been called to the necessity for selecting the content and adapting the form and language to the purpose and to the age and educational status of those for whom it is to be used. Availability requires further elaboration. How, after the initial collection is well under way, shall the material be classified, indexed, and filed so that its availability may be reasonably assured?

This is a difficult problem for any guidance service whether the volume of its material be large or small. Books, pamphlets, clippings, maps, charts, and pictures must all be provided for: there must be some way to know where they are and what their content and utility are. Books and unbound pamphlets which are large enough to stand on shelves will be easily found in cases and may be catalogued by author and title according to the local library system. But title indexing is not usually indicative of content, and almost universally it will be found necessary to institute some classification system which will cover the main categories of guidance and personnel and which will be sufficiently elastic to permit expansion both by category additions and by division into subcategories. One volume may require a dozen cross references in order adequately to indicate its content. College catalogues can usually be arranged on shelves and will not need to be indexed if they are returned to the same position after each use. But pictures, pamphlets, business reports, maps, and clippings are truly troublesome assets, which "vex the soul of the librarian day by day."

The present writer has over ten thousand pieces of such material in her library, and it is a constant struggle to reduce the labor involved in indexing and cross-referencing without losing the ability to locate material quickly when needed. Therefore she fully appreciates the difficulties involved in the preservation as well as in the proper classification, indexing, and filing of this most valuable type of material, and in doing so with the least expenditure of time, money, and energy. Since her present filing system was started approximately thirty years ago in a small way just as any new system would be started, since it might be sufficiently elaborate for permanent use in rural or small city collections, and since it has proved satisfactory over a considerable period of years in handling an ever-increasing amount of material, there may be some useful suggestion for others in an outline of its main features.

A PRIVATE PERSONNEL LIBRARY SYSTEM

The equipment of the library has remained practically the same throughout the thirty years: steel has displaced wood; some improvements have been made in folders for vertical files; and the quantity of equipment has greatly increased. It comprises adjustable shelves or cases, cardboard boxes, and holders for vertical file materials. The shelves or cases are used for books and for those pamphlets which will stand without curling and becoming dog-eared and which are sufficiently large to be labeled, thus making it unnecessary for a person to thumb through many pamphlets in order to find a particular one. The boxes, which were made to order in the vocational classes of the public schools, are similar to the usual library boxes except that they are open at the top and for about one third of the way down the back, the style which was found to be most satisfactory. They are designed to hold twenty-five to thirty pamphlets from six to eight inches wide and from ten to twelve inches long. The label with a subject classification, e.g., Education — Employee, is pasted on the front. Sometimes as the number of pamphlets increased, it was found to save time and constant handling as well as some superfluous indexing if a list of the contents was pasted on the right side of the box. If filing categories are clearly defined, it is not necessary to index such material until the number of items has increased to such an extent that a card index (1) saves time in locating material in the same categories which is filed in different places, (2) assists one in determining from card annotations which pieces of material shall be withdrawn from the files for any given purpose, or (3) gives an opportunity to students and others to make up a reference list which is to be used elsewhere.

Holders for vertical file material such as clippings, maps, small pamphlets of irregular size, and similar material are the third type of equipment needed. Manila folders are satisfactory for the first files; later on extension folders of better material with tabs and guides may be added. This is mentioned because many schools which have sought assistance in planning some system of preserving occupational material have frankly stated that even the cost of manila folders was an important item. All too often there seems to be a feeling that a beginning of classification and filing must await a full complement of book sections, files, folders, boxes, and cards. Any counselor will do well to start with the equipment which is available even though it be homemade shelves and boxes. Paraphernalia is important, but it should not be allowed to overshadow the importance of the educational purpose it is designed to serve. Pupils will take considerable pride in equipment which they have made, while the knowledge that pupils are making it may serve to focus the attention of parents and teachers on the fact that an embryo guidance service exists and that they are potential co-operators in its development.

Scrapbooks and inexpensive binders are useful for preserving pictures, clippings, and magazine articles. A number of binders are used in the author's library. Sometimes they contain articles on several subjects, all from various issues of a single magazine such as *Harper's* or *School Life*. Since the articles fall into a number of categories, it is necessary to index each and to note in the lower left-hand corner of the index card "Harper's Binder," as a means of locating the articles. If binders contain articles dealing with a single topic taken from several magazines, e.g., Apprenticeship, it is not necessary to index each article; one card indicating that a collection of articles on that topic will be found in the binder so labeled will suffice. Binders, labeled as to content and sometimes carrying a typed list of the articles on the inside cover, stand on shelves and are easily handled.

Library indexes and guides are just as essential as containers although their introduction will usually follow rather than accompany the provision for shelves, boxes, and holders for vertical materials. It takes a little time to start a collection and to find receptacles for its items. Then come the problems of listing and of devising some method whereby desired material may be quickly located. An index file of 3 x 5 cards and a library guide are both used in the writer's library. The index file, originally one small box on the counselor's desk, now comprises eighteen drawers with approximately eighty thousand cards. It includes both author and subject cards and is adequately cross-referenced. Author cards are made for all books, and for pamphlets, articles, and even clippings when the author is of paramount importance or would be a spontaneous first thought when information in some special field is sought. For instance, someone wants to know the status of research in factor analysis; Thorndike and Thurstone come to mind. Ben Wood and W. S. Learned have won national recognition in the testing field and in certain areas of college education; W. S. Gray and Arthur Gates write with authority on reading experiments.

When a call comes for the last word on tools for the study of individual differences, one instinctively turns to the index file, Educational Records Bureau. If the latest pronouncements on any one of a large number of topics in the area of business personnel are desired, the file for the American Management Association is the first recourse. On the other hand, the author card may be dispensed with whenever the topic is of outstanding importance and the author either unknown or one of many who have written on the same topic. Local follow-up surveys are good examples. Their main value, outside their own community, is in their contribution to the analysis of trends and to mass or comparative statistics. Quick location is assured if they are indexed under Surveys — Follow-up, since the topic card always carries the author's name.

For a time occupational monographs may be filed without indexing either in boxes or folders, provided such receptacles are labeled and classifications are clear-cut. As their number increases, and especially if the collection is available to strangers who desire to use the material for a variety of purposes, it will become necessary to make an index file for Occupations, expanding the subheads from time to time, indexing each item, and indicating by annotations the character of the content and the purpose for which it is designed. As an illustration, under Occupations — Fingerprinting, the annotation might be:

Of value to secondary and college students. An expanding field in which men are preferred. For the most part position requirements and salaries are adjusted to the secondary level.

Another annotation might read:

The best presentation to date. Based on research conducted by well-trained men. Inclusive as to topics. Adapted in form, content, and language to the college age.

The final piece of equipment is the Guide which lists all the categories and subheads in use. Gradually this comes to be an indispensable tool, both as an aid to the classification and indexing of material and as a means of locating it after it has been filed. One sheet served as a first guide. Today it comprises 39 pages, 147 categories, and many subcategories, one of which is usually Miscellaneous or General in order that from time to time it may be subdivided and new subtitles added. Some categories have, as yet, required no subdivisions. Among these are Handbooks, House Organs, Time and Motion Study, Unemployment, and Work Experience — Educational Value of. But Education has 25 subheads, Colleges and Universities, 19, Occupations, 181, and Psychological Tests, 13.

A few categories from the Guide indicating how material is classified, indexed, and located, and a sample index card are included for their possible suggestive value. As any index expands, the guide will grow; therefore, each counselor will need to formulate some basis for determining what should be indexed, how much should be cross-indexed, when to subdivide or add new categories, and the like. Usually it will save time and be more convenient in locating material if card topics and file categories are identical, but this is sometimes difficult, especially when the number of items to be filed is small. Since the number of boxes is few while folders are many, it is understood by those who use the library that no box is in use for any category unless the word "box" appears in connection with it.

INDEX TOPICS	VERTICAL FOLDERS AND BOXES
Apprenticeship	Apprenticeship — Box also
(including Internship)	
Certification and Licensure	Certification and Licensure
(see also Legislation — Education)	
Personnel Records	Personnel Records
Business	Business
Employment Office	Employment Office
General	General
Schools and Colleges	Schools and Colleges
(including Anecdotal)	
Surveys	Surveys
Educational	Educational — Box also
Elimination — Retardation	Elimination — Retardation
Employment Opportunity	Employment Opportunity
General	General — Box also
Mental Hygiene	Mental Hygiene — Box only
Methods of Making	General
(see also Research)	
Occupational	Occupational — Box also
Personnel	Personnel — Box also
(Old Vocational Guidance)	
Social	Social — Box also
Training Opportunity	Training Opportunity
Teachers	Teachers
College	College
(including Tenure)	
General	General
(including Academic Freedom)	
Student Opinion of	Student Opinion
(including Student Ratings. See also College: Student Opinion)	

INDEX TOPICS	VERTICAL FOLDERS AND BOXES
Supply and Demand	See Placement — Teacher
Preparation of	Preparation of
(including In-Service and Work-	
shops)	
Wages	Wages — Box also
(see also Salaries and Labor — Con-	
ditions of)	
Junior	Junior
Methods of Payment	Wages
Minimum	Minimum Laws and Rulings
Scales (standardization)	Wages
	(see also Job Classification)
Systems	Wages

The tabulation should be read as follows: Apprenticeship is an index topic. It includes Internship. Material on the topic is found in both a folder and a box. Certification and Licensure material is found in a folder only, but this topic should be considered in connection with data indexed under Legislation — Education. Personnel Records has four sub-heads each with a folder for material. Because there was little knowledge of, or call for, Anecdotal Records when the records categories were established, it was not made a separate category. If attention were not called to the fact that there is material available on this topic and where it is filed, it would soon become difficult, even for those who do the indexing, to remember from time to time where such material belonged. The same thing may be noted under Teachers where Workshop, a recent term, has not yet received an independent listing. Under Surveys — Personnel, "Old Vocational Guidance" has been added since many of the younger generation do not know that the type of survey which is today rather universally called "personnel" is the same sort of survey which in the period from 1900 to 1916 was called a "vocational guidance" survey. Under Wages it will be noted that there is not a separate file category for each index topic, that several subheads under wages are filed in a common folder or box.

The present method of indexing, cross-referencing, and indicating the location of material uses a "parent"-card system. This was introduced by Florence Chapman, of Cleveland, an experienced and very successful placement counselor. Acting on the advice of a special librarian who was familiar with the type of material to be classified and filed in a personnel library, Miss Chapman adapted her suggestions to private library needs, and the system has been in continuous use since 1921.

A sample parent card follows:

[*Front of card*]

Publication by Organization   Carnegie Corporation
[*in red*]   •   [*in black*]

Report of Carnegie Foundation for the Advancement of Teaching, June 24, 1932:
State Higher Education in California. Recommendations of the Commission.
Sacramento. State Printing Office. 1932. 82 pp.
Defines a profession and advocates limitation of members.
Associate in Arts title—in use since 1891.
Cost of adult education should be paid by the individual.
Recommendations on counseling.
Does not favor life certificates, or permanent tenure.
Box: California

[*Back of card*]

[*in red*]   [*in black*]

Colleges	Junior
Education	Higher Degrees
Personnel Departments	College
States	California
Surveys	Educational
Terminology	Educational

The Publication by Organization card is the lead, parent, or master card. The dot under Carnegie Foundation indicates this, and it also indicates that there are one or more cross references, the index topics for which will be listed on the opposite side of the card as is shown in the second illustration. The parent or master card need not be either an author or an organization card, but it must always carry some title, name, or subject which can legitimately be repeated on every cross reference. Sometimes the author is the only possible word to repeat and must be used, but in the illustration either California or Education could have been substituted for Carnegie Corporation. It is not necessary to list the other index topics on the opposite side of cross reference cards, although some special librarians always follow this practice. It is not done in the author's library because experience indicated that the labor involved was not justified by the benefits received. But, if one wishes to use a parent-card system, there are certain mechanical procedures which must not be overlooked. Failure to place a dot under the identifying word or words on each card may result in several ineffectual attempts to locate the parent card before it is discovered. Failure to list cross reference topics on the opposite side of the parent card may result in a chaotic condition if one wishes to discard material, reclassify it, transfer it to new receptacles, or reorganize the category files. It is the list on the parent card which gives assurance that every cross reference card has been withdrawn or reclassified. Failure to note the place where the material is filed (**Box: Cali-**

fornia) in the lower left-hand corner of each card foreshadows a frantic hunt for material, usually when it is needed in a hurry.

The annotations on each card should characterize the type of information found in the book or other material, which deals with the specific topic indexed. Page references should be included. Sometimes the annotations will note where criticisms, reviews, abstracts, or comparative material may be found. This has been particularly helpful in indexing important articles which have been well abstracted, digested, or critically reviewed in such publications as the *Loyola Educational Digest*[1] and the published work of the American Management Association.

OTHER SUGGESTIONS FOR INDEXING AND FILING

As the volume of material published has increased, demands for assistance in classifying, indexing, and filing it have also increased and are being responded to by specific efforts to meet specific needs. The emphasis has usually been on occupational categories with comparatively few efforts to include the many marginal and broader aspects of personnel and guidance. But there are descriptions of several systems, both complete and occupational, which may profitably be studied and from which suggestions may be adapted for local use.

A Pamphlet about Pamphlets by Lester Condit[2] will serve as a basis for any system. In a very simple but inclusive way which reveals on every page the spirit of the "forefathers of bibliography," methods of collecting, preserving, and using pamphlet material are discussed. Among the salient topics are: What pamphlets should be preserved? Where may current pamphlets be obtained? How should pamphlets be arranged? How should pamphlets be catalogued? A bibliography for each topic and a list of articles of library equipment with the names of manufacturers and dealers are included.

Three index systems which include guidance and personnel as well as occupational categories are: John M. Brewer's "A Filing List for Vocational Guidance," which was published in 1925;[3] Marguerite W. Zapoleon's *A Source File on Vocational Guidance,* published in 1940;[4] and W. H. Cowley's *The Personnel Bibliographical Index,* published in 1932.[5]

[1] Published monthly at 3441 N. Ashland Ave., Chicago, Ill.

[2] Chicago: University of Chicago Press, 1939.

[3] *Vocational Guidance Magazine,* XIII (1925), 277–280. This list was reprinted by Frederick J. Allen in *Principles and Problems in Vocational Guidance* (New York: McGraw-Hill Book Co., 1927), pp. 350–354.

[4] U. S. Office of Education, Misc. no. 2310; Washington, 1940.

[5] [Columbus, Ohio:] Ohio State University, 1932.

Brewer's and Zapoleon's systems are designated for "vocational guidance," but both include topics well within the broader field of guidance and personnel. Brewer's list is very brief but is as inclusive as could be expected at the date of publication. Zapoleon's system is rather elaborate, but it can easily be adapted to local needs and it is recent enough to warrant the assumption that it will be useful for a considerable period of time.

Cowley's *Index* is a scholarly work, which, while too elaborate for local use, has major values for large libraries on the college or adult level. It is comprised of three parts: Part I, a Subject Index; Part II, Annotations; and Part III, an Authors' Index. Annotations are divided into two parts: the descriptive annotation which deals with the nature of the material and the index annotation which is concerned with the appraisal of its scope. Even though few may follow Cowley's system, it is well for everyone to be familiar with the type of scholarship required to prepare such an index and to appreciate the time and expense involved in such an undertaking.

Among the indexes which deal with occupational topics *The Dictionary of Occupational Titles* is by far the most inclusive. It was prepared for the use of the U. S. Employment Service and published in Washington in 1939.[6] Two helpful works for those who wish to use this dictionary as a basic guide to classification are Franklin R. Zeran's *The Occupational Dictionary as a Tool in Vocational Guidance Work*[7] and William H. Stead's "The Dictionary of Occupational Titles."[8]

The Bureau of Guidance of the New York State Education Department has recently issued a bulletin on the filing of unbound occupational material.[9] The method has been described in some detail by Raymond Handville in an article entitled "Filing Your Occupational Information."[10] Principal E. A. La Fortune has set up a filing system based on the New York plan for the Ithaca, New York, High School and is finding it very satisfactory.

Even simpler and more easily organized systems are described in detail by Science Research Associates in *Basic Occupational Plans*.[11] After describing how to build a vocational book shelf, plans are outlined for filing

---

[6] It consists of three parts: Part I, "Definition of Titles," Part II, "Group Arrangement of Occupational Titles and Codes," and Part III, "Conversion Tables."

[7] U. S. Office of Education, Misc. no. 2528; Washington, 1940.

[8] *Occupations*, XIX (1940), 16–19.

[9] *A Plan for Filing Unbound Occupational Information* (Albany, N.Y.: University of the State of New York, 1939, mimeo.).

[10] *Occupations*, XVIII (1939), 101–104.

[11] Chicago: The Associates (First Quarter), 1939.

unbound occupational material using three bases, the Census classification, the Parker classification,[12] and an alphabetical classification.

EDUCATIONAL VALUES INHERENT IN INDEXING AND FILING

The content of Chapter VIII may seem to the reader to be concerned with useless, mechanical, and very uninteresting aspects of guidance and personnel, and he may be wondering who is to do the classifying, indexing, and filing.

There are three very specific values which derive from classifying, indexing, and filing informational material. One is the purely practical value expressed in the word "availability." But there are two major educational values for the instructional corps which are inherent in the processes as well as in the results: (1) the in-service education of those who have no real understanding of the purposes of guidance and personnel, little or no knowledge of its tools and techniques, and no feeling of responsibility for sharing in the performance of its functions; (2) the maintenance of interest among those who have some basic information but who would soon lose contact with the development of the work and the results of experimentation unless some definite procedure to counteract this natural tendency were followed.

An experienced individual who is familiar with the various categories included in the field of guidance and personnel and knows how to determine which are immediately useful in any given system will, of necessity, assume or be given leadership in classifying and annotating material. And any man or woman who is fortunate enough to have an opportunity to direct this work will be assured of a liberal education—an education broad enough to articulate all the fields of knowledge, all the areas of life, and all the agencies which serve humanity.

Perhaps classification will begin with a counselor, director, or supervisor who reads or skims (and he must know how) all the material which comes to the office. Some will probably be consigned to the wastebasket. Some will be found of temporary value only and it will soon be discarded. Some material may be preserved primarily for its historical value. The remainder will be indexed under appropriate categories. The counselor or director will practice annotating each piece of material in such a way that significant data regarding content, purpose, and value may be secured from the card, not only by himself but by others for whom the collection is being made. Naturally he will appreciate the educational values inherent in this experience and he may be loath to delegate the respon-

---

[12] The twenty-eight occupational groups used by W. D. Parker in *Books About Jobs* (Chicago: American Library Assn., 1936).

sibility to teachers or assistants, but he must learn to do so for very specific reasons: (1) Time will limit his ability to compass the entire task. (2) He must not be selfish. He has a major responsibility for educating others as well as himself and for stressing the values of shared responsibilities in this as well as in other phases of personnel service. And so he will bring others into the evaluating and classifying picture as rapidly as is feasible. He may accomplish this by any method which shares with them his own opportunity for development and progress and enhances their ability to assume a larger share of guidance responsibility without lowering the standards of evaluation or confusing category assignments. The choice of methods is a local matter, but a few practices which have stood the test of time for either novitiate or in-service training are offered.

The initial classifying, the assigning of index topics and subtopics, the preparing of annotations, the determining of parent cards, and the allocating to file categories is done by an experienced person. Rough notes comprising all card data which cannot automatically be included by the typist are jotted down on a slip of paper. A clerk or a commercial-course student, following a sample setup and completing the bibliographical data according to universal library practice, may make the permanent index card. There is frequently considerable guidance value in the familiarity with terms which accrues to the copyists who handle indexing. The completed index card may next be placed inside, or be attached to, the material which it describes, and be available on a table or in a file box for the period of one week. During that period teachers and others are invited to look over the material, noting its content, its classification, its cross references, and its characterization in the annotations. If the content does not seem to have been clearly or adequately described or if additional cross references or comments are desired, a slip to that effect may be attached to the material. Sometimes periodic informal conferences are held to discuss new material and the contribution which it makes to progress in the field. At the close of the week the original classifier again reviews the material, makes such additions or changes as seem desirable, and files both index cards and material.

Gradually the procedure may be reversed. The assistants and teachers may take over the responsibility for the original classifications and annotations with the director or counselor securing a large part of his current information from checking their work and making suggestions for additions or changes. The results will be satisfactory only if the basic work has been so thoroughly done that the categories are clear-cut and clearly understood and if there is a fair degree of unanimity regarding the type of material which belongs in the different categories.

If this systematic and rather elaborate method of training and of keeping up to date by means of classifying, indexing, and filing informational material be reduced to its lowest terms, it may not extend beyond the filing aspect of the program. Indexing and annotating may be eliminated and the incoming material placed without comment on a table or in a box for a period of time. Perhaps now and then a discussion regarding its content and use may be possible. Some system of preserving informational material can be worked out for even the smallest school system. And some method of using this system for in-service training of the instructional corps as well as for assuring availability of material is possible in even the smallest school system. But there must be inspirational leadership by a principal, district superintendent, teacher, or counselor or it will not be done, whether the school system be large or small, poor or rich. Once a program is under way, teachers, principals, part-time counselors, and all others who have major responsibilities in other fields of educational service can, by checking over material or material accompanied by index cards, vastly increase their knowledge of the personnel field and its possibilities. Frequently such first steps act as incentives to further study and further personal interest in pupils in all their activities and in all the phases of their developmental growth.

SELECTED SUPPLEMENTARY READING

[Those who desire information on defense occupations should place their names on federal mailing lists.]

Babcock, Lawrence F. *The U.S. College Graduate*. New York: Macmillan Co., 1941. Based on research conducted by *Time* magazine with the co-operation of 1000 colleges.

Chapman, Paul W. *Opportunities in Farming*. Chicago: Science Research Associates, 1941. (American Job Series of Occupational Monographs, no. 8.)

Fleming, Ralph D. *The Service Station Attendant*. Albany, N.Y.: Bureau of Guidance, State Education Department, 1940. Mimeo. An example of the type of occupational material supplied by some state departments for local use.

Greenleaf, Walter J. *Economic Status of College Alumni*. Washington, 1937. (U. S. Office of Education Bulletin, 1937, no. 10.) A research study which includes 31 colleges and 46,000 bachelor-degree students from the classes of 1928–1935.

Junior Employment Service of the School District of Philadelphia. *How Fare Philadelphia Public School Graduates?* Philadelphia: The School District, 1939.

Keliher, Alice V., ed. Picture Fact Books. New York: Harper and Bros., 1939–. A series designed to help youth find its place in the world of work. The titles include: 1939, *Air Workers, Movie Workers, News Workers, Nurses at Work, Textile Workers;* 1940, *Farm Workers, Library Workers, Office Workers, Radio Workers;* 1941, *Doctors at Work, Household Workers, Machinists at Work,*

Railroad Workers, Retail Sales Workers. The material is carefully selected and very attractively presented. Junior-high-school age.

Kingsbury, Susan M. *Economic Status of University Women in the U.S.A.* Washington, 1939. (U. S. Women's Bureau Bulletin, no. 170.)

Kuller, Ruth. "Occupational Information in Simple Form," *Occupations,* XX (1942), 586–591. An introduction to occupations for pupils of low reading ability in the Cincinnati schools. Classified for grades 3 to 8. Annotated as to content.

Pence, Edith E. "Social Trends and Vocational Guidance," *Occupations,* XIV (1935), 139–146. Indicates how economic and social phenomena are related to occupational opportunities. Has a desirable method of presentation.

U. S. Office of Education. *An Outline of Steps in a Community Occupational Survey.* Washington, 1941. A valuable contribution to procedures involved in collecting local occupational information. Deals with survey methods as applied to communities of varying size and includes an annotated bibliography on survey methods.

U. S. Women's Bureau. Series on Labor Laws for Women in the States. Washington, 1941. Prepared at the request of the U. S. Office of Education for use in vocational classes for women and girls.

BIBLIOGRAPHICAL AIDS

Fortune. *Vocational Index.* [New York:] Lecturer's Bureau of *Time, Life, Fortune,* [1941]. A bibliography of vocational articles selected from *Fortune* magazine, Feb., 1930, to Dec., 1940.

National Urban League. *Vocational Guidance Bibliography.* New York: The League, 1940.

Orata, Pedro T. *Occupational Information and Guidance Bibliography, 1939.* Washington, 1941. (U. S. Office of Education, Vocational Division Bulletin, no. 218, Occupational Information and Guidance Series, no. 8.)

——, and Cookingham, Waldo B. *Occupational Information and Guidance Bibliography, 1937–38.* Washington, 1941. (U. S. Office of Education, Vocational Division Bulletin, no. 212, Occupational Information and Guidance Series, no. 5.) An annotated list of approximately 4500 titles classified under 17 main headings. Includes a directory of sources of occupational pamphlets and both a subject and an author index. No other bibliography is needed for the years covered.

Wilcox, Jerome K., ed. *Manual on the Use of State Publications.* Chicago: American Library Assn., 1940. A directory of bulletins, reports, and statistical publications of state governmental agencies.

PERIODICALS

My Weekly Reader: The Children's Newspaper. Editorial board: Wm. S. Gray, Arthur Gates, *et al.* American Education Press Inc., 400 South Front St., Columbus, Ohio. Published in several editions: No. 1 for Grade One, No. 2 for Grade Two, No. 3 for Grade Three, etc. Exceptionally desirable for the lower grades.

Occupations—The Vocational Guidance Magazine. National Vocational Guidance Association, 425 W. 123rd St., New York, N.Y. Published monthly, October to May, inclusive. Primarily for educators.

Personnel. American Management Association, 330 W. 42nd St., New York, N.Y. Published quarterly. Primarily for businessmen but very helpful in broadening the vision of educators.

Monthly Labor Review. U. S. Department of Labor, Bureau of Labor Statistics, Washington, D.C. Includes material on industrial relations, labor conditions, national income, co-operation, labor laws, costs and standards of living, minimum wages and maximum hours, wages and hours of labor, employment offices, trends of employment, and pay rolls.

The Employment Security Review (formerly *Employment Service News*). Published monthly by the Federal Security Agency, Bureau of Employment Security, Washington, D.C. Contains articles on population trends, unemployment, employment security problems, job opportunities, and co-operative training.

PART III
Information about the Individual
(Individual Inventory)

CHAPTER IX

Data on Health, Activities, Teachers' Marks, References and
Recommendations, and Work Experiences

CHAPTER X

Data Secured from Psychological Testing

CHAPTER XI

Data Secured from Personality Measurement and Appraisals

CHAPTER XII

Classifying, Recording, and Filing Information about the Individual

A SECOND PREREQUISITE TO COUNSELING

"A clear understanding of yourself, your aptitudes, abilities, interests, ambitions, resources, limitations, and their causes."—FRANK PARSONS, 1908.

"Self-appraisal of one's interests, aptitudes and abilities."—DAVID G. RYANS, 1941.

CHAPTER IX

Data on Health, Activities, Teachers' Marks, References and Recommendations, and Work Experiences

PART II dealt with facts about educational and occupational opportunities and the types of developmental facilities and social experiences which are available within individual communities. Review of these chapters, and of such reference material as may have been used, will serve to recall the fact that all educational and occupational information, no matter what its form, gives some attention to the demands which the task makes upon the student or the worker. And it is quite obvious that knowledge of the requirements which a given undertaking makes upon an individual, plus knowledge of the demands of the larger work or service unit with which he is to be associated, is prerequisite to consideration of the desirability of any individual's entering any field of endeavor. It is equally obvious that the capacities, proficiencies, tendencies, and traits possessed by individuals must be known and considered in conjunction with the demands of the contemplated undertaking before the counselor can fully meet his obligation to the counselee.[1]

Part III is designed to indicate how this second and complementary series of facts may be secured and made available for counseling purposes. It deals with Parsons' and Ryans' second series of facts—facts about the individual, the abilities, achievements, and personal qualities which help to picture individuals in their developmental growth and as successful work units contributing to the efficiency of larger units or social groups.

The methods of determining individual differences both as to native and acquired traits, of analyzing mental traits, and of determining how different traits are combined and related are still in the experimental stage. The best technicians have, however, discovered much of factual value—enough to encourage the belief that better analysis techniques are developing and that constant refinement of such techniques foretells increasingly valuable contributions to counseling procedures. Therefore,

[1] The matching of individual qualifications against job demands can be carried too far. Jobs as well as individuals have modifiable personalities. While the character of low-grade employments may be fixed, the duties of many jobs may be modified by the incumbent to such an extent that the original specification is materially altered.

neither the elusiveness of reliable data nor the clamor for more information, accurate or inaccurate, which arises from every level of education and from every walk in business life should trouble us too greatly. Psychologists plod on. They are continually giving to both fields the best factual evidence at their command. They are continually regretting that uncritical use of inadequate criteria by well-meaning but ignorant advisers is doing positive harm to individuals and blocking the path to ultimate success. They recognize, where the layman may not, that an uncritical attitude toward measuring techniques is a serious handicap to progress in analyzing the individual, and they are constantly warning counselors to wait for professional authorization before assuming the reliability and validity of any single measuring tool.

Part III is prepared for the general, not for the psychological, counselor, and it is assumed that those who desire to perform psychometric or clinical services will make special preparation for such work. The chapters on educational and occupational information were also written for the general counselor, and attention was called to the necessity for special preparation before engaging in occupational research. Mastery of the content of Part III should give the student:

1. A clear conception of job specification as applied to clinical procedures and the demands which the job makes upon psychologists, social workers, teachers, counselors, visiting teachers, and all others who undertake to develop or apply analysis techniques or to utilize their results for counseling purposes.

2. Familiarity with the various types of information which help to acquaint counselors with the abilities, interests, and probable achievements of individuals.

3. Knowledge of the sources from which such information may be secured and methods of determining its value.

4. Knowledge of the various tools available for use in acquiring information about the individual.

5. Definite understanding of what is meant by reliable, available, adaptable personnel records and the best methods of maintaining such records.

6. Understanding of the dangers of assuming that the best diagnosticians, using the best techniques, can discover and segregate all the factors or combinations of factors which constitute any given personality.

General Sources of Information about the Individual

In some respects sources of information about individuals are similar in character to those from which occupational information is secured, and their value is tested by the same fundamental principles:

(1) Direct observation of individuals in different situations and under different environmental conditions is an excellent source of information. Observation in the home supplements observation in school activities, and observation of behavior in community activities and in employment situations affords additional supplementary information.

(2) Interviews and conferences, ranging from the most informal consultations with teachers, counselors, parents, employers, and others to the more specific and purposeful conferences relative to health conditions, mental capacities, achievement in relation to ability, and abnormal behavior problems, are a second important source of information. The clinical or case conference, based upon knowledge of the values of both objective and subjective data and their interrelation, is a method of coordinating and interpreting data secured from many sources, and if its findings or conclusions be entered on the record, they become a source of inestimable value for the understanding of the individual.

(3) Records of various types including routine identification data, facts regarding physical and mental health and school progress, scores on psychological tests, ratings on personality traits, facts on work experiences and records of participation in activities. Personnel records correspond to the various types of printed, or otherwise recorded, material discussed under occupational information and should be approached in the same scientific attitude.

GENERAL PRINCIPLES FOR DETERMINING THE VALUE OF INFORMATION ABOUT INDIVIDUALS

Reliability, availability, and adaptability were cited as musts in determining the value of occupational information for counseling purposes. Information about the individual should in general be tested by the same standards.[2]

If it is to be available, this information about individuals—information of different kinds collected from a variety of major and minor sources— must be pooled and co-ordinated in a master record to form an individual inventory. This record should be cumulative and up-to-date and be easily accessible to all who have any legitimate use for it. It should be supplemented by such confidential records as may be needed to aid in the complete analysis of any given individual but which, for one reason or another, are filed separately, often under other jurisdiction, e.g., certain medical records.

Adaptability implies that the record consists of material adequate to

[2] Validity, an essential criterion of psychological tests, is discussed in Chapter X.

serve the several purposes for which information about individuals is sought. It becomes the responsibility of teachers, administrators, or counselors to draw off from the cumulative record whatever data may be adapted to the purpose at hand. Among the several purposes for which data might be used are the following:

(1) To help in self-analysis; to check self-evaluation.

(2) To help in uncovering individual abilities and success factors.

(3) To help in uncovering individual weaknesses and failure factors.

(4) To help in explaining behavior problems and mind sets.

(5) To indicate to what extent desirable work habits and personality traits are being cultivated.

(6) To maintain a progress chart which will indicate how nearly the individual is attaining his goal.

(7) To help in determining qualifications for specific occupations which have aroused interest.

(8) To aid school authorities in right curricular placement and replacement.

(9) To suggest the use of cocurricular or other activities and agencies for overcoming or minimizing revealed deficiencies or for developing desirable qualities.

(10) To aid placement offices in right job placement and replacement.

(11) To aid employers in selection, placement, adjustment, promotion, and transfer.

The reliability of information about individuals can be determined only after microscopic scrutiny. Such information may be purely objective in character, purely subjective, or it may partake of both characteristics. Objective data usually comprise routine identification data such as name, age, residence, and nativity; much of the school history such as courses taken, skips, and repeats; attendance records; results of standardized achievement tests; participation in school and in out-of-school activities; apparent physical defects or conditions affecting free movement of arms, hands, legs, and feet; endurance; ability to lift, stand, walk, or sit for considerable periods of time; records of physical tests and personal hygiene; and other data comparatively free from errors due to personal bias. On the other hand, gross inaccuracies often creep into records on such simple items as age unless they are secured directly from the birth registry. Counselors should be ever alert to the fact that data secured from any form of self-record such as questionnaires and application blanks may be influenced by a variety of factors such as a desire to evade laws, family or personal pride, social ambition, or a wish to secure admission to a given school or occupation. Changes in name, variations in age, and false statements as to experience, training, nationality, religion, or residence frequently occur on educational forms and are quite commonly found on application blanks and employment questionnaires.

Subjective data are known to be more or less influenced by personal bias, prejudice, interest, experiences, or individual philosophy of life. Subjectivity enters into all personal observations whether expressed in anecdotal or rating forms or as personal opinions and guesses relative to physical or emotional conditions. There are those who would brand all subjective data "gossip" and advocate its discard. Others feel that subjective impressions are often more important for guidance service than objective information *if one realizes that they may not be used with equal assurance.* Counselors are advised, at this point, to turn back to Chapter VI and reread, with evaluation of this type of data in mind, the rules for testing the reliability of an author including the list of "intellectual immoralities." They should also consider with reference to each bit of information how the character of the source and the influence of time and place may affect the value of personal information.

ESSENTIAL INFORMATION ABOUT THE INDIVIDUAL

As has been indicated, information essential for one counseling situation is not necessarily equally essential for all other purposes. Topics discussed in this section have been chosen to meet as many as possible of the normal everyday needs of educational systems which can and should have at hand at least a minimum of factual data for every registrant. The importance of the cumulative character of such data for postschool as well as for school development and the additional types of data essential on the adult level have been given some attention—enough, it is hoped, that elementary, secondary, and college teachers and counselors may realize the importance of continuity in records paralleling continuity in developmental growth, and, looking beyond the confines of the formal educational world, may catch a vision of the postschool requirements which will surely be made upon individuals when they pass beyond educational jurisdiction.

Desirable information on Health, Activities, Teachers' Marks, References and Recommendations, and Work Experience will be considered in Chapter IX. Data secured from Psychological Tests, and from various methods of Personality Appraisal will be offered in some detail in Chapters X and XI respectively. Routine identification data, certain types of information dealing with family background and preschool history will receive incidental attention only. The many important unclassifiable items derived from counseling interviews, which serve to fill in the gaps in the total picture and furnish "leads" for inquiry and inference, logically pertain to Chapter XIV which discusses the interview as a major method of counseling.

1. *Health Data.* These form a part of the developmental history of an individual. Under ideal conditions they include: (1) Records of congenital, oftentimes observable, defects. Such items are a timely warning of possible vocational limitations. They indicate the need for carefully planned educational programs and the use of discriminating judgment as to whether rehabilitation services are available and warranted and whether institutional or local facilities will best meet the individual's need. Left-handedness, facial disfigurements, limb deficiencies, and other congenital defects require early attention.

(2) Records of preschool examinations followed by remedial treatment, if necessary; of periodic re-examination throughout school life with special effort to diagnose conditions accurately at the time of entry into employment; and of continued periodic re-examinations during adult life.

(3) Records of illness and accidents and of absences or inefficiencies legitimately credited to poor health; also records of frequent calls for attention from doctors and nurses. The causes of illness and accidents and the costs incidental thereto are of interest to both educator and employer. They help to explain school and college failure and warn potential employees that susceptibility to illness and proneness to accident foretell difficulties in employment adjustment.

(4) Records of physical tests and measurements which have both guidance and employment value. Among the most commonly used are tests of height and weight, of lung capacity, of color sense and color blindness, of visual and auditory acuity, of muscular strength of hands, arms, legs, and back, and of pulse rate, body balance, steadiness, motor agility, and motor co-ordination. Records of such tests have revealed a close relationship between physical deficiencies and social and emotional adjustments and educational achievement. They have long been used for the light which they throw on educational and vocational possibilities and for their value in understanding delinquent, incorrigible, and mentally backward youth. The role of the endocrine glands in personality development is the newest field in which physical measurement plays an important part. Colleges are testing the physical fitness of students for the work they desire to undertake in both the intellectual and activities aspect of the curriculum. Placement officers and employment departments in business and industry include the physical requirements of each position in job requi-

sitions and job specifications, and all industries which employ any number of workers administer their own physical tests.[3]

Counseling individuals within the limitations imposed by physical strength and physical conditions is a highly expert job. It would be too much to expect general counselors to be informed on the physical requirements and physical effects of all jobs. They can be familiar with some generally applicable requirements, and experience will result in additional knowledge. Strength of arms, legs, and back is essential for jobs which involve shoveling, carrying, or lifting. Tests for quick and accurate arm, hand, and finger movements (manual dexterity) indicate ability to handle certain types of punch presses, office calculating machines, and similar machines requiring speed and precision of movement or touch. Defective vision or defective hearing frequently bars men from teaching and from positions in law, medicine, and the ministry. Facial cripples are usually barred from salesmanship and other types of work where their disfigurement would detract from their usefulness. Counter sales, laundry work, and restaurant service require constant standing, while telephone operating requires constant sitting. Observation by teachers and others supplements, and often suggests the desirability of, physical examinations. Signs of malnutrition, excessive nervousness, irritability, fatigue, headaches, failure to see and hear readily, and pupils' or workers' own statements that they are suffering from physical causes are all helpful sources of information even though subjectivity may dominate. Frequently they throw light on the mental as well as on the physical condition of individuals.

Neither lay nor professional opinion is entirely in sympathy with extensive physical examinations under public-school auspices, and the expense seems prohibitive. Inspection for surface defects, for signs of contagious disease, and for bodily cleanliness is fairly common. It may disclose susceptibility to certain types of physical and nervous strain, suggest counteracting activities, explain retardation and school failure, furnish basic information for guidance service, and at employment protect both employer and employee. On the adult level physical examinations are gaining in popularity. Colleges and business houses in increasing numbers are including such examinations in their selective process and are recording the results. Programs for the mental and physical health of students are going forward in a number of colleges; records on health data are becom-

---

[3] The best sources of information on the physical and health data required by business organizations are the periodic surveys reported in the publications of the American Management Association, the National Industrial Conference Board, and the National Association of Manufacturers.

ing more accurate and scientific and are being used to indicate the influence of student employment as well as to aid in educational, vocational and social guidance.

Under the stimulus of workmen's compensation laws, health data and physical examinations have become important factors in the selection of employees. Industrial health, sanitation, and safety have grown in importance; complete medical corps with adequate facilities for many services have been installed; and research into the causes of industrial instability and disease are liberally supported. Recent social-security legislation is tending to draw the selection lines still tighter and to encourage periodic re-examinations after employment. The health records of modern business houses, to the extent that their information is open to counselor follow-up, have value for indicating the specific physical demands which specific positions make upon the worker and the type of person who has been able or unable to meet these demands.

2. *Activities Data.* Organized activities of various types, some of which have long been conducted under philanthropic, social, or commercial auspices, have in recent years found a place in educational systems which are now showing a tendency to accord them a cocurricular status. This situation is partially due to a broadening conception of the objectives of education and to a desire to make available for educational purposes all the facilities and experiences which may contribute to the realization of these broader objectives. It may also be accredited, to some extent, to the interest which business scouts have shown in the activities record of senior-college students and to the fact that requisitions for teachers have increasingly sought specific information regarding student-activities records and the professional courses which have been taken dealing with the organization and values of such activities. These evidences of value have not always been interpreted correctly; they have been abused as well as used. Hence the business world has felt called upon to clarify its position somewhat, to explain that each experience must be considered in the light of position requirements. A long list of heterogeneous activities is not per se an appealing recommendation. From educational circles, too, there comes now and then a warning that "a bundle of activities" is not a legitimate substitute for an education.

The problems involved in the introduction and operation of activities and in the establishment of the basic principles which should control permission for the introduction of any given activity are administrative and supervisory; they are not guidance responsibilities. The counselor is justified in assuming that each activity operating in connection with an educational institution has passed some selective test, has received the approval of the administration, and is at his or her command as need arises. Activities whose objectives are in harmony with the objectives of an educational institution afford a great variety of opportunities for new experiences; they increase provision for the recognition of individual differences; and they are valuable tools for carrying to successful conclusions individual developmental programs which may result from student counseling.

Counselors should be familiar with the different activities sponsored by the institution they serve and should be aware of the guidance values inherent in each. It should be both a privilege and a responsibility to assist the individual to interpret activity opportunities in terms of his personal needs and to choose as wisely as possible such activities as will best supplement his course and curriculum choices and enhance his personal qualities. All students may profit by membership in organizations which afford opportunities to practice teamwork, to develop morale, desirable character qualities, appreciations and ideals, and effective citizenship standards, to acquire social poise, to evaluate and choose leaders, to understand minority groups, to practice tolerance of others' opinions and beliefs and the like. Some students will need counselor advice and assistance in selecting activities to meet specific needs. One student because of shyness, timidity, or lack of self-confidence may profit by membership in a certain organization. The overenergetic, self-assertive type of student will probably make a different choice. Vocational clubs, subject clubs, debating, dramatic, and music clubs are each a valuable adjunct to some student's educational program, and they often afford desirable motivating influences.

Sometimes it has seemed that too much stress has been laid upon the fact that a specific student was not interested in any activity. Are there not some people, perhaps not many, who find work and play synonymous, who prefer to be alone, and who enjoy concerts, theaters, and other pleasures without group association? If physical and mental health are good, if home conditions are normal, may it not be wise to let well enough alone until advice is sought or until there is some evidence that change in interests would be beneficial?

Activities membership, carefully chosen to supplement rather than to dominate educational life, increases developmental assets. Recorded information regarding activities pursued, individual satisfactions derived, and social contributions made are significant items for guidance and employment purposes. That activities have permanent values and should be pursued beyond the years of formal education is evidenced by the number of industrial and business organizations which foster activities programs and by the variety of community programs provided on the adult level.

3. *Data Secured from Teachers' Marks.* In spite of progress in the preparation of standardized subject tests and their recognized contribution to more objective and comparable measurement of pupil achievement, in spite of the fact that research reports have destroyed much of our former confidence in teachers' marks, school records usually carry such marks, and the best thought of the day advocates the continuance of this practice. Ben Wood, upon whose pronouncements in the field of measurement many of us have learned to wait as for signal lights, has after thorough investigation suggested the retention of local marking systems. He bases his suggestions on (1) the utility of marks in achieving individualized standards by "tempering the wind to the shorn lamb" and rating "bantams on bantam standards," (2) on his conviction that teachers' marks have "overtones of moral, personal and social approval" which outweigh their academic elements as an influence in community attitude toward the school, and (3) on his belief in a dual system of marks. One system comprising comparable measures—norms based on standardized tests—should be used for certification and transfer purposes, for recommendations for employment, and for aid to students in setting up appropriate and feasible educational and vocational goals. The other system comprising teachers' marks—stressing their moral and equitable element—should be used to evaluate pupils' achievement in relation to individual powers and needs.[4]

The determination of pupil evaluation systems and the particular items to be included are administrative responsibilities. If teachers' marks are included it becomes the duty of counselors (1) to understand their advantages and disadvantages from the administrative viewpoint; (2) to avoid the dangers involved either in assuming that they are a dependable source of factual, comparable data or in discarding them as valueless for guidance purposes; (3) to recognize that individual differences among the teaching corps are bound to find expression in all subjective measurements and to use discriminating judgment in interpreting marks for advisory purposes; (4) to practice weighing the value of marks against other items of information about the individual, especially if wide discrepancies are revealed; (5) to familiarize themselves with the various ways in which pupils and parents, under different circumstances, react to teachers' marks; (6) to search for the possible guidance values of marks and for methods whereby

[4] See Ben D. Wood, "The Need for Comparable Measurements in Individualizing Education," *Educational Record*, XX, Suppl. no. 12 (1939), 14–31.

youth may be assisted to recognize these values and to make use of them for personal growth.

At all times it is well for counselors to be prepared for such illegitimate uses of marks as the giving of low grades as spurs to achievement or as disciplinary measures, and the giving of high grades as rewards for approved conduct or for purely personal reasons. High grades are encouraged per se and they are overemphasized in the awarding of scholastic honors, whereas grades should be stressed as indicators of growth and as revealers of individual needs. The unfortunate results of these and other misuses of teachers' marks are frequently expressed in inferiority and superiority complexes, in intellectual snobbery, in cheating, or in the formation of other undesirable habits including the "get-by" habit which often accompanies ability to reap high rewards for a minimum of effort. Parental disappointment and displeasure are all too often visited upon children who do not and perhaps cannot realize their expectations. And victims of "complimentary" grades [5] are often penalized for teacher generosity when employers accept such marks as bona fide indications of accomplishment only to discover that they have no significance as measures of present status of efficiency or as signs of potential growth.

College advisers may not be unmindful of the wide gap between high-school and college grades which often alarms and discourages freshmen students. The causal factors require immediate and discriminating attention. High-school counselors who advise on college courses and curricula should remember that during recent years colleges have been raising their standards of achievement, and some institutions are rather mercilessly eliminating all who do not come up to their standards, while high schools have been under considerable pressure to lower standards and, if necessary, provide for awarding "complimentary" grades.

Of course, counselors may not discipline teachers and parents no matter how desirable disciplinary action may seem to be. But frequently, by the use of tact and judgment, they may help teachers to minimize the personal element in marks, assist parents to give more intelligent and more honest consideration to the talents of their children, and guide pupils in understanding how to interpret marks more constructively. They may also show constructive leadership in differentiating more sharply between the purposes of norms on standardized tests and grades on teachers' examinations.

4. *Data Secured from References and Recommendations.* References

[5] Cloy S. Hobson, "The Complimentary Mark," *Elementary School Journal,* XXXIX (1938), 195–199.

and recommendations are another source of subjective information relative to individuals. They are sought by a variety of persons for a variety of purposes—admissions committees selecting applicants for educational institutions, businessmen seeking employees, placement offices checking up on efficiency and character, social and business organizations protecting the integrity of their personnel, boards of education and college boards seeking faculty additions, politicians seeking to preserve the unity of their party, and the like.

The form, value, and method of obtaining recommendations has changed materially with the introduction of more formal and inclusive application blanks, improved record systems, and demands for specific evidence or trait actions to support specific ratings on both skill and character. The "To whom it may concern" blanket recommendation has been largely discarded. Such recommendations usually were, and still are when given, without meaning or value. All too often they served to lighten the blow of dismissal, were colored by friendship or prejudice, were the easiest way out, or were the custom. Many a prayer that he whom it might concern would be sufficiently experienced to read between the lines accompanied these unsealed messages.

One method of securing recommendations is through references listed on the application blank. Such blanks rather generally ask for the names and addresses of a number of persons, former employers or teachers, bankers, ministers, and others to whom one may write for personal opinions relative to the applicant. References secured in this fashion are frequently followed up by educators and by employers who are seeking employees for upper positions or for positions requiring some outstanding or unusual qualities. Naturally, the names furnished by applicants are of those to whom they are favorably known. Many factors tend to detract from the value of personal recommendations secured in this way, and as a rule they must be rather liberally discounted.

Returns on rating scales are increasingly available and valuable as the basis for recommendations. Their very definiteness and formality tend to bring out evidence which might be overlooked in a general recommendation. Some institutions are using recommendation blanks which are based upon the same fundamental principles and are very similar in form to modern rating scales. Recommendation forms prepared for employer use aim to secure the information needed with the minimum demand upon his time and effort. Qualities and habits essential for one position may have little value for another. Delivery men, meter readers, window washers, and others who enter private homes must be able to assume certain responsibilities not required of workers in some other lines.

Cashiers, bank messengers, and others who handle money are required to be strictly honest with reference to financial matters. Business houses ask only for the information needed. Questions which have been found to bring helpful information include: Would you re-employ the applicant? If not, why? If so, in the same or in another capacity? Occasionally a copy of the exit slip is offered prospective and inquiring employers or trusted placement bureaus.

Counselors and placement officers who accumulate ratings and recommendations in anticipation of demand frequently find themselves unable *to interpret their data in terms of specific evidence of fitness, for specific things, in specific situations.* It is a difficult matter to meet the requirement both for immediately available data and for specific data applicable to specific situations. Counselors will need to use all recommendations, no matter what their source, with extreme caution lest their contribution to guidance be negative rather than positive and at times even destructive and misleading.

5. *Data Secured from Work Experiences.* Information relative to work experiences, either in full- or part-time jobs, is always valuable data for counselors. It helps to determine interests, supplements aptitude tests, affords opportunities to combine the practical with the theoretical, and suggests educational programs and exploratory avenues. Remunerated work experiences do not, usually, enter the picture until the requirements of compulsory education and child-labor laws have been met, but there are some opportunities for exploratory and co-operative courses on the secondary level which have definite guidance values. On the college level a large percentage of registrants are engaged in wage-earning occupations. The objectives vary from the purely financial purpose of semi or total self-support to the desire for exploratory experience in various lines as aids to arriving at a vocational choice. Co-operative courses may serve to clinch vocational choices already made. Returns on periodic tests of proficiency, ratings by co-ordinators or employers, and any comments or suggestions which throw light on the vocational potentialities of the individual should be entered on the record.

CHAPTER X

Data Secured from Psychological Testing

A CLEAR-CUT definition of a psychological test is not yet ready for the counselor's dictionary although it is becoming increasingly important that one should be included therein. Not that the use of tests is a recent addition to counseling procedure, for they have, as contemporary documents show, been in use from the inception of the organized guidance movement. But the multiplication of tests, the differentiation of objectives, and the progress in the refinement of all types of tests have been accompanied by the sort of confusion in terms which sooner or later leads to stocktaking, followed by clarification and more explicit definition of terms. The teacher's or general counselor's first difficulty as a novice in the testing field is likely to be found in the not uncommon use of "intelligence test" and "psychological test" as synonyms. The best authorities as a rule do not approve such usage. They grant that a properly constructed intelligence test is a psychological test, but since intelligence is not thought to be the only mental function measurable by psychological tests, they do not agree that a psychological test and an intelligence test are interchangeable terms. It is hoped that the discussion in this section may help to clarify thinking with respect to test relationships, especially relationships between psychological tests and all other types of tests with which counselors should be familiar.

DEFINITION OF A PSYCHOLOGICAL TEST

The following definition of a psychological test seems to be in harmony with the best thought of the time, and, properly interpreted, it meets the needs of counselors and teachers who are laymen in the field of psychology: A psychological test is one which (1) measures samples of an individual's behavior and (2) satisfies the well-known psychological criteria of objectivity, validity, reliability, and established norms.

Objectivity implies that the test is so constructed as to eliminate as far as possible the subjective element involved in the individuality of the examiner. Validity is concerned with the degree to which the test measures what it purports to measure. Reliability is concerned with the degree to which test results remain constant, either with repetition of the same test or with administration of equivalent forms of the same test. Established norms imply that the test is so constructed that it furnishes a basis for the comparison of an individual's score with the scaled scores of a large group of individuals of similar age or grade status. Intelligence scales, as well as many other types of achievement and aptitude measures, if they satisfy these four criteria, are legitimately considered psychological tests. On the other hand, by the application of the same criteria, a number of published tests, especially those dealing with character and personality, are ruled out.

CLASSIFICATION OF PSYCHOLOGICAL TESTS

Psychological tests are classified in a number of different ways according to the purpose for which the classification is made. Among the most common methods are classification according to (1) the sources of ability tested—whether abilities to be tested are supposed to be dependent, in the main, upon native or inherited characteristics or whether they are assumed to represent acquired abilities or proficiencies; (2) the kinds of ability tested, abstract, concrete, or social; (3) the form in which the test content is presented—whether it is an oral, written, picture, or performance test; and (4) the method of administration, to an individual or to a group.

Classification on the basis of source of ability has proved satisfactory for counselor use and will be followed in this chapter. An outline on this basis is included to assist in guiding the study of the reader and also to give a visual demonstration of the ease with which any one of the other classifications may be substituted for the one chosen.

CLASSIFICATION OF PSYCHOLOGICAL TESTS

1. Tests of capacity
   a. Intelligence tests
      (1) Types measured—abstract, mechanical, social
      (2) Forms of test—oral, written, picture, performance
      (3) Method of administration—individual, group
   b. Tests of special aptitude
      (1) Aptitudes measured—manual, mechanical, clerical, professional
      (2) Form of tests—pencil and paper, form board, assembly, etc.
      (3) Method of administration—individual, group
2. Tests of proficiency
   a. Trade tests
      (1) Occupational proficiencies measured—manual, mechanical, clerical

(2) Form of tests—oral, pencil and paper, performance
(3) Method of administration—individual, group
b. School achievement tests
(1) Subject achievement
(2) Form of test—usually written
(3) Method of administration—individual, group

Tests of Capacity: (a) *Intelligence Tests*

The intelligence test is the most highly developed, most widely used, and most severely criticized of all the psychological tests on the market today. It has long since demonstrated its usefulness in assisting parents, teachers, counselors, psychologists, and other interested persons to better understand an individual's mental characteristics. Its validity is acknowledged, its practical utility tried and not found wanting. Wherein, then, lies the basis of so much criticism? In the following two facts:

(1) *Intelligence has never been acceptably defined.* How, then, can tests be constructed to measure it? Moreover, it is currently assumed that there may be more than one kind of intelligence. Thorndike suggests the recognition of a threefold but not mutually exclusive division—abstract, mechanical or concrete, and social. Abstract intelligence is the type of intelligence which is challenged in the mastery of ordinary academic subjects in secondary schools and colleges. It involves ability to deal with ideas and principles, to differentiate the relevant from the irrelevant, to form judgments, and to arrive at logical conclusions. The scales which test this type of intelligence are frequently called "tests of scholastic aptitude," a far more acceptable term than "intelligence test" to both parents and pupils, especially if scores happen to be extremely low. "Mechanical" or "concrete intelligence" is used to designate ability to respond to things rather than to verbal symbols. On various levels mechanical intelligence is exemplified by the plumber, the carpenter, the inventor, the surgeon, etc. Social intelligence is involved in the understanding and managing of human beings. Tests of social intelligence are exceedingly difficult to standardize, and hence less progress has been made in this phase of intelligence testing than in the other two phases. Normally it would be found at a high level among salesmen, social workers, and politicians. Many psychologists feel that the generally intelligent man will rank relatively high in all three of the phases of intelligence cited.

(2) *There is no basis as yet upon which to determine how much of an individual's "intelligence" should be credited to inherited characteristics and how much to environmental factors.* Closely related to this is the

ever-present and unsolved problem of the constancy of the I.Q., the final solution of which is very important for the future of the testing movement. Walter V. Bingham advises us not to worry about constancy but to go forward with testing as a useful tool in helping to plan educational and occupational futures, assuming that the ability of a person to think and act intelligently is neither unalterably fixed at birth nor subject to wide variations if tests are properly administered. He considers intelligence the product of at least three factors, heredity, maturity, and opportunity for educative experience.[1]

In spite of many criticisms and obvious deficiencies, psychologists have authorized the green light with reference to the use of intelligence tests, and at the same time they have warned all who take advantage of the signal to be alert for the yellow light. Thus it happens that in hundreds of public schools, colleges, psychological laboratories, clinics, and various types of social and business organizations intelligence tests are being administered to individuals and to groups in an effort to measure, as far as possible, the degree of intelligence possessed by the subject or subjects. Therefore teachers and counselors, especially those who neither administer nor interpret tests, will find it convenient to understand the difference in the character, purpose, and method of administration of the various forms in which not only intelligence tests, but most other types of psychological tests, are available.

The individual test of intelligence is the outgrowth of the experiments of Alfred Binet, a French psychologist, who in 1905 constructed tests designed primarily to single out individuals lacking in the general ability necessary to master the curriculum of the elementary schools. Several revisions of Binet's tests have been made by American psychologists: by Goddard in 1911, by Kuhlmann in 1912 and 1922, by Terman in 1916 and 1937, and by Herring in 1922. Of these the most widely used and the most valuable scale for measuring an individual's intelligence is the one constructed by Terman, usually known as the Stanford-Binet Test. It is flexible, can be used with individuals having sensory or motor handicaps, does not unduly penalize slowness, and affords a relatively accurate measure of general intelligence, brightness, and ability to learn. The exercises of an individual test prepared for the lower age levels are largely oral, involving manipulative and nonlanguage activities, while linguistic activities are involved on the higher age level. The test is one of power rather than of speed with the usual testing time ranging from forty to ninety minutes.

[1] *Aptitudes and Aptitude Testing* (New York: Harper and Bros., 1937), p. 40.

Since the individual test is a clinical instrument administered privately to one person at a time, satisfactory results are dependent upon carefully controlled testing situations and keen observation of the subject's reactions, which are frequently of more importance than his total score. These requirements mean that the test should never be administered by the untrained classroom teacher or general counselor, but always by one who is adequately trained in psychology, including individual-test administration and interpretation. The experienced tester will observe such personal characteristics as emotional stability, perseverance, motor co-ordination, physical handicaps, peculiarities of behavior, and the like, and he will understand the methods and the necessity of eliminating to the utmost possible degree the subjectivity which is involved in observations and their recordings.

There are two obstacles limiting more widespread use of individual intelligence tests: (1) the time required to test a single individual, forty to ninety minutes, with the consequent cost involved and (2) the harmful results of the attempts of untrained school administrators, teachers, and counselors to administer such tests. The dangers involved in such practice make necessary the repetition of the warning that only those who have had a considerable training in psychology, including supervised practice in the giving of individual tests, should be permitted to administer such tests or to supervise others who administer them.

The group test of intelligence came into the picture later. It was the outgrowth of the urgent need in 1917, when the United States entered World War I, for testing large numbers of men ranging from illiterates to college graduates, and the necessity for accomplishing this task in the shortest possible time with a minimum of equipment under examiners with a minimum of training and experience. Starting with the previous experimentation of A. S. Otis in the construction of a group test, the army psychologists, under the direction of Robert M. Yerkes, devised the Alpha test for literates and the Beta test for illiterates. During the war the Army Alpha test was administered to 1,700,000 men, and an intelligence classification was made by letter grades. The use of these tests in the elimination of men unfit for military service and in the distribution of those retained in the service is a separate story well told by C. S. Yoakum and Yerkes.[2] The three most significant results for counselors are found in the fact that the army testing program (1) gave prestige and impetus to psychological testing, (2) developed the technique of paper and pencil testing to a degree which otherwise might have required many years, and (3) suggested the possibility of establishing occupational intelligence

2 *Army Mental Tests* (New York: Henry Holt and Co., 1920).

standards or "occupational levels of intelligence," which evoked the interest of psychologists, educators, and employers.

This last-mentioned result is worthy of counselor consideration since both values and dangers for educational and vocational guidance are inherent in the factual data upon which the assumption of "occupational levels" rests. Tables 1 and 2 and Chart I have been introduced to assist in the visualization of these dangers and values. The first three columns of Table 1 classify the results of the Army Alpha test as administered to 1,700,000 men with scores ranging from 0 to 212. Data are taken from Yoakum and Yerkes and the classifications, definitions, and interpretations are theirs.[3] Column 4, Mental Ages, shows the army norms worked out by the Division of Psychology of the Surgeon General's Office on the basis of Stanford-Binet and performance tests administered to men who had taken the Army Alpha test.

TABLE 1

CLASSIFICATION OF ARMY PERSONNEL ON THE BASIS OF ALPHA SCORES AND MENTAL AGE

1	2	3	4
Intelligence Grade	Score	Definitions and Interpretations	Mental Age
A	135–212	very superior, marked intellectuality, able to make superior record in college	18.0–21.0
B	105–134	superior, capable of average grade in college	16.9–17.9
C+	75–104	high average	15.0–16.6
C	45–74	average, rarely capable of finishing high school	13.0–14.6
C–	25–44	low average	11.6–12.6
D	15–24	inferior, rarely able to go beyond 3rd or 4th grade	10.6–11.0
D and E	0–14	moron grade of feeble-mindedness	9.0–10.0

Table 2 is based on material published by the Government in 1918 [4] which included a chart showing the results of the Army Alpha as administered to approximately 36,500 men classified by occupational groups with raw intelligence scores ranging from 0 to 212. Original data were taken from the soldiers' qualification cards; key numbers of occupations were given; and the range and median for the middle 50 per cent for each of the 72 occu-

[3] Ibid., p. 17.

[4] Army Mental Tests: Methods, Typical Results, and Practical Application (Washington, 1918).

pations were indicated. The table comprises a fivefold occupational classification on the basis of intelligence scores.

TABLE 2

OCCUPATIONAL GROUPING BASED ON ALPHA SCORES—36,500 MEN

Occupational Group	Range of Middle 50 Per Cent	Median Score
1. Unskilled	21–63	35
2. Semiskilled	23–70	42
3. Skilled	26–95	61
4. Business and clerical	58–145	96
5. Professional	98–184	140

Chart I, based on the same data, brings out even more clearly the score spread of the middle 50 per cent of the cases which fell within each occupational group and stresses the wide overlapping among such groups.[5]

The table and chart should be read as follows, keeping in mind that 25 per cent of each occupational group is omitted at each end of the scale. The scores for the middle 50 per cent of unskilled laborers ranged from 21 to 63 with a median of 35. The overlapping in scores with other occupational groups indicates that on the basis of intelligence as measured by the Army Alpha a large number of unskilled workers falling in the middle 50 per cent might have entered occupations supposedly requiring higher intelligence.

Citations from the original tabulations are not complete, but several examples of occupations which fall within the other groups have been drawn off to indicate the types of occupations which are comprised in each. Among the semiskilled are found cobblers, teamsters, farmers, concrete workers, barbers, and horseshoers. Among the skilled are bricklayers, cooks, laundrymen, bakers, painters, butchers, locomotive engineers, plumbers, detectives and policemen, and stockcheckers. The business and clerical group covers telephone operators, stockkeepers, photographers, telegraphers, filing clerks, mechanical draughtsmen, stenographers and typists, and accountants. The professional group, with a median of 140, includes civil engineers, medical officers, army chaplains, and engineer

[5] Kohs and Proctor translated Army Alpha scores into I.Q.'s by testing 930 secondary pupils using both the Army Alpha and the Stanford-Binet tests. They then worked out the mental age equivalent of the army score, computed I.Q.'s, and found a correlation ranging from 0.80 to 0.92, thus making the "occupational levels" of the army score a rough estimate of the intelligence essential to succeed both in college and in occupations. See W. M. Proctor, *Psychological Tests and Guidance of High School Pupils* (Bloomington, Ill.: Public School Publishing Co., 1921).

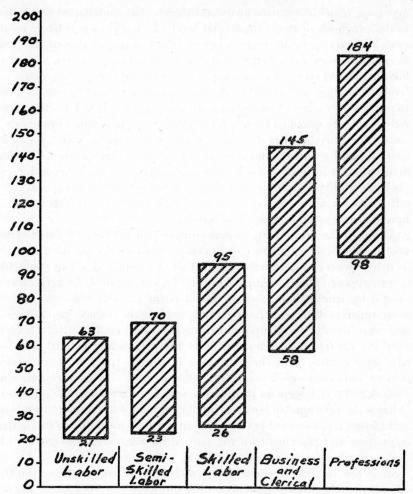

CHART 1.—Occupational grouping and spread of middle 50 per cent of 36,500 cases.

officers. Approximately one half of the business group qualified on the basis of test results for entry into this latter group.[6]

Postwar progress in the testing field has stressed the value of intelligence scores as an indication of the amount of schooling which an individual

[6] For further material on the subject of the relationship of intelligence and occupations, see Douglas Fryer, "Occupational Intelligence Standards," *School and Society*, XVI (1922), 273–277; D. G. Paterson, Gwendolen Schneidler, and J. Spencer Carlson, *Minnesota Occupational Rating Scales* (Minneapolis: University of Minnesota, 1936); and Irving Lorge and Raphael D. Bean, "Broad Occupational Grouping by Intelligence Levels," *Occupations*, XX (1942), 419–423.

may hope to achieve satisfactorily and thereby has contributed one factor to the prognosis of the occupational level which a person is likely to attain. However, pending more accurate information relative to the relationship between intelligence scores and occupational success, the army findings should serve as a warning that the assumption of "occupational levels of intelligence" is still in the assumption stage and cannot be used to predict the success of any given individual on any given job—too many individuals are qualified for too many different occupations. On the other hand, the army findings do have considerable negative value and may well be used by teachers and counselors to warn students against choosing occupations which have basic educational requirements beyond their probable ability to achieve. To choose, educationally or occupationally, either too far above or too far below one's ability to achieve is apt to have harmful social and personal results.

Although the army occupational grouping on the basis of intelligence was the first wide-scale effort so to classify individual capacities, as early as 1910 reports of similar efforts on behalf of mentally deficient youth began to appear. These attempts were the logical result of the activities of mental hygiene societies and of institutes for juvenile research. Studies were supervised by experienced and thoroughly trained psychologists and were usually based upon institutional cases, comparatively few in number. Therefore their findings were not particularly helpful to those who were dealing with the placement of similar types of youth under normal industrial conditions. But, influenced by the army report, employers and social agencies instituted a search for replies to the question: What is the relationship between intelligence and success on a given job? Satisfactory replies meant better selection practices for industry and better counseling and placement on the part of all who were concerned with both normal and subnormal individuals.

Since low intelligences are always with those of us who serve public-school clientele, a few comments on the studies of the Vocational Adjustment Bureau [7] with reference to the occupational possibilities of women and girls of low intelligence may suggest useful sources of information for those who desire to pursue the subject. The purpose of the bureau was to discover the lowest mental level satisfactory for retention on the job. The

[7] The Vocational Adjustment Bureau of New York City is a privately supported, noncommercial, nonpartisan agency interested in the study and placement of maladjusted girls. It was organized in 1919 and has had the advantage of outstanding leadership and painstaking scholarship. Emily T. Burr has been its single director and Edna W. Unger an able research assistant. The publication upon which these comments are based is entitled *Minimum Mental Age Levels of Accomplishment, A Study of Employed Girls of Low-Grade Intelligence*, by Edna W. Unger and Emily T. Burr (Albany, N.Y.: University of the State of N.Y., 1931).

importance of manual dexterity and many personality qualities such as emotional stability was not overlooked, but the single purpose of the study was to find an "irreducible minimum" of intelligence for referral to a job. Moreover, by 1919 it was generally recognized that mental inferiority was an asset for certain routine jobs or repetitive processes, and there was felt to be a social obligation on public and philanthropic agencies to distribute all levels of intelligence to the best occupational advantage.

The bureau study, covering 2649 cases, with mental ages of 5 to 12 years, complemented the findings of the army in the following ways: (1) It covered women and girls. (2) It extended the lower end of the range of ability below that of the army. (3) In the main individual rather than group tests were used. Findings were reported for six types of work, showing percentages and numbers for each mental age group employed in each type and indicating the minimum level at which satisfaction might be expected. Unskilled, light factory jobs took the larger percentage beginning at the six-year level and reaching a peak of absorption toward the close of the eighth year. At the seven-year level the range of possibilities broadened to include assembling, errand-girl jobs, inspecting, and pasting. At eight years hand sewing and garment machine operating were major additions; at nine years three or four more opportunities came into the picture, and at the ten-year level routine clerical jobs and press operating were available. A glance at Table 1 reveals that approximately all the members of the bureau group would fall below the C— of the army classification and that many would fall below the lowest age group, nine years, comprised in that classification.

In the practical application of such findings one should keep in mind the cautions which have been cited with reference to the interpretation of army findings: (1) Even on the very lowest levels there is sufficient overlapping to make occupational success possible in more than one line. (2) Counseling values are negative rather than positive, to guide away from occupations for which an individual's intelligence is too low to warrant hope of success. (3) That intelligence is only one factor contributing to occupational success or failure.

Counselors may find another way of picturing the relationship between job levels and intelligence levels of assistance in advising with run-of-the-mine pupils, especially those who are capable of being up-graded but who need to be alive to their own responsibility for being prepared for promotion. Many business organizations have prepared charts which show job classifications in relation to the personal qualities required to meet the specifications at each promotional level. Among the list of qualifications are both educational status and intelligence level. Several typical charts for clerical and executive occupations are available for counselor use. One by Hugo L. Clary [8] and a second prepared specifically for educational purposes by Ralph S. Rowland and Earl P. Strong [9] are examples. The latter, which is very elaborate, offers twenty-one items of qualification analysis for each of twenty-five office occupations. Educational status and personal qualities are stressed; intelligence scores are omitted.

During the last twenty years a number of group tests, both verbal and nonverbal and measuring the same types of abilities, have been placed on the market. The majority have been verbal, and language facility has been essential to successful performance. Well-known representatives, in addition to the Army Alpha, are the Terman Group Test, the Henman-Nelson Test of Mental Ability, the American Council Psychological Examination, the Otis Self Administering Test, and the Otis Quick-Scoring Test. The administration of group tests requires from 20 to 60 minutes. Individual business houses have done considerable experimenting to secure shorter and less time-consuming tests. The scores of some of these tests correlate sufficiently well with those of one or more of the more elaborate tests to warrant their substitution for purposes of employment selection.

Nonverbal group tests require a minimum of written or spoken language, problems being presented by means of pictures, diagrams, charts, and the like. Such tests are very useful in estimating the mental capacity of young children before language facility has been acquired and in testing adult illiterates. Illustrative of nonverbal abstract-intelligence or scholastic aptitude tests are the Army Beta Intelligence Examination, the Detroit First Grade Intelligence Test, the Pintner-Cunningham Primary Mental Test, and the Pintner Non-Language Mental Test.

When should the group test of intelligence and when should the individual test be used?

Both have value for counseling. The group test will usually be used for ordinary educational and occupational purposes. It has the advantage of economy in time both for administration and for scoring. The cost is less; norms have been established on a broader basis; objectivity is usually high; and a minimum of specialized training is sufficient for those who administer it. It is fairly accurate for superior individuals although results frequently indicate one's minimum intelligence. On the other hand,

[8] "The Zoning of Jobs," *Industrial Management,* LXI (1921), 324–329. Also in National Association of Corporation Training, *Report of the Ninth Annual Convention,* 1921.

[9] *An Analysis of Office Occupations* (Indiana, Pa.: The Authors, State Teachers College, 1934). The chart is supplemented by an interpretative discussion and a classified occupational bibliography.

it is apt to rate inferior persons too low, to penalize unduly the slow, and to give inaccurate results in cases of illness, environmental or emotional disturbance, failure to understand directions, etc. As a rule it is not satisfactory for use with individuals having sensory or motor defects.

The individual test, as has been stated, is a dangerous clinical instrument in the hands of other than thoroughly trained and widely experienced administrators. It has much greater value for individual diagnosis and prognosis because during its administration it permits the observer to watch for many valuable qualities and attitudes which are entirely out of the picture in group testing, and it usually measures maximum intelligence. As a summary one may say that the group test is the only feasible intelligence test for general use—the numbers to be tested prohibit the use of the individual test—and except for special or doubtful cases it may be used advantageously. When there is doubt, if the agency or institution offering testing has no provision for clinical service, an outside agency should be asked to give and interpret an individual test. No agency or individual should assume the responsibility for misguidance based on the misuse or the misinterpretation of test results.

Tests of Capacity: (b) *Special Aptitude*

Educational institutions on the higher level, private schools of all types, and trade or vocational schools are alive to the necessity of utilizing methods of admission which will act as a sieve for the selection of applicants who are qualified to take advantage of their offerings and to become a marketable product when the prescribed curriculum has been completed. Business and industry are also actively engaged in discovering selective devices which will bring into their organizations the best qualified and most promising promotional material. Aptitude tests, which predict ability for acquiring a skill or achieving academic success, are designed to assist the educator and the employer in their quest for desirable training material and to help the individual forecast the avenues through which his special abilities may best be capitalized. The primary purpose of such tests is the measurement of one's potential ability prior to opportunity for special training, but very frequently it happens that their results include also measures of ability or skills which have already been achieved. The types of special ability or aptitude, measured to a greater or less degree by aptitude tests, are usually classified as (1) manual, (2) mechanical, (3) clerical, and (4) professional. As with other test classifications, however, there is no clear line of demarcation between the types mentioned, e.g., manual aptitude is desirable in several of the professions and in many of the semiskilled and skilled occupations.

Measuring Manual Aptitude. Occupations requiring manual skills of one type or another range from heavy manual labor to the work of the dentist or surgeon, with the nature of the manipulative skill required differing markedly from one occupation to another and often being highly specialized. The great field for predictive testing for manual skills is found in the unskilled occupations which enroll thousands of workers annually and for which it is relatively easy to construct pre-employment tests which are predictive of success on the job. The word "unskilled" characterizes the many undifferentiated industrial processes and jobs which are found at the lower end of the army classification, all of the occupations included under potential opportunities for subnormals, and the majority of occupations which fall below the status of semiskilled or skilled trades. It is these occupations which open the door of opportunity to thousands of youths who enter business life on the lowest rung of the ladder irrespective of educational achievement or level of intelligence. It is also these same occupations which afford a livelihood for millions of adult workers and their families.

As a rule unskilled occupations are characterized by the repetitive nature of the work and by the very short time required for proficiency in their tasks—a few hours to two or three weeks at most. They comprise all types of assembling, examining or inspecting, folding, packing, boxing, wrapping, marking and shipping, elevator operating, telephone operating, filing, operating press, office, and garment machines, and the like. Qualifications include manual dexterity, motor co-ordination, steadiness, delicacy of touch, speed, good vision, neatness, precision, ability to follow directions and patterns, and sometimes specific physical qualities. A number of standardized tests are available for measuring perception, dexterity, and manipulative skills of various types, usually called "key skills." Employers are constantly endeavoring to perfect new tests which will have selective values for their own production processes. A recent report from the Western Electric Company indicates the results of its efforts to analyze jobs in terms of nine factors, intelligence, eye and hand co-ordination, finger dexterity, manual dexterity, small-tool dexterity, repetitiveness of work, accuracy, range of observation, and visual memory, for which the Company felt that adequate tests were available. The experiment resulted in the selection of satisfactory employees for six representative jobs: coil winders, solderers, relay adjusters, cable formers, testers and inspectors, and junior draftsmen.[10]

[10] David W. Cook, "Psychological Tests for Unskilled Jobs," in *Psychological Aids in the Selection of Workers* (Personnel Series, no. 50; New York: American Management Assn., 1941), pp. 18–29.

A high score on manual aptitude tests is, however, no guarantee of job proficiency, for there still remains that troublesome residuum of temperamental qualities which cannot be measured and which, under certain environmental conditions, might easily counteract all the predictive values of both intelligence and manual aptitude tests. An interviewer, if he be a skillful questioner and observer, will sometimes discover the individual's probable reaction to long-continued repetitive manual tasks, to the continuous noise which is involved in some lines of work, or to the close association with fellow workers in still other lines. The results of the interview may save the useless giving of tests.

Measuring Mechanical Aptitude. Aptitude for mechanical occupations is much more complex and broader in scope than manual aptitude. The essential difference is found in the fact that mechanical occupations usually consist of semiskilled or skilled trades requiring ability on the part of the workers to think through the problems which arise in connection with their work, whereas the successful performance of manual tasks is largely dependent upon ability to perform repetitive operations rapidly and dexterously.

In the early years of the guidance movement and to some extent today, industrially illiterate teachers and counselors have been prone to assume that deficiency in scholastic aptitude as determined by classroom achievement was prima facie evidence that an individual possessed mechanical aptitude; he belonged in the trades. Boys and girls who listened to such advice based on ignorance of mechanical occupations and their requirements were often misguided. To choose or not to choose, to attempt to prepare for a skilled or semiskilled field is in the final analysis an individual's responsibility. But counselors, labor unions, and employers each play some part in determining who shall be admitted to the ranks of skilled labor. The part of the employer has been mentioned in connection with training opportunities in employment; the influence of labor unions will be discussed later.

The counselor functions during the choice-of-occupation stage. He knows that genuine interest in an occupation, especially one which requires a long period of training or apprenticeship, is an important fundamental consideration, and he is prepared to aid the individual in analyzing the quality and quantity of his interest by means of the best available methods. If interest is established, he turns to the school records for information which will throw light on fitness to undertake training. The high-school average and class rank will reveal something of the individual's intellectual level, and the use which he has made of his opportunity and abilities. Achievement in mathematics, science, mechanical drawing, and industrial arts is indicative of potential mechanical assets. Perhaps the school record will carry an intelligence score. This may or may not have value, depending upon recency, type of test, and details of administration. As a rule scores obtained from nonverbal tests such as the Army Beta are better indicators of the concrete type of intelligence necessary to master a trade than are those obtained from verbal tests. There seems to be a consensus of opinion that the intelligence rating is valuable primarily as confirmatory evidence of school achievement data, since these alone reveal a minimum safe level of intelligence below which effective achievement in a skilled trade is doubtful.

After these two prerequisites, a genuine interest and a degree of concrete intelligence which could be brought to bear upon preparation for the trade, are established, specific mechanical aptitude may be investigated by means of paper and pencil tests. Such tests are inexpensive and comparatively easy to administer, give a rough indication of ability to perceive spatial relations of objects, reveal knowledge of and familiarity with tools and common mechanical contrivances, and correlate well with performance on the job. The Minnesota battery is widely used for this purpose, while the Bennett Test of Mechanical Comprehension gives promise of being a helpful future supplement.

The special measurement of manual aptitude may or may not be desirable at this point. If the trade under consideration is highly skilled, dependent largely upon intelligence and mechanical aptitude, it may be omitted. If manual skills are essential to success it should be given.

Measuring Clerical Aptitude.[11] The clerical worker performs many functions which spread their tentacles into every educational, civic, industrial, philanthropic, and business sphere of activity and which are everywhere indispensable. From the file clerk or office boy, to the private secretary, and on up to the executive, there are both vertical and collateral lines of promotion. But clerical workers as a rule, especially those who enter as beginners, will have rather uniform primary functions to perform and will deal with much the same materials and handle much the same tools. The clerical worker will be concerned with written material of one sort or another, memoranda, correspondence, records, reports, abstracts, and briefs. He will read, evaluate, compare, classify, transcribe, edit, and interpret words, symbols, and numbers. He will use many tools

11 Leonard W. Ferguson in "Ability and Aptitude Tests for Clerical Workers" (*Office Organization and Personnel Problems*, Office Management Series, no. 94; New York: American Management Assn., 1941, pp. 17 ff.) outlines the functions of tests in the selection, placement, promotion, and transfer of clerical employees and discusses the three types of tests which have had practical value in office personnel procedures, mental alertness, trade, and aptitude.

from the pencil and pen to the most intricate research devices; speed, accuracy, and neatness will be prime requirements for the effective manipulation of all. Finally, if his occupational progress continues, he will be called upon to use discretionary judgment in granting interviews, admitting visitors, making purchases, preparing publicity, employing subordinates, and in organizing and supervising the work of others. Intelligence and good judgment are additional prime requirements.

A review of the heterogeneous functions to be performed reveals four types of ability which should be discussed with an individual who is interested in discovering his clerical potentialities: (1) Perceptual ability. The O'Connor Number Checking and Word Checking Test and the O'Rourke Clerical Tests are examples of the type of tests which measures the perceptual abilities needed in the performance of such clerical functions as filing, typing, bookkeeping, and accounting. When interpreting the results of such tests, counselors must remember that a negative score is of greater significance than a high score and that a high score is usually most significant for the lower levels of clerical work. (2) Specific mental skills, e.g., arithmetic and English, are essential for any clerical function and can be rather accurately determined by reference to school marks in these subjects plus performance on standardized achievement tests. Interpretation of the ratings helps the individual to understand his immediate status, indicates weaknesses, and suggests where improvement is needed. (3) Motor skills include ability to manipulate papers, cards, pencil, typewriter, and other office machines adroitly. Observation, the reports of commercial instructors, and one or more of the tests designed to measure manual ability will give the essential information on this type of ability. (4) Intellectual ability or abstract intelligence which may be measured by any of the intelligence or scholastic aptitude tests previously mentioned largely determines success and advancement.

Measuring Professional Aptitude. The word "profession" was for many years regarded as the private property of the ministry, law, and medicine. Gradually use of the term has been extended to cover other occupations until now it is claimed by engineers, teachers, dentists, architects, journalists, librarians, registered nurses, musicians, and other groups. As yet no definition of "profession" has been formulated which is both sufficiently inclusive and sufficiently exclusive to warrant the assumption that it will include the potentially most promising individuals and exclude the potentially least desirable. All professions are supposed to be "service" occupations, and the desire of each group to protect its integrity and maintain its standards is legitimate and laudable. But how do it? Obviously by more rigid selection for preparation, higher standards for continuing preparation, and additional selection requirements for admission to practice.

A beginning has been made in medicine, law, and engineering.[12] Just at present there is much activity and nationwide interest in the field of teacher-selection, while social workers, nurses, and others are taking steps which they hope may lead to progress. Most of the experiments which are going forward in the professional-aptitude field are based upon the assumption that an individual should possess (1) mental capacity sufficient to master basic academic and professional curricula; (2) specific mental, and in some cases manual, abilities which are peculiar to the field; (3) genuine and sustained interest; and (4) the type of personality and temperament which characterizes successful practitioners.

A professional man must, as a rule, do more than complete a college course. Satisfactory scores on scholastic aptitude tests and on subject achievement and teacher examinations from the secondary school on are indices of ability to enter upon and to complete the essential scholastic requirements for a profession. Obviously, specific mental and manual requirements will vary considerably from profession to profession. Evidences of the possession of such specific abilities may be uncovered by thorough analysis of an individual's school record, subject achievement, cocurricular activities, out-of-school interests, and the like. Some admissions officers and counselors are using special aptitude tests such as the Ferson-Stoddard Law Aptitude Examination, the Aptitude Test for Medical Students developed by the Association of American Medical Colleges, the Coxe-Orleans Prognosis Test of Teaching Ability, the Seashore Measures of Musical Talents, and the McAdory Art Test. In the main such tests are still in the speculative stage. If they are used, high scores should be interpreted to mean that an individual is likely to be successful in preparing for a chosen profession, but not that he is likely to be successful in the practice of the profession. Nor should low scores be construed as a definite bar to successful preparation, but rather as a warning that more careful checking before final decision is desirable.

Skillful interviewing, interest inventories, practical experiences or tryouts, analysis of the school record, and persistent interest in spite of all obstacles, including the long and expensive road which must be traveled to attain the goal, are helpful methods of determining the extent to which real interest is present. But all efforts thus far to measure personality and temperament objectively have met with such limited success that there

---

12 A summary of the use of aptitude tests in the professional field is given by I. L. Kandel in *Professional Aptitude Tests in Medicine, Law, and Engineering* (New York: Teachers College, Columbia University, 1940).

is little which can be done at present except to continue to recognize their importance for the majority of the professions.

Tests of Proficiency: (a) *Trade Tests*

The second subdivision under psychological tests is concerned with proficiency or achievement tests. Such tests are designed to measure the extent of knowledge or degree of skill or both possessed by an individual in a given subject or occupation at the time of testing. Although such tests differ materially in their fundamental purpose from the purpose of aptitude tests, it is often difficult to determine whether tests constructed to attain the one purpose do not at times also attain the other, and thereby become interchangeable. Therefore attention is again called to the fact that psychologists do not attempt to draw sharp lines between the various types of tests. Classifications are convenient and flexible, and are an aid to logical thinking in connection with the practical application of all tests.

Achievement or proficiency tests comprise two major subdivisions, trade proficiency tests and school achievement tests, each of which is a resultant of the refinement of earlier subjective ratings; the one, the refinement of previously used selective devices for employment purposes, and the other, the refinement of subjective grading by educators.

Trade proficiency tests are a second type of test for which we are indebted to the United States Army. They are the outgrowth of the necessity for effective distribution of the trade-trained men included in the enlisted personnel. Satisfactory accomplishment of this task required more objective measures of competency than either the man's own statement regarding his qualifications or the opinion of interviewers who were often quite unfamiliar with the various occupations involved.

The same three types of trade tests instituted by and employed for the army personnel are in use in 1943: (1) oral tests, (2) picture tests, and (3) performance tests. Oral tests comprise questions concerning machines, tools, materials, processes, and basic principles involved in their use. The questions call for brief, specific answers, and when single-answer questions are used it is not necessary for examiners to have trade knowledge. Civil service commissions have both constructed and used many such tests, while in abbreviated forms they are valuable substitutes for or adjuncts to the less formal employment interview. Picture tests combine the use of pictures with an oral examination. The introduction of pictures is thought to bring the actual trade situation more vividly before the individual, thus assisting him to recall information of which otherwise he might not think. Pictures also help to accent the practicability of the test. Picture tests are more expensive than oral, and it is not always possible, where many makes of machines are on the market, to be sure that the picture is representative of the machine or tool with which the workman is familiar.

It will be noted that both oral and picture tests measure skills indirectly through ascertaining the amount of information the individual possesses. They are, therefore, very useful when there is high correlation between information and trade efficiency, but oftentimes such relationship is quite insignificant and the degree of skill is the dominant factor. In such cases the performance test, which measures skill directly, is superior to either the oral or picture test. However, it presents certain difficulties of administration: (1) There is a lack of opportunity to test performance under normal work conditions, especially to test the degree of skill possessed by school attendants either during or at the completion of courses preparatory to classification and recommendation for employment. Nor are even the largest employment offices able to offer test situations which approximate normal. (2) A single performance, probably in connection with an employment interview, is not an adequate measure of proficiency. (3) It is impossible to have at command all makes of machines or tools which perform the same operations, a fact which frequently invalidates both the picture and performance tests, especially if the worker has had limited experience or has become rusty, and is confused when confronted with the handling of strange tools.

Trade tests find their major field of utility in business and industry where they provide a quick means of eliminating poorly qualified applicants for jobs. Their counseling value derives from the fact that failure to make an acceptable score is not a permanent measure of disability for the job. If the individual made a wise original choice, and it is part of the counselor's business to know how to help him determine this, failure may suggest that he needs additional study or improvement in some special skill.

Tests of Proficiency: (b) School Achievement Tests

Achievement tests in the educational field parallel in purpose the trade proficiency tests in the industrial and business field. Where industry seeks rapid and accurate methods of determining the knowledge and skill of workers, educators seek methods of determining the skill and knowledge of their pupils at way stations along their educational pathway. A series of achievement tests and the record of their results makes a major contribution to the history of an individual's developmental growth and has outstanding values for counseling purposes.

There are many subject achievement tests on the market which are entitled to full psychological test status. Experimentation in the construction and interest in the use of such tests antedated the army trade tests. By 1910 a good beginning had been made. Unfortunately before such tests had gained a foothold their quality deteriorated; abuses and misuses crept in; and conservative educators suspended both judgment and use until values were more definitely established. The use of such tests, revived in recent years under the leadership of recognized experts, is rapidly gaining ground. A number of individuals and organizations are participating in the preparation of subject tests on different levels of education. Two types of tests are available on the basis of content: (1) A single subject test which is broken down into separate tests for special aspects of the field. The Co-operative Achievement Tests for secondary and college students are examples.[13] (2) A several subjects test comprised within a single test (a battery). The Stanford Achievement Test, Form Z, including ten items and designed for grades four to nine, and the Sones-Harry High School Achievement Test which covers four fields and is intended for use from the ninth grade through college exemplify the second type.

The relationship between scores on standardized achievement tests and teachers' marks on the same subjects, with some evaluation of their supplementary and comparison values, has been discussed earlier in this section and does not require further elucidation. Bibliographies of tests, classified by subjects and annotated by experts, are available and render additional information on the character and value of different tests unnecessary. The Co-operative Test Service of the American Council on Education and the Educational Records Bureau are very valuable sources of information on the uses and interpretation of achievement tests. A few publications issued under their auspices which are musts for up-to-the-minute counselors are mentioned here and there in this book. Once these volumes have been placed on library shelves there should be no rest periods in their use.

GUIDANCE VALUE OF RECENT RESEARCH BASED ON ACHIEVEMENT TESTING

Several researches based on the administration of achievement tests to large numbers of students in specific situations have been undertaken in recent years. The purpose of each, the tests administered, and the results with their interpretations are equally valuable for administrative, instructional, and guidance use. The object of this work precludes detailed

[13] *The Co-operative Achievement Tests: A Handbook Describing Their Purpose, Content, and Interpretation* (New York: Co-operative Test Service of the American Council on Education, 1940).

presentation of these investigations. But attention may well be called to a few of the counseling values which have derived from the findings and to the probability that additional benefit will accrue to those who make a careful study of the complete findings.

The first of these studies, initiated in 1927 and reported in 1938,[14] is usually known as the Pennsylvania Study because it was concerned with the growth in knowledge, as measured by standardized achievement tests, of a large number of individuals as they progressed through the secondary and collegiate institutions of that state. Among its findings and conclusions especially valuable to counselors are:

(1) Two types of variability were found, variability among institutions and variability among individuals. A classification of colleges on the basis of the results of the achievement tests showed wide variability in rank, and the rank thus indicated tended to place each college in the category which experienced and impartial observers would have expected. The same situation carried over to special departments and curricula. A second type of variability was revealed in the range of knowledge possessed by different individuals in any given college; for example, among students classified as sophomores, the range of knowledge extended from a level of inferior high-school achievement to the level attained by the best 10 per cent of college seniors. Assistance in the choice of the college best suited to the abilities and needs of individual students is admittedly a counselor responsibility. It is, therefore, very important that the general level at which different colleges operate and the categories within which different departments and curricula fall be known to counselors. Without such information it is impossible to give effective assistance to individuals who are trying to select the college which, in the light of their previously demonstrated ability to achieve, offers the maximum opportunity for intellectual growth.

(2) A second significant finding is concerned with the distribution of secondary students who achieved high scores on subject tests. The scores of 26,548 seniors, tested in May, 1928, and again two years later, revealed that college does not act as a selective agency in so far as intellectual achievement is concerned. The group of students who entered wage-earning occupations after completion of high school included many whose abilities and achievement equaled or exceeded the achievement of those who went to college. These findings, confirmatory of the earlier findings of Book, Colvin and MacPhail, and others, raise many questions which have significance for colleges, counselors, individuals, and society at large.

14 William S. Learned and Ben D. Wood, *The Student and His Knowledge* (New York: Carnegie Foundation for the Advancement of Teaching, 1938).

Is college always the best avenue for continued growth in intellectual achievement? Should college attendance be discouraged for those whose level of achievement is low but not low enough absolutely to preclude the possibility of entry and success? Since economic pressure closes college doors to some who rank high in intellectual ability, should not colleges be more careful in the distribution of all forms of student-aid, so that there may be a better guarantee that financial assistance is used to the best possible advantage? Such queries always call forth both pros and cons, but always the experienced counselor will remember that intellectual ability is only one individual variability factor.

Doubtless there are many students who reside at colleges who are not college students; doubtless some aid is given to individuals who by no stretch of the imagination could be called "students." And there are no doubt many young people who are college material but who cannot afford to attend college. It is also conceded that many bright minds are thoroughly disgusted with the intellectual mediocrity which characterizes both college students and the instructional corps. Shall counselors deplore self-guidance away from a college environment when they know that for some students it is a handicap to achievement rather than an opportunity for intellectual growth? And how shall they advise the youth who possesses many desirable personal qualities but does not have the type of intellectual ability which permits achievement above mediocrity? Perhaps he needs the self-confidence which comes from being a college man in order to make the best use of his mediocrity! Anything which teachers, counselors, or colleges can do better to distribute postsecondary students among the opportunities available is clear gain to all concerned, but the basis of distribution must always be broad enough to allow for many types of individual differences.

(3) A third significant finding, confirmatory again of previous findings but always resented by teachers, is concerned with the intelligence and knowledge of high-school teachers. Statistical comparisons of the scores on various subject tests revealed that those made by college seniors, who were preparing to teach, were, in a number of cases, at a lower level than those made by high-school seniors, the group they were preparing to teach. The authors conclude that such a situation renders learning very difficult if not impossible for many. The selection and preparation of prospective teachers is a live topic in the educational world today. Do the high-school and college counselors have some responsibility for sharing in the constructive solution of the teacher-selection problem?

And so we come to the second, recently instituted study which is based upon the use of achievement tests as a factor in the selection of secondary school teachers. The National Committee on Teacher Examinations of the American Council on Education gave its first examination in March, 1940.[15] The committee definitely recognizes, as did the Pennsylvania Study, that there are many vital factors in teacher selection, some tangible, others intangible. Knowledge is an indispensable, tangible factor, and it can be objectively measured. Therefore, it is the purpose of this committee to investigate the place of the objective examination as a factor in teacher selection. What degree of knowledge is possessed by those who have completed preparation and been certified for secondary teaching? What value have the results of such examinations in fostering the selection of better teachers? Counselors on both secondary and college level will be interested in learning the results of this use of achievement tests as they are given to the public.[16]

One step higher in the educational hierarchy is the Graduate Record Examination, a project begun in 1937 and reported on for the first time in February, 1941.[17] The question to be answered is: To what extent do students entering on graduate study possess the working knowledge prerequisite to successful graduate work? The purpose is to find some practical means of selecting the best qualified applicants for admission to graduate study. The criterion is written tests in the various divisions of knowledge usually comprised in arts college curricula. Again, the limitations of the study are explained; the importance of immeasurable qualities is pointed out; and the fundamental importance of knowledge is emphasized. The Individual Report of the Examination comprises a chart showing the individual's "test score profile," in comparison with the average "profile" for all beginning graduates majoring in the same subjects. This report is sent to the individual as well as to college and university authorities. Since a similar report may be secured for senior-college students who are contemplating graduate work, the self-appraisal and self-guidance values of the examination for the individual student are even greater than are the selective examination values for the graduate schools.

Two other projects dealing more specifically with secondary schools have been, and are, making valuable contributions to counseling procedures. Both give consideration to personality intangibles and are there-

---

15 See the *Report of the First Annual 1940 Administration of the National Teacher Examinations and Announcement of the 1941 Examinations* ([New York:] The Committee, [1940]).

16 David G. Ryans gives the results of the 1940 examination in *School and Society*, LII (1940), 273–284. In the same and other educational periodicals have appeared arguments pro and con relative to this type of teacher-selection examination.

17 See the Carnegie Foundation for the Advancement of Teaching, *The Graduate Record Examination* (New York: The Foundation, 1941).

fore broader in scope than the previously discussed projects. But both include achievement testing in their program, and both indicate confidence in the value of testing subject-mastery as a means of revealing intellectual growth and of pointing out strengths and weaknesses in scholastic achievement.

The Public School Demonstration Project in Educational Guidance was instituted in 1934 and reported on in 1939.[18] Seven selected public schools collaborated in an effort to develop guidance programs suited to their local needs. Chapter X of the Report is entitled "How a Testing Program Contributes to Guidance." A few of its conclusions are cited: (1) Systematic employment of tests for guidance purposes should cover measurement of academic aptitude, reading ability, and achievement in academic subjects. (2) The general level of scholastic aptitude in any given school is of value in determining standards of achievement to be expected in that school. (3) Wide variability and overlapping in reading ability suggest that some pupils are in need of remedial work while others should be expected to read more extensively and at a higher level of difficulty than the average. (4) The relation between academic aptitude scores and academic achievement scores suggests that, other things being equal, students should be able to achieve in proportion to ability to learn. (5) Growth in achievement is an individual matter. It seems probable that those at the lower end of the distribution will never reach the level already attained by abler students.[19]

A second project, known as The Eight-Year Study of the Progressive Education Association, was instituted to facilitate the transition of students from secondary schools to college, to determine the feasibility of establishing transfer programs adapted to individual needs and objectives without regard to the formal pattern of entrance requirements. The study was conducted under a commission organized in 1930. Work began in 1933. Thirty-four secondary schools and a large number of colleges participated. The first students entered college in 1936, and the original experiment was concluded in 1941. It is needless to state that achievement testing was one of its outstanding tools.

It has been a shock to many educators to learn from the printed page [20]

18 See Arthur E. Traxler, ed., *Guidance in Public Secondary Schools* (Educational Records Bulletin, no. 28; New York: The Bureau, 1939).

19 See also Donald E. Super, "Occupational Level and Job Satisfaction," *Journal of Applied Psychology*, XXIII (1939), 547–564. In this study covering 273 employed adult workers Super found that 70 per cent of the total never changed their occupational level regardless of the number of times they changed jobs.

20 See Wilford M. Cukin, *The Story of the Eight-Year Study* (New York: Harper and Bros., 1942). This is Volume I of the report of the Progressive Education Association Commission on the Relation of School and College.

how little real value the students included in the project have derived from counseling, and how wide the gap between catalogue promises and actual performance has been. Each such study points the way toward better counseling service.

CHAPTER XI

Data Secured from Personality Measurement and Appraisals

IT HAS long been recognized that psychological tests, intelligence, aptitude, and achievement, do not measure all the qualities which comprise personality. Nor do the other items of information about the individual mentioned in Chapter IX supply the deficiency. There is still a residuum of information which is very important for success, not only in educational and occupational life but also in the intimate life of the home and in the social life of the community. This residuary aspect of personality and the procedures which are being used to understand and interpret it, helpful as they may be, are not entitled to rank as psychological tests or to be used with the same degree of assurance as standardized tests whose value has been more definitely established. However, since the well-known difficulties which handicap the development of such measures may stand across the path of progress for many years, it is important for counselors to be familiar with the purpose, status, and value of the most commonly used tools and techniques in this field.[1] Four such devices will be described in this chapter: (1) the anecdotal record, (2) the rating scale, (3) the adjustment and interest inventory, and (4) the objective test.

Separate treatment of these devices does not imply that there is no interrelation. Indeed, they have one very important requirement in common which may well be brought into the foreground at this point— the technique of observation, a technique which has major values for practically every phase of counseling services. The importance of observation in detecting personality characteristics, behaviorisms, and attitudes during the administration of all types of individual tests has been mentioned. The value of anecdotal records and rating scales is directly dependent upon observation consciousness and observation accuracy on the part of parents, teachers, counselors, and others who participate in the making of such records and ratings. The value of adjustment in-

---

[1] For a valuable summary of the status of personality appraisal, see Arthur E. Traxler, *The Use of Tests and Rating Devices in Appraisal of Personality* (Educational Records Bulletin, no. 23; New York: The Bureau, 1938). This is nontechnical in character and includes both an annotated list of tests and a reading list.

ventories is greatly enhanced when their specific findings are checked and supplemented by various forms of casual or systematic observation.

THE ANECDOTAL RECORD

The anecdotal record is not a new device for recording the observations of school authorities, employers, detectives, and others regarding the efficiency, behavior, or attitudes of those who come under their jurisdiction. But the anecdotal method as a consciously planned, formal method of studying personality has a more legitimate claim to modernity, even though the earmarks of the method are to be found in the early American college records. The faculty records of William and Mary for 1817 carry copies of the reports which were summarized from instructors' comments and sent to parents, assurance being given that the "demeanors and improvement of each of the Students" during the course just terminated have been given consideration: "Mr. ——. Has made some progress but has been by no means as attentive as he ought to have been." "They have learnt little or nothing and we believe on account of escapaid and Idleness." "They have evinced some Improvement since the last Examination, but are certainly not as attentive as could be wished. We are doubtful as to the habits of both." Nor was faculty attention focused solely on problem cases. Certain young men were listed as "first in their respective classes, orderly and attentive and have made the most flattering improvement." [2] Mount Holyoke during the 1890's also used descriptive adjectives as one part of its grading plan. Faculty conferences were held on the reports concerning each individual.[3] In 1921 when the author joined the faculty of the University of Chicago, she found W. C. Reavis enthusiastic regarding the potentialities of the anecdotal method of studying and recording pupil behavior. Each teacher in the University High School contributed at frequent intervals one or more anecdotes for each pupil under his jurisdiction. Conferences for discussion of individual pupils' progress and needs were held, and reports were sent to parents. Several series of these anecdotal reports were taken to New York University in 1924, where, pending the publication of Reavis' book [4] which described his experiment in some detail, they made a helpful contribution to class discussion of guidance procedures. Although at the present time several schools are using the anecdotal method of studying pupil personality, leadership in the current revival of interest rightfully belongs to the

[2] Mary L. Smallwood, *An Historical Study of Examinations and Grading Systems in Early American Universities* (Cambridge: Harvard University Press, 1935), pp. 44–45.

[3] *Ibid.*, pp. 52–53.

[4] *Pupil Adjustment in Junior and Senior High Schools* (Boston: D. C. Heath and Co., 1925).

Rochester Athenaeum and Mechanics Institute and to the Progressive Education Association, both of which have issued publications describing procedures in detail from the training of the corps for participation to the possible contribution of their data to cumulative records.[5]

Since the anecdote is an informal, unstandardized comment or story regarding a teacher-chosen phase of a pupil's behavior, it does not require an elaborate record form—space for identification items such as the name of the pupil and observer, and the date and place of occurrence; space for objective description of the behavior; and, entirely separate from it, space for any comments, interpretations or explanations, recommendations, or remedial measures already instituted. Certain difficulties are apparent. Some are shared in common with other forms used for estimating personality and need not receive separate attention. Others are peculiar to the anecdotal method and are of sufficient importance to merit special consideration. A number center around teachers' ability to prepare such records. Comparatively few teachers have either the background or training to make free or undirected choice as to when to observe, what to observe, what to select as significant for recording, or how to record what is selected so that a clear picture of the observation may be given, supported by factual data without distortions due to the interpolation of subjective material.

From the administrative angle difficulties extend from one extreme to the other. At one extreme there are too few anecdotes, or too few teachers write anecdotes, or those which are written are concerned with too few pupils and those mainly of the teacher-annoying type.[6] At the other extreme, an unwieldy mass of good, bad, and indifferent anecdotes pours into the central office, clutters files, defies classification, permits neither logical nor constructive interpretation, and resists summarization without violation of both purpose and content. And finally, there is the question of teacher time. Overburdened or uninterested teachers tend to be careless in observations, in choice of anecdotes, and in accuracy in recording. Often they totally ignore the constructive use which could be made of such data. In his account of the Eight Year Study Raths states that in some schools teachers write six anecdotes a day without spending more than

---

[5] For studies on the anecdotal method, see L. L. Jarvie and Mark Ellingson, *A Handbook on the Anecdotal Behavior Journal* (Chicago: University of Chicago Press, 1940); Arthur E. Traxler, *The Nature and Use of Anecdotal Records* (rev. ed.; New York: Educational Records Bureau, 1940); Progressive Education Association, Reports and Records Committee, *Manual of Directions for Use in Trait Study* (The Association, 1934); and Louis Raths, *Anecdotal Records* (Progressive Education Association Bulletin, no. 1; Columbus, Ohio: Ohio State University, 1935).

[6] See E. K. Wickman, *Children's Behavior and Teachers' Attitudes* (New York: Commonwealth Fund, 1928). Wickman's findings are always useful.

fifteen minutes.[7] Alberta Munkres, in a fairly recent elementary school study, cites helpful suggestions regarding the types of observations which are possible for classroom teachers.[8]

On the whole, it would seem that several of the specific difficulties inherent in this basic method of studying personality might be eliminated or at least lessened were its use to be largely confined to the elementary schools where constant association with one teacher would tend to increase opportunities for observation, reduce the number of anecdotes necessary, and permit a more careful selection of those to be recorded.

Behavior Journals are the continued stories of the anecdotal method. At their best they furnish a valuable picture of the developing personality of individuals and are exceedingly important for cumulative records.

Behavior Descriptions stand midway between the informal, unrestricted anecdotal record and the formal rating scale. The major difference between these descriptions and the best type of rating scales is found in the forms used for ratings and for recording observations, hence it is unnecessary to discuss both methods in detail although counselors should be familiar with all the terms which are used to designate the tools and techniques of counseling.

Those who desire more specific information on behavior description forms will find illustrations in the Detroit Scale for the Diagnosis of Behavior Problems by Baker and Traphagen; in the Vineland Social Maturity Scale by Doll, who indicates that the technique of administering the scale is no less important than that of administering the Stanford-Binet Test, and in the Manual of Directions for Use in Trait Study prepared by the Progressive Education Association. The forms instituted by the Progressive Education Association were designed to overcome some of the objections to the anecdotal method, to lessen the work of teachers, and to focus attention on and largely confine observation to a few selected personality traits which are sufficiently concrete to be supported by reasonably objective evidence and to afford some unity as a behavior pattern or as a picture of the individual. Two forms are used for the expression of judgments. One sheet lists the names of students, and opposite the names provides space for a rating on each trait, while in the final column there is space for teachers to note the trait upon which they wish to make a statement or write an anecdote. A second form is provided for such statements or anecdotes. Very elaborate explanations and directions are given for observing and recording observations.

[7] Op. cit.

[8] Alberta Munkres, Personality Studies of Six-Year-Old Children in Classroom Situations (New York: Teachers College, Columbia University, 1936).

RATING SCALES

Rating scales as a method of measuring or estimating the extent to which an individual possessed or was deficient in supposedly desirable traits, qualities, or characteristics were in use long before standardized tests were developed or measurable and unmeasurable qualities differentiated. Teachers, employers, social acquaintances or coworkers, ministers, and even total strangers have always passed judgment, or expressed personal opinions on their fellow men. Many years ago educators were supposed to be able and willing to indicate the extent to which pupils were honest or dishonest, reliable or unreliable, industrious or lazy, and the like. Employers, supervisors, and foremen consciously or unconsciously formed and expressed opinions relative to traits possessed by their subordinates. As a rule observational accuracy was unchallenged; opinions crystallized unconsciously and were informally expressed.

But there were exceptions which anticipated later developments. A formal rating scale of parliamentary merit used for appraising the characteristics of legislators was reported in the *Dublin Evening Post,* January 25, 1784.[9] The qualities rated were independence, general knowledge, political knowledge, argument, temper, influence, and grace. The form of this scale bears striking resemblance to some of the forms used in postwar experimentation in our own country. A comparison of the ratings of the nine eighteenth-century legislators with the verdict of history reveals that the three who were rated highest made no contribution significant enough to merit historic mention, while of the three rated highest in history, two fell among those rated lowest by their contemporaries. Such accidents still happen after almost two centuries of progress.

In this connection the reader may recall the somewhat different basis of, and may anticipate a somewhat different historical verdict on, a recent attempt at legislator-rating in our own country. On March 20, 1939, *Life* magazine reported on the ratings of the ten ablest members of each house of Congress. The scorers were fifty-three Washington correspondents, whom no one would accuse of being other than trained observers. The qualities appraised were: (1) Integrity. Did he have principles and stick to them regardless of political expediency? (2) Intelligence. Did he have a good head and a sound stock of information, historical and current, to use it on? (3) Industry. Did he give his conscientious best to his job? (4) Influence. Did he have the political wisdom and the personal charm and tact to put his ideas across and get things done?

[9] On the authority of J. D. Hackett. See the *Journal of Personnel Research,* VII (1928), 130–131.

The formal rating scale in the United States was another army-inspired measuring device. Exodus from the army was immediately followed by increased applications for admission to colleges and to occupational pursuits. A more formal method of estimating unmeasurable qualities which would help to separate the sheep from the goats was an immediate necessity. Army experimentation suggested that personnel ratings might be the way out, and from that time to the present research psychologists have made continuous efforts to construct scales which would combine maximum objectivity with a minimum of time, expense, and effort in administration.

Problems which have challenged psychologists. In the course of its evolution the modern rating scale has passed through several stages. It is not necessary at this time to discuss each evolutionary step in the history of ratings, but there may be some value to counselors in mentioning a few of the troublesome questions which have puzzled psychologists as they have struggled to develop formal scales which would fill in some of the personality deficiencies in the picture of an individual, and to accomplish this by means of descriptions based on systematic observations made by trained observers and recorded by methods designed to eliminate as many as possible of the untrustworthy features of opinion records.

Several questions, some still unanswered, have centered about the character of traits. Did not such terms as industry, honesty and reliability represent abstract qualities? Did ratings on abstract qualities have any valid significance unless they were given in connection with specific situations, e.g., might not a boy be lazy with reference to one duty and most industrious with reference to some other duty? Was overlapping among traits necessary or was there some method of determining their simple components and then making sure that each trait selected for rating was mutually exclusive of all others? [10] Might objectivity dominate a trait in one situation, and subjectivity dominate the same trait in another situation? How could control traits be determined? When a boy was industrious in one activity and lazy with reference to another, was it legitimate to assume that the control factor was industry or might it be interest? Were there some qualities, such as co-operativeness and sociability, which were traits of two or more people rather than of individuals? To what extent is co-operation on a boy's part dependent upon corresponding co-operation

[10] Psychologists and psychometricians are attacking this problem by what is known as the factor analysis method. Procedures are too technical for laymen, but if and when results are attained, the findings may have important bearings on the value of personality traits for guidance purposes. See L. L. Thurstone, *The Vectors of the Mind* (Chicago: University of Chicago Press, 1935) and *Primary Mental Abilities* (Chicago: University of Chicago Press, 1938).

on the part of the teacher, parent, or other person? Did average ratings on specific traits, with reference to different activities, give a fair picture of the extent to which such traits were possessed in the abstract?

Individual differences operating among raters have presented another series of problems. Differences in age, sex, educational, social, and economic background, experiences, the sort of people one worked with, was supervised by, or supervised, position relationships, social relationships, and all sorts of personal prejudices and emotional attitudes colored individual interpretation of traits and controlled rating standards. Moreover, experience soon revealed that raters were prone to form a sort of synthetic impression of an individual which influenced their rating on each separate trait. This influence was usually termed the "halo effect," or "halo of general merit." All too often the "halo" was based on a single observed incident, favorable or unfavorable, as the case might be.

A third series of questions was focused upon fundamental principles, tools, and techniques which might be brought to bear upon the solution of at least some of the apparent difficulties. For what type of qualities were rating scales a justifiable measuring instrument? How might greater unity in interpretation of qualities and in standards of rating be secured? To what extent could subjectivity be reduced? How could accuracy of judgments be increased? How could "halo" ratings be controlled? Should limitations be placed on the use of ratings? How could the results be evaluated?

Progress in Scale Development. There was considerable fruitful experimentation in the immediate postwar years. In the educational field progress is exemplified by the Pasadena Public School Blank, devised by W. Hardin Hughes,[11] by the Joliet Township High School and Junior College Blank, prepared by Joseph V. Hanna,[12] and by the personality rating scale of the American Council on Education, based on elaborate investigation and designed primarily for college freshmen.[13]

Between 1920 and 1930 many scales were prepared for the use of different business houses. Forrest A. Kingsbury constructed a scale for rating machine operators and routine workers employed by the Continental and Commercial National Bank of Chicago which caused much favorable comment because of the extensive research upon which it was based and

[11] Described in detail in the Pasadena Public Schools Educational Research Bulletins, 1923–1925, *passim.*

[12] See his article, "Variable Factors Encountered in the Rating of Students," *School Science and Mathematics,* XXV (1925), 481–488.

[13] Discussed in detail in *Educational Record,* IX (1928), 53–64, and by F. F. Bradshaw in "American Council on Education Rating Scale," *Archives of Psychology,* CXIX (1930), 1–80.

the exceptionally helpful manual which directed its use. The Goodyear Company introduced a number of scales designed to serve different purposes; the Research Bureau for Retail Training, Pittsburgh University, devised a scale for rating salespeople; and there were many others.

As a result of these experiments considerable advance in the construction and use of rating scales has taken place. Teachers and counselors, unless they are experienced psychologists, are not supposed to be qualified to construct scales, but some of the less technical phases of scale making are of practical value to all who use scales for any purpose. Progress in replying to some of the questions which have been propounded is indicated: (1) Rating scales should cover only those qualities for which no valid objective measures are available; they are intended to supplement, not supplant, more objective devices. (2) Unity in standards of rating and in interpreting ratings has been much improved by (a) a reduction in the number of traits—three to seven with five a common choice—to be rated and much more careful choice of such traits, (b) a reduction in the number of categories or ranks—three to ten with five a usual choice—into which an individual's degree of possession of a trait might fall, (c) the tendency to discard the name of the trait in favor of a brief and very concrete description of the trait or, if the name be retained, to add a definition expressed in terms of behavior or trait actions and to indicate the degree of the trait which should be considered under each category in the same way, and (d) the wide use of the graphic scale.

Three suggestions for overcoming or lessening the "halo" tendency have been made: (1) Concentrate on one trait at a time and complete ratings on that trait for the entire group before passing on to a second trait. (2) Do not compare present ratings with previous ratings until the entire task has been finished. (3) Vary the order of rank or of descriptions on different qualities so that each end of the line carries at one time the highest and at another the lowest rank, thus forbidding automatic checking of each quality at a similar position on the line.

Since counselors may find it convenient to have at hand illustrations of two or three commonly used scales, one unit from each of three different forms is offered, and complete scales may be secured by those who desire.

The first unit is taken from the graphic form of the American Council Scale. It retains the horizontal line, which characterized the early linear scale, to represent the possible range of trait possession. The extent to which, in the estimation of the rater, the individual under consideration possesses this trait is indicated by placing a check at the appropriate place along the line.

THE FIRST UNIT

How are you and others affected by his appearance and manner?

<table>
<tr><td></td><td></td><td></td><td></td><td></td><td></td><td></td><td></td><td></td><td>X</td><td></td><td>No opportunity to observe</td></tr>
<tr><td colspan="2">Avoided by others</td><td colspan="2">Tolerated by others</td><td colspan="2">Liked by others</td><td colspan="2">Well liked by others</td><td colspan="2">Sought by others</td><td></td></tr>
</table>

Please record here instances that support your judgment.

1. I was attracted to her when I first saw her. Others have noted her dignity and sweet manner as she worked in the office and room and passed through the halls. The children seemed from the first to do what she wished.

2. She was generally among a small knot of people before class time, talking and working, and not sitting idly by herself.

3. Attitude of class generally positive toward her.

THE SECOND UNIT

Does he need constant prodding or does he go ahead without being told?

☐ Seeks and sets for himself additional tasks

☐ Completes suggested supplementary work

☐ Does ordinary assignments of his own accord

☐ Needs occasional prodding

☒ Needs much prodding in doing ordinary assignments

☐ No opportunity to observe

Please record here instances that support your judgment.

Needs more than a desire to learn. Does work assigned, no more. Easy going, often lags behind class. Very timid about reciting, seldom, if ever, volunteering. Gives answers which at best are guesses. Fails to get books back on time.

THE THIRD UNIT

Can he be depended on to carry out obligations or is he unreliable and irresponsible?

☐ Scrupulously fulfills obligations.
☒ Habitually willing and responsible.
☐ Usually fulfills obligations.
☐ Fulfills obligations when convenient.
☐ Constantly neglects all obligations.
I have had no adequate opportunity to observe this trait. ☐

Please give here specific instances to illustrate your estimate. What has he done?
Keen, agreeable, dependable. A high type of youth.

The second unit, also an American Council form, is a variation of the same principles.

The third unit is one of ten which comprise the Ohio College Association Scale.

Comparison of the characteristics of these units with one another and with the items of progress previously cited reveals that the same fundamental principles have prevailed in the construction of each form.[14]

Attention is called to two features common to these scales which help to lessen snap judgments and increase more carefully considered ratings. The *"No opportunity to observe"* accomplishes two objectives: it removes the former stigma which attached to teachers who had not observed everything and everyone and at the same time, unless numbers are so large that they preclude the possibility of observation, it raises questions in the mind of the rater regarding the extent to which he is meeting his observational responsibilities. The value of the second feature, which requires supporting evidence in justification of ratings, needs no comment, but it may be noted that most of the supporting evidence, if it has value, will be submitted in the form of anecdotes and must be secured by the anecdotal method. Comments on the three units submitted are bona fide notations as they appear on used scales.

Training of Raters. The very best of anecdotal programs or of rating devices are only tools. They are one factor in the effectiveness or ineffectiveness of personality ratings. Other decisive factors are the attitude of raters toward the program, the ability of raters to observe and record accurately, and the interpretation and use which is made of the record. Since such factors are of common importance to all personality rating schemes, their discussion is pertinent alike to the anecdotal method, to behavior descriptions, to rating scales, or to any other similar device by whatever designation it may be known.

The Attitude of Raters. Once the administrative authorities are completely sold on the desirability of a rating program, have a clear understanding of its general purposes and modus operandi, and have formulated the benefits which they expect to accrue from the installation of a program in their institution, then the program should be explained to the entire personnel of the organization, both raters and individuals to be rated, and their co-operation should be enlisted. Whenever the program is superimposed without being fully understood, teachers and pupils, foremen and employees are apt to resent its introduction. Reports from

[14] For other examples of rating scales, see the American Council on Education, Central Committee on Personnel Methods, *Measurement and Guidance of College Students* (Baltimore: The Council, 1933) and the Metropolitan Life Insurance Company, Policyholders Service Bureau, *Forms Used in Employing and Training College Graduates* (New York: The Bureau, 1938). The latter is a valuable collection of business forms prepared for the use of policyholders in the Group Insurance Division but distribution is limited.

various agencies indicate that this resentment has been expressed by college faculties, secondary pupils, and employees in all occupational fields, and is universal. In order to be successful the program must be welcome, it must be participated in by all, and some evaluation of results must be made.

Training to observe, record, and use follows the decision to introduce. If any of the devices mentioned are to be used, it is well to remember (1) that opinions must be based on observations, accurately made and accurately recorded, and (2) that for the most part observation and recording will be done by laymen who have not been specifically trained for this function, teachers, parents, counselors, employers, admission officers, placement clerks, and the like. This means training—training to observe accurately; training to differentiate between behavior which is significant as indicative of growth or needs and behavior which has no permanent or meaningful value; training to record what has been observed, not what one thinks he has observed, nor an interpretation of an observation. Accuracy of observation and accuracy in recording are requirements of many occupations and are by no means peculiar to personality rating. Both have been mentioned as prerequisites for the collection of occupational information, and a number of personal traits which disqualify a person for observational responsibilities have been cited. The same general statements apply to collection of information about the individual. Also a number of individual differences which bear specifically on the accuracy and impartiality of ratings have been cited. All of these influencing factors should be taken into consideration by those who prepare training programs. A few suggestions regarding such programs are summarized:

1. Reading assignments are useful in educational and philanthropic agencies since most of the participants are accustomed to securing information from the printed page. They are, perhaps, less useful in industry and business where time is an important factor and many participants are not book-minded, or have grown away from such sources of information under the pressure of practical affairs. If commercially prepared scales are to be used the *Manual of Directions* should form the basis of instructional material.

2. Staff conferences are useful in all agencies. Many topics should receive consideration: the anticipated values to rater, ratee, and institution; the meaning of terms such as "objective," "subjective," "observation," and "interpretation"; the dangers of confusing opinions with observed behavior; the importance of basing anecdotes or ratings on observed behavior and on usual behavior or trait actions; the desirability of bringing home and community as well as school and industry within the observa-

tional field; and the value of recording both favorable and unfavorable items.

3. Drill in the use of anecdotal records and ratings might include drill in selecting and writing anecdotes and in the use of scales; in checking individual ratings against those of others; in pooling independent judgments for the study of values; in noting individual tendencies to rate too low or too high, coupled with practice in methods of overcoming these tendencies such as checking reports before turning them in; in observing one pupil at a time until familiar with the best methods; and in reviewing trait descriptions and rank descriptions immediately before rating.

4. Case studies and case conferences, an outstanding method of helping counselors and others to interpret and use advantageously all the types of information which bear upon the individual, should not be neglected. The interpretation of anecdotes and ratings is open to the same sort of errors of judgment as any other type of recorded material. A sharp distinction should be made between objective recording of observed behavior or performance and opinions or interpretations of observations. Once this is thoroughly understood and the two types of material are always allocated to different positions on the record, the usual rules for appraising historical data apply. If they are complied with, many experienced counselors feel that anecdotal records, behavior descriptions, and scales which require supporting evidence for ratings have more value for counseling purposes than do most of the personality devices which are called "tests."

INVENTORIES AND QUESTIONNAIRES

Inventories and questionnaires afford a third approach to the study of personality. Under various terms devices which should be included in this category have been in vogue from the beginnings of the organized guidance movement. They were freely employed by Parsons whose list of 138 questions included considerable content of the same character and for the same purposes as that found in the more recent and refined inventories. Those who are familiar with the historical development of the guidance movement will recall the close relationship between Parsons' work and the work of the Boston Y.M.C.A. and the fact that the character of their clientele was very similar. This in turn may help to explain the continuous leadership which the Y.M.C.A. has shown in the construction of self-analysis blanks and self-rating scales, and the purposes for which these devices have been used.

In the course of their evolution self-ratings have appeared under such designations as "adjustment inventories," "adjustment questionnaires," and "self-inventories," and also under a number of other terms such as "personality inventories," "interest inventories," "personality schedules," "neurotic inventories," "introversion-extroversion tests," "ascendance-submission scales," "school inventories," "survey of opinions," "case inventories," "vocational interest blanks," and "inventory of activities and interests." Such devices are available for all levels of education and for both sexes. Some follow the form of the graphic rating scale previously described, and for the most part they are, as the name implies, self-administering. The rater and the ratee are one, and both are therefore subject to the same idiosyncrasies, modified somewhat by the fact that they are one.

Representative of such inventories, questionnaires, and scales are the Bernreuter Personality Inventory, the Bell Adjustment Inventory, the Thurstone Personality Schedule, the Allport A–S Reaction Study, the Strong Vocational Interest Blank, the Humm-Wadsworth Temperament Scale, which is widely used in the aviation industry and is proving very satisfactory, and the Brown Personality Inventory for Children. A list of additional devices and their purposes together with a brief appraisal of each is available in *Bulletin No. 23* of the Educational Records Bureau. Before using any one of these devices teachers and counselors should seek information from some authoritative source relative to its purpose, validity, reliability, and legitimate uses. It is totally unsafe to depend upon the fact that a device is cited in this, that, or the other general publication, or that it has been favorably reviewed somewhere. It is equally unsafe to assume that numerous press references enhance the value of a device.

Those who deal with the vocational aspect of counseling will desire to be familiar with the Strong Vocational Interest Blank, which for several years has been carried on the recommended list of the Educational Records Bureau, and with the more recent Kuder Preference Record, which is also being extensively used. They will also wish to keep in touch with any results which may derive from Thurstone's efforts to apply factorial analysis methods to vocational interests.[15]

All personality inventory devices have two common purposes, to secure the individual's opinion relative to his interests, abilities, aptitudes, and temperamental qualities, and to aid the individual in the better understanding of himself. The scores serve to identify the individual, temperamentally, socially, or otherwise, with a more or less well-defined group which thinks much as he does or has the same attitudes toward the same things.

[15] L. L. Thurstone, "Factorial Analysis of Vocational Interests," presented before the American Psychological Association, Sept., 1935.

The impossibility of assuming that factual data or even worth-while information is to be derived from any form of self-inventory makes it very difficult to realize the first purpose. If responses be truthful, there will undoubtedly be some facts; but which statements are facts? Unless supporting evidence from more reliable sources is available, one does not know. Up to the present, consistent lack of validity has been shown by all such measuring instruments. Frequently questions are answered in ways designed to secure a desirable score or make a favorable impression; tendencies to err in self-judgment are notorious; and the suggestiveness of terms contributes its bit to the unreliability of this method of analysis of the individual.[16] On the other hand, realization of the second purpose is within the realm of possibilities. Any device which encourages and directs self-activity is in harmony with the fundamental principles of both education and guidance. Therefore, whenever these devices are used to encourage systematic habits of self-inventory or to give incentive to self-study and self-improvement, or when they furnish leads for counseling and employment purposes, they become of value as guidance tools. A general summary of the value of such instruments was admirably expressed by Joseph V. Hanna some years ago in the final paragraph of an article dealing with the guidance values of self-analysis:

As a formula self-analysis cannot be a success; as a means of summing up hints and indications to be faced in the interview, it may be helpful. Perhaps the greatest value of conservative self-analysis, that of subjective effect on the rater, cannot be appreciated because it cannot be measured.[17]

TESTS OF PERSONALITY

Some authorities classify certain of the standardized inventories and questionnaires which have been included under the previous classification as tests. Since there is no universally accepted classification of measuring devices, it has seemed simpler for layman purposes to exclude from tests all the personality instruments whose purpose is obvious to the subject, even though in other respects they may be very similar. Therefore, under

16 The wording of many vocational interest blanks serves to focus the attention of students on the work which they would like to do or prefer to do rather than on work for which they feel that they can qualify or for which they have some tangible evidence that they can qualify. The occupational pattern of today is not particularly adapted to occupational choice on the bases of personal likes and dislikes, and since present-day youth will be obliged to conform to the present-day occupational pattern, perhaps individual choices might more nearly approximate national and local demands if inventories were to avoid suggesting that "most like" or "prefer to do" were the foundation stones of occupational choice.

17 "The Self-Analysis Device as an Aid in Guidance," *Transactions of the Illinois State Academy of Science*, XVI (1923), 451–469.

the category tests of personality there are two types—disguised, or partially disguised, paper and pencil tests, and free association tests.

Disguised Tests. There are comparatively few disguised tests of personality. The Downey-Will-Temperament Test stands first from the point of view of enthusiastic reception; the Pressey X–O Tests are perhaps the most widely used; while the Character Education Inquiry Tests are the most comprehensive. Each will be briefly described.

The Downey-Will-Temperament Test attracted wide attention soon after its publication in 1921. It deals with a subject's responses to situations involving handwriting and purports to measure twelve traits: four concerned with speed and fluidity of reaction, four concerned with aggressiveness, and four with carefulness and persistence of reaction. The purpose of nearly all the subtests is hidden from the subject; in fact, in certain parts of the test the reactions which seem most desirable actually result in the lowest scores. In recent years the original enthusiasm for the test has subsided, principally because a number of studies reported low coefficients of validity and reliability, the results varying to such an extent that there was little warrant for assuming the presence of the traits the test purported to measure. In general it may be said that the test has little practical value for guidance or for school use. However, in the hands of an expert who is thoroughly familiar with its limitations it may occasionally serve as a valuable laboratory tool.

The oldest of the disguised tests of personality and perhaps the most widely used is the Pressey X–O Tests, which were developed for use in studying sex and individual differences, affective and moral judgment, and emotional make-up. The distinguishing feature of the test consists of having the subject cross out, from a rather long list of words, those which are distasteful to him. The test is scored by counting the number of items to which the individual reacted and by recording the difference between these items and those to which a standard group responded. The Pressey test is probably as valid, reliable, and useful as any of the disguised tests of personality. Properly interpreted it presents significant material which may be of service in analyzing the individual. The best opinion, however, indicates that the results should be used only to supplement other data, that total scores are of little or no importance, and that it is less useful with the dull person since a premium is placed on vocabulary comprehension, the test thus becoming one of intelligence rather than of personality.

The largest group of disguised personality tests available are those of the Character Education Inquiry. Five years of experimentation resulted in tests to measure honesty, trustworthiness, helpfulness, inhibition, persistence, moral knowledge, and attitude. The tests reproduced life situations; for example, a child was placed in a situation where he had an opportunity to steal or to be dishonest, and his conduct was observed and noted. Again, a child was given a test which purported to measure achievement but which was, in reality, a test of honesty in taking the examination. Undoubtedly the Character Education Inquiry Tests provide a very comprehensive measure for surveying various types of behavior of school children. The use of the tests, however, will probably always be restricted to experimental work, if for no other reason than that they are extremely expensive in time and money, much too elaborate for school use.

Free Association Tests. This method of personality appraisal stands apart as unique among experimental techniques and as one of the most potent tools for the diagnosis of conduct. It is not a new technique, Sir Francis Galton having experimented with a free association test in 1879 and Münsterberg having used the association method in the detection of guilt in 1889. In recent years, however, it has received new emphasis, and is looked upon by some psychologists as the most promising method of personality analysis now available.

One of the oldest and best-known tests of this type is the Kent-Rosanoff Free Association Test which first attracted attention in 1910 and concerning which there has recently been a revival of interest. The method of the test consists of presenting orally to the subject a list of one hundred words to each of which he is requested to respond by saying the first word which occurs to him. The test is given individually with the examiner recording the response, the reaction time, the general behavior, etc. The classification of responses permits the detection of various emotional difficulties, peculiarities, eccentricities, guilt, and milder psychopathic states. Although this test may eventually be used in a practical way for discovering the immediate emotional problems of students, difficulties in interpretation of scores have limited it thus far to clinical procedures.

The free association test which is attracting the most attention at the present time is the Rorschach Ink-Blot Test. The extraordinary interest which has been manifested in this test is partly due to the uniqueness of its approach to the study of personality and partly due to the fact that because of all the various instruments used it is more nearly in harmony with the tenets of the Gestalt school of psychology. The stimuli of the test are a series of ten ink blots which are presented to a subject with a request that he state what each blot suggests to him. It is claimed for the test that it will provide information regarding emotional stability, originality of thinking, adaptability, and other traits, and at the same time will indicate the general intellectual level of the subject. The scoring is subjective, and interpretation should not be attempted except by those who are well versed in psychology. The consensus of opinion indicates that while standardization of the test is still imperfect, in the hands of an expert examiner it does constitute a useful and penetrating clinical device for a diagnostic approach to personality study.

Personality tests, on the whole, do not rate very high in the opinion of psychologists and should be used with great caution even for the purposes for which they do have counseling values: (1) to serve as a point of departure during a counseling interview and (2) to arouse interest in critical evaluation of one's own personality qualities.

CHAPTER XII

Classifying, Recording, and Filing Information about the Individual

CHAPTER XII, which deals with methods of classifying, recording, and filing information about the individual, parallels Chapter VIII, which dealt with methods of classifying, indexing and filing information about various types of opportunities which are useful, now one and now the other, to individuals seeking educational, social, occupational, or other outlets for their capacities and interests.

Certain items of information about the individual which are rather universally desirable have been discussed, and the tools and techniques which are available for their collection have been described. Opportunities for the misuse of such tools and techniques, and for inaccuracies in information which must be guarded against, have already been mentioned. The logical next step is the presentation of methods of integrating these data about individuals in order to make them available in the most convenient form for counseling and administrative purposes. This involves consideration of different types of educational records, their purposes, the items of information essential to realize the purposes of each, the best methods of integrating the chosen data, and the most convenient forms of recording them.

A minimum of space has been allotted to this topic because there is no phase of personnel practice which has received, and still is receiving, the attention of such eminent authorities. Generous dissemination of the results of their experimentation has made it possible for every teacher, counselor, or school library to have at hand the most reliable and most recent information on records and their uses, and to do so with a minimum of expense. Moreover, it is both unprofitable and unfair for those of less experience in the field to substitute their secondhand summaries for original accounts which are so easily accessible. Therefore, while it has seemed wise to include a few definitions, fundamental principles, and suggestions in order to round out the picture of guidance tools and techniques, it is hoped that every person who is charged with instituting, interpreting, or using personnel records will go directly to one of the authoritative

204

studies [1] for descriptions of the best methods of planning and introducing record systems and of interpreting and using their data for the better understanding of, and for more intelligently advising with, individual students.

TYPES OF RECORDS

There are several types of records, designated by different terms, which are of more or less interest to counselors and between which it is sometimes difficult, if not impossible, to distinguish. Some are inclusive of other types; others are mutually exclusive. Among current designations applied to records comprising rather inclusive data are "personnel records," "administrative records," "cumulative records," "integrative records," "personal inventories" and "case histories." Examples of terms used to designate records concerned with more specific and usually more technical data are "placement records," "medical records," "accident records," "attendance records," and the like. According to the character of its content, any one of these latter may be a confidential record.

Personnel Records. All records which comprise information about the individual are personnel records in the sense that they are personal; they are all-inclusive so far as the name is concerned, but not necessarily inclusive with reference to certain types of administrative data, to some items essential to the understanding of the individual, or to items of a confidential character which it would be unwise to enter on the record. The most meaningful use of the term stresses the guidance purpose of the record and the accumulation on the record of such personal items as will facilitate this purpose. Other purposes may be served, but individual counseling, or guidance service, is the primary purpose of a personnel record.

---

[1] The Educational Records Bureau, 437 West 59th Street, New York City, is the best source of information on records. One of their publications to which reference has already been made (see p. 185 n.), *Guidance in Public Secondary Schools,* is the best single book on the subject of records and should be in the library of every counselor. Chapter IV, "The Cumulative Record and Its Uses," includes illustrations of cumulative records and interprets their data in terms of a case study of the individual. The use of the record for guidance in the Plainfield High School is described in Chapter III. Undoubtedly the experienced counselor will challenge some of the procedures advocated, but that is only one indication that the material is thought-provoking as well as helpful. Chapter V, "Developing a Cumulative Record for Local Use," contains valuable suggestions for those who are instituting or revising a record system.

A second publication which deals authoritatively with the cumulative record is the work of Giles M. Ruch and David Segel, *Minimum Essentials of the Individual Inventory in Guidance* (U. S. Office of Education, Vocational Division Bulletin, no. 202, Occupational Information and Guidance Series, no. 2; Washington, 1940). The time sequence in this study extends from school entrance to the placement bureau and occupational life.

Administrative records antedated personnel records. They entered the school system to facilitate teacher-principal co-operation in securing data for many routine administrative purposes such as the preparation of various types of reports and as bases for the promotion and transfer of pupils. In most respects the form and content of administrative records did not differ materially from the form and content of the first records which were used to furnish counseling data. The differentiating factor was purpose rather than either form or content. The major purpose of an administrative record was, and still is, to facilitate the solution of administrative problems; the primary purpose of personnel records is to help solve student problems and also to guide developmental growth. Data used for either purpose may appear on a record called by either term, and since the collection of data specifically for counseling purposes is a comparatively new educational practice, it is logical to assume that much of the data which appeared on the earlier administrative records was useful only incidentally for guidance purposes.

During recent years there has been some tendency to differentiate administrative records and personnel records on the basis of content, availability, and guardianship. Various plans have been suggested or are in use. One regards the administrative record as the permanent record and allocates to it all data, both administrative and personnel, which is essential to the educational guidance of the individual or which is useful for administrative and research purposes. Filed in the main office and under clerical supervision, it is easily accessible to teachers and is thought to be adequately protected against misuse. The personnel record may, or may not, duplicate much of the information on the administrative record, but its distinguishing characteristic is the inclusion of temporary confidential data which should be known to the minimum number of persons necessary both to counsel the individual and to protect the welfare of the institution. Such information it is obviously unwise either to place in open files or to entrust to clerical supervision. Personnel officers, deans of students, counselors, or similar officials who understand its purposes are the safest guardians. When its usefulness is ended it should be destroyed.

A second plan does not differ materially from the first. The nomenclature varies; "personnel record" is substituted for "administrative record," which is dropped, and "confidential record" is substituted for "personnel record," which has taken on a broader significance. Undoubtedly some provision should be made, irrespective of the terms used, whereby teachers may have access to all information essential to the educational guidance of pupils in the usual course of their development, and they should be encouraged and assisted to make the best possible use of such data. It is also wise to make suitable provision for a strictly confidential type of personnel record which is so protected that its content is available only when needed for service to the individual or for protection of the welfare of others.

An *integration record,* whether its subtitle be administrative or personnel, is exactly what the expression implies. Records and record forms have been mentioned from time to time in connection with specific items resulting from observation, measurement, and personality appraisals. This development of records and record forms for separate bits of personnel data followed the precedent established by administrators who, as more and more administrative data were called for, instituted a multiplicity of forms for collecting and recording them. An integration record pools all the worthwhile data on all of these contributing records in one master record. The object of integration is to afford the clearest possible picture of the individual's assets and liabilities, interests, activities, and capacities. The accomplishment of this objective is greatly facilitated by proper arrangement of the various items on the record form, a point which should be given due consideration when choosing a commercial record form or when instituting one to meet local needs.

An administrative-integration record or a personnel-integration record may or may not also be a cumulative record. In order to merit classification as cumulative it must comprise data covering more than one unit of a definite period of time, e.g., the life span of an individual, the entire period of his formal education, or his four college years. A record which is both integrative and cumulative pools all the significant data which throws light on the individual's development and needs over a definite period of time, and it integrates and presents these data by time sequences so that it affords a picture of the individual's accomplishments at any given time as well as shows trends in his development. An increasing number of educational systems are using integrated-cumulative records, but the majority are still content with just records, frequently carrying a minimum of information for both administrative and guidance purposes, without much integration, and with no claim to cumulation.

Case histories are the final and most inclusive type of records with which personnel workers should be familiar. Sometimes inexperienced counselors are confused by the fact that writers use "case history" and "cumulative record" synonymously. They are synonymous in a way, although there is considerable difference in the quantity and quality of their data. It would seem logical and might help to clarify thinking if records designed to serve the typical or normal individual were to be called "cumulative personnel records," while records concerned with atypical individuals who require expert service in one or more areas of life were to be called "case histories." Child guidance clinics, neurological institutes, psychopathic hospitals, and social workers write many such case histories and are dependent upon their integrative and cumulative character for the proper treatment of their clientele. "Case study," as an interchangeable term, is less confusing and is rather commonly used with reference to a study of an individual made from any type of record, educational or clinical, preparatory to an interview with the individual or to a conference regarding him with others who are interested in his welfare.

RECORD FORMS

All teachers and counselors are familiar with the record card which has been cited as an early and rather persistent form designed primarily to preserve routine administrative data. Agitation for the improvement of educational records was coincident with the beginnings of the organized guidance movement although this investigator has not been able to find any relation between the two movements. All the evidence at hand, including the name of a committee of the N.E.A. which reported in 1912,[2] indicates that administrative problems and needs were the dominant interest and that the major objective was to facilitate accuracy in national reports by means of uniformity in methods of local record keeping. Nor should this be occasion for either surprise or comment, since the original records of local guidance bureaus, upon which Chapter IV is based, also seem to indicate that the bureaus were totally unfamiliar with most, if not all, of the guidance values of the records which they advocated.

Interest in the improvement of record forms as a means of facilitating guidance services came to a focus in 1928 when Ben D. Wood, under the auspices of the Committee on Personnel Methods of the American Council on Education, devised what is familiarly known as the American Council Record Folder. This folder was a bona fide cumulative personnel record. Four forms have been published, one each for the elementary, secondary, and college level, and one which may be used on either the elementary or secondary level.

Several different forms of cumulative records are in use. One comprises both a cumulative card and a cumulative folder. The card provides for data frequently used by administrators and teachers and is placed in visible files in the general offices where it is easily accessible. The folder, in a

2 See the U. S. Bureau of Education, *Report of the Committee on Uniform Records and Reports* (Bulletin, no. 3, whole no. 471; Washington, 1912).

separate letter file, permits the filing of loose sheets of miscellaneous data which are too valuable to discard and too expensive to copy. This folder material is particularly useful for counseling and for the preparation of more meaningful case studies. A second record form substitutes a printed folder for the printed card, dispenses with the card and visible file, and uses the printed folder also as a filing unit. Frequently used data are not quite as accessible under this plan. Sometimes a cumulative card arranged for annual entries is deemed sufficient, or a plain folder within which miscellaneous data and minor records are accumulated is the chosen form.

Two procedures will doubtless be helpful to administrators, counselors, and teachers whether or not they are interested in establishing or in revising record forms. Study of several of the best record forms is recommended as it will serve as an inspiration to more purposeful observation of individual pupils even though there be no possibility of instituting similar forms. For, although present-day emphasis is placed on the cumulative aspect of record forms, it must not be assumed that schools which for one reason or another have not instituted or cannot institute an up-to-date cumulative form are by virtue of that fact eliminated from sharing in the recent progress which has been made in the better understanding of individual pupils. Perhaps some school, rural or small town, may be using a record form which provides for only the most meager administrative data, entirely overlooking the educational value of other possible items. If teachers are seriously interested in this aspect of modern education they need not mourn lack of facilities nor wait for their introduction. An 8½ x 11 sheet of plain paper is always available, the addition of identifying data will transform it into a "face sheet," and a simple cumulative personnel record form is ready to receive guidance data. Just as was suggested in Chapter VIII with reference to initiating a system of classifying and filing educational and occupational information with whatever facilities were at hand, so it is now suggested that the best record form immediately possible be instituted and that improvements be made whenever opportunity offers.

A second procedure, which may push forward the attainment of an ultimate goal, consists of listing criteria which should characterize what would seem to be a locally desirable record form. Several criteria which are suggestive are found in the references previously cited. The records should be (1) substantial enough to permit frequent handling; (2) convenient in size to handle and file, neither undersize, oversize, nor folded over; (3) easy to read; (4) easy to reproduce by photostating, blueprinting. etc.; (5) large enough for the anticipated items to be presented in concise language and arranged to show trends in growth; (6) designed to require a minimum of clerical work; (7) planned to save space with clear-cut main topics and no duplication; (8) arranged to separate objective from subjective data, facts from opinions; and (9) colored to permit differentiation of sex or of various class groups, thereby facilitating the handling of the records.

The Plainfield experiment describes the method whereby the criteria found in the *Provisional Manual* for the use of the American Council folder were applied to a local situation; [3] Scarsdale familiarized its corps with a variety of criteria and, on the basis of those which promised best to facilitate its guidance function, instituted a cumulative form for community use.

RECORD CONTENT

Record content has been mentioned here and there in connection with the collection of information about the individual. For the most part comments have been concerned with the reliability and utility of data, with the necessity for subjecting all items designed for personnel records to the universal rules for documentary criticism, and with the desirability of checking the personal qualifications of all who contribute subjective data to such records against the list of possible "intellectual immoralities" which might invalidate their evidence. Discussion of the content of the record is confined at this point to consideration of the items which are usually thought to be most useful for cumulative records.

Several studies of record content have been made in order to ascertain if there were any agreement as to the most important items, and if there were, to discover upon what principles the selections were based. The results have not been very helpful; frequency lists show little agreement beyond a few essential items, while elaborate local lists often include many items of questionable usefulness. All records of necessity contain identification items. Sometimes they are exceedingly meager, and again rather complete. They include the name of the school, of the pupil, and of the parents, the date, the residence, the age or date of birth, and rather often other significant family items. Accuracy must be assured, and the data must be sufficient to identify the individual should there be more than one pupil registered under the same name. Among other items which are generally thought to be significant and for which citations in the previous chapters have indicated specific practical values are:

(1) Health data—for health guidance and for consideration in connection with occupational choice.

[3] See p. 208.

(2) School marks—for local values and for certain personality factors which are not measured by standardized tests.

(3) School achievement test scores—for which there are no substitutes for comparative purposes, for transfers, or for business recommendations.

(4) Data on personal characteristics so arranged that objective statements are entirely separated from opinions and subjective data.

(5) Reports on social and occupational experiences.

(6) Returns on psychological tests and inventories of various kinds.

(7) Records of interviews with, and conferences with others on behalf of, the individual.

Perhaps it is just as well to avoid too much uniformity in record content. If content is to be selected to meet local needs, the adaptability of the record may be enhanced by variability beyond the minimum essentials for comparisons, transfers, etc.

Anyone who has attempted to determine which items are significant for record inclusion realizes the difficulties involved. It is much easier to decide that any given item, upon its first appearance, has no guidance value than it is to decide whether continuous recording of data on the same item may, over a period of time, give it considerable value. It is far easier to discard single items offered for entry on the ground that they have no meaning in isolation than it is to realize that the value of any particular item lies in the way it ties up with other items, or to foresee that major values sometimes derive from an accumulation of low value items. It is not always easy to scrutinize, evaluate, interpret, and choose items for entry. It is not always possible to be alert enough to detect misrepresentations in data or errors in vocabulary translations. It always requires rare discriminating judgment to rule out the type of anecdotes which someone has well said either places an undeserved crown of thorns on a student's head or circles his brow with an unearned halo. Such stories, once admitted to the record, tend to accumulate additional disgraces or glories without much reference to merit or validity.

And finally, those who are charged with responsibility for determining the form and content of records may not be unmindful of the demands which their upkeep makes upon contributors. A safe channel between the Scylla of too much useless or questionable form-filling-out and time-consuming questionnaires and the Charybdis of woeful deficiencies in personnel data should be diligently sought. With a full recognition of all the administrative and guidance values which are inherent in carefully prepared records, there is a very real danger that too much stress may be put upon the possession of records per se; that all the outward indications of a full-fledged record system may be present, but that the interest and energy of the corps may have been so depleted in preparing the tools that in the hour of need they are unable to discern their functioning values or to make use of them for individual growth. The end must not be over-shadowed by a desire to perfect the means.

EVALUATION OF RECORD SYSTEMS

Just as the systematic and purposeful collection of reliable information about individuals implies that such data will be integrated, recorded, and filed where it is easily accessible for administrative and guidance pur-poses, so the time and effort expended in preparing and making such records available imply that there will be some method of determining the extent to which they are affording a maximum of service with a mini-mum of lost time and motion. Therefore, after a certain amount of prac-tical experience with the use of the records, it is well to re-examine the purposes that they were supposed to serve and to draw some conclusions regarding the extent to which they have proved to be the satisfactory tools anticipated. A rather wide range of general purposes for which record data are useful is mentioned in Chapter IX, but for evaluating any given system these broader purposes should be broken down into more specific purposes, and local objectives should be stressed. Continuous or periodic surveys participated in by the various beneficiaries of and contributors to record systems will reveal their strengths and weaknesses, point out useless data, and call attention to data deficiencies. A few points which might be included in, or upon which information might be secured by means of, an evaluation survey are suggested:

1. Does the personnel record afford a unified picture of the individual's progress, his accomplishments, deficiencies, and problems, or is it a col-lection of unintegrated raw data?

2. Are the items arranged in the order best suited to the purpose? Does arrangement show trends? Is it convenient for interviewers and for com-parison of facts?

3. To what extent has the instructional corps contributed to the records? What has been the character of its contribution? Has it been comparatively free from the influence of the "intellectual immoralities"? Has the selection of anecdotes and comments revealed discriminating judgment in recognizing what was significant behavior?

4. What has been the frequency of use by instructors as a whole? By individual instructors? For what purposes have data been used?

5. Has the record been helpful to students in better understanding themselves and in charting the direction of their growth? Has it been an incentive to best effort or a discouragement?

6. Has the record afforded basic information for reports to parents, the type of information which gives them an intelligent understanding of their children and enhances their ability to counsel wisely with them?

7. Has duplication been reduced to the minimum? Is only the information which contributes to the development of the individual, or to the efficiency of the school as a unit, recorded?

8. Have significant items been omitted? Are there useless items which could be dispensed with? Where have errors of judgment in interpretation been found? Where has inadequate or unclear evidence been found?

9. Have the data been adequate to provide for transfers to industry or to other educational units? To help differentiate the good from the poor college risk? To identify those who should receive preference in scholarship allotments? To identify the good business risk? To distinguish between the casual and the consistent failure, and the like?

10. Are routine personal data high-lighted by anecdotes and other data which indicate how the individual reacts to his personal qualities, e.g., the fact of oversize or undersize may have no apparent significance, but the student's reaction to his variation from the normal may be of considerable importance. The fact that Mary has been admitted to a girls' school may influence her entire academic and social record. A comment to the effect that John is marking time until he has met compulsory education requirements may be very illuminating with reference to his consistent failures. The fact that a pupil habitually goes without lunch in order to contribute his share toward the activities program may suggest a desirable change in activities management.

There is nothing final about either record forms or record content. Evaluation surveys should reveal useless items and the omission of desirable items; undoubtedly they will reveal errors of judgment in many phases of record making and record interpreting. They are bound to reveal the need for constant in-service training of the instructional corps with ever-increasing responsibilities for progressive leadership allocated to the administrative authorities.

SELECTED SUPPLEMENTARY READING

American Educational Research Association. *Educational Tests and Their Uses.* Washington, 1938. (Review of Educational Research, vol. VIII, no. 5.) This publication gives an annual review of progress in educational testing.

——. *Pupil Personnel, Guidance, and Counseling.* Washington, 1939. (Review of Educational Research, vol. IX, no. 2.)

Beck, Samuel J. *Introduction to the Rorschach Method.* New York: American Orthopsychiatric Assn., 1937. A very complete treatment of the subject.

Bingham, Walter V. *Aptitudes and Aptitude Testing.* New York: Harper and

Bros., 1937. Written for the layman. Presents a very comprehensive treatment of the subject.

Buros, Oscar K., ed. *The Nineteen Forty Mental Measurements Yearbook*. New Brunswick, N.J.: School of Education, Rutgers University, 1940. A biennial publication which evaluates all types of measuring instruments.

Carter, Harold *ↄ*., and Jones, Mary C. "Vocational Aptitude Patterns in High School Students," *Journal of Educational Psychology*, XXIX (1938), 321–334.

Columbia University, Teachers College. *Studies in the Nature of Character*. New York: Macmillan Co., 1928–1930. 3 vols. *Studies in Deceit* appeared in 1928, *Studies in Service and Self-Control* in 1929, and *Studies in the Organization of Character* in 1930. These studies are concerned with a series of Character Education Tests developed under Hugh Hartshorne and Mark May.

Eurich, Alvin C., and Wrenn, C. Gilbert. "Appraisal of Student Characteristics and Needs," in *Guidance in Educational Institutions*. Ch. 2. Bloomington, Ill.: Public School Publishing Co., 1938. (National Society for the Study of Education, Thirty-seventh Yearbook, pt. I.)

Flanagan, John C. *Factor Analysis in the Study of Personality*. Stanford University, Calif.: Stanford University Press, 1935. Helpful to and readable by the average teacher.

Freeman, Frank N. *Mental Tests: Their History, Principles, and Application*. Rev. ed. Boston: Houghton Mifflin Co., 1939.

Garrett, Henry E., and Schneck, Mathew R. *Psychological Tests, Methods, and Results*. New York: Harper and Bros., 1933. One of the best general works on psychological tests.

Hay, Edward N., *et al. Psychological Aids in the Selection of Workers*. New York: American Management Assn., 1941. (Personnel Series, no. 50.)

Knowles, Asa S. *Merit Rating in Industry*. Boston: Northeastern University, College of Business Administration, Bureau of Business Research, [1940]. (Northeastern University Publications, Bulletin, no. 1.) A very complete treatise on the use of the rating scale in industry.

Link, Henry C. *Employment Psychology*. New York: Macmillan Co., 1919. An early account of psychological testing as a practical means of determining the fitness of industrial workers. Subnormal workers are included.

Messenger, Helen R., and Watts, Winifred. "Summaries of Selected Articles on School Report Cards," *Educational Administration and Supervision*, XXI (1935), 539–550.

Moore, Bruce V., Taylor, Harold C., and Hay, Edward N. *Values of Psychology in Industrial Management*. New York: American Management Assn., 1940. (Personnel Series, no. 43.)

National Society for the Study of Education. *Educational Diagnosis*. Bloomington, Ill.: Public School Publishing Co., 1937. (Thirty-fourth Yearbook, pt. I.)

Pechstein, L. A. "The Measurement of Social Maturity in Children," *Elementary School Journal*, XL (1939), 113–123.

Pullias, E. V. "Should an Individual Know His Own I.Q.? A Mental-Health Problem," *Elementary School Journal*, XL (1939), 277–283.

Stead, William H., Shartle, C. L., *et al. Occupational Counseling Techniques*. New York: American Book Co., 1940. Published for the Technical Board of the Occupational Research Program of the U. S. Employment Service. The title is misleading. The major contribution of the volume is in the field of special aptitude.

Strang, Ruth. *Counseling Technics in College and Secondary School.* New York: Harper and Bros., 1937. A summary of expert opinion and an integration of information from various sources on the personnel record, the case study, the interview, observation, and the rating scale.

Symonds, Percival M. *Diagnosing Personality and Conduct.* New York: Century Co., 1931. Very comprehensive.

Terman, Lewis M. "The Vocational Successes of Intellectually Gifted Individuals," *Occupations,* XX (1942), 491–498. A report on the vocational achievement of the gifted children who belonged to the 1920 group retested in 1940. "Intellect and achievement are far from perfectly related."

——, and Merrill, Maud A. *The Measurement of Intelligence.* Boston: Houghton Mifflin Co., 1938. A clinical manual for use in administering the individual test of intelligence.

Traxler, Arthur E. *The Use of Tests and Rating Devices in the Appraisal of Personality.* New York: Educational Records Bureau, 1938. (Educational Records Bulletin, no. 23.) Brief but very satisfactory treatment. Consists of a list of annotated tests and a bibliography.

OBJECTIVES

To help the individual in "true reasoning on the relation of these two groups of facts."—FRANK PARSONS, 1908

To evaluate "the potentialities of the individual in the light of the requirements of the activity under consideration with a view toward enhancing the possibility of a choice satisfactory to the individual and to society."—DAVID G. RYANS, 1941

CHAPTER XIII

Group Methods

THE materials suggested in Part II, if collected by accepted research procedures, will provide teachers, counselors, and others with a series of data which have been continuously considered prerequisite to counseling and guidance from 1908 to 1943.[1] The data discussed in Part III, if collected and recorded by legitimate methods, will go a long way toward furnishing the basic information for deliberative personal consultation and will meet the requirements of the second series of essential information.

But collecting, recording, and filing these two series of data are only preparation for the real task. The tools, or an important part of them, are at hand. It now remains to discuss the techniques which set such tools in motion and, if they be skillfully manipulated, result in guidance and personnel service for many persons at different age and educational levels and in many areas of life. Consideration of the various methods whereby these two series of information may be advantageously utilized is the purpose of Part IV.

As a preliminary to how informational data may be used, it may lessen, or at least help to explain, present-day confusion and oftentimes acrimonious discussion as to when, where, why, and by whom this information should be used if attention is called to the fact that two movements, both designated "guidance," have been developing in this country side by side, and as time goes on promise to become both more closely unified and more definitely differentiated. One of these movements has been stressed, although the other has not been neglected, in this book. Its origin has been briefly ascribed to the practical application of two theories—the one sociological and the other psychological. Its operating information was secured from surveys which were rather inclusive of sociological, educational, economic, and occupational data, and, although their procedures included the use of information about the individual, the status of psychological

---

[1] Recently, perhaps owing to overenthusiasm for analysis of the individual as well as to lack of familiarity with the development of the guidance movement, there was a fleeting tendency to extol the value of data about the individual and to decry the value of occupational information. Since it is obvious that values attach to both types of data, this temporary aberration hardly produced a ripple on the surface and the main trend was not interrupted.

knowledge was such that the sociological information far exceeded the psychological.

Simultaneously, the way was being prepared for the introduction of a second guidance movement. Education was the sponsor; the psychology of individual differences was the keynote; and statistical surveys confined to pupil elimination and retardation, illuminated by the findings of the testing movement, furnished most of the informational data. This second movement was nameless until after the psychological inspiration of World War I had had time to become effective.[2] Gradually the movement has acquired momentum, owing, at least in part, to its liberal financial support and to the high type of scholarship which has been engaged in collecting, evaluating, recording, and demonstrating the possible uses of its operational data. Consciously or unconsciously this movement, too, has come to be called "guidance."

It seems very logical that this second type of guidance service, which originated within the school system instead of being "fastened" upon it, which is due to educational rather than to business or philanthropic initiative, and which deals almost entirely with educational data, should be primarily concerned with those aspects of guidance which are accented during the period of formal education rather than with the more inclusive type of guidance which extends into the areas of adult educational and occupational life. And, while documentary evidence has been submitted to prove that this more recently christened movement did not originate or make the first attempt to put into practice the slogan, "Every teacher a counselor," one would seem justified in assuming that it is the only movement which can hold out any hope of making good on that slogan. Its informational data comprises material which every person qualified to teach should know, to which he should be able and willing to contribute, and which he should be prepared to interpret and use. Moreover, since the education of the individual is more or less dependent upon the effective use of this information, those who wish to consider this phase of guidance as synonymous with education might well be conceded this privilege, even though others may feel that it would be more logical either to consider it as a facilitating service or to drop the word "guidance" and include the procedures which it connotes as an undifferentiated factor in all educational procedures.

2 Since all the elements stressed in this second movement were present in the original movement, it may seem more logical to some to consider that the original movement was divided during the 1920's, each unit accenting specialized aspects of guidance. Analysis of the evidence on the origin and development of both movements, or both units, seemed to this student to favor the two-movement idea, although she could offer considerable documentary support for the two-unit idea.

There would seem no legitimate basis for disagreement up to this point, but when the original, broader guidance movement is under consideration, teacher limitations are so very obvious that it seems unfair to both teachers and students that the one should be expected to counsel or the other to derive much benefit from such counsel. If youth and adult are to be adequately served, as well as protected from actual misguidance, every teacher cannot be assumed to qualify as a counselor.

And now to revert to the promise of the future. Does a unified, effectively functioning guidance service depend upon recognition of the differentiated functions of these two guidance movements? Should every encouragement be offered to those who are interested in expanding and in improving the second movement, which has been so ably directed by the Educational Records Bureau and to whose literature one instinctively turns for authoritative pronouncements in the areas with which it deals? Should an effort be made to restore something of the early prestige which characterized the original guidance movement [3] so that its differentiated functions may adequately supplement and carry forward the educational work begun by the second? Could each movement, specializing in its own area, contribute to a unified guidance service covering the entire life span of individuals?

Study of the literature which has dealt with one or more aspects of these two guidance movements during the last decade will do much to explain the past and to illuminate the future.[4] For instance, it will be noted that literature primarily concerned with the second movement focuses on the individual differences found among students and the implications of these differences in terms of educational opportunities and educational potentialities. To be sure, the leading representatives of the movement usually recognize that there are other aspects of guidance

[3] This loss of prestige has been due to many causes which are without the purview of this work and which may not be charged to any particular person or group. The original vocational guidance movement has not as yet been superseded either in purpose or in effectiveness, but it has lacked the type of scholarship which commands respect and the type of organizational leadership which fosters growth. Moreover, it must not be forgotten that the task of the original movement was both more inclusive and more difficult than is that of the more recent movement.

[4] An effort has been made to select the most authoritative references on both movements in order, among other purposes, to give the reader assistance in answering to his own satisfaction the three questions which have been propounded. As an initial step in arriving at independent conclusions one might compare the two major references cited in Chapter XII, one issued by the Educational Records Bureau and the other by the U. S. Office of Education. Both deal with the cumulative record and are an exposition of its uses. Also it is well to note the difference in the wording of Parsons' and Ryans' prerequisites to guidance, which are carried side by side as indicators of the focal points of the various parts of this volume. Practically identical in their statement of the essentials, they differ noticeably in the inclusiveness of their application.

worthy of consideration; there is at least casual mention of the importance of occupational choice, and occupational data appear on the cumulative records and in the case studies used for demonstration purposes. But in the main developmental growth is concerned with growth during the period of life devoted to formal education and does not carry over to life possibilities and individual potentialities in the postschool world and in adult occupational life.

And herein one finds the major weakness of this second, and primarily educational, guidance movement if it be assumed to function independently. Every public-school pupil, throughout the entire period of his formal education, should be considered a potential entrant to the occupational world. Since both the theory of individual differences and the facts on cumulative records indicate that the points at which different individuals should transfer from the educational to the occupational world vary considerably, one wonders how much dependence can be placed upon each student's receiving the type of guidance best adapted to his needs if teachers alone are to be entrusted with furnishing guidance service? Will the teacher, whose preparation for guidance service has been largely derived from graduate-school instruction and whose experiences have been limited to educational areas, know when the time for transfer has arrived? What will he have contributed that will help the student to choose his occupation and anticipate the problems involved in entering occupational life?

These are the queries for which this counselor has found no satisfactory answer. But, in spite of this major shortcoming which at some time and in some way will have to be overcome, might not leadership in this basic aspect of guidance be conceded to those agencies which have demonstrated such marked leadership therein, thus freeing other agencies to concentrate on other aspects of guidance which are crying for leadership and for which no leadership is available? Thus a foundation might be laid upon which a more secure superstructure could be reared.

The original movement is found to be much more inclusive in scope and to give much more definite recognition to the necessity for the life-continuity of guidance service. But it has lacked a focal point of interest and effort, has made sporadic, often abortive, attempts to function effectively in one or more of the areas embraced in its purview, and has furnished no authoritative leadership to which one might turn with the same assurance of expert assistance as has been the case with the second movement.

Since its inception it has sponsored or been sponsored by several organizations, one of which, the National Occupational Conference, was liberally financed but failed to provide the type of scholarship or leadership essential to command the confidence of its potential beneficiaries. It closed its doors. The National Vocational Guidance Association, which was the parent guidance organization in this country, has maintained its entity, except for one brief interlude, from 1913 to the present.[5] Its objectives have wavered; it has been the victim at one time or another of publicity-seeking individuals or groups within its own ranks, and it has not attracted the type of critical scholarship which alone can and will evaluate, select, and recommend reliable information, and unhesitatingly discredit, discard, and discourage the publication and dissemination of that great mass of nondescript material which flows from the pens of commercially motivated writers. Although it has enrolled many of the instructors who offer university courses for the preparation of counselors,[6] little has been done to improve the content of such courses, to insist that they be staffed only by instructors who are as familiar with the pages of life as they are with the pages of books, or to give practical support and assistance to state departments which are trying to provide guidance services for their schools. Of course, some good work has been done but in the large the scholarship of the movement has been weak, and if the documentary evidence covered in Part I be considered item by item and compared with the status of the movement today, ineffectiveness is found to be a dominant characteristic.

Can an awakened National Vocational Guidance Association assume responsibility for building the broad guidance superstructure which is its legitimate area of service? Active and scholarly leadership in this differentiated area has never been more in demand, and the opportunity for service has never been greater. During recent years a large group of pupils with whom the educational system has previously had little contact and about whom educators will have to do considerable "learning" before they will attain much "understanding," has been forced back under educational supervision. These same pupils were the very group to service whom the original guidance movement was instituted and the National Vocational Guidance Association was formed. They were the retarded and eliminated or dropped pupils to whom, when education closed, philanthropy opened, its doors. It should not require much learning for those who are familiar with out-of-school problems to understand this type of youth and, taking up the responsibility where the second movement leaves off, to offer him effective guidance service. Can the vocational guidance

---

[5] Malcolm Mussina, *The Origin and History of the National Vocational Guidance Association* (unpublished thesis, New York University, 1931).

[6] This instructor accepts her share of the blame.

movement harmonize and utilize, in their proper areas of life, the countless guidance services of philanthropic agencies which were first in the
field and have, on all levels of education and at all age levels, rendered
important guidance service to, and often functioned as salvaging stations
for, the outcasts of education?

This writer is sympathetic with both guidance movements, with both
points of view, and with both methods of approach; but she believes that
both will be better understood if they are studied in the light of their
origin, development, purpose, and the qualifications and training required for the type of special guidance service each purports to give. It
would seem, also, that if the why of guidance at the different way stations of life were thoroughly understood, the questions of when, where
and by whom would be more easily resolved, and all types of functionaries could concentrate on the ever present, and always possible-of-
improvement, problem of how. An intensively cultivated superstructure,
erected on a well-laid foundation, would guarantee both a specialized
and a unified guidance service for all individuals.

"Methods of Utilizing Informational Data" has been chosen for the title
of Part IV because, the situation being what it is and there being as yet
no last word on either nomenclature or distribution of functions, it was
felt that such a title would be inclusive enough to embrace all the methods
of utilizing the previously discussed informational data without implying
that the use of any method was the exclusive prerogative of any agency
or of any specific functionary.

There are two major methods of utilizing such information: (1) methods adapted to group use and (2) methods which serve one individual at
a time. Referring again to the first period in the history of the guidance
movement, one finds that both methods were used by Parsons, Weaver,
and other early leaders, that the values of each were recognized and stated,
and that both have been continuously in use. Chapter XIII will be concerned with certain group methods whereby informational data may be
used. Chapter XIV will consider the use of these tools during the counseling interview, the only technique available for the personal assistance of
an individual in analyzing the various choices and problems which con-
front him and for which he must find some solution. Chapter XV will deal
with placement procedures and the series of interviews which are, at one
moment, a tool for securing up-to-the-minute information and, at the
next, a technique for counseling with the two principals involved in any
placement or employment situation. Chapter XVI carries the uses of in-

formation over to the postschool areas of employment induction and adult life.

It is obvious that, except as general information may be applicable to, or have suggestive guidance values for, individual members of a group, the second series of data which comprises the individual inventory plays no important part in group methods of guidance. On the other hand, skillful leaders may and will select universally applicable data for presentation and will utilize techniques which create desires in individuals to ask themselves questions and to challenge their abilities, aptitudes, attitudes, and behavior. Do I have this quality? Do I make this sort of impression on others? Can I meet the requirements of a college course? Can I qualify for this occupation? Thus, indirectly, challenging data presented through the medium of group activities may assist individuals to understand better their own personal inventories and may result in very effective self-guidance.

Bibliographical material on the media, content, and techniques of group guidance is abundant, and printed material is so easily accessible that it is unnecessary to present these topics in detail, especially those phases which are marginal to rather than within the legitimate field of personnel and guidance and might by some be more logically considered as extraguidance, or coguidance. For, regardless of the personal opinion of many writers, especially in the field of secondary education, it must be conceded that group methods of guidance, combining as they do instructional and advisory functions, are a shared responsibility, drifting about as yet in the no-man's-land of education.

Guidance responsibilities are, of course, always shared responsibilities if they are properly performed, but co-ordination is essential to proper performance, and it is to lack of co-ordination that much of the chaotic condition is due. Everyone is doing it, but no one is preparing everyone to do it, and no one is co-ordinating what is done. Provision for in-service training of functionaries and for co-ordination of services is an administrative responsibility, and no great amount of progress may be anticipated until administrators assume these responsibilities. It seems most profitable under the circumstances to limit the present discussion to a recapitulation of fundamental purposes and principles and to the presentation of a few methods and topics which have been found to have practical value. Four subtopics have been chosen: (1) the purposes of group guidance, (2) media for group guidance, (3) course content or topics for group discussion, and (4) techniques of group guidance.

THE PURPOSES OF GROUP GUIDANCE

There are several purposes for which the group is a satisfactory guidance unit, and there are many topics which are suitable for group discussion which have guidance implications. On the other hand, there is much beneficial group work which is questionable "guidance," and for which some other term would be more appropriate. Argumentation for this or that as guidance is not the province of this publication, but since group methods of guidance are in common use, a presentation of their purposes and procedures is within the scope indicated by the title of the volume. Determination as to what type of group discussion constitutes guidance is left to the discretion of the reader, counselor, or administrator.

The following five purposes will usually be sufficiently inclusive to cover group guidance objectives, whether the group is a school or college unit, a Y.M.C.A. or other community adult unit, or an industrial or business aggregation:

1. To afford an opportunity for the dissemination of information which is a worth-while addition to each person's storehouse of knowledge and upon which he may draw for making immediate or future decisions.

2. To afford an opportunity to get the point of view of the group, to understand its attitudes, reactions, thought processes, etc. Practical application of the principles of group psychology should result in a sort of *group inventory,* as useful for group guidance as is the personal inventory for counseling.

3. To afford an opportunity to resolve common problems through the pooling of experiences and opinions, to set up group standards, to develop attitudes agreed upon as desirable, to plan composite programs, and to promote horizontal co-operation.

4. To afford guidance in the reconciliation of different or conflicting viewpoints, interests, or policies. Attainment of objectives three and four requires modification of the viewpoints of some or all in the interest of teamwork. It also requires very astute leadership which is capable of guiding the development of skill in analysis of evidence and in thought processes.

5. To afford an opportunity to observe participants and to note behavior or responses which suggest the need of, or desire for, individual guidance.

MEDIA FOR GROUP GUIDANCE

The documented story of the early years of the guidance and personnel movement in philanthropy, education, and industry reveals that several media, designated by different terms, were used to realize the purposes of group guidance. Educational media were regarded as vehicles for the transmission of extraclassroom data considered essential for all members of the group and as opportunities for the consideration of common problems, as well as for the analysis and discussion of policies which required decision looking toward united action on the part of the group. The procedures involved and the results supposed to be attained were rather uniformly considered "guidance." The educational media mentioned in Chapter I, and still used, comprise: (1) classes in educational guidance and orientation classes, either as separate courses or as units of a single course; (2) subject courses which include the vocational implications of and the possible occupational outlets for proficiency in their content; (3) life-career or occupation-study classes; (4) tryout courses; (5) part-time and co-operative courses; (6) plant visitation, usually in connection with classes in occupations; (7) vocational addresses and conferences; (8) group study of personal characteristics; and (9) homeroom programs.[7]

On the adult level philanthropy, education, business, and various social organizations sponsor media which in purpose approximate those which have been mentioned and which are usually confined to secondary schools or to youth level groups. Conferences, round tables, symposiums, forums, and panels are among the most common media. The Y.M.C.A., the Y.W.C.A., the Y.M.H.A., the Knights of Columbus, Rotary, Kiwanis, Altrusa, and Zonta clubs, the National Federation of Business and Professional Women's Clubs, labor organizations, professional organizations, chambers of commerce, the American Management Association, the National Association of Manufacturers, and others all utilize one or more of these media either for the in-service benefit of their own group or for service to other groups. Sometimes their purpose is instructional, sometimes both instructional and advisory, and again purely advisory.

Further elaboration of two types of media included in the list of those which have been continuously approved will furnish sufficient background upon which to consider the selection of appropriate course content and discussion topics, to review the techniques available for group guidance, and to weigh the extent of their effectiveness in the light of the five major purposes cited. These two types are (1) courses which require considerable informational data as a prerequisite to the type of advisory service for which they are designed and which carry major responsibility for realizing the first purpose and (2) homeroom programs which represent the

[7] Many other media such as clubs, assembly programs, college weeks, and freshman camps might be mentioned.

informal type of group guidance designed to realize the second, third, and fourth purposes. Each type, of course, contributes to the realization of the major purposes of the other, and all group methods of guidance afford opportunities to contribute to the realization of the fifth purpose.

COURSES DESIGNED TO OFFER GUIDANCE SERVICES

Examples of the first type of media are courses in orientation, in educational guidance, and in occupations or vocational guidance. These courses may be independent units, or their content may be combined in one or more courses or with other educational units. Often they involve class assignments, examinations, and credits, and of a necessity their programs must be more or less formal. Their content will be largely controlled by the fact that their functions are both instructional and advisory; that the essential information which forms the subject matter of the course is assumed to have been collected by the means discussed in Part II and to be available for use; and that certain of these data must be disseminated in the group before the advisory function can operate effectively. Each institution will, therefore, select from the many possible stock topics and problems those which time has shown to have anticipatory and preventive values, and to this list will be added those which are inherent in the specific educational unit plus those which have special values for the type of student associated with the unit. This composite list of topics will be the key to the type of informational data best adapted to the needs of the specific group.

Orientation courses [8] as distinctive features of guidance programs are a comparatively recent practice, but the topics covered in the early educational guidance courses indicated that they were inclusive of much material which gradually came to be called "orientation," and which is sometimes allocated to separate courses. It is now generally recognized that each individual on his journey from the cradle to the grave will meet some orientation problem each time that he passes from accustomed conditions, familiar acquaintances, and known requirements, to a new situation, new human contacts, and unknown requirements. It is recognized also that the need for orientation is not confined to the educational areas of life but extends to every social and occupational area with which the individual has contacts.

The ease with which adjustments are made in later life is largely determined by the type of orientation service which has been at hand to assist an individual in making adjustments within the home circle and in solving the orientation problems involved in contacts with new play-

[8] There are, of course, many informal induction procedures which are in common use.

mates. The type of guidance which welcomes him to the kindergarten and accompanies him at each new upward step along the general education ladder is of equal importance. Fortunately, knowledge of group methods of orienting new pupils to school situations and to fellow pupils is an important part of the preparation for kindergarten teaching. Although all elementary school teachers have not had similar advantages, gradually the importance of the lower schools as factors in the guidance and adjustment of youth is being realized, and before long the gap between the kindergarten and the more or less formal efforts which are programed at different points from the sixth grade on should be filled.

On the college level the freshman year has rather uniformly been chosen as the best place to introduce orientation courses, and their objective is in harmony with that of the lower schools—adaptation to time, place, persons, and conditions. Some college personnel officers have advocated orientation courses for sophomores [9] and cite in defense of their proposition the considerable number of students who are eliminated during the sophomore year after having completed the freshman year satisfactorily. A study of the causal factors of these failures in the second year is reported to reveal that there are almost as many new situations in the sophomore as in the freshman year, prominent among them being a false sense of security caused by passing in the freshman year.

Immediately after the close of World War I, the writer interviewed a number of young men who had entered the service prior to completion of their senior year although their degrees had been granted. Some of these men, when discussing what they felt had been missed by leaving before the close of the year, revealed that there were two or three colleges which offered a last-semester senior-year orientation course which was rated very high by those who had attended it. Such courses were concerned with the orientation of the college man to the life of the world outside.

Another type of orientation course, which is more legitimately educational guidance, has had its ups and downs in college circles—orientation to the various fields of knowledge. Certain inherent weaknesses have been found to characterize such courses not the least of which may be credited to the inability of a highly specialized faculty to relate its own field to other fields and in so doing accord it neither more nor less prominence than it deserves. Unfavorable student reaction to what was considered a conglomeration of badly integrated knowledge, which not only

[9] See F. Isabel Wolcott, "The Sophomore Year—A Scholastic Crisis," *Proceedings of the Eleventh Annual Meeting American Association of Collegiate Registrars*, 1922, pp. 87–90. The author pleads for a special counselor and for the inclusion in every sophomore's program of one subject about which the student is enthusiastic.

failed to "orient" but tended to confuse, has resulted in improvement in such courses or in their elimination. The faculty pronouncement on one of the early experiments with such courses was, "Never again." This decision was motivated by a reading of the themes in which students had evaluated the course. Some had been helped; but the majority had been "thrilled," "dazed," or "confused"; and by unanimous consent the course had been christened "Chaos 1."

It would seem that each college year has specific orientation problems for which some provision, but not necessarily by group methods, should be made. And when the period of general education is completed, at whatever point on the educational ladder that may be, provision should be made for anticipating and preventing orientation difficulties peculiar to the different groups with which individuals align themselves as they are redistributed in the specialized fields of higher education or as they enter the occupational world.

Schools of nursing sometimes have both a preacceptance and a post-acceptance orientation program, the preacceptance program being an intermediate step between admission and final acceptance, a sort of in-residence tryout period. Law, medical, engineering, library, trade, and vocational schools, and industrial apprenticeships all have orientation problems peculiar to their objectives and clientele.

Those who have had advisory experience on the graduate-school level will testify to the fact that persons of considerable experience, who may have been responsible for advising others in the interval between their undergraduate study and their return to the graduate school, often have greater difficulties in orientation than do the younger students.

First, there is the reduced income and the consequent lower standard of living; sometimes there is continual financial worry.

Second, when these experienced matriculants are placed in classes with undergraduates and subjected to undergraduate requirements such as prompt assignment completion and mid-term examinations which interrupt serious independent study and often result in low and rather mortifying grades as compared with those of younger students, unfortunate emotional reactions are apt to occur. The undergraduate senior and the previous-year graduate are both pretty well broken in, are still in harness, and conform to faculty expectations more readily. Their theses, projects, and term papers are more satisfactory in form and language and, depending upon the point of view of the instructor, are apt to be more satisfactory as to content. This is inevitable. Administrators, whose functions have not enhanced their literary abilities, and classroom teachers, who have lost a certain amount of perspective owing to constant reading of the written work prepared by secondary school pupils, may upon their return to student life quite unconsciously tend to approximate lower-school standards. And it is the last straw in a series of humiliating episodes if "readers" are charged with responsibility for the appraisal of graduate efforts.

Third, the position of leadership and of social prestige, which is frequently automatically accorded educators in their own community and to which they have become accustomed, is just as automatically denied them in the larger educational circle, and they miss something which seems to be their due. Family separations entail orientation to entirely different living conditions and sometimes cause constant worries and uncertainties as to the welfare of the family which may be living elsewhere. This counselor has, during years of experience, come to appreciate and understand many of the long list of embarrassments, disappointments, and emotional disturbances which are attendant upon graduate work, which handicap the prompt orientation of graduate students, and which often return them to the world from which they came, with or without a higher degree, but with an accumulation of "chips on the shoulder" which it is difficult to dislodge.

Induction has long been recognized by business and industry as a sufficiently important aspect of personnel procedure to make it a frequent topic of in-service conference discussion and to warrant provision for its successful accomplishment in individual companies.[10]

Courses in educational and occupational information are usually predicated on the assumption that they are not needed prior to the normal time at which educational choices are permitted or required, and at which occupational preparation or choice is determined upon. But again, as in orientation procedures, the beginnings of guidance need not be delayed until the introduction of formal courses. The elementary schools afford many opportunities for the informal beginnings of all aspects of guidance. Nowhere in the entire educational system is there as much freedom to introduce pupils to vocational life through its cultural and service aspects. Geography, history, science, literature, means of transportation and their cultural influence, community life in comparison with community life in other times and in other lands, and the like contribute basic data, which are gradually elaborated and specialized and upon which later occupational choice may be made.

For occupational choice is not made at a predetermined age or grade

---

[10] George E. Yeomans, "The Induction of New Factory Employees," *Personnel,* XVIII (1942), 390–398. This is condensed from an extensive report of a study sponsored by the Massachusetts Institute of Technology. Both formal and informal induction procedures are appraised.

level. It is a growth, dependent upon the gradual accumulation of a body of knowledge, adequate enough and accurate enough, to provide a sufficient basis for choice. Teachers in the elementary schools have rare opportunities, limited only by the limitations of their own knowledge, not only to lay the foundation for the more formal courses of later years but also to open up to all youth sources of knowledge and avenues for the enjoyment of leisure time which otherwise might remain closed.[11] This golden opportunity of the elementary school to broaden the horizon of its charges, especially of those who for one reason or another do not complete the secondary school course and never attain a degree of occupational competency which combines leisure pleasures with work satisfactions, if lost on this level of education may never come again under educational auspices.

The major criticism on such informal guidance programs as are at present found in the elementary grades is that they are too apt to offer in a perfunctory way material obviously designed to improve the personality and conduct of the pupils. If material of permanent cultural value were substituted for disguised lessons in manners and morals, and were interestingly presented, and if the pupils were allowed to draw and discuss their own conclusions, "guidance" might acquire a better reputation and be more welcome as a course when the time was ripe for its admission to the curriculum.

Guidance courses are admitted to the curriculum at different grade levels, either as separate units or as a composite course. If educational guidance and occupational guidance courses are differentiated from one another and from orientation courses, it would seem logical to assume that orientation courses would comprise all topics specifically concerned with transfers or breaking-in procedures and problems—the immediate adjustment to the new situation; that educational guidance would deal with topics concerned with educational choices, educational relationships, and continuous educational adjustments; and that topics concerned with the dissemination of occupational information and its interpretation in terms of occupational choice and occupational adjustments would be the domain of occupational guidance. But assignment of topics and differentiation of course content on a theoretical basis, no matter how logical, is one thing; the practical working out of curricula so constructed is another. When an attempt is made to differentiate the educational function of assisting in course selection from the occupational function of determining the occupational objective to be attained by means of the course

---

[11] Part II suggests a number of sources of information suitable for elementary school use.

selected, the separation of such courses falls into the category of theoretical distinctions without practical differences.

A few school systems have instituted carefully thought through programs which distribute guidance-value topics in such fashion that, with a minimum of both duplications and omissions, each pupil is assured of assistance in making immediate decisions and of a reserve fund of information anticipatory of future needs. This is an ideal situation, and one to be worked toward by all schools. But the decision as to what courses or combinations of courses will best help to attain the ideal locally is a local problem. In general, for example, determination of the specific course to which the orientation problems of employed youth shall be allocated is not nearly as important as to be sure that it is given a position somewhere in the curriculum where it will serve novitiates about to enter occupational life at the time they need it, and that it will be offered neither so early that it has no appeal nor so late that its value is nil.

This indivisibility of guidance-course content and the necessity for joint functioning was recognized and commented on during the early years of the guidance movement, and it has always posed an unanswerable question for those who feel that any classroom teacher may be assigned to orientation and educational guidance courses, while only specially prepared occupational counselors should be assigned to occupational guidance courses. How many individual occupational futures will be handicapped by educational guidance which has no vision of the occupational end results of education? Herein this counselor finds another articulation problem which is most difficult of solution and which certainly cannot be solved by administrative edict.

Topics Suitable for Guidance Courses

Since the content of the courses, though implied in the three titles under consideration, cannot be settled by theory and has not yet been resolved by practice, it has seemed best to cite the major group-guidance topics for which every school system should make some provision and to assume that each system which finds them suggestive will allocate them to whatever curriculum position may best serve local objectives. Obviously, some topics will stand out as primarily orientative in character, some as rather definitely educational, and others as occupational, but the composite and indivisible character of a large number will also be impressive. Since the courses under consideration have been chosen to represent the type of group media which combines informational and advisory functions, each topic deemed worthy of inclusion in a guidance course should be implemented with educational, occupational, and community information which paves the way for the advisory function to operate. Outstanding among topics considered important for inclusion in some guidance course, irrespective of its title, are the following:

1. *Orientation Topics.* Topics which deal with induction to the new educational, work, social, religious, or other unit logically receive first consideration. Routine information at entry to each new unit would include such topics as the organization and operation of the unit and the place of group members therein; its opportunities and requirements; its instructional, supervisory, and associational personnel; its objectives and the responsibility of each individual for contributing to their realization; its traditions, their origin and meaning; and the like. Subtopics, each with an explanation as to its purpose, would comprise rules and regulations; the use and protection of property; service facilities such as libraries, lunchrooms, transportation facilities, activities, safety precautions and devices, lockers, publications, pensions, unemployment insurance, and all legislative enactments which concern the unit involved; company schools with their uses, purposes, and eligibility requirements; the use of extra-company educational facilities such as evening schools, private schools, and correspondence schools; health provisions; and labor-union membership if required. The orientation problems of business and industry parallel those of education much more closely than counselors realize. Both have specific information to impart which is prerequisite to satisfactory initial relations with their clientele, and the educational responsibility for articulation is fundamental.

The instructional material for orientation topics includes handbooks and house organs, bulletins, student or employee publications, legislative enactments, health and safety bulletins, news items from the local press, and courses of study. For many items dependence must be placed on the personal knowledge of the instructor. Some useful data for this unit have been mentioned in Part II.

The advisory function finds an opportunity for service in connection with lunchroom etiquette and the health value in wise choice of menus, student and employee responsibility for making safety devices effective, bus and other public conveyance etiquette and responsibilities, school buildings and supplies as public property, the cost of public education for each member of the group, and his individual obligation as a citizen to insure the best use and protection of public property. The private school and the industrial concern would approach the same problem from another angle. Facts about traditions permit discussion as to the influence of tradition, its desirability and undesirability, the methods of determining which traditions have permanent values and should be retained, which might be advantageously discarded (hell week, for instance), when, and why. Novitiates have a threefold responsibility with reference to traditions, to observe and help to retain some, to join in the abolition of others, and to support the introduction of desirable new ones. The routine instructional data essential for orientation may, in the hands of a skillful instructor, be made exceedingly interesting and inspirational; it may be an asset in morale building and at the same time perform group advisory services.

2. *Educational Topics.* A second series of topics which requires information as a prerequisite to advisory service or to self-guidance in the intelligent making of educational programs comprises such data as types of diplomas, certificates, and degrees, units for graduation, different types of college-admission requirements, requirements for entrance to and graduation from graduate, law, medical, trade, military, naval, secretarial, nursing, and commercial schools—whatever is called for to meet the needs of the group no matter what the educational level. Full information as to scholarships and fellowships available through different institutions and business organizations, with details as to application eligibility, should be at hand. All too often educators regret the economic handicap which prevents an able student from continuing in some special field of study, not knowing that an ideal scholarship or fellowship for meeting the needs of the student is available.

It is amazing how many scholarships and fellowships there are, and by how many agencies they are offered. State scholarships and individual college opportunities, fellowships offered by the American Association of University Women, the Social Science Research Council, the Guggenheim, Rosenwald, and Rockefeller Foundations are usually well advertised. But the Harvard National Scholarships, the Houghton Mifflin fellowships, the Walter Hines Page traveling scholarships, the scholarships at Princeton and the University of Pennsylvania open only to sons of Pennsylvania Railroad employees, the Westinghouse research fellowships, the internships of the National Institute of Public Affairs, the fellowships of the Du Pont Company, and many others are less well known. Scholarships on the elementary and secondary levels and for various types of atypical youth are also available. Audubon camp scholarships on the secondary level are very attractive to Boy and Girl Scout members. And oftentimes most important of all are the previously mentioned training facilities under federal and state auspices for physically handicapped persons. Some of the opportunities are available annually, some are temporary; and educators charged with the conduct of courses which require such data will need to be very alert lest they overlook opportunities which might further the educational ambitions of worthy students or offer suggestions which are already passé.

Courses, curricula, electives, and their occupational outlets should be clearly set forth in educational guidance courses. At every point of transfer to a new unit, after statutory educational requirements have been met, course topics should include not only the next steps in full-time educational programs but also educational opportunities in business and industry and combinations of study with work experience.

Instructional material for courses in educational guidance is abundant, but rather discriminating judgment is required to make the best selection and to guarantee that the latest editions are used. Data for assistance in making immediate choices from offerings within the institution or the community will be much the same as orientation data. But most of the essential information for use at way stations will be selected from the type of sources enumerated in Part II. It will have been collected in advance of need and will have been mastered by those who are charged with its dissemination and interpretation.

The advisory function is so intimately related to the instructional function that were it not for the fact that it cannot operate effectively without a modicum of preliminary information the two functions might well be considered inseparable. A teacher who qualifies for only the instructional phase of group guidance will not be a success in the advisory phase. Only those who know how to interest and guide a group in studying and in interpreting data on educational opportunities, and in discussing a variety of hypothetical or illustrative programs in relation to the abilities and needs of selected types of individual inventories, should be entrusted with the advisory function. If hypothetical cases are well chosen and instructional material is accessible, a number of students will derive from such group methods sufficient assistance to make their own educational choices. But there will always be some who desire, and others who would be lost without, counseling on a purely individual basis. During the performance of his group guidance functions the qualified educational counselor will be ever alert to observe these personal needs and will see that they are provided for through some suitable channel.

3. *Occupational topics* should be given some place on every educational level and in every school year. Nor should opportunities under public auspices for keeping informed about shifting occupational patterns be denied on the adult level. The purpose and character of occupational information and therefore the topics chosen will vary according to age and educational status. Properly arranged sequences of topics and suitable techniques of instruction should gradually accomplish the dual objective

(1) of enhancing the cultural background of pupils sufficiently so that in adult life their resources for self-guidance and for resolving the occupational issues of citizenship may not be limited to the "funny page" of the current press and to emotional political appeals and (2) of opening the door of knowledge regarding requirements and opportunities wide enough to make wiser personal choices possible.

In order to help lay the foundation for the accomplishment of this dual objective, it has been the custom of this instructor to ask graduate students engaged in or preparing for counseling to present the results of their occupational researches on three educational levels designed to serve three differentiated purposes: (1) The story of the occupation prepared for the elementary schools and so reported on that all the subject ramifications, geography, science, history, literature, etc., were woven into the picture. The tools available for the assistance of those who use occupational data for their cultural values were to be included. (2) Preselection information designed to broaden the secondary student's knowledge of the opportunities and requirements of a number of types of occupations and to challenge his interest in further study of any which may seem to offer personal possibilities. Many students make their occupational choice and others enter the occupational world on this level. (3) Data suitable for those who expect to enter occupational life on the college or professional level. Aspects of the work requiring college degrees, curricula, courses, institutions which are recognized as outstandingly successful in the preparation of candidates, and possible employing agencies were to be included.

Approximately one hundred such research studies were prepared and revised during the years 1932–1939. Each group member, as an introduction to the class discussion, briefly presented the findings of his study, speaking from an outline a copy of which was in the hands of all other members. Complete findings were available to any who wished to borrow them for counseling purposes. Teachers and counselors as a rule selected occupations not commonly reported on, and all studies were based on plant visitation,[12] observation, and interviews of employers and workers,

---

[12] These pooled, individual studies, supplemented by visits to four or five concerns representative of the most commonly entered occupations, were found to be more satisfactory as a method of acquainting teachers and counselors with the occupational world than were a larger number of plant visits without an opportunity for intensive individual study. Occupational visits, if worth while, must be prepared for in advance, conducted by instructors who are thoroughly familiar with the occupation visited, and discussed in some detail after the visit. Of course all visitation, singly or in groups, will be prepared for in advance and discussed afterward, but there are few instructors who can qualify equally well as conductors in all occupational fields. Some instructors who prepare counselors for certification are not familiar enough with any field to interpret what they observe correctly; some are so thoroughly at home in one field that they un-

as well as on published material. Fingerprinting, camouflaging, food tasting, soapmaking, training Seeing-Eye dogs, goat raising, plastics, glass furniture, ghostwriting, and silk substitutes were among the very popular reports.

If opportunities for the introduction of occupational topics as a contribution to general education have been used to the best advantage in the lower grades, pupils will be more responsive to the offerings of the formal courses designed to serve as a basis for occupational choice. Such courses have been included in public-school curricula from the very beginnings of the guidance movement. Boston was offering systematic instruction in business opportunities in 1906, and the Committee on Vocational Guidance was urging "a place for vocational information of an educational character in the regular school curriculum." During the early years of the movement, when large numbers of pupils were eliminated between the fourth and the eighth grades, it was necessary, if such courses were to benefit those whom philanthropy had revealed to need them most, to introduce them in the elementary school. As time has passed and the age for compulsory education has been advanced, the position of such courses in the curriculum has also been advanced. At present there is no uniformity in practice; they may be found in any grade from the seventh to the twelfth.[13] The school year is not of particular importance, but it is of importance that their curriculum position be such as to avoid giving them so early that their informational data have grown stale or been forgotten before they are needed. On the other hand, in some communities there is real danger that they may be offered so late in the curriculum that they fail to benefit those who enter wage-earning life as soon as the law permits.

Sometimes courses in occupations are offered on the college level,[14] but

consciously stress it to the neglect of other fields of equal importance; while very few are qualified to direct group visits designed to give their classes a bird's-eye view of the major occupational fields. Institutional trip conductors who know how to approach employers and who have picked up a wide range of general information regarding suitable concerns to visit can usually conduct tours more impartially and with better results than can either inexperienced instructors or those who are too highly specialized. Preparation for the trip and discussion after the trip will be a group conference problem. If the instructor is deficient in some phase of knowledge, someone else in the group may supply the deficiency.

[13] For a discussion of the history and status of such courses in 1934, see Maris M. Proffitt, *Courses in Occupational Information* (U. S. Office of Education Bulletin, 1934, no. 11; Washington, 1934).

[14] In "A College Class in Occupational Information" (*School Review*, XLV [1937], 123–129) E. G. Williamson reported that members of a class in Vocations in the General College of the University of Minnesota, who were paired with a control group, acquired better and more reliable occupational information than did the members of the other group. The final examination consisted of 203 questions.

conferences are the more usual method of serving college students. In order to give each student an opportunity to consider as many occupations as possible, some colleges program the topics so that over a four-year period students who attend each annual conference will obtain a fairly broad overview of opportunities with comparatively little duplication.[15] Colleges which maintain company contacts are able to offer students an opportunity to hear many speakers describe the opportunities and requirements of specific companies.

In addition to course topics, which frequently stress occupational opportunities and their requirements, there are other important occupational topics for which some provision should be made and some time for discussion be arranged. If not included among course topics, they may be considered in clubs, assemblies, conferences, or homerooms. A few such topics are listed. The list is suggestive rather than selective or inclusive, and no effort has been made to allocate any topic to any specific position in an occupational information program.

(1) Each youth prior to entering the work world has a right to some fundamental knowledge regarding the purposes of industry, its organization, and its problems, which are by no means all on the worker's side. He also has a right to understand the social responsibilities of industry, the contribution to the fulfillment of these obligations which is demanded from management, labor, and capital, and the factors governing a fair distribution of the rewards of successful business enterprises. Courses in economics and in social science may provide adequate opportunity to discuss such topics, but if not, those who have charge of occupational courses should be sure that they are included somewhere. And, regardless of previous study, a few refresher conferences on such topics are desirable at the moment of the first opportunity for their practical use.

(2) The orientation and adjustment problem of occupational novices may well be reviewed; or if they have not been previously discussed, they are worthy of considerable attention. The transfer from school to industry is a major adjustment no matter at what point on the educational ladder it occurs. School is apt to regard absence and tardiness rather leniently; it

---

[15] The New Jersey College for Women, under the auspices of the Personnel Bureau, conducts annual vocational conferences with due attention to standardized occupational outlets, potential outlets, and temporary opportunities. Summary reports of the conference are printed.

A number of colleges, some since before 1920, have issued bulletins which indicate occupational outlets for the various curricula and courses. Hunter College, New York City, issues and frequently revises bulletins of this type. The Champaign, Illinois, senior-high-school occupational chart is the outstanding example of secondary school efforts to help students visualize the possible occupational outlets for different school subjects and combinations of subjects.

operates five days a week for five or six hours a day; it has several short vacations and one very long one; it provides semiannual promotions for all and even grants "complimentaries" to some who do not regularly qualify; it does not always stress the necessity for care and economy in the use of public property. And always, during the ten to sixteen years that youth has been employed on the job of acquiring an education, school has made him the center of consideration, observation, and service. Unless someone helps to pave the way for the changes which he will find in the work world, a rude awakening will be due. In the business world absences will be frowned upon; tardiness will not be tolerated; the hours of work will be longer and hourly shifts to different scenery and different duties will not break the monotony of routine processes; noise, speed, and constant repetition of the same process will cause shop fatigue and entail new muscular adjustments. The young worker will cease to be the center of attraction and will take his place in the assembly line as a co-operator in attaining the objectives of industry. Periodic vacations will be missed, and the one or two weeks substituted for the long summer vacation will limit previous vacation programs. Promotions will be rare and will come irregularly; near failures will be discharged; and often, with great regret, the management will be obliged to hold up merited promotions because no promotional position is vacant. Students who have been, or who think they have been, continuously bedeviled by the eccentricities of teachers and costudents may now find their experiences valuable assets in understanding and contending with the idiosyncrasies of foremen, supervisors, and coworkers.

(3) A third group of topics which deserves pre-employment attention is concerned with methods of applying for and securing wage-earning opportunities. Among such topics are the choice and value of secondary occupations; the various media for securing positions and the avoidance of unreliable counseling and placement agencies; the dangers involved in signing commercial placement contracts without reading their content; how to choose an employer; when to change positions; how to write letters of application, fill out application blanks, and prepare for an employment interview; how to use news ads; and how to study both vertical and horizontal lines of promotion.

(4) Preparation for the first day's work comprises a number of topics suitable for group discussion. A successful first day at entry to industry as well as upon entry to any new position thereafter requires a certain physical and mental alertness which results from a good previous night's rest and clothing in complete readiness the day before, a feeling of leisureliness which comes from allowing plenty of time to dress carefully, eat a proper breakfast, and arrive at the appointed place with time to spare.

Those who plan to be on duty at exactly nine o'clock will usually find themselves arriving just a little to one side or the other of the hour. Since arrival on the wrong side means discharge, the person who habitually arrives a few minutes before the hour is the better planner and is more likely to retain his position. The wise use of rest and lunch periods is also of first-day importance. Those who sit continuously at their work may use rest periods for exercise; those whose work requires long periods of standing should either lie down or sit down. This is always a difficult point to get across to young workers; they just do not accept it. Bodily cleanliness, overlooked the first day, brands the newcomer an undesirable to team with, to stand or sit next to, or to welcome socially. Clock watching, overstaying the luncheon period, too frequent use of vanity kits during work hours, and use of an employer's time to prepare for leaving all result in demerits for the beginner.

While girls are apt to be the worst offenders in many of these personal matters, it must not be assumed that young men are blameless. This counselor has had many complaints about men whose body and clothing odors were offensive, whose personal habits disqualified them as coworkers. In a few instances young men have lost positions because they persisted in absenting themselves from work during the late afternoon hours when rapid use of their tonsorial kits permitted them to leave the office with a fair start toward preparation for the social activities of the evening.

College graduates are well advised to soft-pedal college degrees, experiences, achievements, and social life—to forget during work hours the social and financial status of their family and their "junior league" affiliations. If one is a superior worker, no label of notification will be necessary for either employer or coworkers; if one falls down on the job, degrees, honors, and social prestige will only add to the disgrace. The novice may well be very humble. With his diploma bag filled to overflowing, he still lacks something which the youth in the factory and the girl in the ten-cent store have in their bag of work tricks and which he desperately needs as he starts on his business career.

Instructional material for use in connection with occupational topics is voluminous. Much of it has little or no value, and some is actually detrimental to those who are seeking constructive, wholesome, and reliable advice and information. A vast literature, commercially profitable and usually very readable but fallacious in suggested methods of attaining success and popularity or of securing positions, has flooded the market during depression years. Seminars for the review and appraisal of counseling material often result in the discard of unreliable publications and of unethical suggestions which are considered smart and which, while they may succeed in one particular instance, result most disastrously in many others. Raising questions which challenge material of dubious value is not blacklisting, and it accomplishes a much more useful purpose.

Chapter VI discussed in some detail seven types of sources with which counselors should be familiar and from which they might select material worthy of course inclusion. A few publications discuss methods of determining course content and conference topics, and several state and city departments of education issue course syllabi which frequently contain suggestions for workers in other states. Workbooks [16] have had considerable popularity in some school systems, and whether or not they are favored for use in connection with occupational courses, it is well to be familiar with three or four which are sponsored by recognized authorities and which contain more than a reproduction of previously published forms and methods. Company charts which break down the income dollar, showing how it is distributed among the various factors essential to the operation of the concern, are available. A comparison of dollar distribution by several concerns engaged in different lines helps students to understand that the relative importance of the different elements varies from one industry to another; in some cases labor will be found to be the major item of cost; in others materials may absorb the largest portion; while there are other concerns in which capital is the dominant item. Information secured from such comparisons has a number of values. Not the least important for future wage-earning citizens, income-tax payers, and small investors are the interest aroused in logical and illogical bases for levying corporation and individual income taxes and an understanding of the relation between the distribution of dollar costs and the type of industry in which employment promises to be most permanent and investments most profitable. Placement contracts, application blanks, and news ads are excellent instructional material and can be easily procured.

If plant visitation [17] is used as a method of acquainting pupils with occupational processes and opportunities, two types of preparatory discussions are essential in order to make the visit a profitable learning period:

(1) Study of the concern and its product or of a similar concern from such printed material as may be available, so that the group may have some knowledge as to what to observe, how to observe, and how to ask intelligent and pertinent questions. Processes, sources of material, machines, safety devices, use of foremen and supervisors, types of workers, age

[16] Richard J. Williams discusses the advantages and disadvantages of workbooks and gives a list of available workbooks in "The Workbook in the Study of Occupations," *Occupations*, XVII (1938), 28–32.

[17] See Carl M. Marcy, "How to Conduct Field Trips," *Journal of Higher Education*, XI (1940), 204–208.

and sex which predominate, team and individual work processes, posture at work, etc., should be observed. Questions which are pertinent and permissible should be clearly differentiated from those which savor of impertinence or suggest spying. Some outlines designed for the use of seventh graders include such topics as hiring methods, labor relations, promotional methods, wage determination, and methods of payment. Obviously seventh-grade students have no immediate use for such information, and there is often a suspicion that they have been coached by adults who have other than educational motives in mind.

The doors of many business concerns have been opened to this writer as a guest student of occupational life; the freedom of many plants has been gratuitously given as well as admittance to staff conferences on some of the most controversial problems of the business world. Sometimes, during her stay in a given plant, school children have arrived to investigate and, notebooks in hand, have been turned over to her for assistance in gathering data. Among the rapid-fire questions asked were: Do you have welfare work? Do your girls have rest periods? How long does it take to be promoted here? Do the workers get supper money Saturdays? How much? Do you approve of labor unions? What kind of soap do you use in the lavatories? Do your boys work overtime? Do they get pay for it? Are you engaged in interstate commerce? (They did not know what interstate commerce was.) Persons who ask such questions should either be considering immediate connection with the concern, or they should be labor inspectors. Recently a whole flock of college investigators has descended upon business like the locusts of Egypt in bands. They are usually foraging for term-paper or thesis material, or to get source information on occupations. Some employers are amused, some are irritated, some wonder where educators were educated; but all are courteous and glad to give information on any suitable topic.

(2) A second type of preparatory discussion, unless the group is already familiar with the requirements for courteous visitors, should be concerned with this topic. It costs money to show any group through any concern; it consumes valuable time, interrupts work, and is trouble.[18] Among the considerable list of dos and don'ts which might be profitably discussed are the necessity for observing to the letter all plant rules, of arriving on time, of never wandering away from the main group, of never touching or meddling with plant property, of never talking to workers, and of never talk-

---

[18] In "Make Factories Your Sales Tools" (*Forbes*, XLII [Oct. 15, 1938], 18–19, 40), Edwin Laird Cady describes preplanning of visits on the part of industry. Counselors will find it helpful to understand the industrial viewpoint before they send too many groups to visit.

ing with or annoying others in the group during explanations. Be appreciative, look, listen, and ask intelligent questions are good general rules to follow.

All plant visits require postvisit discussions and afford excellent opportunities for oral or written English exercises. Letters of appreciation afford another opportunity for appropriate "experiences."

The advisory function is, or should be, a constant accompaniment of the instructional function. It helps students to interpret statistical surveys in terms of changing occupational patterns and to question the exent to which their own occupational ambitions are in line with such patterns. It helps them to watch for current changes which may affect their occupational opportunities and to understand how, even in a democracy, freedom of choice is limited by legislation, labor-union restrictions, industrial change, and the like.[19] A sufficient number of hypothetical individual inventories should be considered both to bring out the influence of such factors and to furnish each member of the group with a basis upon which to visualize his own inventory in the light of possible occupational opportunities, to discern and accept his disqualification for one opportunity and to realize his abilities for successful entry to another.

Placement problems require extensive advisory service; therefore, as the age for induction to the work world approaches, they should receive their full share of attention. At the same time it is to be hoped that, long before their transfer to the occupational world, pupils may have come to realize that there is no abrupt transition from school to work; that school is not one thing and work something entirely different, but rather that school, as a job, has been a tryout and a preparation for the next job; and that their ability to take responsibility and to accomplish satisfactorily the tasks of the first job is a valuable forecast of their ability to tackle the new job effectively.

4. *Activities.* Cocurricular activities might perhaps be considered under educational topics, but there are three reasons why the general topic seems to warrant separate discussion: (1) Not all activities are cocurricular and not all are under educational auspices. (2) There are so many activities available with such varied objectives that it would require a considerable time allotment in a course to present adequately informational data alone. (3) Rather technical knowledge of educational opportunities, occupational requirements, and activities is required in order to assist a group in understanding how important it is to base activity choice on the contribution

19 "The Trade Unions and Vocational Service" by Harold Siegel and Louis H. Sobel (*Occupations*, XX [1942], 343–347) contains important information for counselors on matters which are rarely as well understood as they should be.

to the total developmental program. This statement implies that the advisory function in the activities area must be performed by those who have a broad knowledge of all three opportunity areas, educational, extracurricular, and occupational, and can select type activities for discussion in their relation to hypothetical educational programs and their occupational outlets. This aspect of activity choice has too long been neglected, but the day of activities for activities' sake is passing under a cloud, and in the new day which is at hand it is hoped that choice of activities will receive the same type of advisory assistance as does the choice of educational programs or occupational objectives and that each student will be helped to understand how to integrate the activities phase of his program with its other developmental aspects.

Sources of information on activities are in the main local, school and community. Part II has indicated how such information may be collected and filed. If the instructional function only is to be performed, the majority of the teaching corps should qualify for service. If the advisory function is to be included, the choice of instructors becomes a very important matter, for not only will it be necessary to discuss unitary programs which visualize each opportunity in its proper relation to other opportunities but it will also be necessary to help students weigh a variety of hypothetical personal inventories in the light of such programs. The advisory procedure is the same as that mentioned under educational and occupational topics, but one more opportunity has entered the picture, so one more series of basic information is required; and the analytical and integrative functions are just that much more difficult to perform effectively.

5. *Personality Topics.*[20] Principal Giles in his 1913 address reported that he was giving systematic instruction in Personal Characteristics with satisfactory results. Institutions which offer formal courses in guidance usually allot some portion of the course to a consideration of personal qualities as assets or liabilities in attaining educational and occupational objectives and in making social adjustments. Prevention or solution of the many problems which arise in connection with such topics is of great

[20] The importance of personality—whatever the word may mean—has recently received so much attention that no personnel course or list of personnel topics is considered complete which does not include it. Neither teachers nor counselors are qualified to deal with the technical aspects of personality. Moreover they need to deal very cautiously with its nontechnical aspects lest they cause technical problems. There are several psychiatrists who are admirably fitted by training and experience to help teachers understand the type of personality problems developing in the school room and to show them how to take some responsibility for anticipatory prevention. "The Psychiatrist Looks at Today's School Child" (*Educational Record*, XXIII, Suppl. no. 15 [1942], 69–82) by James S. Plant is a recent and very helpful article.

importance. Personal qualities often handicap successful accomplishment of educational undertakings, eliminate employees or deny them the promotional opportunities which they feel are their due, brand individuals as unwelcome or undesirable members of social groups, and the like. The physical and emotional disturbances which result from frustrations caused by personal characteristics are difficult to anticipate and guard against by group methods, but a beginning must be made, for unless some means of counteracting their influence is found, they may become sufficiently serious to nullify the effectiveness of the best methods of educational and vocational guidance.

Group methods may well be focused upon such topics as habits of work; time and financial budgets, including the protection of time against the inroads of others, which in some situations is fully as important as is the wise use of time; health habits which enhance the efficiency and personal attractiveness of individuals; and basic principles which are helpful in choosing companions, in avoiding identification with groups which engage in gambling, drinking, late hours, roadhouse visitation, borrowing, and installment buying, and in meeting the many other social, moral, economic, and ethical problems which are apt to arise in making new friends.[21] The fundamental principles of social conduct and the importance of maintaining home ties and religious affiliations are also worthy of group consideration.

Many persons, older as well as younger, changing from one unit of education to another, from education to occupational life, from one work situation to another, or from one environmental situation to another, find that they are also changing from one set of social and moral standards to another and that it is difficult to meet the demands of the new situation without the violation of principles which seem fundamental to them, and often are fundamental.[22] Adaptability has recently received so much attention that some individuals have come to feel that adaptation to the "god of things as they are" is the prime requisite for a successful life. Counselors may well consider with youth the extent to which adaptability is always wise. May a person be too adaptable, and if so, under what circumstances? Upon what bases may one decide to adapt or to refuse to

---

21 Hanson W. Baldwin in "The Making of the American Officer" (*The New York Times Magazine*, Dec. 7, 1941, pp. 3-4) describes the army procedure for selecting men for the Officer Candidate Schools. Thirty-nine qualifications of an officer are used as a sort of rating scale. Just at present a profitable personality discussion can be built around these qualifications.

22 See Willard Waller, "Counseling and the Mores," and Hilda Taba, "The Contribution of the Personnel Worker to Social Sensitivity Among Students," *Journal of the National Association of Deans of Women*, IV (1940), 51-62. These articles are good presentations of the problems of advising when changing mores are involved.

adapt? Does universal adaptation "to what is" have any influence on social progress? Such topics, if confined to the aspects which are within the experience and comprehension of the group, are thought-provoking and lay the foundation for more advanced thinking in later life.

Who shall determine what personality topics and personal problems are to be included in group guidance programs? This is a perennial query. Some argue for student selection; others feel that students lack the experience to determine relative values and argue for faculty selection as the better method of assuring topics which time has shown to be desirable. Many surveys of student problems on all levels of education and of worker problems in various occupations have been made. Experience indicates that the opinion of the group to be served does not always coincide with the selections of its overlords but that it is usually a better criterion of immediate need. Moreover a live and fruitful discussion is apt to result from group-chosen topics, while the "I'm-going-to-be-guided" attitude handicaps the effectiveness of the most carefully chosen topics of superiors. Undoubtedly the mature judgment of those whose experiences have been broad enough to recognize both permanent and relative values should have an important part in the determination of topics in this area, but student- or employee-felt needs, which have immediate importance for them, should also be awarded a considerable share in the program.

A fortunately timed visit to a primary room in a strange city brought the importance of group-chosen topics home to this writer in a very forceful manner. The city had received considerable publicity because of its thoroughly outlined grade to grade, day to day, line upon line, precept upon precept guidance program, with "personality culture" stressed in the lower grades. As the children began to assemble it was apparent that something unusual was on their minds; a few tears were shed; and after a corner consultation one child came to the teacher's desk and asked, "Teacher, could we skip our guidance lesson this morning and talk about Alice? We want to know where Alice is." Alice, who had been a much loved member of the group, had died the previous day. There was no hesitation on the teacher's part; she had sensed the children's problem and knew how to meet it. The guidance lesson was skipped, and instead a group of very tense and eager little six-year-olds were helped to face the first crisis which had occurred in this area of their lives. No laws regarding religious instruction were violated, but a rare opportunity for spiritual guidance had been recognized and had been so used that its influence will be felt as long as life lasts. As the discussion proceeded, the tension was eased. Suddenly one little girl relaxed, leaned back in her seat, smiled, and exclaimed, "I'm a lot happier now." "So am I," said another, "but I think—I mean, I want to do something real good, too." The teacher knew how to capitalize on this situation, too. And, considering the personality of the teacher, it did not seem probable that this lesson would join its predecessors on such abstract topics as honesty, obedience, courtesy, cleanliness, and godliness, each of which had been studied diligently and inattentively during the "period," dramatized during the allotted time, and then passed down the assembly line to oblivion.

It has been surprising to some that when junior-high-school groups are allowed to select personality topics or that when surveys of junior-high-school needs are made, so many topics fall within the social-conduct area. This is not a surprise to those who are familiar with the social sensitivity of this age and the minor delinquencies of which it is frequently the cause. It is a normal expectation. Nor is it a surprise to those who are in constant contact with the social frustrations of out-of-school youth, either unemployed youth, partially employed youth, or those who, for one reason or another, are unable to attain the type of economic independence which permits the gratification of natural social impulses and needs.

The early years of the twentieth century were characterized by humanitarian enthusiasm for service to youth. As a result there was a steady increase in educational opportunities forced upon youth by statutory enactment and a steady decrease, also by statute, in opportunities for employment. The depression years, interested in facilitating the employment of older workers, accentuated what was already a dangerous trend, widening the gap between the attainment of physical maturity and economic independence and breaking what psychiatrists call the "normal developmental rhythm." And then metropolitan newspapers regret the increase of delinquency among youth! And educators and laymen agree that idleness among youth is a menace to the country. "It packs too much political dynamite!" [23] Yes, indeed, and it packs too much moral dynamite too!

Acceptable social conduct and attractive personal appearance are major interests of youth from early adolescence on. To both sexes such things frequently mean successful or unsuccessful competition with their mates for the approval and companionship of the opposite sex. When a boy sixteen years of age cites as his major problem, "I can't get me a girl, a decent one, I mean"; when a girl, even younger, admits that she has stolen tawdry jewelry because, "I wanted to be invited and I had to dress nice"; and when such instances are on the daily counseling calendar, traceable

[23] See Edmund Ezra Day, *Oncoming Changes in the Organization of American Public Education* (Ithaca, N.Y.: Committee on Teacher Education of the Association of Colleges and Universities of the State of New York, 1941).

almost without exception to social frustrations caused by social-conduct deficiencies or to the fact that biological maturity has outdistanced economic independence, it is not very difficult to understand why frequency tabulations place youth's greatest needs in the category of "personality improvement and social conduct." *Truly, it often seems tragic that man-made laws and pronouncements can so easily control the timing of youth's intellectual and employment experiences, and are so helpless in timing his physical maturity and controlling his social impulses!*

Counselors who have the confidence of youth meet these frustration problems in many forms. They are watching with much interest the methods whereby educators and others hope to stem the tide of broken developmental rhythms. The CCC is concerned with unmarried men.[24] Their need for recreation is recognized, but the location of most of the projects prohibits provision for normal social life and needs. The Educational Policies Commission is battling over the "jurisdictional" aspects of youth's educational experiences.[25] A list of the outstanding educational suggestions for further service to youth, suggestions which might be said to be for the preservation and protection of the "American way of life," follows: (1) the addition of two years to the period of public education, making in all fourteen years to the completion of the junior college; (2) the provision of bona fide pre-employment work experience; (3) further expansion of educational opportunities especially along vocational lines; (4) better teachers; (5) counseling service which can suggest, persuade, and if need be, force parents and students to recognize the values and accept the dicta of selective education.

Such a program provides for additional educational experiences, includes work experience as a factor in education, and assumes the ultimate willingness of the public to pay the bill. But it widens, rather than narrows, the gap between physical maturity and economic independence, and therefore does nothing to alleviate the attendant social problems. The counselor is disturbed because he thinks there are other more important arcs to the circle of youth's needs. Permitting youth to select his own discussion topics confirms this belief. The counselor also believes that the social and moral dangers to the individual develop side by side with the social and political dangers to the country, and he feels the need of more virile educational leadership—leadership of the kind that passes over

24 It has been abolished since this chapter was written.

25 See the National Education Association, Educational Policies Commission, *The Civilian Conservation Corps, The National Youth Administration, and the Public Schools* (Washington: The Commission and the American Association of School Administrators [1941]).

trivia and concentrates on the types of work programs which are most promising both in eliminating idleness and in fostering economic independence.

Informational material most helpful to teachers and counselors in understanding the personality and social-conduct needs of students is found in such periodicals as *Mental Hygiene, Progressive Education, Understanding the Child,* and in the *Journals of Psychology, Psychiatry,* and *Sociology;* but current literary magazines must not be overlooked. A very illuminating story, "Small Tragedies," by Agnes Repplier,[26] has perennial values for both parents and teachers and might well be substituted for some assignment of lesser value in teacher-training courses. The power of example, the challenging by youth of the principles and practices of adults, and the disappointment and disillusionment which accompany loss of confidence in the integrity of parents and teachers are forcefully expressed.

Time budgets and instructions for making such budgets are available for every age and every purpose. Bronson Alcott's time card for his children is a good introduction to the topic in the lower schools. Financial budgets are timely as soon as children receive their first weekly allowances. Sample budgets for college students and for wage-earners are abundant, and profitable discussions among girls may be based on a comparison of the budgets set up for college girls and those prepared by minimum-wage commissions for establishing wage rates in various industries.

Discussions on good grooming and appropriate dress for different occasions may be based on data received from college personnel offices, business organizations, magazines, and books designed to serve as guides to those who do not trust their own judgment. The advice in such publications as *Esquire* and *Mademoiselle* may be considered in comparison with suggestions secured from such sources as the Personality Chart prepared by the Transcription Supervisors' Association of New York City and the pamphlets and charts distributed by the Bristol-Myers Company. Benjamin Franklin's personality chart, with a rather detailed description of its purpose and methods of use, is another bit of useful material for the elementary schools.[27]

Social conduct is interestingly approached on the elementary and secondary levels from the historical or historical-traditional point of view. Sources suggested for data on the cultural aspects of occupational information furnish a multiplicity of opportunities to discuss the meaning of

---

[26] *Atlantic Monthly,* CLXI (1938), 805–812.
[27] *Personal Growth Leaflets,* nos. 42 and 43 (Washington: National Education Assn.).

mores—how they are instituted, how maintained, when changed, and how offended. Copies of ancient rules of conduct, of rules and regulations for social conduct among former college students, or in other areas of life, will often deliver a counseling message in its most effective form. Some counselors advocate the use of social etiquette tests, a number of which are on the market. If the mores of the group are sufficiently uniform, such tests, in spite of their inherent faults, may afford the basis for improvement in the emily-post aspects of social conduct, but as a rule there are so many different social cultures represented in American educational units that oftentimes social conduct which would be entirely in harmony with one milieu would be taboo in another. The *American Mercury,* so long ago that credit cannot be given either to author or issue, adequately illustrated the difficulty of assuming that stereotyped rules of social conduct were equally applicable to all places and purposes:

Question. What is the proper way to eat a sandwich?
Reply. Depends on what makes it a sandwich and where it is eaten. If at the St. Regis leave it on your plate and use your knife and fork. If at a lunch counter and a tomato has played an important part in creating it a sandwich, grasp it firmly with both hands, use your teeth and be sure the tomato doesn't evade its responsibility.

The advisory function, if personality topics are meaningful and inspirational and informational data abundant and accessible, will be in operation even though there be neither teacher nor counselor in the picture. A great deal of superb self-education and self-guidance results from suitable topics implemented by suitable reading and illustrative material. But the advisory function in connection with all topics which deal so largely with the emotional life cannot well be eliminated from the picture; it is omnipresent, at least in the background, and is expressed in manner and example as well as in word and deed. Dr. Plant, in the article previously mentioned, indicates that although teachers may tell lies in the intellectual field and the children accept the deception, they cannot do likewise in the emotional field and get away with it. "We do not impatiently teach patience—nor falteringly call for faith." *The way we speak, dress, walk, talk, and act is an important and continuous performance of the advisory function.*

Informal Group Guidance Programs

The homeroom program, sometimes called the "guidance period," has been chosen to represent the second, the less formal and more definitely advisory, type of media for group guidance. History reveals that "homeroom" is a secondary school term, and that it has been the most continuously and universally used of all group guidance media. Statistical tabulations indicate that, at the present time, it is the most common and very frequently the only group guidance medium provided by administrative authorities. Several publications confined to homerooms, their objectives, programs, organization, problems, and values, are to be found on educational shelves in most libraries, and hours of time are annually devoted to the preparation of local programs for the use of homeroom teachers.

In spite of their age, universality, and abundant program implementation, the consensus of student opinion, with more than a modicum of support from parents and teachers, suggests that homeroom programs are the most universally criticized and the most universally disliked of all the supplements to the educational curriculum. Homerooms, as guidance media, have been successful in a few instances, near-failures in some school systems, and dismal failures in others. This generalization can be verified, although it will doubtless be challenged by the type of administrator who automatically accepts each emerging educational fad, who has a good paper program for homeroom guidance on file in his office, who has pronounced every teacher a homeroom teacher and feels that he has thereby created a sufficient supply of such functionaries, and who honestly believes that all's right in his guidance world. Those who have had practical and long-continued association with the teachers who must carry the responsibility for conducting group guidance through homeroom media know that this type of educational service has earned the right to rank, in the educational job hierarchy, as a hazardous occupation.

When pupil after pupil, each a registrant in homeroom-guided schools, calls upon outside agencies for exactly the type of information which is supposed to be, and in many instances could be, provided in homerooms; when one finds on the blackboards of homerooms, or surreptitiously distributed on dodgers, such pat comments as,

> Oh, dear! What can the matter be?
> Dear, dear, what can the matter be?
> Guidance has come to our School.

or

> Guides, philosophers, and friends for sale. Inquire of any student.

or when inquiry after inquiry as to what is done during the guidance period, brings such replies as,

> Oh, that's our joke period.
> We just study, the teacher rests.

Busy work of most any kind.
Only teachers who are "tops" know what to do.
Pretty tame stuff. Worse than Sunday School.
It all depends on the teacher. I had one that was awfully good.
Sometimes we get the teacher awfully fussed.

it is relatively easy to fill in the rest of the picture—poorly selected topics, deadly dull and uninspiring sermons, ignorant leaders of discussions unworthy to be led, horseplay and clever impertinence in the ascendancy at one time and disgust at another, with the whole business a dread nightmare to the teacher.

It is tragic for a school or a community to consider such nonsense "guidance," and it is a caricature of guidance to permit it to go on. Most of the ineffectiveness or worse is due to obvious causes. Some could be removed; others are probably inherent in the situation.

1. School administrators have not grasped the full significance of the guidance movement, have not realized that it is a major administrative responsibility, and are too often oblivious to its local opportunities for disservice.

2. Every teacher is not qualified to be a leader in realizing the five objectives of group guidance which have been mentioned. To make a guidance period both pleasurable and profitable to every member of the group is one of the most difficult tasks assigned to secondary teachers. Inquiries and surveys on both secondary and college levels have consistently revealed that administrators themselves do not consider over one third of their instructional corps qualified for guidance service. If guidance is an every-teacher assignment it must be credited to one of the following: (1) a totally inadequate conception of the functions of guidance and the requirements it makes upon those who attempt to serve youth in this area, (2) an inflated idea of the teacher's capacity to perform any assigned function, or (3) the carry-over from the original use of the homeroom as a minor administrative unit.

3. The functions allocated to homerooms are too diversified; if implemented for minor administrative duties they cannot be equally well implemented for guidance functions.

4. When homerooms are the only guidance media, it is hopeless to expect any worth-while assistance in occupational choice or in educational guidance beyond the boundaries of the community. Orientation to local conditions, immediate educational choices, and problems of social conduct is as wide a range of service as it is justifiable to expect. A very good classroom teacher may lack the broad liberal education which is essential to the sort of impromptu readiness demanded of those who perform guidance

functions. Another teacher, equally good in her own field, may lack the time, energy, alertness, or interest essential to keep abreast of current happenings in which guidance values inhere and which serve as co-ordination topics for knowledge in many fields. It is quite safe to assume that the majority of even the best of teachers are illiterate in occupational subjects.

5. Classroom instructional methods are not adapted to the type of group discussion which accents the advisory function, and few teachers understand the techniques of group conferences which keep this function in the foreground.

6. The utilization of whatever goes on during the homeroom period for parliamentary practice is the last straw which voids the possibility of its functioning as a guidance medium.

7. Programs are too stereotyped, too much like the old normal-school lesson plans, and topics are neither interesting nor instructive.

However, even with the odds against them, homerooms at their best have possibilities as useful media for the exercise of informal group guidance functions. If the word "guidance" has fallen into such disrepute that it will stigmatize any service which carries its name, the word may be dropped and the guidance period be renamed the "conference period" or something similar which will imply that all participants, the teacher included, will confer or consult together. If the topics have been lacking in appeal or have savored of ulterior purposes, a definite understanding relative to student participation in the selection of topics can be arrived at, and assurance can be given—and must be lived up to—that the period is not set aside to teach, to preach, or to guide; to slip something over; to correct bad manners; or to hit somebody over the head of somebody else. There must be full realization of the fact that there are two types of control in any well-conducted school system. Some rules and regulations must be imposed from above through the vertical or line organization; a second type of control may be exercised through horizonal co-operation. The conference period is the time to discuss the *why* of vertical control and the *what* and *how* of horizontal control. If group guidance techniques have been limited to teaching, preaching, boondoggling, and learning parliamentary procedures, the first three techniques might be discarded, parliamentary practice might be allocated to clubs, and some one or more of the most successful group-conference techniques might be studied by the group and chosen for tryouts. But with the best of names, topics, and techniques, the teacher holds the key to the outcome; only her guiding hand in the conference glove can save the situation.

Many of the topics suggested under course content are equally satis-factory for homeroom discussion. In general topics should have both in-spirational and educational values; they should be timely, within the experience of the group, and appropriate to its age and educational level. Since there will be no stereotyped program to cover, no tests, and no credits, the members will be free to select the most interesting topics and will gladly include those suggested by their advisers. Gradually they will learn to select only purposeful topics—those which throw light on com-mon problems, open up new avenues for information and new lines of thought, lead to unity or loyalty in supporting school, college or com-pany policies, and the like. They will also learn to avoid unsuitable topics or personal topics which reflect on individual group members and cause resentment, often a defense reaction.

If it be agreed that homeroom topics should be selected primarily to meet the needs of youth as youth sees them rather than as educators as-sume them to be, informational data for use in connection with their con-sideration will be exceedingly varied and cannot, as has been advocated for specific courses dealing with orientation or educational and occupa-tional data, be collected in advance and filed. Frequently, both with ref-erence to pupil- and adviser-suggested topics, it is the accidentally found informational data which suggest the topic rather than the reverse. As an example, one sees a cartoon in the paper; it suggests a line of thought which results in a discussion topic; the informational data which bring out the cultural ramifications of the topic are rounded up and integrated, and finally are translated into occupational information, revealing among other things how dependent the commercial artist is upon a broad cultural background.[28] The training in mental alertness and in discriminating judgment which is acquired in recognizing and selecting suitable current topics is very valuable.

The advisory function in a group guidance or homeroom situation very definitely outranks the informational function, although both are essential. It is a most difficult function to perform effectively, and its diffi-culties are commensurate with its importance. It is omnipresent and in continuous operation, but never conspicuous and rarely obvious. Its rep-resentative is in absolute control, always by virtue of his advisory func-

[28] Pupils in the elementary and junior-high-school grades have, to this writer's knowl-edge, initiated group conferences based on newspaper items dealing with current hap-penings under such captions as The Children's Crusade, The Trojan Horse, The War Service of (any one of several animals), and The Value of Trade-Marks. With the advice and assistance of broadly educated teachers the guidance possibilities of such topics are unlimited.

tion and never by display of his control function. Its representative is the leader, but he always leads through the led. He imposes no dicta and makes no decisions, but his modus operandi is such that group dicta and decisions are wisely made. He is eternally vigilant for opportunities to serve individuals whose group reactions indicate personal needs. He sees to it that the advisory function does not confine its service to times of crises, but that by its continuous operation it builds up a reserve of anticipatory knowledge and experiences which tend to prevent useless crises, or if they are unavoidable, to meet them as they come with added strength for new trials rather than with disastrous defeat. Moreover, those who are best qualified for group guidance responsibilities realize that every group guidance activity has a dual educational objective, namely, to see that each member of the group grows with the group as a member of the group and at the same time develops his own individual powers which differentiate him or make him unlike the other members of the group. This is what Dr. Plant has so aptly called the "artist's balance" between the values which derive from being lost in the group and those that come from remaining an individual.[29]

With bona fide leaders or advisers, student-programed conferences, whether under the aegis of homerooms or other agencies, have exceptional possibilities for productive self-guidance as well as for preparing members of the group for the assumption of co-operative civic responsibilities.

TECHNIQUES OF GROUP GUIDANCE

Part II has included a number of references which deal with the tools and techniques available for offering guidance service through group media, and frequent reference to such implements has been made. Some have served at one time as tools and at another as techniques. This work does not purport to consider all the tools and techniques available for group guidance. Other publications have done so and no supplementation is, at present, necessary. This section, therefore, is concerned with instructional methods and conference methods, plus such combinations of the two as may be desirable for the accomplishment of any given guidance objective.

Previous sections of this chapter have noted that instructional methods are apt to be stressed when classes and courses are the media and when dissemination of fundamental information is prerequisite to the operation of the advisory function. They have also noted that the guidance values of some topics are better realized through informal discussions in which

[29] *Op. cit.*, p. 78.

the instructional method has a minor role while the conference technique becomes of major importance. This latter technique entails exchange, comparison, and evaluation of the opinions, experiences, and knowledge of the members of the group. The necessary information is woven in as the discussion proceeds and as statements made by different individuals are accepted or challenged. The more informal the group medium, as a rule, the less the instructional method will be used and the more definitely the conference technique will gain ascendancy. Some topics included in course content are admirably adapted to conference methods, while much homeroom guidance should proceed by conference rather than by instructional techniques.

Instructional Techniques. The instructional techniques in the guidance areas of education do not differ materially from those used in imparting information in other areas of education and require no special treatment. The use of radio, moving pictures, occupational workbooks, and self-evaluation books and the preparation for visits to industrial plants and to community service organizations followed by discussion on what was observed and learned during such visits involve well-known methods of instruction.

Addresses on various topics, "college days," and occupational conferences have been in vogue many years, always with the informational objective dominating. Certain difficulties have been encountered, and where possible are being lessened or eliminated; more attention is being given to the selection of suitable speakers; instructions and address outlines are being issued to those who accept invitations to speak; and discussion topics and questions are being prepared in advance. The latest innovation, which promises well if it can be carried out successfully, is the institution of a program for the appraisal of all phases of the conference including the contribution of the guest speakers—both those who give the opening inspirational address and those who lead occupational or choice-of-college discussions. Roughly the procedure is about as follows: three guest appraisers are chosen all of whom attend the opening address and rate the speaker on certain qualities; group discussions are apportioned among the appraisers to be sure that all are covered and each leader of a group discussion is rated on certain qualities; and the general atmosphere of the conference is noted, its organization, the attitude of attendants, both parents and students, etc. After the conference the appraisers join the responsible local authorities in consideration of the strong and weak points and in tentative determination of dos and don'ts for the succeeding year. It is needless to state that it is exceedingly difficult to secure appraisers who are competent to appraise and that considerable embarrassment on both sides is involved in the rating of speakers who are gracious enough to donate their services.[30]

Many colleges and secondary schools hold annual vocational conferences. Some publish their reports; others make stenographic reports or summaries of the high points for their own files.

From the many conference reports available, a student summary of the personal qualifications to be considered by one who is contemplating preparation for the profession of dentistry has been selected for presentation. The address, stenographically reported in toto, was made in 1939 at the Oneonta (New York) High School by Dr. Joseph Pondolfino, a former student at the school.[31] The summary is characteristic of the type of material which was offered on all aspects of the occupation:

Now the question—"What are the personal qualifications for Dentistry?" You are not excluded from the profession if you have big hands or do not have a light fingered touch. For example, one of the doctors at the University's Dental School had larger hands than Primo Carnera and yet he always got out of a mouth what he went after. Dentistry is comprised of a multitude of occupations. If I am to prepare a cavity for a gold inlay, I must be an engineer and designer. If I make a plate, I must be a cabinet maker. In designing the plate I must be a molder. In polishing a gold filling I must know the work of a goldsmith. To remove teeth, I must be a surgeon. When I diagnose a malady in a person's mouth, I must be a physician. In matching a tooth for color when putting in artificial teeth, I must be an artist. As a dentist is sole owner of his business and equipment, I must be a businessman and therefore have to handle the business end of the profession. I must be a good bookkeeper, a filing clerk, a stenographer and a telephone operator. I must be a teacher to educate my patients how to care for their teeth and sometimes a dentist is called upon to do such seemingly impossible things that perhaps he should also be a magician.

So don't ask yourself what qualifications you must have. The qualifications are so numerous that I might say that the first qualification should be adaptability —adaptability to any and all kinds of work. And remember that dentistry is a vocation that plays tag with the nerves.

Conference Techniques. Conferences which are based on informational addresses followed by discussion stand midway between instructional methods and another type of conference technique which, although by no

---

[30] This writer has never attended a conference so conducted but she has assisted in the programing of three or four. Richard J. Bailey, a colleague in the Personnel Department at New York University and an assistant in the preparation of this volume, served as an appraiser at two conferences. Without overlooking the difficulties involved, he considered the experiment worthy of trial.

[31] Annual conferences are held in the Oneonta Senior High School, Edna M. Lawrence, Vice Principal and Counselor in charge. This material is published with her permission and that of Dr. Pondolfino.

means new, has in recent years received considerable attention from leaders in the adult education movement, and which it would seem might be modified and more generally used as a group guidance technique on the college and secondary school level. Designations vary, the most common being "round table," "forum," "symposium," "conference," and "panel." Techniques also vary, but procedures are sufficiently alike to permit their consideration as a unit under the single topic, conference techniques. This technique is given major attention, not because it is more useful than other group methods but because it is less familiar to teachers and counselors and therefore may have a suggestion which will be new to some.

The writer's first contact with a conference of the type reported in the following pages occurred about twenty-five years ago when foremen's conferences were becoming increasingly popular and were proving to be effective methods of accomplishing several tasks which have counterparts in education. For example, the objective of such a conference might be to upgrade foremen transforming them from old-time production taskmasters into teachers. "Every foreman a teacher" was a plant slogan before "Every teacher a counselor" became a slogan in the educational world. The Federal Board for Vocational Education assumed leadership in this field, and hundreds of conferences were held among and within different industries. The conferences were usually reported, and the results were used both for their content and as examples of methods of conducting such meetings. Mimeographed sheets for the analysis of problems to be discussed were distributed before the conference, and sheets for evaluating the outcome were distributed at the close.

Reports of conferences held under federal, state, and private auspices were collected by the present writer and studied for suggestions which might be helpful in group guidance discussions under educational auspices, which then as now were not very successful. These experiences, examples, and reports indicated that the problems common to industrial workers and their superiors were very similar to the problems continuously arising in educational groups, and that the possibilities of developing effective horizontal co-operation were shared alike by both groups. Enough suggestions seemed pertinent to warrant a tryout in education, both in courses preparing teachers for educational personnel work and in student groups, if counselors were interested in experimentation. For more than a decade all teachers and counselors who attended the course in Counseling Methods given by the author at New York University from 1924 to 1939 had an opportunity to participate in a demonstration conference patterned after these industrial conferences, and a number of counselors tried the procedure in secondary school programs. Only one, however, carried the experiment through a full semester,[32] and therefore no positive results can be stated. A brief presentation of the procedure with a summary of the opinions of counselors who have tried it, plus the opinions of students who have participated, may have value for those who are seeking experimental methods.

The minimum essentials for a conference are (1) interested participants, (2) a suitable topic, (3) a qualified leader, (4) a summary or report, and (5) some method of co-operative evaluation of the results.

If the participants are present under duress, if for one reason or another they have no interest in the programs, or if they handicap the procedures in one or more of the ways so well known to high-school students, the homeroom teacher's first task is to find some way to change the attitude of the group so that he may have an interested and a co-operative group to deal with. Ability to win and hold the confidence and co-operation of students is a major requirement for any teaching position; therefore, it requires no specific attention with reference to homeroom teachers. But there are inherent in the conference procedure some opportunities which, if diplomatically used, may make important contributions to winning the support and arousing the interest of the group. These opportunities will be revealed as the procedure unfolds, and other specific opportunities may also be uncovered locally.

There is no necessity for further comment on suitable topics since the purposes and topics of conferences are practically the same as those of homeroom programs and are usually conducted with homeroom groups. A suitable topic is always meaningful and within the comprehension of the group, neither too easy nor too difficult. Any topic worthy of discussion should accomplish one or more of the following: broaden the vision, increase knowledge and experience, develop logical thinking, afford opportunities to alter opinions and change attitudes, and lead to effective horizontal co-operation in arriving at decisions and in formulating plans for action. "Cases," analyses of which bring out a variety of choices and afford the basis for consideration of several possible decisions with their probable or possible outcomes, make good topics if the cases ring true. Hypothetical cases are available in print in considerable variety.[33] Local

32 A. Norman Davis, of the Frederick E. Bellows High School, Mamaroneck, New York, in a Field Course Report for 1936–1937 gave a very unusual account of his work with a homeroom group. The methods were presented in detail, and stenographic reports, participation charts, and evaluations of each conference by the students were included. The results were very promising, and had the report been published, it would have contained many suggestions for others who have charge of homeroom programs.

33 There are two fairly common criticisms on hypothetical cases: (1) They are too easy or do not fit the local situation. (2) If they are re-used, pupils, via the grapevine method, are forewarned as to their content and lessons, lose interest, and grow to regard the whole program as fictitious.

cases involve the risk of identification with attendant unfortunate consequences, but if any individual in the group desires to prepare his own case study from the personal inventory and ask the group to advise with him on his next step, there is sure to be an enthusiastic response. In a number of instances several senior students one after the other have brought their own cases before their fellows for consultation.

Should controversial problems be avoided? This is a perennial question which cannot be answered without knowing the type of controversy involved and something of the local situation with reference to the controversy. There would seem to be no reason for side-stepping controversial topics which have general value if they are within the comprehension of the group, nor would it seem wise to avoid all local controversies; but discriminating judgment is essential in determining which to include and which to reject. When such topics are permitted, it requires very alert leadership to insist that the discussion be maintained on a strictly objective, nonpartisan basis and that each participant be obliged to defend his position. Well handled, such topics are very challenging and thought-provoking, and an excellent preparation for the assumption of the duties of citizenship.

Since qualified leadership is an essential factor in an effective conference and since broad knowledge, wide experience, diplomatic skill of a high order, and a personality which invites confidence and commands respect are important components of a qualified leader, it is obvious that club organization focused on parliamentary training objectives is taboo in such a setup. If the teacher can qualify as a leader, the conference method will be successful; otherwise it will fail.[34] And the teacher has no easy job. The usual classroom devices for motivation of students are discarded; the teacher-pupil relationship fades into the background, but the leadership responsibility for motivation and for stimulation and guidance of thought toward the realization of the objective by the group must be performed from the side-lines. Orders imposed from above may be challenged or rejected by subterfuge, while a conference group under proper guidance, if given a chance, will often convince itself of the desirability of the same order and will be active in its enforcement.

The leader sees that the problem or topic is clearly stated and placed on the blackboard and that unfamiliar words are defined; he sees that no time is wasted, that no local gossip creeps in, that no personal slams or

[34] Davis (see p. 260 n.) reported that the possibility of leading a conference had great motivation value among his students. Those who were allowed to try worked very hard for the opportunity, and he felt that were the teachers to act as leaders long enough to have the methods and responsibilities thoroughly understood, gradually students would be able to assume leadership.

cheap jokes lower the tone of the conference or defeat its purpose. The group analyzes the situation, suggests possible courses of action, distinguishes between subjective and objective contributions, determines which factors shall be given consideration in arriving at a decision, weighs the probable or possible outcomes of the different courses of action, and suggests methods of meeting difficulties which might arise. A chart showing the relationship between the courses of action suggested, the difficulties which may be involved in carrying out each, and possible ways of overcoming each difficulty may be placed on the board and will serve to focus the attention of the group on each item in relation to all other items.

TOPIC OR PROBLEM:

Subtopics or units involved	Possible solutions or methods of handling	Obstacles likely to be met in each effort at solution	How each difficulty may be overcome
1			
2			
3 etc.			

CHART II.—Problem analysis sheet.

Chart II, similar to the sheet used by the Federal Board for Vocational Education immediately after the passage of the Smith-Hughes Law for training foremen and vocational teachers, has been very satisfactory for this purpose and is usually copied in student notebooks. Of course it must be adapted to each topic.

During the collection of the evidence the leader is very busy. Among his important responsibilities are: (1) To think ahead of the group; to anticipate difficulties and, where possible, to prevent sins of omission and of commission. (2) To avoid short-circuiting the thinking of the group or showing impatience when the discussion proceeds too slowly; students must be given a chance to think through their own problems. (3) To hold the group to the subject or to bring it back if it wanders or gets lost. This may be done by an "overhead question," by citing a "case," by the use of illustrative material, or by filling in some gap in knowledge—whatever serves to reintroduce the main thread of the discussion. (4) To utilize the talent of the few for the benefit of all and, at the same time, to promote the participation of all and prevent a small minority from monopolizing the period, thus defeating the purpose of the conference. The weaker members must grow with the group. (5) To be on the alert for personal reactions which are danger signals or suggest counseling needs. (6) To help the group develop habits of listening, challenging, and appreciating the opinions of others, of being good sports under criticism, of differentiating between facts, opinions, and wishful thinking. Growth in ability to determine when opinions are worthy of consideration, whose opinions and why is also important.

An alert leader will keep the discussion alive and moving in the direction of an ultimate objective until all the facts have been assembled. When the evidence is all in and decisions are to be reached or conclusions drawn, he will suggest and encourage methods of evaluation which involve growth in discerning real issues in spite of flowery language and fluent tongues. Rules for weighing evidence, determining upon valid inferences, and recognizing and rejecting common fallacies, will be brought up continuously until students are thoroughly familiar with them and at home in their use.

A report of some kind which gives the results of the conference is the next step. Conference reports play a very important part in the ultimate success of any conference, and they make a major contribution to the satisfaction of the participants. Two types of reports are cited. The first includes the contributions of the different members to the discussion. This may be a stenographic report if some member of the group is qualified and willing to undertake the task; if not, the accepted data and the summary or conclusion may be taken from the blackboard and from student notebooks. The second type of report, presented in chart form, is primarily a record of participation.[35] It has considerable motivation value for the entire group, corrective values for monopolists, and inspirational values for those who may aspire to attempt leadership. Even in counselor-training groups when the two-hour period ended and the clear-the-building signal rang, no one wanted to leave until the participation chart had been shown.

Chart III on page 266 represents a demonstration conference. The participants comprised teachers, counselors, and social workers; one member

---

[35] The use of the chart in this form to report classroom participation was suggested by the chart used by Frank Cushman to represent foreman conferences. The group concerned was small, consisting of adults, and was seated around a table with the leader one of the group. Obviously the table-seating is a great asset as it tends to force interseat exchange of opinions rather than exchange through the leader and it does not set the leader apart from the group and give him so much undue prominence as does the classroom method of seating.

was chosen as leader. "Minority Groups" was the topic. It was selected by the group because, just at the moment, several participants were facing troublesome problems in school or community and wondered to what extent others were similarly situated and how best to meet the difficulties. There was no stenographic report; the blackboard was extensively used, and each individual took such notes as he desired. The summary had four sections; two were given to describing or contrasting minority and majority groupings, and two dealt with personal or group and community responsibilities for understanding that there were both desirable and undesirable features of such groupings, and for making co-operative efforts to foster the former and to discourage the latter. About one half of the items under the first two divisions are reproduced; divisions three and four contained rather long statements and several cases, hence bare facts as to the type of material are all that it is feasible to include.

Section 1. Minority and majority groups are not static. They are frequently regrouped so that each of us, under one condition or another, may at one time belong to a minority group and at another to a majority. Or at the same time we may belong to several groups, some minority, others majority. As examples of groups to which one might belong and at one time be a minority and at another a majority member, the following were suggested:

(1) Married or single people; men or women; young, middle-aged, or old people.
(2) Tall or short people; fat or thin people.
(3) People of black, white, yellow, or red races.
(4) Blonds or brunets.
(5) People born in or citizens of different countries.
(6) Religious groups.
(7) Special ability groups, music, art, debate, etc.
(8) Students or working people; college or noncollege people.
(9) Handicapped groups of various types to some one of which most of us would belong.
(10) Political parties, now minority, again majority.
(11) Social and service clubs, Rotary, Daughters of the American Revolution, Masons, local clubs, etc.
(12) Labor organizations, nonunion groups.

Section 2. Both groups and individual members of such groups are apt to face problem situations, sometimes pleasant and sometimes unpleasant, caused by the fact that they are members of majority or minority groups. One is not justified in assuming that a stigma attaches to a minority. Many times great credit is attached to membership in a minority group while the stigma goes to the majority. The enlargement of some groups, e.g., service clubs, college clubs, sororities and fraternities, destroys the value of membership. The minority group is more selective, sometimes for better, sometimes for worse.

(1) Sensitiveness to low grades, as an individual or as a minority, when a majority have high grades, might change to indifference or to complete satisfaction were the groups reversed. One who was quite indifferent to high standing in a large group might feel quite distinguished as a member of a small group.

(2) Overweight or excessive height leads to embarrassment if all or most of the others are of average height and weight. If the majority have the same physical characteristics, there is no embarrassment.

(3) Religious preference may put a person in a very favorable position at one time, at another the situation may be unfavorable.

(4) A lone man in a group of women feels "like a fish out of water"; he feels like a "man among men" in another situation.

(5) An older woman may be the preferred applicant for one position, a totally unsuitable applicant for another.

(6) Membership in the minority political party may exclude a person from certain types of positions. When the situation changes his former competitor joins the minority group and he takes over majority duties and rewards.

Section 3. This section gave suggestions to relieve the tension and mitigate the evils which sometimes arise in connection with minority-majority groups. The summary covered two major topics. Many highly interesting cases were cited, and a variety of solutions depending, to some extent, on local conditions were discussed.

(1) If I were in an embarrassing situation due to membership in the "wrong" group, what would I like members in the "right" group to do?

(2) If the situation were reversed, what would I be willing to do?

Section 4. How can an individual or a community counteract or minimize a tendency to form majority and minority groups on undesirable bases and foster their development on desirable bases?

The meanings of "undesirable" and "desirable" received attention, and criteria were discussed. What makes a youth gang desirable or undesirable? Passion, unkind and thoughtless comments, prejudice, suspicion, sensationalism, etc., all play some part in group formations.

The second form of report, Chart III, shows the extent to which each member of the group participated, and the contribution made by the leader. It should be read as follows: there were sixty-one seats in the classroom; fifty-three were occupied; the leader occupied the instructor's seat. Two charts were made, by the occupants of seats 36 and 51 neither of whom otherwise participated in the discussion. The occupant of seat 58 volunteered for the blackboard work and did not participate in the discussion. Arrows on each line extending from a seat to the leader or from one seat to another indicate the number of contributions made by each

participant. As a rule arrows which point toward the leader mean tha[ ]
the comment or question was general and not directed to any particula[r]
individual; arrows which point away from the leader usually indicate tha[t]
the comment or question was in response to some statement by anothe[r]
participant. Interseat lines indicate direct communications between tw[o]

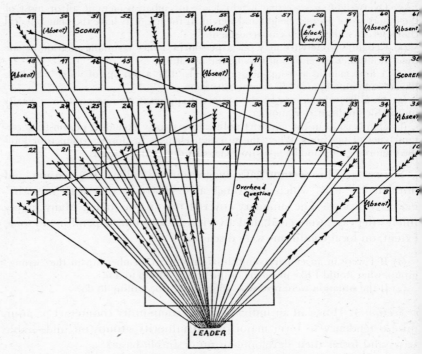

CHART III.—Conference participation (teachers and counselors).

participants. "Overhead questions" show leader contributions, replies t[o]
questions, informational statements, and questions designed to shut o[ff]
personal controversies, lead the thinking back to the original topic, hea[d]
off a too talkative participant, and the like.

From the point of view of participation this was a satisfactory confer[ ]
ence; twenty-five out of a possible fifty persons participated; neither se[ ]
dominated; none abused the participation privilege; the leader's part wa[s]
reduced to the minimum; and there was as much direct seat to seat di[s]
cussion as could be expected in so large a group with classroom metho[d]
of seating.

Chart IV shows a second participation report. It represents the fifth i[ ]

Davis' series of semester reports which were in his project. The classroom method of seating is again a handicap, but the group is smaller and participation more general; twenty-three out of twenty-five members were present; two were used as reporters, and fifteen of the remaining twenty-one took part. The leader, who was the homeroom teacher, made few per-

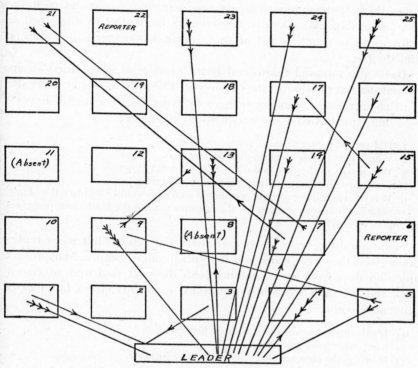

CHART IV.—Conference participation (secondary homeroom).

sonal contributions while seat to seat participation was above the average for secondary school groups.

Co-operative appraisal is an interesting and beneficial phase of a secondary school conference. It might begin with the showing of the participation chart by the member of the group who has made it. Of course it is self-explanatory, but memoranda of high-school conferences indicate that if the situation is favorable, the showing may be accompanied by an interpretative remark now and then to very good advantage. The following are copied from comments which, the conditions being what they were, were thought to be helpful:

Look at this! I'm afraid we let the teacher do too much talking.

Right here [no names mentioned but pointing to the location on the chart] someone was having a sort of soliloquy.

Here are three who didn't have a chance today. Let's give them the first chance next week. Shall we?

The chart gives both the group and the leader a good participation picture—the proportion who took part; how many too often or not at all; the sex, scholarship, and interseat distribution; the number of suppressed or unco-operative members and of antagonistic or too aggressive members, and the like.

Davis also followed the federal board practice of distributing an appraisal sheet at the close of the conference. The purpose was to secure student co-operation in making homeroom programs more useful. Reports were not signed. Among the ten questions asked were:

1. Did you like the program? Why, or why not?
2. Which part of the program did you like best?   Why?
3. Which part of the program did you like least?   Why?
[Several questions omitted here dealt with material.]
9. Was the conference a waste of time? If so where would you place the blame?
10. Have you any suggestions for the improvement of the homeroom programs, in topics, methods, etc.?

Some questions received comparatively few replies, but when replies were given they were frank and helpful. Replies from the Mamaroneck question sheet have been combined with those received from other centers, and the most frequently mentioned comments give a fair idea of student response:

(1) It's the first program we've all been interested in.
(2) I got some good new ideas.
(3) It brings the class members [seniors] closer together.
(4) I like other people's ideas.
(5) Keep on with more occupations, banish stunts.
(6) A more interesting question than usual today.
(7) The boys need a program on etiquette.
(8) The problems should be more complicated.
(9) Many boys are looking for an answer to what we discussed today. It helped.
(10) There are many such cases every day.
(11) Many girls face just this situation; it helped me.
(12) It didn't have anything to do with my life.
(13) About a girl for a change, and very near home.
(14) We have our own problems, and such topics help us to find our way.
(15) More diversified topics, please.
(16) It wasn't an interesting topic.
(17) Not enough sides to this topic.
(18) A question I may need to decide soon. We're all going to work somewhere.

(19) We are the same age as that girl; we know how she felt.
(20) There wasn't time enough to discuss all sides.
(21) A good topic. There's too much graft around.
(22) Topics are too easy; we don't have to think much.
(23) Let's never go back to jokes and stunts.
(24) It seems a long time between discussions.
(25) Could we cut out officers and let each leader work for his chance?
(26) Could we bring in our own cases? Talk about ourselves and get help for ourselves?

Three topics were so frequently suggested that they are quoted:

How can we get along better with our teachers?
What makes a person popular?
Why do people who fail in school often get the best jobs later?

Student appraisal will, logically, be supplemented by teacher or leader appraisal. A one-conference appraisal does not usually extend beyond a comparison of reactions to the new procedure with habitual reactions to the old, the extent and character of participation, the general atmosphere including the attitude and interest of the group, and any appraisals or comments which may be secured from the students. Listening for student comments as they pass from the room is an excellent initial method of appraisal.

If repeat conferences are carried on over an entire semester, appraisal facilities will be expanded and the extent of their use will depend upon the individual teacher or leader. Some appraisals will not extend beyond a few items such as the attendance, the eagerness expressed for the arrival of homeroom day, the disappearance of the atmosphere of boredom accompanied by a tendency to frown on previously enjoyed jokes and stunts, or a constantly growing interest in guidance—or in the new techniques, for one must not overlook the fact that the conference method uses techniques which can be made very fascinating to youth irrespective of any guidance objectives or values. Other appraisals will include evidences of group and individual growth and of interest in and willingness to work to qualify for tryout as a leader, to prepare cases for discussion and to make suggestions for increasing the value of the discussions.

The faculty leader will also appraise his own leadership. He knows that there is a chance for development at every stage of conference procedure from choice of topic to appraisal of results, and he will extend his appraisal system to himself, continually challenging the quality of his leadership: Did I secure and hold the attention of my group? Did I adequately control participation? Did I impose my opinion, or did I guide group thinking toward realization of the objective? What evidence have

I that my charges are making progress in analytical habits of thought, in weighing evidence, in uncovering fallacies, and in arriving at valid conclusions? What evidence is there that conference content and method have guidance values and are being used by students in making personal choices and solving personal problems?

CHAPTER XIV

The Counseling Interview

CHAPTER XIII has cited several group methods which are used for the purpose of disseminating certain types of information and of affording opportunities for general consideration of topics which may, or may not, have guidance implications. No claim has been made for the inclusion of such activities in toto as bona fide guidance or personnel services. On the other hand, it seems legitimate to assume that such conferences and such classes, when properly implemented and conducted, have not only instructional and informational value, but open the door to many ways of self-guidance, lead participants to question their choices and challenge their abilities to meet the requirements of their educational and occupational preferences, and suggest the desirability of seeking personal advice. Group activities also afford observant leaders an opportunity to detect individual needs and to present to the group hypothetical individual inventories in such fashion that here and there some student may be helped to visualize more clearly his own problems and their possible solutions.

Chapter XIV is devoted to the elaboration and the further implementation of Parsons' third, and last, guidance service requirement: "To help [the individual] in true reasoning on the relation of these two groups of facts." This procedure Parsons called "counseling," and his term seems to be in harmony both with the traditional and the presently prevailing point of view. "Counseling" implies consulting together, examining and interpreting together such portions of the two series of data as are pertinent to the problem at hand. It assumes deliberative judgment on the data opening the way for self-decision on the part of the client. And, since the ultimate objective of all counseling is the progressive development of the individual in ability to make choices and solve problems independently, counseling has an educational objective and is an educational technique. However, since education includes many other services and procedures, some of which neither require nor include the counseling function, it does not seem either logical or desirable to consider counseling synonymous with education.

Interviewing,[1] which is the only technique available for counseling, is so intimately related to it in its personnel or guidance significance that the two words are sometimes used singly and interchangeably rather than conjointly: interviewing implies counseling, and counseling cannot take place without interviewing. It is hoped that the content of Chapter XIV—

(1) May be helpful to counselors in determining what is and what is not counseling.

(2) May make it clear that doing a stereotyped list of things called "counseling" does not necessarily mean that they are "counseling."

(3) May motivate interest in the art of interviewing and encourage conscious practice in the application of the art.

(4) May be an incentive to continuous evaluation of the effectiveness of counseling.

(5) May indicate how the two series of tools available to counselors used, now one and now the other, during the interview may result in suggesting new leads and opening up additional opportunities for service.

CLASSIFICATION OF INTERVIEWS

Interviews are of many types, are held for a variety of purposes, and take place under very different conditions as to environmental factors. They may be classified according to purpose: (1) to get information, (2) to give information, (3) to get or to give advice, (4) to secure an employee or a position, (5) to secure or grant some favor, or (6) to get or to give therapeutic aid. Such a classification seems to be sufficiently inclusive to cover interviews with physicians, lawyers, priests, G-men, and politicians, as well as with teachers, counselors, visiting teachers, psychologists, friends, employees, and employers. Again interviews may be classified according to the major area or field in which the topic of the interview seems to lie: physical, medical, or health, educational, religious, social, mental, vocational, economic, and the like.

Such modifiers as "survey," "initial" or "preliminary," and "exit" or "dismissal" are sometimes used to indicate at what stage of the institutional or personal relationship any given interview has taken place. "Voluntary" and "involuntary" or "compulsory" are used to indicate with which party the initiative lies. Classification as "planned," "anticipated," or "prepared" interviews and as "cold" interviews distinguishes between those for which the interviewer has had access to previously collected data regarding the individual, with time and opportunity to study it, and

---

[1] For an outstanding treatment of many types of interviews, see Walter V. Bingham and Bruce V. Moore, *How to Interview* (3d ed., rev.; New York: Harper and Bros., 1941). Chapter II contains fifty-five general suggestions for beginners.

those for which he must rely upon collecting his data as the interview proceeds.

Classifications on the basis of the age, sex, education, or economic status of interviewees are also common and useful. Any experienced interviewer who has maintained classified records of interviews knows that it is unprofitable and useless to attempt to make either one inclusive classification or a number of classifications which will be mutually exclusive. Overlapping is unavoidable and even desirable if it be an indication that interviewers are cognizant of the Hydra-headedness and interrelation of all personal problems and of the necessity for utilizing procedures which tend to aid the individual in the integration of personality.

Statistical records of interviews classified on one or more bases are usually desirable, but there is no rule as to how many or what classifications shall be used. Since they are maintained primarily for their research values, the items to be classified should be determined by the information useful to the agency or institution concerned. During the decade, 1929–1939, the author served in the dual capacity of Professor of Education at New York University and Director of the Bureau of Personnel Service maintained by the National Personnel Service, Inc. The two functions were performed from the same office at the University and approximately eighteen thousand counseling interviews were held during the ten-year period. Various classifications of interviews were made, each designed to serve some specific purpose or reply to some specific question, e.g., Did a free consultation service operating at a university center attract only registrants or alumni of that institution or did it appeal to the clientele of other institutions? Did its location tend to eliminate noncollege persons who otherwise might have sought and profited by its services? What percentage of the interviewees fell into each educational level group? What percentage fell into each age and sex group? What motivated application? In what field or area of life did the specific objective for which the interview was sought primarily belong, and what were the secondary or allied areas? To what types of problems was the Service able to respond without the assistance of other agencies? When referral was desirable, what were its main adjunct agencies? Analysis of the various statistical replies served to indicate trends, suggest changes and improvement in policies, and eliminate useless duplications of local and national services.

Much more important, however, than any classification of interviews is the obligation of remembering that the counseling interview, irrespective of its classifications, is always a method of education, always personal, always purposive, and should be always professional. Many times it has a sales element, an element of motivation or persuasion, even though such element be carefully concealed. It is also important to remember that no sharp line can be drawn between the different purposes for which interviews may be used. They are always at the command of parents, teachers, counselors, and interviewers, and they may be used either as tools for fact collection or as a technique for counseling. Sometimes their very convenience leads to abuses in their use. Counselors are urged to avoid such abuses, but to be ever alert for opportunities to use the interview to reveal facts which verify or supplement previously collected information about the individual. It is hard to conceive of a "cold" counseling interview which does not serve in a dual capacity as a tool for fact finding and as a technique for counseling.

PREPARATION FOR COUNSELING INTERVIEWS

Two types of interviews with reference to opportunity to make specific previous preparation have been mentioned: the one is based upon more or less abundant and previously collected information regarding both opportunities and facilities for service and regarding the individual to be interviewed; the other is dependent upon general knowledge comprised in both series of data plus what the counselor is able to uncover through observation and the content of the interview. Is it then impossible to make any previous preparation for the second type of interview? Of course not. *Previous preparation is possible for any interview, but in one case it is general,* preparation for *an* interview, *while in the other instance it is specific,* preparation for *the* interview.

Were the possibility of previous preparation for interviewing to be denied, efforts to assist beginners in laying a foundation for future interviewing would be futile. For even though there is general agreement that successful interviewing is the result of experience rather than of instruction, no one has denied that many simple interview mistakes, resulting from the trial and error system, might be avoided by familiarity with certain fundamental principles and universally successful practices which are available as the result of the experience of others. University courses in Counseling Methods, Case Conferences, and Practicums are offered on the supposition that basic principles and successful procedures will provide a helpful background on which each counselor may build up his own practices as experience furnishes suggestions. Preparation for interviewing may, therefore, be approached from two points of view— the general or long-term and the specific or immediate.

General preparation for an interview presupposes all the background knowledges which derive from familiarity with the two series of data described in previous chapters. And in addition to mastery of these materials it may well include (1) familiarity with types of individuals with whom interviews are likely to be held; (2) knowledge of the major agencies which help to cause or to prevent maladjustments and of the major areas of life within which problems seem to come to a focus on different age and educational levels; (3) understanding of the various influences, both personal and environmental, which form the matrix of problems; and (4) the setting up of some criteria for evaluating one's own potential strengths and weaknesses as a user of the interview technique. Some valuable assistance in this general preparation may be obtained by attending university courses in personnel, by visiting demonstration interviews, case conferences, and guidance clinics, and by taking advantage of every opportunity to gain practical experience in guidance procedures.

The home, the school, and the office, shop, or factory are the three outstanding agencies which form the matrices within which each individual cultivates habits, develops personality traits, and undergoes experiences which forecast ability to make easy and happy adjustments or vice versa. Under the dominance of each of these agencies in turn, many persons are forced to make puzzling choices or solve more or less serious problems. Factors are inherent in all three agencies which at one time and under certain circumstances tend to help individuals make adjustments without friction or emotional strain. Different, or possibly the same, factors at another time and under other circumstances are found to be causal factors in originating or enhancing maladjustments. All three agencies may well be studied for both their positive and negative influences.

Early conditioning in the home has a lifelong influence on youth and more often than not carries over to another generation. During the early years of childhood attitudes are fixed; likes and dislikes are developed; standards of culture are established; attachments, hostilities, or aversions toward races and individuals are absorbed from the attitudes and comments of adults in the home; and an habitual attitude toward authority is fostered by parental attitude toward legal regulations and the mores of the community. Relationships within the family between parent and parent, between parent and child, and between siblings are exceedingly important. Antisocial behavior of parents which mortifies children, divorce or separation of parents which entails divided allegiance, economic insecurity of the home or unemployment of the father, selfishness and overindulgence of one member of the family at the expense of the other members, parental insistence upon educational achievement beyond the abilities of children, and efforts to prolong dependency beyond reasonable limits are suggestive of the unfortunate home situations with which all social interviewers are familiar long before the children are old enough to enter school. And it is in such home situations that children become problems to their parents, parents become problems to their children, and both become problems to themselves, to their friends, and often to their community.

While from the very nature of their work social workers and visiting teachers have less opportunity for contact with the type of home which provides the framework for happy, constructive living, they all realize that every negative home picture has its positive counterpart. Vacillating parents, who make promises on one day only to break them on the next or who from day to day change their policies to such an extent that children never know what to expect, vie with parents whose consistency is expected, respected, and supported by the children. Neglectful parents, whose social or other engagements leave unguided young children to form undesirable habits and make undesirable friends, are in sharp contrast with parents who are always their children's best and most sympathetic friends:

Sally's mother was an ardent Red Cross worker and, with two cars in the family garage, it was her regular habit to leave home before Sally had gone to school. In due course of time, evidences of immoral conduct on the part of six-year-old Sally were reported to the school. Repeated visits by the visiting teacher failed to secure an interview with the mother. Finally Sally delivered an oral communication to the effect that, "Mother is so busy with the Red Cross that she hops into her car right after breakfast and doesn't come back until dinner time." But Mary's mother, who was a widow, became a visiting housekeeper, caring for one apartment between nine and twelve in the morning, and for another between one and three in the afternoon. By such an arrangement she remained at home until Mary had gone to school, was home to prepare lunch for her, and was ready to welcome her at three o'clock and share in the joys and sorrows of her school day.

It is a mistake all too often made to assume that the economic status of the home is the main determining factor in neglectfulness of parents or that the underprivileged child is always the child of the poor. Nervous, nagging, or quarrelsome parents tend to transmit nervousness to children, arouse feelings of resentment toward, or dislike of, the home, induce quarrelsomeness in children, influence them to take sides with or play off one parent against the other, and finally to instill unfavorable attitudes toward marriage and home life. On the other hand, recent research suggests that those who had the advantages during childhood of a harmonious home life and were the witnesses of happy parental relationships are, in their turn, prone to reproduce such desirable relationships in their own homes. Parents who deceive children or teach children to deceive in order to escape criticism or discipline are contrasted with parents who painstakingly help their children to understand the reason for criticism and discipline and the conditions which would be likely to prevail in home and community were all discipline to cease. Emotionally disturbed or emotionally immature parents and well-balanced, mature parents are in evidence in countless American homes and both, through the media of their own personalities, condition the parents of the future. Cold and unsympathetic parents force their children, whose affections are frozen in the home, to seek sympathy and appreciation outside the home and sometimes to develop crushes or to make early and ill-advised marriages. But here too, as in many other illustrations which might be cited, there is a contrasting picture with constructive results.

Parents' associations and other similar organizations are making increasingly fruitful efforts to bring the guidance message home to those who are responsible for starting youth on the road to self-guidance. Educators who are prepared for service on but one level of education are beginning to realize that guidance does not begin in the junior high school, in the senior high school, in the college, or wherever they may happen to be teaching, but in the home. And more and more literature is appearing which throws light on the status of the home in the total guidance picture. As it is usually sponsored by the best research scholars in the child guidance field, it affords would-be interviewers an overview of the many types of homes from which public-school and college students come and of the many types of parents who are potential interviewees.

The school is the second major agency within which youth meets and solves or fails to solve problems and make adjustments. The school in its own right may rival the home in helping to solve, to intensify, or to create problems. However, when the pupil enters school, he usually takes with him a bundle of habits, attitudes, prejudices, and passions which he has accumulated in the home. These are his personality assets and liabilities. Sometimes they fit into the atmosphere and harmonize with the policies of his particular school home and sometimes they do not. If the mores of the one are in harmony with the mores of the other, there need be no break in developmental growth even though, at times, its direction may be deplored. But if the child faces conflicting mores, he may break under the strain or, as frequently happens among children of keen insight into situations and whose home experiences have made them experts in adaptability, he may ease both situations and clear both atmospheres by checking his home-asset bundle when he enters the schoolroom door and by alternately picking up or checking, as he comes and goes, whichever bundle best meets the situation. And who shall say that such youthful insight and foresight may not be an important factor in ability to make successful life adjustments!

Experience, even vicarious experience, with the variety of home standards which have influenced personality development prior to school admission will better prepare teachers and counselors to cope with the many types of interviews which they must conduct as the result of school situations. A number of lists of types of youth and types of problems on different levels of education have been published, sometimes with frequencies. Some are the result of the experiences of counselors, teachers, and social workers; others are made by youth and are expressive of their needs from their own point of view.[2] A study of such lists helps the prospective counselor to realize that he must be prepared to interview all types of youth, who are confronted by choices and problems in every area of life. The longest list, often the most important although frequently entirely overlooked, is concerned with the needs of so-called "normal" or "average" youth. Such youth, if they remain normal in a world which is anything but normal, form the stabilizing element in American life. But because they are or appear to be normal, their everyday problems are often forgotten, and most interviewers are inducted into counseling via the problem child who has already wandered so far astray that immediate attention is necessary.[3]

The restless, bird-witted girl who flits from one task to another and from one thought to another without mastering anything and the imaginative, daydreaming girl both need help in harnessing their abilities to reality. The boy who knows it all and resents authority and control needs

---

[2] See John M. Brewer *et al., Case Studies in Educational and Vocational Guidance* (Boston: Ginn and Co., 1926) and Zoe Emily Leatherman and Edgar A. Doll, *A Study of the Maladjusted College Student* (Columbus, Ohio: Ohio State University, 1925). Brewer discusses 138 problems of various types which youth face in education and employment. Leatherman and Doll list the student problems which came to the dean's office for solution. This is a pioneer study which has been widely used. Its value is not altered by its age as problems remain much the same.

The New York City Y.M.C.A. several years ago prepared a list of 57 questions upon which young men frequently sought advice. The Girl Scouts have a list of the types of girls with which leaders may expect to deal, and there have been many local studies of student problems. This writer has lists of freshman orientation problems in both segregated and coeducational colleges, many lists dealing with working youth, several enumerating sorority and fraternity problems, and a number made out by adult employed groups.

[3] Even though his assigned counseling load be composed entirely of maladjusted or problem cases, the experienced teacher or counselor will find a way to invite the confidences of every pupil and will be concerned with many simple, everyday, spontaneous calls for assistance in making simple, everyday choices and in solving simple, everyday problems.

assistance in understanding that the only substitute for external control is self-control. The boy who longs for personal attention and has longed so long without satisfaction that he cries aloud for some way of gratifying his desire—"How can I get poplicity? I want poplicity. I want to be like Lindbergh. I want to see my name in all the papers" [4]—needs some suitable outlet for his desire for recognition.

On every list the problem of motivation looms large. Failures to achieve educationally, socially, or vocationally are the usual objectives of educational interviewers on the secondary and college level. Financial problems enter the picture in their own right and are contributing factors to other problems. And, duplicating the home situation, students in both secondary schools and colleges include in their list of problems problem teachers—teachers who have never made happy and satisfactory adjustments and whose unsolved problems have just as unfortunate an effect on pupils as do the unsolved problems of parents in the home.

Unless satisfactory adjustments are made prior to adult life, the problems of youth grow up, and the circle of maladjustment is completed when behavior expressive of maladjustment is repeated in adult work life, among teachers and professional workers, and by a second generation of parents. Employees become problems to their supervisors and foremen; employers become problems to employees; governmental authorities and law enforcement officers become problems to citizens; while citizens are problems to them.

As the embryo interviewer studies people, problems, and environmental influences, he will come to appreciate more fully the practical implications of individual differences. He will realize that their number is legion, that "all the world's a stage" and all the individuals thereon are players, and that it will be his duty to aid as effectively as possible this colorful pageant of individualized America to make its adaptation to the realities of American life. In the light of all that will be required of him, how shall he guide himself in determining whether to move ahead in the direction of professional counseling or to fade out of the picture entirely?

One can only advise with him, as he in turn will advise with others, or suggest a few questions which, if they be answered honestly and conscientiously, may help him to arrive at a wise decision: Am I willing to take humanity as it comes, the educationally, socially, emotionally, and morally halt, lame, and blind; the agreeable and the disagreeable; the normal, the neglected, and the spoiled? Will I be able to differentiate the school-dull and life-bright from the school-bright and life-dull and to help discern the potentialities of each? Will I understand both the college

[4] Taken from a list made by young working boys.

student who would, but cannot, and who could, but will not; both the student who is socially and morally literate, whose spirit is willing although the flesh is weak, and the one who is socially and morally illiterate? Will I understand both the irresponsible and the overresponsible parent? Will I realize that delinquencies may be both caused and forestalled by environment? Am I emotionally stable: can I meet and counsel with all these curious human specimens with sympathy and understanding but without sentimental outbursts or emotional upsets? Will I have the patience to help each individual, whether it be his lot to travel the high road or the low road, to find his road to the dawn of day?

From time to time individuals who have sought assistance in determining whether or not to prepare for the counseling field have been asked to bring to the interview two lists—one entitled "My Potential Strengths as a Counselor" and the other entitled "My Potential Weaknesses as a Counselor." Out of approximately two hundred statements under each title a few have been selected for consideration by any who may find them helpful. They have been very useful to this counselor in understanding the motives for choice of this vocation and the personal characteristics of the individual and in guiding toward self-elimination many who would be totally unsuited to the personnel field.

POTENTIAL STRENGTHS AS A COUNSELOR [5]

1. I am courteous and listen to what is said but try not to commit myself.
2. I have had considerable experience in several occupational fields.
3. It is easy for me to get the confidence of people.
4. I have studied the various phases of guidance so that I appreciate that there are more than one or two ways to handle a guidance program.
5. The older I get the more I appreciate how little I know.
6. I have a liberal philosophy of life and respect for the opinions and beliefs of others.
7. I have a love for people and what might be called a psychological insight into behavior.
8. I maintain good nature no matter what the obstacles.
9. I am easily adaptable.
10. I have the ability to get along with the teachers.
11. I have perseverance; if one kind of program won't work, I try another.
12. I am sensitive to attitudes.
13. I have a fairly broad educational background.
14. I have a happy family life.

[5] Does the reader feel that all the statements listed under assets are assets and that all under liabilities are liabilities? Are there conditions under which a listed asset might become a liability and vice versa? Which single statement in either list gives the most significant information regarding the character of the would-be interviewer?

15. I have a fairly wide range of interests.
16. I am free from emotional disturbances and physical defects.
17. I think very rapidly.
18. I am a good listener and learn a lot that way.
19. I am certain I would appreciate the problems of youth, for I doubt if I shall ever grow up.
20. I am willing to accept or ask for criticism.
21. Constant reading along personnel lines has given me a better understanding of the causes of maladjustments.
22. I am a fluent talker.
23. I am patient in manner and attitude.
24. I have the ability to stimulate by questioning.
25. I am interested in people and have some ability in evaluating them.
26. I have the ability to summarize arguments.
27. I have a good personality and am above the average in intelligence.
28. I have ability to lead without forcing my opinion.
29. I carefully review every undertaking, summarize the results, and try to improve on my methods all the time.
30. I am young. Students would rather talk to the young.
31. I am intelligent but not intellectual.
32. I am impartial, not easily prejudiced.
33. I usually grasp an opportunity to render even a little service.
34. I want to get ahead.
35. I can use illustrative material without forgetting the original problem.
36. I am able to help others organize thought by guiding questions.
37. I can keep a confidence.
38. I understand racial differences.
39. I adjust easily to unusual situations.
40. Boys that I try to help always come back.

POTENTIAL WEAKNESSES AS A COUNSELOR

1. I have an aggressive personality which is often misunderstood.
2. I have an inclination to be pedantic.
3. I fail in judging time and so lose the force of summary.
4. I frequently talk too much.
5. I am unable to keep the whole of the subject well in mind as the parts are developed.
6. My background is narrow for vocational counseling.
7. I am a poor "terminator" without a feeling of apology.
8. I sometimes tell a person my opinion of what he ought to do rather than merely help him to readjust his own thinking.
9. I do not like to have to fight continually for my point of view.
10. I lack contacts.
11. I have a rather excitable nature; I am apt to be carried away.
12. I get impatient with the inflexible attitude of some teachers.
13. I have an inferiority complex.
14. I am very self-conscious until I have gotten well into whatever I am doing.

15. I try to be open to conviction but am rather a positive creature.

16. I give too much of myself to certain people, a habit which after all may weaken them.

17. I have a somewhat dogmatic manner.

18. I failed last week in a motivating interview through inability to convince.

19. I lack patience with individuals who "beat about the bush."

20. I use "snap judgment" at times.

21. I cannot see things from the other fellow's side.

22. I am unable to keep records in a systematic manner.

23. I tend to be self-conscious in any sort of interview, particularly with people in any way superior to me, and it is fairly easy for them to beat me out of the dominating position in the interview.

24. My personality is nothing outstanding. While it may not be a liability, it probably belongs more on this side of the ledger than on the other.

25. I have a little "missionary spirit."

26. I have too many ideals.

27. I lack poise.

28. I have a tendency to believe books or instructors even when they disagree with common sense.

29. I have a tendency toward cynicism and sarcasm when disappointed.

30. I am fond of praise.

31. My voice is slightly nasal when I am careless.

32. I am a poor judge of character.

33. I take dislikes to people which I do not hide very well.

34. I have somewhat of a temper.

35. Sometimes I am very challenging in my speech.

36. I have not yet had wide enough experience in counseling. With wider experience I would improve, I believe.

37. I lack ability to bring an interview to a successful, tactful close, fearing that I may hurt the feelings of the interviewee.

38. I am a poor talker.

39. I lack insight into human nature.

40. Sometimes I jump at a conclusion.

Individuals who have taken advantage of as many opportunities as possible to prepare for any type of interview which may fall to their lot have done the best they can to qualify for "cold" interviewing. Since readiness to handle such situations is cumulative, the mental alertness which is developed and the experience acquired in this more difficult type of interviewing will add greatly to the effectiveness with which background information is used in planned interviews.

AN EXAMPLE OF A COLD INTERVIEW

John entered the office unannounced and asked if he might have an interview. The first glance suggested physical and mental inferiority. John stated his problem: he was twenty years of age, a college freshman preparing to teach; his grades were poor; and he was afraid he would flunk at the end of the first semester.

Where might he find a college that would accept him? He talked freely and frankly, and the details for the background of the picture were soon taking shape: infantile paralysis had held up school work and left him with a crippled left arm; there were younger children and there was economic pressure in the home, but his parents wanted him to have a chance for college so that he could earn his living; he had not done well in high school, he had had no "good" subject and he got a bare passing average for his diploma (one of the "complimentary" diplomas the counselor thought); he had taken one test and did not know what it was for, but he got a low mark (probably an intelligence test, and there seemed to be observable evidences that it had been accurately scored); the teachers thought that if he wanted to go to college a teachers' college was best. [Are teachers trying to increase the already sufficient and legitimate criticism of the profession or are they "passing the buck"?]

As he recited his story, visions of similar types of youth who had made their occupational adjustment crowded into the foreground of the picture. The counselor began to soliloquize. Was he interested in this? Probably not. Could he do that? No. Possibility after possibility was eliminated until the routine clerical field stood alone. Perhaps simple filing, letter or numerical. While filing used a wide range of abilities, a low intelligence was acceptable in the simpler operations. The left arm might be strong enough to manipulate files.

John's reactions were consistently unfavorable toward any occupation which did not require a college education. A little salesmanship, a change to the interview of persuasion, seemed wise. It was made. In due course of time John reached the point where he was interested in testing his physical ability to handle files. He was obviously pleased when he found that he had no trouble with drawers or boxes. Then the accent shifted to the useless sacrifice which his parents must make if he went to college, to the probable difficulty of employment, to the large number of school systems which rule out cripples, to the well-known persons who had commenced at the bottom as file clerks and become head of files or file organizers, to the fact that once started in some line of work he could go to evening sessions and complete a college course if he wanted to, to the fact that rehabilitation boards were prepared to train and place physical defectives provided the right sort of training could be agreed upon.

One at a time, at opportune moments, such comments were interjected. The attitude of hostility was disappearing! Would John like to take a rather large number of tests to see if the results would help him to decide because it was such an awfully important matter? Oh, yes! He trusted tests, so did his parents, but they had no money to pay for them. Co-operation was in the offing! It was time to drop persuasion and shift back to counseling together. A program which greatly pleased John was agreed upon.

Three adjunct agencies were called in: (1) a first-class testing bureau offered to give John a battery of tests without charge; (2) a bureau for placing the physically handicapped agreed to interview John for placement
possibilities; and (3) the Rehabilitation Bureau made an appointment
for an eligibility interview.

The testing report rated John in the lowest quartile on every test
except routine clerical where he approached the average. The Rehabilitation Bureau pronounced him eligible for routine clerical training, and
the placement bureau had nothing better to suggest. John and his parents
were pleased, and the story of the cold interview with the test results was
turned over to the Rehabilitation Bureau which took future responsibility
for the case.

Special Preparation for the Interview. General preparation for any interview is the only preparation possible for cold interviewing. This general preparation is just as important as a preliminary for prearranged
interviews, but the situation is somewhat different. Additional specific
information relative to the interviewee and his problems or to the purpose of the interview will be available and will permit specific preparation on the part of the counselor. Of course the quantity and quality of
such information will vary markedly and the form in which it will be
available will also vary. Sometimes tools will be abundant, keen-edged,
and easily handled; at other times they will be few, dull, and difficult to
use. But in any case they will be all that the counselor has, and he must
develop techniques which use to the best advantage even the poorest of
tools. An interesting incident illustrative of the inability of a highly skilled
user of high-grade tools to cope with a situation where only inferior tools
were available comes to mind.

A rather serious problem which was approaching maturity was brought
to a graduate seminar for advice and suggestions. The group, with one
exception, comprised general counselors. One woman had had the very
best of opportunities for professional training. She was appealed to for
leadership. One or two questions regarding the case as reported were
asked, and then came the very decisive statement: "You can't do anything
with that case. It should never have happened, and you haven't a particle
of authentic information. A string of teacher opinions don't mean anything." Too much training if allowed to substitute for something more
important, too much reliance on plenty of first-class tools which are far
from universally available, and too many stereotyped techniques which
operate successfully only in a matrix adjusted to them may presage
failure, where less training, better judgment, and a more resourceful personality might bring at least a modicum of success.

Whatever the information, be it much or little, poorly recorded or re-corded in the most desirable cumulative or case history form, it gives the counselor an opportunity to consider it on the background of his general preparation and he will usually do so. He will analyze it for causal factors, for positive and negative characteristics, for indications of growth or retrogression, for deficiencies in evidence, for leads for the inter-view, for clues to attitudes, and the like. He may also, prior to the inter-view, desire to seek additional information about the individual, to confer with others as to best procedures, or to refresh his memory regarding available community services and educational and occupational oppor-tunities.

Four interviews based on a minimum of advance information are cited, one each from the elementary, secondary and college level, and one on the adult level. No examples of counseling on the basis of approxima-tion to maximum information are offered because many excellent educa-tional cases with rather complete cumulative records are available. A step-by-step analysis of the contribution which each recorded item makes to understanding the total personality of the subject usually accompanies such cases. Counselors who have had professional training will be fa-miliar with such material and appreciate its value. On the other hand, there is a dearth of material on minimum information cases, which after all do, and for many years to come will, form the bulk of counseling cases. There is an equal deficiency in examples in the field of adult counseling where no records can be secured and where habits and patterns of life are already well established and re-education often most difficult. Counselor ability to obtain during the interview a picture of fixed and fluid assets and liabilities and to visualize what may be capitalized on, rather than to assume potentialities as the fundamental factor even though many may be revealed, is an essential to successful counseling on the adult level.

AN ELEMENTARY SCHOOL CASE

Louis' parents moved to a distant town in the same state during the summer. When school opened Louis, who was ten years old and in every way appeared like a normal boy, presented his transfer card and was admitted to the specified grade, 7A. He did not accomplish assigned tasks; he developed personality difficulties, showed signs of emotional upset, avoided class participation, and finally at test periods became nauseated and was obliged to leave the room.

Interview after interview with the father and the boy failed to locate any explanation, but there was cumulative evidence that when the difficulty was located it would be found in the father-son relationship. Louis was obviously afraid of his father and was setting up defense mechanisms against a situation which he could not face. The illness was transferred to the home: on any previously announced examination day nausea developed as soon as Louis left his bed. Medical assistance was refused. Louis was forced to go to school under threat of severe punishment.

The principal took a hand. A very carefully handled interview secured enough leads to indicate that a letter to the former school might bring information which Louis' father had forbidden him to reveal. The leads were followed. Correspondence showed Louis to have been a normal, well-adjusted boy in school; he had been promoted to 5A and should have been able to do entirely acceptable work. His father had made every effort to force "skips" each year since he entered school, but since the school felt that from every angle it would be detrimental, the principal had been adamant. The father had taken advantage of the change in residence to falsify the record and had threatened Louis with various punishments if he either revealed the falsification or failed to do the work.

The facts at hand, a counseling interview with the boy followed. Then came a very difficult interview with the father which passed through several stages before it reached the counseling phase. At last, after subject tests had been given and the results interpreted to the father, he granted the boy's request to enter 5A and agreed to drop all further efforts to push the boy beyond his ability.

A SECONDARY SCHOOL CASE

Caroline wrote for an interview stating that she desired help in choosing a college for the coming year. She was prompt for her appointment, presented herself well, and wasted no time in coming to the point. She was eighteen years of age, lived with her mother, who was the wage-earner, her two sisters, and her grandmother, who had a small income. She was graduating from the girls' high school in June and had brought her complete school record, including scores on achievement and intelligence tests, with her. All grades were far above the average, and she was graduating with honors. Her grandmother had laid away enough money to send her to college if she could live on $750 per year. Her school did not advise on college selection, but on her own initiative she had selected four segregated colleges in different sections of the country and had used catalogue statements to make a budget for each, adding her own figures for travel. Since she could find no information as to the relative standing of either institutions or departments, she hoped she could get help on that point from the counseling service.

In such a case the counselor turns to the files on educational information. He will, perhaps, discuss Class A colleges and show her where the institutions on her list stand. She will reject the two colleges which are not recognized by accepted accrediting authorities. He will, perhaps, show her some of the Pennsylvania Study charts which indicate relative standing and interpret their importance. He may show her a list of scholarship possibilities and suggest that she enlist school help or possibly a college club if there be one, in securing one. Since Caroline's personality is such that she might profit by attending a coeducational institution and since her home and school circle thus far has comprised only her own sex, he may ask why a segregated college has been chosen. As the interview proceeds he will help Caroline to choose two or three colleges which are in a category corresponding to her abilities and needs and which are financially within her possibilities, and he will suggest that in talking them over at home she bring up the question of the values of college association with both sexes. A second interview will usually follow.

A COLLEGE SOPHOMORE'S PROBLEM

James was a scholarship man. The counselor had enjoyed the admissions interview with him the year before and had noted his excellent secondary record, and his freshman year had been a success. Quite suddenly his work in English fell below average; then other subjects showed evidences of some sort of disturbance. Before the matter became too serious James sought an interview. He had been totally unable to concentrate on his work and was losing interest in continuing in college. He was not, he said, a pious boy, nor was he adverse to criticisms and discussions on religion; he often participated in friendly comparisons of the relative merits of different religions. But it had hit him pretty hard when his English instructor, for whose intellectual ability he had great respect and whom he had admired very much, had in a most irreverent and sarcastic tone spoken of his religion as "a sacred cow." Admitting that it was foolish to allow himself to feel as he did, he said that at that moment he seemed to lose all respect for or confidence in what he thought his instructor was, and what he was trying to become, an educated man.

Did he want to go on? Would it be better to leave college? The counselor knew that he was dealing with a very intelligent boy temporarily upset because his confidence had been shaken in something which had seemed worth-while. The success of the interview depended upon the ability of the counselor to help James see the incident in its true light. Discussion brought out that James's disillusionment was natural; that life has many in store for most of us and that we must be prepared to meet them; that the instructor was not a fair example of an educated man; he lacked the all-round culture, intellectual, social, spiritual, etc., that characterizes the educated man. His remark was an example of supremely bad taste, of a lack of reverence and social culture deplorable in one holding a faculty position. It was well for everyone to regret that those who were so well informed in their subjects should be so illiterate in other ways, but such comments were not worthy of notice. James decided to continue on his path toward becoming a better educated man than the one who had so shaken his confidence.

AN UNEMPLOYED ADULT

Mrs. S. applied for admission to a commercial school where she hoped to prepare for stenography. The interviewer questioned the advisability of registering a woman forty-two years old, for even were she able to do the work as well as younger women, she would be very difficult to place. So she asked Mrs. S. to have a talk with the Personnel Service before she made a definite occupational decision and made the appointment for her by telephone, stating that age, a total lack of previous business experience, and the long period of time between her early education and the present would mean the formation of new study habits and that finally there would be the serious problem of placement.

Shortly Mrs. S. appeared. She introduced herself, connecting her visit with the commercial school's telephone call, expressed appreciation of the counselor's willingness to talk with her, realized the legitimacy of the school's hesitancy, but wondered what a woman situated as she was could do to earn her living. She talked freely of her past so that a picture of capacities and incapacities began to take shape and observation filled in a number of gaps, but no leads were offered as to occupational possibilities.

Here was a rather competent-appearing, well-poised, emotionally mature woman, who had made a good home for her physician husband until his recent death but who appeared to have no occupational assets. The questioning continued: What had she done before marriage? Just school work; she had a secondary school education. Since she had no children how had she used her leisure time since marriage? Many activities were mentioned, among them that she often went to the office and helped during rush hours. Here at last might be a clue. Did she enjoy helping in the office? Did her husband think her efficient? Just what things had she done about the office? Finally, in a most casual manner she stated that she could do a number of things which most office assistants could not do because she had had training for nursing and was a registered nurse. It had taken a long time to get this information. Why had she not mentioned it before? She had never practiced and didn't think it meant anything; she had just entirely overlooked it.

In her case it meant practically everything; many possibilities opened up. One at a time they were considered in the light of personal assets. Radiology was her first choice, and her sex seemed to be her major liability. There was a tendency, which seemed to have increased during the depression, to prefer men who were physicians. Did she know what the situation was in her home city? A list of hospital courses was discussed; cities which employed women were gone over, and an appointment was made for a conference with one of the leading hospitals in the city where the interview was being held. The conference resulted in agreement upon a training program after which, if she made good, she would be employed in the hospital.

MATERIAL AND PSYCHOLOGICAL FACTORS WHICH CONDITION INTERVIEWING

The setting for the interview, or the environment in which it takes place, is an important factor in success. Provision for a suitable location easily accessible and free from the implications of disciplinary functions, adequate office equipment, bookcases, and files for the various types of informational material which have been collected, heating, lighting, etc., are regarded as business functions and are mentioned under Part V, which is concerned with administrative responsibilities. If material facilities be adequate and satisfactory, they will be helpful assets; but it is encouraging to remember that contact between mind and mind is the crux of the counseling situation and that this aspect of interviewing environment is largely controlled by the counselor. The counselor creates the atmosphere. His personality is the dominant factor in the first impression which counseling makes upon interviewees, whether they be public-school and college students or adult callers. A personality which radiates cordiality, invites confidence, removes fears and inhibitions, leaves the impression of shock-proof qualities owing to familiarity with the entire range of human strengths and weaknesses, and implies that broad information and wide experience are available on any topic the interviewee may care to discuss will counteract almost any material deficiency which is conceivable. On the other hand, too elaborate equipment, the presence of too many clerks, too many open files displaying cumulative records of deeds and misdeeds, too much formality, and too much overprofessionalism create a feeling of social distance and inhibit the desire to "counsel with" which is essential to success.

The desirability of counseling in the home is frequently questioned. Home visiting and parental interviews have unquestioned values, but if the purpose be to counsel with the pupil or to secure the co-operation of the parent in carrying forward a program, there are many who feel that interviews will be more profitable if held in the counselor's office. The home environment is apt to be too personal; there are likely to be many distractions; and the hostess may take advantage of her position unfairly to press her point of view. Counseling appointments at the residence of the counselor are open to the same objections and, in addition, to the fact that every individual needs some freedom for relaxation and recuperation. Once the habit of calling upon counselors in their leisure hours is established, especially on the college level, it is very difficult to change the custom. College advisers are, in many ways, *in loco parentis* and of a necessity are subject to emergency calls to which they must respond, but there is no occasion for an open-door policy twenty-four hours a day. Flexibility of practice is necessary: rules are frequently discarded before they are put in operation.

A woman who had had considerable college-teaching experience was appointed dean of women in a large university. While an instructor she had noted how many parents called upon the dean at her residence, and also that from time to time the dean left the campus in order to confer with parents. This she thought was useless. Therefore among the rules which she determined to lay down at the start was, "No interviews with parents except in my own office." The first test came in a situation where parental appearance on the campus, to say nothing of in the dean's office, would have been fatal. The dean and the parents met halfway between the university and their home, and the rule was never promulgated.

Thus it happens with many theoretically desirable efforts to standardize counseling procedures.

An opportunity for privacy is another important conditioning factor. The counter interview and the open room, with people passing in and out, telephones demanding attention, spectators interestedly observing procedures, and fellow students wondering what the occasion and the outcome may be, are always unfortunate. A counseling interview implies two persons consulting together. The presence of a third party for re-search, observational, or training purposes is not endorsed by experienced interviewers. Nor is it advisable for any purpose which does not con-tribute to the welfare of the interviewee. It is frequently both desirable and necessary to invite parents, teachers, husbands, wives, or others to attend a conference in the interests of an individual or a family group, but separate interviews will usually precede a general conference, and the environmental conditions will guarantee each participant perfect free-dom to express his individual point of view. Oftentimes such procedure is essential as a fact-finding method. Mothers who accompany their sons to college and insist upon controlling the interview make both fact-finding and counseling impossible, and it is sometimes necessary to ask them to leave the room temporarily.

Secondary students whose home and school relationships have been happy sometimes ask if they may bring a teacher or parent with them. Such a request the counselor will welcome and honor. Even though the interview be strictly private in that no third party is present in person, the counselor rarely deals with the individual only. Indeed there are few counseling situations which do not reveal silent and invisible participants in the form of parents, teachers, companions, and employers, while the total situation, including environmental or other influences on all parties, is often an important control factor in the outcome of the interview.

The physical condition of both parties has much to do with the out-come of the interview. Counseling with tired, ill, worried, or hurried individuals is not usually very profitable. Nor can physically unfit coun-selors be as alert as is necessary if they are to search for facts and pick up leads.

Appointments made too close to one another or to other obligations to permit a reasonable amount of time for orientation result in a feeling of unrest on the part of counselor and counselee. Some counselors habitu-ally allow from fifteen to thirty minutes for interviews, and if the allot-ment proves insufficient a second appointment is made. This practice has some serious disadvantages, but each "disadvantage" must be con-sidered with reference to the type of clientele served. Routine interviews with persons who are close at hand might be interrupted without detri-mental results. But if the situation is critical, if an element of persuasion is involved, if success depends upon continuity of thought and the gradual selling of an idea or the development of a course of action, failure to com-plete the interview at one sitting may result in negative values. Also if an individual has traveled some distance, has skipped college or secondary classes, or taken time off from work to keep an appointment, or if a parent has inconvenienced himself to accompany a son or daughter, failure to complete the interview because of lack of time is often a serious disappointment and may entail considerable additional expense.

There are, of course, many cases which require more than one interview, and consultants are glad to return even at some inconvenience and expense. If tests are to be administered, records investigated, additional information secured, or outside assistance sought before the desired objective can be attained, there need be no hesitancy about asking the interviewee to return. Always the interviewer should be careful to close the first interview at the right point and in the right way so that progress in arriving at the final solution may not be impeded. Physicians, priests, psychiatrists, and others who conduct many critical interviews are all aware of the importance of preserving the continuity of thought and plan their interviews accordingly.

Calling pupils out of classes for counseling purposes is a practice which often creates conditions which handicap harmonious teacher-counselor relationships. From the teacher and pupil point of view such action seems to be predicated on the assumption that counseling is more important than classwork, while the counselor, if he has an exaggerated conception of the place of counseling in the total educational process, may actually encourage that point of view. If class activities have value, pupils should not be denied participation therein. When this is done teachers are often forced to give additional time to help pupils make up the work which was explained during their absence. Moreover, if pupils resent the summons, the potential values of both educational procedures are lost. Some way should always be found to give pupils the advantage of both methods of education without sacrificing the values of one in order to derive values from the other.

One more factor in the general conditions which set the stage for constructive counseling should be mentioned, the assignment of counselees to counselors. If there be more than one counselor available, the assignment authorities will probably have arranged to have sufficient variety in the personality of interviewers to guarantee suitability for dealing with all types of clientele. Clashes in personality are great inhibitors. Local conditions are important factors in determining whether, on the secondary and college level, men counselors should always interview men and boys, and women, women and girls. An ideal situation would provide several counselors, comprising younger and older members of each sex, who could be assigned according to the character of the case. Adults should always be approached from the adult point of view, and if unemployed, never as unemployed but rather as individuals seeking work. Sometimes older persons are very sensitive about being interviewed by school boys.

THE APPROACH TO THE INTERVIEW

The counselor's approach to the interview will depend to a considerable extent upon the category into which the interview falls, whether voluntary or involuntary. If a voluntary interview, a few words of greeting will open the way for the interviewee to state his purpose. If there should be occasion to refer to records, there will be no hesitation on either side in suggesting that they be consulted. Some counseling agencies require the applicant to fill out a blank, a questionnaire, or an interest or adjustment inventory prior to granting a first interview. The blank is then given to the counselor who uses its content as the basis of the interview and as a guide in conducting it. If the applicant had not anticipated such a requirement, suspicion is apt to be aroused: Who will see what he writes? What is the purpose? Why pry into such personal matters? What is to become of his data? Is he to be "a statistic" for some project? Perhaps he will be unwilling to comply and will leave; perhaps he will fill it all out, cannily and frequently untruthfully.

During the last decade when many foot-weary adults went from agency to agency, always hoping to strike someone who could give practical assistance, the counselors in the National Personnel Service were frequently asked: "Do I have to tell you all my past history and write down every thought I ever had? If I do I don't want your help." Always the reply was the same: "You do not even need to tell your name if you prefer not to. We shall do our best to be useful to you on the basis of what you wish to tell, but you are the one to determine what that shall be." This has been the approach to many very satisfactory cold interviews. After the ice was broken and confidence was gained, all the information needed was always given, if the case was a genuine counseling case, with now and then an offer to write it out. The adult is peculiarly sensitive about putting in writing facts bearing on personal matters, especially if a younger person in a clerical capacity hands out a blank and indicates that filling it out is a prerequisite to the interview.

The compulsory interview, declared by one experienced college youth to be "a common instrument of torture," finds its broadest field of operation in connection with educational agencies. It may be either a routine admissions or orientation interview or it may originate in any one of the variety of purposes for which students are "referred" to, or compelled to consult with, some member of the advisory staff. When the sole purpose

of the interview is routine, to check up on graduation or certification requirements and the like, the term "counseling" is a misnomer. Also,
judged by student reaction, there is some danger that the orientation
interview, which seemed so promising as a factor in college personnel service, is degenerating into a routine procedure, so casual and so stereotyped that it may soon have no legitimate claim to rank as "counseling."
In other instances it seems to be taking on the character of a patronizing
talkfest which breeds contempt among students rather than wins friends
and paves the way for future services.

Counseling contacts with students in twenty-one different collegiate institutions during longer or shorter periods of time have revealed to this
interviewer an attitude of resentment due to the multiplicity of inventories, blanks, life histories, etc., which have been called for in order "to
study their personality." They feel that on the basis of such data they are
being prejudged and pigeonholed, and that a total picture which they
can do nothing to change has been formed prior to any personal contact. They want to sell themselves to the dean, and they expect him to
sell himself to them. At present resentment seems to be changing to a sort
of blasé attitude: Fill them out; they don't amount to anything, but
write cautiously and make the best impression possible because it's going
to stick. An interesting side light on the reaction of students is found in
the replies of deans, counselors, and advisers to queries regarding the
possibility that the cited student reactions do occur. With four exceptions,
very emphatic negative replies have been received. This obliviousness
to the real situation is rather unfortunate, to say the least.

The use of cumulative records and reports as the source of suggestions
for approach to a compulsory but bona fide counseling situation is generally approved, especially if the problem be one which lies in that
no-man's-land where adjustment and discipline are struggling for possession. But even in such cases some will prefer not to have any records or
reports visible, at least during the immediate approach to the problem.
They will so conduct the interview that the student has the right of way
so far as giving information about himself is concerned: How does he
feel about what has happened? How does he think it came about? What
part did he play? What part did others play? What seems to him to be
the best way out? After the initial approach, if it seems best, records may
be brought in. Experience indicates that students on all levels of education feel that they have had a squarer deal, a better chance to be considered not guilty until guilt has been proved, if they are the first witness
and the solution of the problem is approached via their evidence.

THE CONTENT AND CONDUCT OF THE INTERVIEW

In general, interview content will comprise material designed to establish rapport, material definitely related to the problem at hand, material which is a by-product of the main theme but connected with some broader aspect of the individual's interests, and parting comments of the type which tighten the knot of confidence. The specific content will be in harmony with the purpose of the interview. If reliable information on some subject and help in interpreting it be the purpose, then the content will conform. If assistance in the analysis of a problem of which the consultant is aware but which he has not been able to analyze and solve alone be the purpose, then the content will be focused upon data and suggestions which will help to bring intangibles into the open, reveal hidden factors, and clarify thinking regarding cause and effect relationships. If the purpose be changing unawareness of personality defects on the part of an individual to awareness, then the content of the interview will be directed to self-analysis, self-realization of personality assets and liabilities, and the importance of immediate efforts for self-improvement. Nor must it be forgotten that some interviews are sought for the sole purpose of securing an experienced listener, an opportunity to solve one's own problem by thinking it through aloud. It is quite conceivable that the interviewer may contribute little or no content to such an interview except silence; that a solution may be arrived at by the consultant playing all the parts himself: he questions himself, answers himself, presents alternatives to himself, etc. Conducting such an interview consists in listening and thereby exerting a silent concentration pressure on the other party.

The *conduct of an interview* depends upon its type and purpose and upon whether the two personalities involved clash or are able to find a common ground of interest and understanding. Every experienced interviewer can make some suggestions on the basis of practices which he has found good, but few would attempt to tell another exactly how to conduct an interview. There are, however, certain practices involving both dos and don'ts which are freighted with significance for novices if they will pick and choose and adapt rather than adopt.

Several years ago W. W. Charters suggested five one-word rules which he felt were the essence of good interviewing, relax, listen, question, decide, and quit. Each of these words furnished a starting point for the discussion of some major essential in the conduct of a counseling interview. Obviously relaxation tends to create a friendly atmosphere, to invite confidence, and to imply sufficient time for proper orientation and for the

individual to tell his own story in narrative form without too many interruptions or too much short-circuiting. Attentive listening enhances the
beneficial influences of relaxation; gives time for sizing up the personality
of the individual and for observing both mental and physical characteristics; and affords an opportunity for noting consistencies, inconsistencies,
and gaps in his story, for selecting leads, and for determining the type of
questioning best adapted to the situation.

Intelligent questioning is one of the most important techniques in successful interview procedure. It aids in securing, elaborating, or corroborat-
ing facts, opinions, and attitudes; it affords an opportunity to guide and
keep control of the interview, to prevent useless rambling and get to
the main theme as soon as is legitimate. Questioning on the basis of what
the consultant has revealed is a much more satisfactory procedure than
is questioning on the basis of information received from others. The ability of the counselor to select the questioning technique which is best
adapted to the personality of the interviewee is the key to the art of
questioning. Ramblers will require close questioning; the timid and
self-conscious will require an approach which takes their minds off themselves; the dull, slow-thinking will require questioning adjusted to their
mental alertness and thought speed. A self-sufficient egoist frequently
distorts the truth; a lying interviewee may be such through innocence,
carelessness, or intention; the flippant will often give themselves away if
they have sufficient opportunity; the hesitant may be cautious for a number of reasons; the overpositive often contradict themselves; the immature
show immaturity in their attitudes and statements; the nervous must be
questioned in such fashion that tension will be relieved; the cunning need
to be questioned so that they discover their own deficiencies in cunning-
ness; the dogged should be questioned so that as someone has said, one
"gets little answers by asking little questions."

Among the questioning techniques available for counseling with these
varied personalities are:

The direct question. Why did you cheat on examination? This form of
question frequently takes a person by surprise and challenges him in
such a way that denial of the act is a spontaneous defense mechanism.
Parents and teachers are frequent sinners in such questioning. By their
very technique they invite lying and then mete out discipline for both the
lie and the deed. The direct question should be used infrequently and with
caution. The indirect interrogation seeks information by the use of comments and chance remarks. Scraps of conversation from an orientation
interview with a freshman a couple of weeks ago furnish an illustration:

Student. It doesn't make a bit of difference whether I study or not. I'll get good grades if I kowtow to the right birds. Don't you think? [Rising inflection, facial expression, and tone very significant.]

Counselor. Perhaps. I don't believe we knew what kowtow meant when I was in college.

Student. What did you call it—bootlickin'? You know there's lots of ways of sayin' that same thing. And lots of ways of doin' it. [Leaving the impression that he considered himself well-versed in the one and a master of arts in the other.]

Counselor. Yes. I suppose so if one is young and spry [regarded as a personal compliment] and knows how to pick out the right birds. [Regarded as an invitation to enlighten a benighted soul.]

He at once launched into quite a dissertation on methods of selecting "birds" and how best to influence the different varieties. It was a golden opportunity for the counselor to listen and observe. Here was a very bright, sophisticated, self-confident, and exceptionally likable youth. Doomed to many disappointments, of course, but in the long run he would master them all. When he left the office he was in a happy, friendly state of mind. A few parting comments throw light on his personality and are prophetic of the future: "Say, if you want me to I'll come back some day and tell you how I'm making out," and, "If I slip up on my program or if I don't put the salt on the right tails, I'll be interested to see what this advisory business knows about the art of getting a fellow out of tight places," and, "Don't you kid yourself into thinking you've put any salt on this bird's tail today." The freshman will be back in about four to six weeks, and the counselor will not embarrass him by recalling any portion of his "program."

Useless questions waste time and make no contribution to the content of the interview. Repeat or verification questions are often helpful because different wording recalls different associations and is likely to add new information. Antagonistic questions such as, "Do you drink?" "Why are you so lazy?" "Do you and your wife get along well?" are rarely necessary in a counseling interview and are usually considered undesirable. "Yes or no" questions furnish no leads and bring forth no enlightening comments. Implicative questions such as, "Would you do better if you could transfer to another teacher?" are very dangerous to truth because they imply the expected answer. Disjunctive questions offer alternatives but imply that one or the other will be chosen, thus excluding the possibility of a third choice.

Whatever the form of interrogation, the basic rules for interviewing require the interviewer to avoid: (1) Hostility, argumentation, sentimentality, interruption, impatience, aggressiveness which puts the individual on the defensive, partisanship, and threats. (2) The necessity for settlement of incidents at the moment, whether in class, as classes are passing, or while either party is angry or overtired. (3) The betrayal of confidences. If data given in confidence ought to be known by others, some way should be found to convince the individual that such is the case. It is often well to discourage too much confidential information lest afterthoughts by the interviewee bring regrets and inhibit essential future confidences. (4) Any action which may destroy the counselor's self-respect or cause the interviewee to lose confidence. The expectation on the part of pupils of a square deal is a vital teacher asset and should be carefully maintained. (5) An assumption of a right to probe into personal opinions, attitudes, and private affairs in general. Psychiatrists and other specialists in physical and mental disease may do this but never the general counselor except to the extent that it may help the individual make wiser choices and arrive at better solutions of problems. (6) An attitude of superiority or inferiority. (7) A slighting or avoidance of unpleasant facts. (8) Expressions of surprise or annoyance at revealed facts or undesirable behavior. All facts should be faced professionally and neither sentiment nor antipathy should be allowed to enter.

Inability to avoid surprise or disapproval when immoralities of various kinds are revealed has cost a number of too naïve counselors their positions. It is well, of course, to select counselors whose own lives are above criticism, but counselors whose knowledge, as well as their own experiences, are above the clouds are not very well equipped to help those who are "of the earth, earthy" to analyze and to interpret the *how* and *why* of their behavior.

A very fine woman of the highest intellectual, social, and spiritual caliber resigned her position as adviser for women because her cumulative experience warned her that she did not, and probably never could, understand the motives which prompted certain types of human behavior. Quite recently college authorities who were seeking an adviser for men in a segregated college emphatically stressed as one qualification *a knowledge of both the best and worst sides of life and ability to face the worst "without batting an eye."* Colleges usually represent a cross section of American standards, and counselors must be prepared to cope intelligently and effectively, and without betraying astonishment, with all whom the institution accepts.

Charters' fourth verb, "decide," brings the interview to the object for which it is held—to arrive at some conclusion and to formulate some plan with alternatives so that the door of hope may not be closed if the preferred program proves a disappointment. All the facts and opinions will be marshaled, possible courses of action will be related to the facts, possible outcomes of each alternative will be considered, and the student will decide. The counselor at this point sometimes experiences great difficulty in putting the responsibility for the decision on the student. Without eternal vigilance, it is very easy for the counselor to proceed from information to advice, and from advice to decision or dictation of decision.

Charters' last verb, "quit," is sometimes the most difficult to put into motion. To miss the psychological moment to close a counseling interview is often a tragedy. It may result in overselling the counselee on his decision, in renewing vacillation with reference to discarded alternatives, or in changing the program for no real reason. A brief summary of the decision and the method of carrying it into effect, made if possible by the consultant; a word of congratulation on the decision and of encouragement regarding its effectiveness; and an invitation to renew the acquaintance, accompanied by a rising gesture, if needed, will usually close an interview satisfactorily. But the interview is not closed until the door is closed. Sometimes, if the mental strain of telling the story, of replying to questions, and of making the decision has been severe, the by-product of the interview expressed in attitudes or chance comments may be of more value than information secured during the interview. Every counseling interview should close with the feeling that something definite has been accomplished and that both parties will be pleased to meet again.

RECORDING THE INTERVIEW

There is general agreement on at least two points relative to interview records: (1) That records of interviews are an essential and legitimate part of the cumulative records of students on all levels of education and that the items recorded should comprise all statements, observations, or interpretations which throw light on growth or suggest guidance values. Since no cumulative records are available for cold interviews and since they are usually on the adult level, the circumstances surrounding the interview will determine what and how much shall be placed on any record. (2) That the various types of material selected for the record should be distinguished from one another in the same fashion that has been suggested with reference to data secured from other sources.

There is no agreement regarding the desirability of note taking, or recording significant statements and attitudes, during the progress of the interview. Until recently the weight of opinion, based largely on the experience of social workers, was against such a practice. But as all counseling procedures have become more scientific, a change in attitude has been noted with an increase in the number, still a minority, of those who feel that the most salient statements and most significant observations may usually be recorded by an efficient interviewer without causing inhibitions or in any way lessening the effectiveness of the interview. This counselor has consistently followed this practice for thirty years with satisfactory results. She has been exceedingly careful in counselor-training classes, however, not to advocate it as the preferred method but rather to state the majority point of view, to summarize the pros and cons of both procedures, and to indicate that personality is an important factor in the success or failure of either technique. If the interviewer prefers not to make notes in the presence of the interviewee, recording should take place as soon as possible after the close of the interview. There is also some division of opinion, as has been noted, regarding the extent to which confidential information should be recorded on the cumulative record, on a confidential record, or anywhere.

Appraising the Interview

Records of the content and conduct of counseling interviews are still "laboratory material in the rough" so far as scientific attempts to determine their validity and reliability are concerned. Empirical methods are helping to increase the objectivity of interview data and are making contributions to the improvement of self-appraisals and to methods of appraisal by others. Since the interview is one of the most potent, most readily available, and most universally used techniques for aiding another in understanding and solving his problems, it is desirable to make use of any methods which are a help to counselors in systematically challenging their interview techniques and the effectiveness of the outcomes. Appraisals must, however, be made within certain limitations which are understandable and will be appreciated by teachers and counselors alike.

Appraisal of a counseling interview may be approached from either the long-term or the short-term point of view. The long-term point of view regards the interview as one factor in the total counseling procedure, the value of which cannot be judged apart from the ultimate value of all combined factors. This type of appraisal is not a counselor responsibility and is, at present, without the purview of scientific investigation. Among the obvious reasons are: (1) The time element does not permit it. The ultimate results of service to others lie too far in the future to warrant the assumption that all the evidence is in or that any intermediate results will become ultimate results. (2) Techniques for segregating each influencing factor and judging its value independently are not available. (3) There are too many subtle variables which are unrecognized and unrecorded to assume the possibility of quantitative determination. The short-term or immediate appraisal, which regards the interview as an in-

tegrating technique responsible for pooling all the data from all external
sources and helping the individual to interpret and use it to accomplish
the immediate objective of the interview, while subject to some of the
same limitations, may be undertaken by empirical methods either by the
counselor or by others who are qualified for such a task.

The latter, it must be remembered, was the only available method of
appraisal during the early years of the organized guidance movement.
And it was both a more difficult and an easier task than it is under present
conditions. More difficult, because there was a dearth of printed material
on interviewing and what little there was was based on the outdoor relief
interviewing of social workers rather than on the counseling interview;
because there were few discussions of basic laws or psychological principles to help interpret human behavior and explain the fundamental drives
which directed it; and because there were few contributing or adjunct
services available for the diagnosis of different aspects of an individual's
personality, which would have helped to make the picture more intel-
ligible. Easier, because the very absence of such aids and services tended
to concentrate major responsibility for fact gathering, fact interpretation,
fact co-ordinating, and the success or failure of interviewing in a single
individual. What there was could be brought under one microscope; it
could be seen as a whole and interpreted as a unit.

So, as was to be expected, the counselor of thirty years ago was prone
to institute his own appraisal systems without benefit of guidance or
supervision. Most of these, to judge by those which have been preserved,
comprised a series of questions with reference to the content and conduct
of each interview as it was recorded at the close of the day. The questions
followed in logical order and were not different from those asked in the
same sort of appraisal today: What was the purpose of the interview?
What data which had a bearing on the purpose were available? Did the
counselor and the counselee interpret the data correctly? Did they integrate the data in such fashion that courses of action which might be
feasible were brought out? Did they weigh the pros and cons of each
course carefully? Did they select the most promising? Did they outline
a program for carrying it out? Did they plan an immediate first step
toward realization? Was the purpose of the interview attained or to what
extent was it attained? On the basis of replies, the day's interviews were
classified as productive and effective or as unproductive and ineffective,
though sometimes there were several intermediate grades.

Then followed an analysis of the interview procedure to determine in
each case the causes of effectiveness or ineffectiveness, to find possible
strengths and weaknesses, to question what alternative techniques might

have brought more favorable results, etc. Self-interrogation of this type brought many fruitful suggestions, and their variety increased with experience. A few are suggested: (1) Was the purpose of the interview clear-cut and understood by both parties? If not, was the foggy conclusion due to a wrong start? (2) Was the information adequate? If not, what was lacking? Were the missing data of such character that they should have been secured and a second interview suggested? Should they be secured now in preparation for possible future needs? (3) Were all the possible courses of action brought out? Were data or records introduced at the propitious moment? Were free and unrestrained responses secured? Was the decision co-operatively chosen or was it forced? (4) Did the physical or emotional condition of either party influence the outcome? (5) Just what were the weak spots or failures? The strong points? In what respects did the interview improve the situation? In what, leave it worse than before? (6) Was the interview so conducted that both rapport and confidence were won, or was friendship won but respect and confidence lost and vice versa? (7) Did the interview tend to facilitate desirable relationships, teacher-pupil, pupil-parent, pupil-pupil, etc.? Did the interview contribute anything toward better teacher understanding of pupil problems? Did it improve the student's attitude toward school and school responsibilities? Did it contribute to a better understanding of institutional purpose and policy? Did the interviewer do anything to lessen the pupil's respect for the opinion of the classroom teacher? Anything to build it up? Anything to lessen the teacher's authority? Anything to uphold it?

Another early and still useful method of self-appraisal, especially if the work load was too heavy to permit covering of each interview in detail, consisted of selecting two sample interviews, one thought to have been effective and the other ineffective. A comparative analysis was then made for cause and effect factors. These early methods of self-appraisal can be used advantageously by any rural schoolteacher today. And if several teachers or counselors co-operate in an appraisal program, self-appraisal may be supplemented by appraisal by others. Sometimes several individuals appraise the same interview and compare appraisals; sometimes each selects, from a number of reports, what he considers the best and the worst, and discussion follows. Such procedures were forerunners of today's case conferences used as teaching devices. New viewpoints and suggestions are bound to be accompanied by an increase in efficiency, while a review of the records over a sufficient period of time should show growth in certain phases of counseling and reveal weaknesses in others.

CHAPTER XV

Placement Interviews

THE story of placement in these United States and the steps whereby it has attained its present status require a volume rather than a few paragraphs. The present discussion is limited to data essential to connect the old era and its viewpoints with the new theories and practices which are receiving attention today. This, it is hoped, will help counselors to determine the legitimate position of placement in the total personnel program.

Placement agencies, philanthropic, commercial, and public, antedate the beginnings of the organized guidance movement. Interest in the establishment of such agencies is one of the forms in which the humanitarian theories of the eighteenth and nineteenth centuries gradually found practical expression. A comparison of the dates of the wave crests in the rise and fall of public support of placement services with the dates of successive business cycles accompanied by unemployment reveals a definite connection between these cycles and interest in placement services. It was no mere accident that in 1834 New York City established a free employment service designed to protect immigrants against the abuses of commercial distribution agencies; that during the same period the settlement house movement should have moved forward; and that the philanthropic beginnings of both the Bowery and the Emigrant Industrial Savings Banks should have been securely laid.

Placement bureaus in connection with educational institutions came later. Before their advent public and commercial services were fairly common although there was considerable criticism of their standards and methods. Part I has mentioned the collegiate bureaus which were sponsored by the Association of Collegiate Alumnae and has indicated that during the early period of the guidance movement there was no uniform policy on the secondary level of education regarding the inclusion of placement among the functions performed by local guidance bureaus. Contemporary documents consisting of official reports, conference discussions, addresses, and articles reveal considerable difference of opinion on the part of both educators and philanthropists as to the desirability of its inclusion. Boards of education questioned the legitimacy of using school funds for placement services. In some instances the educational corps was openly hostile to any type of service which might tend to facilitate school leaving or bring the attractions of school life into unfavorable competition with those of the work world.

Nor were educational agencies very co-operative in aiding the public and philanthropic agencies which accepted the school discard and attempted to distribute it as advantageously as possible. Data are available to warrant the general conclusion that those who advanced the idea that there were educational values in "juvenile" [1] jobs if educators would assist young workers to uncover them, that work avenues for education should be opened to those who for one reason or another had not profited by the schoolroom type of education, and that supervision under educational auspices should be provided for school eliminates by earmarking a proportionate share of public funds for this purpose were in the minority and were *persona non grata* to the majority of educators. Weaver was greatly concerned with what he called the "vocational adjustment" of youth and was persistent in his efforts to assist young students in their transfers from school life to occupational life. Leavitt and Mrs. Reed were strong advocates of the recognition of work experience as a factor in education, and Leavitt more than once called attention to the fact that educational exploitation of children was as much to be deplored as was labor exploitation.

A comparison of ideas, point by point, from the published statements of Bloomfield and Mrs. Reed furnishes a good illustration of the early period cleavage of opinion regarding the desirability of including placement among educational responsibilities. The comparison was made some years ago by a student attending a placement course:

Bloomfield: Placement means fitting a boy's attainments into the best job.
Reed: Placement is not confined to the narrow meaning of closing a deal in the employment process, but involves training for promotion, employment supervision, etc.
Bloomfield: Placement has been given too much attention.
Reed: Placement is an important function of a vocational guidance bureau.
Bloomfield: Placement is the last phase of vocational guidance to which we should give attention.
Reed: Placement is the Alpha and the Omega of vocational guidance and as such is worthy of considerable attention.
Bloomfield: Placement is a function not to be undertaken by the public school system.

[1] "Juvenile" was used to designate jobs open to youth 13–15 years of age; "junior" to indicate openings for those 16–18 years of age. The terms were dropped when the Junior Section of the United States Employment Service was organized in 1918. Already a considerable number of state labor laws had eliminated wage-earners under 16 years of age and both "child" and "juvenile" had become obsolete with reference to employment.

Reed: Placement is a necessary function to be assumed by any public school system.

Bloomfield: It is not the function of a public school system to maintain an employment agency.

Reed: It is the function of an educational system to maintain a distribution as well as a production center, to market as well as to prepare its pupils. The entire supply of juniors should be distributed through one office, or a chain of offices.

Under the postwar regime of the U. S. Employment Service, a Junior Section [2] was established to serve youth under twenty-one years of age who had been employed in war industries, many of whom, it was felt, would face difficult adjustment problems. Those who had left school prematurely, either for patriotic reasons or because of the alluring war wage, were to be invited and assisted to renew their educational contacts and complete their education. Those for whom formal education had little attraction and promised little benefit were to receive assistance in securing positions and in making employment adjustments.

Obviously this program, were it to be successful, must have the cooperation of educational systems. It was organized on this basis. The local director was always a regular employee of the educational system. "A Statement of General Principles Underlying the Development of Junior Guidance and Employment Service" was issued by the Junior Division of the Employment Service,[3] and was accepted by about twenty school systems with whom contracts were signed although it had no appreciable influence on the almost universal attitude of educators: school, per se, was always beneficial to youth; work, per se, always detrimental. Five of the eight principles comprised in the "Statement," which was issued more than twenty years ago, are interesting in the light of present-day educator pronouncements on the value of work experience:

1. Work experience should be coupled with school experience in affording a well rounded training program for productive service.

[2] The final order establishing this section was prepared for official signature by Anna Y. Reed who suggested three changes in the tentative draft which had been discussed by Jesse B. Davis and William Edwin Hall prior to her arrival in Washington: (1) that "juvenile" be dropped and "junior" be substituted in both title and context; (2) that the upper age limit for registration be raised from 18 to 21 years; and (3) that the proposed boys' section under Mr. Davis and the girls' section under Mrs. Reed be united in a single Junior Section with Mr. Davis as chief and Mrs. Reed as assistant chief. The suggestions were accepted. Before the order was promulgated Mr. Davis resigned and Mrs. Reed became chief. Shortly thereafter, the word "Section" was changed to "Division," and the title "chief" to "director." (The history of this first federal junior employment service has not yet been written. The data used in this work are taken from contemporary records in the private files of the author.)

[3] This statement was formulated by Emery T. Filbey, Assistant Director, now Vice-President of the University of Chicago.

2. In order that junior work experience may function effectively, it should be supervised just as study and play must be supervised if satisfactory results are to be expected.

3. Since junior work experience is to be thought of primarily in terms of educative values, it should be supervised by that agency best suited to provide educative leadership. That agency is, or should be, the public schools.

4. Effective preparation for, and satisfactory interpretation of, early work experience necessitates continuous supervision beginning during the school period and extending through the period of junior employment.

5. Satisfactory control of a guidance and placement program will be dependent upon superior administrative provision. The inclusion of service for all juniors in the community greatly extends the public school function and brings to this department responsibilities almost as great as those delegated to the Superintendent of Schools. This necessitates the recognition of such responsibility by appointment carrying authority second only to that of the superintendent.

The years which lie between these early controversies and the present have witnessed an interesting series of events culminating in a direct reversal of educator opinion.[4] Among these events and trends may be noted:

(1) Persistent efforts to protect "children" through enactment of progressively higher age and grade requirements for school leaving and through corresponding legislation (called "child"-labor) which denied youth the right to work even though he had entered upon man's estate.

(2) Increasing mechanization of certain types of processes which were usually rated as "juvenile" jobs.

(3) During the recent prolonged period of unemployment, a direct reversal of the earlier objective of child-labor legislation has taken place. Its major protagonists now admit that maintaining or raising the legal age of entry to employment in order to protect adult workers against the competition of youth has been substituted for protection of "children" against exploitation.

(4) After a prolonged period during which it considered "work experience" detrimental to the intellectual, physical, and moral development of youth, the educational world is now issuing pronouncement after pronouncement in defense of work experience as an indispensable factor in the all-round education of youth. Out-of-school youth are receiving the solicitous and competitive attention of various departments of the federal government, while the public is paying a large amount to give youth an opportunity to "learn by doing."

(5) A similar situation exists with reference to responsibility for the placement of youth. After years of refusing to recognize placement as an educational function or at best expressing a dilatory interest in it, educational circles are now vigorously asserting that the placement of their own product is both their right and their responsibility. But the National Youth Administration [5] is not under the aegis of the United States Office of Education!

---

[4] Clippings and references in the author's files permit tracing the development of this change in educator attitude from the early years of the guidance movement to the present.

[5] Now liquidated by order of Congress.

It is very profitable to glance backward over a quarter of a century and note in review that leadership in service to out-of-school youth has come from philanthropy and business rather than from education and that leaders in education have systematically and intentionally "missed the bus." Then note how presently eager educators are to bring all youth within the educational fold. There is no profit, however, either in blaming educators for their tardiness or in praising them for their ultimate awakening to their responsibilities. We have waited a long time for work experience to be recognized as a part of education and for placement to be considered an educational responsibility. This is now a *fait accompli*, and those who have recently become interested may join with those who were once educational outcasts in turning these newly recognized responsibilities into practical benefits for youth.

If we assume that all are now agreed that placement is an educational service, that it should be available under public auspices, within the framework of the laws, and at any time when it offers a better avenue for individual growth than does school work, the next question is, Under what public agency shall the service be organized? Shall the agency which produces be responsible for the distribution of its product or shall marketing be allocated to another agency? Shall the production agency market only graduates and alumni and turn over to another agency its irregulars and damaged goods? Shall the producing agency confine its activities to the first distribution of its product leaving any necessary redistributions to other marketing agencies? Is it desirable to distribute youth under twenty-one years of age through one avenue and adults through another? What should be the relation of public placement agencies to the large number of philanthropic agencies which were first in the field and which have made a very important contribution in that field? What place, if any, have the commercial or fee-charging agencies? What about placement through labor unions, employers' associations, professional organizations, and the like? How about college and university bureaus? What about informal methods of securing positions through newspaper advertising, the recommendation of friends, personal application, and nepotism?

The labor market of our country is highly decentralized. This situation involves a correspondingly highly decentralized labor reserve or employable unemployed and difficulty in knowing at any given time the number of unemployed who belong in the labor reserve as distinguished from the unemployed who are, for one reason or another, unemployables. The provision of the Social Security Act concerned with the payment of unemployment benefits requires registration of the beneficiaries at a public employment office. Here we have the beginnings of a centralized labor reserve. What the future will bring forth is uncertain, but it is to be hoped that the public employment offices will prove so effective in the redistribution of the workers registered under the provisions of this law that a firm foundation may be laid for future progress in centralization.

Solution of the various problems which have been raised is of great public importance. They cannot be solved in a day, nor are they primarily the responsibility of school and college counselors. But all counselors are responsible for an intelligent understanding of such problems and for the performance of their own official duties in such fashion that they contribute to, rather than handicap, progress in the improvement of methods of distributing the entire wage-earning population of the country.

DEFINITIONS OF PLACEMENT

Placement of the novice fresh from formal educational experiences and placement of the occupationally experienced proceed from a somewhat different point of view and with some variation in techniques, although routine procedures are much the same. Since this publication is designed primarily to serve teachers and counselors and since placement may not be given more than its proportional share of attention, it is necessary to omit many important details connected with the placement of experienced workers by noneducational agencies and to be content with casual references to such placement.

For the purpose of differentiating between the junior and adult approach and at the same time connecting them sufficiently to indicate that eventually the junior is supposed to take his place in the adult field and assume adult responsibilities, two definitions of placement are offered:

Placement is the process of assisting an individual to transfer from one field of educational opportunity to another.

Placement is assisting an individual to find his most suitable place in the work world, a place where he will have the best chance to use his abilities, to satisfy his interests and needs, to contribute to realization of the objectives of the employing agency, and to the well-being of the social order.

Both definitions recognize placement as a major personnel function, a phase of personnel service based on recognition of individual differences in both clients, the applicant and the employer. The first or "junior" definition recognizes that education does not end when formal schooling is over, that jobs as well as books are potent influences in shaping a budding career and in assisting a student to bring to fruition the knowledge and skills which he has acquired under education auspices.

As has been noted, educators have been very slow to recognize the educative value of bona fide work experience. Recently, perhaps because other agencies are threatening to reduce both their clientele and their income by taking over this function along with certain other "no-man's-land" services, the bars have been lowered and here and there educational systems are offering placement functionaries a seat at the educational table. Placement officers are indeed educators. They know that youth acquires both knowledge and experience when he goes out to hunt a job; when he loses a job and is obliged to explain, at least to himself, why he quit or was discharged; when he is unemployed; when he is promoted, or denied promotion, and the like. They recognize as well as any teacher, and very often better, since they always deal with individuals, that their clients are not cast in the same mold, that paralleling there is "no such thing as an average or normal pupil" is there is "no such thing as an average or normal employee." Pupil and employee, each will show some quantitative or qualitative deviation from the theoretical norm. They know that each employee, just as each pupil, has different problems and is a different problem to his superiors, and they know that problem employers are just as puzzling to employees as are problem teachers or problem parents to pupils and to children.

The second or "adult" definition of placement implies that the applicant has already had opportunities to acquire knowledge and experiences in the work world, whether or not he has made the best use of them. The placement worker always helps to inventory assets and liabilities and to line up the most promising occupational outlets. But, in the adult field he functions more specifically as an information and contact man, middleman, or salesman than as an educator. The accent is reversed in the junior field. The adult placement worker knows that individual differences are apt to intensify with age, that potentialities usually decrease as one grows older, that not infrequently by middle life the ability to increase them has been lost, and that main reliance must be placed upon the capitalization of present assets. He is always alert, however, to the possibility that his legitimate expectations may be agreeably disappointed, and the adult may prove to be an excellent learner; or that they may be disagreeably disappointed when the younger applicant refuses to be interested in the development of potentialities until the day of grace is over. This youthful attitude is due, at times, to temporary relief that "education" is finished and to failure to realize that unless learning be continuous workers soon degenerate into nonpromotional material.

Placement Functions

Placement like education may be carried on under public or private, philanthropic or commercial auspices, or under any combination of such auspices. Its functions may be conceived of narrowly or broadly, depending upon the supervising agency and the extent to which allied preliminary functions are either not performed or are allocated to other agencies, departments, or individuals. Logically, placement comprises counseling only to the extent of the immediate situation, i.e., assisting an applicant to weigh his qualifications in the light of opportunities to make the best immediate use of them, to choose the employer to whose requirements he seems best adapted and to whom he wishes to apply, and to make use of the best methods of salesmanship in the interview with the employer.

Under ideal conditions placement counseling is the final step in the series of guidance procedures which have been outlined in previous chapters. Personal counseling has been initiated in the home and has continued throughout school life. Educational counseling has entered the program at the moment of induction into the school world. The educational foundation for occupational counseling has been laid by the informal inclusion of occupational information in the elementary curriculum and, as time has passed, group conferences and class discussions have been used to unify the theoretical and the practical and to bring occupational information within the realm of general education. General information has gradually become more specific, and educational and occupational counseling have gone forward side by side until, at the termination of formal education on any level, each individual has attained a combined educational and occupational objective and is ready for the next step, placement either in advanced study or in occupational life. Since the situation is what it is, which is far from utopian, if any occupational information is to be consciously disseminated or any occupational counseling done, it frequently happens that those functions are combined with the placement function.

For the present discussion, it will be assumed that occupational information has been adequately disseminated, that educational advisers have given occupational efficiency its rightful place among the objectives of education, that they have given consideration to the occupational potentialities of students and have interpreted cumulative records in terms of occupational as well as of educational guidance, and that occupational counselors, if available, have worked co-operatively together. Furthermore, it will be assumed that at the termination of formal education each individual is potentially desirable for some field of work which may be entered either with or without specific vocational training; that the entire instructional corps is alive to the fact that its task is not finished when it has produced a "product" but it must contribute to the marketing of its product by classifying individuals as firsts, seconds, and irregulars or damaged goods; and that there is a placement office equipped to receive and distribute this product in accordance with recognized placement procedures. To sell the product of any given institution or group of institutions or to sell the services of individuals who are permitted to register at any given placement office is the major function of placement.

PLACEMENT TOOLS AND TECHNIQUES

The tools and techniques available for the performance of placement functions are practically the same as those available for counseling purposes. But the accent is different. The peak of demand for specific knowledge about occupations and individuals has now been reached, and it is the function of the placement interview to bring together a job and an individual whose specifications and qualifications are in harmony. Among the types of occupational information cited in Chapter VII placement interviewers will have major interest in statistical and employment opportunity surveys and in records of usage and job specifications. They will secure a job specification for each job for which they receive an "order," and eventually their accumulated knowledge of local, or frequently filled, jobs and their requirements will constitute a valuable source of faculty, counselor, and student information. Their records will provide locally useful statistical and employment opportunity surveys. Their most useful educational information, aside from thorough and comprehensive knowledge of the offerings of their own institution, will cover opportunities for training in employment and for supplementary education through evening and correspondence courses. Where the counseling interview dealt with relating different types of opportunities to the developmental growth of individuals, the placement interview is concerned with relating specific employment opportunities to the qualifications of specific registrants. The media, in addition to those useful to counselors, are registration blanks, employer orders, and referrals.

All the information about prospective registrants which promises to facilitate transfer from educational responsibilities and their surroundings to business responsibilities and their varied atmospheric conditions should be collected in advance and be at hand when needed. An experienced placement officer knows how to read a cumulative record, and he knows how to translate its different items into job potentialities and probable employee ratings. Subject achievement scores, activities records, personality ratings, and anecdotes are first aids in forecasting business and professional success or failure. Achievement scores equated with aptitude scores give evidence of capacity for growth and of willingness to grow, and they indicate the extent to which continuous growth may be expected. The activities record serves as a measure of the student's selective ability or discriminating judgment: are his choices related to his total educational program and its ultimate objectives or have they just accumulated without purposive direction?

In addition to these essential tools, which may to a considerable extent be kept in stock, there will be some information which must be obtained as occasion demands. Securing this additional information and filling in any gaps which may be found in the cumulative records are placement responsibilities. They are usually accomplished by means of personal interviews or by written communications.

PLACEMENT PROCEDURES

Placement procedures center about interviews, interviews with employers, registrants, educators, counselors, and others, and between any combination of such individuals. During these interviews facts are gathered, challenged, interpreted, and co-ordinated, and information is given in exchange. Any or all of the following may be resultants: the registration of an applicant, the recording of an employer's order, the referral of an applicant to an employer, the closing of a bargain between an employer and an applicant, and the recording of a placement.

Placement procedures do not usually go forward one by one, tandem style, but more often side by side, while details vary considerably depending upon the auspices under which the work is organized. Since procedures must be discussed in turn as though they were separate, the following order is as satisfactory as any: (1) the interview or interviews between the placement counselor and the applicant which presumably will ultimately involve both registration and referral, (2) the interview or interviews between the employer and placement worker which may result in securing job information, an order for a worker, or both, or an expression of satisfaction or dissatisfaction with a previously employed worker, (3) the interview or interviews between the employer and the applicant during which an application blank may be filled out, tests and examinations may be taken or arranged for, an offer of employment may be made and either refused or accepted, or an agreement may be reached and a contract made.

The interviewing of the applicant by the placement functionary usually consists of more than one interview. "Reinterview" is a common term in public placement offices. The approach to such interviews depends upon whether the purpose be immediate placement, with opportunities for preliminary preparation well over, or whether it be an anticipatory interview seeking to ascertain trends in the labor market, the probable demand for employees with certain subject combinations, the extent to which one's own educational program is in harmony with employment prospects, the possibility of educational programing or reprograming which will result in both primary and secondary employment possibilities, and the like. Also, especially in large city institutions, there is a demand for annual interviews in order to be sure that each academic year is a unit toward the completion of an educational objective and at the same time will function as a terminal course if immediate employment should become necessary. Commercial agencies do not usually offer counseling interviews except in connection with registration, but services operated under philanthropic or educational jurisdiction frequently consider long-term counseling an inherent part of placement responsibilities.

Secondary school and college bureaus expect their clientele to seek initial interviews in advance of readiness for placement and usually in advance of desire to register. If occupational counseling has been continuously available during the entire school course, registration early in the final semester before school leaving is usually satisfactory for secondary school youth. They are younger and have spent less time and money on preparation than college youth; they are usually qualified only for unskilled or semiskilled processes, and the opportunities open to them require fewer specific individual recommendations which, however, must be filled without delay. General recommendations as to character, industry, and ability to do teamwork and items regarding scholastic success may be taken from the cumulative record or if such items are insufficient, teachers are easily reached for additional data. Boys seeking apprenticeship opportunities require very careful preplacement counseling. Potentialities for success should be painstakingly appraised since requirements for training involve an investment of time which the boy can ill afford to lose and a financial investment which the company cannot afford to lose. Moreover, even when potentialities seem to be in harmony with interests, it is sometimes difficult to locate just the right opportunity in just the right location.

If the secondary school clientele is distributed through public placement services, school counselors should assume responsibility for seeing that students report for initial and registration interviews whenever and wherever placement authorities suggest, that any portion of the cumulative record pertinent to placement is transferred in time for use, and that additional information requested is promptly secured and transmitted.

On the college level one finds quite a variety of placement regulations, their character depending, to some extent, upon whether or not the placement office is the main source of information on occupational opportunities and their requirements, and whether or not it is the policy of the institution to try to pool and distribute its entire product—the excellent, good, fair, poor and undesirable. In some institutions an initial interview is obligatory during the freshman year, in others it is obligatory at the close of the sophomore year before senior college majors are chosen. Some institutions make no requirement regarding initial or registration interviews, but, if students have not presented themselves for consultation and completed their registration prior to the opening of the final semester in their course, they are denied the assistance of the office in securing a position.

There are logical arguments to support each such regulation. If students are allowed to consult the placement office at will and it is the major source of occupational information, many students will drift along until the last month of their senior year before they give any serious consideration to postcollege possibilities. When they do register, they all too often find that they are encumbered with excess baggage in one field and have traveled far too light in another. It is then too late to rectify such errors. Moreover, during the closing weeks of the year faculty members are too busy to reply to emergency calls for recommendations; the time available for the collection of data about individuals is over; and the placement office is focusing attention on product distribution. It is making referrals, sending out credentials, arranging interviews with prospective employers, and advising with students on their choice of positions.

If colleges—and this applies to any type of educational institution—desire to distribute their entire product, the obligatory interview seems to be the only feasible way of giving the distribution agency adequate knowledge of the quantity and quality of the product it is to distribute and adequate time to perform its functions properly. Some institutions prefer not to take responsibility for distributing their inferior product and have a definite policy, not of refusing to register "difficult to market" students, but of tactfully suggesting that for one reason or another they will be more apt to secure a position if they register with a commercial agency. Reports would seem to indicate that up to the present the commercial agencies have been more successful in marketing academic mediocrity and inferiority than have the educational bureaus; perhaps experience has endowed them with a gift for translating "school dull" into "life bright."

It is unnecessary to mention the various ways in which students are made aware of the fact that placement facilities are available. Nor is it essential to go into detail relative to initial, interim, registration, and referral interviews. In many respects the techniques are the same as those used in the counseling interview, and as a rule initial and interim interviews are counseling rather than placement interviews. They are focused on a somewhat different, and perhaps narrower, objective, and the interviewer's observations will be more intimately concerned with personality traits which he knows will make the individual easy or difficult to place. The first impression made by the personal appearance, the tone of voice and the use of English, the alertness of mind during the interview, the attitude toward business and business responsibilities, mannerisms of various kinds, evidences of social culture, height, weight, and posture both when standing and when sitting are usually worth-while observations for addition to student records. After each interview the interviewer will add his observations to the cumulative records calling attention to any specific assets or liabilities for any particular type of position in which his experience may have permitted him to visualize the individual during the interview.

This ability to visualize individuals in a considerable number of different work situations is an invaluable placement interviewer qualification. Some feel that it is an inherited characteristic and cannot be acquired. Even though it be inherited to some extent, it is the part of wisdom to assume that it can be consciously cultivated by constant practice in observing individuals who are satisfactory and satisfied, or the reverse, in their different work units and then visualizing student registrants as coworkers in the same type of units. This point is worthy of serious consideration by those who are considering placement as a career, for it is universally conceded that success or failure on any occupational level is not attributable solely to the worker but often to the fact that he has been associated with the right, or the wrong, work unit. Teachers who are failures in one situation are pronounced successes in another; ministers who serve one community effectively and happily are neither successful nor happy in another. College presidents and presidents of business corporations are no exception to the general rule, while at the lower occupational levels foremen and coworkers often set the stage for success for one individual and for failure for another.

The *registration interview* is concerned with an appraisal of what, at the moment of registration, the applicant has to sell, for what sort of position he would like to sell it, and what evidence there is to support the assumption that he has the qualifications for such a position. It is a cooperative inventory of assets and liabilities. It should result in the registrant's allocation to a primary and secondary classification for the market. The registration blank is an indispensable tool for this procedure. When completed it contains the record of the final stocktaking upon which referrals are to be based. Records of usage, which it will be remembered are a sort of universal job specification, are also indispensable tools for use during the registration interview, their function being to guide the consultants in determining upon primary and secondary classifications.

There is no universal practice governing when and where the registration blank is filled out. Personal preference, the volume of business, the number of interviewers available, and the time at which registration takes place are among the determinants. Whether or not preliminary interviews have been held, some prefer registrants to fill out the blank prior to the interview. Others prefer partial filling out with completion during or after the interview. A third preference, if time permits and registrants are very inexperienced, is for filling out the entire blank during the interview. Completion before the interview saves time, reveals accuracy in details, and indicates ability to follow instructions, to formulate replies in clear, acceptable language, and to spell and write correctly and legibly. But it often fails to get all the pertinent information, and frequently the experience area of the blank fails to reveal just what work has been done in such a way that its contribution to potentialities is interpretable.

Registration blanks are continuously being revised, and each revision obviates some difficulty and promises others, but even the best blank is a poor substitute for an interview during which statements are verified as they are recorded. Total or partial filling out during the interview, especially if it be an initial interview, is time consuming, but it affords an opportunity for observation, for securing by-product information and side lights which are slowly revealed as the different topics are discussed. This author has secured the best results by allowing the registrant to fill out the blank after the interview, but from notes made while it was in progress. Such a procedure permitted the registrant to formulate his replies in the light of the latest information on opportunities and with a clearer understanding of the importance of secondary occupations and extra-departmental qualifications and experiences as assets for promotion.

The objective of the registration interview will have been attained when the blank is satisfactorily completed and a decision has been reached regarding the classification of the registrant for immediate or future referral. An index card will indicate that another registrant is available for referral. Any index system, visible or not, which permits a quick review of available candidates as orders from employers come in is satisfactory.

The *referral interview* is the acid test of placement efficiency. The placement office is at this point serving in a dual capacity and rendering a joint service. The interviewer is an agent for the employer, handling his order and making preliminary judgments for him. He is also an agent for the registrant, seeking to make appropriate preliminary selections for his consideration. Both parties must be equally well served, and both must be satisfied patrons or the placement service cannot live. Throughout previous procedures the educator has dominated the scene. He has selected the raw material, controlled the production processes, and all of his efforts, presumably, have been focused on service to the student. But when the distribution stage is reached, the employer comes into prominence demanding that an equal share of attention be given to his needs. This is a very important point since experience reveals that many students who have been served continuously for from twelve to sixteen years utterly fail to realize that business is not just another service station for them. The idea that the time has come for them to serve has not yet registered. Secondary school and college faculties whose academic duties have monopolized their energies and interests also often fail to grasp the full significance of the transfer to business and do not understand the new element in personnel procedures which is involved in referral.

Another important change in personnel procedures also takes place in connection with referral interviews. One of the fundamental counseling principles, to assist the individual to interpret all possible opportunities but to hold him responsible for his own choice, will frequently be violated. The placement interviewer may observe the rule, but only after he has predetermined from which opportunities the registrant shall be allowed to choose.[6] Otherwise because of ambition, ignorance, or wishful thinking many registrants would choose to apply for the same position or for totally unsuitable positions and would ask for referrals which, if given, would be in direct conflict with service to employers and would ultimately be a disservice to both the registrant and the institution.

The object of the referral interview is to assist the registrant to determine the extent to which his own qualifications pair with the job specifications accompanying one or more employer orders. This interview may

[6] Sometimes in the course of the referral interview conditions will arise which cause the interviewer to feel that a referral would be unwise. In such cases it is always best and frequently possible so to interpret the total situation that the would-be applicant eliminates himself. Helping a candidate to decide against himself is far wiser than waiting for an employer to decide against both him and the service.

be concurrent with the registration interview and frequently is so in public and commercial agencies. It is less likely to be so in educational service except as the season for availability draws to a close and last minute calls come in. Concurrency is markedly influenced by the condition of the labor market: a sellers' market may bring these interviews into close proximity while a buyers' market may result in wide separation in time.

The employer's order, accompanied by a job specification for the specific position to be filled, is the new tool essential for a referral interview. If an order is in the file at the time of the registration interview and the registrant seems to fit its specifications, a referral may be determined upon during a single interview. If no suitable orders are on hand, the registrant will be called in later as suitable opportunities open. In passing, it may be well to warn novices in the placement game regarding the dangers of referring immediately available registrants to positions without first canvassing the entire file of previous registrants for the same type of positions. It is easier and often quicker to send out the bird in hand rather than to try to summon one from the bush who may never respond to the summons, but it is not considered good placement practice and will sooner or later result in loss of prestige. Nor is it considered wise, lest openings be broadcast indiscriminately and often filled by competitors, to give the name of the employing agency prior to definite decision on the part of the registrant that he wishes to become an applicant. Everything but position identification is discussed. The registrant is told all the details, but not unless and until he has replied affirmatively to a few final questions is he given this last item of information. Now and then the final position information changes an affirmative decision to a negative one, which is entirely legitimate but not frequent if the placement interviewer knows how to question intelligently.

As the process of matching qualifications and specifications goes forward, the educator may come back into the picture and become a vital factor in arriving at a decision as to whether to refer or not to refer. The difficulty previously noted in connection with securing faculty estimates of personality qualities for the cumulative records no longer obtains. The teachers who know the applicant best and who are at the same time best qualified correctly to interpret the job specification will be asked to express an opinion on the fitness of a given individual for a given job. They face a concrete situation. Not, "Please check along the dotted line to indicate the amount of initiative, aggressiveness, industry, resourcefulness, etc., which you think this student has," but, "Does he have sufficient initiative to warrant his recommendation for ————?" "Is he too aggressive to fit into this situation?" "Will this teacher be a good cog in the wheel at ———?" "Will another be resourceful enough to meet the type of problems which arise at ———?" "Does this man bear the earmarks of a future executive or will he always be on the receiving end of business orders?" etc.

After the evidence is all in and has been interpreted, after the referral interviewer is sure that legal enactments will not forbid employment if the applicant is satisfactory, and after agreement has been reached that a given registrant, who desires to apply, shall receive the endorsement of the office, then the final step in referral procedure is taken: an interview between the employer and the applicant is arranged. If both parties are community residents, appointments may be made by telephone or by a referral card which will be presented at the time and to the person indicated on the order. But if the office handles mainly a mail-order business, the applicant will probably communicate his interest in the position to the employer by letter; an application blank will be received with a request that it be filled out and returned accompanied by full credentials from the placement office. A placement is not made until after the employment interviewing is over and the applicant has been definitely engaged and has accepted.

It is not fair to leave the impression that the course of referral always runs smoothly, follows normal, routine procedures, and ends in a placement satisfactory to all. All sorts of situations, disagreeable as well as agreeable, may be anticipated in connection with referrals. The author has had considerable experience in all phases of personnel service and she still finds placement one of the most enjoyable, most challenging, and most educative of all personnel procedures. Collecting and using the data which culminate in a satisfactory referral is a perennial fountain of knowledge for those who are looking for higher education via occupational routes. On the other hand, gadflies that defy description swarm around placement offices and pester referral interviewers.

It is impossible in this cursory overview to discuss the many problems and interferences which complicate efforts to serve adequately and impartially both employer and registrant. The few which are given may afford discussion suggestions for those who are interested in further study of this subject. It will be noted that some owe their origin to public policy and to legislative enactments, others to defects in our educational system, to poor student programing, to inadequate or unfortunate counsel, to parental ignorance, and to ineffective instruction or institutional policies. Some are traceable to those who dictate referrals by virtue of the financial support which they give to the operating agency, others to employer sins of omission and commission, others to labor-union domination and regulations, others to political overlordship, and others to the registrants or to the referral interviewers themselves:

(1) Continued education as a method of unemployment relief and the use of monetary motivation for encouraging such continuance tend to confuse welfare work with education, to create false educational standards, to promote unrealizable occupational ambitions, and to unfit certain individuals for referral to the only type of occupations for which they can qualify.

(2) Public offices, as a rule, may not refuse to register an application. If no referral follows, registrants, parents, friends, and others brand the office a failure. Commercial agencies do refuse registrations and they also at times refer applicants whom they know do not qualify. Are educational institutions which admit students who are over the compulsory education age and permit them to invest their time and money to completion of the course, justified in refusing to refer them to positions? If teachers, engineers, laboratory workers, stenographers, vocational-school graduates, etc., are not referred, the office will be criticized. On the other hand, it takes but a few ill-advised referrals to turn the employer to other sources of labor supply.

(3) Referrals negotiated by the financial supporters of philanthropic bureaus, by individual instructors on secondary and college faculties, by political henchmen, or through pressure from similar sources without reference to qualifications are thorns in the flesh of professional placement interviewers and nails in the coffin of the service they are charged with operating.

(4) The ability of an educational placement office to distribute the majority of its registrants satisfactorily is largely dependent on the admissions policy of the institution.

(5) Excessive decentralization of inter- and intrainstitutional placement efforts handicaps selective referrals, uselessly increases the labor reserve, antagonizes employers, wastes time and money, and discredits the entire institutional program. "Clearance" is the only logical method of counteracting the evils of decentralization.

(6) The referral of an applicant who, no matter how well he may meet employer specifications, is unemployable because of legislative enactments or labor-union regulations can be avoided only by thorough familiarity with all regulations which have a bearing on the distribution of workers.

(7) The placement of minority groups is a vexatious problem intensified by the random and often sentimental or sensational opinions of those who have never faced the practical problems involved. Chapter XIII has considered this topic as an educational problem and has pointed out the absurdity of assuming that legislative enactments can force either referral or employment of an individual who does not fit the position, regardless of the particular factor to which undesirability is due. If employers prefer blonds, the wise placement office will refer blonds and not brunets. On the other hand, after the full confidence of an employer has been gained, it is quite possible to secure his co-operation in the distribution of difficult-to-place individuals, and he will willingly employ members of any minority group who can do the work required and whose employment the internal conditions of his company do not forbid. An intelligent placement interviewer knows that there are any number of types of minority groups whose members cannot be used under certain conditions. The moment he ig-

nores this fact he loses the respect, confidence, and business of his employing clientele.

(8) Another problem, similar in some ways to the minority group problem because, of course, all handicapped groups belong to one or more minority groups, is the placement of physical and mental defectives or substandard groups. Special bureaus should always be used when they are available since familiarity with types and degrees of disability, with legislative enactments which affect such workers, and with types of positions in which employment is possible require detailed information. This subject has been discussed in previous chapters and the references there given will be helpful to those who are responsible for such referrals without expert assistance.

(9) A considerable number of problems center around the use of references. What shall be done with exaggerated or high-pressure recommendations? How shall one meet persistent demands from faculty, social workers, politicians, and others that their candidates have preference? To what extent shall the candidate be informed as to the character of his references? Shall unfavorable references be destroyed? Shall unfavorable comments be expurgated? Are there applicants whose references are so unsatisfactory that one is justified in refusing to place them?

The *interviewing of the employer* by a placement office representative is usually for one or more of the following objectives, to get job information, to get orders for workers, to confer regarding previously recommended employees, and, incidental to all three but by no means of minor importance, to establish rapport, win confidence, and sell the service which the interviewer represents.

The first objective has been partially covered in Chapter VI where the collection of more general occupational information for counseling purposes was considered and a list of rather important Dos and Don'ts for plant visitors was enumerated. These lists may well be reread and their admonitions and suggestions observed by those who are engaged in placement work. A supplementary list which applies more specifically to placement visitors is added:

1. Don't solicit so often that you become a nuisance.
2. Avoid pressure selling.
3. Don't expect special consideration for your referrals.
4. Don't assume that social or family relationships will guarantee positions.
5. If you are a woman, don't make a man of yourself. Businessmen respect and are inclined to favor womanly women.
6. Don't engage in arguments regarding criticisms of your referrals.
7. Don't comment on wages, hours, or labor policies of your employing clientele.
8. Don't offer gratuitous suggestions for the improvement of company personnel policies.
9. Always stand ready to confer regarding the improvement of your referrals or to aid them in preparing for promotion.

10. Learn to accept "heel cooling" as a part of placement procedure, and appear to accept it graciously

The second objective of plant visitation or of employer interviewing, solicitation or the receiving of orders, is essentially a placement function. Either party may take the initiative in seeking the interview. Some will prefer to make appointments, others to take their chances and drop in. When travel is involved, it is always advisable to make an appointment lest a repeat journey for the same purpose be necessary. When the initiative is taken by the employer, the approach is very simple, for, whether it be a first contact or one of many, he seeks the interview as a prospective buyer. Since the placement office exists to serve him, he is always a welcome guest even though he may have come unannounced and have chosen a very inconvenient time for his visit. When the placement service takes the initiative, the situation is radically different and the approach must be adjusted to the situation and personalities involved, otherwise the account of a present or prospective customer may be lost.

It is a fundamental principle of salesmanship that customer-interviewers make themselves as familiar as possible with the business interests and personal idiosyncrasies of those whom they are about to approach. If previous contacts have resulted in sales, succeeding contacts are usually initiated as follow-up interviews and terminated as sales interviews. Job solicitation is a sales proposition and is subject to the same fundamental principles. It pleases the employer to find someone in labor marketing who understands his business, the various types of legislative enactments which control its operation, and its sources of labor supply. It pleases him, too, to note that the interviewer avoids controversial issues and refrains from commenting on a competitor's problems or policies. Rapport is established, and he feels that he can trust the interviewer to recognize confidential information and to see that it remains such.

The timing of employer visits is another factor to which an experienced solicitor always gives consideration. Unless sent for, he tries to avoid the busy seasons of the year and the rush hours of the day. If an appointment has been made, he arrives on time, recalls his appointment, and presents proper credentials or identification cards. His manner is dignified. He has called to see if he can be of service; in some cases the employer is taxed to support the service which is being put at his disposal. He never presents himself in the capacity of a charity worker or a beggar for unemployment relief, nor does he ever make the mistake, which public officials sometimes do, of classifying himself or allowing others to classify him as an investigator, inspector, or law enforcement officer.

Philanthropic agencies have sometimes made the mistake of sending out interviewers who in the guise of solicitors are really "reporters" or even "social snoopers." Every reputable agency is penalized for such errors of judgment.

Most interviewers feel that they learn more, that employers' preferences, needs, and peculiarities are more readily revealed if, after indicating the purpose for which the appointment has been sought, the employer does most of the talking. They keep their eyes open for opportunities to visualize settings and the different types of workers employed in different work units. They are alert to note such observable items as the general appearance of workers, their social and educational status, their personality and the personality of those who hold supervisory positions, sex predominance, any apparent age or nationality preference, physique of workers, etc. They also observe processes and their requirements, repetitive work, team work, special machines with their maker, and who operates them, and the like. Intelligent but not impertinent questions may be asked and will almost invariably receive courteous and informative replies provided they are properly timed and properly worded.

It is more than likely that solicitor interviewers will be the recipients of a variety of criticisms on their methods and on the qualifications, attitudes, and personalities of their nominees. They will also receive some praise. It is not wise to assume the defensive no matter how much illegitimate criticism there may be; but if one is forced to defend his school system, college, philanthropic organization, or public service agency, he should try to view the total situation fairly, to accept and recognize criticisms which are just and to offer a dignified defense when they are unjust. He may or may not find it feasible to take notes during the interview, but he will always keep a record of both commendatory and condemnatory statements and will be alert to make the best possible use of them. He will pass them back to the production agency and to the nominating parties; he will see that teachers, counselors, and registrants have an opportunity to share in their benefits.

The interview with the employer at his place of business has been accented because it is the major method of obtaining employers' orders and has the advantage of affording visualization opportunities which can be secured in no other way. Interviewing for employment is carried on under a number of other conditions. Labor scouting on college campuses has been considered in some detail in Chapter VI, and the function of the placement office, as an assistant to business representatives in making contacts and selections and to registrants in evaluating opportunities and arriving at decisions, has been discussed and requires no elaboration. Interviewing is frequently initiated by correspondence. Usually it involves preliminary negotiations concluding with a personal interview at the place where the work is to be performed before a final agreement is reached. Some colleges and professional services invite orders by sending out lists of available, or presently to be available, applicants accompanied by biographical and qualification data. If any registrant interests the recipient further information is sent on request.

Secondary and vocational schools frequently solicit orders and increase their calls for substandard or mediocre workers by sending to their entire employing clientele a complete list of all prospective workers very carefully classified on the basis of degree of proficiency in the various qualities required in their occupation. If applicants are listed in tabular form, relative proficiency and proficiency in major requirements can be seen at a glance. If a final column entitled "Current Wage Range" be added, and if each applicant, in consultation with the placement office, allocates himself to one of these wage-range groups, an employer will sometimes find that one person in the wage range of $25–30 and another in the $15–20 range will meet his purpose just as well as two persons at $18–20. This markets a less desirable employee as supplementary to a more desirable. Where numbers of registrants are few, this plan has proved an excellent method of order getting.

There are some institutions which do not approve any solicitation on the part of their placement bureaus. They maintain that their product should be sought for, not advertised, and they permit no effort to open up opportunities either by the distribution of lists of registrants or by inquiry regarding vacancies reported to exist. Interviewing initiative must always come from the employer. Such procedure is not salesmanship but order taking, largely mail-order taking, based on the assumption that the institution is turning out a self-selling product. This may be a justifiable assumption if the reputation of the institution be such that its product is in universal demand, but competition is very keen and institutions which are not well established can hardly afford to adopt a laissez-faire policy with reference to the distribution of their product. When there is a sellers' market as at present, no one needs to make much distribution effort; but when the situation changes and buyers dominate the market, the institution which supports an alert sales agency will have many advantages.

The *interview between the applicant and the employer* follows the referral interview and is the next logical step in placement procedure. If there be no placement service acting as an intermediary, it may and often does proceed along the lines of a cold interview, with the company interviewer observing the applicant and collecting the initial information during the interview. Prior to reinterview additional information may be secured.

The purpose of such interview or interviews is to give each party an opportunity to weigh what he has to offer in the light of what the other has to offer. If previous sifting has been done, the offerings of the one will fall into the same category as the offerings of the other, but final consideration of individual qualifications in comparison with job requirements and of applicant personality in relation to job personality are the shared privilege and responsibility of the applicant and the employer. The major tools used during the course of such interviews are whatever general or special information the one party may have secured about the other, observation, application blanks, physical examinations, mental, aptitude, and performance tests, and sometimes personality inventories.

Company interviewers are usually trained in the use of the interview technique. They know how to put the applicant at ease, what to observe, how to word and time questions, how to evaluate secondary occupations, how to close an interview, and how to focus their entire procedure on the single objective, the securing of an employee whose personality, character, education, physical qualities, and experiences indicate that he will fit into the job with the least friction or adjustment. They are familiar with the six to ten points which are usually considered with reference to the qualifications of any applicant,[7] and they know how to vary the order of their importance according to the character of the business and of the specific job. Although personal appearance usually has first place in any list, trained employment interviewers do not transfer qualities of appearance to qualities of ability. If their company is looking for promotional material, they know how to interpret academic records in terms of replies to such questions as: Can he be taught? Will he be willing to learn? Will he help to maintain, raise, or lower the morale of the company personnel? Does he have enough ability? Too much? Too little? Is he looking for a job or for an opportunity?

The applicant's approach to the interview is much more difficult. He is a guest on company ground; he has had limited or no experience in carrying his share of responsibility for employment interviews; and he may not have had even the theoretical assistance which derives from the

[7] Most company personnel departments have lists of "to be avoided qualities" in their hiring specification for different positions. *American Business* (Aug., 1941, pp. 21–22) gives a list of eleven things to watch for in hiring salesmen. The three which are most significant for college students are: Has the applicant had more than five previous jobs; has he gone to college more than three years without graduation; and has he "reformed" in regard to financial affairs or personal habits?

type of group conferences and interview demonstrations mentioned in Chapter XIII or from a few suggestions during a referral interview. All too often secondary or college graduates face the most important sales situation of their lives with little understanding of the techniques involved in successful candidacy for a position. They may have painstakingly outlined their careers and made adequate preparation for entry only to be denied admission because of faulty sales techniques. Indeed, some very able men remain in mediocre positions all their lives because they cannot sell their services nor even close a sale when the preliminary steps have been taken for them. Fortunately this type of deficiency is well known to business interviewers who, if outstandingly desirable qualities are detected, can so utilize their own techniques that the difficulty is partially overcome. But while underselling is a disadvantage to one type of applicant, overselling or talking one's self out of a job is an equal disadvantage to another type. Boasting of accomplishments, calling attention to honors, acting affected in speech and manner, and referring to the number of positions which one has had an opportunity to consider, this being one, are all dangerous practices.

A neatly and properly dressed applicant who presents himself promptly at the time and place designated, tenders his credentials or states the purpose of his call, refrains from loud talking, smoking, gum chewing, or asking to use the telephone while waiting in the reception room is headed in the right direction.[8] If he approaches the interview in a dignified, unassuming manner with full understanding of what he has to sell and its market value, if he maintains the poise that grows out of realization of the fact that he is one of two parties who are engaged in a selective procedure, if he observes his prospective employer and the work situations to which he must adapt himself, and if he replies intelligently to questions and asks intelligent questions, he has no cause to feel nervous or apologetic. When asked to fill out an application blank or to take a test, he will cheerfully comply, asking necessary but not foolish questions and being especially careful to avoid facetious remarks no matter how favorable the opportunity.

---

[8] A young woman was advised to refrain from gum chewing during this rather crucial stage in her career. Energetically she replied, "Oh, I can't do that. I'm so happy chewing gum." A college senior was informed that stockingless women were not considered assets in business offices. Nonchalantly she replied, "That's too bad, but I don't think they'll mind when they see me. Socks are very stylish." A business executive of wide experience but one whose educational advantages had fallen far below those of either of these women was asked what placement interviewers could do with such cases. "You can't get no jobs for them kind of girls," he replied. The business world recognizes many varieties of ignorance!

An upper executive who had been solicited to assist a friend's son in securing a position with his company sent the young man to the personnel department to comply with routine procedures. In due course of time the report of the interviewer reached his desk accompanied by several anecdotes. A second interview took place. With the record before him the executive said, "Well, James, you do not seem to have made much of an impression on the personnel department." Instantly the reply came back, "Yes, I did, too, but it wasn't favorable." Another anecdote graced the cumulative record, but James was not invited to join the company!

Among the many questions which may be asked an applicant during an employment interview are: Why do you want to work for us? What makes you think you can do the work? What salary do you expect, or what is the lowest salary which you will accept? The applicant should be prepared to reply very definitely and adequately to the first two questions. The third, in its second form, creates a very unfavorable impression of the company, but if it is asked, an applicant may ask in return, "What is your current salary for such a position?" If the salary stated is much below the market and if there are no compensating factors, the applicant is free to refuse what he recognizes as an obviously unfair offer. If it is in harmony with current salaries, it is easy to recognize that fact and to so indicate. A positive statement, such as, "Current salaries for such work seem to be about ————. I had hoped to qualify for that range," is another way of replying to such a question. It is always desirable, at least for mature applicants, to word their replies to indicate that they have investigated market conditions and know the current values of the services they have to sell. It is also advantageous to word such statements so that they leave the way open to accept a lower salary if for any reason one wishes to do so or is obliged to do so. The applicant may also ask questions. Most companies will give him abundant opportunity to do so before he accepts a position.

The interview or the series of interviews will culminate in definite decisions on the part of the participants—to employ or not to employ on one side; to accept or not to accept on the other. It makes a very happy ending, of course, if both minds run in the same channel, i.e., if neither desires to make a contract or if both do. But it does not always turn out that way. If the employer decides against the applicant, no matter how great the disappointment it is unwise to argue, criticize, or demand reasons. Sometimes it is harder for an employer to refuse an applicant who has won his respect and confidence but who cannot meet position requirements than it is for the applicant graciously to accept refusal. An expression of disappointment that one does not qualify and of appreciation for the consideration given to his application always leaves a favorable impression and is not infrequently recalled at some future time when it has important asset value:

Recently a university professor had occasion to employ an assistant for some rather technical phase of office work. Among the young women summoned for interview there was one who showed evidence of unusual culture and refinement but she could not qualify for the position. Both parties were, for the moment, a little embarrassed. The applicant was first to grasp the situation and tactfully to eliminate herself by recognizing her deficiencies and regretting that she had taken the employer's time to interview her. Instantly the professor remembered that one of his colleagues was also looking for an office assistant who could do the type of work for which she seemed best qualified. He offered to introduce her, adding that he never liked to see the university lose a chance to add a young woman of her type to its corps. And so social culture, standing out under disappointment, secured a position which had passed out of the mind of the interviewer until the poise and courtesy of the applicant recalled it.

On the other hand, suppose an offer of employment is made. The applicant by his method of acceptance or refusal has an excellent opportunity to enhance his desirability in the eyes of the employer. It is always legitimate to decline an offer of employment, but expressions of appreciation for consideration, thanks for the compliment of the offer, and regrets that it seems unwise to accept should be a part of the refusal. Should reasons for refusal be given? This is not a "yes" or "no" question. If the reasons are personal, it may be wise at times to do so; if they are focused on company shortcomings or practices, it is almost universally unwise. One does not offer gratuitous criticism of a company which offers him a position. If an offer is accepted, a few words of thanks for favorable consideration, of anticipated pleasure in working for the company, and of assurance that he will make every effort to live up to its expectations is a dignified way to close the interview. And then never, even if one is the youngest, greenest and least sophisticated of all employees, fail to report promptly on the date, at the hour, and at the place designated for entrance upon service.

When the applicant is on the job, a placement has been made.

The *induction interview* and induction procedures are company prerogatives. But just as articulation between the various units of the educational system is a shared responsibility, so articulation between the last formal educational unit and the first employing agency is a shared responsibility. The placement office is the integrating agency and should remain at the service of both company and employee until initial adjustments have been made. Oftentimes it is the placement office which helps the business novice to see and to contribute "that little something more" than the required service which means so much in terms of promotional opportunities.

CHAPTER XVI

Postschool Facilities and Methods

CHAPTER XIII has dealt with group methods of guidance, Chapter XIV with counseling, and Chapter XV with placement. Service to individuals who have not yet completed the period of formal education has been emphasized, although each chapter has made it clear that personal problems do not automatically cease to exist at the close of one's formal educational career.

Not only are many unsolved personal problems carried over from the educational to the occupational world, but at each way station on life's journey new problems arise and new adjustments are required. Occupational and educational information may be needed at any age or experience level; community resources which were of no value in early life may become exceedingly valuable as family responsibilities increase; opportunities which require careful appraisal of capacities and abilities frequently come at or after middle life; oftentimes a one-position, thoroughly competent worker is completely at sea when changed conditions force him to write a letter of application or prepare for an employment interview. And, finally, one must not overlook the very great change which has taken place with reference to the older generation and the extremely difficult adjustments which many of this group are forced to make. The detached house, which usually had a place and a welcome for the postwork parent and grandparent, is largely nonexistent today. The superannuated wage-earner and homemaker who has given his best for the younger generation finds it hard to adjust to a world, or a home, which looks upon him as a useless burden. Nor is the adjustment to such a situation on one side only; sometimes it involves a real tragedy for every member of the family circle. Chapter XVI is concerned with postschool guidance and personnel services, including employment supervision and follow-up.[1]

1 The logic of devoting a separate chapter to postschool guidance service may well be challenged. Although the adult has been definitely included in the guidance circle in previous chapters, it has seemed best to utilize one chapter to gather up the loose ends which tell the story of adult guidance, to accord it its legitimate place in the development of the movement, and to lay the foundation for a more detailed future study of this phase of personnel service.

"Postschool" has been chosen to designate the time sequence with which this chapter is concerned because it seemed more nearly to provide for the inclusion of the many types of guidance and personnel work which have been instituted to serve those who have severed their connections with definite educational units and whose primary undertakings lie in the areas of occupational, home, or social life. The group to be served under such a classification is, of course, much larger than either the school group which has been stressed or the preschool group which has been given little attention. Without distinction as to age, sex, or educational, social, and economic status it would comprise three major subdivisions: (1) the beginners in the broader areas of life including occupational life; (2) experienced wage-earners and those who have attained what is usually called adulthood or maturity; and (3) those who have met the responsibilities of life with more or less success and, controlled to some extent by the degree of economic security which accompanies retirement, must adjust to entirely new types of problems and situations. Possible subclassifications under each subdivision are many, while the personal problems of individuals who fall within each classification are legion.

Principles and Practice of Postschool Guidance. The fundamental principles which derive from biology, psychology, sociology, and other knowledges, and upon which counselors rely for guidance in dealing with humanity, apply alike to preschool, school, and postschool groups. But the practical application of principles is bound to vary with the status of the individual concerned. As strengths and weaknesses are revealed, as ability patterns crystallize and shift, as environmental factors change in character and influence, and as adolescence is either prolonged or more rapidly attained than usual, guidance practices will be adapted to the situation whatever it may be, and later in life declining mental and physical powers will demand additional alterations in the application of principles. That such differences in practices are assumed is implied in the difference in the wording of Parsons' and Ryans' statements as to the objectives of guidance which precede Part IV and upon which comments have previously been made.

Word usage conforms to that explained in preceding chapters. Guidance is used in the broad general sense, extensive rather than intensive, and may result from any number of activities or services so numerous in quantity and so diverse in quality that they defy classification, though they are far too important to be ignored as youth passes from the jurisdiction of the educational system to the jurisdiction of the world. These postschool guidance influences which surround youth during the transition period play a very large part in the adult adjustments which are daily taking place.[2] "Counseling" retains its usual significance; it is a personal interview sought for the purpose of securing assistance of some kind in making a choice, interpreting a situation, or arriving at a decision. The counselee may seek an interview on his own initiative or he may be advised to do so by an employer, friend, or parent. "Personnel service" in the technical sense, based on a complete personal inventory, is not often available on the adult level. Cumulative records are rare in connection with adults except for a few beginners as they pass from the educational system to initial employment, and always, as yet, technical services are apt to be more complete for atypical than for normal individuals. Some clinical services are available, however, and here and there experienced interviewers render very helpful guidance service with comparatively meager records or tools of any kind at their disposal. "Employment supervision" and "Follow-up," both definitely postschool terms, have a dual objective, personnel service to the individual supervised or followed up and informational service for administrative authorities who desire to appraise the end results of their productive efforts.

That postschool guidance covering the entire span of adult life antedated and, as time passed, paralleled similar services for school attendants is a well-known fact in the history of the guidance movement. It has, however, been largely overlooked because so many of the early period postschool guidees were in the lower age level groups. In recent years this apparent neglect may, to a considerable extent, be justified by the assumption that if guidance functions are adequately performed by the home,

2 On page 281 of *When Youth Leave School* (see p. 65 n.) there is a classification of types of organizations to which a cross section of New York State youth who have severed their connection with secondary schools belong: Approximately 50 per cent belonged to no organization; the church groups stood first in enrollment of former pupils (about 1 in 16) and character building groups stood fourth (fewer than 1 in 16). The former did not necessarily involve church membership, but membership in groups sponsored by churches such as the Epworth League and Altar Boys' Club; the latter comprised such organizations as the Y.M.C.A., Y.W.C.A., and Boy and Girl Scouts. About one in forty belonged to organizations interested in civic affairs. On pages 29 and 32 of *High School and Life,* another volume in the New York State Regents' Inquiry series published also in 1938, Francis T. Spaulding comments on these statistics as indications of the failure of school-sponsored activities to function in later out-of-school life, especially with reference to civic responsibilities. Good citizenship is, of course, the outstanding objective of public education, but good character based on a spiritually grounded philosophy of life is fundamental to good citizenship. Experienced counselors know that many secondary school youth are seriously concerned about their spiritual life and are struggling to work out a satisfying philosophy of life. Since out-of-school activities are self-chosen from a wide range of offerings, it may be worth while to consider the type of activities chosen, even though chosen by a small percentage of the total. May failure to help students attain their fundamental spiritual objective be one factor in failure of the schools to attain their ultimate civic objective?

church, and school, increasing ability to guide one's self will be a normal outcome and will eliminate the need for guidance services on the adult level. In many cases this should be and is true. In other instances the type of problem upon which the adult seeks service originates in rapidly changing social and economic conditions, in lack of the latest educational and occupational information, or in some family situation which could hardly have been anticipated during school life. There are many choices to be made and many problems to be solved in the different areas of adult life for which there may have been no suitable carry-over knowledges and suggestions, and there is also considerable individual difference in the ability of adults to make practical application of such carry-overs.

As the problems of life increase in number and in complexity, as new knowledges are available, as occupational patterns shift more frequently, bringing new requirements in their wake, as new legislation influences old patterns of life, and as the mores under which the family unit is established and develops change, it seems probable that there will be an increasing demand for adult guidance centers, centers of information on the many items mentioned in Part II, for assistance in their interpretation, and for help in determining their applicability to the individual's immediate need.

Guidance Services for Beginning Wage-Earners

Guidance service for wage-earning novices must be accorded first place in the consideration of service to the three groups included in the postschool category. This group comprises the product and the by-product of our educational systems. The 1908–1916 public-school discard—educational failures who, as soon as the law allowed, eliminated themselves from an intolerable situation and attempted to find a more suitable outlet for their abilities in the occupational world—were child adults, ranging from twelve to fifteen years of age. They made a strong appeal to philanthropy and were vividly portrayed in the considerable number of "vocational guidance" surveys [3] which characterized the early years of the guidance movement and laid the foundation for philanthropic-sponsored guidance bureaus whose objective was service to youth as he severed his connection with education and stood on the threshold of his occupational career. Several agencies which sponsored surveys and fostered guidance bureaus have been mentioned in Part I. The 1911 Chicago survey is particularly

[3] One hundred forty-eight of these surveys covering two periods of "surveying" have been summarized and interpreted by the author in *Human Waste in Education*.

significant because, if not the first, it is among the earliest surveys to call for employment supervision for the working child.[4]

Soon the time was ripe for the extension of interest in employment supervision for beginners beyond philanthropic groups. Education, industry, and public employment services, either because of interest or necessity, began to assume some responsibility for this group.

The revision of compulsory education laws forced educational administration to realize that there were many fourteen- to sixteen-year-old educational undesirables who could no longer be discarded. The introduction of the continuation school resulted in the formation of a new group of occupational beginners who were neither in-school nor out-of-school but were entitled to classification in both groups. Co-ordinators appeared, charged with the employment supervision and follow-up of this new group. A cursory analysis of the character of these functions and the effectiveness of their performance seems to indicate that follow-up was concerned mainly with the enforcement of that portion of the law which required a definite number of hours of day-school attendance during each week, while employment supervision implied co-operative planning and supervision of a co-ordinated program for educational and vocational guidance. The first function appears to have been fairly adequately performed; sometimes the second was also, but many times it was a dead letter. In any event the introduction of the continuation school had given employment supervision and follow-up an opportunity to worm their way, theoretically at least, into the lower-school educational dictionary.

This accomplishment must not be interpreted to mean that placement, employment supervision, and follow-up had been accepted by school authorities as educational functions. They had not. Nor is there today any universal realization of the fact that public education must assume all the responsibilities of an effectively operated production agency or some other agency will encroach upon its prerogatives. Signs of the fear of such encroachment are increasing and may awaken those who are capable of leadership before it is too late. In the meantime, in view of the immediate jurisdictional controversy, it might illuminate the present and cast a ray of light into the future if educators and counselors could

---

[4] In his 1912 address entitled, *The Child, the School, and the Job,* Hiatt declared that more than 50 per cent of Philadelphia youth fourteen and fifteen years of age were employed and that they were as much entitled to their proportionate share of public funds for employment supervision and practical help on the job as were the slightly smaller number of the same age groups who remained in school. A very impressive pictorial presentation of the situation is found in the original pamphlet. It is reproduced in *Human Waste in Education,* page 97.

obtain a forty-year retrospective overview of *When Youth Leave School* and year after year hear *Youth Tell Their Story.* What is the twentieth-century story of *When Youth Leave School?* In other words, what is the twentieth-century history of placement and employment supervision under educational auspices? What is the history of postschool guidance for novitiates?

Piecing together the records, one finds a rather sad story—a truly amazing story to one who has watched it unfold from a vantage point half within and half without the educational system, who has seen *Youth Leave School* and heard *Youth Tell Their Story,* much the same story, year after year, while the majority of important educational eyes have not seen and the majority of influential educational ears have not heard.[5]

For the most part eliminated pupils have always been self-distributing; the schools have always been a negligible factor in the distribution of either graduates or discards. The graduate has received more educational assistance in postschool adjustment than has the discard; the vocational school pupil more than those leaving from other courses. A survey of women and child wage-earners in the United States was authorized by Congress, January 29, 1907, and was reported on in nineteen volumes in 1910.[6] At the date of authorization the vocational guidance movement and its terminology were both unborn; no one expected the public schools to advise, place, and follow-up their school-leaving population; and philanthropic bureaus were hardly above the horizon. In some states employment was legal at twelve years of age and prior to completion of the eighth grade. As an indication of the incidental way in which youth entered industry, this report stated that about five-sixths of the school leavers took the first place that offered, usually through the influence of relatives or friends.

Chapter XV has noted that during the early period of the guidance movement, there was considerable sporadic interest in, and sometimes rather heated controversy relative to, placement as a function of public education. The topic was very definitely before the educational authorities. Philanthropy was trying to "fasten" the function on education, and the

---

[5] It is time for a long-term study of this topic. A thoroughly documented publication should be available for the use of current surveyors who start from scratch. Forty years of background information would result in the omission of some rather naïve statements, in more scholarly and helpful interpretations of data, and in comparisons which would indicate trends. All the essential data for such a publication are available in the author's personal library, which is open to research students upon request.

[6] *Report on the Conditions of Women and Child Wage Earners in the United States* (19 vols., 61st Congress, 2d Sess., Sen. Doc. no. 645; Washington, 1910–1913). A summary of this report may be found in U. S. Bureau of Labor Statistics Bulletin, no. 175 (Washington, 1916).

National Association of Corporation Schools was anxious to co-operate in the postschool adjustment of both product and by-product. Scores of surveys were made during this period. The findings revealed that friends, relatives, and window signs were the most satisfactory methods of securing positions, while no estimate based on statistical surveys placed the services rendered by the schools above 2 per cent.[7]

The postwar years witnessed another period of enthusiasm for surveying. Again the findings showed no general progress in the utilization of school placement bureaus as distribution centers by either the product or the by-product of the public schools.[8] After years of interest and effort the Chicago bureau reported that 2.77 per cent of school leavers had been aided to secure positions by the schools.[9] It is even more surprising to find that Pittsburgh, which was exceptionally alert with reference to school responsibility for the distribution of its clientele, which was closely allied with both the Junior Division of the United States Employment Service and the local chapter of the National Association of Corporation Schools, and which had almost ideal facilities for a genuine junior labor market, admitted that for the most part school leavers were self-distributing.

This second survey period included the survey made under the New York Military Training Commission which covered 245,000 sixteen-, seventeen-, and eighteen-year-old employed boys and was usually considered to have brought together in one volume the most comprehensive description of employed youth ever attempted.[10] It is very helpful for comparison with the findings of the recent New York State Regents' inquiry, especially since Burdge reported his findings by groups, Greater New York, cities over 25,000, under 25,000, villages over 5000, under 5000, and employed farm boys. In Greater New York 1.8 per cent reported school assistance while approximately 90 per cent had been self-distributing; in the remainder of the state less than 1 per cent had received school assistance and about 94 per cent had been self-distributing.

By 1930 the country had entered upon its third survey period. This new period, which has been interested in youth from sixteen to twenty-four years of age, has been briefly characterized by Floyd W. Reeves, who as

---

[7] The Minneapolis Survey of 1913 revealed that 1.7 per cent were assisted by the public schools, and Superintendent Spaulding was a strong supporter of guidance services. Industrial surveying during this same period revealed close agreement between school leavers and employers regarding the best methods of securing positions.

[8] In *Human Waste in Education* the author summarizes the survey findings separately for each period.

[9] See Charles M. Larcomb, *Survey of Free Junior Placement in Chicago* (unpublished thesis, University of Chicago, 1921).

[10] Howard G. Burdge, *Our Boys* (Albany, N.Y.: New York State Military Training Commission, 1921).

Director of the American Youth Commission has been in charge of three surveys and has been in a position to consider the findings of many current local surveys. Reeves concludes that not over 5 per cent of the schools are responsible for effective placement services.[11] Edward Landy reports that only about 4 per cent of those comprised in the Secondary-School study secured their first jobs through the schools.[12] The New York Regents' Inquiry credits the schools with service to less than 3 per cent of the withdrawals and slightly better service (5–9 per cent) to graduates.[13]

Closely connected with the service of the schools to youth is the question of service to employing concerns, for placement is a middleman's function. What confidence does the employer have in the school's appraisal of the marketable qualities of its product? One or two citations will open the way for those who desire to continue their study of this topic.

The Regents' Inquiry found that many employers felt that they could not accept the recommendations made by the schools.[14] Perhaps some explanation of the attitude of employers may be found in the findings of a rather remarkable section entitled "Readiness for Vocational Responsibilities."[15] Almost 50 per cent of those who withdrew from the general high school were denied job recommendations by the school authorities; from 10 to 15 per cent of those who were granted certificates of academic proficiency were considered unready to attain job proficiency.

Supporting this evidence of negative educator appraisal is a breakdown table which counselors will need to study very carefully in order to appreciate its significance. A list of the youth qualifications which are considered by employers at the time of application in comparison with those which make for success on the job is also offered.[16] The fact that personality ranks first in securing a job but is superseded by industry in making good on a job is cited as the possible basis of a "strange conclusion" that many poor employee selections are made, that those who are good at getting jobs may not be good at keeping them. Is this a "strange conclusion" or is it a perfectly normal condition, well understood by every employer and every experienced placement worker? *What proportion of the jobs avail-*

[11] "After the Youth Surveys—What?" *Occupations*, XVIII (1940), 243–248. Those who read Reeves's article will realize that this writer does not agree with his characterization of the surveys made prior to 1929. She does agree that it is time to summarize what we have learned, not only since 1930 but since 1900, and to note any constructive trends which may have resulted from the use of our knowledge.

[12] Edward Landy *et al.*, *Occupational Adjustment and the School* (Bulletin, XXIV, no. 93; Washington: National Association of Secondary-School Principals, 1940).

[13] Eckert and Marshall, *When Youth Leave School*, p. 232.

[14] *Ibid.*, p. 233.

[15] *Ibid.*, 110–114.

[16] *Ibid.*, 236.

able for high-school novitiates require any job readiness other than that which should have been acquired in the mastery of everyday school work? —industry, ability to take school-job responsibility, promptness, co-operation, mastery of assignments, especially the fundamentals, etc. It is practicing job readiness in school that prepares for readiness on the job which follows.

What an awful indictment of public education these findings are! Almost 50 per cent of our youth are branded by those who educate them as unready to take the next step! A rereading of E. W. Butterfield's "School Dull and Life Bright" [17] sometimes relieves the tension and helps to counteract the depressing influence of such academic pronouncements.

TABLE 3

TEACHERS' AND EMPLOYERS' ESTIMATES OF GENERAL CAPACITY OF CHILDREN

Capacity of Children	Teachers' Estimates		Employers' Estimates		Agreeing Estimates	
	No.	Per Cent	No.	Per Cent	No.	Per Cent
Bright	47	26.1	89	49.4	23	12.8
Average	86	47.8	77	42.8	38	21.1
Dull	47	26.1	14	7.8	9	5.0
Total	180	100.0	180	100.0	70	38.9

Looking backward thirty years to the survey authorized by Congress, one finds another use of teachers' and employers' opinions as a method of appraising the general capacity of young wage-earners. By means of personal interviews it was possible to secure employers' estimates of the mental capacities of 180 youths under sixteen years of age who were eliminated before reaching the high school. A comparison with teachers' estimates is shown in Table 3, and that comparison is defended in these words:

> Of course too much weight must not be laid on mere estimates, but the fact that so many of these children who were looked upon as dull and unintelligent in the schoolroom became eager, alert, and interested when they entered the industrial world seems to show that the school was at least partly in fault. And this inference is strengthened by the fact, already commented upon, that so large a proportion of the bright scholars were dissatisfied.[18]

Interim efforts to secure employers' and educators' estimates of desirable youth qualities and to bring such requirements into closer harmony on

[17] *Journal of the National Education Association,* XX (1931), 111–114. Also helpful to teachers is Owen Young's "Examinations in the University of Life," *Educational Record,* XII (1931), 408–416. This also appeared in the *American Scholar,* I (1932), 65–71.

[18] *Report on the Conditions of Women and Child Wage Earners,* VII, 122. This material has been reprinted in Reed, *Human Waste in Education,* p. 83.

the basis of general civic and social requirements for which public education is supposed to prepare are reported here and there in the literature of the guidance movement. The *Report of the Committee on Public Education of the National Association of Corporation Training*, 1916, made a valuable contribution from the employers' point of view. The Seattle *Vocational Guidance Report*, 1913–1916, cited an investigation which secured the opinions of over two hundred business concerns and about fifty of the largest school systems in the country. It also reported on a local device used to bring the appraisals of teachers and employers into closer agreement. Two of the objectives are quoted:

(1) To ascertain how far our teaching corps is estimating character and ability on the same or on a different basis from that of the business house.

(2) To ascertain what percentage of the school product is able to make and maintain a creditable standing in the business world.

Can the public schools distribute their product and by-product? Should they undertake to do so? There seems to be no greater unanimity in replies in 1943 than there was in the early years of the guidance movement. Obviously the record of the public schools as a placement agency is not encouraging. Whether the practical aspects of placement can and should be mastered by the educational system or whether they should become a definitely shared responsibility with some other agency is a matter pressing for decision. The solution of this problem is closely related to another problem. Do the schools wish to delegate employment supervision, or postschool adjustment services, to another agency?

Employment supervision has never implied supervision of occupational adjustments only. It has always implied maintaining contact with postschool youth in order to serve him in any area of life, and this is very definitely an educational function. It would be uselessly repetitious to cite the many pleas which have been made throughout the life of the guidance movement for the educational supervision and guidance of wage-earning youth. There seems to be more current support for the allocation of this function to the schools than there does for accepting placement as an educational function. One of the best, if not the most representative, statements of educational responsibility for postschool adjustment service is found in connection with the Occupational Adjustment Study recently completed under the auspices of the National Association of Secondary-School Principals.[19] The organization advocates the assumption by edu-

[19] All counselors and teachers will be interested in the two bulletins which are concerned with this study. Bulletin no. 93, *Occupational Adjustment and the School*, has already been cited. No. 101, also by Edward Landy and others, is entitled, *The School Follows Through: A Post-School Adjustment of Youth* (vol. XXV, 1941). The four forms recommended for follow-up surveys are included in the latter bulletin.

cation of responsibility for assistance to postschool youth and a counseling service equipped to advise in all the areas of life. It differentiates more clearly than most reports between employment supervision designed for the assistance of youth and follow-up, often synonymous with perpetual or periodic educational surveys, designed to ascertain the whereabouts of former school pupils, their progress, and whatever suggestions they may offer for the improvement of educational programs and procedures. Five years of postschool experience is suggested as an essential period of time before youth can tell a story which will have guidance values for school administration.

Students who read the current follow-up surveys and then turn back to the large number of similar surveys in which former youth have told their story will find much illuminating comparative data on the amount and causes of unemployment, the volume of shifting in juvenile (age 12–15) jobs and the type of youth who does the shifting, the factors which differentiate juvenile jobs from junior (age 16–18) jobs, and the personal qualities which determine what juveniles should be promoted to junior-job status and which, on attaining physical maturity, should be relegated to the ranks of common labor. *The educative value of juvenile and junior jobs stood out very clearly in the early surveys, but there was no one at hand to hear youth's story or help him to make use of the values revealed. Perhaps someone may be at hand as future stories are told!*

In the meantime youth will probably continue to tell his story. It is gradually becoming an epic. The more items that are selected for comparison from period to period the more epiclike the story becomes. There is not very much that is new. The storyteller has grown older; he has attained, by achievement or by "lifting out," a higher educational status; his chances of idleness are perhaps no greater proportionately; there is less chance that he is an alien; but there are some changes in his social and economic status as well as in his community environment. The social implications of his story in its influence on our way of life have changed as he has grown older. In former years idleness seemed closely related to juvenile delinquency; today "social dynamite" is the threat. The outstanding remedy for the ills of youth in former years has been the extension of residential requirements in the schoolroom. It did not check delinquency; it brought it within the schoolroom door. In 1943, additional years of education are suggested as one of the remedial efforts for the ills of older youth. Will this check the increase in social dynamite or will it bring it, too, within the classroom door?

Facts support the conclusion that over a considerable period of years the beginner in postschool life has turned to other than educational agencies for securing positions and for assistance in making his immediate adjustments. The facts do not indicate that any other agency has made any concerted move to pre-empt the field. Several have made helpful contributions, but none has made any effort to assume leadership. Practically all philanthropic bureaus, even though organized to serve older groups, opened their doors to the youngest wage-earners, while a considerable number were instituted primarily for neophytes.

Attention has been called to the keen responsibility for the educationally discarded youth which was shared by public employment officials, and to some of the problems which were occasioned by the presence of this group in offices designed to serve older, even though equally inexperienced, workers. Some of these officials were very persistent in their advocacy of state provision for "minors with a vocational counselor in charge." The Boston office reported a "juvenile" department in 1913, and this writer has yet to find a vocational guidance and placement service for school-leaving youth which was rendering better service than the Cleveland-City-State Bureau, organized in 1915 as a development of the 1908 bureau sponsored by the Consumers' League. It made local occupational studies, had a definite program for the immediate dissemination of current occupational information, co-operated with the public schools, followed up its placements, and had the complete confidence of both youth and employers.

The New York State law of 1914 provided for a certain number of "juvenile" offices and several were in operation in the larger cities. Some of these offices made serious efforts to render adjustment services to school leavers as well as to continuation school youth. A number of clever devices were used to encourage periodic calls at the employment center to report on progress, discuss problems, and maintain an advisory contact which would be helpful in making the transfer, at sixteen years of age, from juvenile jobs to junior jobs. Through the National Association of Corporation Schools, corporations were interested in co-operative supervision of youth programs, and in a number of cities local chapters worked very harmoniously with the public schools.[20]

The depression years witnessed two new federal agencies instituted primarily to serve beginners in the occupational areas of life and to relieve the pressure of unemployment, the Civilian Conservation Corps (1933) and the National Youth Administration (1935). Both programs were emergency efforts. As would be expected, there was considerable duplication of services, not only as between these two agencies but also in con-

[20] Pittsburgh is an outstanding illustration of the possibilities of such co-operation. See J. D. Stark, "How School Personnel and Vocational Guidance Departments Plan to Keep in Touch with Industry," *Vocational Guidance Magazine*, II (1924), 192–196.

nection with services rendered by long-established agencies operating under normal conditions. The wide powers granted the American Youth Commission and the liberal use which it has made of these powers have, with the war program well under way, raised a number of jurisdictional questions which are being widely discussed and which will doubtless lead to a delimitation of its activities if Congress decides to perpetuate the agency.[21]

Counselors who realize the contribution which placement and post-school counseling can make to the immediate adjustments of youth and to the ultimate social well-being of the entire adult population will naturally deplore any decrease in support of the junior placement offices which have been set up co-operatively by the public schools and the United States Employment Service. These junior offices are a revival of the program and procedures of the Junior Division of the United States Employment Service which was a post-World-War I emergency effort to tide youth over the evil effects of unemployment. This original federal effort was a flash in the pan, a bright flash while the money lasted, with great possibilities of service, but it was a very expensive agency if adequately staffed, and after three or four years financial support was withdrawn by Congress. There was continual objection, moreover, on the part of the federal authorities to giving financial support to the counseling or adjustment phase of the Junior Division Program. Placement was the sole function. That the same situation has obtained with reference to the present Junior Placement Service is now and then noted in current literature and prevents too great optimism relative to the future.[22]

---

21 This book has systematically avoided discussion of emergency guidance problems and programs. The author's interest lies in a long-term program which will embrace all individuals and be concerned with all areas of life—a program so fundamentally sound in theory and so successful in practice that it can be adapted to whatever unforeseeable demands society may make upon it.

The general report of the American Youth Commission, *Youth and the Future* (Washington: American Council on Education, 1942) is the most comprehensive, scholarly, farseeing, and nonpartisan presentation of youth emergency programs and their possible utility in an unpredictable future with which this writer is familiar. She commends it to the attention of counselors.

22 See Warren K. Layton, "The Junior Placement Service and the N.Y.A.," *Occupations*, XV (1937), 729–731. A number of points in this article will interest counselors. The contract for financial assistance to the Detroit Public Schools required "that placement rather than guidance be stressed," but soon afterwards the N.Y.A. subsidized a Junior Consultation Service which operated under the Detroit Council for Youth Service and worked in close co-operation with the schools.

The November, 1942, issue of the *Bulletin of the Committee on Youth Problems,* American Council on Education, stated that junior placement services were still being operated in a few cities on a streamlined basis; separate junior counseling services had been curtailed or eliminated.

GUIDANCE SERVICES FOR EXPERIENCED OR MATURE INDIVIDUALS

The second group of individuals allocated to the postschool classification comprises that always large number of persons whose age, mental and physical attributes, and educational and occupational status range from the lowest level of youth recently initiated into the out-of-school world to the highest level of adults who are about to enter upon retirement.

The previous section has noted that philanthropic organizations, business concerns, and employment offices opened their doors to wage-earning recruits even though their services may have been designed for more mature groups. The situation was true in reverse. Adults were often warmly welcomed by agencies whose normal clientele was youth. There never have been, so far as the majority of services are concerned, any sharply drawn lines between services to youth and services to adults.

The Boston bureau was established primarily to serve out-of-school young men. Parsons reported an age range from fifteen to seventy-five years. The majority were of high-school age, but college men, both graduates and undergraduates, and older and more experienced persons, both college and noncollege, were frequent applicants. The Boston Y.M.C.A. and the Women's Educational and Industrial Union worked closely with Parsons and maintained much the same standards and practices. The Collegiate Bureaus of Occupations, sponsored by the Association of Collegiate Alumnae, served both college students and alumnae. The Omaha Vocation Bureau, under the auspices of the local branch of the same organization, responded to appeals from school attendants, beginning wage-earners, and adults. Its director regretted the elimination of service to all over twenty-one when the bureau was taken over by the public schools. Although the Hartford Vocational Guidance Committee was charged with study of the conditions surrounding the fourteen- to sixteen-year-old worker, the report for 1911–1913 drew a very interesting distinction between the type of services desirable for school pupils who were preparing for occupational life and those which best met the needs of more mature persons. The closing statement of the report suggested that "as a *piece* of *educational work*" guidance be provided for children through the labyrinth of vocational and academic courses, and that a second line of development consist of a study of opportunities for minors of a more advanced age and guidance for the older worker.

Guidance Programs of Employing Concerns. All employees came within the corporation school purview. Of necessity the apprentice and the part-time or fulltime youth, whether he entered from the college or the noncollege level, has always received considerable attention; this group is the source of much of industry's promotional material. But a newly inducted employee soon ceased to be a novice and, if he continued with the concern, his developmental growth in a specialized field became of as much moment to his superiors as did the developmental growth of young pupils to educators. The publication of E. L. Thorndike's findings on adult learning [23] aroused much interest in the potentialities of older workers, gave impetus to the training of older employees, fostered their transfer to tryout activities, and expanded guidance facilities to counsel with them regarding preparation for promotion.[24]

The Industrial Relations Association of Chicago is a good example of a local agency acting as a clearance and information center for the personnel problems of its clientele. Its reports included the character and extent of the guidance procedures used and advocated by its various members. The report of the Committee on Education and Training for 1928 was entitled *Educational Guidance of Employed People*.[25] Part I reported on educational guidance practices among Chicago employers: the extent to which educational counsel was offered to all, to those who evidenced promotional possibilities, or to those who applied; the extent to which financial encouragement was customary, and the like. Some of the statements found in this and similar reports of the time read much the same as educator pronouncements. A few are summarized:

It was the policy of some concerns to counsel any employee who aspired to a better job and to let him learn at the expense of the company.

Stimulation to study, offered in groups rather than to individuals, left freedom of choice entirely to the individual. He ought to take responsibility for deciding whether to take advantage of educational opportunities and whether he could profit by doing so.

Some companies kept educational records, gave personal counsel, paid all or part of course expenses, and gave company publicity to educational achievements.

Some concerns made a systematic search for promising promotional material and assisted in making educational programs for promotion.

Other companies favored taking the initiative in advising all employees who held steppingstone jobs. If they did not care to equip themselves for promotion, they were not allowed to remain in such jobs.

The burden rests upon the individual. It is for him to make the decision and make known his desire to study. [A frequent statement.]

23 *Adult Learning* (New York: Macmillan Co., 1928).

24 Counselors who desire to secure an adequate conception of the early guidance activities of corporations should read the reports, especially the 1916 reports, of two committees of the National Association of Corporation Schools, the Committee on Public Education and the Committee on Vocational Guidance, the latter of which stressed the needs of older workers.

25 In the files of the author.

Two sections in the Industrial Relations Association report are as pertinent for educational counselors in 1943 as they were in 1928. In some respects they are more inclusive, more carefully thought through, and more specifically helpful than are similar lists used for guidance in the choice of institutions, curricula, and courses today. The first section mentioned items to consider in selecting an institution or a course. The second and more valuable section was a list of Other Standards for Measuring Schools. This list included such items as the history of the school, its commercial rating, its officers, its policies, its instructional staff, the character of its curricula, its textbooks and other instructional material, and its services to students and employers. Each item was discussed, and there were twenty-six subitems which were explained and their importance noted.

Further information regarding the adult guidance services afforded by business and industrial concerns and by professional and technical organizations is obtainable from annual reports of corporations, from current technical publications, from the research publications of the National Industrial Conference Board, and from the local surveys, reports, and services which are carried on independently or in co-operation with other community agencies.[26] A number of current educational programs primarily for high-school and college youths have been mentioned in Part II.

Adult Services under Philanthropic Auspices. While adult services provided by employing concerns are fairly easy to locate and to study in retrospect if one has both the time and the inclination, there is no national record of the rise and fall, the functions, and the quality of all the adult services which have been in operation during the years of the organized guidance movement. Some have been philanthropic in origin and character, others have been semiphilanthropic; some have been subsidized by the public, others have been purely commercial; some have been in existence many years, others are newcomers or have responded to some temporary need and have closed their doors when the demand was over. Now and then an adult service has been operated mainly for experimental or research purposes.

All things considered, although other agencies with similar objectives would be essential for a complete picture, the adult counseling and guidance services of the Y.M.C.A. seem best to represent the accomplishments

---

[26] During a discussion of grievance procedures A. P. Lancaster, Superintendent of Industrial Relations of the Hawthorne Works of the Western Electric Company, described the counselor system of his company (*Working with Unions—Grievance Procedures*, Personnel Series, no. 57; New York: American Management Assn., 1942, pp. 19–20).

of philanthropic or semiphilanthropic personnel services.[27] Its guidance work is an integral part of its total service but, as was the case with schools and colleges, its early day counseling was incidental and nonprogramed. Prior to the twentieth century, specific calls for occupational information and advice were usually responded to by employment secretaries. After that date programs and reports began to appear, and there is abundant material available to indicate that the organization has always been in step with the best thought in the personnel field and has carried its full share of the load both as to legitimate theory and progressive practice. Its services have always been spiritually grounded, and as the narrower religious aspect which characterized its earlier years has been dropped and nonmembers as well as members have been welcomed without reference to age or religious affiliation, it has taken on more or less the character of a community guidance center.

While the young businessman represents the typical Y.M.C.A. client, local organizations have usually adjusted to local demands, serving men from both the higher and the lower levels of social, educational, and occupational life. For years the organization filled in the gaps in personnel services provided by college authorities for their registrants, while in many high schools the Hi-Y has been the forerunner of, or a supplement to, guidance services under educational auspices. As colleges and secondary schools have assumed responsibility for their own personnel services, Y.M.C.A. secretaries have been withdrawn or their functions redistributed.

Nor have the guidance needs of rural youth been forgotten. C. C. Robinson, reviewing the various features of the organization's guidance program in 1925, mentioned the special services required in country communities, especially in rural regions, in order to aid boys in determining whether their abilities were better adapted to city or to rural occupations and, if their decision led to environmental change, in helping them make the adjustment and find suitable occupational outlets.[28] That the Y.M.C.A. has maintained its interest in the problems of rural youth and is contributing to the recently inaugurated national movement to serve such youth better is evidenced by the complimentary reports on a currently functioning program which come from northern Vermont where, under

27 Some branches of the Y.M.C.A. charge a small fee for counseling or placement. The basis and amount vary, but it is always sufficiently below current commercial rates to warrant the term "semiphilanthropic." A common charge where complete clinical service is required is $7.50, which is approximately the cost per client of the rather heavily subsidized—by volunteer and relief-wage services as well as by financial support —Adjustment Service of New York City. See Jerome H. Bentley and Helen Kelley, *Costs of the Adjustment Service* (New York: American Association for Adult Education, 1935).

28 "The Vocational Guidance Program of the Y.M.C.A," *Vocational Guidance Magazine*, III (1925), 174–176.

the leadership of A. C. Hurd, the schools of that section are the beneficiaries of a carefully planned, locally applicable, guidance service.

World War I gave the Y.M.C.A. an excellent opportunity to acquire new experiences and to enhance its readiness to respond to the demand for personnel assistance in the demobilization of servicemen and their remobilization in civilian occupations. When the call came it accepted the challenge and moved forward in company with other organizations which have been mentioned as evidencing readiness to meet postwar conditions. Under a Bureau of Vocational Guidance, established at the national headquarters in New York City as a service of the United Y.M.C.A. Schools with Eli W. Weaver, Director, a chain of operating units provided varied aspects of guidance service for men as they were released from war service. By virtue of this wide-scale activity, the guidance interest of the Association was nationally expressed. This may be said to mark the beginnings of its efforts to give direction to all of its guidance activities.

Considered from the point of view of tools and techniques the Y.M.C.A., in spite of the financial ups and downs which recur in such organizations with the regularity of business cycles, has not lagged in comparison with other agencies and at times it may legitimately claim leadership.

As an indication of comparatively early responsiveness to progress in the area of clinical counseling, attention may be called to the clinical vocational guidance services instituted by the Camden Y.M. in 1925 and its six-year report, issued in 1931.[29] The laboratory was reported to be thoroughly equipped with materials for a complete psychological analysis. Dr. Morris S. Viteles was in charge. Outside agencies were used for medical or other essential examinations. Placement was done by other agencies, for while it was not needed in the solution of all problems, in some cases it "was sorely needed to complete the recommendation." Analytical reports of each case were made; follow-up was practiced; and careful records for adjustment purposes were maintained.

Two clinical services with which this writer is personally familiar are usually rated among the best in the United States today, the Personal Counseling Service of the West Side Branch of the New York City Y.M. and the Occupational Services of the Huntington Branch of the Boston Y.M.[30] The New York Service is under the supervision of Dr. Joseph V.

[29] "Report of the Psychological Clinic for Vocational Guidance, Conducted in the Camden Y.M.C.A., by the Civic Clubs Council," 1931. In the files of the author.

[30] The services of the Psychological Corporation are neither forgotten nor unappreciated. The origin of the Corporation is interesting, its standards unquestioned, and its services well known among students. As a clinical service for the average individual, it is not particularly useful to counselors because comparatively few individuals can meet the expense involved.

Hanna, who has had wide experience in personnel work on both the secondary school and college level. All ages are accepted, and a wide variety of cases apply—maladjusted individuals, rural youths with no conception of their abilities or their market value, men who need assistance in evaluating different educational opportunities or in relating their own desires and capacities to educational and occupational opportunities, and always a number of emotionally unstable persons. Dr. Hanna has attained considerable proficiency in so conducting interviews that they serve as segregative factors in determining which individuals can be as well, or better, served without clinical procedures and which can be better served by the addition of a more or less detailed psychological analysis, supplemented as occasion demands by other types of analyses.

This is specifically mentioned because many, perhaps the majority at present, seem to feel that all counseling must follow a uniform procedure with a somewhat superficial interview accompanied by filling out a blank, a full battery of tests, and a counseling interview presumably with a clinical psychologist or a case worker who is competent to interpret the results of the tests in all their interrelations in the light of the schedule and interview data. It is obvious that if every normal everyday counseling problem must go through this detailed and expensive procedure, few agencies can afford to support counseling. But it is not necessary. There are hundreds of persons who visit a counseling bureau in search of the sort of assistance which can be given by a well-informed, experienced interviewer without recourse to tests of any kind. The important point is—to be able to determine which tools and techniques are needed for each case and to be sure that no agency and no individual not properly equipped to do so attempts clinical services or disseminates information which is not authentic.

The clinical work of the Boston Occupational Service is but one phase of a rather elaborate program which approaches in scope the work of the Psychological Corporation, including services to employing concerns and the construction of tests to meet specific needs. The guidance services for young men and adults comprise individual and group guidance, vocational round tables, conferences on job seeking, promotions, personality development, and the like. An unusually complete clinical laboratory is available, the result of a generous bequest to the organization, which in turn was more than generous with the clinical department.

The postwar alertness of the Y.M.C.A. and its sensitivity to the guidance needs of both youth and adult are revealed in the literature of that time and have continued to date. Problems have crystallized, deficiencies in service have been revealed, and provocative discussions have opened up new lines of thought and suggested improvements in personnel and in the application of tools and techniques to the diversified groups which have sought its assistance. A few evidences of organization activity are mentioned, and one or two milestones which have significance for the progress of the guidance movement are cited:

Training courses for counselors have been a continuous part of the program of the Y.M.C.A. from the inception of the organized movement. The first course was given under its auspices in 1908 in Boston, and from that date on courses and conferences for the preparation and in-service training of counselors have been included among its functions. The curricula of its professional schools have included guidance units. Current evidence indicates not only that in some respects the preparation afforded by these schools compares favorably with that offered in our largest university centers, but also that it may ultimately excel such centers unless their objectives be more clearly defined, limitations of the field be determined upon, course relationships be harmonized, and useless duplication of course content be avoided.

Association in manageable groups for the exchange of experiences and discussion of common problems has tended to progress and has led to uniformity where uniformity was advantageous, e.g., in 1924 thirty-eight locals were accenting the development of effective vocational guidance centers and were co-operating in such fashion that each received the benefit of the experience of the others.[31]

Records and reports issued by the Y.M.C.A. reveal an early and continued interest in differentiating counseling procedures adapted to adults from those more suitable for youth. There is an increasing challenging of procedures, testing of techniques, and building up of differentiated skills and procedures. A very brief and meaty statement from the Minneapolis Y.M. in 1924 [32] is equally applicable to the counseling of adults of today and is characteristic of advanced thinking in the field of adult guidance. It cites the necessity for speedy "reorganization of the counseling mind" as it jumps from one adult interview to the next; notes the hopelessness of standardized procedures when "the menace to the usual is only equalled by the destruction of the monotonous"; mentions deficiencies in the personnel inventory situation and the greater demands made upon the observational ability of the interviewer.

Some years ago the Y.M.C.A. became aware of the fact that if the vocational aspect of its educational work was to be a success it must move "out of the educational area into closer contact with the industrial and business concerns of the community." Several locals acted upon this conclusion.

The Y.M.C.A. has also participated in some of the experimental guidance activities which are usually thought of as public-school or college functions. The Y schools joined in the wave of life-career-class enthusiasm which permeated secondary education in the 1920's, and Weaver prepared a book for the use of such schools.[33] The Find-Yourself Campaigns were forerunners of much of the present-day interest in self-inventories of various types, and their use was

[31] Robinson, *loc. cit.*

[32] A. H. Speer, "Vocational Guidance in the Young Men's Christian Association," *Vocational Guidance Magazine*, II (1924), 185.

[33] Eli W. Weaver, *Building a Career* (New York: Association Press, 1922).

provocative of much organization discussion regarding the dangers of introspection. Orientation classes are in use in its professional colleges [34] and the maintenance and use of cumulative records is approved and in fairly general use. Group work has always been emphasized in Y programs—group work with full appreciation of the fact that it has the dual purpose, which has previously been mentioned in connection with group guidance or homeroom programs, of guidance in and through group work processes and of guidance which is the result of group work processes.

Adult Services under Public Auspices. Two major public agencies which participated in instituting the guidance movement have continued to make contributions to one or more phases of adult guidance and personnel, public employment services and public education.[35]

All guidance services, irrespective of the auspices under which they operate, have their ups and downs with reference to the interests of their sponsors, to financial support, and to patronage. The efforts of all have been sporadic as to time and effectiveness; all have been influenced by the prevailing economic conditions. Public agencies have lacked the clear-cut objectives which are found in connection with business and industrial concerns and which have provided the Y.M.C.A. with an ultimate goal to be attained in spite of interruptions to progress.[36] This lack has been a handicap to effectiveness and makes it very difficult to find a single thread upon which to string the story of their contribution, especially when space is limited.

Public Employment Services. Here and there throughout this study mention has been made of certain specific guidance contributions made by public employment offices, municipal, state, or federal, especially for the benefit of junior workers. As a rule, in the adult office placement has been the sole function, and any counseling which may have been done was so incidental, so cursory, or so totally dependent upon the interest and qualifications of the individual functionary that the office, as a unit, would

[34] The orientation class at Fenn College, Cleveland, is described in *A Primer of Guidance Through Special Work* (New York: Association Press, 1940). Fenn College is also credited with operating an outstandingly successful guidance clinic under the direction of Dr. Joseph Kopas.

[35] Public libraries should not be eliminated from consideration. They were co-operators in the occupational information phase of several early guidance programs. Their major function of necessity involves some incidental guidance service, but so far as this writer is aware St. Paul was the first public library to provide a full-time counselor for its patrons. (See Nancy S. Loehr, "Occupational Guidance Service in a Public Library," *American Library Association Bulletin,* XXXV [1941], 18–22.) That librarians do not appreciate their own early contribution to guidance is evidenced in the proceedings of a recent *Conference on Guidance through the School Library* at Simmons College, School of Library Science, Boston, 1940.

[36] The same would be true of other organizations which have long-term objectives, e.g., The National Federation of Business and Professional Women's Clubs.

not merit classification as a guidance agency. Some outstanding exceptions have come to the personal attention of this writer, e.g., one in the years 1918–1921 when she was engaged in national supervisory work under the United States Employment Service.

The Philadelphia office for the placement of adult women employed a full-time, high-salaried counselor to advise with women who had been released from war industries in that area. The following is characteristic of the type of placement which she was supposed to prevent by counseling: A woman forty years of age, a shoe factory operator in Massachusetts, had been lured by patriotism and high wages to accept munitions factory work in Philadelphia. The war ended. Tryouts in five to ten lines of work followed. Each time the woman reregistered, the reception clerk assigned her to the desk representing her last job. She was referred again and again for similar work until she either refused to apply or an employer refused to consider her. Then she was sent to another desk and referred to another occupation. This procedure was repeated several times. The experienced counselor was supposed to prevent this counter placement procedure, to find out which workers had been employed in skilled work, and to redistribute them in keeping with prewar occupations. The idea was good, but the counselor was not functioning, and this writer was sent to Philadelphia to find out why there was an extra salary for a minimum of service. The counselor seemed competent, but the location of her desk at the end of a very long room practically prohibited her from functioning. No one appeared to remember that she was available, while she was so far removed from the activities of the office that she had no opportunity to find her own chance to serve. When her desk was moved to the front of the room and the reception clerk was instructed to ask two or three questions which would tentatively differentiate counseling cases and placement cases, she became a very useful person.

It is often the little thing, moving a desk, which changes ineffectiveness into effectiveness. This instance has been mentioned in order to stress that point as well as to call attention to the fact that definite provision for counseling has occurred in adult as well as in junior offices.

The late unemployment crisis brought the usual renewal of public interest in provision for public employment services. The Wagner-Peyser Act of 1933 re-established the old temporary emergency service of World War I, this time by Congressional action on a "matching of state and federal funds" basis. Soon after, additional funds were available under the Works Progress Administration, and the National Reemployment Service was inaugurated on a temporary basis supported by federal emergency funds. The enactment of unemployment compensation laws resulted in closer co-operation between federal and state agencies and in further expansion of state employment services.

Since 1939, when the U. S. Employment Service was transferred to the newly established Federal Security Agency, which also acquired the

U. S. Office of Education, the U. S. Public Health Service, the National Youth Administration, the Social Security Board, and the Civilian Conservation Corps, it has had the advantage of being associated in the same department with several other agencies which have major interests in personnel services and among which duplications on the adult level are most likely to occur. Already alert educational and occupational counselors are turning to its Employment Service Division for reliable occupational information and are benefiting, at least indirectly, from the assistance which it offers states in establishing or improving services for special groups such as inexperienced workers, older workers, juniors, farm workers, and the like. Up to the present, public offices have made no suitable provision for the distribution of professional and technical workers. There are many reasons, some of which will doubtless be overcome as time goes on and the offices acquire experience and efficiency and gain in prestige.

Undoubtedly the public employment offices have traveled a decidedly uphill road, with political exploitation and all its attendant evils a major stumbling block. But civil service has done something to change the picture, and it is amazing, as one reviews the history of the movement, to note how many well-qualified personnel workers have maintained their confidence in the ultimate success of such services and have continued to make personal contributions to the attainment of that goal. The immediate contributions of the federal service to occupational information, to selection techniques, and to the training of placement personnel [37] plus the improvements which have been made in state and local office practices, considered in connection with responsibilities for the proper administration of unemployment compensation legislation, warrant the assumption that public employment services will continue to function as one of the outstanding agencies in the field of guidance and personnel.

Adult Services under Public Education. The quantity and quality of the contribution of public education to guidance services for adults is even more difficult to determine than is that of public employment services. In general the statement regarding the incidental, cursory, and individually controlled guidance services offered by placement offices is equally applicable to educational services. There are certain additional reasons why it is more difficult to offer an authentic picture of adult

[37] The annual *Proceedings* of the International Association of Public Employment Services are valuable sources of practical suggestions in many areas of guidance and personnel. The 1939 meeting accented training, the 1941 meeting discussed fifty-nine functions of an employment service and gave considerable attention to rating employees. These proceedings supply the practical element so often missing from discussions among educator groups.

guidance under education auspices: (1) There is no specific function of guidance and personnel service which is a major responsibility of adult education. Any guidance functions which may accompany adult instruction are usually incidental; possibly there may be education as guidance without any very definite objective for either and with neither receiving much public praise or public blame. On the other hand, public employment services are charged with responsibility for one of the outstanding functions of guidance and personnel service. They have received some public praise, plenty of public blame, and enough merciless criticism to prevent complacency and to inspire to progress. (2) The U. S. Office of Education has given its major attention to youth interests whereas the U. S. Employment Service has been primarily concerned with the adult needs. (3) State departments of education have been charged with the education of adults, but the measuring stick of the occupational efficiency of its clientele has been allocated to the labor departments. (4) It is safe to assume that the employment services have a better equipped staff for both the educational and occupational guidance of adults than do educational systems. Whereas the educator-counselor is, to a large extent, shut off from accumulating the type of information essential to an adult guidance service, opportunities for acquiring such knowledge are abundant for employment-counselors.

Although there are no available data which warrant conclusions regarding the past accomplishments or present status of adult guidance services, it seems desirable to cite certain types of published material which contain forward-looking suggestions and to call attention to a few satisfactorily operating adult services.

Public Rehabilitation Services. From the point of view of continuity of service, promise of permanency, satisfactory performance, and general contribution to the improvement of all educational and personnel services for physically handicapped persons, whether the handicaps be congenital or the result of labor, war service, or accident, the Rehabilitation Division of the U. S. Office of Education stands first. Prior to the entry of the United States into World War I, the Red Cross Institute for Crippled and Disabled Men had instituted a program for the guidance and training of war-disabled men and had published a number of guidance bulletins. Vocational guidance began during hospitalization for its psychological value and as a therapeutic measure. Each case was studied, tested, counseled, and as soon as physically able allowed whatever tryouts were possible.

In 1918 the rehabilitation services for disabled soldiers were allocated to the Federal Board for Vocational Education; in 1920 civilian rehabilitation services were added; and in 1921, the Veterans' Bureau. Although training may be considered the core of the re-education program, counseling, placement, and employment supervision are essential to success. Case studies precede acceptance for training, at every step guidance accompanies training, and the most careful placement procedures are followed in the distribution and supervision of individuals who have completed training. Charles A. Prosser, the first director of the Federal Board, frequently gave others the benefit of a guidance procedure which he had found to be satisfactory, especially with disabled individuals who were inclined to scrap all previous occupational assets. Interviews were followed by a tabulation of assets and a tentative program; classes might be attended as auditors or visitors; students and instructors in different shops could be asked the questions that occur to one who is considering a new line of work. If an individual felt that it would be helpful in determining the effect of his handicap, he could put on overalls and try himself out.

In addition to the guidance services rendered to disabled persons, the surveys and other types of research data which are available through rehabilitation agencies contribute valuable knowledge regarding the importance of psychological factors as well as physical variables in predicting and in attaining occupational success or failure. This statement is also applicable to special placement services which register only the blind, deaf, mental defectives, delinquents, or other variations from normal. It is absolutely essential that education be accompanied by counseling, placement, and employment supervision, and that periodic follow-up surveys be made. All the information secured through such channels contributes to the knowledge needed by less highly specialized counselors, who are frequently required to advise with handicapped persons.

Public Evening Schools. At the state level, adult education has not yet been granted the type of federal-state co-operation which has been so beneficial to public employment services, to vocational rehabilitation services, and to youth education. Logically, one would not expect to find much guidance in connection with adult education offered by public evening schools and other types of educational activity designed primarily to serve adults. Such agencies sometimes advertise guidance service, but as a rule, admitting the usual exceptions which reveal a few schools rendering exceptionally meritorious service, the type of guidance accompanying public adult education does not warrant classification as guidance,[38] and

38 ". . . One of the greatest deficiencies in the total adult education program in New York State is the almost complete lack of adequate and satisfactory facilities for educational and vocational guidance" (F. W. Reeves, T. Fansler, and C. O. Houle, *Adult Education*, New York: The Regents' Inquiry, McGraw-Hill Book Co., 1938, p. 125). The final chapter of this study contains specific recommendations for the improvement of adult education and for the inclusion of guidance services in the program.

to the extent of this deficiency the main objectives of public adult education are defeated or but partially realized.

The difficulties involved in inaugurating and conducting adult guidance services are much greater than are those encountered in connection with the installation of similar services for day-school attendants. The lack of co-ordinating and supervisory services has been mentioned. A second outstanding handicap is the almost universal practice of utilizing the day-school corps as evening instructors. This procedure results in teachers and counselors whose attitudes, methods, and outlook on life are attuned to day-school conditions and the problems of youth and whose knowledge of the occupational and other responsibilities of the adult registrant is inadequate to appreciate his need and understand how best to serve him through the medium of the educational system. Again evening-school salaries are usually supplementary rather than single salaries, which means that the instructor's first obligation is elsewhere and the adult student receives the residuum of mental and physical ability, a major variable among evening instructors.

One feels much sympathy for the tired minds and tired bodies of evening-school students as they struggle to pick up a few intellectual crumbs, a little technical skill, or a bit of helpful guidance from the equally tired and empty minds, in the equally tired bodies of their would-be instructors and counselors. Agility of mind, mentioned by the Y.M.C.A. counselor as an essential in dealing with the diversified problems of adults, is even more essential when it must perform a two-shift duty (1) from immature day-school minds to the mature minds of adults, some of whom have studied long and profitably from the pages of life and (2) from one adult mind to another. Even did the day-weary teacher retain the mental elasticity to shift from group to group and from adult to adult, how many have the fundamental knowledge which permits them to interpret course offerings in terms of immediate occupational needs, of possible promotional opportunities, or of ever-changing occupational trends? How many can interpret the recreational, health, or cultural opportunities of the school in terms of beneficial contributions to the individual's total program? Adult guidance services imply broad experiences with life and familiarity with present occupations and trends in occupational patterns. They also imply familiarity with the types of stress and strain which press so heavily upon adults and which may often be, at least partially, relieved by careful choice of educational activities.

This inability to grasp postschool situations and to be of assistance in the solution of problems involved was a reputation early acquired by day-school teachers assigned to adult classes. The Seattle report of 1913–1916 called the superintendent's attention to the fact that pupils who had but recently left full-time school returned to adult evening classes with an entirely new point of view based on their new experiences and that they reported to the central office that the teachers no longer understood them. To this same characteristic may be attributed one of the main reasons why every "youth-tell-their-story" survey, from Mrs. Woolley's first Cincinnati report on the elementary level [39] to W. S. Learned's recent report on graduates ten years out of college,[40] indicates that although there may be considerable educational assistance in securing first jobs, guidance and placement facilities do not function as agencies for adjustment or for future placements. Ability to distinguish between the psychology of the inexperienced and the experienced, the mature and the immature, and to treat the adult as an adult is one of the arts that must be mastered by school counselors if, when the die is cast, postschool community counseling falls to the public-school system.

If a single illustration of adult guidance in connection with public education were to be chosen as worthy of commendation, probably most observers of the guidance movement would nominate the Denver Opportunity School. The School has been operating since 1916 as an integral part of the Denver public-school system. It is not an experiment, a work-relief project, or a war-emergency program. Day and evening classes are open to any adult resident tuition free. Guidance was not formally recognized in its original program, but when this writer made her first visit to the school in 1917, Emily J. Griffith was not visualizing "opportunities" in the abstract but in connection with definite means of assisting each individual to determine what constituted an opportunity for him. The objectives of the school could never have been so definitely realized by so many individuals [41] without effective guidance services. Mutual confidence was early established between Denver employers and the school; specific educational needs of employees for retention or promotion have been reported to the school and have received attention; and always the school has kept in close touch with community life. For a time there was limited guidance and placement assistance from the adjustment service of the National Youth Administration. The placement bureau of the

39 *Charting Childhood in Cincinnati* ([Cincinnati:] Bureau of Vocational Guidance, Child Labor Dept., Public Schools of Cincinnati, 1913).

40 "The Wages of Scholarship," *Thirty-sixth Annual Report of the Carnegie Foundation for the Advancement of Teaching*, 1940–1941, pp. 42–55. This is a follow-up report on the Pennsylvania students included in Learned and Wood's *The Student and His Knowledge*. Of the 2992 men who participated in the original study, 1227 gave the financial data for the later report.

41 In 1917 the registration was approximately 2500, in 1940–41, 14,200.

U. S. Employment Service also helped, although in Denver as in most other cities guidance bureaus under, or co-operating with, public education usually accent service to high-school eliminates or graduates.

Adult Guidance Services and the Economic Depression. The late economic depression may be credited with responsibility for several adult guidance projects. The objectives varied. Services to the unemployed, utilization of the unemployed as a source of research data, and the reduction of social unrest among the unemployed were among the main ones. Both taxpayers and philanthropists contributed to the financial support of such projects. Many interesting returns are now available, but since a certain historical perspective is essential in order to appraise results and assign new ventures to their legitimate place in the development of any movement, the immediate task must be limited to that of reporting basic facts. Moreover, the impact of the war emergency on the unemployment situation has, to some extent, handicapped the bringing of these projects to their normal fruition. When the time is ripe, future students of the guidance movement must assume responsibility for completing the picture of the current period by giving their legitimate credit and logical place to at least two major philanthropic projects, to the various public projects which were a part of the Adult Education Program of the Works Progress Administration and to such recently instituted community projects as may prove worthy of inclusion in future historical accounts.

The reports of the Minnesota Employment Stabilization Research Institute described three major projects concerned with unemployment in a given locality, one with the economic aspects of unemployment, one with individual diagnosis and retraining, and one with the development of public employment agencies. The University of Minnesota assumed responsibility for leadership in the researches. Liberal subsidies were received from the Rockefeller Foundation, the Spelman Fund, and the Carnegie Corporation. Work began in 1931.[42]

Among the stated objectives was one which had guidance implications, namely, to ascertain what selective principles determined who should join the ranks of the unemployed. Individual diagnoses, industrial, psychological, and medical, were used in order to arrive at conclusions. Case studies, occupational tests, interviewing, and placement practices, all received considerable attention, and here and there throughout the reports many possible values for adult guidance were revealed. It must be remembered, however, that it was an emergency project, that the accent

---

[42] Russell A. Stevenson in *The Minnesota Unemployment Research Project* (Minneapolis: University of Minnesota Press, 1931) states the objectives and outlines the three projects in some detail.

was on research—it was an effort to understand the influence of the depression on the lives of the unemployed, to appraise the various devices used in diagnosis, and the like—and that the ultimate value of the project is for the future to decide.[43]

The second emergency project in the interests of adults was the Adjustment Service of New York City. Where the Minnesota project was primarily interested in research, the objective of the New York experiment was service, but service which included demonstration values. It was a free community counseling service, open to the adult unemployed of both sexes from twenty to forty years of age. It was instituted in January, 1933, financed by the Carnegie Corporation through the medium of the American Association for Adult Education, and directed by an unusually able and experienced group of individuals including some who had been connected with the Minnesota project and were familiar with its findings, its successes and failures, and the criticism of it.

The program of the Service was a counseling one. It was not a complete guidance or personnel service. It gave counsel in the educational, social, recreational, vocational, and avocational areas of life. Its service functions included dissemination of information in the areas mentioned, individual diagnoses, and personal interviews. Records were carefully kept; case conferences were used both for the benefit of clients and for the assistance and training of counselors. The interest of the Service in appraising its accomplishments and having them appraised by others is rather unusual and therefore worthy of mention.[44] When the entire project is considered, favorable and unfavorable comments are about what experienced individuals would expect.

There were several handicaps, perhaps unavoidable, inherent in the contract for financial support of the Service and in its setup. Among those which should be given consideration before history pronounces its final verdict are:

(1) The establishment of a counseling service involves a time element; it is a gradual growth. Twenty months covers the entire history of this experiment.

(2) The quality of the service is the acid test of the effectiveness of counseling. Quantity and quality do not team well together in counseling. This was a mass production job, 16,726 clients.

(3) A work-relief project and a counseling project make a poor combination.

[43] A complete list of the reports may be secured from the University of Minnesota Press, Minneapolis, Minnesota.

[44] See J. A. and Florence Lee Fitch, C. S. Coler, and D. G. Paterson, *General Appraisals of the Adjustment Service*, and L. S. Hawkins, *Clients' Opinions of the Adjustment Service*, Adjustment Service Reports, nos. IX and XII. Paterson's appraisal is especially worthy of study.

The directors, by the terms of their contract, were obliged to select the counseling corps from the ranks of the unemployed.

(4) The major interest of the unemployed is in a job. Placement was not included among the functions of the Service, nor were appropriate employment outlets through other agencies made available.[45]

(5) Adequate tools and skillful operating techniques are indispensable in a counseling service. Tools seem to have been quite adequate, but techniques were too newly acquired and too insecurely grounded to have been used with the skill and assurance which long experience and thorough basic training provide. This, of course, was one of the inevitable results of making unemployment a prerequisite to a position. On the other hand, it must be remembered that this same lack of basic training has long been a common and legitimate criticism of a large number of educational counselors selected under more favorable conditions.

In spite of these admitted handicaps and their logical results, there are some very practical values to be derived from studying the reports of this Service,[46] and as time goes on these values will crystallize and become an integral part of the evolution of adult guidance services.

The Works Progress Administration,[47] through its state emergency education programs, provided the outstanding experimental adult guidance services under public auspices. As a rule its projects were under the direction of local boards of education and were open to out-of-school unemployed of all ages and both sexes. They were financed from relief funds and suffered even more severely than the Adjustment Service from being obliged to combine a work-relief project with a counseling service. In some communities individuals were required to be able to qualify for the pauper's oath before they could qualify as counselors.

Sometimes the educational authorities provided supervisory service, but when the dearth of effective personnel supervision is taken into consideration, it does not require much stretch of the imagination to visualize the majority of these services as purely relief projects. All the apparatus for individual diagnosis might be in stock, money was available for it, and it provided visible evidences of counseling readiness; but the damage done

---

[45] In *Adventures in Giving* (New York: Dodd, Mead and Co., 1939), William H. Matthews remarks on the absurdity of interviewing the unemployed on every possible topic except a job. The incident which Matthews, who spent forty years in social work, offers as illustrative of his point could be duplicated many times by those who have witnessed stereotyped interviews conducted without regard to their applicability to the needs of the applicants. A job-seeker who had patiently replied to endless nonessential questions brought the interview to a close with the comment: "Lady, there's nothing wrong with my family that a job won't cure. If I can get that, I shall be glad; if I can't then I'll be on my way."

[46] There are twelve reports in the series. As long as they are available a special price has been made for the full series. Write to the American Association for Adult Education, Teachers College, Columbia University, New York City.

[47] This was later superseded by the Work Projects Administration and liquidated by order of President Roosevelt, December 4, 1942.

to human lives by the random use and misuse of such dangerous tools will never be known. Nor is it possible to estimate the handicap to the progress of counseling as a profession which has resulted from this stress on pauperism as a counselor qualification. Posterity may well marvel that this all-time low for qualifications and public appreciation of the task of a counselor should have occurred in the late 1930's!

That some excellent counseling was done and that now and then a project was well supervised do not alter the fact that guidance services of this sort are a prolific source of practices to be avoided should the wheel of fortune decree that future adult community guidance services are to become a public responsibility.

During the years of their popularity several helpful pamphlets for the conduct of such services were issued under federal or state auspices. Among them were the memoranda in the series, To Administrators of Emergency Education Programs, published by the U. S. Office of Education from January to March, 1934. The series included such titles as Registration and Guidance and The Adjustment Service—Counseling. New York and Pennsylvania issued pamphlets which exemplify two types of adult guidance sponsored by state departments of education.

The New York pamphlet approached the problem of adult guidance from a broad educational point of view. It called attention to the unity of all areas of life and the necessity in counseling for recognizing such unity. It provided a list of types of information which should be familiar to counselors and available for course registrants. A brief manual for interviewers, one for educational counselors, and a final section concerned with counselor training and qualifications completed the pamphlet.[48]

The Pennsylvania pamphlet was devoted to the occupational aspect of guidance and was designed to serve as an outline for a series of discussions or round tables with a direct employment objective for each participant in view. Among the conference topics were: Self-Analysis, Analysis of Community Occupational Opportunities, Fitting into Obtainable Jobs, How to Apply, and the like.[49]

Community Guidance Projects. Guidance projects originating in community interest in one or more phases of guidance service accounted for the establishment of several of the early guidance bureaus. None could legitimately be considered a community project from the point of view of either inclusiveness of clientele or sources of support. That community

48 George E. Hutcherson and Layton S. Hawkins, Counseling Service for Adults (New York State Emergency Adult Education Program, Series 1, no. 1; Albany, N.Y.: State Education Dept., 1936).

49 Pennsylvania, Department of Public Instruction, A Program of Self-Analysis and Job Guidance for Adults (Harrisburg, Pa.: The Department, ?1935).

centers, county units, social units, rural community buildings, community churches, rating scales and score cards for community self-appraisal were all fairly popular in this country in the early 1920's is evidenced by the current literature of the period as well as by the pronouncements of civic organizations and service clubs.[50] But such activities were not primarily for guidance purposes, and if the guidance aspects were accented, it was for the benefit of school youth rather than for the adult population.

As the years have passed it has become increasingly difficult to differentiate a bona fide community service from such services as those supported by local Y.M.C.A.'s, or other similar organizations, which are to some extent community services and receive their support from individual community residents or from community chests. The author does not know of a single all-inclusive—as to aspects of guidance, public financial support, and clientele—community guidance service in the United States. There are many fragmentary beginnings which may furnish the composite experience for the later development of more complete programs.

Recently there has been considerable interest in community guidance projects organized as independent units or as units in state services cooperating with the Occupational Information and Guidance Service of the U. S. Office of Education. There has also been a revived interest in the development of community placement services in co-operation with state and federal employment services. For the most part, services instituted under educational auspices stress service to youth; those instituted in connection with employment services serve all wage-earning age groups.

Three brief references to limited community services which are largely confined to postschool or adult registrants will afford the reader a background for further investigation.

The Pasadena Employment and Vocational Bureau is suggested for study because it is in no sense a work-relief or a war-emergency bureau. It was organized in 1919 under favorable auspices and experienced leaders and was well grounded before the depression years. Its development has kept pace with social and economic change, and its practical co-operation with local adjunct agencies has revealed the unrealized possibilities of community service through community agency co-operation.[51]

[50] See the National Chamber of Commerce, *Social Agencies and the Community* (1922). See also the following publications of the U. S. Bureau of Education: Bulletin, 1915, no. 11, *The Community Association;* Bulletin, 1918, no. 11, *A Community Center: What It is and How to Organize It,* by Henry E. Jackson; and Misc. Publ., 1924, *Community Score Card Designed for Self-Appraisal and Self-Improvement.*

[51] For a brief account of the status of this bureau in 1937, see Winifred Hausam and George V. Moser, "Community Vocational Guidance for Adults," *Occupations*, XV (1937), 399–402.

The second organization suggested for study will remind the reader that the Pittsburgh Personnel Association is always in the forefront of activities for guidance services for adults. As a result of its recent survey it states that "needs for adult guidance and adjustment are not being adequately met," and recommends an independent service setup to co-operate with all existing agencies. Such a community service, it feels, would benefit individuals and "the community as a whole would share in the resulting improvement in social adjustment.[52]

The Providence Institute for Counseling and Personnel Services was very definitely a community project, although its accent on the sixteen to twenty-five age group would classify it as a service to out-of-school youth rather than to adults. It opened its doors in December, 1936, as an expression of the interest of a considerable number of community agencies in alleviating the evil influences of the economic depression. It was not tax-supported. The overhead was low; administrative service and housing space were contributed, and either the referral agency or the individual applicant paid a covering fee for testing and counseling service.[53]

Many of these recently organized guidance services will serve a temporary purpose and be dissolved when the purpose has been accomplished. Others will shift their purpose and adapt themselves to social and economic changes as they come. All, even the most transitory, will leave some residuum of value for the guidance movement providing there is an alert leadership to take advantage of such suggestions.

GUIDANCE SERVICES FOR OLDER OR RETIRED PERSONS

The third group of individuals entitled to consideration in a complete postschool guidance service comprises the superannuated or retired group. Statistical tabulations of any postschool guidance service will record adult registrants up to, and now and then over, seventy years of age. Those who have done extensive general counseling will bear witness to the fact that the postwork years of the aged are characterized by adjustment problems as peculiar to their age, experience, and varying situations as are the adjustment problems which characterize the years of childhood. Child guidance clinics have received public endorsement as starters along the uphill journey of life; only here and there is there any realization of the fact that counselors qualified to advise with those who are traveling

---

[52] See Glen U. Cleeton, *Occupational Adjustment in Allegheny County* ([Pittsburgh]: Pittsburgh Personnel Assn., 1935).

[53] For a brief description of this organization and its work when it was first instituted, see Wilbur I. Gooch, "A Non-School Youth Counseling Institute," *Occupations*, XV (1937), 396–398.

the downhill journey might render a valuable social, if not educational, service.[54]

Just as the word "child" was for years legitimately used only with reference to youth under fourteen or fifteen years of age, so the word "old" was confined to those who had met the obligations of occupational and family life and were candidates for retirement. Loose usage of both terms has led to amusing and illogical situations. A child seventeen to eighteen years of age, under some of our legislative enactments, is subservient to school-attendance laws; he may not work certain hours of the day, and he may not operate dangerous machinery. But the young man of the same age is pronounced by military authorities to be at the best age to prepare for aviation and to take responsibilities for the defense of his country!

Just about the time the age of childhood was being extended upward, the age of the "older" person was being extended downward, until in the occupational literature of the day "older worker" is being interpreted as one "over forty." The factors which account for this illogical shortening of the wage-earning period of life have been discussed by many writers and their social and economic implications stressed. Their guidance implications require that occupationally older or superannuated persons be considered in a somewhat different category from the biologically superannuated who are physically and mentally unfit for further wage-earning occupations or who for one reason or another, even though they retain mental and physical vigor, have ceased to be an important or dominant factor in the maintenance of the home or other institutions.

The plight of the occupational discard has been emphasized during recent years. The pros and cons of hiring, the social and personal causes and effects of unemployment, the allocation of responsibility, and the methods of relieving the situation have furnished themes for many addresses, conferences, and forums, as well as for countless printed pages. A few bureaus have been established primarily to assist the older worker in stocktaking and in making occupational adjustments. Obviously it is a very difficult undertaking, and even the best-equipped counselors will not attain a high percentage of success. The psychology of each displaced worker, his emotional reaction to the fact that he is unemployed, and the family attitude which may complicate the situation must be uncovered with the utmost of tact and patience. Even more tact and patience is required to help some individuals in this category to realize the important part which their own personality and characteristics may have contributed

[54] A writer in the *Adult Education Journal* of April, 1942 (I, 54), calls attention to certain needs of persons over sixty-five and states that studies are being made by Judson T. Landis at Iowa State College which will be reported on later.

to their unemployment and to see the necessity for personal activity looking toward successful re-employment. Job clinics, man-marketing clinics, demonstration interviews, and critical evaluations of applications have been fostered and personally conducted by employers, placement agencies, personnel men, and salesmen who, still holding their own positions, have been able to help the unemployed in the same age groups appraise their assets and liabilities from a sympathetic and practical rather than from an emotional angle.

While the tendency to retire men and women who seemed to be in the prime of life was a very disturbing factor during the late depression, it was a recurrence of an old problem rather than the occurrence of a new. It was a normal accompaniment to certain stages in our industrial progress. Prior to World War I there was a similar period of anxiety regarding the increasing number of middle-aged unemployed and a genuine fear lest prolongation of unemployment might result in the making of unemployables. The situation was temporarily relieved by war demands. In the meantime surveys, discussions, explanations, and preventive and remedial suggestions claimed the attention of employer, employee, and public.[55] A number of organizations interested in the problem of early superannuation were formed, and special bureaus for the placement of individuals handicapped by age were instituted.

The very fact of specialization permits the employment of a more competent staff, counselors who are able to recognize marginal assets and liabilities and the extent to which the one may overshadow the other, not only in a given field or position but even under different types of foremen or supervisors. Specialists also become more proficient in determining when undesirable habits may be changed, and when they must be reckoned with as permanent liabilities. One of the most successful and unique of these bureaus for the redistribution of men past the prime of life was operated by Victor T. J. Gannon for the Employers' Association of Chicago. The author spent several days in 1917 studying its objectives, methods, records, and accomplishments. It is cited as an illustration of what can be done because its success must be credited to the same factors which bring about success today and its uniqueness remains as much of a novelty as it was twenty-five years ago. While registrants were not confined to employer referrals, employers used the agency as a redistribution

[55] An excellent annotated bibliography on this subject is available for the years 1925–1929 with a few earlier references. A four-point requirement for inclusion was set up and uncritical recitals of findings and random opinions of casual writers were eliminated. See *A Bibliography with Notes on the Subject of the Employment Handicaps of Older Persons,* published by the Research Bureau of the Welfare Council of New York City, 1929.

center for the older employees whom they did not care to retain and also as a source of supply for older workers whom they could use. It was a sort of older workers' exchange with the manager acting as middleman and educator for both employer and employee. Its supporters used it as a medium for the exchange of their own employees. Because of the intervention of the war, placement statistics may not be used as a criterion of success—eighteen thousand men from forty-two to ninety-two years of age were placed in twenty months—but there were many indications that discriminating judgment had been used in the assignment of workers, that there was little time lost between registration and placement, and that both parties were satisfied with the service.

The Permanently Superannuated Person. In addition to the occupational discard, many of whom it may be possible by means of adequate counseling, good salesmanship, constant education of employer, worker, and public, and suitable employment supervision to assist in regaining a foothold in the occupational world, there is a second group to whom the occupational door is very definitely closed or who may never have participated in the activities of the wage-earning world. To every counseling and placement bureau there will come a scattering of such persons. Frequently they are looking for some sort of assistance which they do not understand and cannot, or will not, formulate their needs. Secretiveness is sometimes a very noticeable quality, and X-raying their real problems is most difficult.

One thing is certain, however; if they come even in small numbers, they will bring with them a sampling of all the diversified problems and peculiarities of senescence. Some have a horror of being useless or a nuisance, but they are useless, know it, resent it, and are very quick to see insults where perhaps none are intended. Others who are lonely, unhappy, and unwanted respond very quickly to efforts to assist them to develop resources within themselves. Some have been summarily separated from customary duties and environment with no time to prepare for the inevitable adjustments. Mothers and grandmothers, suddenly transferred from positions of responsibility and leadership in their own homes to the chimney corner in someone else's home, fall into this group, and they often suffer acutely. One person may feel set aside, but learn to be at home with himself, to make a new plan of life, and to undertake other tasks, possibly some line of community service. Another may become obstreperous, offer advice on all occasions, meddle with everything, criticize the habits and standards of youth, and resent any attentions or privileges which remind him that he is growing old. Some of these retired persons are rich in this world's goods and realize or imagine that the buzzards are waiting; others are in terror lest their small resources be not sufficient to last. Each who falls in the superannuated category, as long as life lasts, will be hoping for financial security, for a home, and for friends among whom he will be welcome—friends who will be interested in his welfare and who will be willing to overlook his idiosyncrasies. His needs will be similar to the needs of childhood and may well receive the same consideration.

In spite of the present interest in community guidance, in spite of the fact that every community has its quota of superannuated persons, and in spite of our eagerness to stress the necessity for guidance of the whole man throughout his entire life, in the main we give our attention to the productive years of man's life. Mental-hygiene and psychological publications sometimes discuss the plight of retired persons who, no longer able to care for themselves, revert to the needs of childhood and sometimes show childish behavior tendencies. Welfare agencies come in contact with those who are in financial need, but no provision is made for the inclusion of this group in community guidance programs. Looked at cold-bloodedly, perhaps it should not be included in a community guidance program; perhaps time and money could be used more profitably for the assistance of producers or of those whose productive years lie in the future rather than in the past.

What the superannuated person needs most of all is counseling assistance in orientation to the postgraduate school of life. There are many community agencies which could be useful tools in making such orientation and could at the same time afford an opportunity for the individual to carry some small share of the community responsibility for others. Adjustments after retirement would be much easier if postmiddle-life years were not allowed to accumulate without definite provision for the cultivation of mental, social, civic, or other interests which, immediately upon retirement, would close the gap filled by previous obligations and responsibilities.

SELECTED SUPPLEMENTARY READING

[References have been chosen with three specific objectives in view: (1) to familiarize students with the broad range of knowledges and skills essential to counseling, (2) to be thought-provoking with reference to the practical application of such knowledges and skills, and (3) to assist in discerning trends. The annotations have been designed to help students determine which references will contribute most to their needs.]

Aikin, Wilford M. *The Story of the Eight-Year Study.* New York: Harper and Bros., 1942. This is Volume I of the report of the Progressive Education Association's Commission on the Relation of School and College.

Beatty, John D. "Thirty Years of Personnel and Placement Work at the Carnegie Institute of Technology," *Bulletin, The Carnegie Institute of Technology,* 1938. Covers many topics under selection, placement, orientation, and success of college men.

Bell, Howard M. *Matching Youth and Jobs.* Washington: American Council on Education, 1940. Deals with the occupational adjustment problems of youth.

Biddle, George. "As I Remember Groton School," *Harper's Magazine,* CLXXIX (1939), 292–300. Deals with the problems caused by school traditions, customs, attitudes of teachers, etc.

Brockman, Mary. *What Is She Like? A Personality Book for Girls.* New York: Charles Scribner's Sons, 1930. A practical book dealing with habits, manners, speech, grooming, clothes, health, play, etc.

Coyle, Grace L. *Studies in Group Behavior.* New York: Harper and Bros., 1937. Case studies of five groups are presented in detail. The group leader and his functions, his relation to the group and to the individuals, problems of group control, and the relation of the group to the community are stressed.

Doyle, Henry G. "Are You College Timber?" *Bulletin of the Association of American Colleges,* XXIV (1938), 226–228. An outline, based on observations and comments received from various sections of the country, designed to assist secondary students in determining who should go to college.

Dudycha, George J. "The Moral Beliefs of College Students," *International Journal of Ethics,* XLIII (1933), 194–204.

Dunbar, H. Flanders. "Mental Hygiene and Religious Teaching," *Mental Hygiene,* XIX (1935), 353–372.

"Education for Home Building," *Bulletin of the Association of American Colleges,* XXII (1936), 482–500. A series of discussions dealing with preparation for marriage and a happy home life.

Erland, Nelson. "The Effectiveness of Freshman Orientation at Fourteen [Lutheran] Colleges," *School and Society,* LV (1942), 138–139. A test based on college orientation courses was given to 1,118 freshmen at the close of the first semester, 1941. Students in colleges offering such courses received higher grades.

Fitch, John A. *Vocational Guidance in Action.* New York: Columbia University Press, 1935. The major value of this publication is found in its rather elaborate treatment of placement, which has usually been neglected by writers on vocational guidance.

Fry, Clements C. "Mental Hygiene and Freshman Counseling," *Mental Hygiene,* XXIII (1939), 268–276. Practical advice to counselors of freshmen at Yale. The same author in collaboration with Edna G. Rostow summarizes the problems which college students bring to counselors and psychiatrists (*Mental Hygiene,* XXV [1941], 552–567).

Giberson, Lydia G. "Emotional First-Aid Stations in Industry," *Personnel,* XVI (1939), 1–15. Deals with the functions of psychiatric service in industry. Considers ten years of preparation necessary to qualify for such service.

Gruenberg, Benjamin C. "What Youth Wants and What It Gets from School," *School and Society,* XLIX (1939), 220–224. Report before Section Q—Education, at the meeting of the American Association for the Advancement of Science, Richmond, Va., Dec. 29, 1938. The same material with additional data is given in "What Young People Want to Know about Sex" by Dr. Valeria H. Parker

(*Child Study*, XVI [1939], 88–89). Includes questions by all ages and from all levels of education.

Hatcher, O. Latham. *Guiding Rural Boys and Girls.* New York: McGraw-Hill Book Co., 1930. The most complete presentation of all phases of guidance in rural areas to date. Much of the material is as valuable today as in 1930.

Hersey, R. B. "Case Study of a Successful Man," *Occupations,* XVI (1936), 921–926. A good antidote for counselors and teachers who are prone to have preconceived measuring sticks for success.

Hocking, W. E. "Philosophy and Religion in Undergraduate Education," *Bulletin of the Association of American Colleges,* XXIII (1937), 45–54. A broad liberal discussion of the topics indicated in the title.

Hudson, Holland, and Van Gelder, Rosetta. *Counseling the Handicapped.* New York: National Tuberculosis Assn., 1940. Describes the tools and techniques used in discovering and interpreting the aptitudes of the group served.

Jameson, Samuel H. "Certain Adjustment Problems of University Girls," *Journal of Higher Education,* X (1939), 249–255. Areas of adjustment among 341 freshman girls.

Johnson, Roy I. "The Problem of 'How to Study,'" *School Review,* XLV (1937), 577–584. Are there "best" ways of studying?

Kent, Raymond A. "Some Social and Economic Implications of the Youth Problem," *Occupations,* XV (1937), 694–704. A thought-provoking analysis of the American Youth Act of 1936, which the author considers exploitation of, rather than service to, youth. Where and under what conditions shall youth enter the main current?

Klinefelter, C. F. *Social Leadership.* Washington: U. S. Office of Education, 1940. Report on a 3-year course at the College of Puget Sound, Tacoma, Washington. The course was designed to develop the ability of college students to lead discussion groups. An adaptation of the conference method.

Landis, Paul H. "Points of Stress in Adolescent Morality," *School and Society,* LI (1940), 612–616. Based on 1000 autobiographies of college students.

Lawton, George E. *New Goals for Old Age.* New York: Columbia University Press, 1943. A series of lectures given a year or two before publication. Old age is considered to begin at 60 years. Deals with a great variety of problems of the aged but not with occupational ones.

Link, Henry C. "Wheat and Chaff in Vocational Guidance," *Occupations,* XIII (1934), 11–17. Such an article is needed now and then to help vocational counselors keep their feet on the ground.

McClintock, J. A. "Religious Counseling," *Journal of Higher Education,* IX (1938), 145–152. The author thinks that every counselor should be prepared to deal with religious problems.

National Education Association of the United States, Department of Elementary School Principals. *Personality Adjustment of the Elementary-School Child.* Washington: The Department, 1936. (Fifteenth Yearbook: The National Elementary Principal, vol. XV, no. 6.) A good work on guidance services in elementary schools.

National Society for the Study of Education. *Guidance in Educational Institutions.* Bloomington, Ill.: Public School Publishing Co., 1938. (Thirty-seventh Yearbook, pt. I.) Different writers deal with various phases of guidance.

Nelson, Louise A. "Why John Ruskin Never Learned How to Live," *Mental Hygiene,* XII (1928), 673–705. This entire number is concerned with home conditions and parental influence on children's adjustments. Quotations from John Ruskin make the article mentioned especially interesting.

Pennsylvania, Department of Public Instruction, Pennsylvania Curriculum Studies. *Conference Planning and Leadership as Applied to Foremanship Training.* Harrisburg, Pa.: The Department, [1935]. (Pennsylvania Curriculum Studies Bulletin, no. 87.) A helpful pamphlet for teachers and counselors.

Plant, James S. *Personality and the Cultural Pattern.* New York: Commonwealth Fund, 1937. A good book for those who are interested in understanding how cultural pressures influence behavior.

——. "Present Problems in Marriage Counseling," *Mental Hygiene,* XXIII (1939), 353–362. Condensed from an address before the First Conference on Preparation for Marriage, at Philadelphia, Nov. 16, 1938.

Prescott, Daniel A. *Emotion and the Educative Process.* Washington: American Council on Education, 1938. The report of the Committee on the Relation of Emotion to the Educative Process on an exploratory study of the relationship between nonintellectual factors and the aims, methods, materials, and personnel of education. It includes a chapter on the emotional adjustments of teachers.

Reed, Anna Y. *Junior Wage Earners.* New York: Macmillan Company, 1920. Prepared in response to a demand for a manual for the use of employees of the Junior Division of the U. S. Employment Service. Out of print but available in most libraries.

Rivlin, Harry N. *Educating for Adjustment.* New York: Appleton-Century, 1937. Methods of teaching that aid and those that retard adjustment are discussed.

Roethlisberger, F. J., and Dickson, W. J. *Management and the Worker.* Cambridge, Mass.: Harvard University Press, 1939. A final report on the series of research studies which began in 1927 and have become generally known as the Hawthorne experiment. Concerned with the intangible factors which affect morale and productive efficiency. Part II deals with the interviewing of 20,000 employees in order to secure personal reactions to working environment.

Runner, Jessie R. "Social Distance in Adolescent Relationships," *American Journal of Sociology,* XLIII (1937), 428–439.

Steiner, R. W., and Van Haden, H. I. "The Pre-Training Selection and Guidance of Teachers," *Journal of Educational Research,* XXIII (1940), 321–350. A summary of literature which appeared in the preceding five years.

Symonds, Percival M. "Securing Rapport in Interviewing," *Teachers College Record,* XXXIX (1938), 707–722.

Thom, Douglas, and Johnson, Florence S. "Environmental Factors and Their Relation to Social Adjustment," *Mental Hygiene,* XXIII (1939), 379–413. A survey of 120 well-adjusted high-school students.

Traxler, Arthur E. *Case Study Procedures in Guidance.* New York: Educational Records Bureau, 1937. Rev. ed., 1940.

——. *The Use of Test Results in Secondary Schools.* New York: Educational Records Bureau, 1938. (Educational Records Bureau Bulletin, no. 25.) An aid to the use of objective tests in counseling students.

——, ed. *Guidance in Public Secondary Schools.* New York: Educational Records Bureau, 1939. (Educational Records Bulletin, no. 28.) Chapter XII, pp. 203–295, "Contributions to Guidance Through Case Studies by Classroom Teachers," is a detailed presentation of 15 case studies.

Uhrbrock, Richard S. "Attitudes of 4430 Employees," *Journal of Social Psychol-*

ogy, V (1934), 365–377. Cites five methods of studying the attitudes of employees; gives results and an excellent list of references.

U. S. Office of Education. *Rehabilitation of the Deaf and the Hard of Hearing.* Washington, 1942. (Vocational Rehabilitation Series Bulletin, no. 26.) A manual for rehabilitation case workers. Includes a chapter on interviewing and counseling.

——. *Some Factors in the Adjustment of College Students.* Washington, 1937. (U. S. Office of Education Bulletin, 1937, no. 12.)

University of Tennessee, College of Agriculture. *Guidance for Rural Boys.* Knoxville: The University, 1940. (Bulletin, no. 7.) A general guidance pamphlet with special reference to the guidance responsibilities of teachers of agriculture.

Wallin, J. E. Wallace. *Personality Maladjustments and Mental Hygiene.* New York: McGraw-Hill Book Co., 1935. A good volume for the layman. Contains many case studies presented with a minimum of technical terminology.

Wonderlic, E. F. "Improving Interview Techniques," *Personnel,* XVIII (1942), 232–238. An excellent article on methods of employment interviewing. Types of interviews, pattern interviewing, methods of teaching interviewing, and the reliability of the interview are discussed.

Yoakum, C. S. "Motive and Risk in Counseling," *Occupations,* X (1931), 51–56. The years which have passed since this article was published have not lessened its value.

PART V
Organization and Administration

CHAPTER XVII
The Lag in the Assumption of Administrative Responsibility

CHAPTER XVIII
Principles of Organization Applicable to Guidance and Personnel Services

CHAPTER XIX
Building the Guidance or Personnel Service

CHAPTER XX
Evaluating the Guidance or Personnel Service

"The principal is ultimately responsible for the success or failure of all activities within his school."—NATIONAL ASSOCIATION OF SECONDARY SCHOOL PRINCIPALS.

"There is no successful substitute for good personnel administration."—THOMAS G. SPATES, *Spark Plugs of Democracy*.

CHAPTER XVII

The Lag in the Assumption of Administrative Responsibility

CHAPTER XVI completed the presentation of the possible component parts of a program for guidance and personnel services. There will, however, be no program until someone determines which of the possible functions are to be included and defines those functions clearly, until workers are given specific responsibilities, and until relationships are thoroughly understood throughout the entire institution. This phase of a guidance or personnel service belongs to the field of organization and administration, and it is upon the appropriate solution of the problems involved in organization and administration that one must rely for the final step in the perfection of a successful guidance program.

Part V has been reserved for consideration of some of the problems of organization and administration which are involved in changing a group of heterogeneous, disintegrated, overlapping, and often conflicting activities into a co-ordinated program for guidance service.

Guidance literature has given considerable attention to programs of guidance but appears to have had little interest in the basic principles of organization, the types of organization which tend to make programs effective, or in the serious problems involving relationships which arise in connection with the organization and administration of permeating services. Yet administrative negligence and poor organization are primary weaknesses in most of the so-called "programs" for guidance and personnel service. The colleges on the whole seem to have been more oblivious to their responsibilities in this respect than the secondary schools.

A review of the summary of first-period activity in the area of organization and administration indicates that guidance programs and personnel services did not, as a rule, enter our educational institutions on administrative invitation or as the result of administrative initiative. They entered in a variety of ways. On the college level an outstanding characteristic of personnel service for men is their spontaneous origin. Usually they were the logical outgrowth of inherent and voluntary services in which the chief administrator often shared. In due course of time they were partially centralized by the appointment of an official designated by some preferred title such as "dean of men" or "dean of students."

Services for women came into being as the result of a change in institutional policy regarding the admission of women to colleges originally designed to serve men. The success of this new venture was thought to require the presence on the campus of an administrative colleague of the female sex. Intentionally or otherwise the statement of such new policy and the redistribution of functions usually resulted in the allocation of some personnel functions to the new official. The mode of entry has a dual significance for the topic under consideration (1) because it seems to furnish isolated instances in which personnel services were introduced by the administration for the sole purpose of facilitating definitely stated objectives of institutional policy and (2) because, in so far as such pronouncements may be regarded as forerunners of present-day personnel policies, they established the precedent of college personnel services segmented on a sex basis, and combined administrative and personnel functions, thus setting the stage for certain types of problems which continue to handicap the most effective organization for an all-inclusive student personnel service.

On the public-school level a good deal of "fastening upon" was accomplished by committees or philanthropic boards which had their own specific objectives and had established certain precedents relative to policies and functions. Sometimes these were in harmony with educational policies and practices and sometimes they were not. In few cases was there any evidence of a guiding policy, a well-defined objective, or an organization designed to facilitate the realization of an educational objective. Even when an administrator initiated a program, as was the case in Seattle and in New Orleans, the purpose seems to have been the facilitation of policy determination rather than policy realization. This was entirely logical then, and it still is today. Inquiries which are designed to throw light on such questions as, What should be the objectives of a given local guidance service? What policies should control? What type of organization is most promising? What functions should be included? are prerequisite to effective services.

The close of the first period found a number of "heavenly beginnings" going forward in different sections of the country and on different levels of education. There was not much ballast in the shape of objectives, policies, and organization. A few departments had been established; a few directors had been appointed; and the country had been introduced to several new educational terms and titles. Since guidance services and guidance terms were rarely able to stand alone, for the most part they were publicized as appendages to some older, more welcome, better understood, and more liberally financed educational services. Some of these composites were meaningful and appropriate, others were illogical and inappropriate, but each had a *raison d'être*.

Documents dealing with the development of the guidance and personnel movement during the transition period following World War I throw considerable light on the progress of educational administration in the direction of acceptance of the responsibility for guidance service in comparison with that of business management.

The story of the steps by which industrial concerns came to recognize personnel service as an integral factor in management and as a major responsibility of management and the story of their efforts to find the right place for it in the organization setup and to harmonize its functions with other functions have been well told. By 1923 the task was accomplished. This was evidenced by the final change in the name of the old National Association of Corporation Schools to its present name, American Management Association. The organization's future program for personnel service was based on the assumption that every executive, every supervisor, and every foreman, from the top of the line to the bottom, would render personnel services, that training for the proper performance of such duties was essential, and that provision for training was a management responsibility.

The story of administrative interest in the educational areas of personnel service is equally well documented, but it does not read so well. In fact it is only the continued story of the first period without distinctive features to characterize its efforts. There were no evidences of concerted interest on the part of administration. Departments were established here and there; occasionally a director was appointed; and calls continued to come from the rank and file for some centralizing or co-ordinating agency which could unify local beginnings, bring the service more definitely within the educational circle, and give it a chance to permeate all the units and to act as an articulating agency between units and as an induction agency to the postschool world.[1]

There was no decrease in the number of names used, but the tendency

---

[1] Minneapolis is a good illustration of the difficulties involved in perfecting guidance organizations. As the discussion proceeds the student will find several theoretical points practically illustrated in that city's experience. As was related in Part I, the Department of Attendance and Vocational Guidance was established in 1914 under a director and with several subdivisions. In 1924, Victoria McAlmon, describing the study of occupations which had been introduced in the ninth grade, stated that by the end of the year forty-five teachers and two thousand pupils would be inoculated, and painlessly, with some germs of knowledge about occupations; that if the Department of Guidance and Placement could encourage and maintain the enthusiasm it had kindled, "vocational guidance will have become a function of the classroom teacher, *and will, in time, reach out to touch administrators*" (*Vocational Guidance Magazine*, II [1924], p. 177).

to use "guidance" alone was perhaps more common than would be expected in view of the continued use of "vocational guidance" as the generic term. "Guidance and research" was also a fairly popular compound.[2] Possibly increase in both usages may be credited to the growth of the child-guidance movement and the organization of child-guidance clinics which were accenting research in the field of individual differences and were forecasting a shift in emphasis from the humanitarian aspect of guidance services to the more specific and more scientific educational guidance movement recently sponsored by the Educational Records Bureau and affiliated organizations.

Ryan's report,[3] issued in 1918, has sometimes left the impression that during this transition period there was rather widespread interest among secondary school administrators in the introduction of placement services. This is not a justifiable assumption. Ryan did his best to forestall such an interpretation of his statistical data by indicating that at the time of his investigation placement bureaus were largely a response to the demand for boy labor on farms in order to release adult labor for war services of various kinds. The Boys Working Reserve, a national agency instituted to help in meeting the deficiency in farm labor, operated through local high schools which served as recruiting centers. The Reserve was abolished when the emergency ended. So were the majority of the school bureaus which had served as recruiting centers. A few were merged with the Junior Division of the United States Employment Service but there is no evidence of a change of heart on the part of school administration or of any permanent, well-grounded tendency to accept responsibility for induction into the occupational world or for postschool adjustment.

Increase in the number of deans of women might be assumed to indicate a growing appreciation of the importance of including such functionaries in the corps of educational institutions. But a close examination of the situation reveals considerable pressure selling on the part of the American Association of University Women, which functions as an accrediting agency with specific requirements regarding the employment of deans of women and of women faculty members. The National Association of Deans of Women with its slogan, "A dean of girls in every high school," has also been an influential factor in "fastening upon" educational institutions an official who, in many instances, was assigned such hybrid duties and such a questionable status that in accomplishing her task she

2 Unless one has access to the reports and minutes of boards of education, the best single source of information on the rise and fall, changes in titles, and shifts in accent of local guidance services is the *Vocational Guidance Magazine.*

3 *Vocational Guidance and the Public Schools* (U. S. Bureau of Education Bulletin, 1918, no. 24; Washington, 1918).

became a thorn in the flesh of her coworkers without gaining recognition as either an administrative officer or as a functional specialist. Such functionaries were often very unhappy about the predicament in which they found themselves. Educational administration seemed bewildered. It stood helplessly by and allowed the octopus called personnel service to spread its tentacles into every avenue of "line" and "staff," into every area of executive or functional control.

By the time the movement was well under way it could neither be defined, organized, charted, or confined within any known boundaries. Its representatives were, in truth, "permeating" functionaries. A few administrators, when their backs were firmly against the wall, attempted to extricate themselves from their uncomfortable and dangerous position by superimposing, without the clarification of duties and relationships already in existence, a director of personnel service. This, of course, was beginning at the wrong end and only added to the confusion already apparent in the area of organization and administration.

More intensive and extensive research in this transition period tends to confirm the conclusion that educational administration had not recognized personnel service as an integral factor in education or as a major responsibility of education and that little or no effort had been made to allocate it to a suitable position in the educational program or to determine its functions and harmonize them with other educational functions. Research also reveals that educational administration lagged far behind business management in grasping the significance of the personnel movement, was in touch with the progress going forward under management only to a very limited extent, and was a long distance from realizing the intimate relationship which in the interests of society must eventually exist between personnel programs in education and personnel programs in industry and business.

Recently there has come a change, not so much in the general attitude of educational administration, which still lags far behind industrial management in grasping the significance of personnel service, but in the attitude of the public. Discussion of the responsibility of education for guidance and personnel services is very much in evidence today. Principals, superintendents, and boards of education do not need to apologize for or to defend their interest in guidance; they do not need to camouflage their activities in that area. Public pressure is in the opposite direction, and public interest is calling for leadership and direction. Among the several changes which the depression years have effected in the immediate guidance outlook, one of the most significant is the addition of a third motivating factor which has previously been referred to as the avoidance of the dangers of social unrest. This motivation, which is focused on the welfare of society rather than on the need of the individual, is more easily understood and more generously responded to by the average citizen than were the original motivations.

The public, however, is fickle; this new and appealing motivation may have both temporary causation and temporary support and therefore may afford only a temporary opportunity for educational administration to translate it into permanent guidance services. It would seem that the time has come when the educational authorities, both public-school and college, must either assume leadership in the sponsorship of guidance and in the organization of more effective institutional and community guidance services or permit one of the most important functions of education in a democracy to pass into other hands.

With the past as prologue to the future and with a new public interest in the picture, what is the prospect with reference to more effective organization and administration of guidance and personnel services? What fundamental principles and practices have the years revealed which have crystallized sufficiently to be helpful to those who are anxious to assume administrative responsibility for the organization and development of guidance services?

CHAPTER XVIII

Principles of Organization Applicable to Guidance and Personnel Services

DESPITE the lag in administrative understanding, interest, and action, the documentary history of the early years of the guidance movement reveals several formulated principles and approved practices which recognized the importance of organization and administration in the development of the movement. In the sixteen principles and practices summarized in Chapter IV there is definite evidence that leaders in the movement regarded guidance as an integral factor in education with the dual objective of service to the individual and to society. Here and there a forward-looking individual insisted that administration must assume responsibility for the service, must give the entire corps a chance to participate, and must delegate leadership for carrying forward the program to trained workers. Occasionally some experienced counselor suggested that local services would be improved by the practical application of the principle of centralized control and decentralized execution.

Similar pronouncements and demands are abundant today. They may be couched in somewhat different language but in essence they present the same lines of thought, recognize the same unmet deficiencies, and cite similar resultant problems. Five principles which are primarily concerned with organization and administration and their concomitant problems have been selected for discussion in Chapter XVIII.

GENERAL PRINCIPLES OF ORGANIZATION

1. *Guidance and personnel service are a direct responsibility of administration.*

It has long been recognized that the management of any educational institution, business concern, or what not is responsible for all of the activities in which that agency engages, for the success or failure of each unit as well as for that of the whole. It makes no difference whether management be represented by a superintendent, a principal, a general manager, a president, a director, or other official, whether it be entrusted to one official or to a group of officials, whether it be concerned with a material or a human product; this is a universally accepted first principle and requires no further elaboration.[1]

The first principle which requires attention, therefore, when guidance and personnel services are to be instituted is that administration must assume the responsibility. However personified, it must be responsible for the objectives in view, for the policies which bring such services into the institution, for the organization designed to foster the attainment of goals, for the quality of the leadership which directs and capitalizes on the energies, abilities, and activities of the sustaining corps, for the contours of the matrix within which the service strives to attain its objectives, and for the standards whereby achievements are appraised.

Progress in the acceptance of this corollary is well marked and very easy to trace in connection with industrial and business concerns. The evolution of the name of the American Management Association tells the story of how group thinking, covering a period of ten years, had progressed far enough by 1922 to realize that "personnel administration is essentially a unit." As a result, local concerns tended to combine under one high-ranking official the decentralized units which had been concerned with various aspects of personnel work—employment, training, promotions and transfers, and the like. Concurrently national organizations which represented these local decentralized units were merged in the National Personnel Association. In 1923 there was further development in the attitude of management toward the relation of personnel work to other units of the concern. It found expression in such statements as, "There is in reality no personnel problem; there is only a management problem." Thus personnel service fairly early in the history of the movement was accepted as a responsibility of management and the name of its representative association was changed once more, this time to the American Management Association.

Educational institutions have had no similar experience. They have moved more slowly and without direction. There have been a number of educational pronouncements in harmony with this first principle; several previously mentioned slogans have received the approval of school administration; but even today many educators find it difficult to realize

---

[1] Several excellent presentations of the principles of organization in relation to personnel services in business and industry are available. For example, see Major Lyndall Urwick (an authority in British and international management movements), *Scientific Principles and Organization* (Institute of Management Series, no. 19; New York: American Management Assn., 1938); James O. McKinsey, *Organization Problems under Present Conditions* (General Management Series, no. 127; New York: American Management Assn., 1936); and W. J. Donald, "Effective Executive Personnel Organization," *Personnel*, X (1933), 46–63.

that guidance and personnel services are the direct responsibility of the chief administrative officer; that they should enter the institution only upon his invitation; and that the invitation should not be issued until he knows the responsibilities entailed and is both able and willing to accept them.

2. *The personnel objectives and policies of an institution should be in harmony with its general objectives and policies, and in operation they should help to facilitate the realization of such objectives and policies.*

The early history of the guidance movement reveals few instances in which the objectives of guidance service were stated and in which they were in harmony with the general objectives of the introducing institution. Since it is hard to conceive of any line of action without some directing policy which in turn reflects the philosophy of administration and throws light on its objectives, it would be unwarrantable to assume that no policy determines guidance service procedures because none has been formulated. And this should obtain even though propaganda or pressure politics appear to be the sole motivation; even though there be abundant evidence to prove that college personnel objectives, as stated in the catalogue, are not very well supported by college personnel practices.

The situation in 1943 remains about as it has been throughout the years. There are no very clear-cut objectives of education, especially of public education, although vigorous attacks on the subject are periodically made by deliberative bodies. Each year it seems more unreasonable to assume that school administration can harmonize the objectives and policies of guidance services with the objectives of education when such objectives remain unknown.[2] To a considerable extent, moreover, guidance services are still treated as unwanted children although recent financial support for certain units of such services is arousing competition among public agencies and offering them inducements to aspire to foster parenthood.

Perhaps this general tendency to evade the formulation of definite policies, which would permit guidance and personnel services to enter educational systems as facilitating agencies for the realization of definite objectives, is partially due, on the public secondary level, to the fact that education is not only free but also compulsory. This situation automatically eliminates the possibility of introducing certain desirable personnel practices, while it forces the introduction of others less desirable.

The private secondary schools do not face a similar handicap, nor will it long be possible to avoid the establishment of definite personnel policies

[2] This statement does not imply that the objectives of education should be static, only that certain fundamentals may in time come to be more generally agreed upon.

which will be designed to realize the objectives of all public vocational schools and of vocational curricula and courses offered by public education. The public and parents are more in sympathy with selection on the basis of objectives and abilities than was formerly the case, and there is considerable evidence that those who are responsible for the effective functioning of such programs have long been moving in that direction.

Colleges and universities differ markedly in their objectives whether or not objectives are formulated and made public. Large enrollment as an objective requires one type of personnel policy; limitation of enrollment, another. Technical superiority, religious education, the training of the mentally superior, and the provision of opportunities for mediocrity are all worthy educational objectives; but each requires a personnel policy which is in harmony with its general objective. The general objective and the general policy are logically prerequisite to the personnel objective and the personnel policy; therefore they should receive administrative review prior to the introduction of a personnel service.

3. *The principles of organization should be harmonized with the principles of personnel service prior to the installation of the personnel organization.*

The determination of objectives and policies is usually followed by the setting up of an organization which fits in with the total institutional pattern and which is designed to do teamwork with other units already in operation. This is accomplished not by following some general organization pattern but by adjusting the fundamental principles of organization to any peculiarities of the activities to be organized and to the specific situation for which the organization is projected. Such a statement is easy to formulate, very difficult to put in practice in concrete situations, and even more difficult to compass in a purely abstract situation. On the other hand, there are many indications that failure to take into consideration certain attributes of personnel service which make its segmentation somewhat different from the segmentation of the usual educational unit is responsible for much of the bitterness and acrimonious discussions among teaching corps, much of the disloyalty to and refusal to contribute to guidance programs, and much of the negative appreciation, or positive criticism, which comes from the recipients of such services.

Three characteristics of guidance and personnel service which frequently have been overlooked when a guidance organization was projected have caused such intrainstitutional animosities and undercurrents of hostility:

(a) *Guidance service is a shared responsibility.* The usual organizational pattern for units in educational institutions is not applicable in toto to the organization of guidance services because this particular educational unit deals with shared responsibilities to a far greater extent than do the knowledge and skill units with which administrators are accustomed to deal. Guidance services have never been successfully departmentalized on any level of education. They do not lend themselves to line organization, and, as a rule, whenever they have been allocated to line positions or whenever their functionaries have been allowed to assume line responsibilities, explosions have followed.

(b) *Guidance is a permeating function.* Participation by the entire faculty is desirable, but within certain limitations both as to intensiveness and extensiveness, quality and quantity. Some administrators do not yet realize that it is possible to have a guidance-permeated institution with every member of the corps making some contribution without endorsing every newly acclaimed slogan and without requiring every teacher to be a counselor, a homeroom teacher, a health and safety inspector, a visiting teacher, a test administrator, a psychometrist or psychologist, and—at the very end of the list in apologetically small type—to have some knowledge of the subject taught and some skill in methods of instruction.

Students lose their respect for, and their confidence in, too diverse-minded teachers and they readily distinguish between this type of teacher and the broad-minded type. Of late years the author has felt impelled, in conference with administrators, to beg that they so organize their guidance program that good classroom teachers be permitted to focus their guidance activities on the type of services which are inherent in their instructional duties and in their personality. Knowledge and methods of imparting knowledge which inspire to scholarship, to love of truth, to ability to recognize facts and to interpret them in the interest of society, exemplified in the daily attitudes and activities of teachers, are a valuable contribution to any guidance program. Teachers who possess such qualities are rare, and their services should be conserved. They have contributed much to the guidance of leaders in the past, and they will contribute much to the guidance of future leaders provided their normal contributions are not diluted by so many extraneous demands and by the forced worship of so many other gods that their values are lost.

(c) *Functions included in a guidance service should be selected on some specific basis.* Many of the present-day functions, activities, and whatnots that administrators feel called upon to include in a guidance or personnel service have no legitimate claim to inclusion therein. Chapter IV has called attention to the considerable number of heterogeneous functions which, as time has passed, educational personnel services, especially on the college level, have gathered unto themselves, and to the tenacity with which they have clung to each acquisition until there is considerable justification for the assumption that education and guidance are synonymous.

In many secondary schools and in most collegiate institutions a sifting process should precede organization. Guidance functions which are shared or marginal should be differentiated from those for which one individual must assume responsibility. It is too much to expect that any single service unit will be able to digest all the presently available activities and responsibilities and still maintain the physical and mental balance so essential to the effective performance of bona fide guidance services. But the process of selection and rejection cannot be directed from without; it is a strictly intrainstitutional affair. Excess baggage in one institution is often essential equipment in another, and local conditions must be the determining factor as to which functions shall be included and which discarded.

4. *The director of guidance or personnel service should be chosen on the basis of demonstrated or potential ability to carry forward the service in harmony with the objectives and policies laid down by the administration.*

After the administrator has clarified objectives and made reasonably sure that the policies essential to their realization are in harmony with the general policies of the institution, after he has given consideration to the three attributes of guidance service which are often overlooked and to other similar rocks upon which organizational efforts are apt to founder, his next interest will probably be in the type of organization best suited to the accomplishment of his objectives and in the selection of the individual, or the committee, to whom he is willing to delegate his responsibility for carrying forward the program. Perhaps he will prefer to take the latter step first, especially if he be charged with the administrative duties contingent upon large school systems or universities. He may feel the need of the assistance of his ultimate right hand in selling the proposition to the corps, in determining objectives, in selecting functions, and in deciding upon the type of organization best suited to the local situation.

Whatever the modus operandi, committee versus individual leadership will need some attention. There are certain values in committee control, some of which were mentioned in connection with guidance services in the early period. The majority of these advantages continue today; so also do the majority of the disadvantages. In the main, survey reports show a preference for delegating leadership responsibilities to a single individual whose training and experience qualify him for the duties imposed rather than to a committee.[3] In a few instances this writer has found a rotating committee charged with the performance of guidance functions. The method was introduced and was justified, either as a means of training the corps or because corps jealousies were handicapping the development of the program to such an extent that a heavy dose of the hardships of counseling was thought to be a good method of eliminating the undesirables who were competing for the directorship. Sometimes there were indications that these desired objectives were being accomplished, but as a method of providing worth-while guidance services for students it could hardly be called a success.

If a director be determined upon rather than a committee, what training, experience, and personal qualities should be sought? Administrative efforts to solve this problem are often confused by the multiplicity of lists which are available for suggestive assistance. These lists have been constructed in a number of ways. Some are profiles of ideal counselors and of imaginary deans of women, or they may be the brain children of wishful thinkers. Others are composites of opinions.

Anyone who has wide acquaintance with individual deans of women and who attempts to select a dean on the basis of the qualities contained in the various lists issued by the National Association of Deans of Women [4] will be struck by the absence of the qualities mentioned more frequently than by their presence. Sometimes, surprising as it may seem, the dean who lacks the most of the recommended qualities will in practice prove the most effective functionary.

Anyone who has seriously considered the report of the Committee on Professional Standards of the National Vocational Guidance Association [5] will realize that it is in the main an admirable selection of mechanical devices for locating standardized needles in personnel haystacks. It is quite unconcerned, however, with the possibilities of segregating the few rare individuals who discern the spiritual values in guidance and personnel services and who know how to use every opportunity to help their charges arrive at personal convictions regarding the eternal verities in order that they may go forth from educational institutions with a philosophy of life which guides them in living, and in helping others to live,

---

[3] Advisory committees, especially community committees where one trained functionary serves a county or two or more small schools, are quite different from a school committee which is responsible for the performance of guidance functions.

[4] *The Vocation of Dean* by Ruth A. Merrill and Helen D. Bragdon ([n.p.:] Press and Publicity Committee of the National Association of Deans of Women, 1926) deals separately with college and secondary school deans. In her summary of qualifications Bragdon states that the only omission seems to be "one strong pair of wings."

[5] This report is given by Franklin J. Keller in "The Revelation and Nurture of Counselors," *Occupations*, XVI (1938), 728–731.

even under the most unfavorable conditions. The trivia of the supplementary criteria suggested are truly appalling.

In spite of all the efforts which have been made to list distinctive characteristics and to make them available for the guidance of administrative officers, when comparisons are made as to the type of personnel officer "then and now" considerable disappointment is experienced. Part I has called attention in several places to what might be considered the degeneracy of leadership in the personnel field as exemplified in the character and experience of those who fostered the beginnings of the movement compared with the leadership of today. An address on this subject, made in 1941 with special reference to college personnel services, is the most scholarly and arresting presentation of the tendency toward decadence with which the author is familiar. A few points which emphasize previous warnings, and which may not be gainsaid because they are verifiable in the history of higher education, are commented on here; but since it is difficult to conceive of any single article which will be more thought-provoking to an administrator on the eve of selecting a director of personnel services, reading of the entire address is recommended.[6]

The early day personnel worker had "arrived" in some allied field before he assumed personnel duties: he brought to personnel service a rich background of knowledge and experience; he was a bigger and better person than he usually is today. These early leaders had a firm belief in the eternal verities; they had acquired the ability to transfer their sense of spiritual values and educational practices to any field of endeavor; and they possessed a knowledge of human nature which prepared them to deal with its frailties and to aid individuals to select the virtues essential for achievement and for living.

Many of the great educators of the past have had these qualifications for personnel service. Those who have preserved the record for us have told the story of their achievements. Findlay has noted how unerringly students and administrators alike discovered and made use of these gifts. James Hilton in *Good-Bye, Mr. Chips* tried to put the message in such form that even the busiest administrator in the secondary schools could read it as he ran.

A wise administrator will aim high; he will search for and select the best; and he will realize, as he looks about him, that spiritually and professionally many present-day personnel functionaries are not living up to their inheritance. He will discard the idea that his job specification should

---

[6] See Helen M. Voorhees, "The Responsibilities of the Heritage of Personnel Work," in American College Personnel Association, *Report of the Eighteenth Annual Meeting*, 1941, pp. 1–7.

be matched by the dissection of various personalities into ranks, grades, percentiles, or degrees of this, that, and the other. He will turn to men and women who have already left the imprint of an outstanding personality on both youth and colleagues and, if he be proceeding effectively, he will not be troubled by the fear that he may not be employing the latest measuring instruments or be proceeding entirely scientifically.

Most institutions will have at least one member of the corps [7] who qualifies by such standards for leadership in the field of personnel service, who knows that in the spiritual values of such service lies one of education's most priceless opportunities, and that after all the tangibles of education have been acquired, the ultimate measure of an educated man is his possession of a philosophy of life which is good to live by or good to die by, as the case may be. The delegation of leadership to such a one will not create intracorps jealousies but rather joint approval of colleagues and students.

Such suggestions may be idealistic but they are quite possible of realization. They have demonstrated their practicality over a longer period of time than the life of the organized guidance movement; and it is interesting to recall that while they have reached the height of their practical applicability in collegiate services for men, the National Association of Deans of Men is, at the present time, the only personnel organization which stresses the desirability of giving first consideration to the intangible qualifications of personnel functionaries and tends to minimize degrees, professional courses, and the more tangible evidences of qualifications.

Some administrators may be worried lest selection on this basis may result in overlooking what may be called subsidiary qualifications. Personnel workers are human. No one of them will ever possess all the qualifications desirable for his responsibilities. But men and women are not usually classified as "arrivals" unless they have demonstrated a considerable number of the qualifications. They will be both emotionally and intellectually well balanced, broad-minded, open-minded, generous in their appreciation of the efforts and contributions of others, able to secure cooperation in home, school, and community and to assume leadership in the in-service training and professional upkeep of the corps. They will inspire their colleagues to study, to experimentation, and to evaluation of their accomplishments. Their reports to their superiors will be farseeing and their recommendations nonpartisan, and they will automatically conceive of personnel service as a "we" and an "our" service rather than as an "I" and a "my" department. There is nothing left except routine

[7] The pros and cons of selecting guidance functionaries from the institutional corps are discussed in Chapter XIX.

administrative duties. Personalities of the type mentioned might be lacking in those qualities. They often are. But the deficiencies can be made up for by the appointment of executive-minded secretaries or clerks. "Aim high" is the best advice anyone can offer an administrator who would underwrite the success of his personnel service.

5. *The type of organization chosen for the guidance or personnel service should be in harmony with the total institutional setup.*

Satisfactory organization in any concern requires the classification of all functions and the allocation of definite duties to each unit comprised in the organization; the complete understanding and the effective performance of these duties by the units to which they are assigned; and the recognition by the functionaries of each unit of their relation to the functionaries of all other units plus a complete understanding of the interdependence of all the units comprised in the organization.

Nomenclature Confusion and *Organizational Concepts.* Those who would anticipate certain types of organizational problems prior to the introduction of formal guidance services, especially those who desire to prepare a working chart which will guide their thinking with reference to duties and relationships, will encounter nomenclature confusion as a first obstacle to clear thinking. Several terms used to express organization concepts because of their dual usage handicap the clear-cut classification of duties and the statement of relationships which are so essential to effective organization. Examples are "function," "control," "staff," and "line and staff."

"Function" in its general sense refers to all duties and activities of every type performed by any member of the organization. The recent tendency to use it as a modifier of "control" ("functional control") in connection with technical or special services such as personnel, creates the impression that personnel functionaries perform control functions in the same sense as do line officers or operating executives.

"Control" usually implies a formally assigned right to issue orders or exercise authority over others. But "control" used in connection with certain associational relationships, of which personnel service is one, more often refers to an influence control, personally acquired because of valuable ideas, technical skills, recognized knowledge, or personal popularity. Hence, in his efforts to determine what authority, if any, should be delegated to the personnel unit, the administrator is confused by the various usages and combinations of terms such as "functional control" and "executive control," "functional executives" and "operational" or "control executives," and the like. As a rule operational or control functions will be allocated to "the line," principals, heads of departments,[8] and teachers, while technical or functional executives (specialists) such as psychologists, visiting teachers, physicians, and the like are theoretically without authority except in relation to their own immediate subordinates, plus whatever they may have acquired informally through their own demonstrated skill, knowledge, or facilitating abilities.

"Line," "staff," and "line and staff" are organizational concepts with which educational writers have not come to grips. Therefore, in studying the type of formal organization best adapted to a personnel service one must turn to writers who deal with the general principles of organization and to the experiences of industrial management in its attempts to apply such principles to personnel service. Much which has been accomplished in industrial and business areas has valuable suggestions for educational personnel.

"Line," as a concept, is easily understood and easily exemplified diagrammatically. It is not so easy to determine its relationship to personnel service. As a rule, organized, technical personnel service is not regarded as a line unit, but certain aspects of such a service must, of necessity, be performed by line functionaries. To determine and indicate these relationships and to clarify the duties involved are important parts of organizational procedure. The word "staff" is exceedingly confusing when used in connection with specialized services because educational circles are accustomed to use "staff" in the sense of "corps" rather than to confine its use to a group of persons who act as assistants to a general manager, superintendent, principal, president, or other control executive.

"Line and staff" seems to be more or less of a catch phrase among educators. A review of considerable published material which uses the phrase leaves one in doubt as to whether it is considered as two single concepts or as a compound concept. Four different interpretations of educational usage seem equally well supported: (1) That the author has no very clear-cut idea as to the meaning of either word, especially "staff," but believes that both are desirable in the organization of personnel units and that, by following the fairly popular practice of using both, he can advocate both, and at the same time avoid explanations which are admittedly difficult; (2) That there are personnel functions which belong to each line functionary and functional specialist, and that in due course of time relationships will be better defined; (3) That the personnel unit

[8] Classifying personnel service as a department and the director as the head of a department sometimes accounts for the allocation of the personnel service to the line with the resultant interference in the line which will be discussed later.

performs line functions within its own boundaries; staff functions comprise its major responsibilities in connection with line units; (4) That the activities of line functionaries and of functional specialists require both intra- and interunit co-ordination and that interunit co-ordination is the major excuse for bringing bona fide staff functionaries into the organizational picture.[9]

APPLICATION OF THE GENERAL PRINCIPLES TO GUIDANCE AND PERSONNEL SERVICES

Line Concept. Any statistical report on enrollment in the schools and colleges of the United States will indicate that for the most part they are

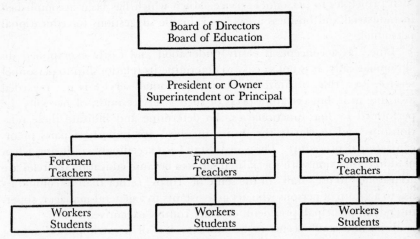

CHART V.—Line organization in a small industry or small school system.

small institutions. The same is true of business concerns. This means that the responsibility for all activities carried on in the majority of educational and business institutions is centralized in the office of the chief administrative officer. The form of organization which prevails in such institutions is usually designated "line" organization. It is the simplest and oldest form of organization, is highly centralized, and is in use in hundreds of concerns today. Chart V illustrates this type of organization as applied to both business and education.

The distinguishing characteristic of this type of organization, and the one from which it derives its name, is the line of authority or executive

9 Urwick discusses true "staff" authority as differentiated from both line authority and technical authority and notes that the concept is at present little used in business. He predicts an increase in its use ("Executive Decentralization with Functional Coordination," *Management Review*, XXIV [1935]).

control, which extends directly from the head of the institution via each executive subordinate in turn to those who ultimately perform the tasks or operations involved—the students in one case, the rank and file of the workers in the other. A highly centralized line organization of this type does not escape the functionally specialized responsibilities assumed by the more elaborate decentralized type of organization, but it may evade their performance, as may any type of organization which does not make definite provision for them. Theoretically at least it is called upon to perform all the functions, operational and service, which are performed by the segmented units of more elaborate organizations. Much of the guidance service in such institutions will be inherent, but when a program is formulated, it will be centralized in all of its aspects under the chief executive, and every teacher or foreman will be a participant.

There are advantages in this type of organization. It pools all special services directly under management and automatically co-ordinates them with one another and with operational units. It is economical and definite, and if the executive can devote sufficient time to a single phase of his total responsibilities, it often proves very effective. Moreover, it is well known that some of the best unrecorded, even unrecognized as such, guidance services are due to the initiative and inspirational leadership of small-school principals and small-college presidents. It is also well known that in response to calls for data for inclusion in statistical tabulations these same small institutions frequently report either no guidance services, or all enumerated on the schedule. In either case there is undeniable evidence that guidance functions are closely co-ordinated, perhaps so closely co-ordinated that existence is not differentiated from nonexistence.

The Expansion of Line Organization Units. As colleges, public schools, and business concerns increased in size, a breakdown of the single administrative unit became desirable. All over the country branch stores, geographically distant manufacturing units, substations of various kinds, uptown and downtown offices, and the like were segregated from the parent unit and set up as decentralized operational units. Responsibility for each branch unit was delegated to a subordinate executive.

In the same fashion, either by segregation from a parent organization or by the acquisition of new units by the parent organization, a group of decentralized educational units came into being. If they were not originally members of a parent unit, they were sooner or later brought together as a school system or as a university. The larger the parent unit and the larger, more numerous, and more widely separated geographically the segregated units were, the more apparent was the desirability of decentralization of executive responsibilities. The principle of centralized control and decentralized execution was rather generally accepted and put into practice.

Chart VI indicates how line organization, as exemplified in the single unit of Chart V, was expanded by the segregation of several similar units and it calls to mind the principle of the span of control. It will be noted that each school or college is highly centralized within its own domain.

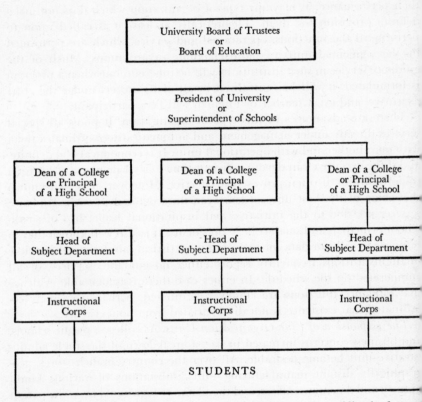

CHART VI.—Expansion of a line organization in a university or in a public-school system.

Each principal or dean stands at the head of his own line, while the superintendent or president stands at the head of the consolidated lines, unifying and standardizing procedures and practices common to all the units. Centralized control of the system or university is exemplified by the superintendent or president; decentralized execution by the principals to whom he has delegated responsibility for subordinate units; in the individual unit centralized control is exemplified by the principals or deans, while decentralization is provided for by the addition of department heads.

The Functional Specialist in Education. The expansion of control or executive responsibility which resulted in the decentralization of operating units was accompanied by the multiplication of responsibilities for certain types of specialized services which were also too burdensome to be carried by a single executive. Increase in the number and the size of operational units entailed similar financial problems within each unit and indicated the desirability of technical advisers who could aid in the unification of tested financial practices. Again, the influx of students, the breakdown in the older fields of knowledge, the addition of new subjects to the curricula, and the ever-narrowing specialization of subject teachers called for the introduction of specialists in the area of instruction—the department head in the single unit and at the central office the subject specialist who had no authority over department heads but was qualified to act in an advisory, leadership, and co-ordinating capacity with reference to all the segmented units. Finally, the addition to educational functions of certain types of services which in former years had been performed by home, church, and community or which were the logical outgrowth of social progress demanded the introduction of such technical specialists as nurses, doctors, psychologists, psychiatrists, visiting teachers, social and religious directors, vocational counselors, and others who are often collectively designated as personnel workers. Such functionaries were not supposed to have any authority. Their activities were purely advisory and facilitative. They served other units and departments and facilitated relationship from the top to the bottom of the line, inter- and intraunit, and inter- and intrafaculty and students.

A group of such services, or facilitating agencies, is shown at the right of Chart VII. One or more is usually found in connection with school systems in the larger towns and cities and in most of the colleges. A considerable number may be added for the larger cities and for universities.

The procedure involved in the introduction of all types of specialists is approximately the same. One at a time functions which have previously formed a part of the duties of line officials are segregated, and their control, or advisory aspects, as the case may be, are allocated to a functional specialist. No one who has been through the mill or who has watched the mill in operation needs to be told that the growing pains which accompany segmentation are always painful and sometimes very severe. Nor do they need to be told that the functionaries chosen to fill the positions so created are often unwelcome, resented as interlopers, unfairly criticized while trying to familiarize themselves with the local situation, refused the co-operation which is essential to success, and subjected by their close associates to prolonged and difficult entrance examinations.

This attitude on the part of the line is quite logical and often vindicated by the incompetence of the appointee, but it can usually be foreseen and at least partially forestalled if administrators, prior to segmentation, will take their subordinates into their confidence, discuss the situation which seems to call for a change, and consult with them regarding policies, procedures, and the type of appointee best qualified to fill the new position. Since much of the animosity is due to fear of a loss of prerogatives and of authority, it is well to make it perfectly clear that functional specialists will not be permitted to interfere with the control functions of line officials, that their duties are facilitative, co-ordinating, and advisory.

And it is just at this point that the author has found administrators, both in secondary schools and colleges, much in fault when inaugurating personnel services. The average administrator who is about to segment (meaning delegate leadership to a functional specialist) personnel service from line functions does not take time to clarify his own thinking on both duties and relationships. He seems to overlook the fact that the moment he segregates any special function from the line, he must not only clearly define the duties which he is segregating but also define the relationships which will come into being as a result of the segmentation or chaos will result. This he all too often does not or cannot do.

A second fault of the average administrator is found in the way he introduces the new functionary to his colleagues and inducts him into office. It makes no difference at what stage in the perfection of the personnel unit he is brought into the picture, whether it be to help determine policy and to assist in developing the organization or later to carry out the policies already determined upon, the administrator will protect both himself and the new official against much sniping if he will make it perfectly clear to every member of the corps that he is assuming full responsibility for the introduction of the service and for the policies to be carried out; that its relation to the line is definitely an advisory, not a control, relationship; and that within the framework of the general institutional policy each decentralized unit is free to work out its own personnel practices, using the assistance of the specialist only when it so desires.[10]

Some of the methods of selection and induction which the author has

---

[10] There is some opposition to this point of view on the ground that not all executives who are in charge of administrative units will know enough to use the assistance of specialists. Undoubtedly that is true. But is it wise to attempt to force advice and assistance on unwilling recipients? Is it not one of the functions of specialists to try to educate such persons to appreciate the value and utility of facilitating services? If they are not educable, the next move is up to the superintendent or president, who will probably know where to find a more co-operative assistant.

had an opportunity to observe or to consider as a mediator between parties after the induction ceremony had taken place are almost beyond belief. For example, docs it seem possible that any administrator would issue a peremptory order that persons who desired to be considered for the position of director of guidance must appear before the board within the week "and tell it what he proposed to do if elected"? The candidate making the best impression on the board and offering what appeared to be the best paper program was to be selected. The methods of educator selection have by no means been exhausted; there are more methods where those which already have been used came from! What sort of co-operation may be anticipated when a principal, or president, introduces his newly appointed specialist to the corps with the comment, "I have asked him to tell you what he expects you to do"?

In contrast, not because all the undesirable methods are used by educators and the more desirable by industry, but because in the author's files the best illustration of effective induction combined with an assumption of full responsibility by the management happens to be an industrial pronouncement, the following quotation is offered:

> It gives me pleasure to announce the appointment of a new member of the General Foods executive organization.
> Effective January 1, Thomas G. Spates becomes Director of Industrial Relations for General Foods. He will report directly to me and will assist the management on problems of employment, training, safety measures, medical service, wage and salary plans, hours, working conditions, retirement and benefit plans and other matters of mutual interest to employees and the corporation. His duties also will include co-ordination of personnel activities, development of more efficient and uniform personnel procedure, and bringing the management into closer touch with the viewpoint of the employees.
> Appointment of a staff assistant to advise and help the management in industrial relations problems involves no change in your present authority and responsibility in these matters, however. Execution of personnel policies and maintenance of satisfactory industrial relations continues to be one of primary duties of each department head, plant manager, and district sales manager.
> Creation of this new executive post is a concrete expression of our recognition that satisfactory industrial relations are among the primary responsibilities of the management.[11]

The Staff Concept in Relation to Personnel Service. When the parent organization has been subdivided into several decentralized units and the demand for specialized knowledge and leadership by both parent organization and its subdivisions has become sufficiently acute to require

[11] C. M. Chester, *Management's Responsibilities in Industrial Relations* (Personnel Series, no. 36; New York: American Management Assn., 1939). "Steps in a Program" are discussed in this address.

the delegation of control or supervisory duties and to call for the introduction of functional specialists, the educational stage is set for interference in the line. It has usually come rather promptly and from the two sources implied, the appointment of assistants to the superintendent, presidents, principals, or deans, and the introduction of functional specialists. The staff concept and the staff terminology are found in connection with both types of officials.

Briefly stated, the first chapter of the story runs about as follows: Executives found it impossible to maintain contact with so many operational units and to co-ordinate so many activities. Staff positions were created. Assistant superintendents were appointed, presumably to act as assistants to the chief executive in the performance of his duties. They had no place in the line, no authority, and no control functions; as usually expressed in military circles from which the staff concept was borrowed, they were "an extension of their chief officer's personality." The commander and his staff were frequently mentioned as a unit, and with reference to the commander's duties they acted as a unit.[12]

But this concept of a "staff" as forming a unit and acting as a unit is not confined to military circles. It is very common in many areas of life and is expressed in a variety of ways. In business one may hear "the authorities," "the executive office," or "management"; in education, "the central office," "the administration," or "the president's office"; in government, "the government," "the administration," "the executive office" or "Washington." Everywhere it is summed up in "the-powers-that-be." All such expressions convey the same concept, a chief administrative officer and his personal assistants.

In many instances these assistants, either through delegation of control function or by the undisputed assumption of such function, became executives in their own right with authority over certain line executives. Thus an intermediate line official stood between the chief administrator and the official to whom he had delegated responsibility for a segregated operational unit. Many opportunities for interference in the line arose. Principals of high schools and deans of colleges asked, Who is to make final decisions, the executive officer in charge of the unit or the assistant to the superintendent or president? Fundamental principles of organization made no provision for the delegation of responsibility for an operational unit to one official and delegation of authority to determine how the responsibilities should be met to a second official.

---

[12] Current news items dealing with the organization and lack of organization among the combat forces of the United Nations is daily focusing attention on certain of these principles of organization.

The second chapter of the story of interference in the line is concerned with the introduction of functional specialists who were supposed to act as technical assistants to the central organization and, if so desired, to the segregated units. Their positions, too, were supposed to be staff positions, their contributions purely advisory or facilitating services; but they, too, either by delegation or usurpation easily acquired the habit of "butting in" rather than "tuning in" on the activities of the line and of assuming functions which belonged to principals rather than of facilitating the better performance of these same functions by principals. A very clear-cut statement of the outcome of interference in the line in industry has recently been made by the personnel relations manager of the Western Electric Company.[13] It is worthy of consideration by educators.

Look back for a moment and consider the high hopes we have had for the specialists of yesteryear—the efficiency engineer, the disciplinarian, the employment manager, the training director, and the safety engineer. There has been the tendency to feel that such delegation of responsibility would relieve the first-line supervisor of many of his difficult supervisory problems. Have many personnel men been wise when they yielded to the temptation of thinking that they could take over those responsibilities? One by one these activities are being handed back to the line organization with a growing recognition that your personnel expert is a staff assistant—helpful, useful and important in all these relationships, but *not* an *operating* man.

Interference in the line is bound to occur whenever either type of relief official mentioned encroaches on the administrative prerogatives of principals, deans, or other executives, whenever they attempt to enter the line, which has no place for them, or to usurp control functions which are assigned to others. In recent years the relationship between principals and assistant superintendents has been clarified and the duties of both have been more clearly defined, but the staff concept, especially in its bearing on personnel service, has not been clarified and is admittedly very difficult to clarify.

It must be recognized that guidance and personnel functionaries have unusual temptations to break in on the technical responsibilities of the line and are more excusable for so doing than are specialists in some other areas. In the first place, as has been noted, guidance service is not a specialized unit in the same sense as is medical service, vocational education, engineering, music, and the like. To a much greater degree it is a shared responsibility demanding that all members of the corps participate, whether or not they have been prepared for or are qualified for, participation. Functions of this type are sometimes called "permeating

13 J. Walter Dietz, "New Trends in Personnel Policies," *Personnel*, XVI (1940), 97–106.

functions" because, while they are under the charge of specialists, the specialists often work out practices and procedures which are used rather universally by the various administrative units throughout the entire institution. Most colleges and secondary schools would probably also consider extra- or cocurricular activities among permeating functions, public relations in universities and business houses, and purchasing departments in connection with all organizations.

Another logical justification for interference is traceable to the fact that, whereas several of the all-pervasive service functions, medical, psychological, and psychopathic, are so highly technical that laymen all down the line are either automatically limited to minor participation or are restrained by law from going beyond certain limits, there is a wide range of personnel functions which are beyond the reach of the law and which lie in the areas of life where ignorance is still bliss. Teachers, teacher-advisers, inadequately trained counselors, and deans are permitted to inflict upon the student personnel the most detrimental types of pseudo-guidance, false guidance, and destructive guidance, which often mar the entire life of an individual; yet they remain on the payroll of educational institutions and are beyond the arm of the law.[14] Thus the responsible personnel functionary is caught between Scylla and Charybdis. He feels that the principle of participation should be endorsed, and he would like to advocate its practice. But he is appalled at the consequent exploitation of youth, and so he tends to salvage what he can even though line interference be involved.

Chart VII represents the application of certain principles with which some institutions, which have exhausted the expansion possibilities of line organization, are trying to utilize the staff concept to relieve pressure in both control areas and in areas of specialization and at the same time to work out some satisfactory relationships between line officials and the specialists who have been employed to facilitate the accomplishment of institutional objectives. Since no chart dealing with this subject can do more than help to focus attention on the many problems involved in perfecting an organization which will allow these comparatively new officials to render a maximum of service to the line with a minimum of

14 Recently the National Vocational Guidance Association appointed a committee which is endeavoring to uncover and eliminate false and pseudo-guidance services offered by commercial agencies. The inspection procedure laid down by the committee leads one to propound several questions: Who among the would-be inspectors can approach this undertaking with clean hands? Is it another case of the pot and the kettle? Wouldn't it be better to clean house in noncommercial institutions first? What danger of libel suits is involved in such a risky business? Would not persistent education of student personnel in methods of appraising and selecting counseling services be both a safer and a more effective method of procedure?

interference in the line, it is with some hesitation that this chart is included. Moreover, it must be remembered that a chart prepared to show relationships in any specific organization is rarely applicable to another organization, and if the organization be a going concern, frequent alterations will be necessary. At best transfer suggestions have limited value.[15]

At the left of the chart, the line organization as discussed in connection with Charts V and VI is shown. The assistant superintendent has been

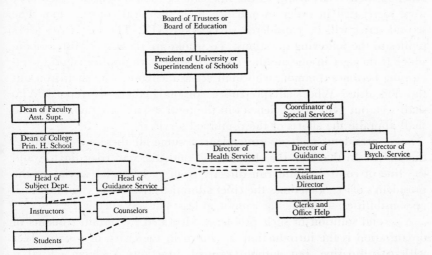

CHART VII. Organization of special services and the interrelationship of line functions and staff functions. (Solid lines show control functions; broken lines show influence functions.)

added and appears to be in the line. Sometimes he is. It depends upon his duties and his relation both to his superior and to other line and technical functionaries.

The group of special services at the right of the chart represents the

[15] About ten years ago, Monograph no. 14, Bulletin, 1932, no. 17, National Survey of Secondary Education, was published by the U. S. Office of Education. It was prepared by William C. Reavis and was entitled *Programs of Guidance.* Ten programs in "places where good guidance programs were in effect" were described. The basis for classification as "good" was not given. Charts accompanied descriptions and during the succeeding years the majority of writers on guidance have either copied its data or drawn heavily upon it for whatever they may have wished to include under organization. Those who desire to examine specific charts will, therefore, find them available in many places. Comparison of these charts and of the terms, with their varying usages, which describe the programs is an interesting and illuminating experience. It will help to stress the problems which have been mentioned in Part V and may possibly help to clarify the thinking of those who are about to undertake the organization of a guidance system.

more or less highly specialized functions which one at a time have been taken from line duties. Some institutions will find one such service sufficient; others will feel the need of several. Each service is provided with a director or a chief officer with some other title, whose rank is co-ordinate with that of all other directors; no one service has authority over any other service. The stage is now set for two series of problems. One series relates to the control and co-ordination of these independent services; the other to their relationship to the line side of the chart from which they were segregated in order to enhance their technical contribution. The second series will be considered in Chapter XIX. The first series seeks replies to the following questions: To whom are these specialists responsible? If they get in one another's way, if efforts are duplicated and overlapping becomes common, who shall act as mediator, who shall iron out the difficulties? Who shall prepare a consolidated service report? Who shall seek out gaps or deficiencies in the total service program? And who shall appraise the efforts of the combined services?

Some presidents and superintendents assume all these responsibilities themselves. In that case the chart would omit the staff co-ordinator, and the line of control would run directly from each special service to the president's office. Sometimes the chief administrative officer can meet such responsibilities; sometimes he cannot, at least not very effectively.

A second solution of such problems advocated by certain students of organization is the introduction, as shown in the chart, of a staff officer with co-ordinating, but without control, functions. Such an official is brought into the organization to compensate for the loss of unity which accompanied disruption of the simple line organization with all functions, control and technical, under one executive. The dovetailing, which foretells the satisfactory accomplishment of all tasks, is his primary job. The titles of such functionaries vary. Assistants to the president, to principals, to superintendents, or to deans are rather common, but some administrators use the same title for both their control and their co-ordinating assistants. The choice of a title would depend somewhat, as it does with the intermediate control functionary at the left of the chart, upon the incumbent's duties and relationships. If control over service agencies has been delegated to him, assistant dean or assistant superintendent are suitable; if he is purely a co-ordinator and adviser keeping all services functioning harmoniously without useless overlappings and duplications and without the omission of important services, if he acquires and passes on to his superior a vision of each service in its relation to other services and to the institution as a whole, if he unifies reports, is a good ghost writer, and adds a "passion for anonymity" to his qualifications, he is majoring in staff functions and his title should so indicate.

In comparison with the type of organization shown in the chart where the efforts of a number of specialists of equal rank are co-ordinated by a staff functionary, a third solution of the co-ordination problem is found in the fairly common practice of elevating the director of one of the services to the directorship of the group. The other services become subordinate, and their directors become assistant directors. This type of organization, which is more often the product of circumstances than of logic, is a potent source of constant complaints which bedevil, instead of relieve, the chief administrator. The reasons are rather obvious:

(1) The more highly specialized a director the more effective he is likely to be as a specialist and the less appreciative of the value of other types of specialization. He is a poor co-ordinator.

(2) The worth-while specialist will brook no interference by other specialists; and it is exceedingly difficult to prevent the assumption being made that the director has authority, or line control, over assistant directors.

(3) It is difficult to determine which service should be given the opportunity to act as co-ordinator. Usually the personality of the director is a safer guide than is the type of service. Sometimes priority of induction is the sole criterion; if there be a psychological service on hand, guidance services may be annexed; or if guidance service happens to be in on the ground floor, the psychological service may be annexed; or, again, guidance is sometimes tacked on to vocational education. Experience has shown that psychologists are especially prone to stress the psychological aspects of personnel services, oftentimes to the serious neglect of other equally important permeating services. Vocational education is a specialized line function operating in a limited sphere, whereas psychological, medical, and guidance services are specialized permeating functions operating throughout the entire system.

(4) Guidance functionaries, as co-ordinators, have been far from acceptable to their colleagues. Dissatisfaction usually centers around their narrow educational background and their limited experiences with life. Were they in truth men who had arrived, men who in their own right could command the universal respect and confidence of their colleagues, they might be the most logical choice because their field is so broad that they are bound to be either less highly specialized on a broader foundation, or if highly specialized in several aspects of personnel service, their foundation for understanding and appreciating the value of other services

is automatically broadened. A good co-ordinator may well know less about the technical aspects of the various services than does the director of each service, but he must know enough about all to be both an intelligent and an impartial co-ordinator.

Committee co-ordination affords a fourth method of providing liaison facilities between technical services and the administrative office. It has the advantage of being the cheapest of all methods and the disadvantages of all committee services including partisanship. For small schools it is often the only feasible method, but it must be remembered that the small school will usually have no functional specialists. Committee co-ordination would be concerned with the efforts of other committees and individuals, none of whom were technical experts.

Every administrator knows that there is no single correct form of organization, that his guidance organization must be projected on local conditions with full consideration of the contribution it is expected to make to the progress of the institution. But he also knows that progressive specialization entails some method of co-ordinating advisory or facilitating services and that neglect to provide it invites chaos. Probably, too, experience will have taught him that to provide a plan does not always mean that the plan will work. Usually plans will need to be revised many times before they approximate perfection.

W. J. Donald, in the address previously mentioned, lays down two main principles which he feels should be accepted by all organizations which set up personnel services. They may be helpful to educators:

1. That an operating executive should make his decisions and assume full responsibility for them and for their execution, subject only to his superior, but with the advice and counsel of staff executives.

2. That the staff executives, such as the budget director, the comptroller, the manager of the personnel department, etc., do not have any responsibility for command in operating departments, and that there is a facilitating relationship between staff and operating departments in the sense that staff men help establish standards of operation by which operating executives may more easily arrive at decisions and by which they may be judged more fairly by the general management. It is not the function of staff executives to control in the sense that they may make operating decisions for the operating executives. If the operating executives make decisions which are contrary to the evidence presented by the staff executive or if they fail to execute decisions made in such a way as to maintain standards that are adopted, the responsibility for control in the sense of command belongs to the general manager and not the staff executives.

Of all the violations of sound organization principles, the failure to observe this latter principle has been the most frequent in management organization. Personnel management went through its violent stages of bad handling in this respect with subsequent deflation of authority and ultimate rise in effectiveness. Budget directors and comptrollers went through a similar period a few years later. Some of them have not yet emerged from the stage of thinking in which they accept the functions of command of the general manager. Until they do they will not serve the operating executives as effectively as they should.[16]

16 P. 57.

CHAPTER XIX

Building the Guidance or Personnel Service

CHAPTER XVIII has discussed the conditions which foster the breakdown of a given operational unit into a number of segmented units all of which are members of the parent organization or system, and all of which, with their principals, deans, or other officers, are under the control of a single chief executive. It has discussed the segregation of various functions which were originally inherent in line responsibilities and their allocation, as special services, to a definite position in the organization. It has indicated how the segregation, first of operational units and second of special services, has revealed the need for co-ordinating and supervisory services and brought the staff concept into the picture.

Furthermore, Chapter XVIII, through the application of the general principles of organization to the organization of personnel services, has indicated how the chief administrator assumes responsibility for partially organizing the central office. That is, he determines the specific functions which he wishes to allocate to the service, and, in many cases by means of committees, or otherwise, he familiarizes the entire corps with the objectives of the service, and seeks the benefit of its suggestions and co-operation as he proceeds. Also, perhaps with the advice of the corps, he appoints a director, sees that he is properly inducted, and that his position as a special functionary without authority over any functionary allocated to any other service or operational unit is made perfectly clear.

Although discussion of the administrative responsibilities and procedures involved in the installation of a guidance or personnel service has centered around a school system or a university comprising an hierarchy of line executives, it must not be assumed that the procedures suggested are applicable only to the larger institutions. The fundamental principles of organization and the initial steps in organization are equally applicable to centralized systems comprising a number of operational units and to unitary colleges or schools which may for the first time be breaking away from the simple line organization. The administrator in charge must take the same responsibilities, make the same sort of decisions, and take the first steps in launching the organization before he delegates responsibility to anyone, a director, chief counselor, counselor, committee, or a teacher-counselor.

However, in spite of this similarity in principles of organization and in the character of administrative responsibilities, it is often difficult in practice to adapt generalizations to local situations, especially when they run the entire gamut of facilities and needs from the well-financed, abundantly staffed, large city system to the most meagerly equipped rural school. For this reason, Chapter XIX will present the problem of building a guidance service under three quite different, but still generalized conditions:

1. Building a centralized organization to serve decentralized operational units.

2. Building a guidance service for a single operational unit.

3. Building a guidance service for small towns or rural communities.

A CENTRALIZED ORGANIZATION TO SERVE DECENTRALIZED OPERATIONAL UNITS

Whenever an educational system or a university has determined to introduce a centralized guidance service with decentralized control allocated to its segregated operational units and whenever the preliminary organizational procedures mentioned in Chapter XVIII have been completed, the appointed director may take over and proceed to carry out the policies and instructions of his superior.

His responsibilities will include the organization of his own service unit; the establishment of cordial working relationships with other service units; and the manifestation of practices, knowledges, judgment, and skills which will advertise the service as a desirable asset to the executives of operational units whether they be contemplating the establishment of a guidance service or whether they have already installed such services. In carrying out these responsibilities he will be confronted by a number of problems which have previously been mentioned as paralleling those encountered in introducing specialists and staff or co-ordinating officers in the parent organization.

Organizing the Central Personnel Service. Setting up within the central unit whatever line organization may be essential, requisitioning supplies and office equipment, and recommending for appointment the necessary assistants are, of course, administrative responsibilities entailing control functions, but control which does not extend beyond the conduct of the single service which has been placed under the jurisdiction of its director. Chart VII shows at the right line organization in connection with a central personnel service. It would be the same for any other service unit which might be incorporated in the system. Since control over all subordinates is assumed, the solid lines correspond to the solid lines used to represent control in the operational units at the left of the chart.

Selecting technical assistants is a major responsibility in any personnel service. It is easy to conceive of situations in which the necessary number and types of line assistants would be so obvious that a director would be justified in proceeding at once with the development of a skeleton corps. Usually the director will prefer to move more slowly, perhaps to work entirely alone while he is studying the situation and forming a clearer picture of the number and qualifications of the assistants needed.

One very important problem, which was also faced by the chief administrator when he was determining upon the director of the central service, is whether, as a rule, personnel assistants shall be chosen from within the system or from without. This issue was not discussed when the selection of a central director was the subject because, while it is of importance at all levels in the personnel hierarchy, it is a more universal problem on the lower levels reaching clear down to the situation which permits only the part-time services of a classroom teacher. The pros and cons of this question require careful balancing for every position which is to be filled. The decision often carries with it either the seeds of discord, hostility, and failure, or of confidence, co-operation, and success.

To state that the best qualified person should be selected is true, obvious, and trite. It is a good pronouncement as far as it goes, but it does not compass the usual situation, nor is it particularly helpful in the light of the many complications involved in the appointment of functionaries whose activities permeate the entire organization and react on every member of the corps.

One approach to a wise solution of the problem is to round up throughout the entire institution all those individuals who informally and unobtrusively have already established nuclei for different phases of personnel service. Almost any institution will reveal two or three. For example, a live psychology department on its own initiative may be experimenting with the clinical approach to student personnel problems, or a commercial department may be placing its own students and accumulating a wide range of contacts and much valuable information which would be useful for the occupational guidance of other students. Again, some instructor in philosophy may have become an expert in recognizing the spiritual thirst so common among college students today, and he may have assisted a sufficient number over the quicksands of religious indecision to have acquired a grape-vine reputation for illuminating the spiritual values of life.

All of these nuclei have values, some more, others less. Every originator of such a nucleus should be given consideration, and some way should be found to show appreciation of his interest and to capitalize on his efforts and achievements, not necessarily, however, as a full-time or as a central office assistant.

Theoretically, some may say, such suggestions read well, but practically they do not work out; many of these self-appointed advisers have assumed these tasks because of mental twists or emotional disturbances in their own lives which have enhanced their humanitarian interests without adding to their scientific equipment. They are frequently harmful rather than helpful to youth.

Such statements are true. It does not take many years of experience to convince one that a considerable number of individuals who are totally unfit temperamentally to advise others are more than anxious to do so and are quite oblivious to their inadequacies.[1]

Some years ago after the author had completed an address bearing on this subject, a personnel director who had had considerable experience with college faculties stressed the difficulties involved in such a procedure. When organizing his faculty for shared responsibilities and attempting to carry out the ideal of personnel service as a permeating function, he had encountered many more difficulties in sidetracking instructors who should not participate, than in persuading those who should participate to do so. How, his question was, can we prevent these well-meaning but obviously incompetent advisers from advising?

That is a difficult question to answer, but it is found in many a director's attention file. Searching for a reply will cause him numerous headaches and will call into play all his ingenuity and resources. But it will continue to be a problem until it is solved. Sometimes a rather detailed job analysis will help. It should include all central office responsibilities, the collection, evaluation, and classification of various types of informational data, the preparation of bulletins and newsletters for distribution throughout the system, the conducting of demonstration interviews or case conferences, the evaluation of the record system, research on some phase of individual analysis devices, publicity and community contacts, and the like.

Analysis of faculty competencies will be facilitated by data on the special fields of knowledge of each person, his greatest strengths as a faculty member, instructional ability, research, off-campus contacts, personal influence, etc. The collective judgment of the student body is often a potent ally in appraising faculty actualities and potentialities in counseling

---

[1] Many inquiries of university and secondary school administrators have brought the common reply, Not over about one third of any faculty is qualified for advisory service.

areas. If students year after year in ever-increasing numbers turn to certain faculty members for assistance in solving personal problems or if students habitually fail to respond to others' bids for confidences, the director will know which type to invite to participate in the advisory aspects of the service.[2]

It should be possible for an alert personnel director to capitalize on some quality possessed by each individual deemed worthy of retention in the instructional corps. Those who fail to qualify for counseling will often prove exceedingly competent in other phases of the work. But all-out faculty participation in organized guidance services should never be accomplished at the expense of real service to students. Now and then there is evidence that principals and presidents as well as directors have unduly stressed their feeling that every good teacher would desire to participate in some formal aspect of guidance services. Good teachers in the classroom and teachers whose example is worthy of emulation by pupils are continually performing informal guidance services, and there is nothing to date which indicates that in ultimate values formal guidance has supplanted inherent guidance. Both are useful.

In the majority of cases when the directors have completed their study of local possibilities, they will find that the pros and cons of local appointees may be summarized about as follows: If some member of the corps seems qualified except for such technical deficiencies as can be remedied after appointment, if he is generally acceptable to his colleagues, and if he desires the appointment, it is wiser to choose the local man. He will be familiar with the traditions of the institution, with its objectives, policies, faculty strengths and weaknesses, and the characteristics of its clientele. He will understand the personality of the corporate community and be familiar with its resources. Promotion from within usually has a beneficial influence on the corps, whereas the selection of an outsider is apt to be resented and to create a "what's the use" attitude.

On the other hand, even though one or more qualified prospects be at hand, if factional support is apparent, if community jealousies and prejudices are rampant, if each possibility is so well known that his deficiencies and previous errors of judgment stand out like porcupine quills, the negative side will probably win, and the director will prefer to secure an assistant from some other source. Whatever the final decision, the serv-

---

[2] Although one occasionally finds a system in which central functionaries do counseling both in the central office and by assignment to decentralized units, it is not considered good practice by authorities on organization. On the other hand, if the central service is supposed to act in a consultative capacity, it would seem wise to appoint as central assistants those who have already received recognition as good counselors.

ice will probably be off to a better start if it is known that local prospects received first consideration.

While the central unit is being built up, now from within, again from without, while functions are being classified and responsibilities assigned, the director will also be giving some attention to his second responsibility, the *establishment of working relations with other service units.*

Chart VII (see p. 397) indicates the co-ordinate positions or ranks of these service units and of their directors. The broken lines imply co-operative effort in the accomplishment of a common undertaking; each service will take major responsibility for the performance of any service which falls primarily within its field of specialization; all other services will recognize its right and obligation to lead. Irrespective of which service may have first received the call or observed the need for service, the specialized service best equipped to lead will lead while other services withdraw to the side lines until one or more are called upon for adjunct services. Requests for adjunct services will be promptly responded to by services marginal to whatever the responsibility may be. They will put their services at the disposal of the leader and work under his direction reporting to him the results of any task which may have been assigned.

A staff co-ordinator who has been delegated control functions may allocate duties to the various services and enforce appropriate distribution of cases or duties, but if he performs facilitating service only, influence becomes an important asset at this point. There is rejoicing in his office when the corps of each service demonstrates its ability and willingness to switch from leader to adjunct, or vice versa as the scene shifts and different types of service are needed. Here is found the key to the ability of any institution to serve each student according to his needs with the person best qualified to deal with the problem at hand.

Where this type of co-operation is lacking, where each service is out with a magnifying glass hunting for cases and pulling them into its own domain, where certain services are always struggling for front-line positions and are never willing to act as adjuncts, there will be only confusion in the co-ordinator's office, only indifferently performed services for students, and always appeals for the settlement of jurisdictional disputes in the office of the chief executive. Now and then an executive has been known to draw a genuine sigh of relief when certain services have faded out of the organization picture.

Establishing service relationships with decentralized units is the third major responsibility involved in the organization of central guidance services. There are so many ways to achieve success in this undertaking, so many purely personal qualities in each situation, so many local factors to be considered in determining upon each course of action, and so many subtle and unforeseen causes of failure that it is useless to attempt to do more than summarize a few of the possible capacities in which a central service director might be expected to show leadership, and continue to call attention to the fact that the types of service which he is supposed to offer are increasingly considered as staff or facilitating functions rather than as line or control functions.

These advisory relationships are clearly brought out in Chart VII where broken lines connect the operational unit executive with the central personnel service, and the decentralized personnel service, under the jurisdiction of this executive, with the central personnel service. The relationships shown are, once again, the result of the application of the fundamental principles of organization to the personnel field. A qualified director will have no difficulty in interpreting them correctly. He will know that violation of such principles has long hindered the establishment of satisfactory relationships between the line organization and the personnel service. He will understand what an impossible situation would result if central service functionaries were allowed to go over the head of unit executives. He will proceed to establish himself on a consultant basis within the framework of these generally accepted principles of organization even though, at times, such principles may appear to handicap his efficiency.

A wise director will not resent, because he will realize that executives are exercising legitimate prerogatives, the installation of personnel services and the appointment of directors without either his advice or approval. He will not attempt to force his advice on either executives or unit personnel directors and, when invited to advise, will show neither surprise nor resentment if his suggestions are rejected.

But if the central director has won recognition in his field, if his opinions are deemed worthy of consideration by the over-all administrative authorities, if his attitude is unemotional, his approach nonpartisan, his sense of fair play obvious, and his willingness to share credit with others and to remain on "tap" rather than strive to be on "top" thoroughly understood,[3] there are few operating units which will not be glad

---

[3] This writer has three favorite expressions which she has used over a long period of years to express what seemed a desirable relation of the personnel director to the corps: he should be always on "tap," but never on "top"; he may "tune in," but never "butt in"; and "he should be willing to open the lines and give a wholehearted cheer as he watches the other fellow go through with the ball." The first two were original; the last is a statement made in the early 1920's by E. K. Hall, then Vice-President of the American Telephone and Telegraph Company, during a conference concerned with qualifications of personnel directors in industry.

to have his assistance. It is on the basis of values, rather than by virtue of position, title, salary, degrees, or authority, that he must win the confidence of the co-operating units which he has been given an opportunity to serve.

During the process of establishing himself as a welcome consultant to the line organization, a central director will act in several different capacities. Attention is called to his duties as a salesman, as a functional specialist, as an educator and leader, as a co-ordinator, and as a research student.

As a Salesman. Any director who is classified as a success will usually have observed that guidance is an acquired taste among educators, frequently very slowly acquired, and he will know that he cannot entirely escape the "show me" attitude. In trying to overcome this attitude, he will have learned that he dare not attempt to conceal the fact that guidance service has by no means as yet validated its claim to the important position and to the wholehearted approval which he is seeking for it. It is one of the outstanding characteristics of guidance services that they can neither be voted in, nor superimposed by edict, but must be sold to the organization by deeds as well as by words. This is the director's job. It will be an easier job if the chief administrator has paved the way during the period of induction.

In accomplishing his task the director will probably find that certain principles of salesmanship outlined with reference to the selling of more tangible things are equally applicable to influence selling. For example, the type of approach to each prospect will be adapted to the specific situation; overselling and underselling, overaggressiveness and underaggressiveness will probably bring approximately the same results in either field. Undoubtedly the director will find it difficult, at times, to reconcile his qualities as a salesman with the passion for anonymity which tends to make him so acceptable as a side-line consultant.

As a Functional Specialist. A director's services will be appraised and his success will be measured by the permeating influence of his scientifically human point of view and by the efficiency with which he assumes his own responsibilities. Although responsibilities will vary from institution to institution, he will usually win the confidence of those who are in executive control of operational units if without butting in he can assist each unit to build, within the framework of institutional policy, a personnel program adapted to local needs and gradually to develop a line organization which understands the implications of a personnel service and is eager to participate in making it a success.

The personnel director in the segregated unit will appreciate assistance in visualizing and putting in practice a well-balanced personnel program. He may desire help on many problems such as collecting and recording informational data, appraising new devices and techniques, and placing proper values on the results of psychological testing as well as on the results deriving from study of the emotions. If the central director will "tune" in whenever he can help, if he will avoid any semblance of usurpation of authority, if he never poses as a specialist but continually strives to be worthy of that rating by others, he will sooner or later become a specialist by common consent.

As an Educator. In order to be accepted as a leader and to receive the right hand of fellowship as an educator, the director must prove that he is informed on both the production and distribution problems of education. He must be aware of personnel activities in every area of life and must keep in touch with social and industrial change, with legislative enactments related to the field, with occupational outlets for various types of preparation, and with shifts in opportunities which affect educational curricula. Furthermore he must be able to help his colleagues evaluate the literature of research and experimentation and of authoritative opinion and pronouncement. Those who seek his assistance will cease to return if the cupboard is always bare.

Since his major educational job, working with and through each operational unit, is improvement of the quality of the work of the corps, he will need to be familiar with the best methods of adult education, to recognize the difference between instructing, and stimulating and guiding, and to be ever alert to discover new methods of keeping up to date and assisting co-operating units.

While it is not fair to burden the director with superhuman leadership responsibilities, it is fair to assume that he will be well informed in his field, that he will be cognizant of the best method of getting his message across, and that he will realize that the degree of Master of Arts in the most innocuous and subtle art of influencing adult educators is more important than the nondescript doctorate. Whether the leadership functions of a central director are confined to executives, other specialists, and directors of personnel service in operational units or whether they extend to the entire corps and to the public will depend upon the administrator's assignment of duties.

As a Co-ordinator. The necessity for co-ordination of service agencies has been mentioned, and it has been suggested that large systems often employ either a staff or a control officer whose major responsibility is the co-ordination of the activities of all such services. The director of the central personnel service is always responsible for co-ordinating the activities of his own unit. Sometimes he is responsible for co-ordinating all the personnel activities which are carried on throughout the system and for articulating such services with those afforded by lower and higher educational units and with community services including those of business and industry.

Since co-ordination of personnel activities within the segmented units of a system may involve eliminations, consolidations, and additions, in its control aspect it is an administrative function full of dynamite and should not be assumed by a central director unless definitely delegated to him with full understanding by both parties of its potentialities for friction. If it is not delegated to him, he must rely entirely on influence to improve what is often a chaotic situation and to win the confidence and support of the various operational units while so doing.

Lack of co-ordination in the secondary schools and in universities clear through the graduate school is a serious handicap to effective work. This deficiency is evidenced by the fact that school clerks, registrars, class advisers, deans of men and women, homeroom teachers, subject teachers and counselors all have a finger in the pie; all make programs, all advise on choice of curricula, and all, often supplemented by psychologists, participate in "guidance in learning." Oftentimes co-ordination is not missed and educational guidance seems to be attaining satisfactory results until suddenly the student, who is about to take the next step, discovers that there has been no co-ordination of his program with possible occupational outlets or with the most desirable advanced educational work. He has had many advisers but no worth-while advice.

Co-ordination is not the result of an act of God. It is the result of organization based on analysis of duties and relationships. All necessary services should be provided. Each service should be performed by the proper functionary. Duplication should be reduced to the minimum. Supplementary service and technical information should be available to assist those who deal with educational, vocational, and personal problems so that all services may be brought to a focus on the program and problems of each student. The possibilities of co-ordination through student personnel records should be exploited. Reports on the activities of segmented services should be co-ordinated for the use of each college, as well as for the information of the central administration. Weaknesses in articulation as between lower and succeeding units should be revealed and strengthened, and the educational facilities of business and industry should be co-ordinated with those of the classroom.

Co-ordinating functions will vary from system to system and from university to university, but every director of a central service should be prepared, either by a combination of influence and delegated authority or by influence alone, to show leadership in the type of co-ordinating activities mentioned.

There will be myriad difficulties to iron out if genuine co-ordination is even semiaccomplished. Part of the difficulties arise from our national tendency, when clouds appear on the horizon, to pyramid officials, each in turn instructed to get the bugs out of the other fellow's efforts, instead of co-ordinating the efforts of those already on the job. Who should be responsible for remedial instruction, the classroom teacher, the psychologist, the counselor? Is remedial reading a personnel function or is it concerned with the psychology of learning? There will be genuine differences of opinion, jealousies, refusals to give up prerogatives or to trust extradivisional specialists, but everybody, prepared or unprepared, should not be performing technical services.

Is it necessary for a student who has received programing assistance from his faculty adviser to have his program validated by the dean of men or dean of women before he or she can register? Is it a mere formality, a waste of time and a duplication of effort? Is it an honest attempt to be sure that everyone participates and that programing is a faculty-permeating function? Is it based on the assumption that faculties cannot be trusted to make educational programs without the oversight of student deans?

When a student wants to change his program to whom does he go for assistance, to his faculty adviser, to the dean of his sex, or to the registrar? How many decentralized placement services are operating on the campus? One for each division, with several departmental supplements? What a duplication of services, waste of money, and serious inconvenience to patrons, both students and employers!

Gaining the confidence and support of operational units and at the same time so co-ordinating the personnel services of the various units that, with the least duplication of effort and expense, they may fit into a unified institutional program is a very difficult, very delicate, and very hazardous responsibility for any central service. Sometimes the best-qualified director fails and loses his position as a reward for his efforts.

As a Research Student. The attitude of the central director toward research, his knowledge of methods of research, and his ability to suggest the practical application of the results of research to the solution of local problems and to the improvement of personnel practices will have considerable influence on the value which the entire institution puts upon his services. On the other hand, it will be easier to win the respect and confidence of the corps if the personnel director poses as a student of problems rather than as a director of research—unless, of course, research is his field of specialization in which case he will not be likely to qualify for the variety of nonresearch functions required of personnel directors, nor will he be interested in assuming them.

Here and there a public-school system combines the functions of educational research with those of personnel service using the title, Director of Guidance and Research. This is unfortunate, since if the holder of the title is a success as a director of personnel services, he is likely to be a poor apology for a director of educational research. Nothing militates against a personnel director more than the assumption of or the assignment to him of responsibilities which many members of the line are better qualified to perform than is he. In general personnel directors may well confine their research activities to the study of local personnel problems, relying upon research specialists who are familiar with the increasing number of highly technical research techniques to furnish research data in the broader field of personnel.

In order to function effectively in the various aspects of his service, the director must be accepted as an upper official in the hierarchy of his own institution. The chief administrator is responsible for opening the inner sanctum of the institution to him. Unless the director knows the problems of the administration, unless he is in touch with important decisions and with trends in thought relative to policies, curricula, social life, and the like, he cannot carry his share of the load. Nor can he even be sure that he is always proceeding in harmony with institutional policy, to say nothing of interpreting it correctly to decentralized units.

Some personnel directors who have not been invited to join the inner circle have resented this omission and have openly expressed their resentment. Some have been bidden to attend but have had neither voice nor vote in the proceedings. Voice and vote do not matter, but if attendance be permitted, even though grudgingly, a firsthand knowledge of the policy-makers' thought and the reasons for ultimate decisions are a great asset to the director in meeting his own responsibilities effectively.[4]

A Service for a Single Operational Unit

Two types of single operational units must be considered, the decentralized unit in the large system and the self-contained unit which is a

---

[4] Women directors and would-be directors will do well to remember that on the college level and in both business and industry, whenever the policy-making group is composed entirely of men, an aggressive woman is *persona non grata* while even the most unassuming is a nuisance. By virtue of her sex she spoils the informality and freedom to relax which relieves tension, rests tired nerves, and makes such meetings less of a burden. Omission should never be regarded as a personal affront.

system in its own right. In some respects the procedures involved in building a guidance or personnel organization in these two types of units do not differ materially from those involved in building a central guidance service, but there are some dissimilarities in functions and objectives which require consideration.

The executive of any system, unit of a system, or self-contained unit must assume responsibility for the service under his control. All executives will face such common problems as setting up a personnel policy and outlining objectives in harmony with the general policies and objectives of the unit or system, selling the guidance point of view to the corps, giving the corps an opportunity to share in the introduction of the service, determining upon functions and relationships, and appointing a director and seeing that he is properly inducted and that his functions and relation to other functionaries are thoroughly understood.

The segregated unit of a system, if it introduces its guidance service prior to the installation of a central service, will take into consideration the general policies and objectives of the parent institution as well as its individual policies and objectives and will build within the framework provided by the system. If the guidance service is instituted after the organization of the central service, its functions and procedures will probably be partially determined by the functions and procedures of the central service, and it will doubtless receive considerable assistance from that source in perfecting its organization. The self-contained unit will have no central service either to assist or to handicap it, but it will also be obliged to assume a number of responsibilities for which the decentralized unit may call upon the central service.

Fundamental Principles of Organization Applicable to Operational Units. Chart V showed a unitary educational system with no special provision for guidance services. Chart VII, assuming the operational unit at the left to represent both a decentralized operational unit and a unitary system, shows a guidance service on its right which is similar in its internal organization and in its line and staff relationships to the central service at the far right of the chart. This chart serves as a prototype, suitable for adaptation but not often suitable for adoption without adaptation.

Solid lines indicate that the decentralized guidance service is definitely under the control of the chief executive of the unit and that counselors attached to it have the same relationship to their director as instructors have to heads of departments. All relationships are "line," as they must be in any well-planned organization, for as has been previously stressed, no functionary can logically serve in any operational unit, decentralized or self-contained, who is not subject to the authority of the executive in charge of that unit. Broken lines indicate the same type of relationships between the guidance service and the heads of subject departments and their instructional corps as was explained with reference to the central service and the executives of decentralized units. They are advisory, facilitative, or consultative relationships—a relationship which in operational units holds clear to the end of the line, where faculty-student relationships are "line," while counselor-student relationships are advisory.[5] Any other relationship is bound to cause interference in the line.

It seems logical to assume, then, that the fundamental principles of organization, as outlined in some detail with reference to the installation of a central guidance service, are a safe starting point for the organization of a service in an operational unit. It also seems both logical and desirable to maintain the same type of relationships between line functionaries and specialists. There are, however, two major differences in the functions and relationships of central directors and operational unit directors: (1) Where the central director functions with and through the executive of each segmented unit, the director in a unit functions also with and through the faculty of that unit. (2) Where direct student contacts make few demands on central services, they are a major responsibility of many decentralized or self-contained services. Because of these differences it seems desirable to present certain additional principles of organization which are concerned specifically with faculty and student relationship. Several of these principles were formulated in the early period and may be reviewed in Chapter IV: [6]

[5] The principle of "line and staff" is given verbal endorsement by many educational writers. In practice, there is little tendency to distinguish between line and staff responsibilities and definitely to clarify relationships. L. A. Appley summarizes the situation as follows: "Where does the authority of the line stop and that of the staff begin, and vice versa? They both have definite places in any organization and if they function properly they are equally important and no friction should result. However, the improper conception that the extent of one's authority governs the amount of prestige that a position enjoys causes deep-seated difficulties. A purely service organization without any authority can be of greater service and importance in an organization than some line positions which have considerable authority" ("Basic Factors in Modern Organization Development," *Personnel*, XV [1938], 49–56).

[6] *Character Education*, the Tenth Yearbook of the Department of Superintendence, National Education Association (Washington, 1932, pp. 246–247) suggests seven tentative principles for a counseling (not a guidance or personnel) service. This is one of the best statements of principles which has come to this writer's attention: principles are not confused with duties, tools, and techniques as is so often the case. The National Vocational Guidance Association issues reprints of "The Principles and Practices of Educational and Vocational Guidance," an article which first appeared in *Occupations*, XV (1937), 772–778.

1. Guidance service should be introduced as a co-operating agency with, and a co-ordinating agency for, all guidance and personnel activities in the unit.

2. All registrants should come within the purview of the guidance service. It should not be limited to those who have mental or physical handicaps, who are delinquent, or who create problems in school. A thought-provoking question for discussion in systems where it is impossible adequately to serve all is, Upon what basis should selection for service be determined? Obviously there will be no uniform answer.

3. Consistent and persistent recognition of individual differences and the maintenance of sympathetic-scientific rather than sympathetic-sentimental attitudes toward human problems are essential.

4. Guidance is a unitary function. All the aspects of an individual's development are interrelated and all of his problems overlap. Advisory services must be concerned with the whole, not a divided, life. Sometimes such a statement is interpreted to imply that one general counselor should be able to advise on any aspect of the life of an individual. This writer interprets it to mean that some one broadly informed and generally experienced person must assume responsibility for the unification of all the information received from various specialists, medical, occupational, religious, psychological, etc., who have highly specialized knowledges and skills. It implies the organismic approach.

5. Continuity of guidance is essential to developmental growth and to the integration of personality. This does not imply that the same person should counsel the same students from year to year. It does imply that each student should be regarded as a growing personality, that his development should be continuous and as full, emotionally, mentally, physically, socially, and spiritually, as his capacities permit, and that gradually he should evolve his own philosophy of life.

6. Educational articulation, vertically and horizontally, is essential to the continuity of guidance. Vertical articulation recognizes that the various units of our educational system are not self-contained and provides for relating new experiences and knowledges to the old in such fashion that there are no breaks between units. Horizontal articulation implies the co-ordination and integration of all services, experiences, and influences afforded an individual at each level of education, both within and without the school system, so that all aspects of his personality may be given proper attention.

7. The ultimate results of a guidance service should be self-guidance. Encouragement of progressive independence from the inspiration and guidance of teachers and counselors should result in the acquisition of

techniques suitable for making adjustments to either desirable or undesirable conditions or for assisting in the modification of conditions which
can and should be changed.

These and any other principles which the chief executive may deem
desirable will be of assistance in outlining the duties and determining
upon the relationships of his prospective director and in selecting the
appointee best qualified to meet such obligations.

Selecting a Director. Executives are called upon to provide leadership
in initiating and carrying forward guidance services under a variety of
conditions. A college or school large enough to warrant and financially
able to support a full-time qualified director, and to provide the necessary
equipment and assistants, granting the interest and co-operation of the
corps, affords an ideal matrix for the gradual development of an effective
guidance service. In a single building or within narrow geographical confines all line functionaries and all specialists are closely associated under
the same executive. The director of the service will be close to the line,
and his relationships with it should be strengthened by frequent opportunity for personal contacts, for firsthand knowledge of assets and liabilities, and for many informal opportunities to lead, train, and demonstrate
by influence as well as through the media of classes and conferences.

The executive will face practically the same pros and cons regarding
the selection of a director from within or from without the unit as does
a central service. The presence within the corps of an obvious "arrival"
who wishes to serve relieves the situation. If there be no such person and
none is otherwise available, sometimes an executive is forced to choose
between the questionably competent person within the corps, whose incompetencies will already be well publicized, and a similar type of individual from without, whose incompetencies will be detected long before
his competencies are appreciated. Either choice is unfortunate. Either is
apt to discredit the service and often to result in its elimination from the
institution for many years.

Another unfortunate condition arises when, for one reason or another, the executive is forced to camouflage his guidance interests and
activities by utilizing as a director some person already attached to the
unit in another capacity but whose duties are such that free time is available or can be made available. A similar situation arises when the unit
is too small or is not financially able to permit the selection of a director
on the basis of qualifications. The executive may feel obliged to appoint
an athletic coach who has the single qualification of free time at certain
periods of the school year, a teacher on tenure whose subject is declining in popularity, a teacher who has failed in class management but who

may be able to cope with one student at a time, or a teacher whose subject demands less out-of-school labor or less daily preparation. Many such control factors enter the appointment picture. Some are almost unbelievable.

Whatever the resources and whatever the provision for leadership, it will prevent much friction if all executives, directors, part-time counselors, teacher-advisers, and others remember that as classroom teachers, whether of history, mathematics, or occupations, they are line functionaries under the authority of their superior in the line. Whenever they step out of the instructional line to perform the duties of a service agency, they become, for the period of time so employed, a facilitating or service functionary under the control and in the line of the director of that service if there be one. If a part-time counselor is the sole official representative of a guidance service, he serves directly under the principal or president. In either case, when performing personnel functions he ceases to be a fellow instructor and assumes servicing responsibilities to both students and teachers.

Part-time directors and teacher-counselors do not always find it easy to fill two such different types of positions simultaneously and to switch from one to the other, oftentimes daily, without overstepping in one position or the other, thereby causing offense and the most annoying type of interference in the line.

Titles and status have much to do with the type of director who will be appointed, who will be willing to serve, and who will be acceptable to other members of the corps. Recent statistical reports indicate a wide range of titles on both levels of education; assistant principal, director, supervisor, chief counselor, counselor, adviser, dean of men, dean of women, all are in common use.[7] The author has no preference and no basis upon which to suggest the most logical or desirable term, but she does feel rather strongly that a great deal of trouble would be avoided if each administrator would see that title and status are appropriate in the light of the duties assigned and the relationships outlined.

This would mean that both should be in harmony with the general titles and status hierarchy in vogue in the institution, and that salary should be fixed within the same category. If the functions are facilitating and permeating, if relationships are consultative and advisory, it would seem wiser to avoid titles which imply executive control. If line functions with authority over line functionaries other than those in their own domain are assigned, a title which carries that implication is desirable and

---

[7] There have been a number of additions to early period personnel titles, but this writer has, as yet, found no discards.

logical. No matter how logical such a procedure may be, it is very difficult to put in practice because practically every title used in connection with personnel service except counselor or adviser, neither of which is applicable to the entire field, carries some implications which clash with the modern conception of personnel service.

In recent years there has been a noticeable trend in secondary schools and colleges in favor of the title of "director," which seems fairly satisfactory for central or unitary systems but causes confusion if used both as a central service and as a segregated unit title. If "assistant director" is used for the units, the principles of organization as applied to personnel service are violated, at least by implication, since the unit functionary appears to be removed from the authority of his principal or president and placed in the line under the authority of the director of the central service. This type of organization is in use in some secondary systems but has not been very successful in practice and is not approved in theory. The best current practice seems to favor "director" for a central or unitary system and "head of guidance service" for the larger segregated units, with "chief counselor," "head counselor," or "adviser" for the smaller units.

"Dean" is an administrative title. It is not difficult to understand that its use as a personnel title was the logical outgrowth of the "lady principal" for one sex and of the segmentation of the administrative dean's duties for the other. As the functions of personnel services are becoming more definitely differentiated from control functions and are requiring special professional preparation, it is difficult to reconcile its use as a service title with its use as an administrative title for those who exercise control over operational units.

There are other difficulties which come to the surface here and there when "dean" is used on the same campus in this dual sense; clashes in priorities and authorities are inevitable. As deans in the line hierarchy deans of sexes outrank heads of departments, faculty advisers, and instructors. They frequently exercise, sometimes with and sometimes without approval but often with the tacit consent of the president, control over every activity of the sex concerned; they wield the disciplinary ax even to dishonorable dismissals, and they may veto an educational program which has been approved by a faculty adviser. It has reached the point where deans of sexes are neither flesh, fish, nor fowl, but all three and then an intangible plus. This situation may be credited to administration.

The emotional reaction of other members of the corps to the activities of the holders of such titles and ranks does not contribute to harmonious faculty relationships. Insult is added to injury when such functionaries are assigned to minor instructional duties with the supplementary title of "professor." Men and women who begin at the bottom of the academic hierarchy and serve full-time apprenticeships before they attain a professorship are astounded and resentful when they find themselves outranked by a service functionary who is also their administrative superior. It is a body blow to faculty morale.

College authorities have been aware of these illogicalities for years; more than twenty years ago the author was approached by a number of college presidents on this subject. Some of them have watched the growing cloud on the academic horizon without complacency, but the majority have made but feeble attempts to stem the tide of irritation and confusion. It is now generally conceded that administrative functions and student advisory functions should, whenever possible, be divorced. Student confidence is not won when deans of sexes perform both advisory and disciplinary functions, nor is faculty co-operation secured by allowing personnel functionaries to determine whether they will "butt in" or "tune in" on faculty-student relationships.

In some institutions administrative officers are trying to alleviate the confusion by substituting "counselors" of sexes for "deans" of sexes. If in so doing they have made no realignment of functions and relationships, they have only eliminated one disturbing factor and added another. Counselor is obviously not an administrative title but counselors who continue to perform administrative duties are in the same sort of anomalous position as were deans. Moreover, the appointment of counselors of sexes as independent personnel functionaries has two rather serious organizational drawbacks: (1) The lack of an official co-ordinating functionary unless the institution is small enough for the president or dean to assume this function. This statement, of course, applies equally to deans of the sexes. If the reader will turn to Chart VII once more and note the service agencies which have been drawn up at the right under a staff or line co-ordinator, and then picture the same setup altered to provide two services under each category, one for men and the other for women, he will have no difficulty in visualizing the first drawback. (2) The second drawback is inherent in the title "counselor." "Counselor" does not rate high in the educational hierarchy. Its use is in direct conflict with the qualifications previously listed for directors of guidance and personnel services. Either the qualifications suggested are too high, or "counselor" rates too low. "Arrivals" will not accept positions carrying that title, but it is quite suitable for those whose experience and professional preparation puts them on a par with instructors. A really experienced man in the field of personnel is entitled to a status and title which will indicate that he stands close to the executive dean and is considered an important helpmate in attaining the objectives of the institution.

Up to the present the most promising efforts to bring titles and status into harmony with duties and relationships are exemplified by institutions which have separated personnel functions and administrative functions, abolished the title of "dean" of sex, eliminated separate personnel services operating on a sex basis, and substituted a unitary service under a director of personnel service with a sufficient corps of counselors to meet all the demands of students, both men and women. This plan unifies all personnel activities, permits a title commensurate with responsibilities but not in conflict with academic titles held by administrative officers, and provides a status which allows the director a seat in the policy-making council.

The appointment of a director during the incumbency of deans of sexes, unless by mutual consent such officials are absorbed in the new organization, is apt to cause partisan division in the faculty. Usually administrators find it wiser to delay reorganization until resignations or retirements permit a fresh start. Both methods have been tried, and at least one institution has maintained both a personnel director and deans of sexes over a long period of years.

The "dean" complex has been a much less troublesome problem in the secondary school. This is partly because "dean" is not a secondary title and there has, therefore, been no clash in usage, and partly because, whereas the college dean of women was originally a "lady principal," which is definitely an administrative title, the dean of girls in the high school was originally elected as a "counselor" or "adviser." Later on the high schools imitated the college title, and the "dean of boys," who came later, followed the precedent. "Counselor" or "adviser" has always been the preferred title in secondary schools.

New York City is an excellent example of a secondary system which has never had to contend with the "dean problem," possibly because there is more machinery connected with titles and status in the very large system. As a rule, positions in large cities are established by administrative action based on demonstrated need and after consideration of the same or marginal duties presently performed by other functionaries. Qualifying examinations follow. The secondary authorities in New York City have never given official endorsement to the title of either "dean of boys" or "dean of girls"; [8] there are therefore no officially recognized positions which carry these titles.

---

[8] They have established the position of "counselor" for which competitive examinations are held, but few appointments have been made and those mostly for junior high schools.

Both titles are used informally among the members of the corps and by certain functionaries themselves in a semiofficial capacity, but they have no legal status. The official title for those who perform the services usually assigned to deans is "administrative assistant," and their duties comprise both administrative and personnel functions. Their relationship to their principal is the nearest to a bona fide staff position of any arrangement with which this writer is familiar. Until very recently this "commander and his staff" relationship was strengthened by the fact that such assistants were selected by the principal to act as his assistants during his pleasure or his incumbency. They were certified as teachers and returned to their former positions when their period of administrative assistantship ended. Recently the principal's freedom of choice has been curtailed by the introduction of qualifying examinations for the position of administrative assistant. But the title remains a much more logical title for the functions and relationships than is "dean" of sexes. Positions are now permanent and salaries have been adjusted.

Duties of Directors of Operational Units. Enumerations of the duties performed by directors of guidance and personnel services, whether their titles be director, supervisor, chief counselor, dean, counselor, or other reveal no interinstitution uniformity and no intrainstitution stability. This situation prevents crystallization of duties and fixation of programs before guidance services have found their most effective place in the educational system and established working relations with other aspects of educational service. On the other hand, it makes it very difficult to discuss organization in any general sense.[9]

No tabulation of duties with performance frequencies is offered here. Many such tabulations showing preferences and trends are available, and the reference list accompanying Part V contains sufficient statistical data for those who wish to study the various titles, the numerous duties, the allocation of duties, and the frequencies of performance to do so. Since there is bound to be some differentiation in duties as they are performed in closer proximity to the ultimate recipients of the service, the broad general responsibilities which have previously been discussed with reference to central directors will be again considered with reference to unit services. Two additional responsibilities, the counseling of individuals and the instructional responsibilities connected with either teaching or

[9] Perhaps these inherent difficulties may account for the fact that few educational writers have attacked the total problem of organization with reference to guidance and personnel services. For the most part they have been content to discuss "programs," including duties and functions, and have overlooked the fact that organization is an essential tool for realizing programs and that it requires clearly defined relationships as well as definitely listed duties.

supervising the teaching of orientation and guidance classes and with group conferences and homeroom programs, will also be considered. Very rarely is either responsibility assigned to a central director; quite often both are allocated to a unit director; and almost universally both are major responsibilities of directors, counselors, or others in charge of guidance services in small units.

The director or counselor will serve as a *salesman* within, and often without, the system. As with all salesmen, his success will depend upon a combination of thorough knowledge of what he has to sell with ability to demonstrate to the corps, to the students, and to others specific ways in which his assistance will be helpful in attaining their objectives or meeting their responsibilities.

As a *specialist* in his field he will be informed on researches and experiments, on new theories and tested practices, and he will, by virtue of his influence, have control of the signal lights in determining upon eliminations, additions, and alterations in current guidance procedures. His office will be the center for the collection, classification, filing, and dissemination of informational data along lines presented in Parts II and III.

As a *leader and educator* of the corps he will need to be familiar with the best and most tactful methods of adult education, the methods whereby he may be reasonably sure that interest in participating in the service is permeating the entire corps and that progress in ability to serve is going forward. There may or may not be considerable difference in the composition of the group for the in-service training of which the central director and the unit director are responsible. Sometimes much of the education of the teaching corps in segmented units is, by common consent, turned over to the central director. In other instances the central director confines his educational efforts to members of the administrative corps and to directors of guidance services in operational units, while full responsibility for the training of all line functionaries is left to the directors in the units. The director in a unitary system will of necessity assume all training responsibilities.

In any case the in-service training of the instructional corps is very important since the ultimate success or failure of the service will depend upon the ability and willingness of each teacher to use the tested tools and techniques available for advising students on the choice of curricula, electives, cocurricular activities, wage-earning opportunities, occupations, and advanced study, and for considering with them the possibilities of improvement in personal characteristics. Item by item the cumulative record may be studied for its counseling values. Item by item each teacher should have an opportunity to understand how he contributes to the making of the records and how the character of his contribution influences its guidance value. As the various items are discussed, directors will find many opportunities to stress the difference between the technical and non-technical aspects of guidance service and to point out the dangers involved when those who are not technically trained attempt to perform technical services. Some methods available for in-service training have been mentioned in connection with specific topics. There are many others, and the list will be supplemented by each director as he accumulates experience.

Since so many directors of guidance services are young, perhaps just out of graduate schools where recent theories, practices, and terms are familiar to all, whereas many members of almost any teaching corps have been in the service some years and are totally unfamiliar with new lines of talk, a word of caution from one who has seen some of these novices struggle to win the confidence and secure the support of older teachers may not be amiss.

Offense, often terminating in actual hostility, is caused by many seemingly trivial acts and attitudes. Sometimes it is caused by what is regarded as a parade of knowledge designed to create the impression that teachers who do not understand personnel jargon are out-of-step with educational progress. The tone of the voice will do it. Sometimes it is caused by creating an impression that the guidance service is a sideshow, the director's show, instead of stressing the fact that the director is trying to help the corps build a permeating function into the line organization. Now and then the die is cast by the director's use of Ph.D. on every scrap of paper which affords an opportunity—always an ill-advised method of salesmanship. The subtly expressed but quickly detected preference for being addressed or mentioned as "doctor" will do the trick, and while it does nothing to enhance popularity, it often focuses the attention of degree-sensitive teachers on their own deficiencies. "Mister" is a very honorable title; scholars and gentlemen need no other. Those who are consistent in its use will find it helpful in the winning of confidence and in the influencing of teachers.

Graduate school instructors who prepare young persons for guidance service have great responsibility for degree complexes, even though there is a growing tendency in academic circles to drop all degree or status titles. Overstress on the value of a degree at the expense of knowing how to use effectively the knowledge acquired in securing the degree turns out many youngsters who, in spite of their degree, have no understanding of oldsters whose feet are firmly planted on the rock of experience. They may have had much advice regarding the best methods of dealing with the inferiority complexes of youth, but no one may have warned them that as guidance functionaries they may meet or create inferiority complexes among those upon whose co-operation their success depends.

On the other hand, confidence is slowly won. A young director or counselor may be well prepared, gracious, and unassuming in the presence of so much mass experience, but still the older teachers may hesitate to betray their ignorance by asking questions of one who is much younger. Age is sensitive. Youth often does not realize that every educational responsibility entails its own upkeep requirements and that at best his major field of specialization is a secondary field for the instructional corps.

The difficulties encountered by young directors and counselors in their efforts to establish leadership relations with older members of the corps are very real and quite understandable, and therefore might be anticipated, even though they are often unavoidable. It will help some if each newly appointed director will stress guidance services as primarily a teachers' show, will tell his story in the simplest layman's language, and will make it easy for any member of the corps, no matter how old he may be, how many or how few degrees he may have, or how convinced he may be that he is already an encyclopaedia of knowledge requiring no supplements, to ask questions, call for explanations, and acquire information with the feeling that he is conferring a favor rather than advertising his ignorance.

On the college level leadership opportunities in personnel service are frequently lost because personnel functionaries meddle in every institutional activity and every instructional responsibility. If administrative authorities would properly perform their duties in allocating responsibilities and defining relationships, such incidents as the following would be less frequent: During a personnel conference a young dean of freshmen reported on the results of visits to classes conducted by freshmen instructors; his objective was to discover the extent to which subject failures should be attributed to faculty incompetence. At the close of the story a dean of men of wide experience and national reputation rose to assure himself that he had "heard correctly." An affirmative reply brought the rejoinder, "Young man, you wouldn't last five minutes in my university, either under the present president, or under me, were I president."

In a round table for the benefit of recently inducted deans one young woman asked how she should deal with a situation in which the mannerisms of an instructor were so annoying that students tried to avoid his classes. The only suggestion, given tacit approval by the advising group, was that she speak to the instructor about it. Such a course of action will win neither faculty co-operation nor administrative support, rather will it result in loss of personnel positions.

The improvement of instruction and the correction of faculty manners are not the responsibilities of student personnel officers who are usually fairly busy dealing with student manners and keeping a watchful eye on their own. Incidents of this type afford opportunities to discuss with students (1) the reaction of others to unpleasant mannerisms and the desirability of acquiring as few, and of eliminating as many, as possible themselves and (2) the necessity of learning to adapt themselves to conditions which they cannot change since they may be forced to deal with many persons who have unpleasant mannerisms later in life. It is a part of education.

The director of a unit in his capacity as *co-ordinator* will have much the same duties as has a central co-ordinator. He will inform himself regarding efforts already instituted and will make a tactful effort to eliminate ineffective nuclei and to combine or co-ordinate the effective ones in which duplicates and overlappings prevail. While accomplishing this not too easy task, he may find some consolation in remembering that many original efforts and false starts are logical intermediate steps on the road to better organized services.

After the informal beginnings have been evaluated and organized, with the co-operation of the corps and the approval of the executive additional services may be introduced until a well-rounded program has been set up. It may then be necessary to take the initiative in co-ordinating the school services with similar community services and with those afforded by lower and higher educational units and by business and industry. These responsibilities are a legitimate assignment for directors in any system.

In addition to co-ordination of the administrative aspects of the service so that some semblance of an organization evolves, there is equal necessity for the type of co-ordination which unifies all the results of the services which have been brought to bear on the development of the individual student. Cumulative records are a major reliance in the individual aspect of co-ordination. The publications of the Educational Records Bureau and of the Co-operative Test Service demonstrate how this type of co-ordination may be achieved. Stanford University makes the record of core items taken from the complete record accessible to all instructors with a provision for additional knowledge on the approval of the official in charge. The University of Minnesota finds the contract desk a good co-ordinating device. On all levels of education case studies and case conferences are considered the best methods of interpreting and co-ordinating the various items found on such records. The director as a co-ordinator will desire to be familiar with and able to show leadership in the use of both techniques.

As a *research student* in the field of local personnel the director will be closer than is a central director to the ultimate beneficiaries of guidance services and closer to the sources of information which deal with the personal aspects of personnel research. Some functionaries will have no time for studies worthy to be called "research." It would be too much to expect that part-time counselors have either the training or the time to do research, much less to direct the faculty in doing it.

Where conditions permit, the unit director may enhance the value of the service by studying or directing the study of such topics as: (1) The relative values of group conferences and individual counseling with reference to the same and different objectives. The results would help to achieve a desirable balance in the total guidance program. (2) The guidance values of extraclass activities and the type of activity which best completes different types of educational programs. (3) The contribution of wage-earning experience to education. (4) Community occupational surveys which reveal immediately available occupational outlets (placement), and indicate possible future outlets (occupational choice and educational programs). (5) Periodic or continuous follow-up surveys of drop-outs and of graduates. The findings have value for both administrators and students. (6) The guidance values of the record system, of reports to parents, and the like.

Since many topics which have guidance values are marginal to, or lie mainly within, other service or line areas, co-operative researches are frequently desirable. In such cases a guidance functionary will move tactfully in order to avoid the assumption of leadership in a field which may more legitimately be considered to belong to another.

As a *teacher of students* or as a classroom instructor and conference leader, the director, counselor, or part-time counselor performs functions which are rarely performed by central directors. If he performs instructional services or acts as a conference leader, either as the sole individual performing such functions or as an experimenter in, and a demonstrator of, procedures, he should be as nearly an exemplar of desirable procedures as is possible in the light of the fact that he too is frequently not a full-time functionary. Only in this way can he hope to win the respect and confidence of the teaching corps and of the students.

The character of group guidance activities, the materials available for assistance in their performance, and some methods which are in use have been discussed in detail in Part IV. It was also noted in Part IV that group guidance activities in the main had not been very successful.[10] Some of the reasons suggested were inadequate and inaccurate informational data, the unsuitability of the homeroom setup for other than routine duties, the use of untrained or inadequately trained teachers, the inappropriateness of programs and topics, the lack of objectives and of co-ordination with other aspects of the educational program, and the attempt to use the guidance period for training in parliamentary usage.

In spite of the growing recognition of its deficiencies, many schools rely entirely on the homeroom as the major or sole method of providing guidance services. Hence the improvement of homeroom programs and homeroom methods may be the first task of the head of a guidance service. This may require in-service training of the faculty or homeroom work with students or both. Definite objectives will need to be set up. They may be few, only such as are possible of realization with the facilities available. Conferences to avoid duplication, to evaluate procedures and materials, and to plan future programs will be necessary.

It may help the director or counselor to look more leniently on the inadequacies of such services if he keeps in mind the fact that the homeroom was instituted as an administrative, not as a guidance, device. At best it is a makeshift and it has never been given a clearly defined position in the guidance organization.[11]

It is not necessary to consider in detail the methods of group activities which a director might be called upon to conduct and in which his abilities might be challenged. If he serves students only, he must so perform his duties that he wins the respect of both students and teachers. If he serves as a teacher or supervisor of teachers, he must be prepared to utilize and to suggest improvements in utilizing all the materials and methods enumerated in previous chapters.

As a *counselor* the director may fit into one of many categories. The hierarchy of counseling qualifications ranges downward from the highly skilled technical counselor, who is prepared to utilize technical skills as a part of the counseling process, to the limited service which the classroom teacher is qualified to perform. Counseling on the intermediate levels does not require a guidance functionary to be a clinical psychologist, a licensed physician, or a psychiatrist, but it does require him, and

10 School administrators are becoming more critical of the rating of the sort of thing that goes on in homerooms as guidance and are admitting that building a guidance program entirely around homeroom teachers cannot be done. It results in a nominal, not a real, program. See Paul B. Jacobson and William C. Reavis, *Duties of School Principals* (New York: Prentice-Hall, 1941), p. 148.

11 Frequency of performance lists indicate that both deans of sexes and homeroom functionaries perform administrative duties more frequently than guidance duties.

his employer, to understand that he may not perform technical services in any line, whether or not he be legally restrained, for which he is not prepared.

Moreover, since there is so much watered stock on the guidance market, does it not seem justifiable for those who are struggling to approach professionalism to ask that no title, not even a diluted one, be awarded those who are not prepared to assume the responsibilities of the status implied in the title? Should any person be designated counselor who cannot select from the type of informational data dealt with in Parts II and III that which promises to be of use in any given case; who cannot interpret it, integrate it, supplement it from either technical or non-technical sources, and so use it that it may have value in guiding developmental growth? Does the teaching corps not have a right to expect that those who are granted personnel titles will be able to assist them in the better performance of their more limited guidance functions and, where counseling is needed beyond the scope of their knowledge and ability, take over the case and complete the service?

A SERVICE FOR SMALL TOWNS OR RURAL COMMUNITIES

There is much interest in rural schools and much regret that while they are serving youth whose needs for and rights to public services are just as legitimate as are those of youth served by larger units, no very satisfactory method of equalizing educational opportunities has as yet been found. The guidance situation is but one factor in the total situation.

The pupil in the rural school needs approximately the same guidance service in quantity and merits the same in quality as does the boy in the best-equipped educational system in the country. He needs occupational information and an opportunity to weigh his own assets and liabilities not only for agricultural pursuits but in other occupational areas. His teacher, with fewer pupils but a wider range of duties, needs the assistance of a guidance director just as much as does the city teacher with more pupils and a narrower range of duties. It is not a question of "either, or." All pupils need guidance services, and all teachers who perform other than routine guidance duties need the assistance of a trained director or supervisor if their responsibilities are to be met.

In making such a generalization one is in danger of overestimating the quality and quantity of genuine guidance service which is available for city boys and of underestimating the value of the type of inherent guidance which rural schools often provide and which may be more helpful to youth than is much of the routine guidance advertised in paper programs and carried on under compulsion. Sometimes the very limitation on services tends to develop a type of resourcefulness, ingenuity, initiative, and industry which guides a boy over the shell holes of life, whereas constant guidance and supervision pave the way for serious difficulties in making later adjustments. There is considerable encouragement for rural youth in the fact that much of our most virile national leadership in the present emergency is coming from these formerly underprivileged "boys grown tall." Sometimes our verbal picture seems to be a bit out of focus, not entirely dependable. Rural youth should understand this.

Interest in rural guidance services is not a product of the recent depression although it was greatly stimulated by surveys which revealed the predicament of farm youth and focused attention on the possibility of better rural services of various kinds, guidance services included. A previous wave of interest in guidance for rural youth came to a focus in 1924 when several philanthropic agencies were disturbed about the steady migration of farm youth from the country to the city. During the early twenties a few state and county organizations had come into being to serve such youth before they left the farm, and some city philanthropic agencies stood ready to assist them after they had arrived in the city.

The most effective work, based on data secured from carefully conducted surveys and other types of research, the service broadest in scope, reaching back into the early years of life and continuing through initial adjustment to postschool life, and the most persistently maintained interest and service must be credited to the Alliance for Guidance of Rural Youth under the leadership of O. Latham Hatcher. Its scholarly and distinctive service entitles it to first place in any historical study designed to give students a fair overview of the development of the guidance movement.

The Alliance was born in 1914 under the same leadership but under the name of the Virginia Bureau of Vocations. Later it was renamed the Bureau of Vocations, and still later it became the Southern Woman's Educational Alliance. During the early years it performed much the same services for southern college women as did the other college bureaus that were mentioned in Chapter II. Miss Hatcher has remained its guiding genius throughout its history and, as would be expected, brought to its rural activities in 1924 a wealth of background knowledge and experience in the guidance field which was a very valuable asset to the rural program.

Miss Hatcher's *Guiding Rural Boys and Girls*, published in 1930, is a much more helpful volume for students of guidance procedures than are many volumes of later date.[12] Part IV, "Setting up the Guidance Pro-

---

12 New York: McGraw-Hill Book Co., 1930. Miss Hatcher has written a number of other books on rural guidance and has been a leader in establishing county services.

gram," is still timely and may well be used to supplement official suggestions afforded by supervisory government agencies. Chapter XVI is an anticipatory presentation of present-day problems. It deals with the co-ordination of all out-of-school community activities with the school guidance program.

The building of a guidance service for rural and small schools will call into play the same fundamental principles as those which have been presented in connection with building a service in large schools, but in order to warrant the employment of a director it will probably be necessary to make some co-operative arrangement with one or more schools conveniently located for sharing services. When this is not feasible, teachers will be obliged to depend on such supervisory assistance as may be available from district, county, or state officials.

Both systems have been practiced here and there in the country, but there has been no widespread use of either until recently when federal funds were made available to support and encourage state programs which in turn are offering assistance to the schools under their jurisdiction. A number of states have accepted federal assistance, have made additional subsidies, and have appointed state and county functionaries who are assisting small and rural schools to perfect some approved type of organization and institute a program which gives promise of being effective.[13]

Information regarding the procedures involved in securing federal and state assistance, the type of assistance which is available, and descriptions of presently operating programs have been generously disseminated and are easily accessible; therefore casual mention here is sufficient. The newly instituted Occupational Information and Guidance Service, established in 1939 under the U. S. Office of Education, is the original source of information on the federal service.[14] Each state department of education is the source of information for schools within the state.[15]

[13] Pennsylvania was in the front rank in interest in and provision for guidance services. Beginning in 1920 with surveys, tryout programs followed, and many valuable and forward-looking bulletins have been issued. For a brief, well-documented account of the program in each state, see Layton S. Hawkins *et al., Occupational Information and Guidance: Organization and Administration* (Washington: U. S. Office of Education, 1940), pp. 45-111.

[14] For the origin of the national service and the procedures involved in securing its assistance, see *ibid.*, pp. 10-43. The scope and functions of the service are described by the U. S. Commissioner of Education, John W. Studebaker, in two articles which appeared in *Occupations*, XVII (1938-1939), 101-105, 586-593.

[15] In June, 1942, the New York State Bureau of Guidance, George E. Hutcherson, Chief, issued a mimeographed pamphlet of nine pages entitled, *Suggestions for Organization and Finance in a Cooperative Plan for Two or More School Districts.* The question and answer method was used. Questions were selected from those which had come to the office frequently enough to warrant the assumption that they had anticipatory

It is obvious that no matter how small the school there must be a line organization and that any specialized services which come from without the line are facilitating services working with and through the line and not in control of the line. This fundamental principle is sometimes more obvious when the director is shared than it is when he is omnipresent and often called upon to assist in the performance of control functions just because he is at hand.

A shared director will need to be familiar with the local situation and with the educational objectives and policies of each co-operating school and to assist in setting up a guidance program which will be in harmony with the policy of each school. Otherwise, the duties of shared directors do not differ in kind from those of full-time directors, while their relationships with other specialists and with line functionaries remain much the same.

As a *salesman* the shared director may have fewer prospects to contact than a full-time city director, but he may have no executive officer to assume leadership in selling the desirability of the service to the board and community or adequately to pave the way for his salesmanship efforts. He may be responsible for selling the program to the board, the community, the one or more teachers, and the students. Rural boards are not notoriously easy to sell new projects, especially if there be no tangible evidence of their value.

As a *specialist* and as an *educator* he will need to be very careful lest his own enthusiasm for his field lead him to advocate more specialized guidance services and to undertake more in-service training than is legitimate or than can be successfully carried out in rural schools. He will educate his colleagues in the theory and practice of guidance service and indicate how each participant plays an important part in its success. For each school, he will accent the in-service needs of *that* school. The teachers have a right to expect considerable assistance in the collection of occupational information, especially nonagricultural information. Not less important is the record system and the study, item by item, of the previously discussed data—how to secure it and how to integrate it for counseling purposes. Rural teachers will probably have less background than city teachers upon which to discuss new experiments and researches, and the wise director will select for presentation the accepted and the locally applicable rather than the new and the provocative.

As a *co-ordinator* the shared director will be responsible for working out some plan by means of which all the available guidance services of

values. This is the most specific and helpful state pronouncement with which the author is familiar.

the community may be co-ordinated. In accomplishing this task he may face a wider range of responsibilities than does the city director, especially in the out-of-school areas. County occupational surveys participated in by several schools or communities require the co-ordination of the services of all contributors. The many excellent services on both the youth and adult level which are offered by governmental agencies, federal, state, and county, and by departments of home economics, agriculture, and sociology in universities should be used to the best advantage. Club activities, Future Farmers of America, Junior Achievement Leagues, Hi-Y, 4-H, and others, have many guidance values which should not be overlooked.

Some co-operative arrangement for the placement of rural youths who do not wish to remain on the farm is desirable. A public employment service conveniently located is one possibility, but youths who are making the transition from rural to city life or from the home circle to a rooming or boarding-house will benefit more from a combination of counseling and placement services such as is sometimes offered by the Y.M.C.A., Y.W.C.A., and other semiphilanthropic organizations.

Part II includes occupational reference material which is applicable to rural life and notes that, other things being equal, some industrial concerns prefer rural boys as apprentices. For more than twenty-five years the author has maintained contact with certain business and industrial concerns which stand ready to make a place for a country boy who shows potentialities. Sometimes such a concern subsidizes an appropriate organization with the understanding that it shall assume guidance responsibilities for rural boys at the point where the responsibility the concern is able to take leaves off. A county or shared director who can establish a reputation with a few business concerns for discriminating judgment in the selection and recommendation of rural youth will open up very desirable opportunities for co-operation and for the co-ordination of rural life with the industrial world.

There is plenty of work, and it is time-consuming work, for a rural director along the lines mentioned, but he will probably have less responsibility for intracorps co-ordination, as the usual rural corps contains few members and undertakes few spontaneous and informal guidance activities.

The shared director as a *research student* will not wander away into the field of clinical and experimental research. He will not attempt to devise tests, construct rating scales, or prepare vocational monographs. His duties will require him to be familiar with the processes involved in the most simple types of research and to know how to apply their underlying principles to the tasks at hand.

Among these tasks will be: (1) The securing of, and the directing of others in methods of securing, the basic facts upon which to plan a guidance program and to perfect an appropriate organization. (2) Periodic surveys which bring out trends in opportunities and reveal new community needs. (3) The collection and evaluation of occupational information of different types, fiction, news clippings, advertising material, business reports, college catalogues, and bona fide occupational researches such as those prepared by the Occupational Outlook Service, Science Research Associates, and others. Boys and girls, as well as teachers, can be interested in the simple research procedures which are used to test the value of verbal and printed statements and to distinguish between hearsay evidence and authenticated data. Part II indicates how any director may be of assistance along such lines. (4) Study of the current record system as to its suitability and utility. If improvements are needed, tools and techniques which seem valuable will need to be considered and selected in the light of the purpose they are to serve. Reports to parents are rarely as useful as they might be.

As a *teacher and counselor* the shared director will follow the basic procedures fundamental to the counseling process and to the conduct of group activities. There are no additional principles and practices to supplement those already discussed. Familiarity with accepted practices and ability to modify them so that they may have a maximum of effectiveness in the given situation are the main things.

Those who make a comparative survey of the duties of directors, counselors, and even part-time counselors who assume the responsibilities of chief functionary in the various types of schools will be struck by the heavy load of duties and relationship responsibilities which must be carried by rural directors. It is almost fatal to select a director without a background of rural experience and assume, as has too often been done with reference to rural teachers, that a beginner, no matter what his background, is good enough for the country and that with the accumulation of experience he may secure a city directorship with a higher salary. As a teacher of rural youth, rural teachers, and rural communities, a director will find, or can find, use for an even broader general knowledge than is necessary in city schools where supplementary facilities are greater. Yet $2500–$3000 is considered an excellent salary for a rural director! This is not peculiar to guidance services; it is a part of the general picture of rural education.

CHAPTER XX

Evaluating the Guidance or Personnel Service

PROBABLY no one will dispute the responsibilities which Part V has allocated to administrative authorities for the formulation of guidance objectives, for the outlining of guidance policies which promise to realize such objectives, for seeing that both objectives and policies are integrated with institutional policies and objectives, for providing proper leadership for carrying forward the program, and for seeing that the entire corps is familiar with the policies and objectives and is ready to participate in the development of the service. Probably also no one will object to the addition of a final administrative responsibility, the evaluation of the accomplishments and weaknesses of the service. What has been done? How well has it been done? What objectives have been attained, or what progress has been made in the direction of attainment? What phases have been neglected? What additions to the program seem desirable? Is the time ripe for undertaking such additions? Should some phases be dropped? These and similar questions should be asked, and answered.

After a project is launched, especially one which requires universal participation and exerts a permeating influence, it is human nature to do considerable wishful thinking regarding values while awaiting the time when sufficient data are available for whatever type of evaluation is possible. The desire of the workers in the early period to know the results of their guidance efforts is noted in Part I. Statistical tabulations of quantitative returns were common, but the difficulties involved in the evaluation of intangibles were recognized to such an extent that workers were resigned to wait for the verdict of time and eternity.

The passage of time has not changed the desire of guidance supporters, nor has it materially altered the character of the evaluation problem. The latter has become more complex as more and more factors, both tangible and intangible, have come to the fore. The techniques for dealing with both types of factors have been refined, and new measuring devices are improving the quality of the data offered for evaluation, but for the most part the early intangibles are still intangibles. On the other hand, there is a steadily growing interest in evaluation as is evidenced by the marked increase in professional literature dealing with the subject. How ever, when one attempts to get therefrom an overview of progress and to select suggestions which seem worth while for those who face the practical problem of evaluation, the harvest is remarkably thin.

Is the evaluation of a guidance service possible? During a recent informal conference relative to the possibilities of evaluating personnel services, a business executive stated: "The returns on any properly organized and adequately implemented project can be evaluated, and sometimes they can be measured." [1]

Guidance and personnel service in education did not start with a "properly organized" project, nor has it now attained that status to any appreciable degree, either in the meaning of the executive or as the expression has been used in this book. Projects were sometimes amazingly well implemented in the light of early period knowledge, experience, and facilities for implementation, but not many then or now could be considered "adequately implemented." The third point in the executive's pronouncement raises a question which students often ask and which is not often clearly answered by those who write on evaluation, What is the difference in the meaning of "appraisal," "evaluation," and "measurement"?

The author is not a technician but she has found enough confusion in the literature dealing with these aspects of guidance services to wish that those who are technicians or who deal with the technical aspects of such services would define their terms so that laymen may know just what they are writing about. For example, "appraisal" and "evaluation" appear to be used synonymously; then suddenly one strikes "appraisal of evaluation in guidance." Perfectly legitimate, according to dictionary authorities, but how confusing under the particular circumstances. Students cannot be blamed for asking if the author's meaning would have been the same had he chosen to write "evaluation of appraisal in guidance."

The use of these terms in this chapter has been influenced by the interpretation of their meanings, expressed or implied, in reports of researches which involve or should involve prior selection of the terminology most applicable to the project at hand, consideration of their use by educational authorities, and authorization by one or more standard dictionaries. Neither research reports nor educational authorities are consistent in their usage, while dictionaries give endorsement to a rather

---

[1] The evaluation of personnel services in connection with a business concern is easier than it is in connection with an educational institution. Business objectives are more definite; degrees of attainment more easily determined; there are more tangible factors in the picture; and results are available in the immediate future rather than indefinitely delayed.

wide range of meanings. The validity of individual choice is, obviously, open to challenge, but students will find it easier to proceed with their study if consistency is used in discussing the topic. They are not asked to accept the definitions or usages which follow:

Appraisal will be considered to be applicable to the considerable number of nontechnical, and frequently very informal, efforts to determine the value of any guidance program or segmented portion thereof, the contribution of any functionary, or the value of any tool or technique. Judgments or estimates of value may be made by individuals or groups and may be based on either or both subjective and objective data. Sometimes the evidence from which estimates are made will be entirely adequate and fairly reliable; again it will be both insufficient and unreliable. Appraisals were the main dependence in the early period of the guidance movement and were based almost entirely on such tangible and quantitative data as the number of persons interviewed, the cost per person, the subject discussed, the number persuaded to return to school, the number placed, mortality statistics, and the like. The objectives of the service were considered in the appraisal. If the objective were to reduce failures or delay entry into the occupational world and statistics showed accomplishment in relation to the objectives, there was nothing left for hopeful functionaries except to recognize that there were valuable intangibles involved in the immeasurable values of guidance and to regret that the spiritual returns on their efforts must remain unknown.

A recent example of the use of "appraisal" is found in the report of the 1941 Sophomore Testing Program entitled, *The College Sophomore Appraises His Curriculum.*[2] This report indicates how individual profile charts were used as a device for assisting students to appraise their own abilities, and how students were asked to appraise the training they had received in various fields. The results of the latter are summarized in what might be called "appraisal language": the students "felt that," indicated that they "believed," "seemed to be," etc. These results were regarded as one factor to be taken into consideration as a college "evaluates its offerings and revises its plans." It will be noted that the first type of appraisal data is primarily objective and used to assist students in forming individual judgment; the second type, obviously subjective, is considered as one appraisal factor to be used in total evaluation.

Measurement will be assumed to imply measurability of the factors involved or of the results of some undertaking—the extent or degree to which something exists, succeeds, or fails, the extent to which some physical

[2] Series III, vol. II, no. 2; New York: Co-operative Test Service of the American Council on Education, 1942.

or mental undertaking has been accomplished, and the like. The use of this term implies that suitable measuring devices are available and will be or have been used in such fashion that results will show a high degree of accuracy and would be confirmed by repetition of the measurement. Only in measurement does one anticipate such a high degree of accuracy. Only in measurement may one express results in terms of assurance: we have found, have shown, or have demonstrated.

Schools and colleges have maintained measurement programs for years which have functioned with steadily increasing accuracy, reaching their peak of dependability in the new type or standardized achievement tests. Civil service boards and state departments of education maintain systems of examination so constructed and scored that they legitimately classify as measurement programs. Improvement in measurement programs has been accompanied by a shift in the original objective, which was standardization of the product of institutions largely for administrative purposes, to emphasis on their use for improvement in methods of instruction and for the guidance of individual students.

It is obvious that many factors which enter into a guidance or personnel service are not measurable according to the standards implied in measurement. The quality of the service, either in its total influence on the individual or with reference to its contribution to the realization of the institutional objective, is ruled out as measurement in this narrow usage. No method has yet been devised whereby a single factor in the total educational program can be completely segregated from all other factors and its value measured. No method is available for detecting the subtle influence of mind upon mind, the results of which frequently do not come to the surface until many years later, or for measuring the value of advice which may have been on reserve for years and which ultimately becomes of inestimable value in time of need. Those who elect to enter service occupations understand that much of their courage to go forward must be based on faith in the worthwhileness of their efforts and that visible, measurable evidences of the value of their contribution may never be their privilege.

Not all factors in a guidance service are immeasurable. Examples of items which are measurable, devices available for measurement, and the guidance values of results have been mentioned in previous chapters in connection with other items whose values can only be appraised or estimated. The more measurable factors there are in a guidance program, the more nearly the total program approaches measurability.

While appraisal and measurement have been refining their tools and techniques and thus enhancing the value of their pronouncements, a comparatively new term has entered the guidance picture, *evaluation*. Although all three terms are frequently used synonymously and although reports of projects, made by those who should have made a deliberative choice of terms before initiating their project, make no distinction, a canvass of considerable recent literature seems to warrant the assumption that "evaluation" stands midway between "appraisal," regarded as a purely informal estimate, and "measurement," as a fairly accurate determinant of quality and quantity. Evaluation seems to be supplanting appraisal [3] and to be using techniques which have not usually and do not necessarily characterize appraisal. In comparison with measurement it seems to have a broader field of applicability and a lesser degree of accuracy. By a process of elimination, the distinctive characteristic of evaluation appears to lie in its control criteria. While it does not measure, neither does it estimate without the assistance of a carefully constructed instrument usually called evaluative criteria, a check list set up by accepted methods and used as a standard of excellence against which individuals or schools may estimate, appraise, or evaluate the extent of their individual accomplishments or those of their institutions.

The outstanding example of evaluation based on the use of evaluation criteria is the recent Cooperative Study of Secondary School Standards [4] which is being used with considerable success as a guide for determining where, on a general scale of excellence, a school may justifiably rate itself. The guidance service was one aspect of secondary school work evaluated. Four major phases of such services were studied: articulation with other schools, information regarding pupils, the guidance program, and post-

[3] In the subject index of *Occupational Information and Guidance Bibliography 1937-38*, compiled by Pedro T. Orata with the assistance of Waldo B. Cookingham (Washington: U. S. Office of Education, 1941) only "evaluation" is listed. About forty items on the subject are given in the bibliography.

Pupil Personnel Services as a Function of State Departments of Education, by David Segel and Maris M. Proffitt (U. S. Office of Education Bulletin, 1940, no. 6, Studies of State Departments of Education Monograph, no. 5; Washington, 1940) distinguishes very clearly between "measurement" programs and "evaluation" programs, but does not use the term "appraisal."

James H. Green of the Retail Merchants Association noted that in 1934 we talked about "evaluation" rather than "measurement," a fact of which he approved ("How Can the Effectiveness of Training Programs Be Evaluated?" *Personnel*, XI [1934], 133-135).

[4] See Walter C. Eells, Co-ordinator, Evaluation of Secondary Schools, *General Report on the Methods, Activities, and Results of the Cooperative Study of Secondary School Standards* (Washington: American Council on Education, 1939). For special reports on significant guidance findings, see Eells, "Pupil Judgment on Value of Guidance Received," *School Review*, XLVI (1938), 265-275; Eells, "Judgment of Parents Concerning American Secondary Schools," *School and Society*, XLVI (1937), 409-416; and M. L. Altstetter, "Guidance Service in Two Hundred Secondary Schools," *Occupations*, XVI (1938), 513-520.

school relationships. The same check list of evaluative criteria was used by participating schools for self-evaluation and by the visiting committees. Composite findings indicated "that guidance service is probably less well organized and is operating less effectively than any other phase of secondary school activity."

Pupil evaluation and parent evaluation were both sought. Neither was complimentary. The reports of the committee conclude that, on the basis of student judgment not only in the two hundred schools studied but "probably in the thousands of other schools which they typify," the guidance service is far from satisfactory and complete. On the basis of parental judgment the vocational guidance provided by the schools was the least satisfactory of all services; educational guidance was reported to be more satisfactory.

The best overview of attempts to determine the value of guidance procedures and programs is found in the two summaries in which Harry D. Kitson has collaborated. Both reports are accessible and will be of assistance to those who seek background information upon which to formulate their own evaluation program.[5]

The problem of evaluation may seem very simple. The pronouncement of the business executive may be accepted, the project may be well organized and implementation adequate, but it does not take long for one who undertakes evaluation to realize that he faces an exceedingly complex and difficult task, a situation which may have been partially anticipated by a review of the literature on evaluation.

EVALUATING A LOCAL GUIDANCE SERVICE

The administrator, or his subordinate to whom he has delegated the task, may approach the evaluation problem from one or from several angles. He may seek answers to specific questions relative to the effectiveness of some phase of the guidance or personnel service or he may hope to compass the total program in the light of the objectives which it was instituted to accomplish. Two or three examples of possible local procedures to satisfy different evaluation desires are suggested.

Determining the relative excellence of a given program. Those who are concerned with secondary schools will find the evaluative criteria provided by the Cooperative Study helpful; those in charge of collegiate institutions will turn to the criteria set up by the North Central Associa-

---

[5] Harry D. Kitson and Edgar M. Stover, "Measuring Vocational Guidance—a Summary of Attempts," *Personnel Journal*, XI (1932), 150–159, and Kitson and Margaret Crane, "Measuring Results of Vocational Guidance: A Summary of Attempts, 1932–1937," *Occupations*, XVI (1938), 837–842.

tion.[6] In using these criteria it must be remembered that both studies were primarily concerned with standards for accreditation, with the improvement of methods of evaluating applicant schools. In the final analysis the results of the application of such criteria are very limited. They will reveal the extent to which in its component parts a given program conforms to a standard pattern of excellence. They will not reveal the extent to which the functions comprised in the program are those best adapted to local needs or the degree of effectiveness with which they have been performed; nor will they indicate the influence of the program, or any part of it, on the development of students.

Determining the extent to which a given program has realized on its avowed objectives. This is the heart of the local evaluation problem. It implies examination of the total program in terms of its objectives, both administrative and personal, and it involves a series of tests and of evaluations, appraisals, and investigations based on the discriminating use of various types of data.

If a paper program transplanted from a standard pattern or from some other system is in vogue, if no administrative and individual objectives have been set up, if no discriminating judgment has been used in the selection of tools and techniques, and if no effort has been made to familiarize the corps with purposes, methods, and informal means of appraising the results of its contribution, it will be very difficult to make other than a rough estimate of what has been attempted and what has been neglected. Nevertheless the attempt may be worth while. It may awaken the administration to the futility of assuming that such desultory procedures constitute a guidance program and it may lead to more intelligent and purposeful guidance activities.

On the other hand, if the service has been instituted in line with procedures previously discussed, if it is well organized, properly implemented, and each participant understands its objectives and the necessity for continuous appraisal of his efforts to help in attaining them, an evaluation program may be undertaken in the expectation that a survey of past procedures will reveal present successes and failures and will illuminate the future.

Stimulated by the Cooperative Study, a number of secondary schools have undertaken evaluative surveys.[7] Different topics, different sources of

[6] See Donfred H. Gardner, *Student Personnel Service* (Chicago: University of Chicago Press, 1936).

[7] The *Occupational Information and Guidance Bibliography, 1937–38* lists among other references a number of master's theses completed in 1937–38 which deal with local evaluation. *The Review of Educational Research,* published five times a year by the American Educational Research Association, Washington, D.C., is a valuable source of information on progress in "evaluation."

information, and different methods of measurement, evaluation, and appraisal have been used. Some have brought helpful returns, others have not been worth while. After all the procedures prerequisite to surveying have been effectively carried out, careful selection of the most appropriate measuring, evaluation, and appraisal devices for each aspect of the survey is a final essential.

Among the various phases of guidance procedures which have received evaluative attention and upon which the director or counselor is able to secure more or less information to guide his own attempts at evaluation are:

1. *The extent to which suitable educational and occupational information is available.* Part II has provided sufficient background data against which any school system, large or small, may check the degree to which it has at hand the type of educational and occupational information with which adequately to serve its clientele. Continuous appraisal of the extent to which such data are available and up-to-date is possible for any director or counselor. The methods of determining the value of all types of such data have been discussed at some length.

No guidance functionary need feel embarrassed if there comes a call for data which are not on hand, but a demerit mark is in order for those who receive repeat calls for the same information without having made an effort to add it to their informational storehouse.

2. *The effectiveness of group activities as methods of disseminating educational and occupational information.* Group methods of guidance, as discussed in Part IV, included group activities designed to serve specific guidance purposes and believed to have major guidance values. Informal and inspirational methods of appraising results and the use of tests to measure the results of course instruction were referred to. A review of the previous discussion will help to suggest methods of approach to evaluation of local results. Additional suggestions may be secured from a study of formal experiments to measure on both levels of education the results of course instruction in educational, occupational, and orientation topics.

It was natural that efforts to measure the results of segmented portions of the guidance program should have commenced with an attack on the more tangible aspects of its procedures. In the early 1920's Brewer was engaged in constructing tests to measure the results of course instruction in terms of information acquired during the course. Similar efforts have been reported from time to time. Kitson and his collaborators have covered these measurement experiments very adequately for the years 1907–1937 and have stated very clearly the difficulties involved in measuring the results of vocational guidance. The most recent investigation, which included the construction of tests, is reported by G. N. Kefauver and Harold C. Hand.[8]

The findings of these attempts at measurement are interesting and thought-provoking for those who have cultivated a comfortable degree of complacency regarding the probable value of course instruction. In the main, however, the results have been disappointing, i.e., the tests do not measure what it was hoped they might measure, the effectiveness of course instruction. It is generally agreed that test scores may be accepted as a measure of the amount of knowledge possessed by a student at a given time, but it is also agreed that, even with the use of control groups and the administration of tests both before and at the close of the test period, it is not justifiable to assume that whatever additional information has been acquired ad interim is creditable to class instruction. Some experiments report a high degree of gain on the part of the instructed group; others report little or no difference between the status of the two groups.

Discouraging reports regarding efforts to measure the results of group activities in educational, occupational, and orientation areas should not act as a deterrent to continued experimentation. Rather, they should encourage the use of additional means of appraising results. Student judgments on values derived from group activities have more appraisal potentialities than educators usually realize. Using some of the available check lists as guides, any school can prepare a list of evaluative criteria adapted to local conditions and is justified in anticipating helpful suggestions.

Comments from a number of recent student "opinionaires" point out remediable defects and indicate some of the helpful aspects of guidance courses:

It all depends on the teacher. Last year it was fine; this year it's awful.
The educational unit is O.K.; cut out the occupational unit.
I like all of it. I have learned to consider my educational program as a personal matter and to think of my abilities in comparison with my program.
Might be very helpful if the homeroom teacher knew anything about occupations.
Taught me not to specialize too young.
Tries to cram an occupation down your throat.
Helps on educational programs, not on vocational.
Classes in guidance tell you over and over what you already know.

This sort of comment, emphasized by frequent repetitions and checked by other methods of appraisal, does not measure anything, but it has considerable significance.

[8] *Appraising Guidance in Secondary Schools* (New York: Macmillan Co., 1941).

3. *The extent to which essential information regarding students is available.* Part III has elaborated the meaning of "essential" and has indicated the tools and techniques usually recommended for securing such data, determining its reliability, and recording it. A list of references which furnish suggestions for setting up evaluative criteria on this aspect of guidance procedures was included.

The degree to which this material is available and accessible may be easily determined. The extent to which it provides data for research and counseling purposes is also comparatively easily determined, and alterations in both content and form of the inventory or record may be made as deficiencies are revealed. The utility of the record content for administrative purposes may be evaluated in terms of the extent to which it provides data, statistical and other, for reviewing and revising the objectives, policies, and practices of the service and of appraising its tangible results.

Analysis of record items should throw light on unmet student needs and lack of facilities for meeting them, on the relation of curriculum regulations to student needs and potential occupational outlets, on methods of selection and induction in relation to retention and elimination, on the successes and failures of transfers, both intra- and interinstitution, and the like.

4. *The effectiveness of the director or chief counselor who is charged with leadership responsibilities in winning the confidence of all parties.* Few appraisals of a director's leadership are available, and no studies which merit classification as evaluations are in print to this writer's knowledge. This situation is rather interesting and tempts one to rationalize. Several explanations which come to mind seem plausible: (1) Few bona fide directors have been appointed and the activities of lower level functionaries are too ill-assorted to assume that their primary duties lie in guidance areas. (2) Duties and relationships have not been sufficiently defined to permit the application of evaluative criteria. (3) The diplomatic risks involved in securing suitable evaluative data are too formidable for the average administrator to face them with equanimity.

If a director has been selected on the basis of his proved or potential ability to accomplish certain objectives and make certain contributions, there is no reason why criteria should not be prepared and applied to his accomplishments. A director's usual functions as a salesman, a functional specialist, an educator and leader, a co-ordinator, a research student, and a counselor have already been discussed. Criteria may be grouped about this or any other list of major responsibilities, and subtopics may be chosen from a number of questions and challenges. A few are noted:

Has he developed, or is he developing, a service based on quantity or quality, on authority or on influence?

Does his strength derive from administrative backing and delegated authority or from his facilitating and leadership qualities?

Does he regard the service as his handiwork or does the "we" spirit pervade all of his activities?

What has he done to facilitate intrainstitution, administration-corps, parent-school, teacher-pupil, teacher-teacher, and other relationships?

Has he shown ability to interpret, within and without the institution, its personnel policy in relation to the philosophy of education which prevails in the institution?

Is progress being made? Because of his activities or in spite of them?

What specific things has he done to improve the quality of the service?

Is the corps actually receiving leadership? What specific contributions has he made to its professional growth?

Is he up to date on researches and experiments and, when feasible, does he make practical use of their results?

Is he continually appraising his own efforts and does he assist teachers to appraise theirs?

Does he use good judgment in selecting measurement, evaluation, and appraisal devices for each specific purpose?

Does he use supervisory clearance or consultative supervision in such fashion that his co-operators may keep informed on and exchange experiences regarding methods, procedures, and problems?

Does he readily assume adjunct responsibilities and assist the corps to welcome adjunct services?

What is the attitude of the corps toward both his personality and his leadership abilities? [9]

Selected statements from four unpublished, confidential teacher opinionaires exemplify the type of data one may expect to secure from such sources, and they stress the institutional upsets which might result from this method of receiving data. Nevertheless the returns might have considerable value.

One survey reported that 85 per cent of the teachers felt that the influence of the director had been a handicap with reference to student attitudes toward both teacher and school. Another reported that 70 per cent of the corps considered his activities a hindrance to desirable student-teacher relationships. Supporting evidence consisted of incidents which tended to break down respect for the advice and judgment of classroom

[9] If the director has direct contact with students, student opinion adds another source of appraisal data.

teachers, to lessen respect for their authority, and to leave the impression that it would be well to disregard teacher advice or would be wise to check teacher opinion with that of the counselor.

With reference to the helpfulness of the director in the better understanding of pupil problems, 60 per cent of one corps had received no help and 40 per cent of a second corps did not feel that the director understood pupil problems well enough to assist anyone; but 50 per cent of a third corps were very appreciative of the new light which the director had thrown on the causal factors of such problems, while 20 per cent of the fourth corps had found the explanation of the cumulative record and the results of case studies of inestimable assistance.

Increase in time-consuming routine duties with no explanation of their purpose and with no apparent results was resented by 80 per cent of one corps and 90 per cent of another, while 75 per cent of a third reported that what might usually be considered routine duties were willingly performed because the director had so clearly described their importance and the various ways in which they were a contribution.

The director's influence on scholarship and on student behavior showed about the same variation in appraisals. General comments which accompanied the opinionaires included:

He is operating a spy system for the principal.
He is a stuffed shirt, window dressing for the institution.
I don't see how we got along without him.
He regards himself as in authority over teachers.
He always takes a back seat and gives the teacher credit.
It is a positive inspiration to work with such a man.
He is helpful in too many ways to mention.
It is an insult to teachers to ask them to work with such a second-class man.
He might be very helpful were he not used as a dumping ground for administrative problems.
He has been most helpful in showing the desirability of an organismic approach to personnel problems.
He is very accessible and always helpful.
He places far too much stress on our limited testing program; he overvalues it.
His methods close the mind of the child to any new possibilities; once his four-year program is made out he is pigeonholed for life.
He is not a director of guidance; he is a clinical psychologist.
We need a better organizer and co-ordinator. There is too much duplication in our school.
He should undertake some comparative studies of the things we are doing rather than keep adding new.
It is well for all of us to remember that at times we may be wrong.

5. *The cost of the service in terms of accomplishment.* The cost of the service, just as all other factors in the service, must be determined in the

light of the objectives and accomplishments of the service. Principals and presidents who are satisfied with paper programs or catalogue pronouncements and who estimate values in terms of the number of personnel activities included in the program or the number of promises made to students and parents will not find the copy writer's and printer's bill any great drain on their financial resources. But if the quality of the service be the major concern, the cost in relation to the ultimate influence on the lives of its recipients may evade statistical analysis for years, perhaps always, and may force administrators to be content with partial cost appraisals and incomplete evaluations.

Some cost studies and cost estimates have been made. Statistics have not been very satisfactory and it is very difficult to secure any that are: (1) Because there is no agreement as to what constitutes guidance or personnel services. They may be so ethereal and so imperceptible that they constitute only a point of view, and points of view, helpful as they may be if properly grounded, are not very expensive.[10] (2) Because if guidance and personnel service are considered shared responsibilities and regarded as permeating functions, they will be so closely interwoven with instructional and other services that it is quite impossible to segregate personnel activities and pro rate their cost. (3) Because a number of administrators still adhere to the early period camouflage whereby those who were allocated to guidance services were labeled "teachers" and carried as such on the instruction payroll. Guidance services cost nothing, but the cost of instruction is increased by the amount of the salaries paid teachers who perform guidance functions. Each administrator, also, may desire to determine whether it is cheaper to employ a trained counselor for full-time service or to release five or six teachers from instructional duties for one period each per day. The cost of the program may or may not prove to be approximately the same.

Another difficulty in attempting to determine costs is found in the fact that although objectives may be set up, the ultimate results of the pro-

10 The author has used the expressions "guidance-minded" and "personnel point-of-view" for years but she has never suggested that either implies an attempt to perform guidance services without implementation. In June, 1937, the American Council on Education published The Student Personnel Point of View. Since that date enough articles have appeared to suggest the possibility that an appealing catch phrase is crowding out realization of the necessity for the tangible evidences of personnel services. Sarah Rogers in "Guidance on a Shoe-String" (School Executive, LX [1941], 14–15) sets up as an objective for an administrator who wants a guidance program but has no funds available the idea that guidance is a point of view and that pupils rather than subject matter should be stressed. When this has been done, the administrator is supposed to have a guidance program without a cent of expense. Of course an idea is not a program, and the author goes on to outline a program based on the idea, which she implements rather well for no expense, including the services of a "director of guidance."

gram against which costs must be appraised are so far in the future that only estimated short-term accomplishments are available for evaluation purposes. There is, however, one generalization which may safely be made without supporting evidence: *effective guidance service is going to add materially to the educational budget.* How much it may save in terms of success rather than failure, better pupil adjustment, smoother intra- and interinstitution relationships, a larger institutional contribution to social progress, and a greater elimination of human waste is anyone's guess.

On the other hand, it is a little difficult to conceive of an administrator who is so totally oblivious to cost that he will advocate one full-time counselor for every three hundred students. No such provision should be necessary or advisable unless he desires to provide a complete clinical service for each student. Unless youth are in need of constant supervision and direction, why accustom them to it during school life? Why make them so dependent on one three-hundredths of the time of a service agency that they cannot make even simple adjustments on their own responsibility?

There can be no standard number of counselors needed in any given school. Some schools and some colleges can advantageously use more counselors per capita than others, and it might be just as harmful to youth to find counseling eternally stalking his activities as it would be to call in vain for a little assistance now and then. One wonders sometimes how much superficial, ill-advised, and conflicting counsel a normal youth can be subjected to without suffering mental indigestion. Those of us who prepare counselors for service need to remember that not all the apron strings are in the home!

6. *Of course every administrator would like to be able to determine the results of the counseling procedure.* If he will take time to examine the problem, however, and to state it clearly, he will realize the inherent difficulties and perhaps be content to center his appraisal efforts on such intermediate steps as lend themselves to the application of presently available techniques.

The intangible, which one would like to evaluate, is the influence of counseling on the total life of an individual. How has it controlled the direction of his developmental growth? Among the obvious obstacles to such an evaluation are the following facts: (1) The ultimate results of counseling lie far in the future; the school cannot maintain contacts long enough to receive the final returns. (2) Even were the end of the road in sight, there are no criteria for determining whether or not another road might have led more happily and more expeditiously to a safer harbor.

(3) There are no criteria by which to determine the extent to which an individual life has been a success or a failure or what contribution counseling might have made to either possibility. (4) There is no way of segregating the effects of social, economic, and cultural influences operating without the school from those operating within; no way of determining the influence of such institutional factors as the character of its policies, of its executive personnel, and of its instructional corps. Sometimes it has seemed that the difference in the influence of in-school and out-of-school factors must account for the fact that so many school-dull youth develop into life-bright workers and citizens.

Probably until technical experts have solved some of the problems connected with the intangibles involved in counseling procedures, the continuous study of case histories will be one of the most helpful methods of estimating counseling returns and revealing deficiencies in procedures. The studies published by the Educational Records Bureau were noted in Part III. They may be supplemented by reports on the evaluation efforts of social case workers and of clinical services of various types.

A discussion, case by case, participated in by the entire corps, may be made the beginning of an appraisal of counseling procedures.[11] It must be remembered that the hierarchy of evaluation begins just where the hierarchy of performance begins, with the line functionaries, the students and the teachers. Each official from the bottom to the top of the line should uncover some things to praise in his counseling work and some things which call for improvement and can be improved. In lieu of an over-all evaluation, achievements and suggestions for progress should eventually reach the chief administrator. In the meantime every educator looks forward hopefully to the time when the organismic philosophy may be successfully applied to guidance and personnel services as they affect individuals.

There are many other factors included in guidance and personnel services which the average administrator would like to appraise, evaluate, or measure. Precedents have been established for some, for others he would be breaking virgin soil. If he seeks to know the value of work experience as a factor in education—really an educational rather than a guidance problem—he cannot afford to overlook the evaluative criteria which have been set up by the National Youth Administration in various states. Ohio has led with eight evaluation studies, covering both college and secondary programs. The studies were supervised by research students of unques-

11 The literature of social work suggests many ways in which cases may be co-operatively evaluated.

tioned ability and their techniques and their findings are extremely valuable.[12] W. W. Charters, Chairman of the Division of Research in charge of the Evaluation Programs, notes that an especial effort was made to clarify intangibles.

Under a committee of experienced research students, New Hampshire followed the techniques of the evaluation program at Ohio University, Athens, Ohio, and produced an evaluation report dealing with the N.Y.A. program on a state-wide basis from the point of view of students, supervisors, and administrators.[13] It is interesting to find the college students calling for closer co-operation among the several student personnel officers in each college and university and for a clearinghouse for data on students so that access to all data on each applicant might be secured in one office.

If the administrator would like to know to what extent problem conferences are being programed around student problems rather than around students' problems as teachers see them, he will turn to student opinionaires and questionnaires for evaluative assistance. If he would like to know whether the follow-up procedures in vogue help to correct deficiencies in the past and supplement previous assets or whether they increase dependency on the institution and foster continuous immaturity of judgment, he will probably find cumulative records and case studies a good starting point.

No matter what aspect of his guidance service an administrator may desire to evaluate, he will turn to the most available device for assistance. He will measure what is measurable, appraise that which lends itself to appraisal, use authoritative opinions on many items which are not now, and may never be, statistically measurable, and evaluate all the admissible returns as a steppingstone for tomorrow. He will emphasize in the presence of his corps the fact that no effectively operated business can afford to ignore the responsibilities and advantages of evaluation; that each unit, the guidance unit included, must justify its existence and that each member of each unit must justify his retention therein. He will ask, and expect, his director of guidance to show renewed interest in helping the corps to stress the appraisal of the ordinary, everyday functions which are susceptible of control and improvement, while they all wait and hope for more accurate methods of determining over-all results.

[12] National Youth Administration in Ohio, Evaluation Studies (Columbus, Ohio: The Administration, 1937–1939).

[13] An Evaluation Study of the N.Y.A. Student Work Program in New Hampshire Schools and Colleges (Concord, N.H., 1940).

SELECTED SUPPLEMENTARY READING

American College Personnel Association. *Report of . . . Annual Meeting.* [v. p.]: The Association, 1925–. [The title varies.] Cover all phases of college personnel work and are uniformly helpful. The reports are in most college libraries.

American Vocational Association, Inc., Committee on Research. *Occupational Adjustments of Vocational School Graduates.* Washington, 1940.

Brumbaugh, A. J., and Emme, E. E. "Principles in the Organization of College Counseling," *Religious Education*, XXVII (1932), 225–229.

Brunner, Edmund deS. *Working with Rural Youth.* Washington: American Council on Education, 1942. A review of the influences which from 1920 on have changed the character of youth problems, especially with reference to migration. Reports on the procedures of the Rural Project of the American Youth Commission and appraises its results.

Chambers, M. M., and Bell, Howard M. *How to Make a Community Youth Survey.* Washington: American Council on Education, 1939.

Chapman, Paul W. *Guidance Programs for Rural High Schools.* Washington, 1939. (U. S. Office of Education, Occupational Information and Guidance Service, Misc., no. 2196.) After a brief statement regarding the problem of guidance in rural schools, a rather complete report of two projects in New York State is presented, one at the Newark Valley Central School and the other at the Nyack and Rockland County Schools.

Gooch, W. I., and Keller, F. J. "Breathitt County in the Southern Appalachians," *Occupations*, XIV (1936, June, sec. 2), 1011–1110.

Hahn, Milton E. "What Price Pupil-Personnel Work?" *School Review*, XLVII (1939), 374–380. Hahn's estimate of costs for an average school of 200–600 pupils is $500–$1,000 per year.

Hambright, Irene. "Creating a Personnel Department," *Personnel*, XV (1938), 39–42. A brief but helpful article for educators who are able to select suggestions applicable to their needs from the experience of others.

Hatcher, O. Latham. *Guiding Rural Boys and Girls.* New York: McGraw-Hill Book Co., 1930. Part IV is "Setting Up the Guidance Program" and Part VI is "Unifying the Guidance Program."

Hawkins, Layton S., *et al. Occupational Information and Guidance: Organization and Administration.* Washington, 1940. (U. S. Office of Education, Vocational Division Bulletin, no. 204, Occupational Information and Guidance Series, 1939, no. 1.) Discusses the newly organized Occupational Information and Guidance Service and its relation to other educational services. Explains procedures for setting up state programs and briefly, but with abundant documentation, gives the status of guidance services in each state. A valuable reference book which should be in every director's library.

Indiana, Department of Public Instruction. *The Present Status of High School Guidance as It Affects the Seniors of 1942 in Indiana.* Indianapolis: The Department, 1942. (Guidance Research Bulletin, no. 1.) Based on a sampling comprising 86,481 students in 371 schools. Questionnaires were filled out by principals who reported on the guidance devices used to assist seniors in various choices. Senior opinion was not sought.

Jacobson, Paul B., and Reavis, William C. *Duties of School Principals.* New York:

Prentice-Hall, 1941. Chapter 5 is "Guidance Functions of the Principal" and Chapter 6 is "Projecting a Guidance Organization." Statistical data collected from 68 secondary schools with reference to titles of functionaries, duties, frequencies of performance, etc., are included.

Jessen, C. A., and Hutchins, H. C. *Youth*, Pt. VI: *Community Surveys*. Washington, 1936. (U. S. Office of Education Bulletin, 1936, no. 18–VI.) Covers a wide range of topics usually included in personnel surveys. Part III discusses survey methods. An annotated bibliography and a survey schedule are included.

McKinsey, James O. *Organization Problems Under Present Conditions*. New York: American Management Assn., 1936. (General Management Series, no. 127.) Tells the necessity for the co-ordination of the activities of all specialists. Functional authority and line authority are clearly distinguished.

Martens, Elise H. *Clinical Organization for Child Guidance Within the Schools*. Washington, 1939. (U. S. Office of Education Bulletin, 1939, no. 15.)

Meriam, Lewis. *Personnel Administration in the Federal Government*. Washington: Brookings Institution, 1937. An inquiry into suggestions for revision of the laws which govern the personnel administration of the federal government. The broad background on which the specific problem is attacked follows the general principles of organization. Very brief but very clear statement of relationships.

Metropolitan Life Insurance Company, Policyholders Service Bureau. *Functions of the Personnel Director*. New York: The Bureau, 1937. An outstanding presentation of personnel policies, programs, and organization based on personal interviews with 40 business executives and on an equal number of questionnaire returns. The place of the personnel department in the organization, the organization within the department, and its functions are discussed. Students may compare this material with the American Council on Education pamphlet, *The Student Personnel Point of View*, 1937, which discusses the philosophy of personnel work, various aspects of co-ordination, and the future of the work.

Milwaukee, Wisconsin, Superintendent of Schools. *The Entire School as an Advisory Agency*. Milwaukee, 1933. (Seventy-fourth Annual Report of the Superintendent of Schools.) The entire report is given to a description of the Life Advisement Bureau in the Milwaukee schools, its historic background, evolution, and function as a co-ordinating agency.

National Association of Deans and Advisers of Men. *Report of Proceedings of the . . . Annual Conference*. Lawrence, Kans., Urbana, Ill., etc.: The Association, 1921–. [The title varies.] The reports are not available for general distribution but they are usually found in large libraries.

National Association of Secondary-School Principals. *Guidance in Secondary Schools*. Cicero, Ill.: The Association, 1928. (Bulletin, no. 19.) Contains a proposed general type of organization for an individual high school.

——. *Evaluating Secondary Education*. Washington: The Association, 1942. (Bulletin, vol. XXVI, no. 106.)

New Jersey State Teachers College, Newark. *Student Personnel Services in the New Jersey State Teachers College at Newark*. Newark: The College, ᶜ1939. Prepared by the Personnel Cabinet of the college.

Niles, Henry E., and Niles, M. C. H. "Assistance in Coordination," *Personnel*, XV (1938), 26–38. An excellent article for school officials. Progressive specialization requires co-ordination; co-ordination as an administrative function;

"staff assistants," line executives, administrative assistants, and functional specialists; a list of functions which a staff assistant can perform for his chief and a list of those which he should avoid.

Root, Robert K. "Problems in Articulating American Secondary and Higher Education," *Proceedings of the Forty-ninth Annual Convention of the Middle States Association of Colleges and Secondary Schools,* 1935, pp. 57–65.

Russell, John D., and Reeves, Floyd W. *Administration.* Chicago: University of Chicago Press, 1936. (The Evaluation of Higher Institutions, VI.) A monograph based on investigations conducted by the Committee on Revision of Standards, Commission on Higher Institutions of the North Central Association of Colleges and Secondary Schools.

Segel, David, and Proffitt, Maris M. *Pupil Personnel Services as a Function of State Departments of Education.* Washington, 1940. (U. S. Office of Education Bulletin.) Part II, pp. 45–60, deals with the development of state interest from 1930 to 1940, the activities engaged in, and the services rendered; p. 61 lists 12 functions for which state departments have special responsibilities.

Stolz, Herbert R. "The Integration of All Guidance Work," *Occupations,* XV (1937), 712–717. Discusses 4 obstacles to the integration of programs.

Sturtevant, Sarah M. "Organizing a Guidance Program," *Teachers College Record,* XL (1938), 5–15.

Symonds, Percival M. "A Plea for the Integration of School Guidance Activities," *Teachers College Record,* XXXVIII (1937), 686–710. Outlines the fields of study which contribute to guidance services. Suggests a plan for instituting a guidance service.

Urwick, Lyndall. *Scientific Principles and Organization.* New York: American Management Assn., 1938. (Institute of Management Series, no. 19.) Principles of organization, classification of functions, line and staff concepts, types of relationships, and methods of securing co-ordination are discussed.

Wonderlic, E. F. "Personnel as a Control Function," *Personnel,* XIV (1937), 31–41. Discusses the relationship of 10 techniques and how they are so combined that the personnel department is both a controlling and co-ordinating unit. The author's use of "control" is interesting: "As a control group a personnel department serves management in an advisory capacity."

PART VI
Retrospect and Prospect

Chapter XXI
Retrospect

Chapter XXII
Prospect

"To every man his chance—to every man, regardless of his birth—his opportunity—to every man the right to live, to work, to be himself, and to become whatever thing his manhood and his vision can combine to make him—this . . . is the promise of America."—Thomas Wolfe, *You Can't Go Home Again,* 1940. (By permission of the publishers, Harper and Brothers.)

"We have made progress in the past and we will continue to, and it will be on the basis of taking forward steps of the right length at the right time, in such ways that we do not skid or slip backward. . . . There has been enough experience and progress in this process called 'personnel work' during the past 30 years to aid us in a look ahead."—J. Walter Dietz, 1940.

CHAPTER XXI

Retrospect

PART I of this volume has been concerned with historical data from which to understand the origin of the guidance movement, to interpret its progress, and to anticipate its future. Parts II and III have been devoted to various types of informational data and the tools and techniques employed in their collection. Part IV has presented a number of methods which have proved valuable for the utilization of informational data, and Part V has discussed the problems involved in organizing, conducting, and evaluating the results of guidance and personnel services. A recapitulation of certain aspects of the guidance movement, especially of those which are of fundamental importance for future progress, is the purpose of Chapter XXI.

1. *Guidance Movements versus A Guidance Movement.* The story of the beginnings of guidance and personnel activities reveals that during the first decade of the twentieth century there were four guidance movements, or four segments of a guidance movement. Three of these movements have been discussed. One of the three has been stressed, the fourth has received passing mention. Since their interrelation has considerable significance for the future, a brief restatement of their spheres of influence seems desirable.

(a) *The Child Guidance Movement,* closely related to the mental hygiene movement and to the development of the nursery school and parental education movements, found expression in its less highly specialized aspects in child-study associations and parent-teacher clubs. In its highly specialized aspects it has served parents and children through child guidance clinics. Leadership has always been in the hands of professionally trained and experienced workers. Current publications have disseminated information and dealt with the type of guidance and personality problems which frequently trouble those who offer guidance services on the pre-school or elementary school level.

Personal and professional qualifications of functionaries who serve on this age level are fairly specific for each type of service rendered. The titles of the workers, among which are "psychologist," "psychiatrist," "physician," "nurse," "psychiatric social worker" and "visiting teacher," indicate functions which are both differentiated and co-ordinated.

Although this division of guidance service has been neglected in this volume, no overview of a unified guidance movement is complete which fails to give it its proper place in the story of the past and in the promise of the future. The student is urged to remember that its beginnings were coincident with the beginnings of the movements which have been elaborated, that it moved forward in the 1920's in company with the other movements, and that in the final analysis it occupies the strategic position of laying the cornerstone.

(b) *The Educational Guidance Movement* traces its origin to the unwelcome revelations of the various school surveys which were so common during the last years of the nineteenth and the early years of the twentieth centuries. It was very disturbing to school administration to learn that so large a proportion of school youths were repeating grades year after year. Some who left at fourteen to fifteen years of age had never completed the first grade; a considerable number had not acquired the fundamental tools of an education.

The testing movement came along just in time to explain some of the failures to learn, partially to make clear the causes of stagnation in grades three to five, to relieve teachers of the entire onus of failures, and to relieve economic pressure of blame as being the major factor responsible for denying an education to many youth. A desultory sort of educational guidance came into being. The school psychologist was the chief professional functionary; the redistribution of pupils whose test scores suggested that they had reached the limit of their scholastic abilities was the major guidance device.

Here and there an alert superintendent was interpreting the findings of psychology in terms of educational service adapted to individual differences, but for the most part it requires quite a stretch of the imagination to assume that educational guidance had been incorporated in the school program. It is well to recall that this was the period of active philanthropic interest in the vocational guidance of these same eliminated school youth —the period during which philanthropy was trying desperately to fasten guidance on the educational system.

In recent years the Educational Records Bureau and co-operating agencies have led in the revival of a well-implemented educational guidance movement. Professional leadership has been assured, and up-to-date information has been made available through publications and conferences. Thus a second segment of a unified guidance movement seems to be established on a solid foundation, and is prepared to move forward whenever local systems provide the type of leadership which is necessary to make use of its facilities. But like the child guidance movement, it is a segment only; it must depend upon other agencies to supplement its educational services with the type of occupational services which are so essential a factor in meeting the guidance needs of secondary school youth.

(c) *The Vocational Guidance Movement* is the third segment of a guidance service which originated in the first decade. It has received major attention in this study and is the one usually meant when "the guidance movement" is mentioned. It is much more inclusive, both of age groups and of arcs of the guidance circle, than is any one of the other three segments. By virtue of the breadth of its interests, its continuous service, its voluminous literature, its diversified sponsorship, and the greater degree of universality of its presence in philanthropic, educational, and business concerns, it has always held a strategic position with reference to leadership in a guidance movement and the possible integration of the activities of its various segments. The two previously mentioned segments cannot offer an integrated service without supplementary assistance from this segment, nor will it be possible to introduce postschool or all-inclusive community services without leaning heavily on its assistance.

On the other hand, something inherent in this segment seems to have prevented it from attaining the type of professionalism which is usually required of an organization or a movement before it is accorded leadership status. It is represented by the National Vocational Guidance Association and by *Occupations: The Vocational Guidance Magazine.* But the Association has never been a professional organization in the usually accepted sense. It has had no requirements for membership and no clear-cut field of service to prevent first one pressure group and then another from dominating its activities. It has set up no acceptable standards for the recruitment or preparation of its operating personnel, nor is its professional prestige such that universities and state departments of education instinctively turn to it for assistance in determining upon selection, preparation, and certification procedures.

(d) *The Personnel Movement in Business and in Industry,* which is concerned with the individual in relation to his work and to his work unit, is the fourth segment and tops the present-day structure as the postschool or adult phase. This and the vocational guidance segment were collaborators in calling the first national vocational guidance conference in 1910, and it has always advocated close co-operation between the two segments. Sufficient attention has been given to its development to indicate the direction in which it has been moving, the type of leadership which has been developing, and the values which will derive from ever closer co-operation between the educational and business segments of the guidance movement.

As the years have passed, these four segments of an over-all service have moved along side by side with some subdivisions,[1] but with comparatively little effort to co-ordinate or to integrate their services. Therefore, at the beginning of the fifth decade of the century there is still no guidance movement, nor will there be one until the activities of these various segments are so co-ordinated that youth easily and automatically passes from one aspect of the service to the next whether he be traveling the highways or the byways of life.

2. *Co-ordination of Service Agencies.* A second significant early day characteristic of the guidance movement, especially of the vocational guidance segment, which has endured throughout the years and must be reckoned with in the future, is the strong appeal which it has made to a wide variety of service agencies and organizations. This pervasive appeal must be capitalized on. As guidance services become more scientific in character and the suggestion of community control appears on the horizon, the dangers of propaganda, of ill-advised but well-meaning guidance and counseling procedures, of the appointment of untrained but popular functionaries, of inaccurate informational data, of the advocacy of unethical methods of approaching employers, and the like may tend to increase rather than to decrease. Professional leadership which can co-ordinate, control, and utilize to the best advantage all types of contributions which service agencies desire to make and at the same time keep guidance activities moving steadily along progressive, scientific avenues may become essential if the promise of guidance is to be realized.

3. *The Dangers of Mechanization.* The underlying philosophy of the early guidance movement—to every man his chance to become whatever his abilities, manhood, and vision can combine to make him—has remained constant. The fundamental principles formulated by the early sponsors of guidance services were not materially different from those of today. The broad classification of tools and techniques still holds, but the refinement of tools and techniques which has been accomplished warrants the assumption that we are engaged in an occupation which is a "continuously growing science and art."

On the other hand, scientific progress has been accompanied by certain dangers which are inherent in the mechanization of any form of personnel service. There was no mechanical guidance in the early period; the time was not ripe and the essential facilities were not at hand. However, retro-

[1] The guidance activities of federal and state agencies during the depression and their more recent defense programs have been regarded as temporary expansions of the activities of the vocational guidance or personnel movements, and not as independent movements. The Civilian Conservation Corps, the Work Projects Administration, and the National Youth Administration were all liquidated by the end of 1943.

spection reveals that conditions were ripening and implementation was under way, so slowly, so insidiously, and so logically that it was invisible even to the most experienced eye. Guidance under philanthropy was always individualized guidance, bona fide personnel service in the fullest sense of the term. There was no desire, no temptation, and no facilities to make it anything else. But when it was taken over by the schools mass instruction was the method in vogue; therefore it was entirely logical that mass methods of guidance should be introduced and modeled on the older, prevailing pattern. At once implementation began. A classroom, a "teacher of guidance," a textbook on guidance, tests of achievement in guidance, credits in guidance, and grades in guidance were introduced here and there before World War I. When the army cleared the way, group psychological tests were added.

As time has passed, tests, questionnaires, inventories, and ratings of many types have increased in quantity and improved in quality, bringing in their wake an increasing tendency to "streamline" guidance. When the very clever and valuable scoring machine was put on the market in 1937, it offered an irresistible temptation to those who were looking to psychometrics as the major factor in the improvement of guidance service for the further streamlining of guidance. D. G. Paterson's final statement in "The Genesis of Modern Guidance" provokes serious thinking and raises some very disconcerting questions:

> In closing permit me to make a prediction. From developments and achievements to date, and from the widespread interest one finds in scientific guidance work here in California, in the Mid-West, in the East, and in the South, I am confident that we are on the threshold of a rapid expansion of guidance service in high schools, colleges, and universities, and in adult adjustment clinics attached to public employment offices. And this prediction is also safe, namely, we are on the threshold of a tremendous acceleration of testing programs everywhere as a result of the introduction at this very moment of an electrical scoring machine that will reduce costs to a negligible figure. . . .
> For all these reasons, I make bold to predict the immediate rapid development of educational and vocational guidance programs. . . .[2]

Not everyone, however, has been equally optimistic either in retrospect or forecast. The signal lights have flashed on and off with a regularity which has warned of the dangers of streamlining for action in an area where assembly lines and streamlining may well be by-passed. Professor

[2] *Educational Record*, XIX (1938), 45–46. That there is some international interest in the dangers of mechanized guidance is evident in Lin Yutang's observation, "I understand there are not only intelligence tests . . . but there is in a certain institution even a machine which gives you the correct percentage of a man's intelligence by just slipping the person's answers into the machine. The machine does everything" ("When East Meets West," *Atlantic Monthly*, CLXX [Dec., 1942], 46).

James some years ago warned his hearers against too great readiness to use the findings of psychology to make predictions for others, and remarked that he did not anticipate that they would permit us to write biographies in advance. After the publication of the *Thirty-fourth Yearbook of the National Society for the Study of Education*, M. R. Trabue suggested the possibility that the tools and techniques mentioned therein might be used to eliminate individual differences rather than to integrate all activities for serving the individual.[3] Miss Voorhees, in the previously mentioned address,[4] expressed a fear that too much stress on the mechanical aspects of personnel service might result in elaborate diagnosis to the neglect of the type of synthesis which included essential intangibles. And Harold Benjamin has recently invited us to join with him in casting "a cold, hard eye at the tools we love," lest we overlook the danger of using the tools and devices of modern guidance programs "for their own sweet sakes." [5]

Testing, of course, is not the only aspect of personnel service which invites mechanization, nor are psychologists and psychometricians the only functionaries who are apt to overlook the individual while they push forward their own major interests. The perfecting of any personnel procedure may easily overshadow the needs of individuals unless the danger be recognized and guarded against; the collection of information, the making of the cumulative record, the conduct of classes, group discussions and counseling interviews, and the organization of the service itself may become ends in themselves rather than helpful means to an end.

4. *The Apathy of Educational Administration* with regard to the objectives, organization, and development of guidance and personnel services is a fourth factor which has had continuous influence on the progress of the movement. There is abundant documentary evidence, covering the entire history of the guidance movement on both levels of education, to indicate that educational administration has never fully grasped the significance of the movement and never assumed the responsibility which it must assume if the movement is to make good on its promise.[6] Part V

---

[3] *Journal of Educational Research*, XIX (1936), 327–331.

[4] American College Personnel Association, *Report of the Eighteenth Annual Meeting*, 1941, pp. 1–7.

[5] *Ibid.*, p. 36.

[6] It will be remembered that in 1931 a conference with superintendents was arranged by the National Vocational Guidance Association in order to discuss with them the values of guidance service. The superintendents admitted that it had local propaganda values. Accounts of the recent Superintendents' Tour, under the direction of the National Occupational Conference, reveal that the tour was a promotional device, but it has never been entirely clear what it was designed to promote. Apparently it furthered vocational education. The latest, and possibly the most effective, prod to interest has

has given extensive consideration to the types of responsibility which are administrative in character and logically devolve on the administrative authorities but which, to a minor degree only, have been taken over by them. Because of their persistent apathy they may be justly credited with a considerable portion of the onus of having delayed progress in the past, of continuing to delay it in the present, and of threatening to delay it in the future.

That educational administration has not been entirely without interest in guidance services is evidenced by a number of publications which have appeared under the auspices of the American Association of School Administrators, the regional standardizing agencies, and the Department of Secondary School Principals, whose excellent bulletins are indicative of the contribution which administrative authorities can make when they are fully aware of the objectives and values of student personnel services. But the publication of bulletins by an organization is not valid evidence that a majority of the membership is practicing or even interested in the suggestions contained in the reports which they have nominally endorsed.

No educational service can make satisfactory progress if the over-all policy makers of the institutions concerned fail to include its objectives in the objectives of the individual institution or to realize that its policies and objectives must be interwoven with those of the institution. *Guidance and personnel services cannot rise higher than their source.*

If guidance and personnel service after approximately thirty years of experimental progress is regarded as an educational and social asset, it does not seem unreasonable to expect that the movement will receive in the near future more intelligent and purposeful assistance from administration in clarifying objectives, relating objectives to policies, clearing up title and status confusion, especially on the college level, coming to an agreement on terms, checking the ever-growing list of hybrid functions included under personnel service, and helping to determine upon some basis for deciding what in general are personnel functions and how best to eliminate, or allocate elsewhere, the intruders.

Relationships, too, need to be more clearly defined and proper provision for the co-ordination and integration of all personnel activities is a pressing demand. Budget provision which permits the appointment of "arrivals" as directors and an administrative setup which recognizes the most elementary principles of organization are responsibilities which can be assumed only by administrative authorities.

If guidance and personnel services have not been worth while, if they

_____
come in the shape of the decision of the federal government to allocate financial support to youth agencies under the jurisdiction of other than educational authorities.

have neither serviced students, facilitated faculty-student relationships, nor contributed to the realization of institutional objectives, it is time for stocktaking, which may result in the elimination of such service from the educational picture.

5. *Adequate Professional Preparation of Operational Personnel* has been a fifth continuous need. Chapter IV has noted that coincident with the beginnings of organized guidance training courses for the preparation of functionaries in both education and industry were instituted and have constantly increased in numbers, although in content they have fallen short of meeting the demand which an effective service usually makes upon its practitioners.

Chapter IV also suggested that it might be worth while, as a basis for estimating progress in the preparation of professional personnel, to compare item by item (1) the personal qualifications required for admission to training courses in 1908 and in 1943 and (2) the curriculum requirements laid down by Parsons, Gilbreth, and Person with those laid down by universities and by the certificating authorities of state departments of education in 1943. The results of such a comparison would be similar in education and industry.[7]

The promise of guidance will hardly be fulfilled without considerable overhauling of the methods of selecting pretraining personnel, of the methods and content of training courses, and of the requirements for the upkeep of functionaries once they have been admitted to the service.

If guidance has accepted values, if it be recognized as a permeating function, and if it is to go forward on this basis, all prospective teachers should have an opportunity to understand its philosophy and principles in their relation to the philosophy and principles of education. They should realize that in connection with their instructional responsibilities and the daily development of their students they will occupy positions of tremendous strategic importance—positions which will permit them to

---

[7] In *The Preparation, Certification and Selection of Personnel Workers for the Secondary Schools of the United States* (unpublished thesis, New York University, 1940) Richard J. Bailey supplies a wealth of material regarding present requirements and certification practices. See also Bailey's article, "Preparing, Certifying and Selecting Public-School Counselors," in *Educational Administration and Supervision*, XXVI (1940), 415–423. "The Education of Personnel Administrators as an Aid to a Sound Human Order," Ordway Tead's conference address before the Bureau of Personnel Administration, December 18, 1930, is an exceptionally good presentation of the problem of the preparation of business and industrial personnel with attention to the past, present, and future. *New Responsibilities of the Personnel Executive* (Personnel Series, no. 45; New York: American Management Assn., 1940) by J. Walter Dietz *et al.* is also a valuable pamphlet for educators.

nullify and vitiate the objectives of guidance or to help in achieving them by example and attitude. They should also be able to differentiate the levels at which teachers, general counselors and functional specialists are qualified to serve, understand their relationship to other contributors to guidance services; and realize the necessity for the integration of all services afforded each individual.

The preparation of guidance functionaries is a very important matter. Were a Gallup Poll to be taken there would doubtless be stiff competition between the indifference of educational administration and the inadequate preparation of functionaries to rank first as the Achilles heel of the guidance movement. Not only is the quality of preparation open to challenge in the best-equipped universities, but the sales value of the word "guidance" has been capitalized on to such an extent that any small college which can entice a few teachers or others to register in a summer session will offer a course in guidance anticipating that it will be accepted by school authorities and that in those states which require the certification of public-school counselors it will be credited toward the accumulation of the "points" necessary to be officially declared "a counselor." *At the present time the professional preparation of guidance personnel has become a full-fledged racket.*

The uncomplimentary reports of the New York State Regents' Inquiry and of the Cooperative Study of Secondary School Standards regarding present-day guidance services have been quoted. The ineffectiveness of guidance practices has been recognized time and again by individuals who have shared in the development of the movement and are interested in its future. For example, Richard D. Allen in an article entitled, "Let's Stop Playing with Guidance," cites nine shortcomings in guidance programs and expresses the opinion that the programs have improved but slightly in the last five years.[8] In "Measuring the Results of Vocational Guidance," Harry D. Kitson and Margaret Crane conclude that the evidences of value are "pitifully insignificant when compared with the momentous aims of vocational guidance." [9] Ray M. Simpson, in *Education,* June, 1930, notes that the results of vocational guidance thus far have not been encouraging.[10] In a discussion of exploratory courses and their various purposes E. C. Cline states that after twenty years of experience we find chaos and apathy.[11] Quite recently Gilbert Wrenn mentioned six

[8] *Education,* LVII (1937), 627–633.

[9] *Occupations,* XVI (1938), 842.

[10] "Vocational Guidance," *Education,* L (1930), 606.

[11] "Junior-High-School Exploratory Units in Practice," *Junior-Senior High School Clearing House,* VII (1932), 152–156.

things that have handicapped guidance and indicated that there was grave danger that it might become an educational fad.[12]

What are institutions of higher education and state departments of education going to do about this? What are guidance and personnel associations going to do about it? What are their plans for the future?

Many of the failures which have been mentioned and of which workers in the field are aware may be charged against the quality of the operating personnel. This in turn may be credited to the apathy of administrators, to the fact that universities are willing to muff their job, and that state departments certify counselors who are obviously inadequately prepared.

Improvement in the quality of personnel is a shared responsibility. Agencies which undertake it will face the same type of difficulties that has always been faced by associations, preparatory institutions, and licensing authorities when they have united their forces to raise the standards of an occupation operating at a lower level than was permissible in the interests of the public. Such problems are not insurmountable, and if the early promise of guidance is to be fulfilled, it is time to make an initial attack, at least to analyze the situation and face the facts.

Universities have not as a rule made the first move to raise selection qualifications or training standards for professions or near professions. Professional organizations interested in raising and maintaining standards and in protecting their membership and the public against inadequately trained and unethical practitioners have usually taken the initiative. Guidance and personnel organizations have never set up any professional requirements for membership; therefore they have no standards to maintain and no membership to protect; and with a large percentage of their enrollment nonprofessional in character it would hardly be expected that a minority group of these organizations could impose more stringent professional requirements upon a majority whose very positions might be at stake.

Individual universities could make an immediate contribution to more effective functionary preparation if they understood the problem and were willing to do so. They could place quality of registrants above quantity. They could deny registration to persons obviously unfit for personnel services and could eliminate promptly, after trial, those who proved to be unfit. If interinstitution competition were to be based on the quality of preparation rather than on the numbers registered in courses, instructors who are close to the problem could make an excellent start in the direction of progress. But here, again, there is the possibility,

---

[12] "The Evaluation of Guidance Practices," *Purdue University Studies in Higher Education*, XXXVII (1940), 51–61.

and often the probability, that the contribution of individual instructors is measured by the number of students rather than by the quality of students who are attracted to their courses.

Universities could refuse to appoint as instructors those who have had no fundamental preparation and no practical experience in the basic knowledges upon which training courses must be built. There are too many instructors, especially in the summer sessions, who are content to offer a course based on a single textbook the preparation of which has, all too often, been commercially rather than professionally inspired.

State departments of education can, and do, establish certification standards, but of necessity they must be minimum standards and are applicable only to public schools. The requirements are usually based on university courses and on experience. The several state authorities with whom the author has discussed the subject seem to feel that they are not in a position to accept courses offered by one institution and refuse those offered by another. They feel rather that they should indicate to teachers' colleges and schools of education the objectives they desire to accomplish and the type of preparation they consider essential and assume that suitable courses under suitable instructors will be provided. State departments can, however, and sometimes do refuse to credit courses given by obviously unprepared instructors or courses the content of which rules them out as guidance courses.

On the other hand, state departments might contribute to progress on their own initiative in at least two ways: They might make more effective use of their prerogatives with respect to the practical aspects of training. The extra something beyond training requirements, which can be secured only through wide and varied contacts with the world of reality, has never received the attention which it merits and which it must receive if, and when, the jurisdictional dispute regarding postschool guidance services is settled in favor of education.

Much more stringent experience and apprenticeship or internship requirements are a crying need of the present, for it is a well-known fact that the majority of counselors are not qualified to advise anyone on either level of education in any area of life which falls without the educational arc of the circle. Unless this situation is changed, the promise of the future is not very bright, but state departments which attempt to change it may expect acrimonious attacks from those whose vision of life is bounded by the educational horizon.

A second contribution for which state departments might assume the initiative is found in control of the rate of speed with which new guidance services are introduced. Recent estimates indicate that possibly seventy-five city systems have some official who serves full time or part time as a director of guidance. This is a very modest beginning. But there are not enough qualified directors to operate even so small a number of services effectively. Therefore there is considerable danger of pushing organization more rapidly than it is possible to secure trained leadership, with the result that incompetent directors will be fastened on systems for years to come.

It is natural, of course, for states which have endorsed guidance services, and especially for the supervisors of such services, to desire to push forward the work as rapidly as is possible.[13] That is their job. Moreover, there is likely to be the same sort of pressure on state officials for tangible evidences of progress that is brought to bear on instructors by university authorities.

Two safeguards against malpractice, which also come within the province of state departments, are concerned with *temporary certificates* and with *half-time counselors*. Both practices, which are carry-overs from teacher certification, are open to challenge in the guidance field. The temporary certificate affords an opportunity for an individual of decidedly limited qualifications legally to engage in a variety of practices which may make mental and moral cripples of some youth and may deny many others their right to participate in the promise of America.

The practice of not requiring a certificate for those who give a limited amount of time to the work, usually less than half time, must be predicated on the assumption that malpractice does not occur except under conditions of full-time practice.[14] Suppose physicians and lawyers, nurses and dentists were permitted to practice their profession up to half time without a license! Guidance services can never become professional services on any such basis.

What can guidance and personnel organizations do to improve the quality of their operating personnel? They can "stop playing with guidance." They can forget personalities and personal interests, and on a strictly nonpartisan basis they can give the full support of their membership to any university which will sacrifice the commercial value of numbers to the selection and preparation of guidance functionaries who know

---

[13] The New York State law of 1935, possibly motivated by the depression revelation of youth needs, made it compulsory for cities of over 100,000 to establish services with directors in charge. The North Dakota statutes require accredited schools to provide effective guidance services.

[14] Only 6 per cent of the public high schools are in states which employ counselors giving at least half their time to guidance work. See Walter J. Greenleaf and Royce E. Brewster, *Public High Schools Having Counselors and Guidance Officers* (U. S. Office of Education, Vocational Division Misc. [Series], no. 2267; Washington, 1939).

how to help youth take advantage of the promise of America. They can uphold state departments, each member in his own state, in every move which promises to enhance the value of guidance services, and sometimes they can initiate changes which, were they to be suggested by state officials, might handicap them in carrying forward other equally important co-operative activities.

Perhaps the time may come when they or some one of them will take the initiative in establishing professional requirements for membership; they will thus be enabled to take their place among other organizations which have a voice in determining the essential preparation of their future operating personnel.[15] When that time comes it should be remembered that it is not training for clinical psychologists which is being provided, but training for the more general and more inclusive arcs of the circle which are generally implied in guidance and personnel services.

6. *Authoritative Professional Leadership* has been a sixth need and one which has been of increasing importance as the years have passed. Movements are not launched by casually interested persons. At least a small group, the members of which are vitally interested in a project, have faith in its value, and can furnish the leadership and prestige to institute it under propitious conditions, is a major prerequisite. The vocational guidance movement was no exception to this general rule.

The documented story of the beginnings of the movement includes the names of enough leading educators, philanthropists, and businessmen who had caught the vision of its possibilities to give it a certain amount of national prestige. But this type of interest and support was short-lived, too short to have established the work on a sufficiently permanent and financially attractive basis to enlist the services of men who had already won their spurs in allied fields and could afford the luxury of insecurity.[16]

---

[15] Bailey in his thesis (*op. cit.*) gives an elaborate discussion of what constitutes a profession and concludes that on several counts personnel and guidance functionaries are not entitled to professional status. The present uncertain professional status of personnel directors in industry was recently described by General Lewis B. Hershey, when, during the Manpower Conference of the American Management Association, he was asked about the draft status of personnel officers: "One hundred and thirty million people know that they cannot doctor other people; they do not attempt to preach from the pulpit or even from the floor, nor do they attempt to build a bridge from blueprints—but they would not hesitate to take over your business any time you are ready to step out." Alvin E. Dodd, President of the Association, commenting on the statement, noted the difficulty of proving essentiality because of the lack of standards against which status could be measured. "It is difficult to determine what qualifies a man to call himself a personnel manager" (*Business Conditions and Forecasts*, XV [Oct. 26, 1942]).

[16] It is hard to build a profession out of an occupation which is characterized by uncertainty and insecurity, and to obtain adequate salaries to attract men "arrivals" in occupational areas dominated by women "arrivals."

The original opportunity for professional leadership was lost. Low-salaried, social-service-trained women, whose interest was great and who for the most part had performed the early remunerated counseling services, were left in possession of the field. The inevitable happened. A woman-dominated movement, except in areas confined entirely to women, does not command the status, salaries, or prestige that a man-dominated, or a shared, movement does. For a number of years men were somewhat of a novelty, not always the highest grade novelty, in the operational field.[17] Gradually the situation is changing, but lack of authoritative professional leadership is a major deficiency at the present time and is badly needed if guidance is to move forward.

Professional leadership from other fields of knowledge and other operational areas has infiltrated the guidance movement and contributed to both its professionalization and progress. Psychology, biology, anthropology, sociology, and economics are major contributors to the enrichment of the soil in which guidance practices are grounded, but their contribution is not a substitute for the professional contributions which are due from an organized leadership within the personnel field, a leadership which represents its most professional group and can speak with authority for, and give direction to, the future of the movement.

Such leadership should be able to join with educational administration in eradicating some of the illogicalities now confusing thought and hampering progress, in agreeing upon appropriate and meaningful titles and terms, and upon functions which are legitimately included under guidance and personnel.[18] It should be helpful in stressing the importance of balance between tangibles and intangibles, and in fostering the organismic approach to personnel problems. It could encourage the type of in-service training which prepares faculties to do more than approve a schedule or choice of a major, look after student conduct, distribute financial gratuities and work opportunities, and perhaps provide courses, or conferences, on orientation and occupational topics. It could instill a professional spirit among the members of its affiliated organizations and give the spiritual values of guidance services the place that they deserve and that students, in too many surveys to be longer ignored, are asking that they be given.

[17] There is plenty of evidence to warrant this generalization although exceptions stand out. When the tide began to turn, it was reflected in the change in character of registration in university courses and in the appointment of advisers for boys in secondary schools.

[18] In a recent article descriptive of a guidance program in a large city high school, six full-time counselors were reported. Prominent among the special duties of these advisers were looking after class cuts, absence from school, poor conduct, class tardiness, unsatisfactory class progress, and failure to make class adjustment.

Professional leadership should be able to help solve the pressing problems of co-ordination and integration which are everywhere in evidence, in connection with the activities of national organizations, and all the way down the line, to co-ordination of personnel services with instruction, and with all other phases of college or secondary school programs.

Another responsibility which can be assumed only by a professional organization is the authoritative appraisal of guidance literature, including all types of informational data used in the counseling procedure, addresses and articles prepared for presentation before the Association, and general publications designed to serve as textbooks and to enlighten and win the support of the public.

The Educational Records Bureau is a reliable assistant in appraising one type of informational data. Its methods are positive rather than negative; the listing of material in its publications may usually be taken to mean that counselors may use it with full confidence in its proved reliability. When listing does not include endorsement, the reader is so informed. Omissions are often more significant than inclusions.

The Occupational Research Section of the National Vocational Guidance Association, which deals with the characteristics of good occupational monographs, recognizes and advocates universally approved research practices, but neither this Association nor any other has assumed responsibility for the appraisal of occupational monographs which are flooding the market.

Some organizations maintain committees to which addresses and articles prepared for delivery before their constituencies, or for publication in their magazines, must be submitted in advance for approval. Members of such committees stake their professional reputation on the manner in which they deal with such material, whether or not they do it intelligently, fearlessly, impartially, and impersonally. Whether contributions are refused or accepted, committees must be prepared to defend their decisions if challenged by those who disagree. There is no guidance and personnel association which is performing this service at the present time.

Book reviewing—of the type of book in which guidance and personnel workers are interested—requires knowledge of the fundamental processes of research and ability to challenge an author's use of procedures which influence the value of his contribution. The usual purpose of such reviews is to help the reader decide whether or not it will be wise to use his time to read the book or to use his money to purchase it. What is its probable value to him?

There is no guidance and personnel organization to which an inquirer may turn for authoritative reviews in this field. The character of reviews ranges all the way from the most conscientious application of scientific principles, including documentation of all comments, favorable and unfavorable, to obvious exchanges of compliments among friends, rewards for those "who play the game," and discipline for those who do not. The time is ripe for some organization to help its clientele establish an "Index Purgatorium" and in so doing show the type of professionalism which makes it a compliment to an author to have his book accepted for review.[19]

Only universities, state departments of education, and guidance and personnel associations themselves can determine the extent to which they are willing to accept the increasing responsibilities which must be accepted by someone if the promise of America is to be fulfilled. Only they can remove the deficiencies which have been inherited from the past and which have intensified with neglect and the passage of time. Only they can meet the pressing tasks of the present and at the same time anticipate the new responsibilities which must be assumed in the near future and, perhaps, be carried on under increasingly difficult conditions for years to come.

[19] Mortimer Karpp, of the New York State Employment Service, in a review of three books, each of which professed to be "the authoritative handbook" on acting and play producing (the prefaces in two of the books were identical) advised that all three be placed "high on the personnel workers' Index Purgatorium." He called for the setting up of "adequate procedures for the appraisal and certification of books, articles, and speeches which profess to be vocational guides" (*Occupations*, XVIII [1940], 313).

CHAPTER XXII

Prospect

THE story of the past and the Hydra-headed problems of the present, the relatively slow progress of the movement with its sudden forward spurt during the depression, the grudgingly given endorsement of educational authorities, the shortcomings of professional leadership and of operating personnel, and the temporary subordination of individual welfare to the salvation of the nation should, in the light of history, be regarded as steppingstones along the road to progress. They should not be allowed to overshadow factual evidences of progress or to appear to refute the assumption that the movement is gradually meeting the historian's test,[1] and is making a sufficiently significant social contribution to warrant its further development in the postwar era.

On the other hand, there could hardly be a more unpropitious time to prophesy with reference to any present-day institution. Truly, as H. G. Wells says, "We live in the end and the beginning of an age. The forces of destruction and the forces of construction are traveling side by side. The old education is dying, the new is still unborn." [2]

No one knows what social changes may follow the close of the war. No one knows how the purpose and content of education may be altered. Ideas and ideals, theories and practices, which have seemed so vital in the dying age, may lose their values in the transition period. Substitutes will be offered. Some may be strangers to our way of life. Others, which may previously have been discarded, may return to the educational doorstep and again be knocking for admission. This has already happened with reference to work experience and doubtless there will be other instances.

Since guidance and personnel services are facilitative in character, they must move forward in the new age, as they have in the old, within the limitations laid down by education and by other control agencies. Their fortunes and their service contributions will rise and fall as the fortunes

---

[1] Three tests to which historians usually subject a movement are: Is it broad enough to cover the field; is it deep enough to reach the heart of the problems involved; is it enduring? Does it deal with permanent values, with the fundamentals of society?

[2] *Mr. Britling Sees It Through.* A statement even more pertinent today than it was in 1917.

of the institutions through which they serve individuals and society rise and fall. Their opportunities for service will be curtailed or expanded within the framework of such institutions and will be influenced by the type of implementation which research agencies afford.

As they stand on the threshold of the new age, guidance and personnel services have some and will have more responsibilities which may not be shifted to other shoulders. It is the guidance functionaries who will keep an eye on the ultimate goal and see that guidance objectives and procedures are continuously facilitating the fulfillment of the promise of America. It is they who will keep the guidance movement in line with the historian's test, never forgetting that periodic contests between the forces of destruction and the forces of construction have characterized the story of civilization, that history records many temporary interruptions as humanity moves forward toward an ever higher goal. It is they who will remember that in every age leadership in any movement has implied readiness—readiness to cope with emergencies, readiness to meet temporary demands with the minimum sacrifice of enduring values, and readiness to face the future whatever it may be.

Readiness involves anticipation of the probable and possible conditions under which youth and adult must make personal adjustments and assume their shares of responsibility for social reconstruction. It involves knowledge of the mold within which the new age is developing and an understanding of the broader problems which condition personnel problems. The growing interdependence of nations will create new international problems, demand new machinery to aid in their solution, and result in new educational opportunities and responsibilities. *Personnel service must be ready to "tune in" on the international aspect of postwar problems.*

Unsolved domestic problems will doubtless be intensified by the impact of the war. A distorted national economy will almost surely claim the foreground of the domestic picture. Technological advance promises to go forward with renewed vigor, and the possibility of a surplus of man power and the return of unemployment with the cessation of hostilities and a less active labor market must be anticipated and prepared for. Population changes, which were engaging the attention of economists and sociologists throughout the depression, will again demand consideration though altered to some extent by the influence of the war. *Personnel service must be "on tap" to assist in solving the domestic aspect of postwar problems.*

Since the effect of the war and of its aftermath on individuals will be the special concern of guidance and personnel workers, readiness to serve will involve anticipatory understanding of the many types of problems which individuals of different ages, with different social, educational, and occupational backgrounds, are likely to face.[3]

Adult groups will include men and women who have shifted from the more or less fixed habits of life to combat service or to war industries, neither of which will have permanent use for them; small businessmen who have lost their business and perhaps also their life savings; and home-makers whose war-industry experiences have created new interests and aroused desires for permanent economic independence. They will include teachers who have grown weary of dealing with immature minds and have sought relief in war industries or who, under the constant pressure of war service calls, may have lost their perspective and forgotten that there is no national or international need which supersedes in service value the leadership of youth. Finally, there will be the older, superannuated worker, who for the second time is forced into retirement.

Youth groups will include individuals who assumed war service responsibilities at all stages of preparedness for entry to adult occupational life. Some who made their occupational adjustment in early youth, if they return mentally and physically sound, may find it comparatively easy to pick up the thread of the old life; others, under the changed economic conditions, may find that retraining is necessary. Some who interrupted carefully planned professional careers may need encouragement and assistance to return to student activities. Others may discard all prewar plans and will need assistance in planning a new educational and occupational program.

A second youth group will consist of those who entered the service before they had made their occupational choice, and quite possibly before having given it any intelligent consideration. War experiences may make valuable guidance contributions to the developmental growth of some members of this group. Others may need considerable educational and occupational information before they are able to make any satisfactory plan for the future.

A third youth group, with whose ideas and ideals the forces of destruction are playing havoc *now*, comprises those who are too young for military service but who, in one way or another, are daily affected, favorably or unfavorably, by the impingement of the war on the home front.

Some of this group, motivated by high wages, economic need in the home, or patriotism, have dropped out of school to enter occupational life. Socially and morally immature and quite undisciplined in the ways

[3] See *Guidance Problems in Wartime* (U. S. Office of Education, Education and National Defense Series, pamphlet no. 18; Washington, 1942).

of adult life, they are exposed to the influences which prevail in newly established industrial centers and camp communities—influences which may result in distorted ideas of values and take a heavy toll of the potential constructive forces which are so essential to the future.

The younger members of this same group are being subjected to destructive influences of other types. With the father in the service and the mother in war industries, normal home life is interrupted, and parental control disappears or is reduced to the minimum. Delinquencies are bound to increase. Unless interpreted as immature expressions of the national emotional attitude, the acts of some of these youths seem almost unbelievable.

Readiness to anticipate the causal factors which result in many overt acts or emotional explosions requires full appreciation of the meaning of hero worship and realization of the fact that war heroes are likely to be those who have exhibited most effectively the baser instincts of man. The model hero for his admiring younger brother is the man who has made the most killings, downed the most planes, torpedoed the most transports. It is he who is lauded over the air, in the printed page, and in award citations. All agencies unite to focus the attention of youth on the desirability of destructive attributes, forgetting except casually to mention the other qualities of the same heroes which are worthy of imitation by youth, and perhaps not even realizing how hero worship in wartime is affecting the ideals of youth.

What could be more natural than that youth should desire to emulate these heroes? Might not teachers, counselors, and others who are dealing with youth do much to direct their thoughts, and thereby their acts, into nobler channels if, without detracting from the military accomplishments of heroes, they would call attention to the other characteristics of these same heroes and indicate the many ways in which men on the fighting fronts are continuously exhibiting the higher and nobler instincts of man? There is much material available which could be used to bring out these characteristics, and the exigencies of war should not be allowed to overshadow them. If they are, the glory of participation in the process of destruction is bound to dominate youth's thinking and to encourage him to express destructive tendencies in the only way available to him, in delinquencies.

The demobilization of these different groups of servicemen and women and their remobilization in civilian life will require many types of readiness, informational readiness, interpretative readiness, readiness with the best tools and techniques for serving adults and returned student groups. Counselors who dealt with the same types of individuals during and after

World War I will easily visualize their immediate and postwar responsibilities. They will recall a variety of effects of war experiences on different types of individuals and be ready to take the right "step of the right length at the right time."

War experience for some has served, and will serve again, as a valuable educational, vocational, and spiritual counselor. It has afforded new learning opportunities, focused attention on the realities of life, and opened the door to progress. For others, who had faced a future full of promise, war has been a disruptive force. They returned to find that their opportunities had slipped away and that they were re-entering a competitive world with the cards stacked against them. Ten years after the close of the last war follow-up studies revealed, and probably will again, that some re-mobilized men had attained an occupational status far superior to any to which they had aspired prior to war. Others whose prewar prospects were bright had never been able to rise above mediocrity. It was difficult then, and it is going to be difficult again, to reconcile the rewards of military service with the promise of America.

Counselors who served during the former war will recall and will, therefore, be able to anticipate to some degree the problems and attitudes of young wage-earners. They will remember the pathetic and ludicrous postarmistice picture of schoolboys, fresh from Hog Island and other industrial centers, sitting calmly and confidently in junior employment offices and declaring, sometimes quite belligerently, that they would not go to school; they needed no more education; they could earn forty to sixty dollars a week with what they had. Labor surplus and unemployment meant nothing to them; they intended to have their previous wage or they would not work. In due course of time disillusionment came, and it will come again; but the quicker the mental attitudes which are engendered by war can be blotted out of the life of the nation after the cessation of hostilities, the quicker youth will be able to make adjustment to the normal responsibilities of life.

Passing from the lower age and occupational level group to the professional group, the counselor will recall the large number of college-trained men and women who had burned all previous educational and occupational bridges to enter war industries and who were cast adrift on November 11, 1918, without rudder or compass. They will remember especially the number of women teachers who were stranded in Washington, dependent for livelihood on the hand addressing of envelopes for various governmental agencies. Returning these professional women to their prewar homes at government expense was a rather humiliating experience. Such World War I memories will do much to fortify counselors in terms of readiness for meeting the aftermath of World War II.

Spiritual readiness to cope with postwar problems must not be overlooked. National neglect of the spiritual values of life has received much printed-page attention in recent years. Youth surveys on both levels of education have repeatedly suggested that a spiritual sector be brought within the guidance circle. Education did not respond while youth was on the home front. Now that these same youths are on the fighting front, there seems to be some concern lest, face to face with death, they may not "know how to die." [4] The educator lost his opportunity for the spiritual guidance of youths who are now on the fighting front. War, which is a great spiritual teacher, has taken over and, as is usual in the crises of life, spiritual values are crowding lesser values into the background. "There are no atheists in fox holes" or in slit trenches. Chaplains in the various branches of the service, some of whom claim that association with the fighting forces has resulted in a "spiritual sharpening of their own faith," and the spiritual influence of men like Generals MacArthur and Montgomery are making up for the educational deficiencies of the past. It seems quite safe to assume that the spiritual life of youth on the fighting front is in better hands than is the spiritual life of youth on the home front.

The counselor's responsibility for assistance in meeting the spiritual problems of life and in helping youth to understand spiritual values is *now, and on the home front*. Those who purport to be leaders of youth may well be concerned lest they fall short in readiness to meet the spiritual needs of youth who are still under their jurisdiction. And they may well be worried lest they fail to sharpen their own faith, or be unable to stretch their own spiritual stature sufficiently to deserve the confidence and respect of youth whom they are hoping to serve when demobilization comes.

Readiness to look ahead and prepare for the new age requires inventory of present-day trends and the use of discriminating judgment in differentiating between those which have constructive values and those which have destructive or negative values. Among the more general trends which have implications, for better or for worse, and which impose additional responsibilities on guidance services are:

[4] See John S. Brubacher, "Education for Death," *School and Society*, LVI (1942), 137–140; John E. Wise, "Education for Life," *School and Society*, LVI (1942), 441–443; Chaplain Edward J. Burns, "The Soldier's Faith," *New York Times Magazine*, Dec. 20, 1942, p. 4; and General Douglas MacArthur, "Only Those Are Fit to Live Who Are Not Afraid to Die," *Association of American Colleges Bulletin*, XXVIII (1942), 353–355. The latter is a brief condensation of a commencement address given at the University of Pittsburgh in 1932.

1. The tendency to abbreviate and accelerate the educational programs of youth. This may prove to be a temporary trend, and one which is essential to winning the war. But whether the trend be short-term or long-term, it is in direct conflict with guidance objectives, with the promise of America, and with the ultimate safety of the nation. The safeguarding of broad general education is essential to effective personnel service, and counselors should be very alert to trends which promise permanently to lower educational standards.

2. The increasing public interest in guidance services. Born of the depression this interest may not survive the war, but if it does it must be directed into constructive channels.

3. State departments of education seem to be endorsing the theory that guidance is a life-long procedure, beginning in the home, carrying over to school life, and going with the school leaver as he enters on his postschool career. Here and there there is evidence that state departments, in cooperation with the new federal service, are becoming actively interested in fostering the development of guidance programs.

4. The recently revealed desire of education to assume responsibility for incorporating work experience in the educational curriculum and for taking on postschool guidance can hardly be considered a trend since it may prove to be only a temporary break in a long-term trend in the opposite direction.

Undoubtedly educational administration realizes that unless more intelligent attention is given to the noncollege group, other agencies will take over. On the other hand, the program outlined in *Youth and the Future* is based quite largely on the assumption that the American way of life needs protection against the socially destructive tendencies of youth. Since that report was prepared, the relationship between youth and the nation has been materially altered. The nation has openly proclaimed its dependence upon youth for protection against the forces of destruction from other lands. Therefore when youth returns from his immediate task—a task well worthy of man's estate—his thinking may be so far ahead of that of home-front planners that what is offered him may seem unworthy of his sacrifice. It may seem the shadow rather than the substance of a youth program.

By this time the lessons of the war should be illuminating the lessons of the depression sufficiently to warn adults that it is no wiser to crucify youth on the cross of unemployment than on the cross of "child" labor; on the cross of occupational illiteracy than on the cross of intellectual illiteracy; on the cross of social exploitation than on the cross of educational or labor exploitation; on the cross of advantage to adults than on the cross of national advantage. Readiness on the part of guidance functionaries to discriminate between youth programs based on service to adults and those planned primarily to serve youth is a new responsibility which the trends of the time have brought into the picture.

5. A trend in the direction of better understanding of the relative values of, and relationship between, cultural and vocational education is increasingly apparent and has constructive guidance implications. It is to be hoped that this tendency may be developed to the point where both types of education may be prerequisites for personnel service. The constructive returns on such a counselor training program would be invaluable to junior-high-school youth.

6. Psychology, sociology, and economics are becoming more scientific and are making more factual and more dependable contributions to the background knowledges upon which personnel and guidance services are based.

Trends which are more specifically under the control of guidance and personnel functionaries include the following:

1. There is a tendency to regard guidance and personnel service as a permeating, a facilitating, and a shared function.

2. There is a tendency toward self-criticism. As the movement becomes more scientific it tends to challenge its procedures, to search for evaluative criteria, and to approximate more nearly the goal of service in breadth, depth, and permanence.

3. The value of and the necessity for co-operation, co-ordination, and integration are becoming more apparent and are receiving more attention.

4. The growing tendency to mechanize guidance and to develop an effective counseling machine is accompanied by a slowly awakening realization of the dangers involved. It is feared that the war may add new facilities for mechanization and thereby encourage destructive mental fingerprinting.

5. There is an increasing tendency to appreciate the necessity for understanding individuals and to encourage the organismic approach to individual development.

6. Teachers and counselors are learning to search more diligently for "the unduplicated excellence" of each individual.

7. There is a tendency to regard more critically the objectives of guidance, to challenge the inclusion of so many nondescript functions among guidance responsibilities, and to question the returns on guidance services.

8. There is a tendency to acknowledge that homeroom programs under

untrained teachers cannot qualify as guidance, and to substitute group activities under trained leaders, which result in group inventories interpretable in terms of guidance values.

9. There is also a tendency on the part of the most potentially promising operating personnel to avoid the guidance and personnel field and to acknowledge that there is no leadership in the movement which is worthy of followership and no university centers properly equipped for counselor training.

Personnel functionaries, in their efforts to study trends for whatever constructive or destructive values they may find and to be prepared for whatever responsibilities the future may impose, will have the assistance of some new and promising agencies, as well as of others that have long been in operation.

Federal assistance in anticipating the future may be secured from the occupational research program of the U. S. Employment Service and from the National Resources Planning Board. The Institute of Rural Youth Guidance in 1942 prepared a co-operative program designed to be helpful to those charged with advising rural youth. The Federal-State Rehabilitation Services can be depended upon to disseminate new knowledge and to be informed as to new opportunities of importance for their particular clientele. Agencies dealing with the selection, classification, and training of defense personnel will collect an enormous amount of valuable educational and counseling material which will flow back into civilian channels. For general information counselors will turn to the Occupational Information and Guidance Service of the U. S. Office of Education, which is concerned with many arcs of the guidance circle, collaborates with state services, and functions as a national clearinghouse, primarily for public-school services. Its excellent publications, including annotated (for content, not for values) bibliographies, are indispensable aids to counselor readiness.

For trends in the area of general education which have important implications for guidance and personnel service, the publications of the American Council on Education are a valuable source of information, especially on the college level. The U. S. Office of Education and the various departments of the National Education Association deal more specifically with public-school problems.

Industry is developing new tools and techniques and is refining the old. In recent years industrial concerns have done considerable research on the personal interview and have made no small contribution to the development of the art of interviewing and to the objectivity of interview results, thereby, on the very eve of the new age, reviving interest in the further development of its possibilities as a personnel technique. Personnel departments are co-operating with educators and psychologists, engaging in war programs, testing new devices, revising vocational training curricula, and improving educational procedures. The publications of the American Management Association are an authoritative source of information on both long-term and short-term trends in personnel service in industrial and business areas.

Guidance and personnel functionaries will watch with interest the activities of psychologists who are engaged in the analysis, classification, and distribution of servicemen and women. Fortunately, enough psychologists who carried on initial mass researches in this area during World War I are again available so that immediate progress can go forward on the basis of previous experiences. Already sufficient tentative returns are available to warrant the anticipation of important contributions to educational and industrial progress. New tests of various types for various purposes are being developed, and the individual inventory, or qualification card, for both privates and officers, is being improved. Thus far the discarding of the Army Alpha and Beta Tests and of mental age units and I.Q.'s in favor of the Army General Classification Test, which is better adapted for adult use, is perhaps of most general interest in relation to educational and industrial progress.

As guidance functionaries, organized groups of guidance and personnel workers, and educators stand on the threshold of the future with the forces of destruction and the forces of construction struggling for supremacy, it is they who will determine whether the guidance movement, as it has been developing, shall pass away with the dying age or go forward with the forces of construction to aid in building the new.

Stocktaking, as the old age passes away, reveals that some of the things which have been done under the auspices of the movement have been well done; others have deserved and have received the censure of all parties concerned, including many personnel workers themselves. Stocktaking reveals the strengths and weaknesses of the movement. It points out deficiencies which have persisted from the inception of the movement and which require immediate authoritative attention. It points out trends which promise to be constructively helpful in meeting the demands of the new age. And it points out new agencies which are at hand to aid the movement in taking "forward steps of the right length at the right time, in such ways that we do not skid or slip backward."

Although as a facilitating agency guidance and personnel service may not cast the decisive vote which determines the character of education in the new age, by its readiness to facilitate whatever education may be decreed it can determine whether it has outlived its usefulness and shall pass into history or whether what has been accomplished in the past is only the prologue to a greater future—whether the present, standing between the old age and the new, is to be "the beginning of the end" of the guidance and personnel movement or whether it is to be "the end of the beginning."

Those who have faith in the objectives of the movement and confidence in its ability to contribute to the fulfillment of the promise of America, will hope and believe that it is "the end of the beginning" which is passing away. They will hope and believe that the movement will broaden its cultural background, strengthen its technical knowledge, and professionalize its services; that it will become broad enough, and deep enough, and enduring enough to meet the historian's test; and that it will become effective enough to justify every educator who speaks with authority on any level of education in endorsing it as a vital force in the fulfillment of the promise of America.

INDEX OF SUBJECTS

INDEX OF NAMES